P9-BBQ-562

Office Home and Student 2010
ALL-IN-ONE
FOR
DUMMIES®

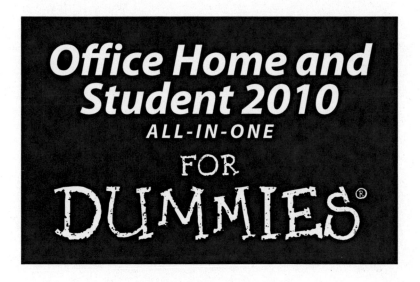

Office Home and Student 2010
ALL-IN-ONE
FOR DUMMIES®

by Peter Weverka

WILEY

John Wiley & Sons, Inc.

Office Home and Student 2010 All-in-One For Dummies®

Published by
John Wiley & Sons, Inc.
111 River Street
Hoboken, NJ 07030-5774

www.wiley.com

Copyright © 2011 by John Wiley & Sons, Inc., Hoboken, New Jersey

Published by John Wiley & Sons, Inc., Hoboken, New Jersey

Published simultaneously in Canada

For general information on our other products and services, please contact our Customer Care Department within the U.S. at 877-762-2974, outside the U.S. at 317-572-3993, or fax 317-572-4002.

For technical support, please visit www.wiley.com/techsupport.

Wiley publishes in a variety of print and electronic formats and by print-on-demand. Some material included with standard print versions of this book may not be included in e-books or in print-on-demand. If this book refers to media such as a CD or DVD that is not included in the version you purchased, you may download this material at http://booksupport.wiley.com. For more information about Wiley products, visit www.wiley.com.

Library of Congress Control Number: 2010935589

ISBN 978-0-470-87951-1 (pbk); ISBN 978-0-470-94880-4 (ebk); ISBN 978-0-470-94881-1 (ebk); ISBN 978-0-470-94882-8 (ebk)

10 9 8 7 6 5 4 3 2

WILEY

About the Author

Peter Weverka is the bestselling author of many *For Dummies* books, including *Office 2010 All-in-One Desk Reference For Dummies,* as well as 35 other computer books about various topics. Peter's humorous articles and stories — none related to computers, thankfully — have appeared in *Harper's, SPY,* and other magazines for grown-ups.

Dedication

For Valentine Wannop.

Author's Acknowledgments

This book owes a lot to many hard-working people at the offices of Wiley Publishing in Indiana. Once again, I want to thank Steve Hayes for giving me the opportunity to write a *For Dummies* book.

I would also like to thank Susan Christophersen, who has edited many of my books, this one included, and is always a pleasure to work with.

Technical editor Lee Musick made sure that all the explanations in this book are indeed accurate, and I would like to thank him for his diligence and suggestions for improving this book. I would also like to thank Rich Tennant for the witty cartoons you will find on the pages of this book and Broccoli Information Mgt. for writing the index.

These people at the Wiley offices in Indianapolis gave their all to this book, and I want to acknowledge them by name: Katherine Crocker, Melanee Habig, Joyce Haughey, Melanie Hoffman and Sheree Montgomery.

Finally, I owe my family — Sofia, Henry, and Addie — a debt for tolerating my vampire-like working hours and eerie demeanor at daybreak. How can I ever repay you?

Publisher's Acknowledgments

We're proud of this book; please send us your comments at http://dummies.custhelp.com. For other comments, please contact our Customer Care Department within the U.S. at 877-762-2974, outside the U.S. at 317-572-3993, or fax 317-572-4002.

Some of the people who helped bring this book to market include the following:

Acquisitions and Editorial

Project and Copy Editor: Susan Christophersen

Executive Editor: Steve Hayes

Technical Editor: Lee Musick

Editorial Manager: Jodi Jensen

Editorial Assistant: Amanda Graham

Sr. Editorial Assistant: Cherie Case

Cartoons: Rich Tennant (www.the5thwave.com)

Composition Services

Project Coordinator: Katherine Crocker

Layout and Graphics: Melanee Habig

Proofreaders: Melanie Hoffman, Evelyn Wellborn

Indexer: BIM Indexing & Proofreading Services

Publishing and Editorial for Technology Dummies

> **Richard Swadley,** Vice President and Executive Group Publisher

> **Andy Cummings,** Vice President and Publisher

> **Mary Bednarek,** Executive Acquisitions Director

> **Mary C. Corder,** Editorial Director

Publishing for Consumer Dummies

> **Kathleen Nebenhaus,** Vice President and Executive Publisher

Composition Services

> **Debbie Stailey,** Director of Composition Services

Contents at a Glance

Introduction 1

Book I: Common Office Tools 7
Chapter 1: Office Nuts and Bolts...9
Chapter 2: Wrestling with the Text...33
Chapter 3: Speed Techniques Worth Knowing About 59
Chapter 4: Taking Advantage of the Proofing Tools...................67
Chapter 5: Creating a Table 83
Chapter 6: Creating a Chart 103
Chapter 7: Making a SmartArt Diagram 141
Chapter 8: Drawing and Manipulating Lines, Shapes, and Other Objects.............159

Book II: Word... 187
Chapter 1: Speed Techniques for Using Word...........................189
Chapter 2: Laying Out Text and Pages......................................207
Chapter 3: Word Styles 229
Chapter 4: Desktop Publishing with Word 245
Chapter 5: Getting Word's Help with Office Chores 263
Chapter 6: Tools for Reports and Scholarly Papers..................281

Book III: PowerPoint 303
Chapter 1: Getting Started in PowerPoint.................................305
Chapter 2: Fashioning a Look for Your Presentation 327
Chapter 3: Entering the Text 341
Chapter 4: Making Your Presentations Livelier 357
Chapter 5: Delivering a Presentation 373

Book IV: Excel 393
Chapter 1: Up and Running with Excel......................................395
Chapter 2: Refining Your Worksheet...413
Chapter 3: Formulas and Functions for Crunching Numbers 425
Chapter 4: Making a Worksheet Easier to Read and Understand..........445
Chapter 5: Analyzing Data 461

Book V: OneNote 471

Chapter 1: Up and Running with OneNote.. 473

Chapter 2: Taking Notes.. 485

Chapter 3: Finding and Organizing Your Notes 501

Book VI: Office 2010: One Step Beyond 509

Chapter 1: Customizing an Office Program 511

Chapter 2: Ways of Distributing Your Work... 523

Chapter 3: Handling Graphics 531

Chapter 4: Decorating Files with Clip Art 551

Chapter 5: Automating Tasks with Macros 561

Chapter 6: Linking and Embedding in Compound Files.................................... 571

Chapter 7: Office Web Apps.. 581

Index 617

Table of Contents

Introduction 1

Home and Student Edition..1
What's in This Book, Anyway?..2
What Makes This Book Different 3
    Easy-to-look-up information 3
    A task-oriented approach 3
    Meaningful screen shots 3
Foolish Assumptions..4
Conventions Used in This Book..4
Icons Used in This Book 5
Good Luck, Reader! 5

Book 1: Common Office Tools 7

Chapter 1: Office Nuts and Bolts 9

A Survey of Office 2010 Home and Student Programs 9
Starting an Office Program 10
Finding Your Way around the Office Interface 13
    The File tab 13
    The Quick Access toolbar.......................................13
    The Ribbon and its tabs..14
    Context-sensitive tabs...15
    The anatomy of a tab...16
    Live previewing 18
    Mini-toolbars 19
    Office 2010 for keyboard lovers 19
Saving Your Files 20
    Saving a file 20
    Saving a file for the first time...............................20
    Declaring where you like to save files 21
    Saving files for use in earlier versions of an Office program...21
    Saving AutoRecovery information................................24
Navigating the Save As and Open Dialog Boxes 25
Opening and Closing Files 26
    Opening a file...26
    Closing a file...28
Reading and Recording File Properties 28
Locking a File with a Password.......................................29
    Password-protecting a file 29
    Removing a password from a file................................31

Chapter 2: Wrestling with the Text **33**

Manipulating the Text 33
    Selecting text 33
    Moving and copying text..35
    Taking advantage of the Clipboard task pane..............................35
    Deleting text..36
Changing the Look of Text...36
    Choosing fonts for text..38
    Changing the font size of text..39
    Applying font styles to text 39
    Applying text effects to text 40
    Underlining text 41
    Changing the color of text 42
Quick Ways to Handle Case, or Capitalization......................................42
Entering Symbols and Foreign Characters...44
Finding and Replacing Text...45
    The basics: Finding stray words and phrases................................45
    Narrowing your search 47
    Conducting a find-and-replace operation 51
Creating Hyperlinks...53
    Linking a hyperlink to a Web page 53
    Creating a hyperlink to another place in your file.........................54
    Creating an e-mail hyperlink..56
    Repairing and removing hyperlinks 56

Chapter 3: Speed Techniques Worth Knowing About **59**

Undoing and Repeating Commands 59
    Undoing a mistake 59
    Repeating an action — and quicker this time 60
Zooming In, Zooming Out 61
Viewing a File through More Than One Window.....................................62
Correcting Typos on the Fly..62
    Opening the AutoCorrect dialog box 63
    Telling Office which typos and misspellings to correct 65
    Preventing capitalization errors with AutoCorrect.......................65

Chapter 4: Taking Advantage of the Proofing Tools **67**

Correcting Your Spelling Errors 67
    Correcting misspellings one at a time...68
    Running a spell-check...68
    Fine-tuning the spell checker 70
Checking for Grammatical Errors in Word...73
Researching a Topic inside an Office Program..74
    Looking at the research services..75
    Using the Research task pane 76
    Choosing your research options 77

Finding the Right Word with the Thesaurus.................................77
Proofing Text Written in a Foreign Language 79
   Telling Office which languages you will use.......................79
   Marking text as foreign language text 80

Chapter 5: Creating a Table 83

Talking Table Jargon...83
Creating a Table...84
Entering the Text and Numbers..86
Selecting Different Parts of a Table.................................86
Aligning Text in Columns and Rows....................................87
Merging and Splitting Cells..87
Laying Out Your Table..88
   Changing the size of a table, column, or rows 89
   Adjusting column and row size.....................................89
   Inserting and deleting columns and rows...........................90
   Moving columns and rows...91
Formatting Your Table..91
   Designing a table with a table style..............................91
   Calling attention to different rows and columns 92
   Decorating your table with borders and colors 93
Using Math Formulas in Word Tables...................................95
Neat Table Tricks 96
   Changing the direction of header row text.........................96
   Using a picture as the table background 97
   Drawing diagonal lines on tables 99
   Drawing on a table...101

Chapter 6: Creating a Chart.................................103

A Mercifully Brief Anatomy Lesson...................................103
The Basics: Creating a Chart..105
Choosing the Right Chart 107
   Ground rules for choosing a chart 108
   Examining the different kinds of charts..........................108
Providing the Raw Data for Your Chart...............................124
Positioning Your Chart in a Workbook, Page, or Slide 124
Changing a Chart's Appearance 125
   Changing the chart type..126
   Changing the size and shape of a chart 126
   Relying on a chart style to change appearances 126
   Changing the layout of a chart 127
   Handling the gridlines 130
   Changing a chart element's color, font, or other particular 132
Saving a Chart as a Template So That You Can Use It Again...........133
   Saving a chart as a template.....................................134
   Creating a chart from a template.................................134

Chart Tricks for the Daring and Heroic 134
Decorating a chart with a picture.. 135
Displaying the raw data alongside the chart........................ 136
Creating an overlay chart 136
Placing a trendline on a chart 137
Troubleshooting a Chart 138

Chapter 7: Making a SmartArt Diagram.....................141

The Basics: Creating SmartArt Diagrams 141
Choosing a diagram.. 141
Making the diagram your own.. 143
Creating the Initial Diagram 143
Creating a diagram.. 144
Swapping one diagram for another 144
Changing the Size and Position of a Diagram............................ 145
Laying Out the Diagram Shapes.. 145
Selecting a diagram shape 146
Removing a shape from a diagram 146
Moving diagram shapes to different positions 146
Adding shapes to diagrams apart from hierarchy diagrams 147
Adding shapes to hierarchy diagrams 148
Adding shapes to Organization charts.................................. 149
Promoting and demoting shapes in hierarchy diagrams 151
Handling the Text on Diagram Shapes.. 151
Entering text on a diagram shape... 151
Entering bulleted lists on diagram shapes 152
Changing a Diagram's Direction 153
Choosing a Look for Your Diagram 154
Changing the Appearance of Diagram Shapes.......................... 155
Changing the size of a diagram shape.................................. 155
Exchanging one shape for another.. 156
Changing a shape's color, fill, or outline............................. 156
Changing fonts and font sizes on shapes............................. 158

Chapter 8: Drawing and Manipulating Lines, Shapes, and Other Objects..................................159

The Basics: Drawing Lines, Arrows, and Shapes...................... 160
Handling Lines, Arrows, and Connectors.................................. 161
Changing the length and position of a line or arrow...................... 161
Changing the appearance of a line, arrow, or connector 162
Attaching and handling arrowheads on lines and connectors 163
Attaching and handling arrowConnecting
shapes by using connectors 164
Handling Rectangles, Ovals, Stars, and Other Shapes............................ 165
Drawing a shape.. 166
Changing a shape's symmetry 167
Using a shape as a text box 167

WordArt for Bending, Spindling, and Mutilating Text 169
    Creating a WordArt image 169
    Editing a WordArt image... 169
Manipulating Lines, Shapes, Art, Text Boxes, and Other Objects........ 170
    Selecting objects so that you can manipulate them..................... 172
    Hiding and displaying the rulers and grid 173
    Changing an object's size and shape..................................... 173
    Moving and positioning objects... 174
    Tricks for aligning and distributing objects 175
    When objects overlap: Choosing
      which appears above the other 178
    Rotating and flipping objects 179
    Grouping objects to make working with them easier 181
Changing an Object's Color, Outline Color, and Transparency 182
    Filling an object with a color, picture, or texture..................... 182
    Making a color transparent 183
    Putting the outline around an object 184

Book II: Word 187

Chapter 1: Speed Techniques for Using Word 189

Introducing the Word Screen... 189
Creating a New Document 191
Getting a Better Look at Your Documents 193
    Viewing documents in different ways 193
    Splitting the screen... 195
Selecting Text in Speedy Ways 196
Moving Around Quickly in Documents................................... 198
    Keys for getting around quickly... 198
    Navigating from page to page or heading to heading 199
    "Browsing" around a document.. 200
    Going there fast with the Go To command............................. 200
    Bookmarks for hopping around 201
Entering Information Quickly in a Computerized Form.................. 202
    Creating a computerized form 202
    Entering data in the form 204

Chapter 2: Laying Out Text and Pages 207

Paragraphs and Formatting.. 207
Inserting a Section Break for Formatting Purposes 208
Breaking a Line... 209
Starting a New Page... 210
Setting Up and Changing the Margins.................................... 210

Indenting Paragraphs and First Lines 212
    Clicking an Indent button (for left-indents)..............................212
    "Eye-balling it" with the ruler 213
    Indenting in the Paragraph dialog box..214
Numbering the Pages 214
    Numbering with page numbers only 214
    Including a page number in a header or footer 215
    Changing page number formats..216
Putting Headers and Footers on Pages 216
    Creating, editing, and removing headers and footers................217
    Fine-tuning a header or footer..218
Adjusting the Space between Lines...219
Adjusting the Space between Paragraphs 220
Creating Numbered and Bulleted Lists 220
    Simple numbered and bulleted lists...221
    Constructing lists of your own...222
    Managing a multilevel list 222
Working with Tabs 223
Hyphenating Text 225
    Automatically and manually hyphenating a document 225
    Unhyphenating and other hyphenation tasks.............................226

Chapter 3: Word Styles 229
All about Styles 229
    Styles and templates 229
    Types of styles 230
Applying Styles to Text and Paragraphs 231
    Applying a style...231
    Experimenting with style sets 233
    Choosing which style names appear on the Style menus 233
Creating a New Style 235
    Creating a style from a paragraph 235
    Creating a style from the ground up 235
Modifying a Style 237
Creating and Managing Templates...238
    Creating a new template 238
    Opening a template so that you can modify it.............................239
    Copying styles from different documents and templates 240
    Modifying, deleting, and renaming styles in templates 242

Chapter 4: Desktop Publishing with Word .245
Making Use of Charts, Diagrams, Shapes, Clip Art, and Photos 245
Constructing the Perfect Table...246
    Repeating header rows on subsequent pages 247
    Turning a list into a table...248
Positioning and Wrapping Objects Relative to the Page and Text........248
    Wrapping text around an object...249
    Positioning an object on a page...250

Working with the Drawing Canvas 251
Choosing a Theme for Your Document 252
Putting Newspaper-Style Columns in a Document 253
    Doing the preliminary work..253
    Running text into columns..253
Working with Text Boxes..255
    Inserting a text box...255
    Making text flow from text box to text box 256
Sprucing Up Your Pages 256
    Decorating a page with a border 256
    Putting a background color on pages 258
Dropping In a Drop Cap 258
Watermarking for the Elegant Effect 259
Landscape Documents..260
Printing on Different Size Paper...261

Chapter 5: Getting Word's Help with Office Chores. 263

Highlighting Parts of a Document..263
Commenting on a Document...264
    Entering a comment 264
    Caring for and feeding comments...............................265
Tracking Changes to Documents..266
    Telling Word to start marking changes.......................266
    Telling Word how to mark changes..............................267
    Reading and reviewing a document with change marks 268
    Marking changes when you forgot to turn on change marks....268
    Accepting and rejecting changes to a document...........270
Printing an Address on an Envelope.....................................271
Printing a Single Address Label (Or a Page of the Same Label) 272
Churning Out Letters, Envelopes, and Labels for Mass Mailings..........274
    Preparing the source file...274
    Merging the document with the source file.................275
    Printing form letters, envelopes, and labels................279

Chapter 6: Tools for Reports and Scholarly Papers 281

Alphabetizing a List..281
Outlines for Organizing Your Work......................................282
    Viewing the outline in different ways..........................283
    Rearranging document sections in Outline view..........283
Generating a Table of Contents 284
    Creating a TOC 284
    Updating and removing a TOC......................................285
    Customizing a TOC 285
    Changing the structure of a TOC 286
Indexing a Document 287
    Marking index items in the document.........................288
    Generating the index 290
    Editing an index..291

Putting Cross-References in a Document 292
Putting Footnotes and Endnotes in Documents 294
    Entering a footnote or endnote.. 294
    Choosing the numbering scheme and position of notes 295
    Deleting, moving, and editing notes 296
Compiling a Bibliography 296
    Inserting a citation for your bibliography 297
    Editing a citation 298
    Changing how citations appear in text 299
    Generating the bibliography 299

Book III: PowerPoint.. *303*

Chapter 1: Getting Started in PowerPoint .... .305

Getting Acquainted with PowerPoint..306
A Brief Geography Lesson 308
A Whirlwind Tour of PowerPoint 309
Creating a New Presentation...310
Advice for Building Persuasive Presentations.............................311
Creating New Slides for Your Presentation.................................314
    Inserting a new slide..314
    Speed techniques for inserting slides 315
    Conjuring slides from Word document headings.................315
    Selecting a different layout for a slide...............................318
Getting a Better View of Your Work...318
    Changing views 319
    Looking at the different views...319
Hiding and Displaying the Slides Pane and Notes Pane 320
Selecting, Moving, and Deleting Slides 321
    Selecting slides..321
    Moving slides..322
    Deleting slides 322
Putting Together a Photo Album..322
    Creating your photo album 322
    Putting on the final touches 325
    Editing a photo album..326

Chapter 2: Fashioning a Look for Your Presentation .... .327

Looking at Themes and Background Styles 327
Choosing a Theme for Your Presentation.....................................329
    Selecting a theme 329
    Tweaking a theme 329
Creating Slide Backgrounds on Your Own 330
    Using a solid (or transparent) color for the slide background....330
    Creating a gradient color blend for slide backgrounds 331

Placing a clip-art image in the slide background 333
Using a picture for a slide background 334
Using a texture for a slide background 335
Changing the Background of a Single or Handful of Slides 336
Using Master Slides and Master Styles for a Consistent Design...........337
Switching to Slide Master view 338
Understanding master slides and master styles.............................338
Editing a master slide...339
Changing a master slide layout 340

Chapter 3: Entering the Text....................................341

Entering Text...341
Choosing fonts for text...342
Changing the font size of text..343
Changing the color of text 343
Fun with Text Boxes and Text Box Shapes 344
Controlling How Text Fits in Text Frames and Text Boxes..................346
Choosing how PowerPoint "AutoFits" text in text frames............346
Choosing how PowerPoint "AutoFits" text in text boxes 348
Positioning Text in Frames and Text Boxes...349
Handling Bulleted and Numbered Lists..350
Creating a standard bulleted or numbered list...............................350
Choosing a different bullet character, size, and color..................351
Choosing a different list-numbering style, size, and color 352
Putting Footers (and Headers) on Slides..352
Some background on footers and headers..353
Putting a standard footer on all your slides...................................353
Creating a nonstandard footer 354
Removing a footer from a single slide...355

Chapter 4: Making Your Presentations Livelier 357

Suggestions for Enlivening Your Presentation 357
Exploring Transitions and Animations 359
Showing transitions between slides 359
Animating parts of a slide 360
Making Audio Part of Your Presentation..362
Inserting an audio file on a slide 363
Telling PowerPoint when and how to play an audio file..............364
Playing audio during a presentation 365
Playing Video on Slides...365
Inserting a video on a slide...366
Fine-tuning a video presentation 366
Recording a Voice Narration for PowerPoint 367
Testing your computer's microphone 368
Recording a voice narration in PowerPoint 370

Chapter 5: Delivering a Presentation **373**

All about Notes 373
Rehearsing and Timing Your Presentation 374
Showing Your Presentation. 375
Starting and ending a presentation 376
Going from slide to slide 376
Tricks for Making Presentations a Little Livelier 379
Wielding a pen or highlighter in a presentation 380
Hiding and erasing pen and highlighter markings. 380
Blanking the screen 381
Delivering a Presentation When You Can't Be There in Person. 381
Providing handouts for your audience 381
Creating a self-running, kiosk-style presentation 383
Creating a user-run presentation. 384
Packaging your presentation on a CD 386
Creating a presentation video 389

Book IV: Excel **393**

Chapter 1: Up and Running with Excel. **395**

Creating a New Excel Workbook. 395
Getting Acquainted with Excel. 397
Rows, columns, and cell addresses. 399
Workbooks and worksheets 399
Entering Data in a Worksheet 399
The basics of entering data 399
Entering text labels. 401
Entering numeric values 401
Entering date and time values. 402
Quickly Entering Lists and Serial Data with the AutoFill Command. . . . 404
Formatting Numbers, Dates, and Time Values 406
Conditional Formats for Calling Attention to Data. 407
Establishing Data-Validation Rules 409

Chapter 2: Refining Your Worksheet. **413**

Editing Worksheet Data 413
Moving around in a Worksheet. 414
Getting a Better Look at the Worksheet 415
Freezing and splitting columns and rows 415
Hiding columns and rows 417
Comments for Documenting Your Worksheet. 417
Selecting Cells in a Worksheet 419
Deleting, Copying, and Moving Data 419
Handling the Worksheets in a Workbook. 420
Keeping Others from Tampering with Worksheets 421
Hiding a worksheet 422
Protecting a worksheet 422

Chapter 3: Formulas and Functions for Crunching Numbers 425

How Formulas Work 425
   Referring to cells in formulas 425
   Referring to formula results in formulas 427
   Operators in formulas 428
The Basics of Entering a Formula 430
Speed Techniques for Entering Formulas 431
   Clicking cells to enter cell references 431
   Entering a cell range 431
   Naming cell ranges so that you
      can use them in formulas 432
   Referring to cells in different worksheets 435
Copying Formulas from Cell to Cell 436
Detecting and Correcting Errors in Formulas 437
   Correcting errors one at a time 437
   Running the error checker 438
   Tracing cell references 439
Working with Functions 440
   Using arguments in functions 442
   Entering a function in a formula 442

Chapter 4: Making a Worksheet Easier
to Read and Understand 445

Laying Out a Worksheet 445
   Aligning numbers and text in columns and rows 445
   Inserting and deleting rows and columns 447
   Changing the size of columns and rows 448
Decorating a Worksheet with Borders and Colors 450
   Cell styles for quickly formatting a worksheet 450
   Formatting cells with table styles 452
   Slapping borders on worksheet cells 453
   Decorating worksheets with colors 454
Getting Ready to Print a Worksheet 454
   Making a worksheet fit on a page 455
   Making a worksheet more presentable 458
   Repeating row and column headings on each page 459

Chapter 5: Analyzing Data 461

Managing Information in Lists 461
   Constructing a list 461
   Sorting a list 462
   Filtering a list 462
Forecasting with the Goal Seek Command 464
Performing What-If Analyses with Data Tables 466
   Using a one-input table for analysis 466
   Using a two-input table for analysis 468

Book V: OneNote *471*

Chapter 1: Up and Running with OneNote .473
  Introducing OneNote..473
  Finding Your Way around the OneNote Screen.......................................474
    Navigation bar 474
    Section (and section group) tabs 475
    Page window 475
    Page pane 475
  Units for Organizing Notes 475
  Creating a Notebook...476
  Creating Sections and Section Groups..478
    Creating a new section 478
    Creating a section group...478
  Creating Pages and Subpages 479
    Creating a new page 479
    Creating a new subpage 480
  Renaming and Deleting Groups and Pages..480
  Getting from Place to Place in OneNote 480
  Changing Your View of a Page 481

Chapter 2: Taking Notes 485
  Notes: The Basics 485
    Moving and resizing note containers 486
    Selecting notes 486
    Deleting notes..486
    Getting more space for notes on a page 486
  Entering a Typewritten Note..487
  Drawing on the Page 487
    Drawing with a pen or highlighter 488
    Drawing a shape...489
    Changing the size and appearance of drawings and shapes........490
  Converting a Handwritten Note to Text 491
  Writing a Math Expression in a Note 491
  Taking a Screen-Clipping Note 492
  Recording and Playing Audio Notes...493
    Recording an audio note...494
    Playing an audio note 495
  Attaching, Copying, and Linking Files to Notes 495
    Attaching an Office file to a note..495
    Copying an Office file into OneNote 496
    Linking a Word or PowerPoint file to OneNote...........................497
    Copying a note into another Office program.......................................498
  Formatting the Text in Notes 498
  Docking the OneNote Screen 499

Chapter 3: Finding and Organizing Your Notes...................501

Finding a Stray Note 501
    Searching by word or phrase 501
    Searching by author 502
Tagging Notes for Follow Up 503
    Tagging a note 504
    Arranging tagged notes in the task pane 504
    Creating and modifying tags 505
Color-Coding Notebooks, Sections, and Pages 506
Merging and Moving Sections, Pages, and Notes 507

Book VI: Office 2010: One Step Beyond 509

Chapter 1: Customizing an Office Program 511

Customizing the Ribbon 511
    Displaying and selecting tab, group, and command names........513
    Moving tabs and groups on the Ribbon...........................513
    Adding, removing, and renaming tabs, groups,
        and commands..514
    Creating new tabs and groups 515
    Resetting your Ribbon customizations............................515
Customizing the Quick Access Toolbar....................................516
    Adding buttons to the Quick Access toolbar 516
    Changing the order of buttons on the Quick Access toolbar.......517
    Removing buttons from the Quick Access toolbar 518
    Placing the Quick Access toolbar above or below
        the Ribbon...518
Customizing the Status Bar 518
Changing the Color Scheme 519
Customizing Keyboard Shortcuts in Word...............................520

Chapter 2: Ways of Distributing Your Work 523

Printing — the Old Standby 523
Distributing a File in PDF Format..524
    About PDF files 524
    Saving an Office file as a PDF 525
Saving an Office File as a Web Page 526
    Choosing how to save the component parts...................526
    Turning a file into a Web page..526
    Opening a Web page in your browser...............................528
Blogging from inside Word..528
    Describing a blog account to Word..................................529
    Posting an entry to your blog..529
    Taking advantage of the Blog Post tab............................530

Chapter 3: Handling Graphics 531

All about Picture File Formats 531
  Bitmap and vector graphics 531
  Resolution 533
  Compression 533
  Choosing file formats for graphics 534
The All-Important Copyright Issue 534
Inserting a Picture in an Office File 535
Touching Up a Picture 536
  Softening and sharpening pictures 537
  Correcting a picture's brightness and contrast 537
  Recoloring a picture 538
  Choosing an artistic effect 539
  Selecting a picture style 540
  Cropping off part of a picture 540
  Removing the background 542
Compressing Pictures to Save Disk Space 543
Using Microsoft Office Picture Manager 544
  Mapping the graphic files on your computer 545
  Displaying the graphic file you want to work with 545
  Editing a picture 546

Chapter 4: Decorating Files with Clip Art .551

What Is Clip Art? 551
Inserting a Clip-Art Image 552
Handling Media Files with the Clip Organizer 553
  Knowing your way around the Clip Organizer 554
  Locating the media file you need 555
  Inserting a media file 556
  Storing your own files in the My Collections folders 557

Chapter 5: Automating Tasks with Macros .561

What Is a Macro? 561
Displaying the Developer Tab 561
Managing the Macro Security Problem 562
Recording a Macro 564
  Enabling your files for macros 564
  Ground rules for recording macros 564
  Recording the macro 565
Running a Macro 567
Editing a Macro 568
  Opening a macro in the Visual Basic Editor 568
  Reading a macro in the Code window 569
  Editing the text that a macro enters 570
  Deleting parts of a macro 570

Chapter 6: Linking and Embedding in Compound Files...........571

What Is OLE, Anyway? 571
    Linking and embedding...571
    Pitfalls of linking and embedding..574
Linking to Data in a Source File 574
    Establishing the link 575
    Updating a link 576
    Editing data in the source file..576
Embedding Data from Other Programs 577
    Embedding foreign data 577
    Editing embedded data 579

Chapter 7: Office Web Apps 581

Introducing the Office Web Apps 581
Storing and Sharing Files on the Internet......................................582
Office Web Apps: The Big Picture 583
Getting Ready to Use the Office Web Apps 584
Signing In to Windows Live 584
Navigating to the SkyDrive Window...584
Managing Your Folders..585
    Creating a folder..586
    Going from folder to folder in SkyDrive 588
    Deleting, moving, and renaming folders 589
Creating an Office File in SkyDrive 589
Opening and Editing Office Files Stored on SkyDrive 590
    Opening and editing a file in an Office Web App 590
    Opening and editing a SkyDrive file
    in an Office 2010 program 592
Managing Your Files on SkyDrive..594
    Making use of the Properties window....................................594
    Uploading files to a folder on SkyDrive.................................596
    Downloading files from SkyDrive to your computer 596
    Moving, copying, renaming, and deleting files.......................597
Ways of Sharing Folders: The Big Picture 597
Making Friends on Windows Live..598
    The two types of friends 598
    Fielding an invitation to be someone's friend...............................600
    Inviting someone to be your friend 600
Understanding the Folder Types...601
    Types of folders 601
    Knowing what kind of folder you're dealing with.........................602
    Public and shared folder tasks...603
Establishing a Folder's Share With Permissions 604
Sharing on a Public or Shared Folder 606
    Sharing with friends on Windows Live....................................606
    Sending out e-mail invitations..607
    Posting hyperlinks on the Internet...609

Writing File Comments and Descriptions 610
Coauthoring Files Shared on SkyDrive 611
　　When you can and can't coauthor 612
　　Finding out who your coauthors are 613
　　Getting locked out of a shared file 614

Index *617*

Introduction

*T*his book is for users of Office 2010 Home and Student edition who want to get to the heart of the program without wasting time. Don't look in this book to find out how the different programs in Office work. Look in this book to find out how *you* can get *your* work done better and faster with these programs.

I show you everything you need to make the most of the different Office programs. On the way, you have a laugh or two. No matter how much or how little skill you bring to the table, this book will make you a better, more proficient, more confident user of the Office Home and Student edition programs.

Home and Student Edition

This book covers the Home and Student edition of Microsoft Office 2010. To find out which edition of Office you have, click the Start button on your computer, choose All Programs, and look for the words "Microsoft Office" on the pop-up menu. If you see "Microsoft Office Home and Student," not "Microsoft Office," you have the Home and Student edition.

This little table shows you which software programs are in the Home and Student edition and other editions of Office 2010.

Program	Home and Student	Standard	Professional
Word	Yes	Yes	Yes
Excel	Yes	Yes	Yes
PowerPoint	Yes	Yes	Yes
OneNote	Yes	Yes	Yes
Publisher	No	Yes	Yes
Access	No	No	Yes

What's in This Book, Anyway?

This book is your guide to making the most of the Office Home and Student edition programs. It's jam-packed with how-to's, advice, shortcuts, and tips. Here's a bare outline of the six parts of this book:

✦ **Part I: Common Office Tools:** Looks into the many commands and features that are common to all or several of the Office programs. Master the material in Part I and you will be well on your way to mastering all the programs. Part I explains handling text, the proofing tools, charts, diagrams, and tables. It explores speed techniques that can make you more productive in most of the Office programs, as well as how to draw and manipulate lines, shapes, clip-art, and other so-called objects.

✦ **Part II: Word:** Explains the numerous features in Office's word processor, including how to create documents from letters to reports. Use the techniques described here to turn Word into a desktop-publishing program and quickly dispatch office tasks such as mass-mailings. You also discover how to get Word's help in writing indexes, bibliographies, and other items of interest to scholars and report writers.

✦ **Part III: PowerPoint:** Demonstrates how to construct a meaningful presentation that makes the audience say, "Wow!" Included in Part III are instructions for making a presentation livelier and more original, both when you create your presentation and when you deliver it.

✦ **Part IV: Excel:** Shows the many different ways to crunch the numbers with the bean counter in the Office suite. Along the way, you find out how to design worksheets that are easy to read and understand, use data-validation rules to cut down on entry mistakes, and analyze your data. You find out just how useful Excel can be for financial analyses, data tracking, and forecasting.

✦ **Part V: OneNote:** Tells you how to take notes and organize notes so that you can find them when you need them. You discover how to use the different OneNote amenities, including how to capture screenshots in notes, take audio notes, and convert handwritten notes to text.

✦ **Part VI: Office: One Step Beyond:** For people who want to take full advantage of Office, Part VI delves into customizing the Office programs, and recording and running macros. It looks into some auxiliary programs that come with Office, including the Picture Manager and the Clip Organizer. It also looks into alternative ways to distribute your work — in a blog or a Web page, for example. Finally, you get a quick tour of Office Web Apps, the online versions of Word, Excel, PowerPoint, and OneNote.

What Makes This Book Different

You are holding in your hands a computer book designed to make learning the Office programs as easy and comfortable as possible. Besides the fact that this book is easy to read, it's different from other books about Office. Read on to see why.

Easy-to-look-up information

This book is a reference, and that means that readers have to be able to find instructions quickly. To that end, I have taken great pains to make sure that the material in this book is well organized and easy to find. The descriptive headings help you find information quickly. The bulleted and numbered lists make following instructions simpler. The tables make options easier to understand and compare.

I want you to be able to look down the page and see in a heading or list with the name of the topic that concerns you. I want you to be able to find instructions quickly. Compare the table of contents in this book to the book next to it on the bookstore shelf. The table of contents in this book is put together to present topics in a way to help you find them in a hurry.

A task-oriented approach

Most computer books describe what the software is, but this book explains how to complete tasks with the software. I assume that you came to this book because you want to know how to *do* something — print form letters, create a worksheet, or create a PowerPoint presentation. You came to the right place. This book describes how to get tasks done.

Meaningful screen shots

The screen shots in this book show only the part of the screen that illustrates what is being explained in the text. When instructions refer to one part of the screen, only that part of the screen is shown. I took great care to make sure that the screen shots in this book serve to help you understand the Office programs and how they work. Compare this book to the next one on the bookstore shelf. Do you see how clean the screen shots in this book are?

Foolish Assumptions

Please forgive me, but I made one or two foolish assumptions about you, the reader of this book. I assumed that:

✦ You own a copy of Office 2010 Home and Student edition and have installed it on your computer.

✦ You use a Windows operating system. All people who have the Windows operating system installed on their computers are invited to read this book. It serves for people who have Windows 7, Windows Vista, Windows XP, and Windows NT.

✦ You are kind to foreign tourists and small animals.

Conventions Used in This Book

I want you to understand all the instructions in this book, and in that spirit, I've adopted a few conventions.

Where you see boldface letters or numbers in this book, it means to type the letters or numbers. For example, "Enter **25** in the Percentage text box" means to do exactly that: Enter the number 25.

Sometimes two tabs on the Ribbon have the same name. To distinguish tabs with the same name from one another, I sometimes include one tab's "Tools" heading in parentheses if there could be confusion about which tab I'm referring to. In PowerPoint, for example, when you see the words "(Table Tools) Design tab," I'm referring to the Design tab for creating tables, not the Design tab for changing a slide's appearance. (Book I, Chapter 1 describes the Ribbon and the tabs in detail.)

To show you how to step through command sequences, I use the ➪ symbol. For example, on the Home tab in Word, you can click the Change Styles button and choose Style Set➪Distinctive to change the look of a document. The ➪ symbol is just a shorthand method of saying "Choose Style Set and then choose Distinctive."

To give most commands, you can press combinations of keys. For example, pressing Ctrl+S saves the file you're working on. In other words, you hold down the Ctrl key and press the S key to save a file. Where you see Ctrl+, Alt+, or Shift+ and a key name or key names, press the keys simultaneously.

 Yet another way to give a command is to click a button. When I tell you to click a button, you see a small illustration of the button in the margin of this book (unless the button is too large to fit in the margin). The button shown here is the Save button, the one you can click to save a file.

Icons Used in This Book

To help you get the most out of this book, I've placed icons here and there. Here's what the icons mean:

Next to the Tip icon, you can find shortcuts and tricks of the trade to make your visit to Officeland more enjoyable.

Where you see the Warning icon, tread softly and carefully. It means that you are about to do something that you may regret later.

When I explain a juicy little fact that bears remembering, I mark it with a Remember icon. When you see this icon, prick up your ears. You will discover something that you need to remember throughout your adventures with Word, Excel, PowerPoint, or the other Office program I am demystifying.

When I am forced to describe high-tech stuff, a Technical Stuff icon appears in the margin. You don't have to read what's beside the Technical Stuff icons if you don't want to, although these technical descriptions often help you understand how a software feature works.

Good Luck, Reader!

If you have a comment about this book, a question, or a shortcut you would like to share with me, address an e-mail message to me at this address: peterwev@gmail.com. Be advised that I usually can't answer e-mail right away because I'm too darned busy. I do appreciate comments and questions, however, because they help me pass my dreary days in captivity.

Book I

Common Office Tools

The 5th Wave   By Rich Tennant

"The odd thing is he always insists on using the latest version of Office."

Contents at a Glance

Chapter 1: Office Nuts and Bolts **9**

A Survey of Office 2010 Home and
Student Programs 9

Starting an Office Program 10

Finding Your Way around the Office
Interface 13

Saving Your Files 20

Navigating the Save As and
Open Dialog Boxes................................25

Opening and Closing Files 26

Reading and Recording File Properties 28

Locking a File with a Password 29

Chapter 2: Wrestling with the Text **33**

Manipulating the Text 33

Changing the Look of Text 36

Quick Ways to Handle Case, or
Capitalization 42

Entering Symbols and Foreign
Characters 44

Finding and Replacing Text......................45

Creating Hyperlinks..................................53

**Chapter 3: Speed Techniques Worth
Knowing About** **59**

Undoing and Repeating Commands 59

Zooming In, Zooming Out 61

Viewing a File through More
Than One Window 62

Correcting Typos on the Fly 62

**Chapter 4: Taking Advantage
of the Proofing Tools** **67**

Correcting Your Spelling Errors 67

Checking for Grammatical Errors
in Word 73

Researching a Topic inside
an Office Program 74

Finding the Right Word with the
Thesaurus 77

Proofing Text Written in a Foreign
Language...79

Chapter 5: Creating a Table **83**

Talking Table Jargon 83

Creating a Table.......................................84

Entering the Text and Numbers 86

Selecting Different Parts of a Table..........86

Aligning Text in Columns and Rows........87

Merging and Splitting Cells......................87

Laying Out Your Table..............................88

Formatting Your Table..............................91

Using Math Formulas in Word Tables........95

Neat Table Tricks 96

Chapter 6: Creating a Chart **103**

A Mercifully Brief Anatomy Lesson........103

The Basics: Creating a Chart...................105

Choosing the Right Chart 107

Providing the Raw Data for Your Chart........124

Positioning Your Chart in a
Workbook, Page, or Slide.....................124

Changing a Chart's Appearance 125

Saving a Chart as a Template So
That You Can Use It Again...................133

Chart Tricks for the Daring
and Heroic 134

Troubleshooting a Chart 138

Chapter 7: Making a SmartArt Diagram . . . **141**

The Basics: Creating SmartArt
Diagrams 141

Creating the Initial Diagram 143

Changing the Size and Position
of a Diagram 145

Laying Out the Diagram Shapes..............145

Handling the Text on Diagram Shapes 151

Changing a Diagram's Direction 153

Choosing a Look for Your Diagram........154

Changing the Appearance
of Diagram Shapes 155

**Chapter 8: Drawing and Manipulating
Lines, Shapes, and Other Objects** **159**

The Basics: Drawing Lines, Arrows,
and Shapes 160

Handling Lines, Arrows,
and Connectors....................................161

Handling Rectangles, Ovals,
Stars, and Other Shapes 165

WordArt for Bending, Spindling,
and Mutilating Text 169

Manipulating Lines, Shapes, Art,
Text Boxes, and Other Objects...........170

Changing an Object's Color, Outline
Color, and Transparency.....................182

Chapter 1: Office Nuts and Bolts

In This Chapter

✔ Introducing the Office programs

✔ Running an Office program

✔ Exploring the Office interface

✔ Saving and auto-recovering your files

✔ Opening and closing an Office file

✔ Recording a file's document properties

✔ Clamping a password on a file

C hapter 1 is where you get your feet wet with Office 2010 Home and Student edition. Walk right to the shore and sink your toes in the water. Don't worry; I won't push you from behind.

In this chapter, you meet the Office Home and Student edition programs and discover speed techniques for opening programs and files. I show you around the Ribbon, Quick Access toolbar, and other Office program landmarks. I also show you how to open files, save files, and clamp a password on a file.

A Survey of Office 2010 Home and Student Programs

Office 2010 Home and Student edition is a collection of four computer programs:

✦ **Word:** A word processor for writing letters, reports, and so on. A Word file is called a *document* (see Book II).

✦ **PowerPoint:** A means of creating slide presentations to give in front of audiences. A PowerPoint file is called a *presentation,* or sometimes a *slide show* (see Book III).

✦ **Excel:** A number cruncher for performing numerical analyses. An Excel file is called a *workbook* (see Book IV).

✦ **OneNote:** A program for taking notes and brainstorming (see Book V).

Other Office 2010 editions

As a proud owner of Office 2010 Home and Student edition, your Office software comes with Word, PowerPoint, Excel, and OneNote. Other editions of Office come with these programs as well:

✔ **Outlook:** A personal information manager, scheduler, and e-mailer (in the Home and Business and the Professional editions)

✔ **Publisher:** A means of creating desktop-publishing files — pamphlets, notices, newsletters, and the like (in the Professional edition)

✔ **Access:** A database management program (in the Professional edition)

The easiest way to find out which edition of Office you have is to click the Start button, choose All Programs, and choose Microsoft Office. The submenu shows which Office programs are available to you.

Office 2010 also comes with the *Clip Organizer,* for managing and inserting clip-art images in files and managing media files on your computer, and the *Picture Manger,* for inserting and editing pictures. These programs are explained in Book VI.

If you're new to Office, don't be daunted by the prospect of having to study so many different computer programs. The programs have much in common. You find the same commands throughout Office. For example, the method of choosing fonts is the same in Word, PowerPoint, and Excel. Creating diagrams and charts works the same in Word, PowerPoint, and Excel. Book I describes tasks that are common to all or most of the Office programs. Master one Office program and you're well on your way to mastering the next.

Starting an Office Program

Unless you start an Office program, you can't create a document, construct a worksheet, or make a database. Many have tried to undertake these tasks with mud and paper-mâché without starting a program first, but all have failed. Here are the various ways to start an Office program:

✦ **The old-fashioned way:** Click the Start button, choose All Programs⇨ Microsoft Office, and then choose the program's name on the submenu.

✦ **The Start menu:** Click the program's name on the Start menu, as shown in Figure 1-1. The *Start menu* is the menu you see when you click the Start button. By placing a program's name on the Start menu, you can open the program simply by clicking the Start button and then clicking the program's name. To place an Office program on the Start menu:

1. **Click the Start button and choose All Programs➪Microsoft Office.**

2. **Move the pointer over the program's name on the submenu, but don't click to select the program's name.**

3. **Right-click the program's name and choose Pin to Start Menu on the shortcut menu that appears.**

   To remove a program's name from the Start menu, right-click the name and choose Remove from This List.

✦ **Desktop shortcut icon:** Double-click the program's shortcut icon (see Figure 1-1). A *shortcut icon* is an icon you can double-click to do something in a hurry. By creating a shortcut icon on the Windows desktop, you can double-click the icon and immediately start an Office program. To place an Office shortcut icon on the desktop:

1. **Click the Start button and choose All Programs➪Microsoft Office.**

2. **Move the pointer over the program's name on the submenu, but don't click the program's name.**

Click a program on the Start menu   Double-click a shortcut icon

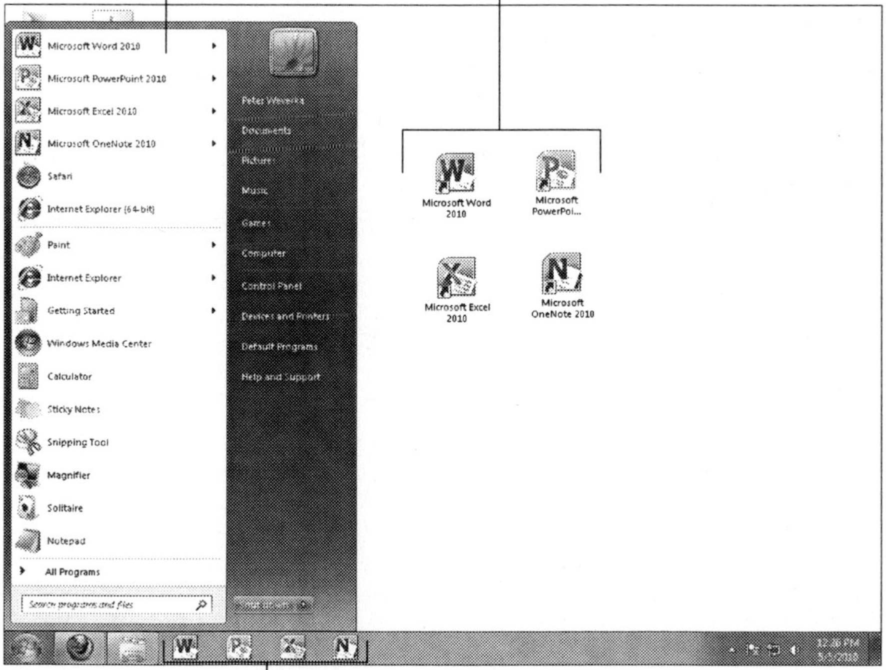

Figure 1-1:
Three of several ways to start an Office program.

Click an icon on this taskbar

3. **Right-click the program's name and choose Send To⇨Desktop (Create Shortcut) on the shortcut menu that appears.**

   To remove a desktop shortcut icon from the Windows desktop, right-click it, choose Delete, and click Yes in the Delete Shortcut dialog box. Don't worry about deleting a program when you delete its shortcut icon. All you do when you choose Delete is remove the program's shortcut icon from the desktop and make your desktop a little less crowded.

✦ **Taskbar (Windows 7 only):** Click the program's icon on the taskbar, as shown in Figure 1-1. To place a program's icon on the taskbar, right-click its name on the Start menu or All Programs menu and choose Pin to Taskbar. To remove a program's icon from the taskbar, right-click it and choose Unpin This Program from Taskbar.

✦ **Quick Launch toolbar (Windows Vista and XP only):** Click a shortcut icon on the Quick Launch toolbar. The Quick Launch toolbar appears on the Windows taskbar and is easy to find. Wherever your work takes you, you can see the Quick Launch toolbar and click its shortcut icons to start programs. Create a shortcut icon and follow these steps to place a copy of it on the Quick Launch toolbar:

1. **Click the shortcut icon to select it.**

2. **Hold down the Ctrl key.**

3. **Drag the shortcut icon onto the Quick Launch toolbar.**

   To change an icon's position on the toolbar, drag it to the left or the right. To remove an icon, right-click it and choose Delete.

Starting a program along with your computer

Yet another way to start an Office program is to make the program start automatically whenever you turn on your computer. If you're the president of the Office Fan Club and you have to run, for example, Word each time your computer starts, create a Word shortcut icon and copy it into the Startup folder.

Note which Windows operating system you have, and copy the shortcut icon into the Startup folder in one of these locations:

✔ **Windows 7 and Vista:** `C:\Users\`*`Username`*`\AppData\Roaming\Microsoft\Windows\Start Menu\Programs\Startup`

✔ **Windows XP:** `C:\Documents and Settings\`*`Username`*`\Start Menu\Programs\Startup`

Finding Your Way around the Office Interface

Interface, also called the *user interface,* is a computer term that describes how a software program presents itself to the people who use it (and you probably thought *interface* meant two people kissing). These pages give you a quick tour of the Office interface and explain what the various parts of the interface are. You will be glad to know that the interface of all the Office programs is pretty much the same. Click along with me as I describe the interface and you'll know what's what by the time you finish reading these pages.

The File tab

In the upper-left corner of the window is the *File tab,* as shown in Figure 1-2. Go to the File tab to find commands for creating, opening, and saving files, as well as doing other file-management tasks. Notice the Options command on the File tab. You can choose Options to open the Options dialog box and tell the program you are working in how you want it to work.

Figure 1-2:
The File tab and Quick Access toolbar are always available.

File tab

Quick Access toolbar

⚠️ WARNING!

To leave the File tab, click a different tab on the Ribbon — Home, Insert, or another tab. Be sure *not* to choose the Exit command on the File tab menu. Doing so closes the Office program you are working in.

The Quick Access toolbar

No matter where you travel in an Office program, you see the *Quick Access toolbar* in the upper-left corner of the screen (refer to Figure 1-2). This toolbar offers three necessary buttons: the all-important Save button, the trusty Undo button, and the convenient Repeat button. You can place more buttons on the Quick Access toolbar as well as move the toolbar lower in the window. I explain how to customize the Quick Access toolbar in Book VI, Chapter 1.

By the way, Microsoft wants you to call the Quick Access toolbar the QAT, or "kwat," but I don't think you should do that. Others might think you have indigestion.

The Ribbon and its tabs

Across the top of the screen is the *Ribbon,* an assortment of different *tabs;* click a tab to undertake a task. For example, click the Home tab to format text; click the Insert tab to insert a table or chart. Figure 1-3 shows what you see in Word when you click the Home, Insert, and Page Layout tabs on the Ribbon. Each tab offers a different set of buttons, menus, and galleries.

Practically speaking, your first step when you start a new task is to click a tab on the Ribbon. Knowing which tab to click takes awhile, but the names of tabs — Home, Insert, View, and so on — hint as to which commands you find when you visit a tab.

To make the Ribbon disappear and get more room to view items onscreen, click the Minimize the Ribbon button (or press Ctrl+F1). This button is located on the right side of the Ribbon, to the left of the Help button. You can also right-click the Ribbon and choose Minimize the Ribbon on the shortcut menu, or double-click a tab on the Ribbon. To see the Ribbon again, click the Minimize the Ribbon button, press Ctrl+F1, double-click a Ribbon tab, or right-click a tab name or the Quick Access toolbar and deselect Minimize the Ribbon on the shortcut menu. While the Ribbon is minimized, you can click a tab name to display a tab.

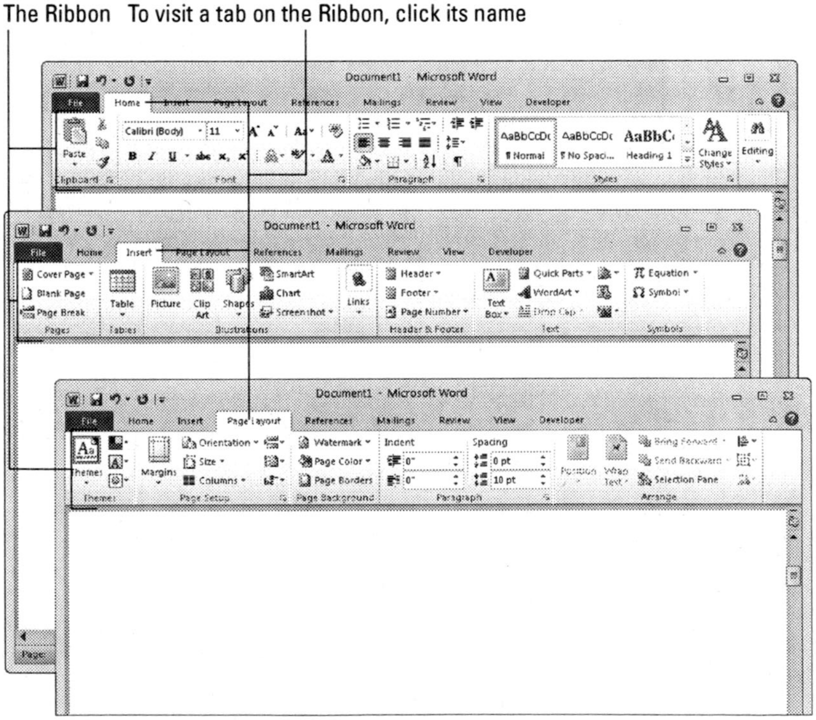

The Ribbon   To visit a tab on the Ribbon, click its name

Figure 1-3: The commands are different on each tab on the Ribbon.

How many buttons appear on some of the tabs depends on the size of your monitor screen. On narrow 800 x 600 screens, Office sometimes can't find enough room to display all the buttons on a tab, so it presents you with a primary button to click in order to get to the other buttons. Throughout this book, I endeavor to tell you which button you click if your monitor has a narrow as well as a wide screen, but if the instructions in this book tell you to click a button and you don't see it, you have to click a primary button first. Look around for the primary button and then click it to get to the secondary button.

Context-sensitive tabs

Sorry for dropping the term *context-sensitive* on you. I usually steer clear of these horrid computer terms, but I can't help it this time because Microsoft calls some tabs context-sensitive, and by golly, I have to call them that, too.

To keep the Ribbon from getting too crowded with tabs, some tabs appear only in context — they appear on the Ribbon after you insert or click something. In Figure 1-4, for example, I inserted a table, and two additional tabs — the Design and the Layout tab — appear on the Ribbon under the heading "Table Tools." These context-sensitive tabs offer commands for designing and laying out tables. When I click the (Table Tools) Design tab, as Figure 1-4 shows, I see commands for putting colors and borders on tables. The idea behind context-sensitive tabs is to direct you to the commands you need and exclude all other commands.

Select or insert an item . . .   and you get context-sensitive tabs

Figure 1-4:
After you insert or select an item, context-sensitive tabs appear on the Ribbon.

Critter Population Levels

	Deer	Bear	Wombat
California	150,000	8,000	42,000
Nevada	45,000	2,000	23,000
Arizona	23,000	2,500	112,000

If you're looking for a tab on the Ribbon but can't find it, the tab is probably context-sensitive. You have to insert or select an item to make some tabs appear on the Ribbon. Context-sensitive tabs appear on the right side of the Ribbon under a heading with the word *Tools* in its name.

Context-sensitive tab names can be confusing because sometimes they repeat the names of other tabs. When I refer to a context-sensitive tab name in this book, I include its Tools heading in parentheses in case there is any confusion about which tab I'm referring to. In PowerPoint, for example, the Design tab that always appears on the Ribbon is the *Design tab,* but the context-sensitive Design tab is the *(Table Tools) Design tab.*

The anatomy of a tab

All tabs are different in terms of the commands they offer, but all are the same insofar as how they present commands. On every tab, you find groups and buttons. Some tabs also offer galleries. Groups, buttons, galleries — what's up with that?

Groups

Commands on each tab are organized into *groups.* The names of these groups appear below the buttons and galleries on tabs. For example, the Home tab in Excel is organized into several groups, including the Clipboard, Font, Alignment, Number, Styles, Cells, and Editing group, as shown in Figure 1-5.

Figure 1-5:
Each tab is organized into groups; some groups offer group buttons.

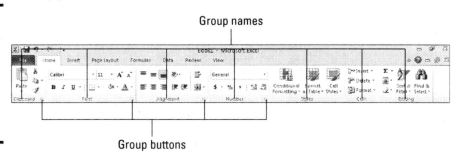

Group names

Group buttons

Groups tell you what the buttons and galleries above their names are used for. On the Home tab in Excel, for example, the buttons in the Font group are for formatting text. Read group names to help find the command you need.

Group buttons

Many groups have a *group button* that you can click to open a dialog box or task pane (officially, Microsoft calls these little buttons *dialog box launchers,* but let's act like grownups, shall we?). Group buttons are found to the right of group names (refer to Figure 1-5). Moving the pointer over a group button opens a pop-up help box with a description and picture of the dialog box or task pane that appears when the button is clicked.

As with tabs on the Ribbon, group buttons are context-sensitive (there's that term again!). Whether you can click a group button to open a dialog box or task pane depends on the context in which you're working. Sometimes the buttons are grayed out because they don't pertain to the task you're currently doing.

Buttons

Go to any tab and you find buttons of all shapes and sizes. Square buttons and rectangular buttons. Big and small buttons. Buttons with labels and buttons without labels. Is there any rhyme or reason to these button shapes and sizes? No, there isn't.

What matters isn't a button's shape or size, but whether a down-pointing arrow appears on its face:

 ✦ **A button with an arrow:** Click a button *with* an arrow and you get a drop-down list with options you can choose.

 ✦ **A button without an arrow:** Click a button *without* an arrow and you complete an action of some kind.

 ✦ **A hybrid button with an arrow:** Some buttons serve a dual purpose as a button and a drop-down list. By clicking the symbol on the top half of the button, you complete an action; by clicking the arrow on the bottom half of the button, you open a drop-down list. On the Home tab, for example, clicking the top half of the Paste button pastes what is on the Clipboard into your file, but clicking the bottom half of the button opens a drop-down list with Paste options.

You can find out what clicking a button does by moving the pointer over it. You see a pop-up description of what the button is for.

Galleries

Built into some tabs are galleries like the one shown in Figure 1-6. The gallery in the figure pertains to charts: the Chart Styles gallery is for formatting charts. A *gallery* presents you with visual options for changing an item. When you move the pointer over a gallery choice, the item on your page or slide — the table, chart, or diagram, for example — changes appearance. In galleries, you can preview different choices before you click to select the choice you want.

Click the More button to open the gallery in a drop-down list

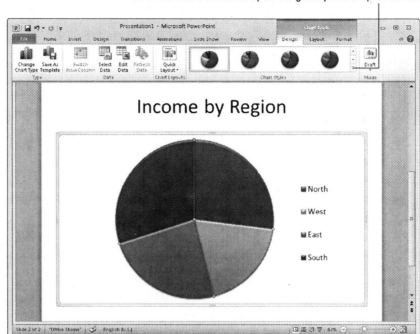

Figure 1-6:
Galleries
present you
with visual
choices.

To view and make choices on a gallery:

✦ Move the pointer over gallery choices and watch how the item or items
on-screen change.

✦ Click a scroll arrow to see more gallery choices on the tab.

✦ Click the More button (see Figure 1-6) to open the gallery choices in a
drop-down list and see many choices at once.

✦ Click a gallery choice to apply it.

Live previewing

Thanks to *live previewing,* you can see the results of a menu or gallery
choice before actually making the choice. Here's how live previewing works:
Move the pointer over an option in a gallery or drop-down list and glance at
your page or slide. You can see the results of selecting the option. For example, you see a different font or shape color. You can judge whether choosing
the option is worthwhile without choosing the option first. Live previewing
liberates you from repeatedly choosing commands, backtracking, and trying
again until you get it right.

Right-clicking to open a shortcut menu

Similar to mini-toolbars are the shortcut menus you get when you right-click. *Right-click* means to click the right, not the left, mouse button. Right-click just about anywhere and you get a shortcut menu of some kind. The shortcut menus differ, depending on what you right-click.

Right-clicking sometimes gets you to the command you need without having to select a different tab. I right-click more than usual in Office to keep from switching from tab to tab on the Ribbon.

Mini-toolbars

A *mini-toolbar* is a ghost-like toolbar that appears on-screen to help you do a task, as shown in Figure 1-7. Move the pointer over the mini-toolbar, and it ceases being ghost-like, as Figure 1-7 demonstrates. Now you can select an option from a drop-down list or click a button on the mini-toolbar to complete a task.

Figure 1-7:
Move the pointer over the mini-toolbar to make it come alive.

The mini-toolbar, as shown in Figure 1-7, appears when you select text and then move the pointer over selected text. Don't be frightened of these ghost-like mini-toolbars. Keep your eyes open for them. Mini-toolbars are very convenient, and they save you the trouble of going to a different tab to complete a task.

Office 2010 for keyboard lovers

People who like to give commands by pressing keyboard shortcuts may well ask, "Where are the keyboard shortcuts in Office?" The answer is: They're still there. For example, you can press Ctrl+B to boldface text and Ctrl+U to underline text.

Office offers Alt+key shortcuts as well. Press the Alt key and letters —
they're called *KeyTips* — appear on tab names, as shown in Figure 1-8. After
you press the Alt key, follow these instructions to make use of KeyTips:

✦ **Go to a tab:** Press a KeyTip on a tab to visit a tab.

✦ **Make KeyTips appear on menu items:** Press a KeyTip on a button or
gallery to make KeyTips appear on menu items.

Figure 1-8:
Press the
Alt key to
see KeyTips.

Saving Your Files

Soon after you create a new file, be sure to save it. And save your file from
time to time while you work on it as well. Until you save your work, it rests
in the computer's electronic memory (RAM), a precarious location. If a
power outage occurs or your computer stalls, you lose all the work you did
since the last time you saved your file. Make it a habit to save files every ten
minutes or so or when you complete an important task.

These pages explain how to save a file, name a file, choose the folder where
you want to save a file, declare where you want to save files by default, save
files for use in 97-2003 editions of Office, and handle files that were saved
automatically after a computer failure.

Saving a file

To save a file:

✦ Click the Save button (you'll find it on the Quick Access toolbar).

✦ Press Ctrl+S.

✦ Go to the File tab and choose Save.

Saving a file for the first time

The first time you save a presentation, the Save As dialog box opens. It
invites you to give the file a name and choose a folder in which to store it.

Enter a descriptive name in the File Name text box. To locate a folder for storing your presentation, see "Navigating the Save As and Open Dialog Boxes," later in this chapter.

Declaring where you like to save files

When you attempt to save a file for the first time in the Save As dialog box, Office shows you the contents of the Document folder (in Windows 7 and Windows Vista) or the My Documents folder (in Windows XP) on the assumption that you keep most of your files in that folder. The Documents folder is the center of the universe as far as Office is concerned, but perhaps you keep the majority of your files in a different folder. How would you like to see it first in the Save As and Open dialog boxes?

To direct Office to the folder you like best and make it appear first in the Save As and Open dialog boxes, follow these steps:

> File

1. In Word, Excel, or PowerPoint, go to the File tab and choose Options.

You see the Options dialog box.

2. Select the General category.

Figure 1-9 shows the topmost options in this category.

3. In the Default File Location text box, enter the address of the folder where you prefer to keep your files.

For example, if you're fond of keeping files in the My Stuff folder on the C drive of your computer, enter **C:\My Stuff**, or click the Browse button (if it's available) and select the My Stuff folder in the Modify Location dialog box.

4. Click OK.

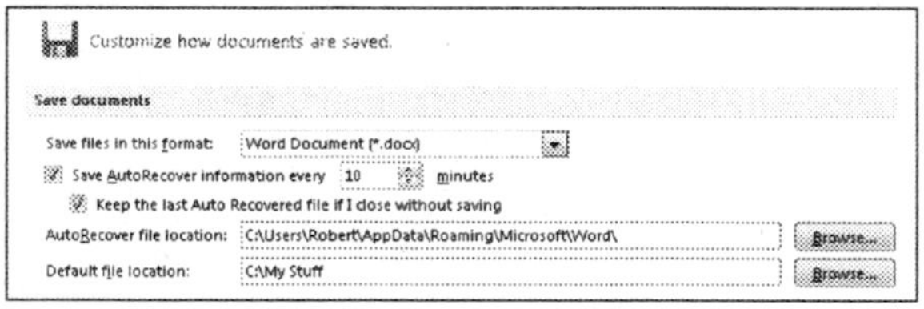

Figure 1-9:
The Save options in the Options dialog box.

Saving files for use in earlier versions of an Office program

Not everyone is a proud owner of Office 2010 Home and Student edition. Before you pass along a file to a co-worker who has Office 2003, XP, 2000, or

97, save your document so that your co-worker can open it. People with versions of Office prior to version 2010 and 2007 cannot open your Office files unless you save your files for earlier versions of Office.

You can tell whether a Word, PowerPoint, or Excel file is formatted for a 2010 program or an earlier version of the program by glancing at its file extension. PowerPoint, Excel, and Word files have four-letter, not three-letter file extensions. Table 1-1 lists Office program file extensions.

Table 1-1	Office program file extensions	
Program	*2010, 2007*	*97–2003*
Excel	`.xlsx`	`.xls`
PowerPoint	`.pptx`	`.ppt`
Word	`.docx`	`.doc`

Saving a file for use in Office 97–2003

Follow these steps to save a file so that someone with Office 97, 2000, XP, or 2003 can open it:

1. **Go to the File tab.**

2. **Choose Save & Send.**

   You see the Save & Send window.

3. **Under File Types, choose Change File Type and then choose the 97-2003 option for saving files.**

   The Save As dialog box opens.

4. **Enter a new name for the file, if necessary.**

5. **Click the Save button.**

   You can tell when you're working on a file saved in the 97–2003 format because the words "Compatibility Mode" appear in the title bar next to the file's name. The title bar is located at the top of the screen.

Files saved in the 97–2003 format have a different file extension. Instead of a four-letter file extension that ends in *x*, they have a three-letter extension without the *x* (see Table 1-1, shown previously).

Saving files by default for earlier versions of Office

If you're way ahead of the pack and you always have to save files in a different format so that co-workers can open them, make the different format the default format for saving all your files. That way, you don't have to choose a new format whenever you pass along a file to a co-worker.

Follow these steps to change the default format for saving files:

File

1. **Go to the File tab and choose Options.**

   The Options dialog box appears.

2. **In Word, Excel, and PowerPoint, go to the Save category.**

3. **In the Save Files in This Format drop-down list, choose the 97–2003 format.**

4. **Click OK.**

   Remember that you made 97–2003 the default format for saving files. At some point, when the world catches up to you and 97–2003 files have become obsolete, return to the Options dialog box and choose the most up-to-date format.

Converting Office 97–2003 files to 2010

When you open a file made in an earlier version of Office, the program switches to *compatibility mode.* Features that weren't part of earlier versions of the program are shut down. You can tell when a file is in compatibility mode because the words *Compatibility Mode* appear in the title bar next to the file's name.

Follow these steps to convert a 97–2003 file for use in an Office 2010 program:

1. **Go to the File tab.**

2. **Choose Info.**

3. **Click the Convert button.**

   A dialog box informs you what converting means. If you don't see the Convert option, your file has been converted already.

4. **Click OK.**

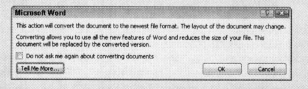

When disaster strikes!

After your computer fails and you restart an Office program, you see the Document Recovery task pane with a list of files that were open when the failure occurred:

- ✔ *AutoSave* files are files that Office saves as part of its AutoRecovery procedure (see "Saving AutoRecovery information").

- ✔ *Original* files are files that you save by clicking the Save button.

The Document Recovery task pane tells you when each file was saved. By studying the time listings, you can tell which version of a file — the AutoRecovery file or the file you saved — is most up to date.

Open the drop-down list for a file and select one of these options:

- ✔ **View:** Opens the file so that you can examine and work on it. If you want to keep it, click the Save button.

- ✔ **Save As:** Opens the Save As dialog box so that you can save the file under a

different name. Choose this command to keep a copy of the recovered file on hand in case you need it.

- ✔ **Close:** Closes the file.

- ✔ **Show Repairs:** Shows repairs made to the file (for use with repaired Word documents).

Saving AutoRecovery information

To insure against data loss due to computer and power failures, Office saves files on its own every ten minutes. These files are saved in an AutoRecovery file. After your computer fails, you can try to recover some of the work you lost by getting it from the AutoRecovery file (see "When disaster strikes!").

Office saves AutoRecovery files every ten minutes, but if you want the program to save the files more or less frequently, you can change the AutoRecovery setting. Auto-recovering taxes a computer's memory. If your computer is sluggish, consider making AutoRecovery files at intervals longer than ten minutes; if your computer fails often and you're worried about losing data, make AutoRecovery files more frequently.

Follow these steps to tell Office how often to save data in an AutoRecovery file:

File

1. **On the File tab, choose Options.**

The Options dialog box appears.

2. **Select the Save category (refer to Figure 1-9).**

3. **Enter a Minutes setting in the Save AutoRecover Information Every box.**

4. **Click OK.**

Navigating the Save As and Open Dialog Boxes

The Open dialog box and Save As dialog box offer a bunch of different ways to locate a file you want to open or locate the folder where you want to save a file. Figure 1-10 shows the Open dialog box. I'm happy to report that both dialog boxes, Open and Save As, work the same way.

✦ **Retracing your search:** Click the Back and Forward buttons (or open the drop-down list on the Back button) to retrace your search for a folder or revisit a folder you previously visited.

Change views   Search for a file in a file folder

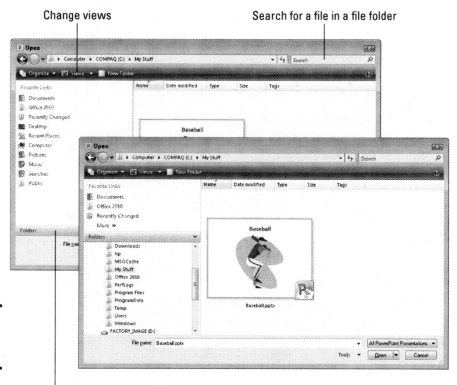

Figure 1-10:
The Open
dialog box.

Click to display the Navigation pane

+ **Searching for files in a folder:** Use the Search box to search for sub-folders and files in the folder you're currently viewing. After you type the first few letters of a filename or subfolder, you see only the names of items that start with the letters you typed. To see all the files and sub-folders again, click the Close button (the *X*) in the Search box.

+ **Changing views:** Display folder contents differently by choosing a view on the Views drop-down list (in Windows 7, look for the View arrow in the upper-right corner of the dialog box). In Details view, you see how large files are and when they were last edited.

+ **Creating a new folder:** Click the New Folder button to create a new subfolder for storing files. Select the folder that your new folder will be subordinate to and click the New Folder button. Then type a name for the saved.

+ **Open one of your favorite folders (Windows Vista):** Select a folder in the Favorite Links list to see its contents. Later in this chapter, "Putting a favorite folder on the Favorite Links list" explains how to place the name of a folder in the list.

+ **Navigate to different folders:** Click the Folders bar (in the lower-left corner of the dialog box) to open the Navigation pane and look for folders or presentations on a different drive, network location, or folder on your computer. If you don't see the Folders bar, click the Organize button and choose Layout⇨Navigation Pane.

Opening and Closing Files

To get to work on a file, you have to open it first. And, of course, you close a file when you're finished working on it and want to stop and smell the roses. The following pages explain all the intricate details of opening and closing files. In these pages, you find many tips for finding and opening the file you want to work on.

Opening a file

Between the two of them, Office and Windows offer many shortcuts for opening files. To open a file, take the standard route — go to the File tab and choose Open — or take advantage of the numerous ways to open files quickly.

The slow, conventional way to open a file

If you can't open a file by any other means, you have to resort to the Open dialog box:

File

1. **On the File tab, choose Open (or press Ctrl+O).**

You see the Open dialog box (refer to Figure 1-10).

2. **Locate and select the file you want to open.**

Earlier in this chapter, "Navigating the Save As and Open dialog boxes" offers some tricks for locating a file in the Open dialog box.

3. **Click the Open button.**

Your file opens. You can also double-click a filename to open a file.

Speed techniques for opening files

As shown in Figure 1-11, the fastest way to open a file is to go to the File tab, choose Recent, and choose the file's name on the Recent Documents list. This list shows the names of the last 22 files you opened. By moving the pointer over a name, you can see which folder a file is stored in. Click the pin next to a name to make the name remain on the list even if it isn't one of the last several files you opened (click the pin a second time to "unpin" a name).

Click to "pin" a name to the list

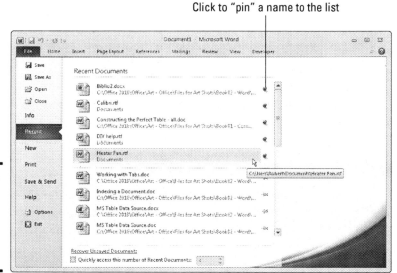

Figure 1-11:
Opening
a file on
the Recent
Documents
list.

To make more (or fewer) than 22 filenames appear on the Recent Documents list, go the File tab in Word, Excel, or PowerPoint, and choose Options. In the Options dialog box, visit the Advanced category, scroll to the Display section, and enter a number in the Show This Number of Recent Documents text box.

Here are other speed techniques for opening files:

✦ **In Windows Explorer or Computer:** Locate the file in one of these file-management programs and double-click its name.

✦ **Shortcut icon:** Create a shortcut icon to a file and place the icon on the Windows desktop. In Windows Explorer or the Open dialog box, right-click the file's name and choose Send To⇨Desktop (Create Shortcut). To quickly open the file, double-click its shortcut icon on the desktop.

Closing a file

Closing a file is certainly easier than opening one. To close a file, save your file and use one of these techniques:

✦ On the File tab, choose Close. The program remains open although the file is closed.

✦ Click the Close button — the *X* in the upper-right corner of the window. (Alternatively, press Alt+F4.) Clicking the Close button closes the program as well as the file.

✦ Click the program icon (in the upper-left corner of the screen) and choose Close.

If you try to close a file without first saving it, a message box asks whether ditching your file is in your best interests, and you get a chance to click Save in the message box and save your file. Sometimes closing a file without saving the changes you made to it is worthwhile. If you made a bunch of editorial mistakes and want to start over, you can close the file without saving the changes you made. Next time you open the file, you see the version that you had before you made all those mistakes.

Reading and Recording File Properties

Properties are a means of describing a file. If you manage two dozen or more files, you owe it to yourself to record properties. You can use them later to identify files.

File

To read property descriptions, go to the File tab and examine the Information window. Property descriptions are found on the right side of the window, as shown in Figure 1-12.

To record even more descriptions, click the Properties button and choose one of these commands on the drop-down list:

✦ **Show Document Panel:** The Document Properties panel appears so that you can enter more descriptions and comments.

✦ **Advanced Properties:** The Properties dialog box appears. Enter information about your file on the Summary and Custom tab.

You can read a file's properties without opening a file. In Windows Explorer, Computer, or the Open dialog box, right-click a file's name and choose

Properties. You see the Properties dialog box. Go to the Details tab to see descriptions you entered.

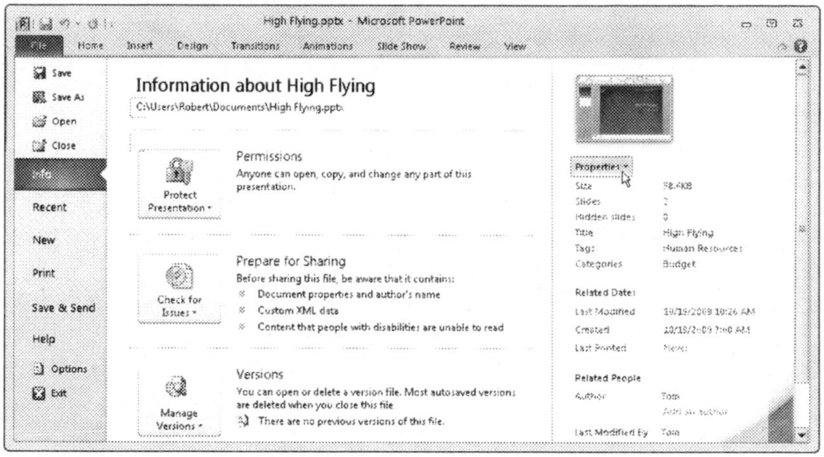

Figure 1-12:
Enter
properties
in the
Information
window.

Word, Excel, and PowerPoint offer a command for erasing document properties. On the File tab, choose Info, click the Check for Issues button, and choose Inspect Document. In the Document Inspector dialog box, click the Inspect button, and then click the Remove All button if you want to remove document properties.

Locking a File with a Password

Perhaps you want to submit your file to others for critical review but you don't want any Tom, Dick, or Harry to look at your file. In that case, lock your file with a password and give out the password only to people whose opinions you trust. These pages explain how to password-protect a file, open a file that is locked with a password, and remove the password from a file.

Password-protecting a file

Follow these steps to clamp a password on a file, such that others need a password to open and perhaps also edit it:

File

1. **Go to the File tab.**

2. **In the Information window, click the Protect Document (or Workbook or Presentation) button, and choose Encrypt with Password on the drop-down list.**

The Encrypt Document dialog box appears, as shown in Figure 1-13.

Figure 1-13:
Enter
passwords
for the file in
this dialog
box.

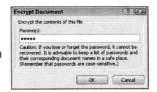

3. **Enter a password in the Password text box and click OK.**

   Others will need the password you enter to open the file. No ifs, ands, or buts. They have to enter the password.

   Passwords are case-sensitive. In other words, you have to enter the correct combination of upper- and lowercase letters to successfully enter the password. If the password is *Valparaiso* (with an uppercase *V*), entering **valparaiso** (with a lowercase v) is deemed the wrong password and doesn't open the file.

4. **In the Confirm Password dialog box, enter the password again.**

   Figure 1-13 shows the Confirm Password dialog box.

5. **Click OK.**

   The Information window informs you that a password is required to open the file.

Putting a favorite folder on the Favorites list

The Favorites list (or Favorite Links list) in the Open dialog box and Save As dialog box gives you the opportunity to go lickety-split to a folder on your computer or network. When you're saving a file for the first time or you want to open a folder, all you have to do is click a folder name on the list to see the contents of the folder. If there's a particular folder you visit often that deserves "favorite" status, you can put that folder on the Favorites list by following these steps:

1. **In the Open or Save As dialog box, locate and select the folder that you want to be a favorite.**

2. **Drag the folder into the Favorites list. That's right — just drag it. Moreover, you can slide it up or down the list to put it where you are most likely to find it.**

To remove a folder from the Favorites list, right-click it and choose Remove Link.

Removing a password from a file

Follow these steps to remove a password from a file:

1. **Open the file that needs its password removed.**

2. **Go to the File tab, and in the Information window, click the Protect Document button, and choose Encrypt with Password.**

   The Encrypt Document dialog box appears (refer to Figure 1-13).

3. **Delete the password and click OK.**

File

Chapter 2: Wrestling with the Text

In This Chapter

✔ Selecting, moving, copying, and deleting text

✔ Changing the appearance, size, and color of text

✔ Changing the case of letters

✔ Inserting foreign characters and symbols

✔ Finding text — and replacing it if you want

✔ Hyperlinking to Web pages and other places in a file

To enter text, all you have to do is wiggle your fingers over the keyboard. Everybody knows that. But not everyone knows all the different ways to change the look and size of text in an Office 2010 file. In this chapter, I explain how to do that as well as how to move, copy, and delete text. You find out how to quickly change a letter's case, enter a symbol or foreign character, and find and replace text in a file. Finally, I show you how to link your files to the Internet by fashioning a hyperlink.

Manipulating the Text

This short but important part of Chapter 2 describes the many techniques for selecting, deleting, copying, and moving text. You find an inordinate number of tips on these pages because there are so many shortcuts for manipulating text. Master the many shortcuts and you cut down considerably on the time you spend editing text.

Selecting text

Before you can do anything to text — move it, boldface it, delete it, translate it — you have to select it. Here are speed techniques for selecting text:

To Select	Do This
A word	Double-click the word.
A few words	Drag over the words.
A paragraph	Triple-click inside the paragraph (in Word and PowerPoint).
A block of text	Click the start of the text, hold down the Shift key, and click the end of the text. In Word you can also click the start of the text, press F8, and click at the end of the text.
All text	Press Ctrl+A.

Word offers a special command for selecting text with similar formats throughout a document. You can use this command to make wholesale changes to text. Select an example of the text that needs changing, and on the Home tab, click the Select button and choose Select Text with Similar Formatting (you may have to click the Editing button first). Then choose formatting commands to change all instances of the text that you selected.

A look at the Paste options

Text adopts the formatting of neighboring text when you move or copy it to a new location. Using the Paste options, however, you can decide for yourself what happens to text formatting when you move or copy text from one place to another. To avail yourself of the Paste options:

- On the Home tab, open the drop-down list on the Paste button to see the Paste Options submenu.

- Right-click to see the Paste options on the shortcut menu.

- Click the Paste Options button to open the Paste Options submenu. This button appears after you paste text by clicking the Paste button or pressing Ctrl+V.

Choose a Paste option to determine what happens to text formatting when you move or copy text to a new location:

- **Keep Source Formatting:** The text keeps its original formatting. Choose this option to move or copy text formatting along with text to a different location.

- **Merge Formatting (Word only):** The text adopts the formatting of the text to where it is moved or copied.

- **Use Destination Theme (Word only):** The text adopts the formatting of the theme you chose for your document (if you chose a theme).

- **Keep Text Only:** The text is stripped of all formatting.

Some people think that the Paste Options button is a bother. If you're one of those people, go to the File tab and choose Options. You see the Options dialog box. Go to the Advanced category and deselect the Show Paste Options Buttons When Content Is Pasted check box.

Moving and copying text

Office offers a number of different ways to move and copy text from place to place. Drum roll, please. . . . Select the text you want to move or copy and then use one of these techniques to move or copy it:

✦ **Dragging and dropping:** Move the mouse over the text and then click and drag the text to a new location. *Drag* means to hold down the mouse button while you move the pointer on-screen. If you want to copy rather than move the text, hold down the Ctrl key while you drag.

✦ **Dragging and dropping with the right mouse button:** Drag the text while holding down the right, not the left, mouse button. After you release the right mouse button, a shortcut menu appears with Move Here and Copy Here options. Choose an option to move or copy the text.

✦ **Using the Clipboard:** Move or copy the text to the Clipboard by clicking the Cut or Copy button, pressing Ctrl+X or Ctrl+C, or right-clicking and choosing Cut or Copy on the shortcut menu. The text is moved or copied to an electronic holding tank called the *Clipboard.* Paste the text by clicking the Paste button, pressing Ctrl+V, or right-clicking and choosing Paste. You can find the Paste, Cut, and Copy buttons on the Home tab.

Taking advantage of the Clipboard task pane

The Windows Clipboard is a piece of work. After you copy or cut text with the Cut or Copy command, the text is placed on the Clipboard. The Clipboard holds the last 24 items that you cut or copied. You can open the Clipboard task pane and view the last 24 items you cut or copied to the Clipboard and cut or copy them anew, as shown in Figure 2-1.

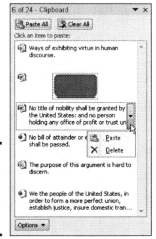

Figure 2-1:
The
Clipboard
task pane in
action.

To open the Clipboard task pane, go to the Home tab and click the Clipboard group button (it's to the right of the word *Clipboard*). Icons next to the items tell you where they came from. To copy an item, click it or open its drop-down list and choose Paste. The Clipboard is available to all Office programs; it's especially useful for copying text and graphics from one Office program to another.

The Options pop-up list at the bottom of the Clipboard task pane offers these options:

✦ **Show Office Clipboard Automatically:** Choose this option if you want the Clipboard task pane to open automatically when you cut or copy two items consecutively or you copy the same item twice.

✦ **Show Office Clipboard When Ctrl+C Pressed Twice:** Choose this option if you want to open the Clipboard task pane by pressing Ctrl+C and Ctrl+C again.

✦ **Collect Without Showing Office Clipboard:** Choose this option to be notified when an item has been cut or copied to the Clipboard by an icon in the system tray and/or a pop-up notice. To be notified, you must have selected either or both of the preceding two options on the Options menu.

✦ **Show Office Clipboard Icon on Taskbar:** Choose this option to be notified when an item has been cut or copied to the Clipboard by an icon in the *system tray,* the part of the Windows taskbar by the clock. (The icon appears after you cut or copy the first item to the Clipboard.) You can double-click the icon to open the Clipboard task pane. After an item is cut or copied to the Clipboard, a tiny page glides across the icon.

✦ **Show Status Near Taskbar When Copying:** Choose this option to be notified when an item has been cut or copied to the Clipboard by a pop-up notice in the lower-right corner of the screen. It tells you how many items have been collected on the Clipboard.

Deleting text

To delete text, select it and press the Delete key. By the way, you can kill two birds with one stone by selecting text and then starting to type. The letters you type immediately take the place of and delete the text you selected.

You can always click the Undo button (or press Ctrl+Z) if you regret deleting text. This button is located on the Quick Access toolbar.

Changing the Look of Text

What text looks like is determined by its font, the size of the letters, the color of the letters, and whether text effects or font styles such as italics or boldface are in the text. What text looks like really matters in Word and

PowerPoint because files you create in those programs are meant to be read by all and sundry. Even in Excel and OneNote, however, font choices matter because the choices you make determine whether your work is easy to read and understand.

A *font* is a collection of letters, numbers, and symbols in a particular typeface, including all italic and boldface variations of the letters, numbers, and symbols. Fonts have beautiful names and some of them are many centuries old. Most computers come with these fonts: Arial, Tahoma, Times New Roman, and Verdana. By default, Office often applies the Calibri and Cambria fonts to text.

Font styles include boldface, italic, and underline. By convention, headings are boldface. Italics are used for emphasis and to mark foreign words in text. Office provides a number of text effects. *Text effects,* also known as *text attributes*, include strikethrough and superscript. Use text effects sparingly.

The following pages look at the different ways to change the font, font size, and color of text, as well as how to assign font styles and text effects to text.

The Format Painter: A fast way to change the look of text

When you're in a hurry to change the look of text and reformat paragraphs, consider using the Format Painter. This nifty tool works something like a paintbrush. You drag it over text to copy formats from place to place. Follow these instructions to use the Format Painter:

1. **Click a place with text and paragraph formats that you want to copy elsewhere (or select the text).**

2. **On the Home tab, click or double-click the Format Painter button (or press Ctrl+Shift+C).**

   You can find the Format Painter button in the Clipboard group. Click the button to copy formats once; double-click to copy formats to more than one location. The pointer changes into a paintbrush.

3. **Drag the pointer across text to which you want to copy the formats.**

   You can go from place to place with the Format Painter.

4. **Click the Format Painter button a second time or press Esc when you finish using the Format Painter.**

   Press Esc or click the Format Painter button again to cease using the Format Painter if you used it to copy formats to more than one location.

At the opposite end of the spectrum from the Format Painter button is the Clear Formatting button on the Home tab. You can select text and click this button to strip text of all its formats, whatever they may be.

Choosing fonts for text

If you aren't happy with the fonts you choose, select the text that needs a font change and change fonts with one of these techniques:

+ **Mini-toolbar:** Move the pointer over the selected text. You see the mini-toolbar. Move the pointer over this toolbar and choose a font in the Font drop-down list, as shown in Figure 2-2.

+ **Shortcut menu:** Right-click the selected text and choose a new font on the shortcut menu.

+ **Font drop-down list:** On the Home tab, open the Font drop-down list and choose a font.

+ **Font dialog box:** On the Home tab, click the Font group button. You see the Font dialog box. Select a font and click OK.

Figure 2-2:
Changing fonts by way of the mini-toolbar.

 Another way to change fonts is to select a different theme font. In the Page Layout tab (in Word and Excel) or the Design tab (in PowerPoint), open the drop-down list on the Theme Fonts button and choose a font combination.

 Avoid using too many different fonts because a file with too many fonts looks like alphabet soup. The object is to choose a font that helps set the tone. An aggressive sales pitch calls for a strong, bold font; a technical presentation calls for a font that is clean and unobtrusive. Make sure that the fonts you select help communicate your message.

Changing the font size of text

Font size is measured in *points;* a point is ½ of an inch. The golden rule of font sizes goes something like this: the larger the font size, the more important the text. This is why headings are larger than footnotes. Select your text and use one of these techniques to change the font size of the letters:

✦ **Mini-toolbar:** Move the pointer over the text, and when you see the mini-toolbar, move the pointer over the toolbar and choose a font size on the Font Size drop-down list (refer to Figure 2-2).

✦ **Shortcut menu:** Right-click the text and choose a new font size on the shortcut menu.

✦ **Font Size drop-down list:** On the Home tab, open the Font Size drop-down list and choose a font. You can live-preview font sizes this way.

✦ **Font dialog box:** On the Home tab, click the Font group button, and in the Font dialog box, choose a font size and click OK.

✦ **Increase Font Size and Decrease Font Size buttons:** Click these buttons (or press Ctrl+] or Ctrl+[) to increase or decrease the point size by the next interval on the Font Size drop-down list. You can find the Increase Font Size and Decrease Font Size buttons on the Home tab and the mini-toolbar. Watch the Font Size list or your text and note how the text changes size. This is an excellent technique when you want to "eyeball it" and you don't care to fool with the Font Size drop-down list or Font dialog box.

Click the Increase Font Size and Decrease Font Size buttons when you're dealing with fonts of different sizes and you want to proportionally change the size of all the letters. Drag the pointer over the text to select it before clicking one of the buttons.

If the font size you want isn't on the Font Size drop-down list, enter the size. For example, to change the font size to 13.5 points, type **13.5** in the Font Size box and press Enter.

Applying font styles to text

There are four — count 'em, four — font styles: regular, bold, italic, and underline:

✦ **Regular:** This style is just Office's way of denoting an absence of any font style.

✦ **Italic:** Italics are used for emphasis, when introducing a new term, and to mark foreign words such as *violà, gung hay fat choy,* and *Qué magnifico!* You can also italicize titles to make them a little more elegant.

✦ **Bold:** Bold text calls attention to itself.

✦ **Underline:** Underlined text also calls attention to itself, but use underlining sparingly. Later in this chapter, "Underlining text" looks at all the ways to underline text.

Select text and use one of these techniques to apply a font style to it:

✦ **Home tab:** Click the Bold, Italic, or Underline button.

✦ **Keyboard:** Press Ctrl+B to boldface text, Ctrl+I to italicize it, or Ctrl+U to underline it.

✦ **Mini-toolbar:** The mini-toolbar offers the Bold, Italic, and Underline button.

✦ **Font dialog box:** Select a Font Style option in the Font dialog box. To open this dialog box, visit the Home tab and click the Font group button.

To remove a font style, click the Bold, Italic, or Underline button a second time. You can also select text and then click the Clear Formatting button on the Home tab (in Word and PowerPoint).

Applying text effects to text

Text effects have various uses, some utilitarian and some strictly for yucks. Be careful with text effects. Use them sparingly and to good purpose. To apply a text effect, start on the Home tab and do one of the following:

✦ Click a text effect button on the Home tab.

✦ Click the Font group button and choose a text effect in the bottom half of the Font dialog box, as shown in Figure 2-3.

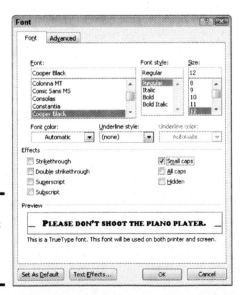

Figure 2-3: Text effects in the Font dialog box (Word).

Here's a rundown of the different text effects (not all these effects are available in PowerPoint, OneNote, or Excel):

+ **Strikethrough and double strikethrough:** By convention, *strikethrough* is used to show where passages are struck from a contract or other important document. Double strikethrough, for all I know, is used to shows where passages are struck out forcefully. Use these text effects to demonstrate ideas that you reject.

+ **Subscript:** A *subscripted* letter is lowered in the text. In this chemical formula, the 2 is lowered to show that two atoms of hydrogen are needed along with one atom of oxygen to form a molecule of water: H_2O. (Press Ctrl+=.)

+ **Superscript:** A *superscripted* letter or number is one that is raised in the text. Superscript is used in mathematical and scientific formulas, in ordinal numbers (1st, 2nd, 3rd), and to mark footnotes. In the theory of relativity, the 2 is superscripted: $E = mc^2$. (Press Ctrl+Shift+plus sign.)

+ **Small Caps:** A *small cap* is a small capital letter. You can find many creative uses for small caps. An all-small-cap title looks elegant. Be sure to type lowercase letters in order to create small caps. Type an uppercase letter, and Office refuses to turn it into a small cap. Not all fonts can produce small capital letters.

+ **All Caps:** The All Caps text effect merely capitalizes all letters. Use it in styles to make sure that you enter text in all capital letters.

+ **Equalize Character Height (PowerPoint only):** This effect makes all characters the same height and stretches the characters in text. You can use it to produce interesting effects in text box announcements.

Underlining text

You can choose from 15 ways to underline text, with styles ranging from Words Only to Wavy Line, and you can select a color for the underline in Word and PowerPoint. If you decide to underline titles, do it consistently. To underline text, select the text that you want to underline, go to the Home tab, and pick your poison:

+ On the Home tab, click the Underline button. A single line runs under all the words you selected. In Word, you can open the drop-down list on the Underline button and choose from several ways to underline text.

+ Click the Font group button to open the Font dialog box (refer to Figure 2-3) and then choose an underline style from the drop-down list. You can also choose an underline color from the Underline Color drop-down list (in Word and PowerPoint). The color you select applies to the underline, not to the words being underlined.

To remove an underline from text, select the text and then click the Underline button on the Home tab.

Changing the color of text

Before you change the color of text, peer at your computer screen and examine the background theme or color you chose. Unless the color of the text is different from the theme or color, you can't read the text. Besides choosing a color that contributes to the overall tone, choose a color that is easy to read.

Select the text that needs touching up and use one of these techniques to change its color:

+ On the mini-toolbar, open the drop-down list on the Font Color button and choose a color, as shown in Figure 2-4.

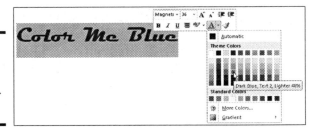

Figure 2-4:
Choosing a font color on the mini-toolbar.

+ Right-click, open the drop-down list on the Font Color button, and choose a color on the shortcut menu.

+ On the Home tab, open the drop-down list on the Font Color button and choose a color.

+ On the Home tab, click the Font group button to open the Font dialog box, open the Font Color drop-down list, and choose a color.

The Font Color drop-down list offers theme colors and standard colors. You are well advised to choose a theme color. These colors are deemed *theme colors* because they jive with the theme you choose for your file.

Quick Ways to Handle Case, or Capitalization

Case refers to how letters are capitalized in words and sentences. Table 2-1 explains the different cases, and Figure 2-5 demonstrates why paying attention to case matters. In the figure, the PowerPoint slide titles are presented using different cases, and the titles are inconsistent with one another. In one slide, only the first letter in the title is capitalized (sentence case); in another slide, the first letter in each word is capitalized (capitalize each word); in another, none of the letters is capitalized (lowercase); and in another, all the letters are capitalized (uppercase). In your titles and headings, decide on a capitalization scheme and stick with it for consistency's sake.

Table 2-1	Cases for Headings and Titles	
Case	*Description*	*Example Title*
Sentence case	The first letter in the first word is capitalized; all other words are lowercase unless they are proper names.	Man bites dog in January
Lowercase	All letters are lowercase unless they are proper names.	man bites dog in January
Uppercase	All letters are uppercase no matter what.	MAN BITES DOG IN JANUARY
Capitalize each word	The first letter in each word is capitalized.	Man Bites Dog In January

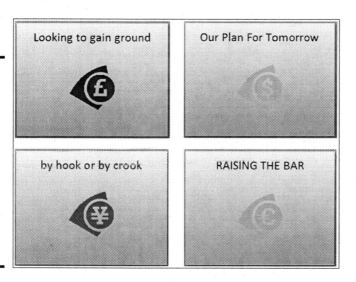

Figure 2-5:
Capitalization schemes (clockwise from upper-left): sentence case; capitalize each word; uppercase; lowercase.

 To change case in Word and PowerPoint, all you have to do is select the text, go to the Home tab, click the Change Case button, and choose an option on the drop-down list:

✦ **Sentence case:** Renders the letters in sentence case.

✦ **lowercase:** Makes all the letters lowercase.

✦ **UPPERCASE:** Renders all the letters as capital letters.

✦ **Capitalize Each Word:** Capitalizes the first letter in each word. If you choose this option for a title or heading, go into the title and lowercase the first letter of articles *(the, a, an)*, coordinate conjunctions *(and, or, for, nor)*, and prepositions unless they're the first or last word in the title.

✦ **tOGGLE cASE:** Choose this option if you accidentally enter letters with the Caps Lock key pressed.

You can also change case by pressing Shift+F3. Pressing this key combination in Word and PowerPoint changes characters to uppercase, lowercase, each word capitalized, and back to uppercase again.

Entering Symbols and Foreign Characters

Don't panic if you need to enter an umlaut, grave accent, or cedilla because you can do it by way of the Symbol dialog box, as shown in Figure 2-6. You can enter just about any symbol and foreign character by way of this dialog box. Click where you want to enter a symbol or foreign character and follow these steps to enter it:

Figure 2-6:
To enter a symbol or foreign character, select it and click the Insert button.

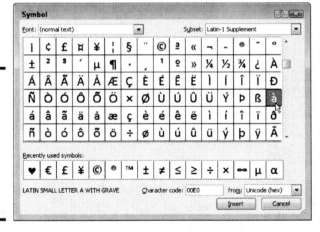

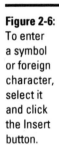 **1. On the Insert tab, click the Symbol button. (You may have to click the Symbols button first, depending on the size of your screen.)**

In Word and OneNote, click More Symbols after you click the Symbol button if no symbol on the drop-down list does the job for you. You see the Symbol dialog box (refer to Figure 2-6).

2. If you're looking to insert a symbol, not a foreign character, choose Webdings or Wingdings 1, 2, or 3 in the Font drop-down list.

Webdings and the Wingdings fonts offer all kinds of weird and wacky symbols.

3. Select a symbol or foreign character.

You may have to scroll to find the one you want.

4. **Click the Insert button to enter the symbol and then click Close to close the dialog box.**

The Symbol dialog box lists the last several symbols or foreign characters you entered under Recently Used Symbols. See whether the symbol you need is listed there. It spares you the trouble of rummaging in the Symbol dialog box. In Word and OneNote, you see the last several symbols or foreign characters you entered on a drop-down list after you click the Symbol button.

Finding and Replacing Text

Use the Find command to locate a name or text passage. Use its twin, the powerful Replace command, to find and replace a name or text passage throughout a file. For an idea of how useful the Replace command is, imagine that the company you work for just changed its name and the old company name is in many different places. By using the Replace command, you can replace the old company name with the new name throughout a long file in a matter of seconds.

The basics: Finding stray words and phrases

To locate stray words, names, text passages, and formats, follow these basic steps:

1. **Press Ctrl+F or go to the Home tab and click the Find button. (In Excel, click the Find & Select button and choose Find on the drop-down list.)**

A dialog box or pane appears so that you can enter search criteria. Figure 2-7 shows the Find dialog box in PowerPoint and the Find and Replace dialog box in Excel.

Figure 2-7:
Conducting
a Find
operation in
PowerPoint
(left) and
Excel (right).

2. **Enter the word or phrase in the Find What or Search Document text box.**

After you enter the word or phrase in Word, the Navigation pane lists each instance of the term you're looking for and the term is highlighted in your document wherever it is found, as shown in Figure 2-8. You can click an instance of the search term in the Navigation pane to scroll to a location in your document where the search term is located.

In Excel and PowerPoint, the Find What drop-down list shows words and phrases you looked for recently. You can make a selection from that list rather than enter a search term.

3. **If you want, choose additional options for narrowing your search.**

To access these options in Excel, click the Options button (see Figure 2-7); in Word, click the Find Options button — it's located to the right of the Search Document text box in the Navigation pane — and make a choice on the drop-down list (see Figure 2-8).

Later in this chapter, "Narrowing your search" explains how to make searches more efficient.

4. **Click the Find Next button if you're looking for a simple word or phrase, or the Find All button to locate all instances of a word or phrase in your file.**

In PowerPoint, the Find All button is available only if you start your search in Slide Sorter view.

Enter a word or phrase

Choose a search option   Choose a search criteria

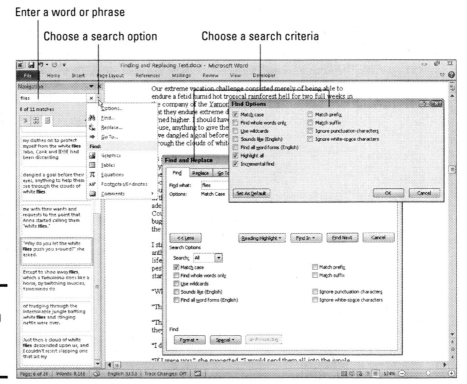

Figure 2-8: Conducting a Find operation in Word.

5. **To find the next instance of the thing you're looking for, click Find Next again.**

   In Word, either click an instance of the search word in the Navigation pane or click the Previous Find/Go To or Next Find/Go To button at the bottom of the scroll bar (or press Ctrl+Page Up or Ctrl+Page Down) to go to the previous or next instance of the thing you're looking for.

Narrowing your search

All the Office programs offer techniques for narrowing a search and making it more efficient. You can choose criteria for narrowing your search as well as search for text that has been formatted a certain way.

To narrow your search in Word, click the Find Options button, choose Options or Find on the drop-down list, and make choices in the Find Options or Find and Replace dialog box (refer to Figure 2-8). In Excel, click the Options button in the Find and Replace dialog box (refer to Figure 2-7).

Match Case and Find Whole Words Only

These options are your first line of defense in narrowing a search:

✦ **Match Case:** Searches for words with upper- and lowercase letters that exactly match those in the Find What or Search Document text box. When the Match Case option is selected, a search for *bow* finds *bow,* but not *Bow* or *BOW.*

✦ **Find Whole Words Only (not available in Excel):** Normally, a search for *bow* yields *elbow, bowler, bow-wow,* and all other words with the letters *b-o-w* (in that order). Click this option and you get only *bow.*

Searching for formats in Word and Excel

In Word and Excel, you can search for formats or text that was formatted a certain way with these techniques:

✦ **In Word:** Click the Format button in the Find and Replace dialog box (refer to Figure 2-8), and on the drop-down list, choose a Format type — Font, Paragraph, Tabs, Language, Frame, Style, or Highlight. A Find dialog box opens so that you can describe the format you're looking for. Select options in the dialog box to describe the format and click OK.

✦ **In Excel:** Click the Format button and choose a format in the Find Format dialog box. You can also open the drop-down list on the Format button, select Choose Format from Cell on the drop-down list, and click a cell to describe the format you're looking for.

After you finish conducting your search for formatted text, don't forget to click the No Formatting button (in Word) or open the Format drop-down list and choose Clear Find Format (in Excel). You can't conduct a normal search again unless you turn format searching off.

Taking advantage of search criteria in Word

Above and beyond the other Office programs, Word offers a bunch of ways to narrow a search. To take advantage of the search options in Word, click the Find Options button (it's located to the right of the Search Document box in the Navigation pane) and choose Options or Advanced Find on the drop-down list:

✦ Choose Options to open the Find Options dialog box and describe search criteria. With this technique, search terms when they are found are highlighted in the Navigation pane (provided that you select the Highlight All check box).

✦ Choose Advanced Find to open the Find tab of the Find and Replace dialog box and describe search criteria. With this technique, you click the Find Next button in the dialog box and locate search terms one at a time.

Word search options

Word offers these check box options for narrowing a search.

✦ **Use Wildcards:** Click here if you intend to use wildcards in searches. (See "Using wildcard operators to refine searches" later in this chapter.)

✦ **Sounds Like:** Looks for words that sound like the one in the Find What box. A search for *bow* with this option selected finds *beau,* for example. However, it doesn't find *bough.* This command isn't very reliable.

✦ **Find All Word Forms:** Takes into account verb conjugations and plurals. With this option clicked, you get *bows, bowing,* and *bowed* as well as *bow.*

✦ **Match Prefix:** A *prefix* is a syllable appearing before the root or stem of a word to alter its meaning. For example, *co, mid, non,* and *un* are prefixes in the words *coauthor, midtown, nonviolent,* and *unselfish.* Choose this option and enter a prefix in the Find What text box to locate words that begin with the prefix you enter.

✦ **Match Suffix:** A *suffix* is a syllable or two appearing at the end of a word that alters its meaning. For example, *age, ish,* and *ness* are suffixes in the words *spillage, smallish,* and *darkness.* Choose this option and enter a suffix in the Find What text box to find words that end with the same suffix.

✦ **Ignore Punctuation Characters:** Search in text for word phrases without regard for commas, periods, and other punctuation marks. For example, a search for *Yuma Arizona* finds *Yuma, Arizona* (with a comma) in the text.

✦ **Ignore White-Space Characters:** Search in text for word phrases without regard for white space caused by multiple blank spaces or tab entries.

Using wildcard operators to refine searches

Word permits you to use wildcard operators in searches. A *wildcard operator* is a character that represents characters in a search expression. Wildcards aren't for everybody. Using them requires a certain amount of expertise, but after you know how to use them, wildcards can be invaluable in searches and macros. Table 2-2 explains the wildcard operators you can use in searches. Click the Use Wildcards check box if you want to search using wildcards.

Table 2-2		Wildcards for Searches
Operator	*What It Finds*	*Example*
?	Any single character	**b?t** finds *bat, bet, bit*, and *but.*
*	Zero or more characters	**t*o** finds *to, two*, and *tattoo.*
[*xyz*]	A specific character, *x, y,* or *z*	**t[aeiou]pper** finds *tapper, tipper,* and *topper.*
[*x-z*]	A range of characters, *x* through *z*	**[1-4]000** finds *1000, 2000, 3000,* and *4000*, but not *5000.*
[!*xy*]	Not the specific character or characters, *xy*	**p[!io]t** finds *pat* and *pet,* but not *pit* or *put.*
<	Characters at the beginning of words	**<info** finds *information, info-maniac,* and *infomercial.*
>	Characters at the end of words	**ese>** finds *these, journal-ese,* and *legalese.*
@@	One or more instances of the previous character	**sho@@t** finds *shot* and *shoot.*
{*n*}	Exactly *n* instances of the previous character	**sho{2}t** finds *shoot* but not *shot.*
{*n,*}	At least *n* instances of the previous character	**^p{3,}** finds three or more paragraph breaks in a row, but not a single paragraph break or two paragraph breaks in a row.
{*n,m*}	From *n* to *m* instances of the previous character	**10{2,4}** finds *100, 1000,* and *10000,* but not *10* or *100000.*

You can't conduct a whole-word-only search with a wildcard. For example, a search for **f*s** not only finds *fads* and *fits* but also all text strings that begin with *f* and end with *s,* such as *for the birds.* Wildcard searches can yield many, many results and are sometimes useless.

To search for an asterisk (*), question mark (?), or other character that serves as a wildcard search operator, place a backslash (\) before it in the text box.

Searching for special characters in Word

Table 2-3 describes the *special characters* you can look for in Word documents. To look for the special characters listed in the table, enter the character directly in the text box or click the Special button in the Find and Replace dialog box, and then choose a special character from the pop-up list. Be sure to enter lowercase letters. For example, you must enter **^n**, not **^N**, to look for a column break. *Note:* A caret (^) precedes special characters.

Table 2-3	Special Characters for Searches
To Find/Replace	**Enter**
Manual Formats That Users Insert	
Column break	^n
Field[1]	^d
Manual line break (¬)	^l
Manual page break	^m
No-width non break	^z
No-width optional break	^x
Paragraph break (¶)	^p
Section break[1]	^b
Section character	^%
Tab space (→)	^t
Punctuation Marks	
¼ em space	^q
Caret (^)	^^
Ellipsis	^i
Em dash (—)	^+
En dash (–)	^=
Full-width ellipses	^j
Nonbreaking hyphen	^~

To Find/Replace	Enter
Optional hyphen	^-
White space (one or more blank spaces)[1]	^w
Characters and Symbols	
Foreign character	You can type foreign characters in the Find What and Replace With text boxes
ANSI and ASCII characters and symbols	^*nnnn*, where *nnnn* is the four-digit code
Any character[1]	^?
Any digit[1]	^#
Any letter[1]	^$
Clipboard contents[2]	^c
Contents of the Find What box[2]	^&
Elements of Reports and Scholarly Papers	
Endnote mark[1]	^e
Footnote mark[1]	^f
Graphic[1]	^g

[1]*For use in find operations only*

[2]*For use in replace operations only*

 Before searching for special characters in Word, go to the Home tab and click the Show/Hide¶ button. That way, you see special characters — also known as *hidden format symbols* — on-screen when Word finds them.

 Creative people find many uses for special characters in searches. The easiest way to find section breaks, column breaks, and manual line breaks in a document is to enter **^b**, **^n**, or **^l**, respectively, and start searching. By combining special characters with text, you can make find-and-replace operations more productive. For example, to replace all double hyphens (–) in a document with em dashes (—), enter – in the Find What text box and **^m** in the Replace With text box. This kind of find-and-replace operation is especially useful for cleaning documents that were created in another program and then imported into Word.

Conducting a find-and-replace operation

Conducting a find-and-replace operation is the spitting image of conducting a find operation. Figure 2-9 shows (in PowerPoint) the Replace dialog box, the place where you declare what you want to find and what to replace it with. Do the options and buttons in the dialog box look familiar? They do if you read the previous handful of pages about searching because the Replace options are the same as the Find options.

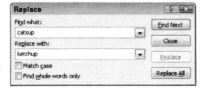

 The key to a successful find-and-replace operation is making sure you *find* exactly what you want to find and replace. One way to make sure that you find the right text is to start by running a Find operation. If the program finds precisely the text you want, you're in business. Click the Replace tab or Replace button in the Find dialog box and then enter the replacement text.

To locate and replace words, names, or text passages with the Find command, follow these steps:

1. **Press Ctrl+H or go to the Home tab and click the Replace button (in Excel, click the Find & Select button and choose Replace on the drop-down list).**

   The Replace (or Find and Replace) dialog box appears (see Figure 2-9).

2. **Describe the text that needs replacing.**

   Earlier in this chapter, "Finding stray words and formats" explains how to construct a search. Try to narrow your search so you find only the text you're looking for.

3. **Click the Find Next button.**

   Did your program find what you're looking for? If it didn't, describe the search again.

4. **Enter the replacement text in the Replace With text box.**

   You can select replacement text from the drop-down list.

5. **Either replace everything simultaneously or do it one at a time.**

   Click one of these buttons:

   • Click Replace All to make all replacements in an instant.

   • Click Find Next and then either click Replace to make the replacement or Find Next to bypass it.

Click the Replace All button only if you are very, very confident that the thing your program found is the thing you want to replace.

Be sure to examine your file after you conduct a find-and-replace operation. You never know what the powerful Replace command will do. If the command makes a hash of your file, click the Undo button.

Creating Hyperlinks

A *hyperlink* is an electronic shortcut from one place to another. If you've spent any time on the Internet, you know what a hyperlink is. Clicking hyperlinks on the Internet takes you to different Web pages or different places on the same Web page. In the Office programs, you can use hyperlinks to connect readers to your favorite Web pages or to a different page, slide, or file. You can fashion a link out of a word or phrase as well as any object — a clip-art image, text box, shape, or picture.

These pages explain how to insert a hyperlink to another place in your file as well as create links to Web pages. You also discover how to enter an e-mail hyperlink that makes it easy for others to e-mail you. By the way, the Office programs create a hyperlink for you automatically when you type a word that begins with *www* and ends with *.com* or *.net*. The programs create an automatic e-mail hyperlink when you enter letters that include the symbol (@) and end in *.com* or *.net*.

Linking a hyperlink to a Web page

It could well be that a Web page on the Internet has all the information your readers need. In that case, you can link to the Web page so that viewers can visit it in the course of viewing your file. When a viewer clicks the link, a Web browser opens and the Web page appears.

Follow these steps to hyperlink your file to a Web page on the Internet:

1. **Select the text or object that will form the hyperlink.**

   For example, select a line of text or phrase if you want viewers to be able to click it to go to a Web page.

2. **On the Insert tab, click the Hyperlink button (or press Ctrl+K).**

   Depending on the size of your screen, you may have to click the Links button before you can get to the Hyperlink button. You see the Insert Hyperlink dialog box, as shown in Figure 2-10. You can also open this dialog box by right-clicking an object or text and choosing Hyperlink on the shortcut menu.

3. **Under Link To, select Existing File or Web Page.**

4. **In the Address text box, enter the address of the Web page to which you want to link, as shown in Figure 2-10.**

Choose a Web page   Click to go on the Internet to a Web page

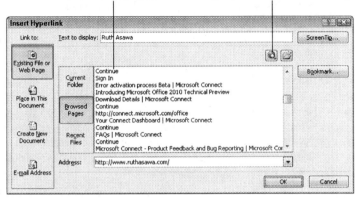

Figure 2-10:
Enter the
Web page
target in the
Address
text box to
create a
hyperlink to
a Web page.

From easiest to hardest, here are techniques for entering Web page addresses:

- *Click the Browse the Web button:* Your Web browser opens after you click this button. Go to the Web page you want to link to and return to your program. The Web page's address appears in the Address text box. (Figure 2-10 shows where the Browse the Web button is.)

- *Click Browsed Pages:* The dialog box lists Web pages you recently visited after you click this button, as shown in Figure 2-10. Choose a Web page.

- *Type (or copy) a Web page address into the Address text box:* Enter the address of the Web page. You can right-click the text box and choose Paste to copy a Web page address into the text box.

5. **Click the ScreenTip button, enter a ScreenTip in the Set Hyperlink ScreenTip dialog box, and click OK.**

Viewers can read the ScreenTip you enter when they move their pointers over the hyperlink.

6. **Click OK in the Insert Hyperlink dialog box.**

I would test the hyperlink if I were you to make sure it takes viewers to the right Web page. To test a hyperlink, Ctrl+click it or right-click it and choose Open Hyperlink on the shortcut menu.

Creating a hyperlink to another place in your file

Follow these steps to create a hyperlink to another place in your file:

1. **Select the text or object that will form the hyperlink.**

2. **On the Insert tab, click the Hyperlink button (or press Ctrl+K).**

You see the Insert Hyperlink dialog box. (Depending on the size of your screen, you may have to click the Links button before you see the Hyperlink button.) Another way to open this dialog box is to right-click and choose Hyperlink in the shortcut menu.

3. **Under Link To, select Place in This Document.**

What you see in the dialog box depends on which program you're working in:

- *Word:* You see bookmarks and headings to which you've assigned a heading style.

- *PowerPoint:* You see a list of slides in your presentation, as well as links to the first, last, next, and previous slide, as shown in Figure 2-11.

- *Excel:* You see boxes for entering cell references and defined cell names.

Select a target

Select Place in This Document   Click to enter a ScreenTip

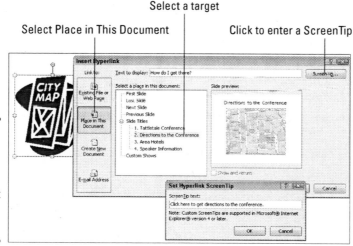

Figure 2-11:
You can
also create
a hyperlink
to a different
place in a
file.

4. **Select the target of the hyperlink.**

5. **Click the ScreenTip button.**

You see the Set Hyperlink ScreenTip dialog box, as shown in Figure 2-11.

6. **Enter a ScreenTip and click OK.**

When viewers move their pointers over the link, they see the words you enter. Enter a description of where the hyperlink takes you.

7. **Click OK in the Insert Hyperlink dialog box.**

   To test your hyperlink, move the pointer over it. You should see the ScreenTip description you wrote. Ctrl+click the link to see if it takes you to the right place.

Creating an e-mail hyperlink

An *e-mail hyperlink* is one that opens an e-mail program. These links are sometimes found on Web pages so that anyone visiting a Web page can conveniently send an e-mail message to the person who manages the Web page. When you click an e-mail hyperlink, your default e-mail program opens. And if the person who set up the link was thorough about it, the e-mail message is already addressed and given a subject line.

 Include an e-mail hyperlink in a file if you're distributing the file to others and you would like them to be able to comment on your work and send the comments to you.

Follow these steps to put an e-mail hyperlink in a file:

1. **Select the words or object that will constitute the link.**

2. **On the Insert tab, click the Hyperlink button (or press Ctrl+K).**

   The Insert Hyperlink dialog box appears.

3. **Under Link To, click E-Mail Address.**

   Text boxes appear for entering an e-mail address and a subject message.

4. **Enter your e-mail address and a subject for the messages that others will send you.**

   Office inserts the word *mailto:* before your e-mail address as you enter it.

5. **Click OK.**

   Test the link by Ctrl+clicking it. Your default e-mail program opens. The e-mail message is already addressed and given a subject.

Repairing and removing hyperlinks

From time to time, check the hyperlinks in your file to make sure they still work. Clicking a hyperlink and having nothing happen is disappointing. Hyperlinks get broken when Web pages and parts of files are deleted.

To repair or remove a hyperlink, right-click the link and choose Edit Hyperlink on the shortcut menu (or click in the link and then click the Hyperlink button on the Insert tab). You see the Edit Hyperlink dialog box. This dialog box looks and works just like the Insert Hyperlink dialog box.

✦ **Repairing a link:** Select a target in your file or a Web page and click OK.

✦ **Removing a link:** Click the Remove Link button. You can also remove a hyperlink by right-clicking the link and choosing Remove Hyperlink on the shortcut menu.

Installing and removing fonts on your computer

If Windows is installed on your computer, so are many different fonts. The names of these fonts appear on the Font drop-down list, Font dialog box, and mini-toolbar. Do you have enough fonts on your computer? Do you want to remove fonts to keep the Font drop-down list from being overcrowded?

Font files are kept in the `C:\Windows\Fonts` folder on your computer. You can double-click the Fonts icon in the Control Panel to open this folder. Here are instructions for handling fonts:

✔ **Installing new fonts:** Place the font file in the `C:\Windows\Fonts` folder.

✔ **Removing a font:** Move the font file out of the `C:\Windows\Fonts` folder. Store font files you don't want in another folder where you can resuscitate them if need be.

✔ **Examining fonts:** Double-click a font file to examine a font more closely. A window opens, and you see precisely what the font looks like. Do you know why "The quick brown fox jumps over the lazy dog" appears in this window? Because that sentence includes every letter in the alphabet.

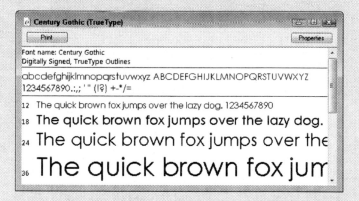

Chapter 3: Speed Techniques Worth Knowing About

In This Chapter

✓ **Undoing mistakes and repeating actions**

✓ **Zooming to get a better view of your work**

✓ **Working with two different files at the same time**

✓ **Instructing Office to correct typos automatically**

✓ **Entering hard-to-type text with the AutoCorrect command**

*T*his brief chapter takes you on a whirlwind tour of shortcut commands that can save you time and effort no matter which Office program you're working in. This chapter is devoted to people who want to get it done quickly and get away from their computers. It explains the Undo and Repeat commands, zooming in and out, and opening more than one window on the same file. You also discover how to display windows in different ways, correct your typos automatically, and enter hard-to-type terminology with a simple flick of the wrist.

Undoing and Repeating Commands

If I were to choose two commands for the Hall of Fame, they would be the Undo command and the Repeat command. One allows you to reverse actions you regret doing, and the other repeats a previous action without your having to choose the same commands all over again. Undo and Repeat are explained forthwith.

Undoing a mistake

Fortunately for you, all is not lost if you make a big blunder because Office has a marvelous little tool called the Undo command. This command "remembers" your previous editorial and formatting changes. As long as you catch your error in time, you can undo your mistake.

 Click the Undo button on the Quick Access toolbar (or press Ctrl+Z) to undo your most recent change. If you made your error and went on to do something else before you caught it, open the drop-down list on the Undo button.

It lists your previous actions, as shown in Figure 3-1. Click the action you want to undo, or if it isn't on the list, scroll until you find the error and then click it.

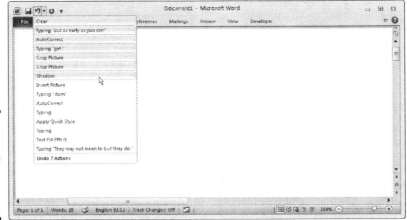

Remember, however, that choosing an action far down the Undo list also reverses the actions before it on the list. For example, if you undo the 19th action on the list, you also undo the 18 more recent actions above it.

Repeating an action — and quicker this time

The Quick Access toolbar offers a button called Repeat that you can click to repeat your last action. This button can be a mighty, mighty timesaver. For example, if you just changed fonts in one heading and you want to change another heading in the same way, select the heading and click the Repeat button (or press F4 or Ctrl+Y). Move the pointer over the Repeat button to see, in a pop-up box, what clicking it does.

You can find many creative uses for the Repeat command if you use your imagination. For example, if you had to type "I will not talk in class" a hundred times as a punishment for talking in class, you could make excellent use of the Repeat command to fulfill your punishment. All you would have to do is write the sentence once and then click the Repeat button 99 times.

After you click the Undo button, the Repeat button changes names and becomes the Redo button. Click the Redo button to "redo" the command you "undid." In other words, if you regret clicking the Undo button, you can turn back the clock by clicking Redo.

Zooming In, Zooming Out

Eyes weren't meant to stare at the computer screen all day, which makes the Zoom controls all the more valuable. You can find these controls on the View tab and in the lower-right corner of the window, as shown in Figure 3-2. Use them freely and often to enlarge or shrink what is on the screen and preserve your eyes for important things, such as gazing at the sunset.

Zoom button

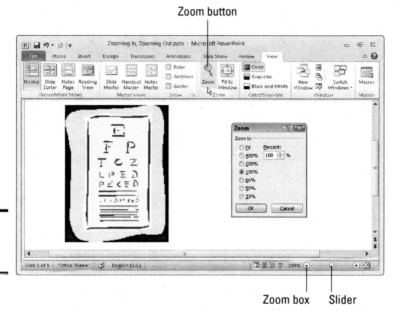

Figure 3-2:
The Zoom
controls.

Zoom box   Slider

Meet the Zoom controls:

✦ **Zoom dialog box:** Click the Zoom button on the View tab or the Zoom box (the % listing) to display the Zoom dialog box, as shown in Figure 3-2. From there, you can select an option button or enter a Percent measurement.

✦ **Zoom button:** Click the Zoom In or Zoom Out button on the Zoom slider to zoom in or out in 10-percent increments.

✦ **Zoom slider:** Drag the *Zoom slider* left to shrink or right to enlarge what is on your screen.

✦ **Mouse wheel:** If your mouse has a wheel, you can hold down the Ctrl key and spin the wheel to quickly zoom in or out.

Each Office program offers its own special Zoom commands in the Zoom group on the View tab. In Word, for example, you can display one page or two pages; in Excel, you can click the Zoom to Selection button and enlarge a handful of cells. Make friends with the Zoom commands. They never let you down.

Viewing a File through More Than One Window

By way of the commands in the Window group in the View tab, you can be two places simultaneously, at least where Office is concerned. You can work on two files at once. You can place files side by side on the screen and do a number of other things to make your work a little easier.

Word, Excel, and PowerPoint offer these buttons in the Window group:

✦ **New Window:** Opens another window on your file so you can be two places at once in the same file. To go back and forth between windows, click a taskbar button or click the Switch Windows button and choose a window name on the drop-down list. Click a window's Close button when you finish looking at it.

✦ **Arrange All:** Arranges open windows side by side on-screen.

✦ **Switch Windows:** Opens a drop-down list with open windows so that you can travel between windows.

You can also take advantage of these Window buttons in Word and Excel to compare files:

✦ **View Side by Side:** Displays files side by side so you can compare and contrast them.

✦ **Synchronous Scrolling:** Permits you to scroll two files at the same rate so that you can proofread one against the other. To use this command, start by clicking the View Side by Side button. After you click the Synchronous Scrolling button, click the Reset Window Position button so both files are displayed at the same size on-screen.

✦ **Reset Window Position:** Makes files being shown side by side the same size on-screen to make them easier to compare.

Correcting Typos on the Fly

The unseen hand of Office 2010 corrects some typos and misspellings automatically. For example, try typing **accomodate** with one *m* — Office corrects the misspelling and inserts the second *m* for you. Try typing **perminent** with an *i* instead of an *a* — the invisible hand of Office corrects the misspelling, and you get permanent. While you're at it, type a colon and a close parenthesis **:)** — you get a smiley face.

As good as the AutoCorrect feature is, you can make it even better. You can also add the typos and misspellings you often make to the list of words that are corrected automatically.

Opening the AutoCorrect dialog box

Office corrects common spelling errors and turns punctuation mark combinations into symbols as part of its AutoCorrect feature. To see which typos are corrected and which punctuation marks are turned into symbols, open the AutoCorrect dialog box by following these steps:

1. **On the File tab, choose Options.**

You see the Options dialog box.

2. **Go to the Proofing category.**

3. **Click the AutoCorrect Options button.**

The AutoCorrect dialog box opens.

4. **Go to the AutoCorrect tab.**

As shown in Figure 3-3, the AutoCorrect tab lists words that are corrected automatically. Scroll down the Replace list and have a look around. Go ahead. Make yourself at home.

Enter a typo and its replacement

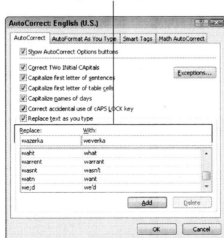

Figure 3-3:
As you type, words in the Replace column are replaced auto- matically with words in the With column.

Entering Text Quickly with the AutoCorrect Command

The preceding part of this chapter explains how you can use the AutoCorrect command to help correct typing errors, but with a little cunning you can also use it to quickly enter hard-to-type jargon, scientific names, and the like. To open the AutoCorrect dialog box, go to the File tab, choose Options, go to the Proofing category in the Options dialog box, and then click the AutoCorrect Options button. Then select the AutoCorrect tab in the AutoCorrect dialog box.

In the Replace column in the AutoCorrect tab are hundreds of common typing errors and codes that Office corrects automatically. The program corrects the errors by entering text in the With column whenever you mistakenly type the letters in the Replace column. However, you can also use this dialog box for a secondary purpose to quickly enter text.

To make AutoCorrect work as a means of entering text, you tell Office to enter the text whenever you type three or four specific characters. Follow these steps to use AutoCorrect to enter text:

1. **On the File tab, choose Options.**

2. **Go to the Proofing category in the Options dialog box.**

3. **Click the AutoCorrect Options button.**

   You see the AutoCorrect dialog box.

4. **Select the AutoCorrect tab.**

5. **In the Replace text box, enter the three or four characters that will trigger the AutoCorrect mechanism and make it enter your text.**

   Don't enter a word, or characters that you might really type someday, in the Replace box. If you do, the AutoCorrect mechanism might kick in when you least expect it. Enter three or four characters that never

appear together. And start all AutoCorrect entries with a slash (/). You might forget which characters trigger the AutoText entry or decide to delete your AutoCorrect entry someday. By starting it with a slash, you can find it easily in the AutoCorrect dialog box at the top of the Replace list.

6. **In the With text box, enter the hard-to-type name or word(s) that will appear when you enter the Replace text.**

7. **Click the Add button.**

8. **Click OK.**

   Test your AutoCorrect entry by typing the Replace text you entered in Step 2 (which, of course, includes the slash I recommended) and pressing the spacebar. (AutoCorrect doesn't do its work until you press the spacebar.)

To delete an AutoCorrect entry, open the AutoCorrect dialog box, select the entry, and click the Delete button.

Telling Office which typos and misspellings to correct

No doubt you make the same typing errors and spelling errors time and time again. To keep from making these errors, you can tell Office to correct them for you automatically. You do that by entering the misspelling and its corrected spelling in the AutoCorrect dialog box (see Figure 3-3):

✦ Enter the misspelling in the Replace text box and its correct spelling in the With text box.

✦ Click the AutoCorrect button in the Spelling dialog box when you spell-check a file. This action automatically places the misspelling and its correction in the AutoCorrect dialog box so that the correction is made in the future.

You can also remove misspellings and typos from the list of words that are corrected automatically. To remove a word from the list of corrected words, select it in the AutoCorrect dialog box and click the Delete button.

Preventing capitalization errors with AutoCorrect

Near the top of the AutoCorrect dialog box (refer to Figure 3-3) are five check boxes whose job is to prevent capitalization errors. These options do their jobs very well, sometimes to a fault:

✦ **Correct TWo INitial Capitals:** Prevents two capital letters from appearing in a row at the start of a word with more than two letters. Only the first letter is capitalized. This option is for people who can't lift their little fingers from the Shift key fast enough after typing the first capital letter at the start of a word.

✦ **Capitalize first letter of sentences:** Makes sure that the first letter in a sentence is capitalized.

✦ **Capitalize first letter of table cells:** Makes sure that the first letter you enter in a table cell is a capital letter. A table cell holds one data item; it's the place in a table where a column and row intersect.

✦ **Capitalize names of days:** Makes sure that the names of the days of the week are capitalized.

✦ **Correct accidental usage of cAPS LOCK key:** Changes capital letters to lowercase letters if you press the Shift key to start a sentence while Caps Lock is on. The idea here is that if you press down the Shift key while Caps Lock is on, you don't know that Caps Lock is on because you don't need to hold down the Shift key to enter capital letters. AutoCorrect turns the first letter into a capital letter and the following letters into lowercase letters and then turns Caps Lock off.

Chapter 4: Taking Advantage of the Proofing Tools

In This Chapter

✓ Fixing spelling errors and customizing the spelling dictionary

✓ Repairing grammatical errors in Word documents

✓ Conducting outside research while you work in an Office program

✓ Looking for a better word in the thesaurus

✓ Working with and translating foreign language text

I was going to call this chapter "Foolproofing Your Work," but that seemed kind of presumptuous because keeping every error from slipping into your work is well-nigh impossible. Still, you can do a good job of proofing your work and eliminating errors by using the tools that Office provides for that purpose. This chapter describes how to proof your work for spelling and grammatical errors. It shows how to conduct research in reference books and on the Internet without leaving an Office program. You also find out how to translate text and proof foreign language text in an Office file. The Office proofing tools are not foolproof, but they're close to it.

Correcting Your Spelling Errors

Office keeps a dictionary in its hip pocket, which is a good thing for you. Who wants to be embarrassed by a spelling error? Office consults its dictionary when you enter text in Word, PowerPoint, Excel, and OneNote. To correct misspellings, you can either address them one at a time or start the spell checker and proof many pages or slides simultaneously. You can even create your own dictionary with the jargon and slang peculiar to your way of life and have Office check the spelling of your jargon and slang.

Don't trust the smell checker to be accurate all the time. It doesn't really locate misspelled words — it locates words that aren't in its dictionary. For example, if you write "Nero diddled while Rome burned," the spell checker doesn't catch the error. Nero *fiddled* while Rome burned, but because *diddle* is a legitimate word in the spelling dictionary, the spell checker overlooks the error. The moral: Proofread your files carefully and don't rely on the spell checker to catch all your smelling errors.

Getting rid of the squiggly red lines

More than a few people think that the squiggly red lines that appear under misspelled words are annoying. To keep those lines from appearing, press F7 to open the Spelling dialog box, and click the Options button. You see the Proofing category of the Options dialog box. Deselect the Check Spelling As You Type check box.

Even with the red lines gone, you can do a quick spell-check of a word that you suspect has been misspelled. To do so, select the word (double-click it) and press F7. The Spelling dialog box appears if the word has indeed been misspelled. Select a word in the Suggestions box and click the Change button.

Correcting misspellings one at a time

In Word, PowerPoint, and OneNote, you can practice the one-at-a-time method of spell-checking. As shown in Figure 4-1, you can right-click each word that is underlined in red and choose a correct spelling from the shortcut menu. After you choose a word from the shortcut menu, it replaces the misspelling that you right-clicked.

Figure 4-1:
Right-click a word underlined in red to correct a typo or repeated word.

Words entered twice are also flagged in red, in which case the shortcut menu offers the Delete Repeated Word option so that you can delete the second word. You can also click Ignore All to tell Office when a word is correctly spelled and shouldn't be flagged, or click Add to Dictionary, which adds the word to the Office spelling dictionary and declares it a correctly spelled word.

Running a spell-check

Instead of correcting misspellings one at a time, you run a spell-check on your work. Start your spell-check with one of these methods:

✦ Press F7.

 ✦ Go to the Review tab and click the Spelling (or Spelling & Grammar) button (you may have to click the Proofing button to get to the Spelling button).

You see the Spelling and Grammar (or Spelling) dialog box, as shown in Figure 4-2. Misspellings appear in the Not In Dictionary text box. As I explain shortly, your Office program offers all sorts of amenities for handling misspellings, but here are options for correcting known misspellings in the Spelling dialog box:

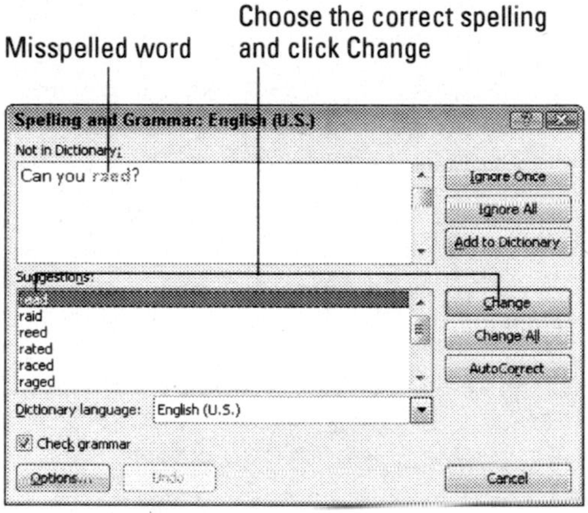

Misspelled word   Choose the correct spelling and click Change

Figure 4-2: Correcting a misspelling in the Spelling and Grammar dialog box.

✦ Select the correct spelling in the Suggestions box and click the Change button.

✦ Click in the page or slide you're working on and correct the spelling there; then click the Resume button, located where the Ignore or Ignore Once button used to be. (You can't do this in Excel.)

✦ In Word or Excel, correct the spelling inside the Not in Dictionary text box and then click the Change button. (In PowerPoint, correct the spelling in the Change To box and then click the Change button.)

If the word in question isn't a misspelling, tell your program how to handle the word by clicking one of these buttons:

✦ **Ignore (or Ignore Once):** Ignores this instance of the misspelling but stops on it again if the same misspelling appears later.

✦ **Ignore All:** Ignores the misspelling throughout the file you're working on and in all other open Office files as well.

✦ **Change/Delete:** Enters the selected word in the Suggestions box in the file where the misspelling used to be. When the same word appears twice in a row, the Delete button appears where the Change button was. Click the Delete button to delete the second word in the pair.

✦ **Change All/Delete All:** Replaces all instances of the misspelled word with the word that you selected in the Suggestions box. Click the Change All button to correct a misspelling that occurs throughout a file. When two words appear in a row, this button is called Delete All. Click the Delete All button to delete the second word in the pair throughout your file.

✦ **Add (or Add to Dictionary):** Adds the misspelling to the Office spelling dictionary. By clicking the Add button, you tell Office that the misspelling is a legitimate word or name.

✦ **Suggest (in PowerPoint only):** Changes the list of words in the Suggestions box. Select a word in the Suggestions box and then click the Suggest button to see whether you can find a correct spelling.

✦ **AutoCorrect:** Adds the spelling correction to the list of words that are corrected automatically. If you find yourself making the same typing error over and over, place the error on the AutoCorrect list and never have to correct it again. (See Chapter 3 of this mini-book for details.)

Office programs share the same spelling dictionary. For example, words you add to the spelling dictionary in PowerPoint are deemed correct spellings in Word documents, Excel spreadsheets, and OneNote notebooks.

Fine-tuning the spell checker

Especially if you deal in jargon and scientific terminology, you owe it to yourself to fine-tune the spell checker. No matter how arcane, it can make sure that your jargon gets used correctly. These pages explain the nuances of the spell checker.

Employing other dictionaries to help with spell-checking

To find spelling errors, Office compares each word on your page or slide to the words in its main dictionary and a second dictionary called `Custom. dic`. If a word you type isn't found in either dictionary, Office considers the word a misspelling. The main dictionary lists all known words in the English language; the `Custom.dic` dictionary lists words, proper names, and technical jargon that you deemed legitimate when you clicked the Add (or Add to Dictionary) button in the course of a spell-check and added a word to the `Custom.dic` dictonary.

From Office's standpoint, a dictionary is merely a list of words, one word per line, that has been saved in a `.dic` (dictionary) file. Besides the `Custom.dic` dictionary, you can employ other dictionaries to help with spell-checking. People who work in specialized professions such as law or medicine can also use legal dictionaries and medical dictionaries to spell check their work. You can create dictionaries of your own for slang words, colloquialisms, or special projects. Before you start spell checking, you can tell Office which dictionaries to use. You can edit dictionaries as well. All this magic is done by way of the Custom Dictionaries dialog box, as shown in Figure 4-3, and explained in the pages that follow.

Click to edit or delete the words in a dictionary

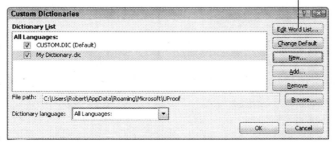

Figure 4-3:
Manage dictionaries in this dialog box.

Opening the Custom Dictionaries dialog box

Starting in the Custom Dictionaries dialog box, you can create a new spelling dictionary, tell PowerPoint to use a third-party dictionary you acquired, edit words in a dictionary, and tell PowerPoint which dictionary to use in a spell-check. Better keep reading.

Follow these steps to open the Custom Dictionaries dialog box:

1. **Press F7 or go to the Review tab and click the Spelling button.**

You see the Spelling and Grammar (or Spelling) dialog box.

2. **Click the Options button.**

The Proofing category of the Options dialog box opens.

3. **Click the Custom Dictionaries button.**

Creating a new spelling dictionary

People who work in law offices, research facilities, and medical facilities type hundreds of arcane terms each day, none of which are in the main dictionary. One way to make sure that arcane terms are spelled correctly is to create or acquire a dictionary of legal, scientific, or medical terms and use it for spell-checking purposes. By Office's definition, a dictionary is simply a list of words saved in a dictionary (.dic) file.

Follow these steps to create a new spelling dictionary or tell Office that you want to use a secondary dictionary to check the spelling of words:

1. **Click the New button in the Custom Dictionaries dialog box (refer to Figure 4-3).**

You see the Create Custom Dictionary dialog box.

2. **Enter a name for your new dictionary.**

3. **Click the Save button.**

See "Entering and editing words in a dictionary," later in this chapter, to find out how to enter terms in your new spelling dictionary.

Using a third-party dictionary

Besides creating your own dictionary, you can acquire one and tell Office to use it by following these steps:

1. **Take note of where the dictionary file is located on your computer.**

It doesn't have to be in the `C:\Users\User Name\AppData\Roaming\Microsoft\UProof` (Windows 7 and Windows Vista) or the `C:\Documents and Settings\`*User Name*`\Application Data\Microsoft\Proof` (or `UProof`) (Windows XP) folder along with the other dictionaries for PowerPoint to use it.

2. **Click the Add button in the Custom Dictionaries dialog box (refer to Figure 4-3).**

The Add Custom Dictionary dialog box appears.

3. **Locate and select the dictionary on your computer.**

4. **Click Open.**

The dictionary's name appears in the Custom Dictionaries dialog box. Ten dictionaries total can appear in the Dictionary List box.

Select a dictionary and click the Remove button to remove its name from the Dictionary List box. Removing a name in no way, shape, or form deletes the dictionary.

Entering and editing words in a dictionary

To edit the words in the `Custom.dic` dictionary or any other dictionary, select its name in the Custom Dictionaries dialog box (refer to Figure 4-3) and click the Edit Word List button. A dialog box opens with a list of the words in the dictionary, as shown in Figure 4-4. From there, you can delete words (by clicking the Delete button) and add words to the dictionary (by clicking the Add button).

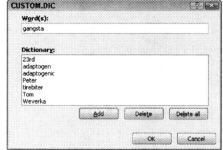

Figure 4-4:
Edit the
words in
a custom
dictionary in
this dialog
box.

Preventing text from being spell checked

Spell-checking address lists, lines of computer code, and foreign languages such as Spanglish for which Microsoft doesn't offer foreign language dictionaries is a thorough waste of time. Follow these steps in Word, PowerPoint, and OneNote to tell the spell checker to ignore text:

1. **Select the text.**

2. **In the Review tab, click the Language button and choose Set Proofing Language on the drop-down list.**

You see the Language dialog box.

3. **Select the Do Not Check Spelling or Grammar check box.**

4. **Click OK.**

Checking for Grammatical Errors in Word

Much of what constitutes good grammar is, like beauty, in the eye of the beholder. Still, you can do your best to repair grammatical errors in Word documents by getting the assistance of the grammar checker. The grammar checker identifies grammatical errors, explains what the errors are, and gives you the opportunity to correct the errors.

Figure 4-5 shows the grammar checker in action in the Spelling and Grammar dialog box. As long as the Check Grammar check box is selected, Word looks for grammatical errors along with spelling errors. To open the Spelling and Grammar dialog box, press F7 or go to the Review tab and click the Spelling & Grammar button.

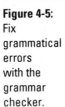

Figure 4-5:
Fix grammatical errors with the grammar checker.

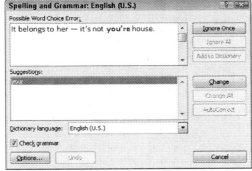

Sentences in which grammatical errors appear are underlined in blue in your document. Meanwhile, the grammatical errors themselves appear in bright blue in the box at the top of the Spelling and Grammar dialog box (along with spelling errors, which are red). When Word encounters an error, take one of these actions to correct it:

✦ Select a correction in the Suggestions box and click the Change button.

✦ Delete the grammatical error or rephrase the sentence in the top of the dialog box, enter a correction, and click the Change button.

✦ Click outside the Spelling and Grammar dialog box, correct the grammatical error in your document, and then click the Resume button (you find it where the Ignore Once button used to be).

Click one of the Ignore buttons to let what Word thinks is a grammatical error stand.

If you want to fine-tune how Word runs its grammar checker, click the Options button in the Spelling and Grammar dialog box. You land in the Proofing category of the Word Options dialog box. Under When Correcting Spelling and Grammar in Word, choose whether to underline grammatical errors in your documents, whether to check for grammatical as well as spelling errors, and in the Writing Style drop-down list, how stringent you want the rules of grammar to be. Choose Grammar & Style, not Grammar Only, if you want Word to enforce style rules as well as the rules of grammar.

Researching a Topic inside an Office Program

Thanks to the Research task pane, your desk needn't be as crowded as before. The Research task pane offers dictionaries, foreign language dictionaries, a thesaurus, language translators, and encyclopedias, as well as Internet searching, all available from inside the Office programs. As shown in Figure 4-6, the Research task pane can save you a trip to the library.

Looking at the research services

Table 4-1 describes the research services in the Research task pane. Use these services to get information as you compose a Word document, Excel worksheet, OneNote notebook, or PowerPoint presentation.

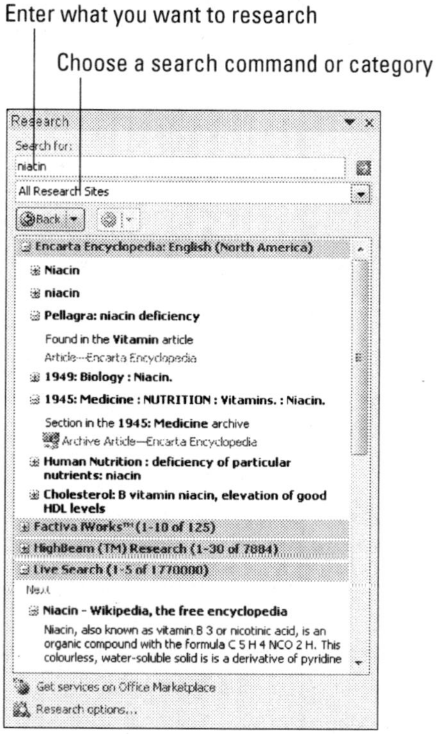

Enter what you want to research

Choose a search command or category

Figure 4-6:
The Research task pane is like a mini-reference library.

Table 4-1	Research Services in the Research Task Pane
Research Service	*What It Provides*
All Reference Books	
Encarta dictionaries	Word definitions from the Microsoft Network's online dictionaries
Thesauruses	Synonyms from the Microsoft Network's online thesauruses
Translation	Translations from one language to another
All Research Sites	
Bing	Results from Microsoft's search engine

(continued)

Table 4-1 *(continued)*

Research Service	What It Provides
Factiva iWorks*	Business articles from Factiva (you must be a paid subscriber)
HighBeam Research*	Newspaper and magazine articles from the HighBeam Research Library (you must be a paid subscriber)
All Business and Financial Sites	
MSN Money Stock Quotes*	Stock quotes from the Microsoft Network's Money Web site
Thomas Gale Company Profiles*	Thumbnail company profiles, including tickers, revenue, and Web site information

Requires an Internet connection.

Your computer must be connected to the Internet to run some of the services in the Research task plane. Bilingual dictionaries and thesauruses are installed as part of the Office software, but the research Web sites and the Encarta dictionaries and encyclopedia require an Internet connection.

In order to use some of the services offered by the Research task pane, you must pay a fee. These services are marked in search results with the Premium Content icon.

Using the Research task pane

The task pane offers menus and buttons for steering a search in different directions, but no matter what you want to research in the Research task pane, start your search the same way:

1. **Either click in a word or select the words that you want to research.**

For example, if you want to translate a word, click it. Clicking a word or selecting words saves you the trouble of entering words in the Search For text box, but if no word in your file describes what you want to research, don't worry about it. You can enter the subject of your search later.

2. **On the Review tab, click the Research button (you may have to click the Proofing button first).**

The Research task pane appears (refer to Figure 4-6). If you've researched since you started running your Office program, the options you chose for researching last time appear in the task pane.

3. **Enter a research term in the Search For text box (if one isn't there already).**

   If you weren't able to click a word or select words in Step 1, enter research terms now.

4. **Open the Search For drop-down list and tell Office where to steer your search (refer to Table 4-1).**

   Choose a reference book, research Web site, or business and financial Web site. To research in a category, choose a category name — All Reference Books, All Research Sites, or All Business and Financial Sites. Later in this chapter, "Choosing your research options" explains how to decide which researching options appear on the drop-down list.

5. **Click the Start Searching button (or press Enter).**

   The results of your search appear in the Research task pane.

If your search yields nothing worthwhile or nothing at all, scroll to the bottom of the task pane, click Can't Find It?, and try the All Reference Books or All Research Sites link. The first link searches all reference books — the dictionaries, thesauruses, and translation service. The second searches research sites — Bing, Factiva iWorks, and HighBeam Research.

You can retrace a search by clicking the Previous Search button or Next Search button in the Research task pane. These buttons work like the Back and Forward buttons in a Web browser.

Choosing your research options

Which research options appear in the Search For drop-down list is up to you. Maybe you want to dispense with the for-a-fee services. Maybe you want to get stock quotes from a particular country. To decide which research options appear in the Research task pane, open the task pane and click the Research Options link (at the bottom of the task pane). You see the Research Options dialog box. Select the research services you want and click OK.

Finding the Right Word with the Thesaurus

If you can't find the right word or if the word is on the tip of your tongue but you can't quite remember it, you can always give the thesaurus a shot. To find synonyms for a word, start by right-clicking the word and choosing Synonyms on the shortcut menu, as shown in Figure 4-7 (you can't do this in Excel). With luck, the synonym you're looking for appears on the submenu, and all you have to do is click to enter the synonym. Usually, however, finding a good synonym is a journey, not a Sunday stroll.

Figure 4-7:
Searching
for a
synonym.

To search for a good synonym, click the word in question and open the thesaurus on the Research task pane with one of these techniques:

✦ Press Shift+F7.

✦ Right-click the word and choose Synonyms➪Thesaurus.

✦ Go to the Review tab and click the Thesaurus button.

The Research task pane opens. It offers a list of synonyms and sometimes includes an antonym or two at the bottom. Now you're getting somewhere:

✦ **Choosing a synonym:** Move the pointer over the synonym you want, open its drop-down list, and choose Insert.

✦ **Finding a synonym for a synonym:** If a synonym intrigues you, click it. The task pane displays a new list of synonyms.

✦ **Searching for antonyms:** If you can't think of the right word, type its antonym in the Search For box and then look for an "antonym of an antonym" in the Research task pane.

✦ **Revisit a word list:** Click the Back button as many times as necessary. If you go back too far, you can always click its companion Forward button.

If your search for a synonym comes up dry, scroll to and click a link at the bottom of the Research task pane. Clicking All Reference Books gives you the opportunity to look up a word in the reference books you installed in the task pane; clicking All Research Sites gives you a chance to search the Internet (see "Researching a Topic inside an Office Program" earlier in this chapter for details).

Proofing Text Written in a Foreign Language

In the interest of cosmopolitanism, Office gives you the opportunity to make foreign languages a part of Word documents, PowerPoint presentations, and OneNote notebooks. To enter and edit text in a foreign language, start by installing proofing tools for the language. With the tools installed, you tell Office where in your file a foreign language is used. After that, you can spell check text written in the language.

To spell check text written in Uzbek, Estonian, Afrikaans, and other languages apart from English, French, and Spanish, you have to obtain additional proofing tools from Microsoft. These can be obtained at the Microsoft Product Information Center at www.microsoft.com/products (enter **proofing tools** in the Search box). Proofing tools include a spell checker, grammar checker, thesaurus, hyphenator, AutoCorrect list, and translation dictionary, but not all these tools are available for every language.

In PowerPoint and Word, the status bar along the bottom of the window lists which language the cursor is in. Glance at the status bar if you aren't sure which language Office is whispering in your ear.

Telling Office which languages you will use

Follow these steps to inform Word, PowerPoint, and OneNote that you will use a language or languages besides English in your files:

1. **On the Review tab, click the Language button and choose Language Preferences.**

   The Options dialog box opens to the Language category.

2. **Open the Add Additional Editing Languages drop-down list, select a language, and click the Add button to make that language a part of your presentations, documents, and messages.**

3. **Click OK.**

Translating Foreign Language Text

Office offers a gizmo for translating words and phrases from one language to another. The translation gizmo gives you the opportunity to translate single words and phrases as well as entire files, although, in my experience, it is only good for translating words and phrases. To translate an entire file, you have to seek the help of a real, native speaker.

To translate foreign language text, start by selecting the word or phrase that needs translating. Then, on the Review tab, click the Translate button and choose a Translate option on the drop-down list:

✔ **Translate Document (Word only):** Word sends the text to a translation service, and the translated text appears on a Web page. Copy the text and do what you will with it. (If the wrong translation languages are listed, choose the correct languages from the drop-down lists.)

✔ **Translate Selected Text:** The Research task pane opens. Choose a From and To option to translate the word from one language to another.

✔ **Mini Translator:** After you choose this option, move the pointer over the word you need translated. (If the Mini Translator command doesn't list the correct language, select the Choose Translation Language option and then select a language in the Translation Language Options dialog box.)

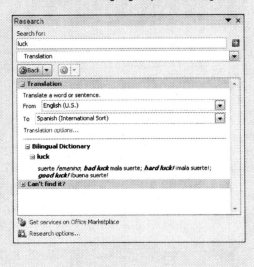

Marking text as foreign language text

The next step is to tell Office where in your file you're using a foreign language. After you mark the text as foreign language text, Office can spell check it with the proper dictionaries. Follow these steps to mark text so that Office knows in which language it was written:

1. Select the text that you wrote in a foreign language.

2. Go to the Review tab.

3. Click the Language button and choose Set Proofing Language on the drop-down list.

   You see the Language dialog box, as shown in Figure 4-8.

4. **Select a language and click OK.**

Figure 4-8:
Identifying
foreign
language
words
for spell-
checking.

Language

Mark selected text as:

Spanish (Argentina)
Spanish (Bolivia)
Spanish (Chile)
Spanish (Colombia)
Spanish (Costa Rica)
Spanish (Dominican Republic)
Spanish (Ecuador)
Spanish (El Salvador)

The speller and other proofing tools automatically use
dictionaries of the selected language, if available.

☐ Do not check spelling or grammar
☑ Detect language automatically

Set As Default   OK   Cancel

Chapter 5: Creating a Table

In This Chapter

⮑ **Understanding table jargon**

⮑ **Creating a table and entering the text and numbers**

⮑ **Aligning table text in various ways**

⮑ **Merging and splitting cells to make interesting layouts**

⮑ **Changing the size of rows and columns**

⮑ **Decorating a table with table styles, colors, and borders**

⮑ **Doing math calculations in a Word table**

⮑ **Discovering an assortment of table tricks**

The best way to present a bunch of data at once in Word, PowerPoint, or OneNote is to do it in a table. Viewers can compare and contrast the data. They can compare Elvis sightings in different cities or income from different businesses. They can contrast the number of socks lost in different washing machine brands. A table is a great way to plead your case or defend your position. On a PowerPoint slide, the audience can see right away that the numbers back you up. In a Word document, readers can refer to your table to get the information they need.

As everyone who has worked on tables knows, however, tables are a chore. Getting all the columns to fit, making columns and rows the right width and height, and editing the text in a table isn't easy. This chapter explains how to create tables, enter text in tables, change the number and size of columns and rows, lay out tables, format tables, and (in Word) do the math in tables. You'll also discover a few tricks — including using a picture for the background — that only magicians know. And to start you on the right foot, I begin by explaining table jargon.

Talking Table Jargon

As with much else in Computerland, tables have their own jargon. Figure 5-1 describes this jargon. Sorry, but you need to catch up on these terms to construct the perfect table:

✦ **Cell:** The box that is formed where a row and column intersect. Each cell holds one data item.

✦ **Header row:** The name of the labels along the top row that explain what is in the columns below.

✦ **Row labels:** The labels in the first column that describe what is in each row.

✦ **Borders:** The lines in the table that define where the rows and columns are.

✦ **Gridlines:** The gray lines that show where the columns and rows are. Unless you've drawn borders around all the cells in a table, you can't tell where rows and columns begin and end without gridlines. To display or hide the gridlines, go to the (Table Tools) Layout tab and click the View Gridlines button.

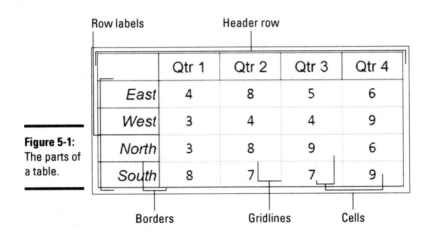

Figure 5-1: The parts of a table.

Creating a Table

Word, PowerPoint, and OneNote offer several ways to create a table:

✦ **Drag on the Table menu.** On the Insert tab, click the Table button, point in the drop-down list to the number of columns and rows you want, click, and let go of the mouse button.

✦ **Use the Insert Table dialog box.** On the Insert tab, click the Table button and choose Insert Table on the drop-down list. The Insert Table dialog box appears. Enter the number of columns and rows you want and click OK. In PowerPoint, you can also open the Insert Table dialog box by clicking the Table icon in a content placeholder frame.

✦ **Draw a table (Word and PowerPoint).** On the Insert tab, click the Table button and then choose Draw Table on the drop-down list. The pointer changes into a pencil. Use the pencil to draw table borders, rows, and columns. If you make a mistake, click the Eraser button on the (Table Tools) Design tab and drag it over the parts of the table you regret drawing (you may have to click the Draw Borders button first). When you finish drawing the table, press Esc.

You can click the Pen Color button and choose a color on the drop-down list to draw your table in your favorite color.

✦ **Create a quick table (Word).** On the Insert tab, click the Table button and choose Quick Tables on the drop-down list. Then select a ready-made table on the submenu. You have to replace the sample data in the quick table with your own data.

✦ **Convert text in a list into a table (Word).** Press Tab or enter a comma in each list item where you want the columns in the table to be. For example, to turn an address list into a table, put each name and address on its own line and press Tab or enter a comma after the first name, the last name, the street address, the city, the state, and the ZIP Code. For this feature to work, each name and address — each line — must have the same number of tab spaces or commas in it. Select the text you'll convert to a table, click the Table button on the Insert tab, and choose Convert Text to Table. Under Separate Text At in the Convert Text to Table dialog box, choose Tabs or Commas to tell Word how the columns are separated. Then click OK.

After you create a table, you get two new tabs on the Ribbon. The (Table Tools) Design tab offers commands for changing the look of the table; the (Table Tools) Layout tab is for changing around the rows and columns.

Constructing your table from an Excel worksheet

Fans of Microsoft Excel will be glad to know that you can construct an Excel worksheet in a Word document or PowerPoint slide. Excel worksheets, which present data in columns and rows, are very much like tables and can serve as such in documents and slides.

To create an Excel worksheet, go to the Insert tab, click the Table button, and choose Excel Spreadsheet. An Excel worksheet appears on the slide and — *gadzooks!* — you see Excel tabs and commands where Word or PowerPoint tabs and commands used to be. The worksheet you just created is embedded in your file. Whenever you click the worksheet, Excel menus and commands instead of Word or PowerPoint menus and commands appear on-screen. Click outside the worksheet to return to Word or PowerPoint. Book VI, Chapter 6 explains how embedded objects work.

Entering the Text and Numbers

After you've created the table, you can start entering text and numbers. All you have to do is click in a cell and start typing. Select your table and take advantage of these techniques to make the onerous task of entering table data a little easier:

+ **Quickly changing a table's size:** Drag the bottom or side of a table to change its overall size. In Word, you can also go to the (Table Tools) Layout tab, click the AutoFit button, and choose AutoFit Window to make the table stretch from margin to margin.

+ **Moving a table:** In Word, switch to Print Layout view and drag the table selector (the square in the upper-left corner of the table). In PowerPoint, move the pointer over the table's perimeter, and when you see the four-headed arrow, click and drag.

+ **Choosing your preferred font and font size:** Entering table data is easier when you're working in a font and font size you like. Select the table, visit the Home tab, and choose a font and font size there. In Word and PowerPoint, you can select a table by going to the (Table Tools) Layout tab, clicking the Select button, and choosing Select Table on the drop-down list.

+ **Quickly inserting a new row:** Click in the last column of the last row in your table and press the Tab key to quickly insert a new row at the bottom of the table.

Here are some shortcuts for moving the cursor in a table:

Press	*Moves the Cursor to*
Tab	Next column in row
Shift+Tab	Previous column in row
↓	Row below
↑	Row above
Alt+Page Up	Top of column (Word and PowerPoint)
Alt+Page Down	Bottom of column (Word and PowerPoint)

Selecting Different Parts of a Table

It almost goes without saying, but before you can reformat, alter, or diddle with table cells, rows, or columns, you have to select them:

+ **Selecting cells:** To select a cell, click in it. You can select several adjacent cells by dragging the pointer over them.

✦ **Selecting rows:** Move the pointer to the left of the row and click when you see the right-pointing arrow; click and drag to select several rows. You can also go to the (Table Tools) Layout tab, click inside the row you want to select, click the Select button, and choose Select Row on the drop-down list. To select more than one row at a time, select cells in the rows before choosing the Select Row command.

✦ **Selecting columns:** Move the pointer above the column and click when you see the down-pointing arrow; click and drag to select several columns. You can also start from the (Table Tools) Layout tab, click in the column you want to select, click the Select button, and choose Select Column in the drop-down list. To select several columns, select cells in the columns before choosing the Select Column command.

✦ **Selecting a table:** On the (Table Tools) Layout tab, click the Select button, and choose Select Table on the drop-down list. In PowerPoint, you can also right-click a table and choose Select Table on the shortcut menu.

Aligning Text in Columns and Rows

Aligning text in columns and rows is a matter of choosing how you want the text to line up vertically and how you want it to line up horizontally. Select the cells, columns, or rows, with text that you want to align (or select your entire table) and then align the text:

✦ **In Word:** On the (Table Tools) Layout tab, click an Align button (you may have to click the Alignment button first, depending on the size of your screen). Word offers nine of them in the Alignment group.

✦ **In PowerPoint:** On the (Table Tools) Layout tab, click one Horizontal Align button (Align Left, Center, or Align Right), and one Vertical Align button (Align Top, Center Vertically, or Align Bottom). You may have to click the Alignment button first.

Merging and Splitting Cells

Merge and split cells to make your tables a little more elegant than run-of-the-mill tables. *Merge* cells to break down the barriers between cells and join them into one cell; *split* cells to divide a single cell into several cells (or several cells into several more cells). In the table shown in Figure 5-2, the cells in rows two, four, and six have been merged and a baseball player's name appears in each merged cell. Where rows two, four, and six originally had nine cells, they now have only one.

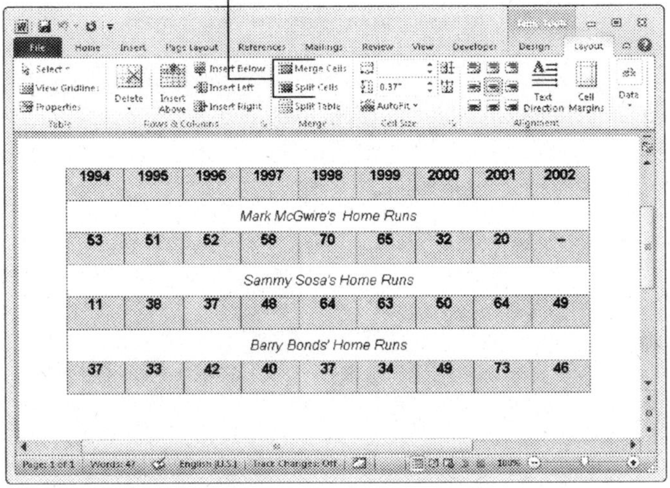

Merge and split cells

Figure 5-2:
Merge cells
to create
larger cells.

1994	1995	1996	1997	1998	1999	2000	2001	2002
Mark McGwire's Home Runs								
53	51	52	58	70	65	32	20	--
Sammy Sosa's Home Runs								
11	38	37	48	64	63	50	64	49
Barry Bonds' Home Runs								
37	33	42	40	37	34	49	73	46

Select the cells you want to merge or split, go to the (Table Tools) Layout tab, and follow these instructions to merge or split cells:

✦ **Merging cells:** Click the Merge Cells button (in Word and PowerPoint, you can also right-click and choose Merge Cells).

✦ **Splitting cells:** Click the Split Cells button (in Word and PowerPoint, you can also right-click and choose Split Cells). In the Split Cells dialog box, declare how many columns and rows you want to split the cell into and then click OK.

In Word and PowerPoint, you can merge and split cells by clicking the Draw Table or Eraser button on the (Table Tools) Design tab. Click the Draw Table button and then draw lines through cells to split them. Click the Eraser button and drag over or click the boundary between cells to merge cells. Press Esc when you're finished drawing or erasing table cell boundaries. You can click the Pen Color button and choose a color on the drop-down list to draw in a particular color.

Need to split a table? In Word, place the cursor in what you want to be the first row of the new table, go to the (Table Tools) Layout tab, and click the Split Table button.

Laying Out Your Table

Very likely, you created too many or too few columns or rows for your table. Some columns are probably too wide and others too narrow. If that's the case, you have to change the table layout by deleting, inserting, and changing the size of columns and rows, not to mention changing the size of the table itself. In other words, you have to modify the table layout. (Later in this chapter, "Decorating your table with borders and colors" shows how to put borders around tables and embellish them in other ways.)

Changing the size of a table, column, or rows

The fastest way to adjust the width of columns, the height of rows, and the size of a table itself is to "eyeball it" and drag the mouse:

+ **Column or row:** Move the pointer onto a gridline or border, and when the pointer changes into a double-headed arrow, start dragging. Tug and pull, tug and pull until the column or row is the right size.

  In Word and PowerPoint, you can also go to the (Table Tools) Layout tab and enter measurements in the Height and Width text boxes to change the width of a column or the height of a row. The measurements affect entire columns or rows, not individual cells.

+ **A table:** Select your table and use one of these techniques to change its size in Word and PowerPoint:

  • *Dragging:* Drag the top, bottom, or side of the table. You can also drag the lower-right corner to change the size vertically and horizontally.

  • *Height and Width text boxes:* On the (Table Tools) Layout tab, enter measurements in the Height and Width text boxes. In PowerPoint, click the Lock Aspect Ratio check box if you want to keep the table's proportions when you change its height or width.

  • *Table Properties dialog box (Word only):* On the (Table Tools) Layout tab, click the Cell Size group button, and on the Table tab of the Table Properties dialog box, enter a measurement in the Preferred Width text box.

Adjusting column and row size

Resizing columns and rows can be problematic in Word and PowerPoint. For that reason, Word and PowerPoint offer special commands on the (Table Tools) Layout tab for adjusting the width and height of rows and columns:

+ **Making all columns the same width:** Click the Distribute Columns button to make all columns the same width. Select columns before giving this command to make only the columns you select the same width.

+ **Making all rows the same height:** Click the Distribute Rows button to make all rows in the table the same height. Select rows before clicking the button to make only the rows you select the same height.

In Word, you can also click the AutoFit button on the (Table Tools) Layout tab, and take advantage of these commands on the drop-down list for handling columns and rows:

+ **AutoFit Contents:** Make each column wide enough to accommodate its widest entry.

+ **AutoFit Window:** Stretch the table so that it fits across the page between the left and right margin.

+ **Fixed Column Width:** Fix the column widths at their current settings.

Inserting and deleting columns and rows

 The trick to inserting and deleting columns and rows is to correctly select part of the table first. You can insert more than one column or row at a time by selecting more than one column or row before giving the Insert command. To insert two columns, for example, select two columns and choose an Insert command; to insert three rows, select three rows and choose an Insert command. Earlier in this chapter, "Selecting Different Parts of a Table" explains how to make table selections.

Go to the (Table Tools) Layout tab and follow these instructions to insert and delete columns and rows:

+ **Inserting columns:** Select a column or columns and click the Insert Left or Insert Right button. If you want to insert just one column, click in a column and then click the Insert Left or Insert Right button. You can also right-click, choose Insert, and choose an Insert Columns command.

+ **Inserting rows:** Select a row or rows and click the Insert Above or Insert Below button. If you want to insert just one row, click in a row and click the Insert Above or Insert Below button. You can also right-click, choose Insert, and choose an Insert Rows command on the shortcut menu.

 To insert a row at the end of a table, move the pointer into the last cell in the last row and press the Tab key.

+ **Deleting columns:** Click in the column you want to delete, click the Delete button, and choose Delete Columns on the drop-down list. Select more than one column to delete more than one. (Pressing the Delete key deletes the data in the column, not the column itself.)

+ **Deleting rows:** Click in the row you want to delete, click the Delete button, and choose Delete Rows. Select more than one row to delete more than one. (Pressing the Delete key deletes the data in the row, not the row itself.)

Moving columns and rows

Because there is no elegant way to move a column or row, you should move only one at a time. If you try to move several simultaneously, you open a can of worms that is best left unopened. To move a column or row:

1. **Select the column or row you want to move.**

   Earlier in this chapter, "Selecting Different Parts of a Table" explains how to select columns and rows.

2. **Right-click in the selection and choose Cut on the shortcut menu.**

   The column or row is moved to the Clipboard.

3. **Insert a new column or row where you want the column or row to be.**

   Earlier in this chapter, "Inserting and deleting columns and rows" explains how.

4. **Move the column or row:**

   • **Column:** Click in the topmost cell in your new column and then click the Paste button or press Ctrl+V.

   • **Row:** Click in the first column of the row you inserted and then click the Paste button or press Ctrl+V.

Formatting Your Table

After you enter text in the table, lay out the columns and rows, and make them the right size, the fun begins. Now you can dress up your table and make it look snazzy. You can change fonts, choose colors for columns and rows, and even land a graphic in the background of your table. You can also play with the borders that divide the columns and rows and shade columns, rows, and cells by filling them with gray shades or a black background. Read on to find out how to do these tricks.

Designing a table with a table style

The fastest way to get a good-looking table is to select a table style in the Table Styles gallery, as shown in Figure 5-3. A *table style* is a ready-made assortment of colors and border choices. You can save yourself a lot of formatting trouble by selecting a table style. After you select a table style, you can modify it by selecting or deselecting check boxes in the Table Style Options group on the (Table Tools) Design tab.

Modify your table   Select a table style

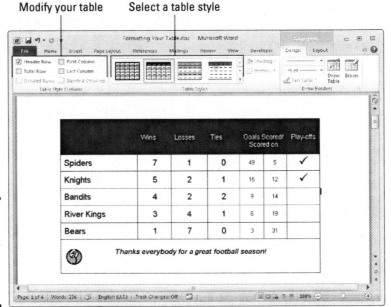

Figure 5-3:
You have
many oppor-
tunities for
designing
tables.

Click anywhere in your table and follow these steps to choose a table style:

1. **Go to the (Table Tools) Design tab.**

2. **Open the Table Styles gallery and move the pointer over table style choices to "live-preview" the table.**

3. **Select a table style.**

> To remove a table style, open the Table Styles gallery and choose Clear (in Word) or Clear Table (in PowerPoint).

For consistency's sake, choose a similar table style — or better yet the same table style — for all the tables in your document or presentation. This way, your work doesn't become a showcase for table styles.

Calling attention to different rows and columns

On the (Table Tools) Design tab, Word and PowerPoint offer Table Style Options check boxes for calling attention to different rows or columns (refer to Figure 5-3). For example, you can make the first row in the table, called the header row, stand out by selecting the Header Row check box. If your table presents numerical data with total figures in the last row, you can call attention to the last row by selecting the Total Row check box. Select or deselect these check boxes on the (Table Tools) Design tab to make your table easier to read and understand:

✦ **Header Row and Total Row:** These check boxes make the first row and last row in a table stand out. Typically, the header row is a different color or contains boldface text because it is the row that identifies the data in the table. Click the Header Row check box to make the first row stand out; if you also want the last row to stand out, click the Total Row check box.

✦ **Banded Columns and Banded Rows:** *Banded* means "striped" in Office lingo. For striped columns or striped rows — columns or rows that alternate in color — select the Banded Columns or Banded Rows check box.

✦ **First Column and Last Column:** Often the first column stands out in a table because it identifies what type of data is in each row. Select the First Column check box to make it a different color or boldface its text. Check the Last Column check box if you want the rightmost column to stand out.

Decorating your table with borders and colors

Rather than rely on a table style, you can play interior decorator on your own. You can slap color on the columns and rows of your table, draw borders around columns and rows, and choose a look for borders. Figure 5-4 shows the drop-down lists on the (Table Tools) Design tab that pertain to table decoration. Use these drop-down lists to shade table columns and rows and draw table borders.

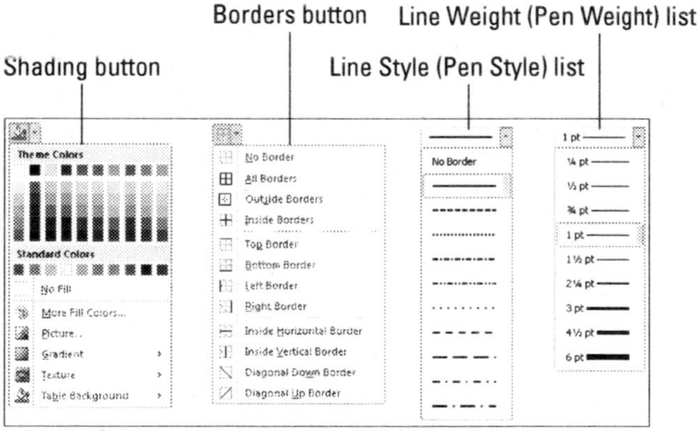

Borders button   Line Weight (Pen Weight) list

Shading button   Line Style (Pen Style) list

Figure 5-4:
Tools on
the (Table
Tools)
Design
tab for
decorating
tables.

Designing borders for your table

Follow these steps to fashion a border for your table or a part of your table:

1. **Go to the (Table Tools) Design tab.**

2. **Select the part of your table that needs a new border.**

To select the entire table, go to the (Table Tools) Layout tab, click the Select button, and choose Select Table.

3. **Open the Line Style drop-down list (in Word) or the Pen Style drop-down list (in PowerPoint) and choose a line style for the border (you may have to click the Draw Borders button first, depending on the size of your screen).**

Stay away from the dotted and dashed lines unless you have a good reason for choosing one. These lines can be distracting and keep others from focusing on the data presented in the table.

4. **Open the Line Weight drop-down list (in Word) or the Pen Weight drop-down list (in PowerPoint) and choose a thickness for the border (you may have to click the Draw Borders button first).**

5. **If you want your borders to be a color apart from black, click the Pen Color button and choose a color on the drop-down list (you may have to click the Draw Borders button first).**

6. **Open the drop-down list on the Borders button and choose where to place borders on the part of the table you selected in Step 2.**

This is the tricky part. The Borders commands have different effects, depending on which part of the table you selected. For example, if you selected two rows and you choose the Top Border command, the command applies only to the top of the uppermost row. If you are anywhere near typical, you have to repeat Step 6 until you get it right.

In Word, you can also change borders by clicking the Draw Borders group button and making selections in the Borders and Shading dialog box, as shown in Figure 5-5.

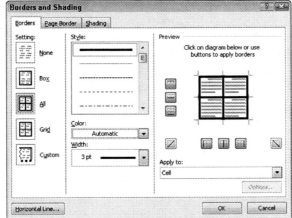

Figure 5-5: In Word, you can draw borders with the Borders and Shading dialog box.

Selecting colors for columns, rows, or your table

Follow these steps to paint columns, rows, or your table a new color:

1. **Select the part of the table that needs a paint job.**

2. **In the (Table Tools) Design tab, open the drop-down list on the Shading button and choose a color (refer to Figure 5-5).**

Later in this chapter, "Using a picture as the table background" explains how to use a picture as the background in a table.

Using Math Formulas in Word Tables

No, you don't have to add the figures in columns and rows yourself; Word gladly does that for you. Word can perform other mathematical calculations as well. Follow these steps to perform mathematical calculations and tell Word how to format sums and products:

1. **Put the cursor in the cell that will hold the sum or product of the cells above, below, to the right, or to the left.**

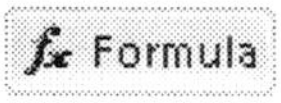

fx Formula

2. **On the (Table Tools) Layout tab, click the Formula button.**

Depending on the size of your screen, you may have to click the Data button first. The Formula dialog box appears, as shown in Figure 5-6. In its wisdom, Word makes an educated guess about what you want the formula to do and places a formula in the Formula box.

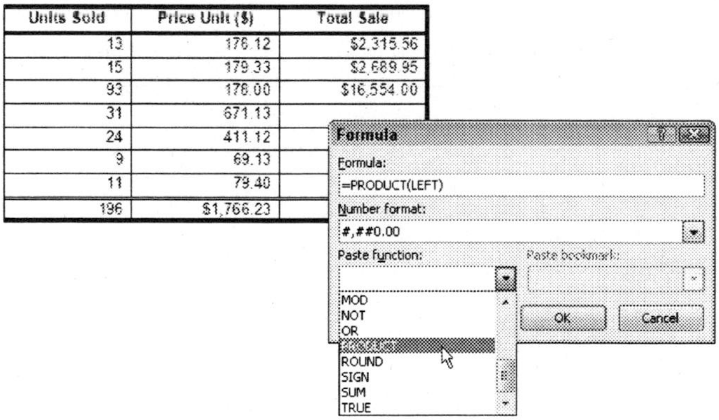

Units Sold	Price Unit ($)	Total Sale
13	176.12	$2,315.56
15	179.33	$2,689.95
93	178.00	$16,554.00
31	671.13	
24	411.12	
9	69.13	
11	79.40	
196	$1,766.23	

Formula

Formula:
=PRODUCT(LEFT)

Number format:
#,##0.00

Paste function: Paste bookmark:

MOD
NOT
OR
PRODUCT
ROUND
SIGN
SUM
TRUE

OK   Cancel

Figure 5-6:
A math formula in a table.

3. **If this isn't the formula you want, delete everything except the equal sign in the Formula box, open the Paste Function drop-down list, and choose another function for the formula.**

For example, choose PRODUCT to multiply figures. You may have to type **left**, **right**, **above**, or **below** in the parentheses within the formula to tell Word where the figures that you want it to compute are.

4. **In the Number Format drop-down list, choose a format for your number.**

5. **Click OK.**

Word doesn't calculate blank cells in formulas. Enter 0 in blank cells if you want them to be included in calculations. You can copy functions from one cell to another to save yourself the trouble of opening the Formula dialog box.

Neat Table Tricks

The rest of this chapter details a handful of neat table tricks to make your tables stand out in a crowd. Why should all tables look alike? Read on to discover how to make text in the header row stand on its ear, put a picture behind a table, draw diagonal border lines, draw on top of a table, and wrap slide text around a table.

Changing the direction of header row text

In a top-heavy table in which the cells in the first row contain text and the cells below contain numbers, consider changing the direction of the text in the first row to make the table easier to read. Changing text direction in the first row is also a good way to squeeze more columns into a table. Consider how wide the table shown in Figure 5-7 would be if the words in the first row were displayed horizontally.

Figure 5-7:
Change the direction of text to squeeze more columns on a table.

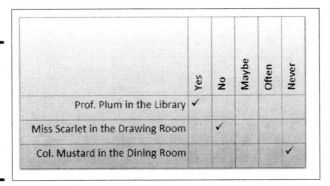

	Yes	No	Maybe	Often	Never
Prof. Plum in the Library	✓				
Miss Scarlet in the Drawing Room		✓			
Col. Mustard in the Dining Room					✓

Follow these steps to change the direction of text on a table.

1. **Select the row that needs a change of text direction.**

   Usually, that's the first row in a table.

2. **Go to the (Table Tools) Layout tab.**

3. **Click the Text Direction button.**

   What happens next depends on whether you're operating in Word or PowerPoint:

   - *In Word:* Keep clicking the Text Direction button until text lands where you want it to land. (You may have to click the Alignment button before you can see the Text Direction button.)

   - *In PowerPoint:* Choose a Text Direction option on the drop-down list. (You may have to click the Alignment button to get to the Text Direction button, depending on the size of your screen.)

4. **Change the height of the row to make the vertical text fit.**

   As "Changing the size of a table, columns, and rows" explains earlier in this chapter, you can change the height of a row by going to the (Table Tools) Layout tab and entering a measurement in the Height box.

Using a picture as the table background

As Figure 5-8 demonstrates, a picture used as the background in a table looks mighty nice. To make it work, however, you need a graphic that serves well as the background. For Figure 5-8, I got around this problem by recoloring my graphic (Book VI, Chapter 3 explains how to recolor a graphic.) You also need to think about font colors. Your audience must be able to read the table text, and that usually means choosing a white or light font color for text so that the text can be read over the graphic. For Figure 5-8, I selected a white font color.

Figure 5-8:
Using a
graphic
as a table
background
(left) and
placing
the same
graphic in
all table
cells (right).

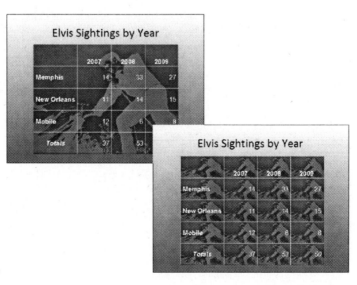

Besides putting a graphic behind a table, PowerPoint gives you the opportunity to make the graphic appear in every table cell, as shown on the right side of Figure 5-8. Sorry, you can't do that feat in Word, but you can place a picture behind a table, as the following pages explain.

Placing a picture behind a table

Placing a graphic behind a table requires a fair bit of work, but the results are well worth the effort. First you insert the graphic and perhaps recolor it. Then you create the table. Lastly, you make the table fit squarely on top of the graphic and perhaps group the objects together.

In Word and PowerPoint, follow these steps to place a graphic behind a table:

1. **Insert the graphic, resize it, and format the graphic.**

   Book VI, Chapter 3 explains how to insert and resize graphics. To insert a graphic, go to the Insert tab and click the Picture button. To resize it, drag a selection handle; make the graphic as big as you want your table to be. To recolor a graphic similar to the job done to the graphic in Figure 5-8, select the (Picture Tools) Format tab, click the Color button, and choose an option.

2. **Insert the table and make it roughly the same size as the graphic.**

   These tasks are explained earlier in this chapter. To change the size of a table, drag a selection handle on its corner or side. Place the table nearby the graphic, but not right on top of it.

3. **On the (Table Tools) Design tab, open the Table Styles gallery, and choose Clear (in Word) or Clear Table (in PowerPoint).**

   With the table styles out of the way, you can see the graphic clearly through your table.

4. **Enter the data in the table, select a font and font color, select a border and border color, and align the text.**

   These tasks (except for selecting fonts) are described throughout this chapter. The easiest way to choose a font and font color for a table is to select the table, go to the Home tab, and select a font and font size.

5. **Move the table squarely on top of the graphic and then make the table and graphic roughly the same size.**

Here are a few tricks that are worth knowing when you're handling a graphic and table:

 ✦ In Word, you have to turn off text wrapping in order to bring the graphic behind the table. To do that, select your graphic, go to the (Picture Tools) Format tab, click the Wrap Text button, and choose Behind Text on the drop-down list.

♦ If the graphic is in front of the table, select the graphic, go to the (Picture Tools) Format tab, open the drop-down list on the Send Backward button, and choose Send to Back (in PowerPoint) or Send Behind Text (in Word).

♦ To make the graphic and table the same size, enter the same measurements for both. Select the table, go to the (Table Tools) Layout tab, and enter measurements for the table in the Height and Width boxes. Then select the graphic, go to the (Picture Tools) Format tab, and enter the same measurements in the Height and Width boxes (you may have to click the Size button to see these boxes, depending on the size of your screen).

Placing a background picture in each PowerPoint table cell

PowerPoint offers a special command for placing a picture in each table cell (refer to Figure 5-8). For this trick to work, you need a graphic of uniform color; otherwise, the text is too hard to read. (You might consult Book VI, Chapter 3, which explains how to alter graphics with the Office Picture Manager.) Follow these steps to place a background picture in each PowerPoint table cell:

1. **Right-click your table and choose Select Table.**

2. **Go to the (Table Tools) Design tab.**

3. **Open the drop-down list on the Shading button and choose Picture.**

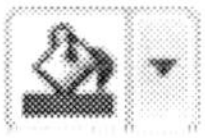

The Insert Picture dialog box opens.

4. **Select a picture and click the Insert button.**

To remove the background pictures from a table, open the drop-down list on the Shading button and choose No Fill or choose Clear Table in the Table Styles gallery.

Drawing diagonal lines on tables

Draw diagonal lines across table cells to cancel out those cells or otherwise make cells look different. In Figure 5-9, diagonal lines are drawn on cells to show that information that would otherwise be in the cells is either not available or is not relevant.

Figure 5-9:
Diagonal lines mark off cells as different.

	Mon.	Tues.	Wed.	Thurs.	Fri.	Sat.	Sun.
McKeef	8:00			3:00		8:00	2:15
Arnez	9:00	6:00	2:30	12:00	8:15		4:00
Danes	9:30		2:00	7:30		3:30	7:30
Minor		12:00	4:15	5:15	2:00		
Krupt	3:30	6:00		12:00	2:30	9:00	9:00
Gough	3:00			7:00	3:30	4:530	3:30
Gonzalez	12:00	7:15	8:30				10:15

Sorting, or reordering a table (in Word)

The fastest way to rearrange the rows in a Word table is to sort the table. *Sorting* means to rearrange all the rows in a table on the basis of data in one or more columns. For example, a table that shows candidates and the number of votes they received could be sorted in alphabetical order by the candidates' names or in numerical order by the number of votes they received. Both tables present the same information, but the information is sorted in different ways.

The difference between ascending and descending sorts is as follows:

- Ascending arranges text from A to Z, numbers from smallest to largest, and dates from earliest to latest.

- Descending arranges text from Z to A, numbers from largest to smallest, and dates from latest to earliest.

When you rearrange a table by sorting it, Word rearranges the formatting as well as the data. Do your sorting before you format the table.

Follow these steps to sort a table:

1. **On the (Table Tools) Layout tab, click the Sort button.**

   You see the Sort dialog box. Depending on the size of your screen, you may have to click the Data button before you see the Sort button.

2. **In the first Sort By drop-down list, choose the column you want to sort with.**

3. **If necessary, open the first Type drop-down list and choose Text, Number, or Date to describe what kind of data you're dealing with.**

4. **Select the Ascending or Descending option button to declare whether you want an ascending or descending sort.**

5. **If necessary, on the first Then By drop-down list, choose the tiebreaker column.**

   If two items in the Sort By columns are alike, Word looks to your Then By column choice to break the tie and place one row before another in the table.

6. **Click OK.**

When you sort a table, Word ignores the *header row* — the first row in the table — and doesn't move it. However, if you want to include the header row in the sort, select the No Header Row option button in the Sort dialog box.

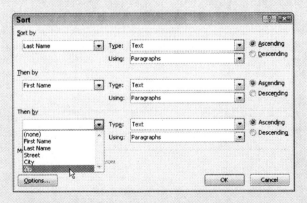

Go to the (Table Tools) Design tab and use one of these techniques to draw diagonal lines across cells:

+ **Draw Table button:** Click the Draw Table button (you may have to click the Draw Borders button first). The pointer changes into a pencil. Drag to draw the diagonal lines. Press Esc or click the Draw Table button a second time when you're finished drawing.

    Click the Pen Color button and choose a color before drawing on your table if you want the diagonal lines to be a certain color.

+ **Borders button:** Select the cells that need diagonal lines, open the drop-down list on the Borders button, and choose Diagonal Down Border or Diagonal Up Border.

To remove diagonal lines, click the Eraser button and click or drag across the diagonals.

Drawing on a table

When you want to call attention to data in one part of a table, draw a circle around the data. By "draw" I mean make an Oval shape and place it over the data you want to highlight, as shown in Figure 5-10. Book I, Chapter 8 explains the drawing tools in detail. To spare you the trouble of turning to that chapter, here are shorthand instructions for drawing on a table in Word and PowerPoint:

1. **On the Insert tab, click the Shapes button and select the Oval shape on the drop-down list.**

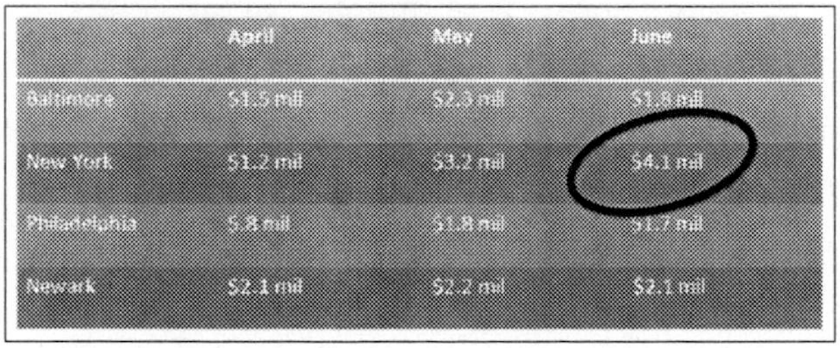

Figure 5-10:
You can circle data to highlight it.

	April	May	June
Baltimore	$1.5 mil	$2.3 mil	$1.8 mil
New York	$1.2 mil	$3.2 mil	$4.1 mil
Philadelphia	$.8 mil	$1.8 mil	$1.7 mil
Newark	$2.1 mil	$2.2 mil	$2.1 mil

2. **On a corner of your page or slide, away from the table, drag to draw the oval.**

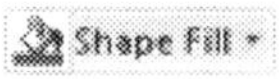

3. **On the (Drawing Tools) Format tab, open the drop-down list on the Shape Fill button and choose No Fill.**

4. **Open the drop-down list on the Shape Outline button and choose a very dark color.**

5. **Open the drop-down list on the Shape Outline button, choose Weight, and choose a thick line.**

6. **Drag the oval over the data on your table that you want to highlight.**

   If the oval is obscured by the table, go to the (Drawing Tools) Format tab, and click the Bring Forward button (click the Arrange button, if necessary, to see this button). While you're at it, consider rotating the oval a little way to make it appear as though it was drawn by hand on the table.

In the course of a live PowerPoint presentation, you can draw on slides with the Pen to highlight data. See Book III, Chapter 4.

Chapter 6: Creating a Chart

In This Chapter

✓ Looking at the different parts of a chart

✓ Creating a chart

✓ Examining the different types of charts

✓ Entering chart data in an Excel worksheet

✓ Positioning a chart in Excel, Word, and PowerPoint

✓ Changing the appearance of a chart

✓ Saving a customized chart as a template so that you can use it again

✓ Exploring some fancy-schmancy chart tricks

✓ Fixing common problems with charts

*N*othing is more persuasive than a chart. The bars, pie slices, lines, or columns show immediately whether production is up or down, cats are better than dogs or dogs better than cats, or catsup tastes better than ketchup. Fans of charts and graphs will be glad to know that putting a chart in a Word document, Excel worksheet, or PowerPoint slide is fairly easy.

This chapter explains how to create a chart. It looks at which charts are best for presenting different kinds of data, how to change a chart's appearance, and how to save charts in a template that you can use again. You discover some nice chart tricks, including how to make a picture the backdrop for a chart and how to annotate a chart. This chapter also addresses common chart problems.

A Mercifully Brief Anatomy Lesson

Throughout this chapter, I show you many ways to tinker with charts, but before you can begin tinkering, you need to know what you're tinkering with. In other words, you have to know what the different parts of a chart are. Here is a brief chart anatomy lesson. Figure 6-1 points out where some of the terms described here are found on a real, live chart:

✦ **Plot area:** The center of the chart, apart from the legend and data labels, where the data itself is presented.

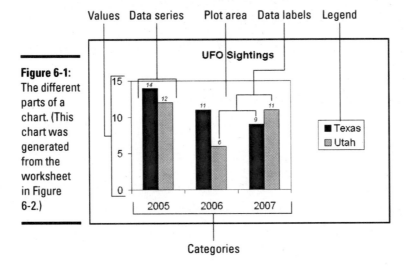

Values Data series   Plot area Data labels   Legend

Figure 6-1:
The different
parts of a
chart. (This
chart was
generated
from the
worksheet
in Figure
6-2.)

Categories

✦ **Values:** The numerical values with which the chart is plotted. The values you enter determine the size of the *data markers* — the bars, columns, pie slices, and so on — that portray values. In the column chart in Figure 6-1, values determine the height of the columns.

✦ **Gridlines:** Lines on the chart that indicate value measurements. Gridlines are optional in charts (none are shown in Figure 6-1).

✦ **Worksheet:** Where you enter (or retrieve) the data used to plot the chart. The worksheet resembles a table. Figure 6-2 shows the worksheet I used to enter the data that produced the chart in Figure 6-1. Notice how the numbers at the top of the columns correspond to the numbers entered in the worksheet shown in Figure 6-2. A worksheet is called a *data table* when it appears along with a chart.

Data labels

Figure 6-2:
The
information
entered
in this
worksheet
produced
the chart
shown in
Figure 6-1.

Categories   Data series

	A	B	C
1		Texas	Utah
2	2005	14	12
3	2006	11	6
4	2007	9	11

✦ **Data series:** A group of related data points presented by category on a chart. The chart in Figure 6-1 has two data series, one for Texas and one for Utah.

✦ **Categories:** The actual items that you want to compare or display in your chart. In Figure 6-1, the categories are the three years in which UFO sightings occurred in the two states.

✦ **Legend:** A text box located to the side, top, or bottom of a chart that identifies the chart's data labels.

✦ **Horizontal and vertical axes:** For plotting purposes, one side of the plot area. In the chart in Figure 6-1, UFO sightings are plotted on the *horizontal axis;* categories are plotted on the *vertical axis.* Sometimes these axes are called the *category axis* (or *x axis*) and the *value axis* (or *y axis*).

Axes can be confusing, but these axes aren't as evil as they seem. All you really need to know about them is this: You can label the axes in different ways and you can rotate the chart so that the horizontal becomes the vertical axis and vice versa (click the Switch Row/Column button).

✦ **Data point:** A value plotted on a chart that is represented by a column, line, bar, pie slice, dot, or other shape. Each data point corresponds to a value entered in the worksheet. In Figure 6-1, for example, the data points for Texas UFO sightings are 14 in 2005, 11 in 2006, and 9 in 2007. Hence the Texas columns in the table rise to the 14, 11, and 9 level.

✦ **Data marker:** Shapes on a chart that represent data points. Data markers include columns, lines, pie slices, bubbles, and dots. In Figure 6-1, columns are the data markers.

✦ **Data label:** A label that shows the actual values used to construct the data markers. In the chart in Figure 6-1, there are six data labels, one on the top of each column. Displaying data labels in charts is optional.

The good news where the anatomy of a chart is concerned is that you can click anywhere on a chart and see a pop-up box that tells you what part of the chart you just clicked. I wish biology class were that easy!

The Basics: Creating a Chart

Throughout this chapter, I explain the whys, wherefores, and whatnots of creating a chart. Before going into details, here are the basic steps that everyone needs to know to create a chart in Word, Excel, and PowerPoint:

1. **Go to the Insert tab.**

2. **If you're working in Excel, select the data you'll use to generate the chart (in Word and PowerPoint, skip to Step 3).**

In Excel, you select the data on a worksheet before creating the chart, but in Word and PowerPoint, you enter the data for the chart in Excel in Step 4. Yes, you heard me right — in Word and PowerPoint. Excel opens after you begin creating your chart so you can enter data for the chart in an Excel worksheet.

3. **Select the kind of chart you want.**

   How you select a chart type depends on which program you're working in:

   • *Excel:* Either open the drop-down list on one of the buttons in the Chart group on the Insert tab (Column, Line, Pie, Bar, Area, Scatter, or Other Charts) and select a chart type, or click the Charts group button to open the Insert Chart dialog box and select a chart there. As shown in Figure 6-3, the Insert Chart dialog box shows all the kinds of charts you can create.

   • *Word and PowerPoint:* Click the Chart button. You see the Insert Chart dialog box shown in Figure 6-3. Select a chart and click OK. The Excel program opens on the right side of your computer screen. (In PowerPoint, you can also click the Chart icon on a placeholder frame to open the Insert Chart dialog box.)

   The next portion of this chapter, "Choosing the Right Chart," describes all the chart types and advises you on which to choose.

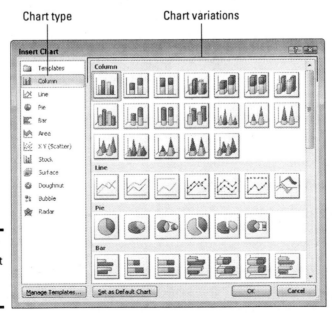

Chart type   Chart variations

Figure 6-3:
Which chart
do you
want?

4. **In Word and PowerPoint, replace the sample data in the Excel worksheet with the data you need for generating your chart.**

   Later in this chapter, "Providing the Raw Data for Your Chart" explains how to enter data in an Excel worksheet. After you finish entering the data, you can close Excel by clicking the Close button in the Excel window or by going to the File tab and choosing Close.

5. **To modify your chart, start by selecting it.**

   Click a chart to select it. Selecting a chart makes the Chart Tools tabs appear in the upper-right corner of the window. Use these tabs — Design, Layout, and Format — to make your chart just-so.

   In Word, you must be in Print Layout view to see a chart.

6. **Select the (Chart Tools) Design tab when you want to change the chart's layout, alter the data with which the chart was generated, or select a different chart type.**

   Later in this chapter, "Changing a Chart's Appearance" explains how to change the design of a chart.

7. **Select the (Chart Tools) Layout tab when you want to change the chart's title, labels, or gridlines.**

   You can add or remove parts of a chart starting on the Layout tab. Later in this chapter, "Changing the layout of a chart" describes how to change around the text and gridlines on a chart.

8. **Select the (Chart Tools) Format tab when you want to change the appearance of your chart.**

   You can change colors and fills on your chart, as "Changing a chart element's color, font, or other particular" explains later in this chapter.

And if you decide to delete the chart you created? Click its perimeter to select it and then press the Delete key.

Choosing the Right Chart

If you're a fan of charts, the huge selection of charts can make you feel like a kid in a candy store, but if charts aren't your *forté,* the wealth of charts you can choose from can be daunting. You can choose among six dozen charts in 11 categories (refer to Figure 6-3).

Which chart is best? It depends on the data you're plotting and what you want to communicate to your audience. The following pages explore the chart categories and give you some gratuitous advice for presenting data in a chart.

Ground rules for choosing a chart

The golden rule for choosing a chart is this: Select the chart type that presents your information in the brightest possible light. The purpose of a chart is to compare information across different categories. Select a chart that draws out the comparison so that your audience can clearly make comparisons.

Try to make your charts simple, even if it means breaking down a complex chart into several smaller charts. The "keep it simple" rule applies as well to charts' appearance. Using a 3-D chart or other fancy chart is tempting because these charts are easy to make, but fancy charts can be confusing to the audience. Imagine you're sitting in the back row of the audience at a PowerPoint presentation and you see a complex 3-D chart dripping with data markers? You might feel cheated at not being able to make sense of the chart. Avoid complex 3-D charts, especially in bar and column charts that compare data in series.

Examining the different kinds of charts

Table 6-1 describes the 11 chart categories and explains in brief when to use each type of chart. The following pages examine the chart types in excruciating detail.

Table 6-1		Chart Types
Symbol	*Chart Type*	*Best Use/Description*
	Area	Examine how values in different categories fluctuate over time, and see the cumulative change in values. (Same as a line chart except that the area between trend lines is colored in.)
	Bar	Compare values in different categories against one another, usually over time. Data is displayed in horizontal bars. (Same as a column chart except that the bars are horizontal.)
	Bubble	Examine data relationships by studying the size and location of the bubbles that represent the relationships. Bubble charts are often used in financial analyses and market research. (Similar to an XY scatter chart except that you can use three instead of two data series, and the data points appear as bubbles.)
	Column	Compare values in different categories against one another, usually over time. Data is displayed in vertical columns. (Same as a bar chart except that the bars are vertical.)

Symbol	Chart Type	Best Use/Description
◉	Doughnut	See how values compare as percentages of a whole. (Similar to a pie chart except that you can use more than one data series and create concentric doughnut rings in the chart.)
⬿	Line	Examine how values fluctuate over time. Data is displayed in a set of points connected by a line.
◔	Pie	See how values compare as percentages of a whole. Data from categories is displayed as a percentage of a whole. (Similar to a doughnut chart.)
✪	Radar	Examine data as it relates to one central point. Data is plotted on radial points from the central point. This kind of chart is used to make subjective performance analyses.
⋰	XY (Scatter)	Compare different numeric data point sets in space to reveal patterns and trends in data. (Similar to a bubble chart except that the data appears as points instead of bubbles.)
⊞	Stock	See how the value of an item fluctuates as well as its daily, weekly, or yearly high, low, and closing price. This chart is used to track stock prices, but it can also be used to track air temperature and other variable quantities.
◈	Surface	Examine color-coded data on a 3D surface to explore relationships between data values.

Column charts

Use a *column chart* when you want your audience to compare data values in different categories. Often the values are compared within a time frame. The column chart in Figure 6-4, for example, compares the number of fish caught over three days in three lakes. Viewing columns of different heights side by side makes it easy to see how values compare to one another.

As shown on the bottom of Figure 6-4, a *stacked column chart* also compares values, except the columns appear one over the other, not side by side. Value comparisons aren't as easy to make in a stacked column chart, but a stacked chart gives you a sense of cumulative values that you can't get from a standard column chart. In Figure 6-4, for example, the stacked chart clearly shows how many fish in total were caught each day in the three lakes.

✦ **Example:** Compare year-by-year sales totals in different regions.

✦ **Similar charts:** The bar chart and column chart serve similar purposes. Both compare values, except the bars in a bar chart are horizontal (they run side to side), whereas the columns in a column chart are vertical (they run up and down). The conventional wisdom is to use a column chart when you want to emphasize how data compare to one another across categories, but use a bar chart when you want to emphasize the largest or smallest values in the comparison. Large and small bars appear prominently in bar charts — they stick their heads out where all can see them.

✦ **Variations:** Nineteen charts comprising various combinations of stacked, 3-D, cylindrical, and pyramid-shaped columns. Imagine you're Dr. Frankenstein and experiment with the different variations when you're feeling ghoulish.

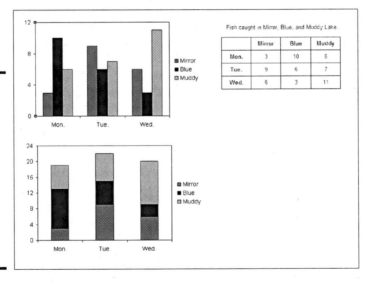

Figure 6-4:
A column chart (top), stacked column chart (bottom), and the worksheet used to generate the charts.

Avoid the third dimension in column charts and bar charts. The purpose of these charts is to compare data in different categories, but when a chart is "tipped" to render it in 3-D, you see the tops and sides of the columns and bars, which effectively makes small columns and bars look bigger than they really are. The comparison between large and small columns and bars can get lost in the third dimension. If you must make a 3-D column chart, use cylindrical, cone-shaped, or pyramid-shaped columns to avoid the problem of making tipsy small columns look bigger.

When many columns appear on a chart, they have to be narrowed so that they can all fit, and this can render the chart useless. Consider what would happen in Figure 6-4, for example, if the chart compared how many fish were caught at the three lakes not on three days, but on 30 days. The top chart would have 90 very narrow columns. Comparing the day's catch on different days would be close to impossible. If you have to compare many data points across different categories, consider using a line chart instead of a column chart.

Line charts

The purpose of a *line chart* is to examine how values fluctuate over time. Each line on the chart, with its peaks and valleys, clearly shows fluctuations. Because each data point in the chart is represented by a dot, not a fat column or bar, you can plot many values without running out of chart space. In Figure 6-5, for example, the chart plots 30 data points, 10 for each lake. The similar chart in Figure 6-4, a column chart, plots only nine data points. Use a line chart when you want to plot many data values to demonstrate a trend or movement in the data.

Figure 6-5:
A line chart and the worksheet used to generate it.

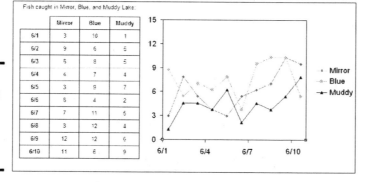

Line charts don't adequately show individual data points — the number of fish caught in a lake, sales in the month of October, the number of people who live in Ohio. Use line charts not to report data but to show data trends over time.

✦ **Example:** Examine how the value of two commodities changes week by week to demonstrate price fluctuations and compare the value of the two commodities in a six-month period.

✦ **Similar charts:** An area chart is a line chart with filled in color. A stock chart is a special kind of line chart designed especially for tracking the value of stocks, including each stock's high, low, and closing prices.

♦ **Variations:** Seven variations, including stacked line and 3-D charts. Instead of criss-crossing, lines in a *stacked line chart* are arranged on top of one another so that you can see the cumulative value of the data being plotted as well as the individual value of each data point. (Consider using a stacked area chart if you want to present data this way.) You can include drop lines and up/down bars in line charts to more clearly distinguish one data marker from the next (see "Examining combination charts," later in this chapter).

In a line chart, each data series is represented by one line. Figure 6-5, for example, charts the number of fish caught daily at three lakes, so there are three lines on the chart. Be careful about plotting too many data series — including too many lines — on a line chart. Put too many lines in your chart, and it starts looking like a bowl of spaghetti!

Pie charts

A *pie chart* is the simplest kind of chart. It shows how values compare as parts of a whole. Use a pie chart to compare values that are associated with one another. For example, the pie chart in Figure 6-6 shows how the number of fish caught at each of three different lakes compares to the total amount of fish caught. Pie charts don't show quantities, but relationships between data.

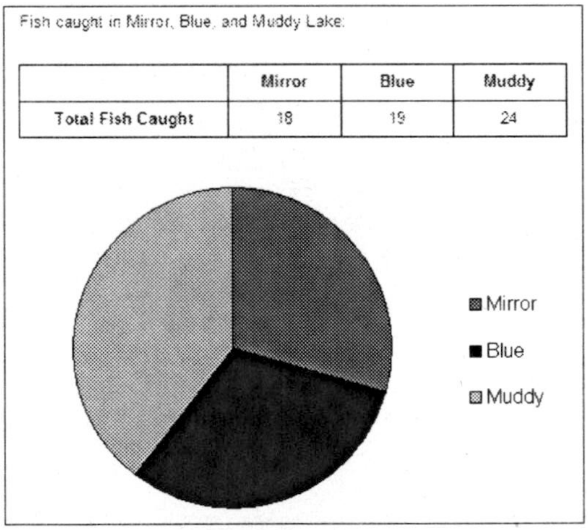

Fish caught in Mirror, Blue, and Muddy Lake:

	Mirror	Blue	Muddy
Total Fish Caught	18	19	24

Figure 6-6: A pie chart and the worksheet used to generate it.

■ Mirror
■ Blue
▨ Muddy

Bear in mind when you enter data for your pie chart in the worksheet that a pie chart plots only one data series. In other words, it has only one category. In Figure 6-6, for example, "Total Fish Caught" is the only category. Pie charts are the only charts that plot a single data series.

✦ **Example:** Discover how different business expenses contribute proportionally to total business expenses.

✦ **Similar charts:** A doughnut chart is a pie chart with a hole in the middle. However, you can arrange to plot more than one data series with a doughnut chart. The column, line, bar, and area chart types offer 100% charts. These charts, as do pie charts, display values as a portion of a whole rather than as values by amount.

✦ **Variations:** Six variations, including 3-D pie charts, exploded pies, and a pie of pie and bar of pie chart. In an *exploded pie chart,* slices are pulled apart to make them more distinct from one another. Pie of pie and bar of pie charts collect small pie slices and put them in a stacked column chart or secondary pie beside the pie chart (see "Examining combination charts," later in this chapter, if you're curious about this subject).

Any data series that presents percentages is a good candidate for a pie chart because a percentage value is by definition part of something bigger.

Don't include more than seven or eight values in a pie chart, and try to avoid small values that make for narrow pie slices, or else your pie chart will splinter into narrow pie slices and be all but useless for comparison purposes. (You can get around the problem of narrow pie slices with a bar of pie or pie of pie chart. These charts place smaller data values in a column chart or secondary pie chart to the side of the pie chart. See "Examining combination charts" later in this chapter.)

Bar charts

A *bar chart* compares values in different categories against one another, usually within a time frame, and emphasizes the largest and smallest values. The bars show you right away how the values compare to one another and which values are largest and smallest. In the bar chart in Figure 6-7, for example, it's plain to see that the most fish were caught on Wednesday at Muddy Lake; the fewest fish were caught on Monday at Mirror Lake and Wednesday at Blue Lake.

A *stacked bar chart* also compares values, but it does so cumulatively. Instead of the bars in each data series being grouped together, they are laid end on end, so you get a sense of the total value of the bars. In the stacked bar chart in Figure 6-7, you can see that more fish were caught on Tuesday than the other two days and you can also tell (sort of) how many fish were caught each day at each lake.

✦ **Example:** Compare cities' population totals in different censuses.

✦ **Similar charts:** A bar chart is a column chart turned on its ear. (To compare a bar chart to a column chart, compare Figure 6-7 to Figure 6-4.) Whereas the bars in a bar chart are horizontal, the columns in a column chart are vertical. Generally speaking, use a bar chart to emphasize which data in the comparison is the largest or smallest; to strictly compare data, use a column chart. The idea here is that the horizontal bars on a bar chart make small and large values stand out, but the vertical columns on a column chart call viewers' attention to the relative differences between all the values.

✦ **Variations:** Fifteen variations, including combinations of stacked and 3-D charts with conical and pyramid-shaped bars.

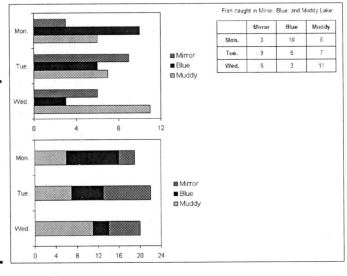

Figure 6-7: A bar chart (top), stacked bar chart (bottom), and the worksheet used to generate the charts.

Fish caught in Mirror, Blue, and Muddy Lake.

	Mirror	Blue	Muddy
Mon.	3	10	6
Tue.	9	6	7
Wed.	6	3	11

 Be careful about plotting too many values in a bar chart. If you do, you'll wind up with many skinny bars and make comparisons on your chart difficult to see and read. To plot many values in a chart, consider using a line chart or an area chart.

Area charts

 An *area chart* is a line chart (refer to Figure 6-5) with colors filled in. Use it to compare data values and track their fluctuations over time. The standard area chart isn't worth very much because the data series' colors obscure one another; you can't compare values easily or make much sense of the chart. However, a *stacked area chart* like the one shown in Figure 6-8 can be very useful. A stacked area chart is similar to a line chart because it shows how values fluctuate over time, but it also shows volume. In Figure 6-8, the colors give you a sense of how many fish were caught daily in each lake, and you can also see the total number of fish caught daily. The chart clearly shows that the fewest fish were caught on 6/6 and the most were caught on 6/9.

Figure 6-8:
A stacked area chart and the data from which it was generated.

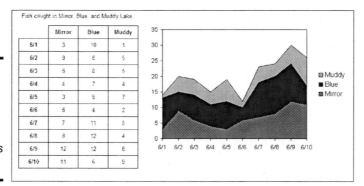

Fish caught in Mirror, Blue, and Muddy Lake

	Mirror	Blue	Muddy
6/1	3	10	1
6/2	3	6	5
6/3	6	8	5
6/4	4	7	4
6/5	3	9	7
6/6	6	4	2
6/7	7	11	5
6/8	8	12	4
6/9	12	12	6
6/10	11	6	9

✦ **Example:** Look at monthly revenue sources from different regions to examine each revenue source and see how much each source contributes to your total revenue.

✦ **Similar charts:** A line chart also shows how values fluctuate over time. A stacked line chart is the same as a stacked area chart, except the area between the lines is not colored in.

✦ **Variations:** Six variations, including 3-D charts and 100% charts. Instead of dealing in amounts, 100% charts show what portion each value is in the sum of all values. You can include drop lines in area charts to more clearly distinguish one data marker from the next (see "Examining combination charts," later in this chapter).

You need many data points to make an area chart worthwhile. If you don't have much data to plot, consider using a column chart rather than an area chart.

XY (scatter) charts

 XY (scatter) charts are used in scientific and financial analyses to discern a trend or pattern in data. These advanced charts are used to find "data clusters" — unforeseen relationships between different data variables. Unlike other charts, XY (scatter) charts point out similarities rather than contrasts between data values. Time is usually not plotted in XY (scatter) charts, nor are any values that occur or increment at regular intervals. Both axes — the X and the Y — require numeric values.

Use an XY (scatter) chart when you suspect a causal relationship between data but you aren't sure what that relationship is. Figure 6-9, for example, shows an XY (scatter) chart that looks into how the number of years of schooling a person has relates to his or her annual income. The chart shows that people with more education tend to earn more money, although a handful of people do quite well without a formal education, and one or two well-educated souls nevertheless have trouble paying the rent.

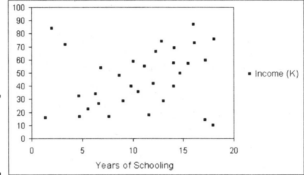

Figure 6-9:
An XY (scatter) chart.

When you enter numbers in the worksheet from your XY (scatter) chart, the values from column A appear on the horizontal axis (x axis) and the values from column B appear on the vertical axis (the y axis). In other words, the numbers you put in the first column will appear along the bottom of the chart, and the numbers you enter in the second column will form the scale on the left side of the chart.

✦ **Example:** Evaluate how the consumption of soft drinks relates to air temperature to see whether people drink more soda in the summertime.

✦ **Similar charts:** An XY (scatter) chart is similar to a bubble chart but points rather than bubbles are the data markers, and you can plot three data sets with a bubble chart. Surface charts also reveal hidden relationships between data values.

✦ **Variations:** Five variations with some charts connecting the data points by lines or smoothed lines, and some charts removing the data markers in favor of lines.

To get any use out of an XY (scatter) chart, you need a lot of data. The more data you enter on your worksheet, the more data markers appear on your chart, and the more likely you are to discover a trend or pattern in the data. An XY (scatter) chart with only a few data markers looks anemic and sad.

If your XY (scatter) chart is too scatterbrained — if the data points are spread seemingly at random around the chart — consider adding a trendline to your chart. A trendline can help indicate trends in data. See "Examining combination charts," later in this chapter, to find out more about trendlines.

Stock charts

A *stock chart* is a line chart designed especially for tracking the value of stocks, including their daily, weekly, or yearly highs, lows, and closing prices. If you're up to it, you can modify stock charts to track data apart from stock prices. For example, you can plot the daily high, low, and average temperature of a city or town. Figure 6-10 shows a stock chart that tracks the high, low, and closing price of a stock over a six-month period. Notice that horizontal lines on the chart indicate closing prices; vertical lines are long if the difference between the high and low price is great.

Figure 6-10:
A stock chart and the worksheet used to create it.

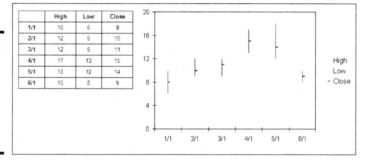

✦ **Example:** Show how the price of a share of Microsoft stock has changed over a 10-year period.

✦ **Similar charts:** A line chart also shows how values change over time.

✦ **Variations:** Four variations, some of which plot the opening price and trading volume as well as the high, low, and closing price.

Surface charts

A *surface chart* provides a three-dimensional, "topographical" view of data, as shown in Figure 6-11. Normally in a chart, each data series is assigned the same color, but in a surface chart, data values in the same range are given the same color so that you can discover where data values are similar and find hidden relationships between data. Use a surface chart to find data patterns and trends.

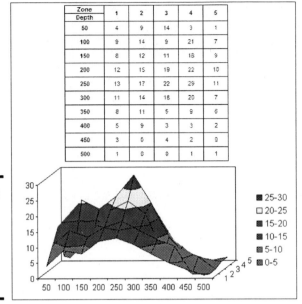

Figure 6-11: A surface chart and the worksheet used to create it.

The surface chart is the only truly three-dimensional chart (the other 3-D charts are merely "tilted" to give the appearance of three dimensions). A surface chart requires three sets of data variables, each with numeric values. The surface chart in Figure 6-11 looks at the number of fish sighted in five different zones to gain an understanding of where fish are most likely to be caught. From the looks of it, the best place to troll for fish is zone 4 at the 250-feet level.

✦ **Example:** To examine a material whose strength increases with temperature but decreases over time, find which combinations of time and temperature produce similar strain results.

✦ **Similar charts:** As do surface charts, XY (scatter) charts and bubble charts uncover unforeseen relationships between data.

✦ **Variations:** Four variations, including a wireframe chart (without the colors) and two-dimensional contour charts.

It might interest you to know that topographical maps, like surface charts, are generated from three numeric data values: altitude, longitude, and latitude. A topographical map is actually a kind of surface chart.

Doughnut charts

Like a pie chart, a *doughnut chart* shows how values compare as parts of a whole. However, a doughnut chart is shaped — you guessed it — like a doughnut, and you can plot more than one data series in a doughnut chart. Figure 6-12 shows two doughnut charts, one that plots a single data series and one that plots two data series. The first chart compares the number of fish caught at three lakes and the second the number of fish caught at three lakes over two days.

Figure 6-12:
A doughnut chart plotting one data series (left) and two series (right), along with the worksheets that produced the charts.

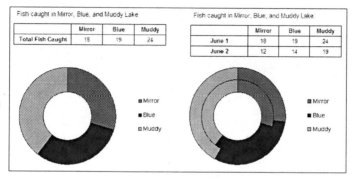

American and European audiences aren't used to seeing doughnut charts and tend to squint and scratch their heads when presented with one. Doughnut charts are a favorite in East Asia. Kind of strange, don't you think, that Americans eat doughnuts but don't care for doughnut charts, whereas East Asians like doughnut charts but don't care for doughnuts?

✦ **Example:** Compare by percentage how income from different sources contributes to total income in three separate years.

✦ **Similar charts:** A pie chart is similar to a doughnut chart, but there isn't a hole in the middle, and you can plot only one data series.

✦ **Variations:** Two variations, including an exploded doughnut chart with the "bites" of the doughnut separated from one another.

Bubble charts

Bubble charts are used in financial analyses and market research to illuminate data relationships, unearth trends in data, and find data patterns. As do XY (scatter) charts, they produce data clusters that emphasize similarities rather than contrasts between data. Use bubble charts to explore cause-and-effect relationships and follow hunches.

The bubble chart shown in Figure 6-13 looks into the data relationship between the size of companies' sales forces, their income from sales, and market share. The object is to get a rough idea of how large a sales force is necessary to increase sales and market share. Notice that the third data series in the worksheet, market share, determines the size of the bubbles.

Size of Sales Force	14	12	10	16	18	14	13	9
Income (in millions)	40	42	59	87	76	58	29	29
Market Share (%)	4	14	12	18	3	21	11	9

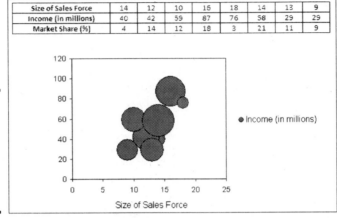

Figure 6-13:
A bubble
chart
and the
worksheet
that
produced it.

+ **Example:** Study how income from sales is influenced by pricing, labor costs, and market share.

+ **Similar charts:** A bubble chart is similar to an XY (scatter) chart in the way data points are plotted, but you can use three data series, not just two, in a bubble chart.

+ **Variations:** Two variations, one having a 3-D visual effect.

Radar charts

A *radar chart,* also called a *spider chart* because of its resemblance to a spider web, compares data values by showing how they relate to a central point in the middle of the chart. The further away a data marker is from the central point, the larger its value is. Radar charts are often used for subjective performance comparisons. The radar chart in Figure 6-14, for example, compares the play of three basketball players using as criteria the number of most valuable player (MVP) awards they received, the number of NBA championships they won, and the number of NCAA championships they won.

Player	NBA MVP	NBA Championships	NCAA Championships
Kareem Abdul-Jabbar	6	6	3
Wilt Chamberlain	4	2	0
Bill Russell	5	9	2

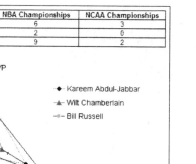

Figure 6-14: A radar chart and the worksheet that produced it.

As are doughnut charts, radar charts are favored in East Asia and can be confusing to Western audiences. It's hard to distinguish the data categories being compared from the lines and data markers on a radar chart. I'm told that in Japan, where radar charts are called spider charts, you can't sit through a PowerPoint presentation without seeing at least one radar chart.

✦ **Example:** Using employee performance ratings in different categories, compare the performance of five employees by studying their "radar rings" on the radar chart.

✦ **Similar charts:** There are no similar charts, as far as I can tell.

✦ **Variations:** Three variations, including one with markers at each data point and a fill chart in which one data series is filled in with color.

Examining combination charts

The bar of pie, pie of pie, and trendline charts do double-duty and combine two charts in one. You can also place error bars, up/down bars, and drop lines on charts. Better keep reading if you want to know about these combination charts. Figure 6-15 shows what two of these charts — a bar of pie and trendline chart — look like.

Bar of pie and pie of pie charts

In *bar of pie* and *pie of pie* charts, the narrow pie slices that represent small values are taken out of the pie and put in a stacked column chart or secondary pie where all can see them (refer to Figure 6-15). A bar of pie chart permits the audience to see what narrow pie slices are made of. To create a bar of pie or pie of pie chart, enter data in the worksheet as you would normally for a pie chart, but enter the smallest values on the bottom rows of the sheet; PowerPoint takes the smallest categories and places them in the stacked column chart or smaller pie.

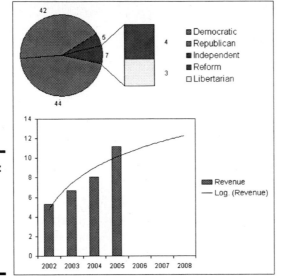

Figure 6-15:
A bar of pie chart (top) and a trendline chart (bottom).

What kind of a name is "bar of pie"? If I went to a bar and they were serving only pie, I would be sorely disappointed.

Trendline chart

A column, bar, area, XY (scatter), line, or bubble chart can be turned into a trendline chart. Use *trendline charts* in regression analysis to reveal trends in data, forecast future data trends, or iron out fluctuations in data to make trends emerge more clearly. Figure 6-15, shown earlier in this chapter, shows a trendline chart that predicts future income.

You can't create a trendline chart from these chart varieties: 3-D, stacked, pie, radar, surface, or doughnut.

Follow these steps to place a trendline on a chart:

1. **On the (Chart Tools) Layout tab, open the Chart Elements drop-down list in the Current Selection group and choose the data series that you want to highlight with a trendline.**

2. **Click the Trendline button and choose a trendline option on the drop-down menu.**

    Your choices are as follows:

    - *Linear:* A straight line that shows the rising or falling data rate.

    - *Exponential:* A curved line that shows how values rise or fall at increasingly higher rates.

- *Linear Forecast:* A straight line that shows the future data rate rising and falling based on the performance reported on the chart. For example, if your chart shows three months' of data, the chart with a trendline shows three more months so that the chart reports six months' of data, three real and three projected.

To change the look of a trendline, right-click it and choose Format Trendline. In the Format Trendline dialog box, choose a line color and line style.

To remove a trendline from a chart, click the chart to select it, go to the (Chart Tools) Layout tab, click the Trendline button, and choose None on the drop-down menu.

Drop lines in line and area charts

In two-dimensional line and area charts, you can include *drop lines* that run from the horizontal axis to each data point. Especially in area charts, the lines help show where one data marker ends and another begins. To include drop lines on a line or area chart, select the chart, go to the (Chart Tools) Layout tab, click the Lines button (you may have to click the Analysis button first), and choose Drop Lines on the drop-down list.

Up/down bars in line charts

In line charts, you can include *up/down bars* that illustrate the difference between data points in the same series. Sometimes up/down bars are useful for helping the audience see data points more clearly. To experiment with up/down bars, select your line chart, go to the (Chart Tools) Layout tab, click the Up/Down Bars button (you may have to click the Analysis button first, and choose Up/Down Bars on the drop-down list.

Error bars

By placing *error bars* on a chart, you can illustrate how each data marker in the chart — each column or bar, for example — deviates from the norm. Error bars show variability in the data being plotted or uncertainty in measurements. The "bars" are actually lines. To apply error bars to a chart, select the chart, visit the (Chart Tools) Layout tab, click the Error Bars button (you may have to click the Analysis button first), and choose an option on the drop-down list.

Providing the Raw Data for Your Chart

Every chart is constructed from *raw data* — the numbers and category names you select in an Excel worksheet (in Excel) or enter in an Excel worksheet (in Word and PowerPoint). If you're operating in Word or PowerPoint, you see, in the Excel worksheet, sample data in a *data range*. The information inside the data range is used to generate the chart. You can tell where the data range begins and ends because it is enclosed in a blue border. Your job is to replace the sample data in the data range with data of your own. As you enter your data, the chart on your slide or page takes shape.

Book IV, Chapter 1 explains in detail how to enter data in an Excel worksheet, but here are the basics of entering data in case you're new to Excel:

+ **Entering the data in a cell:** A cell is the box in a worksheet where a column and row intersect; each cell can contain one data item. To enter data in a cell, click the cell and start typing. When you're finished, press Enter, press Tab, or click a different cell. You can also click in the Formula bar (above the worksheet) and enter the data there.

+ **Deleting the data in a cell:** To delete the data in a cell, including the sample data Excel provides for charts, click the cell and press Delete.

+ **Displaying the numbers:** When a number is too large to fit in a cell, Excel displays pound signs (###) or displays the number in scientific notation. Don't worry — the number is still recorded and is used to generate your chart. You can display large numbers by widening the columns in which the numbers are found. Move the pointer between column letters (A, B, and so on at the top of the worksheet) and when you see the double-headed arrow, click and drag to the right.

To enclose more or fewer cells in the data range, move the pointer to the lower-right corner of the data range, and when the pointer changes into a two-headed arrow, click and drag so that the blue box encloses only the data you want for your chart.

In Word and PowerPoint, click the Edit Data button on the (Chart Tools) Design tab at any time to open Excel and fiddle with the numbers and data from which your chart is generated.

Positioning Your Chart in a Workbook, Page, or Slide

To change the position of a chart, click to select it, click its perimeter, and when you see the four-headed arrow, start dragging. Otherwise, follow these instructions to land your chart where you want it to be:

+ **Excel:** To move your chart to a different worksheet or create a new worksheet to hold your chart, go to the (Chart Tools) Design tab and click the Move Chart button. You see the Move Chart dialog box.

  - *To move your chart to a different worksheet:* Click the Object In option button, choose the worksheet in the drop-down list, and click OK.

  - *To create a new worksheet for a chart:* Click the New Sheet option button, enter a name for the new worksheet, and click OK.

+ **Word:** Starting in Print Layout view, select your chart, and in the Page Layout or (Chart Tools) Format tab, click the Position button (you may have to click the Arrange button first, depending on the size of your screen). You see a drop-down list with text-wrapping options. Choose the option that describes how you want surrounding text to behave when it crashes into your chart. Book II, Chapter 4 looks in detail at wrapping text around charts and other objects in Word.

+ **PowerPoint:** Select the chart and drag it on the slide to the right position.

Changing a Chart's Appearance

Charts are awfully nice already, but perhaps you want to redesign one. Perhaps you're an interior decorator type and you want to give charts your own personal touch. Excel, PowerPoint, and Word offer these Chart Tools tabs for redecorating charts:

+ **Design tab:** For quickly changing a chart's appearance. Go to the Design tab if you're in a hurry. The ready-made gallery choices give you the opportunity to change a chart's layout and appearance in a matter of seconds. You can also choose a new chart type from the Design tab. See "Relying on a chart style to change appearances," later in this chapter.

+ **Layout tab:** For rearranging, hiding, and displaying various parts of a chart, including the legend, labels, title, gridlines, and scale. Go to the Layout tab to tweak your chart and make different parts of it stand out or recede into the background. For example, you can display axis labels more prominently or make them disappear, enter a title for your chart, or display more or fewer gridlines. See "Changing the layout of a chart" and "Handling the gridlines," later in this chapter.

+ **Format tab:** For changing the color, outline, font, and font size of various parts of a chart, including the labels, bars, and pie slices. You have to really know what you're doing and have a lot of time on your hands to change colors and fonts throughout a chart. See "Changing a chart element's color, font, or other particular," later in this chapter.

These pages explain how to change a chart's appearance, starting with the biggest change you can make — exchanging one type of chart for another.

Changing the chart type

The biggest way to overhaul a chart is to ditch it in favor of a different chart type. Luckily for you, Office makes this task simple. I wish that changing jobs was this easy. Follow these steps to change a pumpkin into a carriage or an existing chart into a different kind of chart:

1. **Click your chart to select it.**

2. **On the (Chart Tools) Design tab, click the Change Chart Type button, or right-click your chart and choose Change Chart Type on the short-cut menu.**

   The Change Chart Type dialog box appears. Does it look familiar? This is the same dialog box you used to create your chart in the first place.

3. **Select a new chart type and click OK.**

   Not all chart types can be converted successfully to other chart types. You may well have created a monster, in which case go back to Step 1 and start all over or click the Undo button.

Changing the size and shape of a chart

To make a chart taller or wider, follow these instructions:

+ Click the perimeter of the chart to select it and then drag a handle on the side to make it wider, or a handle on the top or bottom to make it taller.

+ Go to the (Chart Tools) Format tab and enter measurements in the Shape Height and Shape Width boxes. You can find these boxes in the Size group (you may have to click the Size button to see them, depending on the size of your screen).

Relying on a chart style to change appearances

The easiest way to change the look of a chart is to choose an option in the Chart Styles gallery in the (Chart Tools) Design tab, as shown in Figure 6-16. You can choose among 50 options. These gallery options are quite sophisticated. You would have a hard time fashioning these charts on your own.

If your file includes more than one chart, make the charts consistent with one another. Give them a similar appearance so that your file doesn't turn into a chart fashion show. You can make charts consistent with one another by choosing similar options for charts in the Chart Styles gallery.

Select a Chart style

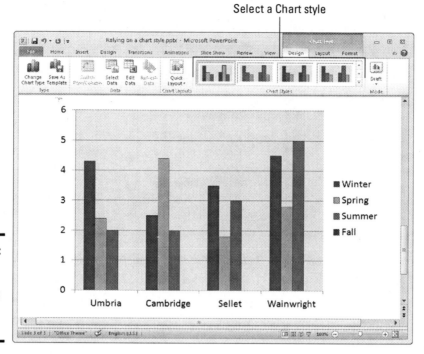

Figure 6-16:
Redesign
your chart
in the Chart
Styles
gallery.

Changing the layout of a chart

Figure 6-17 identifies the chart elements that you can lay out in different
ways. Some of these elements can be removed as well as placed on different
parts of a chart. For example, you can display the legend on any side of a
chart or not display it at all. Some of the elements can be labeled in different
ways. To decide on the layout of a chart, select it and visit the (Chart Tools)
Layout tab.

The following pages explain how to change the layout of a chart starting on
the (Chart Tools) Layout tab. However, before hurrying to the Layout tab to
change your chart's layout, you may consider taking a detour to the (Chart
Tools) Design tab (refer to Figure 6-16). The Chart Layouts gallery on the
Design tab offers ten ready-made layouts, one of which may meet your high
expectations and spare you a trip to the Layout tab.

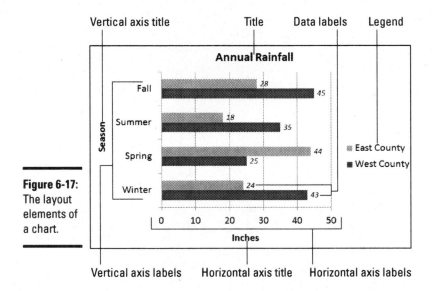

Figure 6-17:
The layout
elements of
a chart.

Deciding where chart elements appear and how they are labeled

On the (Chart Tools) Layout tab, open the drop-down list on these buttons and choose options to determine how and whether chart elements are labeled:

✦ **Chart Title:** The chart title appears above the chart and describes what the chart is about (refer to Figure 6-17). Place a centered title inside or above the chart. The Above Chart option shrinks the chart a bit to make room for the title. Click in the text box and enter the title after Office creates a chart title text box.

✦ **Axis Titles:** Axis titles list the series name and category name of the data being plotted in the chart (refer to Figure 6-17). You can select Rotated Title for the vertical axis to make the axis label read vertically rather than horizontally (refer to Figure 6-17).

✦ **Legend:** The legend is the box to the side, top, or bottom of the chart that describes what is being plotted (refer to Figure 6-17). Choose an option from the drop-down list to place the chart's legend above, below, or to the side of a chart.

✦ **Data Labels:** Data labels show the numeric values by which the data markers — the bars, columns, pie slices, or dots — in your chart are constructed (refer to Figure 6-17). For example, if a bar in your chart represents the number 28, the data label 28 appears in the bar. You can also label the series name or category name by choosing More Data Label Options on the drop-down list and making selections in the Format Data Labels dialog box.

✦ **Axes:** The axes labels are the series names and scale markers that appear in the chart. Choose Primary Horizontal Axis or Primary Vertical Axis and then select None to remove series names and scale markers from your chart. The other axes options are for deciding how to display axes labels (and are explained in the next section of this chapter).

Deciding how the chart's scale and axes labels are presented

The labels and scale on the horizontal and vertical axes of a chart tell viewers what is being plotted on the chart (see Figure 6-17). By clicking the Axes button on the (Chart Tools) Layout tab, you can fine-tune the axes labels and scale on your chart.

 After you click the Axes button, you see options for changing around your chart's horizontal or vertical axis. What the horizontal and vertical axis options are depends on whether the axis you're dealing with presents text labels, expresses numerical values, or expresses date values.

Text axis options

Choose a text axis option on the drop-down list to remove the labels or present category name labels in reverse order from the way in which these labels are listed on the worksheet.

Numerical and date axis options

The axis options that pertain to numbers and dates are for declaring how to present the scale on your chart. You can present the numbers in thousands, millions, billions, or with a log scale. By opening the Format Axis dialog box shown in Figure 6-18, you can get quite specific about how the scale is presented on your chart. To open this dialog box, click the Axes button, select the appropriate axis option on the drop-down list, and choose More Options on the submenu. Which options you see in this dialog box depends greatly on which chart type you're dealing with.

The Format Axis dialog box offers these opportunities for changing around the scale of a chart:

✦ **Changing the scale's range:** By default, the scale ranges from 0 to 10 percent more than the largest value being plotted, but you can change the scale's range by selecting a Fixed option button and entering a new value in the Minimum and Maximum text box.

✦ **Changing the number of unit measurement labels:** Label measurements (and gridlines) appear at intervals on a chart according to the number entered in the Major Unit text box. For example, an entry of 10 tells Office to mark each 10 units with a measurement label. Select the Fixed option button and change the number in the Major Unit text box to draw fewer or more unit labels (and gridlines) on your chart. If your chart displays minor tick marks, do the same in the Minor Unit text box.

✦ **Displaying numbers as thousandths, millionths, or billionths:** If your chart presents large numbers, consider listing these numbers in thousandths, millionths, or billionths by selecting an option in the Display Units drop-down list. You can also select the Logarithmic Scale check box to display numbers as logarithms.

✦ **Changing the tick-mark scale markers:** Choose Tick Mark options to tell Office where or whether to place *tick marks* — small unit markers — on the scale.

✦ **Changing the location of axis labels:** Choose an option in the Axis Labels drop-down list to tell Office where to place the unit labels on the scale.

✦ **Change the axis crosses:** Select the Axis Value option button and enter a measurement in the Axis Value text box if you want to change the baseline of your chart. Usually, the axis value is set to 0, and markers rise from 0 on the chart; but by entering a different measurement, you can make markers rise or fall from the baseline. For example, if the Axis Value baseline is 5, markers less than 5 fall from a baseline in the middle of the chart and markers greater than 5 rise above it.

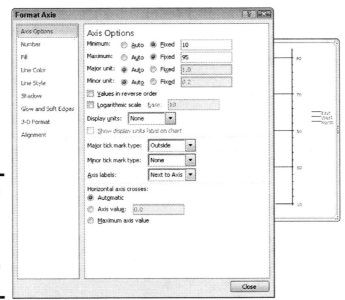

Figure 6-18:
Fashion a numerical scale for a chart in the Format Axis dialog box.

Handling the gridlines

Gridlines are lines that cross a chart and indicate value measurements. Most charts include major gridlines to show where bars or columns meet or surpass a major unit of measurement, and you can also include fainter, minor gridlines that mark less significant measurements. Figure 6-19 shows a chart with gridlines displayed in different ways.

Figure 6-19:
Options for handling gridlines (clockwise from upper left): None, Major Gridlines, Major & Minor Gridlines, and Minor Gridlines.

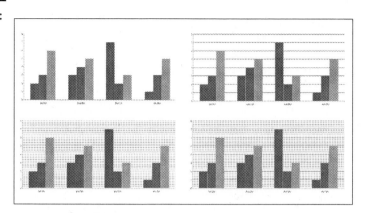

Select your chart and follow these instructions to hide or display gridlines, change the lines' width, or change the lines' color:

✦ **Hiding and choosing the frequency of gridlines:** On the (Chart Tools) Layout tab, click the Gridlines button, choose Primary Horizontal Gridlines or Primary Vertical Gridlines on the drop-down list, and choose an option on the submenu. You can hide gridlines (by choosing None), display major gridlines, display minor gridlines, or display major and minor gridlines (refer to Figure 6-19).

The frequency of gridlines on a chart is tied to the scale. If you want to control the frequency of the gridlines on your own without relying on a Gridlines option, change your chart's scale. The preceding section in this chapter explains how to handle scales.

✦ **Changing gridline width:** On the (Chart Tools) Format tab, open the Chart Elements drop-down list and choose Axis Major Gridlines or Axis Minor Gridlines. (Display gridlines on your chart if you don't see these options.) Then click the Format Selection button, and in the Line Style category of the Format Gridlines dialog box, enter a measurement in the Width text box to make the gridlines heavier or thinner.

✦ **Changing gridline color:** On the (Chart Tools) Format tab, open the Chart Elements drop-down list and select Axis Major Gridlines or Axis Minor Gridlines. (Display gridlines on your chart if you don't see these options.) Then open the drop-down list on the Shape Outline button and choose a color. You can also click the Format Selection button, and in the Line Color category of the Format Gridlines dialog box, select the Solid Line option button and then click the Color button and choose a color there.

Gridlines are essential for helping read charts, but be very, very careful about displaying minor gridlines on charts. These lines can make your chart unreadable. They can turn a perfectly good chart into a gaudy pinstripe suit.

Changing a chart element's color, font, or other particular

Generally speaking, the (Chart Tools) Format tab is the place to go to change the color, line width, font, or font size of a chart element. As I explain shortly, you can do some interior decorating tasks on the (Chart Tools) Layout tab as well.

Follow these basic steps to change a color, line width, font, or font size in part of a chart:

1. Go to the (Chart Tools) Format tab.

The tools on the (Chart Tools) Format tab are very similar to the tools found on the (Drawing Tools) Format tab. You can find all the tools you need here to change the color, outline, and size of a chart element. These tools are explained in detail in Book I, Chapter 8.

2. Select the chart element that needs a facelift.

To select a chart element, either click it or choose its name on the Chart Elements drop-down list, as shown in Figure 6-20. You can find this list in the upper-left corner of the window.

3. Format the chart element you selected.

Use one of these techniques to format the chart element:

- *Open a Format dialog box.* Click the Format Selection button to open a Format dialog box. The dialog box offers commands for formatting the element you selected.

- *Do the work on your own.* Format the chart element as you would any object. For example, to change fonts in the chart element you selected, right-click and choose a font on the shortcut menu. Or go to the Home tab to change font sizes. Or open the drop-down list on the Shape Fill button on the (Chart Tools) Format tab and select a new color.

The (Chart Tools) Layout tab also offers these convenient commands for changing the color of a chart element:

✦ **Plot area:** The *plot area* is the rectangle in which the chart's gridlines, bars, columns, pie slices, or lines appear. In some chart designs, the plot area is filled with color. To remove this color or choose a different color, click the Plot Area button and choose an option. Choose More Plot Area Options to open the Format Plot Area dialog box and select a new fill color.

✦ **3D chart wall and chart floor:** Three-dimensional charts have chart walls and a chart floor. The *chart wall* forms the backdrop of a 3D chart; the *chart floor* forms the bottom of the chart. Click the Chart Wall button and choose an option to remove the chart wall or change its color; click the Chart Floor button and choose an option to remove the chart floor or change its color.

Select a chart so that you can format it

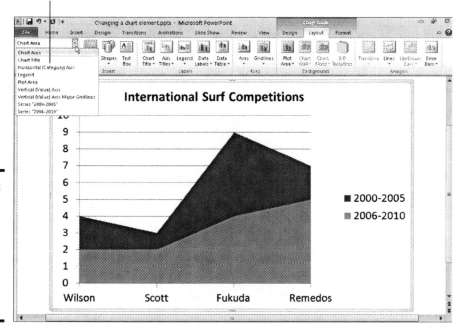

Figure 6-20:
Choose what you want to format on the Chart Elements drop-down list.

Saving a Chart as a Template So That You Can Use It Again

If you go to the significant trouble of redecorating a chart and you expect to do it again the same way in the future, save your chart as a template. This way, you can call on the template in the future to create the same chart and not have to decorate it again. Perhaps you've created charts with your company's colors or you've created a chart that you're especially proud of. Save it as a template to spare yourself the work of reconstructing it.

A chart template holds data series colors, gridline settings, plot area colors, font settings, and the like. It doesn't hold data. These pages explain how to save a chart as a template and how to create a chart with a template you created.

Saving a chart as a template

Follow these steps to make a template out of a chart:

1. **Save your file to make sure the chart settings are saved on your computer.**

2. **Select your chart.**

3. **Go to the (Chart Tools) Design tab.**

4. **Click the Save As Template button.**

   You can find this button in the Type group. You see the Save Chart Template dialog box.

5. **Enter a descriptive name for the template and click the Save button.**

   Include the type of chart you're dealing with in the name. This will help you understand which template you're selecting when the time comes to choose a chart template.

By default, chart templates are saved in this folder in Windows 7 and Windows Vista: `C:\Users\`*Username*`\AppData\Roaming\Microsoft\ Templates\Charts`. Chart templates are stored in this folder in Windows XP: `C:\Documents and Settings\`*Username*`\Application Data\ Microsoft\Templates\Charts`. The templates have the `.ctrx` extension. If you want to delete or rename a template, open the Charts folder in Windows Explorer or Computer and do your deleting and renaming there. You can open the Charts folder very quickly by clicking the Manage Templates button in the Insert Chart dialog box (refer to Figure 6-3).

Creating a chart from a template

To create a chart from your own customized template, open the Create Chart dialog box (click the Chart button) and go to the Templates category. The dialog box shows a list of templates you created. Move the pointer over a template to read its name in a pop-up box. Select a template and click OK.

Chart Tricks for the Daring and Heroic

This chapter wouldn't be complete without a handful of chart tricks to impress your friends and intimidate your enemies. In the pages that follow, you discover how to make charts roll over and play dead. You also find out how to decorate a chart with a picture, annotate a chart, display worksheet data alongside a chart, and create an overlay chart.

Decorating a chart with a picture

As shown in Figure 6-21, a picture looks mighty nice on the plot area of a chart — especially a column chart. If you have a picture in your computer that would serve well to decorate a chart, you are hereby encouraged to start decorating. Follow these steps to place a picture in the plot area of a chart:

1. **Select your chart.**

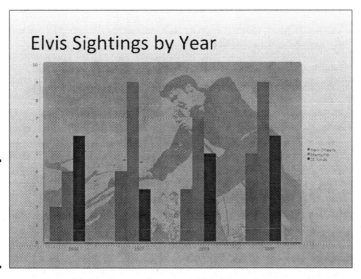

Figure 6-21:
Using a
picture
as the
backdrop of
a chart.

2. **On the (Chart Tools) Format tab, open the Chart Elements drop-down list and choose Plot Area.**

3. **Click the Shape Fill button and choose Picture on the drop-down list.**

You see the Insert Picture dialog box.

4. **Locate the picture you need and select it.**

Try to select a light-colored picture that will serve as a background. Book VI, Chapter 3 explains how you can recolor a picture to make it lighter.

5. **Click the Insert button.**

The picture lands in your chart.

You may need to change the color of the *data markers* — the columns, bars, lines, or pie slices — on your chart to make them stand out against the picture. See "Changing a chart element's color, font, or other particular," earlier in this chapter.

Displaying the raw data alongside the chart

Showing the worksheet data used to produce a chart is sort of like showing the cops your I.D. It proves you're the real thing. It makes your chart more authentic. If yours is a simple pie chart or other chart that wasn't generated with a large amount of raw data, you can display the data alongside your chart in a data table. Anyone who sees the table knows you're not kidding or fudging the numbers.

Select your chart and use one of these techniques to place a table with the raw data below your chart:

+ On the (Chart Tools) Layout tab, click the Data Table button and choose an option on the drop-down list.

+ On the (Chart Tools) Design tab, open the Chart Layouts gallery and select a layout that includes a data table.

To format a data table, go to the (Chart Tools) Format tab, open the Chart Element drop-down list and choose Data Table. Then click the Format Selection button. You see the Format Data Table dialog box, where you can fill the table with color and choose colors for the lines in the table.

Creating an overlay chart

An *overlay chart* is a secondary chart that appears over another chart, the idea being to contrast two sets of data. Create an overlay chart by selecting one data series in a chart you already created and instructing Office to use the data in the series for the overlay chart. To create an overlay chart, the original chart must plot more than one data series. Figure 6-22 shows a bar chart overlaying a stacked area chart.

Figure 6-22:
An overlay chart, in this case a bar chart overlaying a stacked area chart.

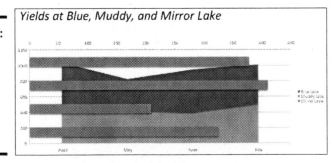

Follow these steps to create an overlay chart:

1. **In a chart you created, click to select the data series that you will use to create the secondary chart.**

The easiest way to select a data series is to click the chart itself, but you can also go to the (Chart Tools) Format tab and select a series in the Chart Elements drop-down list.

2. **Right-click the data series you selected and choose Change Series Chart Type.**

   You see the Change Chart Type dialog box.

3. **Choose a chart type for the overlay chart and click OK.**

   Be sure to click a chart type different from the one in the other chart.

Placing a trendline on a chart

Especially on column charts, a *trendline* can help viewers more clearly see changes in data. Viewers can see, for example, that sales are going up or down, income is rising or falling, or annual rainfall is increasing or decreasing. Figure 6-23 shows an example of a trendline on a chart. In this case, the trendline shows that the deer population in Sacramento County is rising.

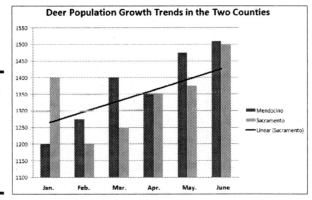

Figure 6-23: A trendline helps viewers recognize changes in data.

Follow these steps to put a trendline on a chart:

1. **On the (Chart Tools) Layout tab, open the Chart Elements drop-down list and choose the data series that you want to highlight with a trendline.**

2. **Click the Trendline button and choose a trendline option on the drop-down list.**

   You can choose More Trendline Options on the drop-down list to open the Format Trendline dialog box and choose additional types of trendlines.

   To change the look of a trendline, right-click it and choose Format Trendline. In the Format Trendline dialog box, choose a line color and line style.

To remove a trendline from a chart, go to the (Chart Tools) Layout tab, click the Trendline button, and choose None on the drop-down list.

Troubleshooting a Chart

Sometimes tinkering with a chart opens a Pandora's Box of problems. You find yourself having to correct little errors that appear in charts. Here are some shorthand instructions for fixing common chart problems:

✦ **The dates in the chart aren't formatted right.** To change the way in which dates are formatted on a chart, go to the (Chart Tools) Format tab, open the Chart Elements drop-down list, and choose Horizontal (Value) Axis or Vertical (Value) Axis. Then click the Format Selection button, and in the Format Axis dialog box, go to the Number category, select Date in the Category menu, and choose a date format.

✦ **The numbers in the chart aren't formatted right.** To change the number of decimal places, include comma separators in numbers, display currency symbols, or do all else that pertains to numbers, go to the (Chart Tools) Format tab, open the Chart Elements drop-down list, and choose Horizontal (Value) Axis or Vertical (Value) Axis. Then click the Format Selection button. You see the Format Axis dialog box. Visit the Number category and select options for displaying numbers.

✦ **"Category 1" or "Series 1" appears in the chart legend.** To direct you to the right place to enter data in Excel worksheets, phantom names such as "Category 1" and "Series 1" appear in worksheets. Sometimes these phantoms wind up in chart legends as well. To remove them, go to the (Chart Tools) Design tab and click the Edit Data button. You see the Excel worksheet, where the data range used to generate the chart is enclosed in a blue box. Drag the lower-right corner of the box so that the box encloses only the data you want for your chart.

✦ **In 3D charts, small markers are obscured by large markers in the foreground.** For all the data markers to be shown in a 3D chart, the smaller ones have to be in the foreground. To rearrange data markers, go to the (Chart Tools) Design tab and click the Select Data button to open the Select Data Source dialog box. Then select a series and click the Up or Down button to rearrange the series in your chart. Series that are high on the list go to the back of the chart; series that are low on the list go to the front.

✦ **The chart doesn't gather all data from the worksheet.** On the (Chart Tools) Design tab, click the Edit Data button, and in the Excel worksheet that stores data for your chart, enlarge the blue data-range box so that it encloses all your data. You can enlarge the box by dragging its lower-right corner.

Annotating a chart

To highlight part of a chart — an especially large pie slice, a tall column, or a bar showing miniscule sales figures — annotate it with a callout text box and place the text box beside the pie slice, column, or bar. The annotation tells you that one sector isn't performing especially well and somebody ought to get on the ball.

To annotate a chart, select a callout shape, enter text in the callout shape, and connect the shape to part of your chart. Follow these steps to annotate a chart:

1. **Select your chart and go to the (Chart Tools) Layout tab.**

2. **Click the Shapes button, scroll to the Callouts section of the drop-down list, and choose a callout.**

Depending on the size of your screen, you may have to click the Insert button to get to the Shapes button.

3. **Drag on your slide to draw the callout shape.**

   Book I, Chapter 8 explains drawing shapes in gory detail.

4. **Type the annotation inside the callout shape.**

5. **Resize the callout shape as necessary to make it fit with the chart.**

6. **Drag the yellow diamond on the callout shape to attach the callout to the chart.**

   You probably have to do some interior decorating to make the callout color fit with the chart. Book I, Chapter 8 explains how to change an object's color.

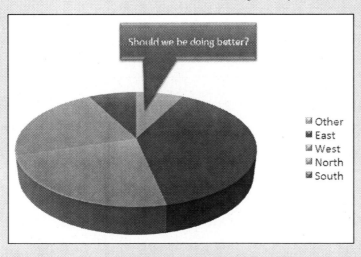

✦ **The scale is too big for my chart.** Especially if the scale range on a chart is small, the scale can be too big compared to the data markers. To change the scale range, go to the (Chart Tools) Layout tab, click the Axes button, choose the appropriate axis option on the drop-down list, and choose More Options. Then, in the Format Axis dialog box, select the Fixed option button and enter a Maximum value to establish the top of the scale for your chart. For more details, see "Deciding how the chart's scale and axes labels are presented," earlier in this chapter.

Chapter 7: Making a SmartArt Diagram

In This Chapter

✔ Creating a diagram

✔ Repositioning and resizing diagrams

✔ Laying out and changing the look of diagram shapes

✔ Entering text on a diagram shape

✔ Changing the appearance of a diagram

✔ Creating a diagram from shapes

*A*long with charts and tables, diagrams are the best way to present your ideas. Diagrams clearly show, for example, employees' relationships with one another, product cycles, workflow processes, and spheres of influence. A diagram is an excellent marriage of images and words. Diagrams allow an audience to literally visualize a concept, idea, or relationship.

This chapter explains how to construct diagrams from SmartArt graphics and how to create a diagram. It shows how to customize diagrams by changing the size of diagrams and diagram shapes, adding and removing shapes, and changing shapes' colors. You also discover how to change the direction of a diagram and enter the text. Finally, this chapter demonstrates how to create a diagram from scratch with shapes and connectors.

The Basics: Creating SmartArt Diagrams

In Word, PowerPoint, and Excel, diagrams are made from *SmartArt graphics*. These diagram graphics are "interactive" in the sense that you can move, alter, and write text on them. In other words, you can use them to construct diagrams. You can alter these diagrams to your liking. You can make a diagram portray precisely what you want it to portray, although you usually have to wrestle with the diagram a bit.

Choosing a diagram

The first step in creating a diagram is to select a layout in the Choose a SmartArt Graphic dialog box, shown in Figure 7-1. After you create the initial diagram, you customize it to create a diagram of your own. About 120 diagrams are in the dialog box. They fall into these eight categories:

Diagram Type	Use
List	For describing blocks of related information as well as sequential steps in a task, process, or workflow
Process	For describing how a concept or physical process changes over time or is modified
Cycle	For illustrating a circular progression without a beginning or end, or a relationship in which the components are in balance
Hierarchy	For describing hierarchical relationships between people, departments, and other entities, as well as portraying branch-like relationships in which one decision or action leads to another
Relationship	For describing the relationship between different components (but not hierarchical relationships)
Matrix	For showing the relationship between quadrants
Pyramid	For showing proportional or hierarchical relationships
Picture	For creating diagrams that include photographs and pictures (This catch-all category presents picture diagrams from the other categories.)
Office.com	For downloading various types of diagrams from Office.com

Diagram types   Select a diagram   Diagram explanation

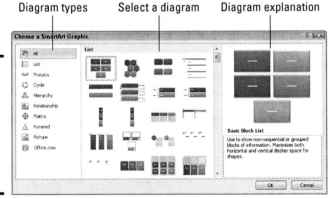

Figure 7-1:
To create a diagram, start by selecting a diagram in this dialog box.

If you intend to construct a "flow chart type" diagram with many branches and levels, go to the Hierarchy category and select the Organization Chart or one of the hierarchy diagrams. As "Laying Out the Diagram Shapes" explains later in this chapter, only these choices permit you to make a diagram with many different branches and levels.

Making the diagram your own

After you select a generic diagram in the Choose a SmartArt Graphic dialog box and click OK, the next step is to make the diagram your own by completing these tasks:

+ **Change the diagram's size and position:** Change the size and position of a diagram to make it fit squarely on your page or slide. See "Changing the Size and Position of a Diagram," later in this chapter.

+ **Add shapes to (or remove shapes from) the diagram:** Adding a shape involves declaring where to add the shape, promoting or demoting the shape with respect to other shapes, and declaring how the new shape connects to another shape. See "Laying Out the Diagram Shapes," later in this chapter.

+ **Enter text:** Enter text on each shape, or component, of the diagram. See "Handling the Text on Diagram Shapes," later in this chapter.

If you so desire, you can also customize your diagram by taking on some or all of these tasks:

+ **Changing its overall appearance:** Choose a different color scheme or 3D variation for your diagram. See "Choosing a Look for Your Diagram," later in this chapter.

+ **Changing shapes:** Select a new shape for part of your diagram, change the size of a shape, or assign different colors to shapes to make shapes stand out. See "Changing the Appearance of Diagram Shapes," later in this chapter.

If you're comfortable creating a diagram of your own by drawing shapes and lines, no law says you have to begin in the Choose a SmartArt Graphic dialog box. Later in this chapter, "Creating a Diagram from Scratch" looks into creating a diagram by making use of text boxes, lines, and shapes.

Creating the Initial Diagram

The first step in fashioning a diagram is to choose a SmartArt graphic in the Choose a SmartArt Graphic dialog box. After that, you roll up your sleeves, change the diagram's size and shape, and enter the text. If you select the wrong diagram to start with, all is not lost. You can choose another diagram in its place, although how successful swapping one diagram for another is depends on how lucky you are and how far along you are in creating your diagram. These pages explain how to create an initial diagram and swap one diagram for another.

Starting from a sketch

You can spare yourself a lot of trouble by starting from a sketch when you create a diagram. Find a pencil with a good eraser, grab a blank piece of paper, and start drawing. Imagine what your ideal diagram looks like. Draw the arrows or lines connecting the different parts of the diagram. Write the text. Draw the diagram that best illustrates what you want to communicate.

Later, in the Choose a SmartArt Graphic dialog box (refer to Figure 7-1), you can select the diagram that most resembles the one you sketched. The dialog box offers 120 types of diagrams. Unless you start from a sketch and have a solid idea of the diagram you want, you can get lost in the dialog box. Also, if you don't start from a sketch, adding shapes to the diagram and landing shapes in the right places can be a chore.

Creating a diagram

Follow these steps to create a diagram:

1. **On the Insert tab, click the SmartArt button.**

You see the Choose a SmartArt Graphic dialog box (refer to Figure 7-1). In PowerPoint, you can also open the dialog box by clicking the SmartArt icon in a content placeholder frame.

2. **Select a diagram in the Choose a SmartArt Graphic dialog box.**

Diagrams are divided into ten categories, as I explain earlier in this chapter. The dialog box offers a description of each diagram. Either select a type on the left side of the dialog box or scroll the entire list to find the graphic that most resembles the diagram you want.

If you want to create a graph with many levels and branches, go to the Hierarchy category and select one of these charts: Organization Chart, Picture Organization Chart, or Name and Title Organization Chart. These three diagrams are much more complex than the others are and allow for branching. See "Laying Out the Diagram Shapes," later in this chapter, for details.

3. **Click OK.**

The next topic in this chapter explains how to swap one diagram for another, in case you chose wrongly in the Choose a SmartArt Graphic dialog box.

Swapping one diagram for another

If the diagram you chose initially doesn't do the job, you can swap it for a different diagram. How successful the swap is depends on how far along you are in creating your diagram and whether your diagram is simple or complex. Follow these steps to swap one diagram for another:

1. **Click your diagram to select it.**

2. **Go to the (SmartArt Tools) Design tab.**

3. **Open the Layouts gallery (you may have to click the Change Layout button first).**

    You see a gallery with diagrams of the same type as the diagram you're working with.

4. **Select a new diagram or choose More Layouts to open the Choose a SmartArt Graphic dialog box and select a diagram there.**

You may have to click the trusty Undo button and start all over if the diagram you selected for the swap didn't do the job.

Changing the Size and Position of a Diagram

To make a diagram fit squarely on a page or slide, you have to change its size and position. Resizing and positioning diagrams and other objects is the subject of Book I, Chapter 8, but in case you don't care to travel that far to get instructions, here are shorthand instructions for resizing and positioning diagrams:

 ✦ **Resizing a diagram:** Select the diagram, move the pointer over a selection handle on the corner or side, and start dragging after the pointer changes into a two-headed arrow. You can also go to the (SmartArt Tools) Format tab and enter new measurements in the Width and Height boxes. (You may have to click the Size button to see these text boxes, depending on the size of your screen.)

 ✦ **Repositioning a diagram:** Select the diagram, move the pointer over its perimeter, and when you see the four-headed arrow, click and start dragging.

Notice when you resize a diagram that the shapes in the diagram change size proportionally. Most diagrams are designed so that shapes fill out the diagram. When you change the size of a diagram, remove a shape from a diagram, or add a shape, shapes change size within the diagram.

Laying Out the Diagram Shapes

At the heart of every diagram are the rectangles, circles, arrows, and whatnots that make the diagram what it is. These shapes illustrate the concept or idea you want to express to your audience. Your biggest challenge when creating a diagram is laying out the diagram shapes.

The following pages explain how to select diagram shapes, add shapes, reposition shapes, and remove shapes from diagrams. They also offer instructions specific to working with hierarchy diagrams.

Selecting a diagram shape

Before you can remove a shape from a diagram or indicate where you want to add a new shape, you have to select a diagram shape. To select a diagram shape, move the pointer over its perimeter and click when you see the four-headed arrow underneath your pointer.

You can tell when a diagram shape is selected because a solid line, not a dotted line, appears around the shape, as shown in Figure 7-2. When you see dotted lines around a shape, you're expected to enter text.

Selected diagram shape

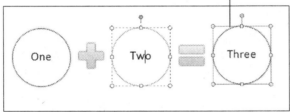

Figure 7-2: A selected diagram shape is surrounded by solid lines.

Removing a shape from a diagram

Removing a shape from a diagram is as easy as falling off a turnip truck as long as you correctly select the shape before you remove it. To remove a shape, select it and press Delete. Other shapes grow larger when you remove a shape, in keeping with the "fill out the diagram by any means necessary" philosophy.

Moving diagram shapes to different positions

If a shape in a diagram isn't in the right position, don't fret because you can change the order of shapes very easily by going to the (SmartArt Tools) Design tab and clicking the Move Up or Move Down button.

Select the diagram shape that needs repositioning and click the Move Up or Move Down button as many times as necessary to land the shape in the right place.

Adding shapes to diagrams apart from hierarchy diagrams

Unlike hierarchy diagrams, list, process, cycle, relationship, and matrix diagrams don't have branches. They always travel in one direction only. This makes adding shapes to these diagrams fairly straightforward. To add a shape, you select a shape in the diagram and then add the new shape so that it appears before or after the shape you selected, as shown in Figure 7-3.

Select a shape and choose an Add Shape option   The new shape

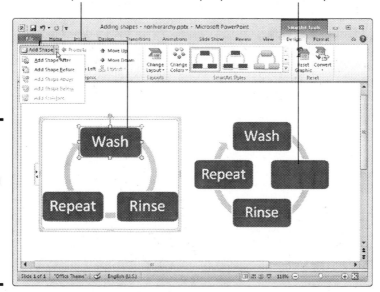

Figure 7-3: To add a shape, start by selecting the shape that your new shape will go before or after.

Follow these steps to add a shape to a list, process, cycle, relationship, matrix, or pyramid diagram:

1. **In your diagram, select the shape that your new shape will appear before or after.**

   Earlier in this chapter, "Selecting a diagram shape" explains how to select diagram shapes.

2. **Choose the Add Shape After or Add Shape Before command.**

   To get to these commands, use one of these techniques:

   • On the (SmartArt Tools) Design tab, open the drop-down list on the Add Shape button and choose Add Shape After or Add Shape Before, as shown in Figure 7-3.

- Right-click the shape you selected, choose Add Shape on the short-cut menu, and then choose Add Shape After or Add Shape Before on the submenu.

Adding shapes to hierarchy diagrams

Hierarchy diagrams are more complex than other diagrams because they branch out such that shapes are found on different levels. This branching out makes adding shapes to hierarchy diagrams problematic.

As shown in Figure 7-4, Office offers four Add Shape commands for adding shapes to hierarchy diagrams: Add Shape After, Add Shape Before, Add Shape Above, and Add Shape Below. What these commands do depends on whether the diagram is horizontally or vertically oriented, because what constitutes after, before, above, and below is different in vertical and horizontal diagrams. Suffice it to say that when you add shapes to hierarchy diagrams, you often have to try different commands, clicking the Undo button and starting all over until you get it right.

Select a shape and choose one of four Add Shape commands

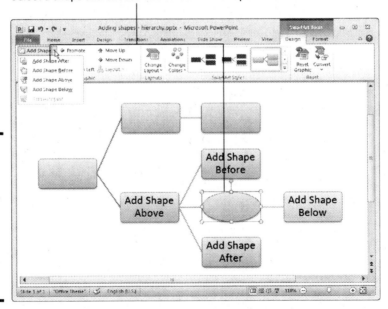

Figure 7-4:
You can add a shape after, before, above, or below a shape in a hierarchy diagram.

Follow these steps to add a shape to a hierarchy diagram:

1. **In your diagram, select the shape to which your new shape will be connected.**

   Earlier in this chapter, "Selecting a diagram shape" describes how to select a shape.

2. Choose an Add Shape command.

Figure 7-4 shows what Add Shape commands do. You can choose Add Shape commands with one of these techniques:

- On the (SmartArt Tools) Design tab, open the drop-down list on the Add Shape button and choose an Add Shape command (refer to Figure 7-4).

- Right-click the shape you selected, choose Add Shape on the short-cut menu, and choose an Add Shape command on the submenu.

Adding shapes to Organization charts

An Organization chart diagram offers many opportunities for connecting shapes. The shapes can branch out from one another in four directions as well as appear to the side in the "assistant" position. When you place one shape below another shape, you can make the new shape *hang* so that it is joined to a line that drops, or hangs, from another shape. These pages explain how to add shapes and create hanging relationships between one shape and the shapes subordinate to it.

Adding an Organization Chart shape

Besides adding a shape after, before, above, or below a shape, you can add an assistant shape to an Organization Chart diagram, as shown in Figure 7-5. An assistant shape is an intermediary shape between two levels. Follow these steps to add a shape to an Organization Chart diagram:

1. Select the shape to which you will add a new shape.

Earlier in this chapter, "Selecting a diagram shape" explains how to select shapes. As shown in Figure 7-5, shapes are surrounded by solid lines, not dotted lines, when you select them properly.

2. Choose an Add Shape command.

You can choose Add Shape commands in two ways:

- On the (SmartArt Tools) Design tab, open the drop-down list on the Add Shape button and choose an Add Shape command (see Figure 7-5).

- Right-click the shape you selected, choose Add Shape on the short-cut menu, and then choose an Add Shape command on the submenu.

Figure 7-5 demonstrates what the Add Shape commands do to a vertically oriented diagram. Notice that Add Shape Before places a new shape to the left of the shape you selected; Add Shape After places a new shape to the right.

Select a shape and choose one of five Add Shape commands

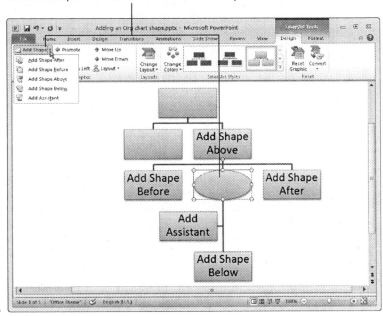

Figure 7-5:
Adding a
shape to an
Organization
Chart
diagram.

Be careful about choosing the Add Shape Above command. This command effectively bumps the shape you selected to a lower level in order to make room for the new shape. In effect, you demote one shape when you place a new shape above it.

Shapes created with the Add Assistant command land on the left side of the line to which they're attached, but if you prefer the assistant shape to be on the right side of the line, you can drag it to the right.

Hanging a shape below another shape in an Organization Chart

Besides the standard relationship between shapes above and below one another, you can create a *hanging relationship* in an Organization Chart diagram. Figure 7-6 shows the three kinds of hanging relationships — Standard, Both, Left Hanging, and Right Hanging. In a hanging relationship, the line hangs from a shape, and subordinate shapes are connected to the line.

You can create a hanging relationship between shapes before or after you create the subordinate shapes. Follow these steps to create a hanging relationship:

1. **Select the shape to which other shapes will hang or are hanging.**

2. **On the (SmartArt Tools) Design tab, click the Layout button.**

3. **On the drop-down list, choose Both, Left Hanging, or Right Hanging.**

Figure 7-6:
Ways that
shapes can
hang in
Organization
Chart
diagrams.

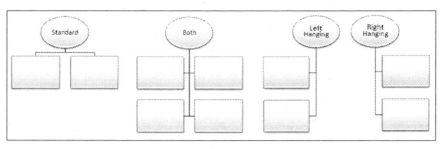

Promoting and demoting shapes in hierarchy diagrams

Shapes in hierarchy diagrams are ranked by level. If a shape is on the wrong level, you can move it higher or lower in the diagram by clicking the Promote or Demote button on the (SmartArt Tools) Design tab. Promoting and demoting shapes can turn into a donnybrook if you aren't careful. If the shapes being promoted or demoted are attached to subordinate shapes, the subordinate shapes are promoted or demoted as well. This can have unforeseen and sometimes horrendous consequences.

Follow these steps to promote or demote a shape (and its subordinates) in a hierarchy diagram:

1. **Select the shape that needs a change of rank.**

You can select more than one shape by Ctrl+clicking.

2. **Go to the (SmartArt Tools) Design tab.**

3. **Click the Promote or Demote button.**

Do you like what you see? If not, you may have to click the Undo button and start all over.

Handling the Text on Diagram Shapes

When you create a new diagram, "[Text]" (the word *Text* enclosed in brackets) appears on shapes. Your job is to replace this generic placeholder with something more meaningful and less bland. These sections explain how to enter text and bulleted lists on shapes.

Entering text on a diagram shape

Use one of these techniques to enter text on a diagram shape:

✦ **Click in the shape and start typing:** The words you type appear in the shape, as shown in Figure 7-7.

✦ **Enter text in the Text pane:** Enter the text by typing it in the Text pane, as shown in Figure 7-7. The text pane opens to the left of the diagram. To open the text pane:

- *On the (SmartArt Tools) Design tab, click the Text Pane button.*

- *Click the Text Pane button on the diagram.* This button is not labeled, but you can find it to the left of the diagram.

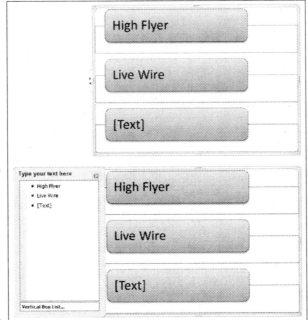

Figure 7-7: Type directly on diagram shapes (top) or enter text on the Text pane (bottom).

The text in diagrams shrinks as you enter more text so that all text is the same size. If you want to make the text larger or smaller in one shape, see "Changing fonts and font sizes on shapes" later in this chapter.

Entering bulleted lists on diagram shapes

Some diagram shapes have built-in bulleted lists, but no matter. Whether a shape is prepared to be bulleted or not, you can enter bullets in a diagram shape. Here are instructions for entering and removing bullets:

✦ **Entering a bulleted list:** Select the shape that needs bullets, and on the (SmartArt Tools) Design tab, click the Add Bullet button. Either enter the bulleted items directly into the shape (pressing Enter as you type each entry) or click the Text Pane button to open the Text pane (refer to Figure 7-7) and enter bullets there.

Turning a bulleted list into a diagram (PowerPoint)

Suppose you're working along in PowerPoint when suddenly the realization strikes you that a bulleted list in a text frame or text box would work much better as a diagram. For those occasions, you can click the Convert to SmartArt button. By clicking this button, you can turn the text in a text frame or text box into a diagram. If the text frame or box contains a bulleted list, each bulleted item becomes a diagram shape.

Follow these steps to turn a text frame or text box into a diagram:

1. **Select the text frame or text box.**

2. **On the Home tab, click the Convert to SmartArt Graphic button.**

   You see a drop-down list with basic diagram choices.

3. **Either select a diagram on the list or choose More SmartArt Graphics to open the Choose a SmartArt Graphic dialog box and select a diagram there.**

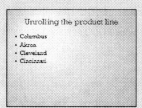
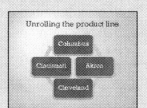

✦ **Removing bulleted items:** Click before the first bulleted entry and keep pressing the Delete key until you have removed all the bulleted items. You can also start in the Text pane (refer to Figure 7-7) and press the Delete key there until you've removed the bulleted items, or drag to select several bulleted items and then press Delete.

Changing a Diagram's Direction

As long as your diagram is horizontally oriented, you can change its direction. As shown in Figure 7-8, you can flip it over such that the rightmost shape in your diagram becomes the leftmost shape, and what was the leftmost shape becomes the rightmost shape. If arrows are in your diagram, the arrows point the opposite direction after you flip the diagram. You can't flip vertically oriented diagrams this way. Sorry, but diagrams that run north to south, not west to east, can't be rolled over.

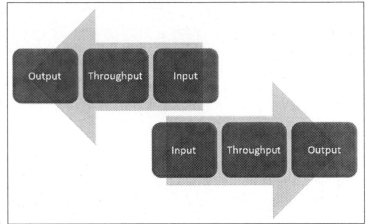

Figure 7-8:
You can flip horizontal diagrams so that they run the opposite direction.

Follow these steps to flip a horizontally oriented diagram:

1. **Select the diagram.**

2. **On the (SmartArt Tools) Design tab, click the Right to Left button.**

If you don't like what you see, click the button again or click the Undo button.

Choosing a Look for Your Diagram

Decide how a diagram looks by starting on the (SmartArt Tools) Design tab. Starting there, you can choose a color scheme for your diagram and a different style. Between the Change Colors drop-down list and the SmartArt Styles gallery, you can find a combination of options that presents your diagram in the best light:

✦ **Change Colors button:** Click the Change Colors button to see color schemes for your diagram on the drop-down list, as shown in Figure 7-9. Point at a few options to live-preview them.

✦ **SmartArt Styles gallery:** Open the SmartArt Styles gallery to choose simple and 3-D variations on the diagram.

If you experiment too freely and wish to backpedal, click the Reset Graphic button on the (SmartArt Tools) Design tab. Clicking this button reverses all the formatting changes you made to your diagram.

Select a color scheme   Select a diagram style

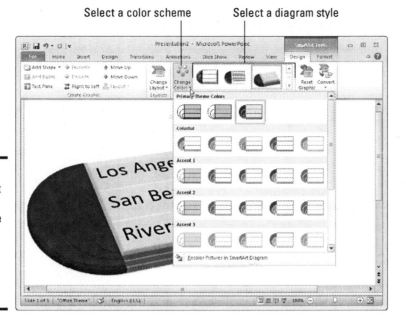

Figure 7-9:
Experiment
freely with
the Change
Colors and
SmartArt
Styles
gallery
options.

If your Word document, Excel worksheet, or PowerPoint presentation includes many diagrams, make sure your diagrams are consistent in appearance. Choose similar colors for diagrams. If you like 3-D diagrams, make the majority of your diagrams 3-D. Don't let the diagrams overwhelm the ideas they are meant to express. The point is to present ideas in diagrams, not turn your work into a SmartArt diagram showcase.

Changing the Appearance of Diagram Shapes

To call attention to one part of a diagram, you can change the appearance of a shape and make it stand out. Any part of a diagram that is different from the other parts naturally gets more attention. To change the appearance of a shape, consider changing its size or color, exchanging one shape for another, or changing the font and font size of the text. These topics are covered in the following pages.

Changing the size of a diagram shape

A shape that is larger than other shapes in a diagram gets the attention of the audience. Select your shape and use one of these techniques to enlarge or shrink it:

♦ On the (SmartArt Tools) Format tab, click the Larger or Smaller button as many times as necessary to make the shape the right size.

♦ Move the pointer over a corner selection handle, and when the pointer changes to a two-headed arrow, click and start dragging.

Notice that the text inside the shape remains the same size although the shape is larger. To change the size of the text in a shape, see "Changing fonts and font sizes on shapes," later in this chapter.

To return a diagram shape to its original size after you've fooled with it, right-click the shape and choose Reset Shape.

Exchanging one shape for another

Another way to call attention to an important part of a diagram is to change shapes, as shown in Figure 7-10. Rather than a conventional shape, use an oval, block arrow, or star. You can substitute a shape in the Shapes gallery for any diagram shape (Book I, Chapter 8 explores the Shapes gallery). To exchange one shape for another in a diagram, select the shape and use one of these techniques:

♦ On the (SmartArt Tools) Format tab, click the Change Shape button and select a shape in the Shapes gallery.

♦ Right-click the shape, choose Change Shape on the shortcut menu, and select a shape on the submenu.

Figure 7-10:
Using different shapes and different-sized shapes in a diagram.

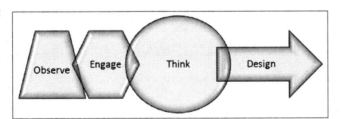

Changing a shape's color, fill, or outline

Yet another way to call attention to a shape is to change its color, fill, or outline border, as shown in Figure 7-11. Select a shape and go to the (SmartArt Tools) Format tab to change a shape's color, fill, or outline.

♦ **Restyling a shape:** Select an option in the Shape Styles gallery to give a shape a makeover.

Editing 3-D diagrams in 2-D

Three-dimensional diagrams are wonderful. You can impress your friends with a 3-D diagram. All you have to do to turn a mundane two-dimensional diagram into a three-dimensional showpiece is go to the (SmartArt Tools) Design tab, open the SmartArt Styles gallery, and select a 3-D option.

Unfortunately, editing a 3-D diagram can be difficult. The shapes and text are all aslant. It's

hard to tell where to click or what to drag when you're editing a 3-D diagram.

Fortunately, you can get around the problem of editing a 3-D diagram by temporarily displaying it in two dimensions. On the (SmartArt Tools) Format tab, click the Edit in 2-D button to temporarily render a 3-D graphic in two dimensions. Click the button a second time to return to the third dimension.

◆ **Filling a shape with a new color:** Click the Shape Fill button and make a choice from the drop-down list to select a color, picture, two-color gradient, or texture for the shape.

◆ **Changing the outline:** Click the Shape Outline button and choose a color and weight for the shape's border on the drop-down list.

◆ **Applying a shape effect:** Click the Shape Effects button to select a shape effect for your shape.

Figure 7-11:
Ways to make a diagram shape stand out.

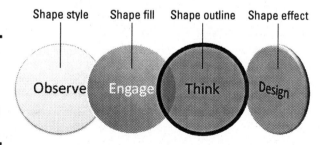

Creating a Diagram from Scratch

If you have the skill and the wherewithal, you can create a diagram from scratch by piecing together shapes, arrows, and connectors. The diagram shown here, for example, was made not from SmartArt graphics but from shapes, arrows, and connectors. Book I, Chapter 8 explains how to draw shapes and lines between shapes. You can enter text on any shape merely by clicking inside it and wiggling your fingers over the keyboard.

Making a diagram from scratch has some advantages. You can draw the connectors any which way. Lines can cross the diagram chaotically. You can include text boxes as well as shapes (this diagram has four text boxes). Don't hesitate to fashion your own diagrams when a presentation or document calls for it.

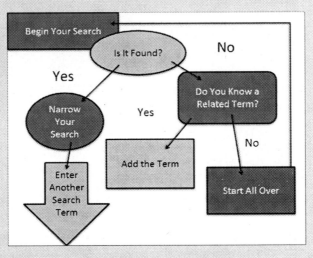

Changing fonts and font sizes on shapes

To make a diagram shape stand out, try changing the font and font size of the text on the shape. Before you change fonts and font sizes, however, you should know that changing fonts in a shape effectively disconnects the shape from the other shapes in the diagram. Normally text changes size throughout a diagram when you add or remove shapes, but when you change the font or font size in one shape, it is no longer associated with the other shapes; its letters don't change their size or appearance when shapes are added or removed from the diagram of which it is a part.

To alter the text on a diagram shape, select the text, go to the Home tab, and choose a different font, font size, and font color, too, if you want.

Chapter 8: Drawing and Manipulating Lines, Shapes, and Other Objects

In This Chapter

- ✔ Drawing and manipulating lines, arrows, and connectors
- ✔ Creating and modifying shapes
- ✔ Creating WordArt images
- ✔ Selecting, resizing, moving, aligning, overlapping, rotating, and grouping objects
- ✔ Changing the color and border around an object

*W*hether you know it or not, Office Home and Student edition comes with drawing commands for drawing lines, arrows, shapes, block arrows, stars, banners, and callout shapes. And Office provides numerous ways to manipulate these objects after you draw them. The drawing commands are meant to bring out the artist in you. Use them to make diagrams, fashion your own ideagrams, and illustrate difficult concepts and ideas. Lines and shapes give you a wonderful opportunity to exercise your creativity. A picture is worth a thousand words, so they say, and the drawing commands give you a chance to express yourself without having to write a thousand words.

In this chapter, you discover the many ways to manipulate lines, shapes, text boxes, WordArt images, clip-art images, and graphics. You discover how to lay out these objects on a page or slide, flip them, change their colors, resize them, move them, and otherwise torture them until they look just right. You discover how to draw lines and arrows, draw connections between shapes, and draw ovals, squares, other shapes, and WordArt images.

Use the techniques I describe in this chapter to bring something more to your Word documents, PowerPoint presentations, Publisher publications, and Excel worksheets: originality. With the techniques I describe in this chapter, you can bring the visual element into your work. You can communicate with images as well as words and numbers.

The Basics: Drawing Lines, Arrows, and Shapes

Figure 8-1 demonstrates how you can use lines, arrows, and shapes (not to mention text boxes) to illustrate ideas and concepts. Sometimes, saying it with lines and shapes is easier and more informative than saying it with words. Even in Excel worksheets, you can find opportunities to use lines, arrows, and shapes. For example, draw arrows and lines on worksheets to illustrate which cells are used to compute formulas.

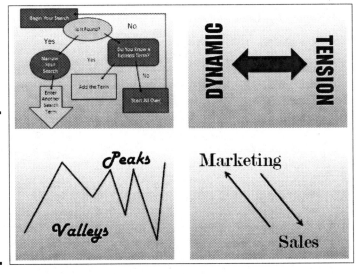

Figure 8-1: Exercise your creativity by including lines, arrows, and shapes in your work.

Follow these basic steps to draw a line, arrow, or shape:

1. Go to the Insert tab.

In Word, you must be in Print Layout view to draw and see lines and shapes.

2. Click the Shapes button to open the Insert Shapes gallery.

As shown in Figure 8-2, the Shapes gallery appears. The shapes are divided into several categories, including Lines, Basic Shapes, and Block Arrows, as well as a category at the top of the gallery where shapes you chose recently are shown. (PowerPoint also offers the Shapes button on the Home tab.)

3. Select a line, arrow, or shape in the Shapes gallery.

4. Drag on your page, slide, or worksheet.

As you drag, the line, arrow, or shape appears before your eyes.

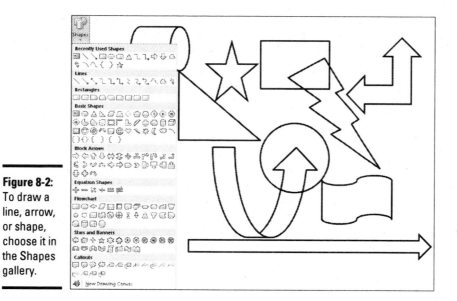

Figure 8-2:
To draw a
line, arrow,
or shape,
choose it in
the Shapes
gallery.

5. **To alter your line, arrow, or shape — that is, to change its size, color, or outline — go to the (Drawing Tools) Format tab.**

   This tab offers many commands for manipulating lines and shapes. (Those commands are explained throughout this chapter.) You must select a line or shape to make the (Drawing Tools) Format tab appear.

   In the upper-left corner of the (Drawing Tools) Format tab is another Shapes gallery for creating new shapes to go along with the one you created.

Handling Lines, Arrows, and Connectors

Earlier in this chapter, Figure 8-1 shows examples of how you can use lines and arrows to present ideas. As well as lines and arrows, the Insert Shapes gallery offers *connectors,* the special lines that link shapes and can bend and stretch as you move shapes around. Use connectors along with lines and arrows to describe the relationships between the people or things in a diagram. These pages explain how to handle lines, arrows, and connectors.

Changing the length and position of a line or arrow

To change anything about a line or arrow, start by clicking to select it. You can tell when a line has been selected because round selection handles appear at either end. Follow these instructions to move a line or adjust its length or angle:

✦ **Changing the angle of a line:** Drag a selection handle up, down, or sideways. A dotted line shows where your line will be when you release the mouse button.

✦ **Changing the length:** Drag a selection handle away from or toward the opposite selection handle.

✦ **Changing the position:** Move the pointer over the line itself and click when you see the four-headed arrow. Then drag the line to a new location.

Changing the appearance of a line, arrow, or connector

What a line looks like is a matter of its color, its *weight* (how wide it is), its *dash status* (it can be filled out or dashed), and its *cap* (its ends can be rounded, square, or flat). To change the appearance of a line, start by selecting it, going to the (Drawing Tools) Format tab, and opening the drop-down list on the Shape Outline button (this button is in the Shape Styles group). As shown in Figure 8-3, you see a drop-down list with commands for handling the appearance of lines, arrows, and connectors:

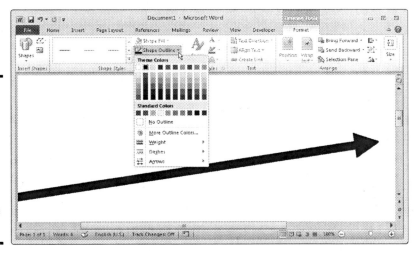

Figure 8-3: Open the drop-down list on the Shape Outline button to change the appearance of lines.

✦ **Color:** Select a color on the drop-down list (see Figure 8-3).

✦ **Width:** Choose Weight on the drop-down list (see Figure 8-3) and then choose a line width on the submenu. You can also choose More Lines on the submenu to open the Format Shape dialog box and change the width there. Enter a setting in points to make the line heavier or thinner.

✦ **Dotted or dashed lines:** Choose Dashes on the drop-down list (see Figure 8-3) and then choose an option on the submenu. Again, you can choose More Lines to open the Format Shape dialog box and choose from many dash types and compound lines.

> ✦ **Line caps:** Click the Shape Styles group button to open the Format Shape dialog box. In the Line Style category, select a cap type (Square, Round, or Flat).

You can also change the appearance of a line on the (Drawing Tools) Format tab by opening the Shape Styles gallery and selecting a style.

Attaching and handling arrowheads on lines and connectors

Arrows, of course, have arrowheads, and arrowheads on lines and connectors can go on either side or both sides of a line. What's more, arrowheads come in different sizes and shapes. To handle arrowheads on lines and connectors, select your line or connector and go to the (Drawing Tools) Format tab. Then use one of these techniques to handle the arrowheads:

✦ Open the drop-down list on the Shape Outline button, choose Arrows (refer to Figure 8-3), and select an arrow on the submenu.

✦ Click the Shape Styles group button to open the Format Shape dialog box. In the Line Style category, choose Arrow settings to describe where you want the arrowheads to be, what you want them to look like, and what size you want them to be.

To attach an arrowhead or arrowheads to a line or connector you've already drawn, select the line and proceed as though you were attaching arrowheads to a line that already has an arrow.

Choosing a default line style for consistency's sake

One of the secrets to making an attractive drawing is to make the lines consistent with one another. Lines should be the same width and color. They should be the same style. Unless you observe this rule, your drawings will be infested with lines of varying width and different colors. They will look like a confetti parade in a windstorm.

You can get around the problem of making lines consistent with one another by creating a model line and making it the default line style.

After you declare a default style, all new lines you create are assigned the style. You don't have to spend as much time making the lines look alike.

Give a line the style, weight, and color that you want for all (or most) lines and then follow these steps to make that line the default style:

1. **Select and right-click the line.**

2. **Choose Set As Default Line on the shortcut menu.**

Attaching and handling arrowConnecting shapes by using connectors

Under Lines, the Shapes gallery offers six different connectors. Use *connectors* to link shapes and text boxes to form a diagram. Connectors differ from conventional lines in an important way: After you attach one to a shape, it stays with the shape when you move the shape. You don't have to worry about remaking all the connections after you move a shape. You can move shapes at will and let the connectors between shapes take care of themselves. Figure 8-4 shows three types of connectors in action. (By the way, if you came here to explore how to make a diagram, be sure to check out Book I, Chapter 7 as well. It explains Office SmartArt diagramming.)

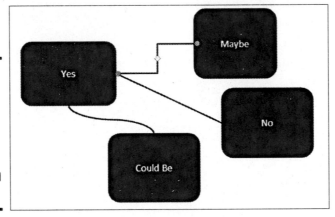

Figure 8-4: The three types of connectors (from top to bottom): elbow, straight, and curved.

To connect shapes in Word, the shapes must be on the drawing canvas. Book II, Chapter 4 describes the Word drawing canvas. (Click the Shapes button and choose New Drawing Canvas to create one.)

Making the connection

Before you draw the connections, draw the shapes and arrange them on the slide where you want them to be in your diagram. Then follow these steps to connect two shapes with a connector:

1. **Select the two shapes that you want to connect.**

    To select the shapes, hold down the Ctrl key and click each one.

2. **On the (Drawing Tools) Format tab, open the Shapes gallery.**

3. **Under Lines, select the connector that will best fit between the two shapes you want to link together.**

4. **Move the pointer over a side selection handle on one of the shapes you want to connect.**

   The selection handles turn red.

5. **Click and drag the pointer over a selection handle on the other shape, and when you see red selection handles on that shape, release the mouse button.**

   Red, round selection handles appear on the shapes where they're connected. These red handles tell you that the two shapes are connected and will remain connected when you move them.

If your connector is attached to the wrong shape, don't despair. Select the connector, and on the (Drawing Tools) Format tab, click the Edit Shape button and choose Reroute Connectors. Then move the pointer over the red handle on the side of the connector that needs to be attached elsewhere, click, drag the connector elsewhere on the other shape, and release the mouse button when you see the red selection handles.

Adjusting a connector

Chances are, your connector needs adjusting to make it fit correctly between the two shapes. Click to select your connector and follow these techniques to adjust it:

+ **Changing the shape of a connector:** Drag the yellow diamond on the connector. As you drag, the connector assumes different shapes.

+ **Changing the connector type:** Right-click the connector, choose Connector Types, and choose Straight Connector, Elbow Connector, or Curved Connector on the submenu.

+ **Handling arrows on connectors:** If the arrows on the connector aren't there, are pointing in the wrong direction, or shouldn't be there, change the arrowheads around using the same techniques you use with standard arrows. See "Attaching and handling arrowheads on lines and connectors" earlier in this chapter.

Make sure that the connector lines in your diagram are consistent with one another. Give them the same style and appearance, or else it will be hard to make sense of your diagram.

Handling Rectangles, Ovals, Stars, and Other Shapes

Figure 8-5 illustrates how shapes can come in very handy for illustrating concepts and ideas. You can combine shapes to make your own illustrations. Apart from the standard rectangle and oval, you can draw octagons and various other "-agons," arrows, stars, and banners. You are hereby encouraged to make shapes a part of your work, and you'll be glad to know that drawing shapes is not difficult. These pages explain how to draw a shape, exchange one shape for another, change a shape's symmetry, and enter words on a shape.

Figure 8-5:
An example
of using
shapes (and
connectors)
to convey
an idea.

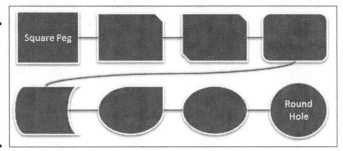

In Word, you must be in Print Layout view to draw and handle shapes. If you intend to draw more than one shape in Word, create a drawing canvas to hold the shapes (click the Shapes button and choose New Drawing Canvas). Book II, Chapter 4 describes the drawing canvas in Word.

Drawing a shape

Follow these steps to draw a shape:

1. **On the Insert tab, click the Shapes button to open the Shapes gallery.**

   You can also insert shapes from the Shapes gallery on the (Drawing Tools) Format tab.

2. **Select a shape in the gallery.**

   If you've drawn the shape recently, you may be able to find it at the top of the gallery under Recently Used Shapes.

3. **Click and drag slantwise to draw the shape, as shown at the top of Figure 8-6.**

   Hold down the Shift key as you drag if you want the shape to retain its proportions. For example, to draw a circle, select the Oval shape and hold down the Shift key as you draw.

Changing a shape's size and shape

Selection handles appear on the corners and sides of a shape after you select it. With the selection handles showing, you can change a shape's size and shape:

+ Hold down the Shift key and drag a corner handle to change a shape's size and retain its symmetry.

+ Drag a side, top, or bottom handle to stretch or scrunch a shape.

Drag to draw a shape

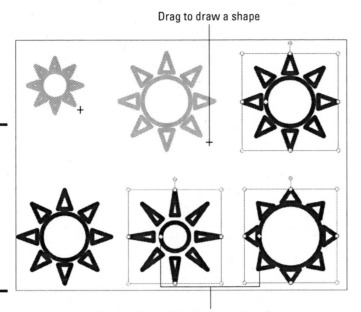

Figure 8-6:
Drag to
draw a
shape
(top); drag
a diamond
to change
a shape's
symmetry
(bottom).

Drag a diamond to change a shape's symmetry

Choosing a different shape

To exchange one shape for another, select the shape and follow these steps:

1. **On the (Drawing Tools) Format tab, click the Edit Shape button.**

You can find this button in the Insert Shapes group.

2. **Choose Change Shape on the drop-down list.**

3. **Select a new shape in the Shapes gallery.**

Changing a shape's symmetry

A yellow diamond, sometimes more than one, appears on some shapes. By dragging a diamond, you can change a shape's symmetry. Figure 8-6, for example, shows the same shape — the Sun shape — altered to show different symmetries. Notice where the diamonds are. By dragging a diamond even a short distance, you can do a lot to change a shape's symmetry.

Using a shape as a text box

Here's a neat trick: Rather than use the conventional rectangle as a text box, you can use a shape. Figure 8-7 shows examples of shapes being used as text boxes. By placing words on shapes, you can make the shapes illustrate ideas and concepts.

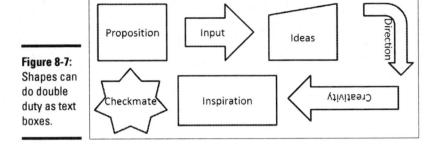

Figure 8-7: Shapes can do double duty as text boxes.

Follow these instructions to handle text box shapes:

✦ **Entering the text:** Click in the shape and start typing. In Word, you can right-click and choose Add Text if you have trouble typing in the shape.

✦ **Editing the text:** Click in the text and start editing. That's all there is to it. If you have trouble getting inside the shape to edit the text, select the shape, right-click it, and choose Edit Text on the shortcut menu.

✦ **Changing the font, color, and size of text:** Right-click in the text and choose Font. Then, in the Font dialog box, choose a font, font color, and a font size for the text.

✦ **Allowing the shape to enlarge for text:** You can allow the shape to enlarge and receive more text. Click the Shape Styles group button, and in the Text Box category of the Format Shape dialog box, select the Resize Shape to Fit Text option button.

Turning a text box into a text box shape

To turn a conventional text box into a text box shape, follow these instructions:

1. **Select the text box by clicking its perimeter.**

2. **On the (Drawing Tools) Format tab, click the Edit Shape button, choose Change Shape, and then select a shape in the Shapes gallery.**

After the conversion, you usually have to enlarge the shape to accommodate the text.

> **Rugby Club Meeting**
>
> Thursday, June 4 — 3:00
>
> *Your presence is mandatory!*

> **Rugby Club Meeting**
>
> Thursday, June 4 — 3:00
>
> *Your presence is mandatory!*

WordArt for Bending, Spindling, and Mutilating Text

A *WordArt image* consists of a word that has been stretched, crumpled, or squeezed into an odd shape. Actually, a WordArt image can include more than one word. Figure 8-8 shows the WordArt gallery, where WordArt images are made, and an example of a WordArt image. After you insert a WordArt image, you can fool with the buttons on the (Drawing Tools) Format tab and torture the word or phrase even further.

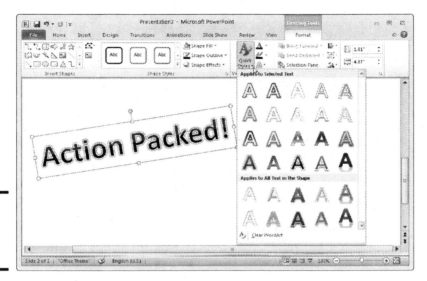

Figure 8-8:
Creating a
WordArt
image.

Creating a WordArt image

Follow these steps to create a WordArt image:

1. **On the Insert tab, click the WordArt button.**

   A drop-down list with WordArt styles appears.

2. **Select a WordArt style.**

   Don't worry about selecting the right style; you can choose a different one later on.

3. **Enter the text for the image in the WordArt text box.**

   Congratulations. You just created a WordArt image.

Editing a WordArt image

Usually, you have to wrestle with a WordArt image before it comes out right. Select the image, go to the (Drawing Tools) Format tab, and use these techniques to win the wrestling match:

✦ **Editing the words:** Click in the WordArt text box and edit the text there.

✦ **Choosing a new WordArt style:** Open the WordArt Styles gallery and select a style. Depending on the size of your screen and which program you're working in, you may have to click the Quick Styles button first (refer to Figure 8-8).

 ✦ **Changing the letters' color:** Click the Text Fill button and choose a color on the drop-down list.

 ✦ **Changing the letters' outline:** Click the Text Outline button and make choices to change the letters' outline.

 To apply color or an outline to some of the letters or words in a WordArt image, select the letters or words before choosing options on the (Drawing Tools) Format tab.

Manipulating Lines, Shapes, Art, Text Boxes, and Other Objects

After you insert a shape, line, text box, clip-art image, graphic, diagram, WordArt image, chart, or embedded object in a file, it ceases being what it was before and becomes an *object*. Figure 8-9 shows eight objects. I'm not sure whether these eight objects resent being objectified, but Office objectifies them. As far as manipulating these items in Office is concerned, these are just objects.

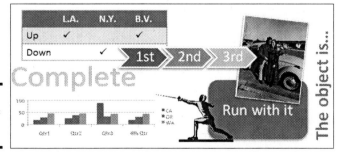

Figure 8-9: Examples of objects.

The techniques for manipulating objects are the same whether you're dealing with a line, shape, graphic, clip-art image, diagram, or text box. The good news from your end is that you have to master only one set of techniques for handling these objects. Whether you want to move, change the size of, or change the outline of a text box, clip-art image, graphic, or shape, the techniques are the same.

In the remainder of this chapter are instructions for doing these tasks with objects:

✦ **Selecting:** Before you can do anything to objects, you have to select them. See "Selecting objects so that you can manipulate them."

✦ **Making use of the rulers and grid:** Rulers (in Word, PowerPoint, Excel, and Publisher) and the grid (in Word and PowerPoint) can be very helpful for aligning and placing objects. See "Hiding and displaying the rulers and grid."

✦ **Changing an object's size and shape:** You can enlarge, shrink, stretch, and scrunch objects to make them wider or taller. See "Changing an object's size and shape."

✦ **Moving and positioning:** You can land objects with precision in a Word document, PowerPoint slide, or Excel worksheet. See "Moving and positioning objects."

✦ **Aligning and distributing:** Another way to move and position objects is to realign or redistribute them across a page, slide, or worksheet. See "Tricks for aligning and distributing objects."

✦ **Overlapping:** When you're dealing with several objects, they're bound to overlap — and sometimes overlapping objects make for an interesting effect. On the right side of Figure 8-9, for example, several objects overlap and give the impression that they were "dropped there." See "When objects overlap: Choosing which appears above the other," to handle overlapping objects.

✦ **Rotating and flipping:** Viewers turn their heads when they see an object that has been flipped or rotated. You can rotate and flip shapes, lines, text boxes, graphics, clip-art images, and WordArt images. See "Rotating and flipping Objects."

✦ **Grouping:** To make working with several different objects easier, you can *group* them so that they become a single object. After objects have been grouped, manipulating them — manipulating it, I should say — is easier. See "Grouping objects to make working with them easier."

✦ **Applying outlines and fills:** Putting outlines and color fills on objects makes them stand out. You can also fill some kinds of objects with a color or pattern. See "Changing an Object's Color, Outline Color, and Transparency."

If you sighed after you finished reading this long list, I don't blame you. But be of good cheer: Most of these commands are easy to pick up, and including lines, shapes, text boxes, WordArt images, clip art, and graphics in your work is a good way to impress your friends and intimidate your enemies.

Selecting objects so that you can manipulate them

Before you can move or change the border of a graphic, text box, or other object, you have to select it. To select an object, simply click it. Sometimes, to align or decorate several objects simultaneously, you have to select more than one object at the same time. To select more than one object:

✦ Ctrl+click them. In other words, hold down the Ctrl key as you click the objects.

✦ On the Home tab, click the Select button and choose Select Objects on the drop-down list. (You may have to click the Find & Select button first, depending on the size of your screen.) Then click on one side of the objects you want to select and drag the pointer across the other objects. In Word, the objects must be on the drawing canvas for you to select them this way. (Book II, Chapter 4 describes the Word drawing canvas.)

✦ On the (Drawing Tools) Format tab, click the Selection Pane button. The Selection and Visibility pane opens, as shown in Figure 8-10. It lists objects on the drawing canvas (Word), slide (PowerPoint), or worksheet (Excel). Click or Ctrl+click object names in the pane to select objects.

You can also open the Selection and Visibility pane by clicking the Select button on the Home tab and choosing Selection Pane on the drop-down list. (You may have to click the Editing button first, depending on the size of your screen.)

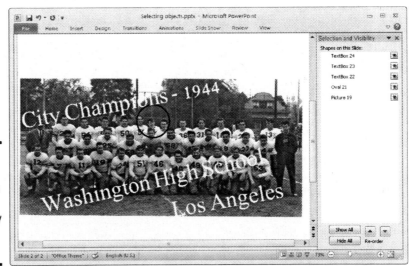

Figure 8-10: Click an object in the Selection and Visibility pane to select it.

After you select an object, its selection handles appear. Objects have eight selection handles, one at each corner and one at each side. To tell whether an object is selected, look for its selection handles.

Hiding and displaying the rulers and grid

Word, PowerPoint, Excel, and Publisher offer two rulers, one along the top of the window and one along the left side. Use the rulers to help place and align objects. To display or hide these rulers, use one of these techniques:

✦ On the View tab, click the Ruler check box. (You may have to click the Show button first, depending on the size of your screen.) To see the rulers, you must be in Print Layout view in Word and Page Layout view in Excel.

✦ In PowerPoint, you can also hide or display rulers by right-clicking a slide (but not an object or frame) and choosing Ruler on the shortcut menu.

In Word and PowerPoint, the grid can come in very handy for aligning objects. On the View tab, click the Gridlines check box to see the grid. (You may have to click the Show button first.) The grid settings in PowerPoint are quite sophisticated (see Book III, Chapter 4 for details).

By the way, fans of the metric system will be pleased to know that you can display centimeters (or millimeters, points, or picas) on the ruler instead of inches. On the File tab, choose Options. In the Options dialog box, go to the Advanced category, open the Show Measurements in Units Of drop-down list, and choose a unit of measurement.

Changing an object's size and shape

Usually when an object arrives on screen, you have to wrestle with it. You have to change its size (and sometimes its shape as well). Figure 8-11 demonstrates how to resize an object. Select your object and use one of these methods to change its size and shape:

✦ **"Eyeball it":** Hold down the Shift key and drag a *corner* selection handle to make the object larger or smaller but maintain its proportions. Drag a selection handle on the *side* to stretch or crimp an object and change its shape as well as its size.

✦ **Enter height and width measurements:** On the Format tab, enter measurements in the Height and Width boxes (see Figure 8-11). Depending on the size of your screen, you may have to click the Size button before you can see these boxes.

✦ **Open the Format (or Layout) dialog box:** Click the Size group button on the Format tab to open the Format dialog box (in PowerPoint and Excel) or the Layout dialog box (in Word). Then change the Height and Width settings in the dialog box (see Figure 8-11).

Drag a selection handle . . .   or enter measurements

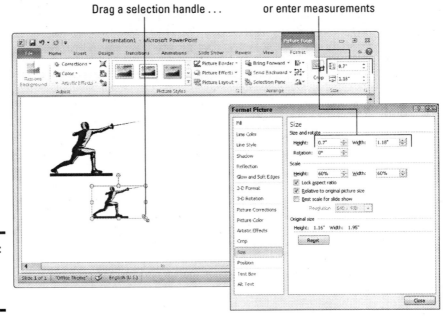

Figure 8-11:
Ways to
resize an
object.

Whether you can change an object's shape as well as its size depends on whether the object's aspect ratio is *locked*. If you're wrestling with an object and it won't do your bidding — if it refuses to change shape or it changes shape, and you don't want it to do that — unlock its aspect ratio setting. Click the Size group button, and in the dialog box that appears, select or deselect the Lock Aspect Ratio check box. When an object's aspect ratio is *locked*, it maintains its shape as you change its size, but when it's *unlocked*, you can change its shape as well as its size.

You can change the size and shape of several objects at one time by selecting all the objects before giving a command to change sizes. Being able to change objects' size this way is convenient when you want to change the size of many objects but maintain their with relationships to one another.

Moving and positioning objects

Moving objects is considerably easier than moving furniture. Select the object you want to reposition and use one of these techniques to land it in the right place:

✦ **Dragging:** Move the pointer over the perimeter of the object, click when you see the four-headed arrow, and drag the object to a new location. Hold down the Shift key as you drag to move an object either horizontally or vertically in a straight line.

✦ **Using a dialog box (in PowerPoint and Word):** On the Format tab, click the Size group button. (Depending on the size of your screen, you may have to click the Size button first.) You see the Format or Layout dialog box. On the Position category or tab, enter Horizontal and Vertical position measurements to place the object on the slide or page.

✦ **Nudging:** If you can't quite fit an object in the right place, try using a Nudge command. Nudge commands move objects up, down, left, or right. Press one of the arrow keys ($\uparrow$, $\downarrow$, $\leftarrow$, $\rightarrow$) to move the object a little bit. Hold down the Ctrl key as you press an arrow key to make the object move by tiny increments.

Use the dialog box method of positioning objects when you want objects to be in the exact same position on different pages or slides.

Tricks for aligning and distributing objects

When several objects appear in the same place, use the Align and Distribute commands to give the objects an orderly appearance. You can make your Word page, PowerPoint slide, Excel worksheet, or Publisher publication look tidier by aligning the objects or by distributing them so that they are an equal distance from one another. Office offers special commands for doing these tasks.

Aligning objects

The Align commands come in handy when you want objects to line up with one another. Suppose you need to align several shapes. As shown in Figure 8-12, you can use an Align command to line up the shapes with precision. You don't have to tug and pull, tug and pull until the shapes are aligned with one another. In the figure, I used the Align Top command to line up the shapes along the top. In Word and PowerPoint, besides aligning objects with respect to one another, you can align objects or with respect to the page (in Word) or the slide (in PowerPoint). For example, you can line up objects along the top of a slide.

Follow these steps to line up objects:

1. **Move the objects where you roughly want them to be, and if you want to align objects with respect to one another, move one object to a point that the others will align to.**

When Office aligns objects with respect to one another, it aligns them to the object in the leftmost, centermost, rightmost, topmost, middlemost, or bottommost position, depending on which Align command you choose.

2. **Select the objects you want to align.**

Earlier in this chapter, "Selecting objects so that you can manipulate them" looks at selection techniques.

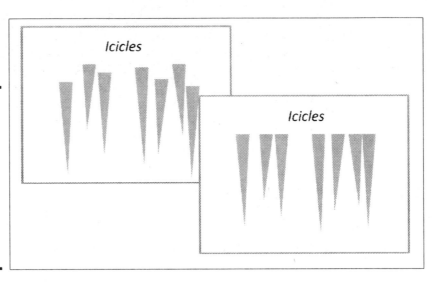

Figure 8-12:
Use the Align commands to align objects. These objects are aligned along the top.

3. **Go to the Format tab.**

   You can also go to the Page Layout tab (in Word and Excel) or the Home tab (in PowerPoint).

4. **Click the Align button, and on the drop-down list, choose whether to align the objects with respect to one another or with respect to the page or page margin (in Word) or a slide (in PowerPoint).**

   Depending on the size of your screen, you may have to click the Arrange button to get to the Align button.

5. **Click the Align button again and choose an Align command — Left, Center, Right, Top, Middle, or Bottom.**

6. **If necessary, drag the objects on the page.**

   That's right — drag them. After you give an Align command, the objects are still selected, and you can drag to adjust their positions.

Distributing objects so that they are equidistant

The Distribute commands — Distribute Horizontally and Distribute Vertically — come in handy for laying out objects on a page or slide. These commands arrange objects so that the same amount of space appears between each one. Rather than go to the trouble of pushing and pulling objects until they are distributed evenly, you can simply select the objects and choose a Distribute command.

Figure 8-13 demonstrates how the Distribute commands work. In the figure, I chose the Distribute Horizontally command so that the same amount of horizontal (side-by-side) space appears between the objects. Distributing objects such as these on your own, perhaps by entering measurements in the Layout or Format dialog box, is a waste of time when you can use a Distribute command.

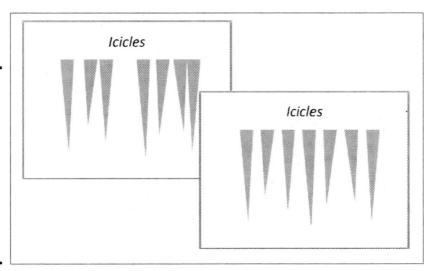

Figure 8-13:
The Distribute commands rearrange objects so that the same amount of space is between them.

Follow these steps to distribute objects horizontally or vertically on a page or slide:

1. **Arrange the objects so that the outermost objects — the ones that will go on the top and bottom or left side and right side — are where you want them to be.**

In other words, if you want to distribute objects horizontally across a page, place the leftmost object and rightmost object where you want them to be. Office will distribute the other objects equally between the leftmost and rightmost object.

2. **Select the objects.**

3. **Go to the Format tab.**

You can also go to the Page Layout tab (in Word and Excel) or the Home tab (in PowerPoint).

4. **Click the Align button and choose a Distribute option on the drop-down list.**

To find the Align button, you may have to click the Arrange button first, depending on the size of your screen.

When objects overlap: Choosing which appears above the other

On a page or slide that is crowded with text boxes, shapes, graphics, and clip-art images, objects inevitably overlap, and you have to decide which object goes on top of the stack and which on the bottom. In a Word document, you have to decide as well whether text appears above or below objects.

Objects that deliberately overlap can be interesting and attractive to look at. On the right side of Figure 8-14, for example, a clip-art image and text box appear in front of a shape. Makes for a nice effect, no? These pages explain controlling how objects overlap with the Bring and Send commands and the Selection and Visibility pane.

Select an object   Choose a Bring or Send command

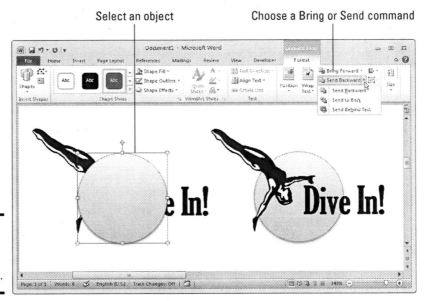

Figure 8-14:
An example
of objects
overlapping.

Controlling overlaps with the Bring and Send commands

Word, PowerPoint, Excel, and Publisher offer these commands for handling objects in a stack:

✦ **Bring Forward:** Moves the object higher in the stack

✦ **Bring to Front:** Moves the object in front of all other objects in the stack

✦ **Send Backward:** Moves the object lower in the stack

✦ **Send to Back:** Moves the object behind all other objects

Word offers these additional commands:

✦ **Bring in Front of Text:** Moves the object in front of text on the page

✦ **Send Behind Text:** Moves the object behind text on the page so that the text appears over the object

Select an object and use one of these techniques to give a Bring or Send command:

✦ On the Format tab, click the Bring Forward or Send Backward button, or open the drop-down list on one of these buttons and choose a Bring or Send command (refer to Figure 8-14). Depending on the size of your screen, you may have to click the Arrange button before you can get to a Bring or Send command.

In Word, Excel, and Publisher, the Bring and Send commands are also available on the Page Layout tab; in PowerPoint, they are also available on the Home tab, although you may have to click the Arrange button first, depending on the size of your screen.

✦ Right-click an object and choose a Bring or Send command on the shortcut menu.

In Word, you can't choose a Bring or Send command unless you've chosen a text-wrapping option apart from In Line with Text for the object. Select your object, go to the Format tab, click the Text Wrap button, and choose an option on the drop-down list apart from In Line with Text. Book II, Chapter 4 looks at text wrapping in Word.

If an object on the bottom of the stack shows through after you place it on the bottom, the object on the top of the stack is transparent or semi-transparent. Transparent objects are like gauze curtains — they reveal what's behind them. If you want to make the object on the top of the stack less transparent, see "Making a color transparent," later in this chapter.

Controlling overlaps with the Selection and Visibility pane

Another way to control how objects overlap is to open the Selection and Visibility pane, select an object, and click the Bring Forward or Send Backward button as necessary to move the object up or down in the stack. The Bring Forward and Send Backward buttons are located at the bottom of the pane. Earlier in this chapter, "Selecting objects so that you can manipulate them" explains the Selection and Visibility pane. (On the Format tab, click the Selection Pane button to open it.)

Rotating and flipping objects

Rotating and flipping objects — that is, changing their orientation — is a neat way to spruce up a page or slide, as Figure 8-15 demonstrates. You can rotate and flip these kinds of objects: lines, shapes, text boxes, clip-art images, graphics, and WordArt images. To flip or rotate an object, select it and do one of the following:

✦ **Choose a Rotate or Flip command:** On the Format tab, click the Rotate button and choose an option on the drop-down list (refer to Figure 8-15). The Rotate commands rotate objects by 90 degrees; the Flip commands flip objects over. The Rotate button is also found on the Page Layout tab (in Word and Excel) and the Home tab (in PowerPoint and Publisher). You may have to click the Arrange button to see the Rotate button, depending on the size of your screen.

✦ **Roll your own:** Drag the object's *rotation handle,* the green dot that appears after you select it. Hold down the Shift key as you drag to rotate the shape by 15-degree increments.

✦ **Open the Format or Layout dialog box:** On the Rotate drop-down list, choose More Rotation Options to open the Format or Layout dialog box. Enter a degree measurement in the Rotation text box.

To rotate several objects simultaneously, Ctrl+click to select each object and then give a rotation command.

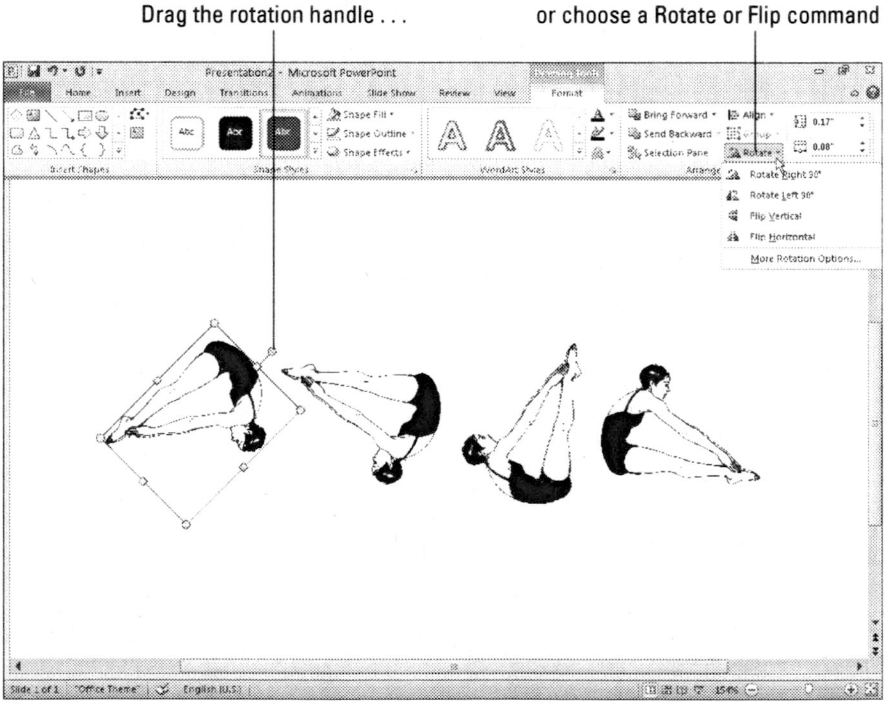

Drag the rotation handle . . .   or choose a Rotate or Flip command

Figure 8-15: Members of an audience turn their heads when objects are rotated or flipped.

Grouping objects to make working with them easier

Consider the clip-art image, shape, and text box in Figure 8-16. To move, resize, or reshape these objects, I would have to laboriously move them one at a time — that is, I would have to do that if it weren't for the Group command.

Figure 8-16:
You can move, resize, and reshape grouped objects as though they were a single object.

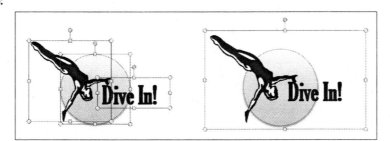

The Group command assembles different objects into a single object to make moving, resizing, and reshaping objects easier. With the Group command, you select the objects that you want to "group" and then you wrap them into a bundle so that they become easier to work with. Office remembers which objects were grouped so that you can ungroup objects after you've moved or resized them.

Grouping objects

Select the objects and do one of the following to group them into one happy family:

♦ On the Format tab (or the Page Layout tab in Word and Excel, and the Home tab in PowerPoint and Publisher), click the Group button and choose Group on the drop-down list. Depending on the size of your screen, you may have to click the Arrange button to get to the Group button.

♦ Right-click one of the objects you selected and choose Group⇨Group.

After objects are grouped, they form a single object with the eight selection handles.

To add an object to a group, select the object and the grouped objects by Ctrl+clicking and then choose the Group command.

Ungrouping and regrouping

To ungroup an object and break it into its components parts, perhaps to fiddle with one of the objects in the group, select the object, go to the Format tab, click the Group button, and choose Ungroup.

Office remembers which objects were in a group after you ungroup it. To reassemble the objects in a group, click an object that was formerly in the group and then choose the Regroup command. You can find this command on the Group button, and you can also give the Regroup command by right-clicking and choosing Group⇨Regroup.

Changing an Object's Color, Outline Color, and Transparency

If an object's color or outline color doesn't suit you, you have the right to change colors. For that matter, you can opt for a "blank" object with no color or remove the color from around the perimeter of the object. As the saying goes, "It's a free country."

Office has its own lingo when it comes to an object's color. Remember these terms when you make like Picasso with your shapes, text boxes, graphics, and clip-art images:

✦ **Shape fill colors:** The color that fills in an object is called the *shape fill*. You can apply shape fills to shapes, text boxes, and WordArt images, but not clip-art or graphics. Besides colors, you can fill a shape with a picture, a gradient, or a texture. (See the next topic in this chapter, "Filling an object with a color, picture, or texture.")

✦ **Shape outline colors:** The line that goes around the perimeter of the object is called the *shape outline*. You can choose a color, style, and line width for outlines. (See "Putting the outline around an object," later in this chapter.)

The easiest way to decorate a shape, text box, or WordArt image is to visit the Format tab and make a selection in the Shape Styles gallery. These ready-made gallery selections can spare you the work of dealing with fill colors, outlines, and shape effects. Just remember not to mix and match different Shape Style options; use them with consistency.

Filling an object with a color, picture, or texture

Shapes, text boxes, and WordArt images are empty when you first create them, but you can fill them with a color, picture, gradient, or texture by following these basic steps:

1. **Select the object that needs a facelift.**

2. **On the Format tab, click the Shape Fill button.**

3. **On the drop-down list, choose a fill color, picture, gradient, or texture.**

Choose No Fill to remove the fill color, picture, gradient, or texture from an object.

Figure 8-17 shows the same object filled with a color, picture, gradient, and texture. Which do you prefer? Your choices are as follows:

✦ **Color:** Applies a single color to the object.

✦ **Picture:** Places a picture in the object. You see the Insert Picture dialog box. Choose a picture and click the Insert button.

✦ **Gradient (Word, PowerPoint, and Publisher only):** Applies gradient color shading to the object. You can choose between various shading styles.

✦ **Texture:** Offers 24 patterns meant to simulate various surfaces. The choices include Granite, Paper Bag, and Pink Tissue Paper. Be sure to use the scroll bar to see all the choices.

✦ **Pattern (Publisher only):** Applies a pattern to the object. Select a pattern on the Pattern tab of the Fill Effects dialog box.

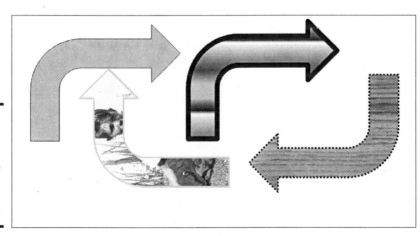

Figure 8-17:
Shape fills (from left to right): color, picture, gradient, and texture.

Making a color transparent

A transparent color is like gauze because instead of being solid, it shows what's behind it. Transparent colors are especially useful in text boxes because the text shows through and can be read easily. Follow these steps to make the fill color in a text box, shape, or WordArt image transparent or semi-transparent:

1. **Right-click the object and choose Format Shape (or Format AutoShape).**

   You see the Format Shape dialog box.

2. **In the Fill category, drag the Transparency slider to choose how transparent a color you want.**

   At 100%, the color is completely transparent and, in fact, not there; at 1%, the color is hardly transparent at all.

3. **Click the Close or OK button.**

You can also make a graphic transparent by recoloring it. See Book VI, Chapter 3.

Putting the outline around an object

The *outline* is the line that runs around the perimeter of an object. Put an outline color around an object to give it more definition or make it stand out. Figure 8-18 shows examples of outlines. What a shape outline looks like has to do with the color, weight, and dash style you choose for it.

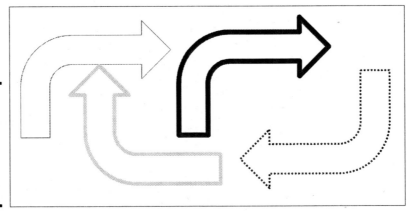

Figure 8-18: An object's outline has to do with its color, weight, and dash style.

Select your object and follow these steps to change its outline:

1. **On the Format tab, click the Shape Outline button.**

   A drop-down list appears.

2. **Choose a color, weight, or dash.**

   You may have to return to the Shape Outline drop-down list more than once to make the outline just so.

- *Color:* Choose a theme color deemed right for borders by the makers of your program or choose a standard color.

- *Weight:* Choose how thick or thin you want the border to be. You can choose More Lines on the submenu to open the Format dialog box. In the Line Style category, you can choose compound lines and enter a point-size width for the outline.

- *Dashes:* Choose straight lines, dashed lines, or broken lines.

The (Picture Tools) Format tab — the one you see when you're dealing with pictures and clip art — offers the Picture Border drop-down list instead of the Shape Outline drop-down list, but the options on the lists are the same.

To remove an outline from an object, choose No Outline on the Shape Outline (or Picture Border) drop-down list.

Designating a fill and outline color for all your objects

Rather than go to the significant trouble of giving all or most of your objects the same look, you can make one object the model for all others to follow and declare it the default style. After that, all new objects you insert appear in the same style, your objects have a uniform appearance, and you don't have to spend as much time formatting objects.

Select an object with a fill and an outline color that you want as your model, right-click the object, and choose Set As Default to make your object the default that all other objects start from.

Book II

Word

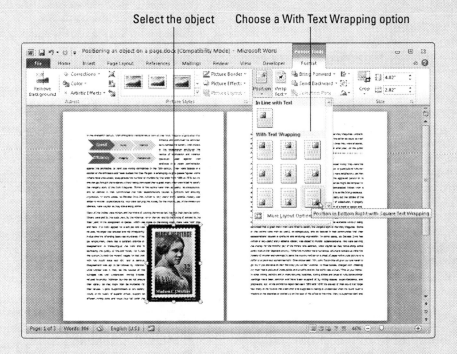

Select the object   Choose a With Text Wrapping option

Contents at a Glance

Chapter 1: Speed Techniques for Using Word 189

Introducing the Word Screen 189
Creating a New Document 191
Getting a Better Look at Your
   Documents 193
Selecting Text in Speedy Ways........... 196
Moving Around Quickly in
   Documents 198
Entering Information Quickly in a
   Computerized Form 202

Chapter 2: Laying Out Text and Pages. 207

Paragraphs and Formatting 207
Inserting a Section Break for
   Formatting Purposes....................... 208
Breaking a Line 209
Starting a New Page 210
Setting Up and Changing
   the Margins 210
Indenting Paragraphs and
   First Lines 212
Numbering the Pages............................ 214
Putting Headers and Footers
   on Pages.. 216
Adjusting the Space between Lines ... 219
Adjusting the Space between
   Paragraphs 220
Creating Numbered and
   Bulleted Lists 220
Working with Tabs................................ 223
Hyphenating Text................................. 225

Chapter 3: Word Styles 229

All about Styles.................................... 229
Applying Styles to Text
   and Paragraphs............................... 231
Creating a New Style 235
Modifying a Style................................. 237
Creating and Managing Templates 238

Chapter 4: Desktop Publishing with Word 245

Making Use of Charts, Diagrams,
   Shapes, Clip Art, and Photos 245
Constructing the Perfect Table 246
Positioning and Wrapping Objects
   Relative to the Page and Text 248
Working with the Drawing Canvas..... 251
Choosing a Theme for
   Your Document................................. 252
Putting Newspaper-Style
   Columns in a Document 253
Working with Text Boxes 255
Sprucing Up Your Pages...................... 256
Dropping In a Drop Cap....................... 258
Watermarking for the Elegant Effect ... 259
Landscape Documents 260
Printing on Different Size Paper 261

Chapter 5: Getting Word's Help with Office Chores 263

Highlighting Parts of a Document 263
Commenting on a Document 264
Tracking Changes to Documents 266
Printing an Address on an Envelope... 271
Printing a Single Address Label
   (Or a Page of the Same Label) 272
Churning Out Letters, Envelopes,
   and Labels for Mass Mailings.......... 274

Chapter 6: Tools for Reports and Scholarly Papers 281

Alphabetizing a List 281
Outlines for Organizing Your Work ... 282
Generating a Table of Contents.......... 284
Indexing a Document 287
Putting Cross-References in
   a Document 292
Putting Footnotes and Endnotes
   in Documents 294
Compiling a Bibliography.................... 296

Chapter 1: Speed Techniques for Using Word

In This Chapter

✔ **Getting acquainted with the Word screen**

✔ **Creating a Word document**

✔ **Changing your view of a document**

✔ **Selecting text so that you can copy, move, or delete it**

✔ **Getting from place to place in long documents**

✔ **Pasting one Word document into another**

✔ **Creating data-entry forms**

This chapter explains shortcuts and commands that can help you become a speedy user of Word 2010. Everything in this chapter was put here so that you can get off work earlier and take the slow, scenic route home. Starting here, you discover how to create and change your view of documents. You find out how to select text, get from place to place, and mark your place in long documents. You also explore how to insert one document into another and create data-entry forms to make entering information a little easier.

Introducing the Word Screen

Seeing the Word screen for the first time is like trying to find your way through Tokyo's busy Ikebukuro subway station. It's intimidating. But when you start using Word, you quickly learn what everything is. To help you get going, Figure 1-1 shows you the different parts of the screen. Here are shorthand descriptions of these screen parts:

 ✦ **Word button:** In the upper-left corner of the screen, the Word button offers a menu for restoring, moving, sizing, minimizing, maximizing, and closing the Word window.

✦ **Quick Access toolbar:** This toolbar offers the Save, Undo, and Repeat buttons. Wherever you go in Word, you see the Quick Access toolbar. Book I, Chapter 1 explains the toolbar in detail; Book VI, Chapter 1 explains how to customize and move the Quick Access toolbar.

✦ **Title bar:** At the top of the screen, the title bar tells you the name of the document you're working on.

✦ **Minimize, Restore, Close buttons:** These three magic buttons make it very easy to shrink, enlarge, and close the window you are working in.

File

✦ **File tab:** Go to the File tab to do file-management tasks.

✦ **The Ribbon:** Select a tab on the Ribbon to undertake a new task. (Book I, Chapter 1 explains the Ribbon in detail, and Book VI, Chapter 1 explains how to customize the Ribbon.)

✦ **Scroll bars:** The scroll bars help you get from place to place in a document.

✦ **Status bar:** The status bar gives you basic information about where you are and what you're doing in a document. It tells you what page and what section you're in, the total number of pages and words in your document, and what language the text is written in. Book VI, Chapter 1 explains how to customize the status bar.

✦ **View buttons:** Click one of these buttons — Print Layout, Full Screen Reading, Web Layout, Outline, or Draft — to change your view of a document.

✦ **Zoom controls:** Use these controls to zoom in and out on your work.

Word button

File tab

The Ribbon

Quick Access toolbar   Title bar   Minimize, Restore, and Close buttons

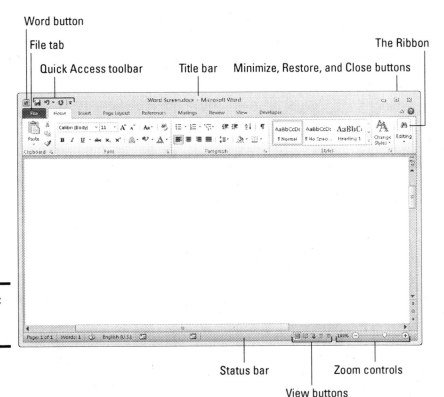

Figure 1-1:
The Word
screen.

Status bar   Zoom controls

View buttons

Creating a New Document

Document is just a fancy word for a letter, report, announcement, or proclamation that you create with Word. When you first start Word, you see a new, blank document with the generic name *Document1*. You can start working right away on this document, or you can create a new document by choosing a template.

A *template* is a special kind of file that is used as the starting point for creating documents. Each template comes with many preformatted styles. If your aim is to create an academic report, flyer, newsletter, calendar, résumé, or other sophisticated document, see if you can spare yourself the formatting work by choosing the appropriate template when you create your document. (Chapter 3 of this mini-book explains templates in detail and how to create your own templates.)

**Book II
Chapter 1**

Speed Techniques
for Using Word

File

No matter what kind of document you want, start creating it by going to the File tab and choosing New. The Available Templates window shown in Figure 1-2 appears. This window offers templates for creating many types of documents. Click a template in this window to see, on the right side of the window, a preview of the document you will create. Double-click a template (or select it and click the Create button) to create a document.

Preview the template you will create

Click to backtrack   Choose a template

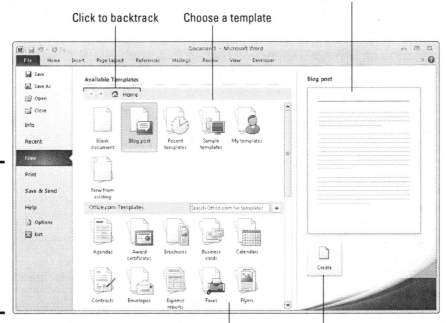

Figure 1-2: Create documents from templates in the Available Templates window.

Click Create (or double-click a template) to create a document

---

Constructing your blank default document

When you open a new, blank document by pressing Ctrl+N or choosing the Blank Document icon in the Available Templates window (refer to Figure 1-2), does the document meet your specifications? When you start typing, does the text appear in your favorite font? Are the margins just-so?

You can get a head start on creating documents by telling Word what you want new, blank documents to look like. To do that, open the Font dialog box (click the Font group button on the Home tab) followed by the Page Setup dialog box (click the Page Setup group button on the Page Layout tab), make your formatting choices in each dialog box, and click the Set As Default button. Changes you make this way are saved to the Blank Document template, the one used to create blank documents. (Chapter 3 of this mini-book explains what templates are).

Use these techniques in the Available Templates window to create a document:

+ **Create a blank document:** Choose the Blank Document icon to create a bare-bones document with few styles. Blank Document is the default template for creating documents. (By pressing Ctrl+N, you can create a new, blank document without opening the Available Templates window.)

+ **Create a brochure, form, invoice, or other specialty document:** Take your pick of these techniques to create a specialty document:

  • *Use a template on your computer:* Choose Sample Templates. Templates that you loaded on your computer when you installed Office appear in the window.

  • *Download a template from Microsoft:* Under Office.com Templates, do one of the following: (1) choose the type of template you want, or (2) make sure your computer is connected to the Internet, enter a search term in the Search box, and click the Start Searching button (or press Enter). Choose a template and click the Download button to download it to your computer.

  • *Use a template you created (or downloaded earlier from Microsoft or acquired from a third party):* Click the My Templates icon. The New dialog box appears so that you can choose a template.

+ **Create a document from a template you recently used:** Click the Recent Templates icon and choose a template.

+ **Create a document from another document:** If you can use another document as the starting point for creating a new document, click the New from Existing icon. In the New from Existing Document dialog box, select the document and click the Create New button.

If your search for the perfect template takes you too far afield, you can click the Home, Back, or Forward button in the Available Templates window to backtrack.

Book I, Chapter 1 explains how to save documents after you create them, as well as how to open the document you want to work on.

Getting a Better Look at Your Documents

A computer screen can be kind of confining. There you are, staring at the darn thing for hours at a stretch. Do you wish the view were better? The Word screen can't be made to look like the Riviera, but you can examine documents in different ways and work in two places at one time in the same document. Better read on.

Viewing documents in different ways

In word processing, you want to focus sometimes on the writing, sometimes on the layout, and sometimes on the organization of your work. To help you stay in focus, Word offers different ways of viewing a document. Figure 1-3 shows these views. These pages explain how to change views, the five different views, and why to select one over the other. (Be sure to visit Book I, Chapter 3 as well; it describes how to view a document through more than one window and how to open a second window on a document.)

Changing views

Use these techniques to change views:

✦ Click one of the five View buttons on the right side of the status bar.

✦ On the View tab, click one of the five buttons in the Document Views group.

Print Layout view

Switch to Print Layout view to see the big picture. In this view, you can see what your document will look like when you print it. You can see graphics, headers, footers, and even page borders in Print Layout view. You can also see clearly where page breaks occur (where one page ends and the next begins). In Print Layout view, you can click the One Page, Two Pages, or Page Width button on the View tab to display more or fewer pages on your screen.

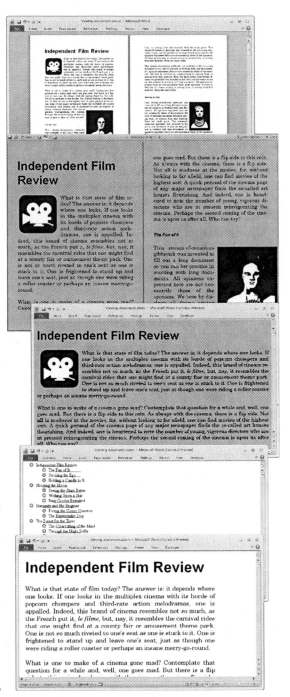

Figure 1-3:
The different document views (top to bottom): Print Layout, Full Screen Reading, Web Layout, Outline, and Draft.

Full Screen Reading view

 Switch to Full Screen Reading view to focus on the text itself and proofread your documents. In this view, everything gets stripped away — the Ribbon, scroll bars, status bar, and all. All you see is the text and artwork in your documents. You can't enter or edit text (unless you open the View Options menu and choose Allow Typing).

Click the View Options button to open a menu with options for improving your view. For example, you can increase or decrease the size of text, show one or two document pages at a time, and display page margins. To get from page to page, click buttons along the top of the window. Click the Close button to leave this view.

Web Layout view

 Switch to Web Layout view to see what your document would look like as a Web page. Background colors appear (if you chose a theme or background color for your document). Text is wrapped to the window rather than around the artwork in the document. Book VI, Chapter 2 explains how to save an Office file, a Word document included, as a Web page.

Outline view

 Switch to Outline view to see how your work is organized. In this view, you can see only the headings in a document. You can get a sense of how your document unfolds and easily move sections of text backward and forward in a document. In other words, you can reorganize a document in Outline view. Chapter 6 of this mini-book explains outlines in torturous detail.

Draft view

 Switch to Draft view when you're writing a document and you want to focus on the words. Clip-art images, shapes, and other distractions don't appear in this view, nor do page breaks (although you can clearly see section breaks). Draft view is best for writing first drafts.

Splitting the screen

Besides opening a second window on a document (a subject of Book I, Chapter 3), you can be two places at once in a Word document by splitting the screen. One reason you might do this: You're writing a long report and want the introduction to support the conclusion, and you also want the conclusion to fulfill all promises made by the introduction. That's difficult to do sometimes, but you can make it easier by splitting the screen so you can be two places at once as you write your introduction and conclusion.

Splitting a window means to divide it into north and south halves, as shown in Figure 1-4. In a split screen, two sets of scroll bars appear so that you can travel in one half of the screen without disturbing the other half. Word offers two ways to split the screen:

✦ Move the mouse pointer to the *split box* at the top of the scroll bar on the right. Move it just above the View Ruler button. When the pointer turns into double-arrows, click and drag the gray line down the screen. When you release the mouse button, you have a split screen.

✦ On the View tab, click the Split button. A gray line appears on-screen. Roll the mouse down until the gray line is where you want the split to be, and click. You get two screens split down the middle.

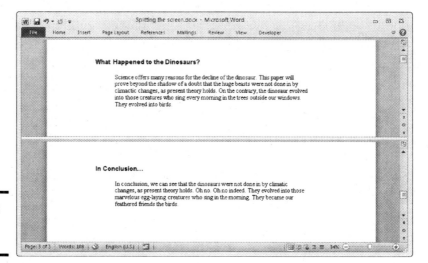

Figure 1-4:
A split
screen.

When you tire of this schizophrenic arrangement, click the Remove Split button on the View tab or drag the line to the top or bottom of the screen. You can also double-click the line that splits the screen in two.

In a split screen, you can choose a different view for the different halves. For example, click in the top half of the screen and choose Outline view to see your document in outline form, and click on the bottom half and choose Draft view to see the other half in Draft view. This way, for example, you can see the headings in a document while you write the introduction.

Selecting Text in Speedy Ways

Book I, Chapter 2 explains how to enter text and change its appearance and size. After you enter text, you inevitably have to copy, move, or delete it, but you can't do those tasks until you select it first. Table 1-1 describes short-cuts for selecting text.

Table 1-1	Shortcuts for Selecting Text
To Select This	*Do This*
A word	Double-click the word.
A line	Click in the left margin next to the line.
Some lines	Drag the mouse pointer over the lines or drag it down the left margin.
A sentence	Ctrl+click the sentence.
A paragraph	Double-click in the left margin next to the paragraph.
A mess of text	Click at the start of the text, hold down the Shift key, and click at the end of the text.
A gob of text	Put the cursor where you want to start selecting, press F8, and press an arrow key, drag the mouse, or click at the end of the selection.
Text with the same formats	On the Home tab, click the Select button and choose Select Text with Similar Formatting (you may have to click the Editing button first).
A document	Hold down the Ctrl key and click in the left margin; triple-click in the left margin; press Ctrl+A; or go to the Home tab, click the Select button, and choose Select All (you may have to click the Editing button first).

If a bunch of highlighted text is on-screen and you want it to go away but it won't (because you pressed F8), press the Esc key.

Viewing the hidden format symbols

Sometimes it pays to see the hidden format symbols when you're editing and laying out a document. The symbols show line breaks, tab spaces, paragraph breaks, and the space or spaces between words. To see the hidden format symbols, go to the Home tab and click the Show/Hide ¶ button. Click the button again to hide the symbols.

Here's what the hidden symbols look like on-screen.

Symbol	How to Enter
Line break (¬)	Press Shift+Enter
Optional hyphen -(-)	Press Ctrl+hyphen
Paragraph (¶)	Press Enter
Space (·)	Press the spacebar
Tab (→)	Press tab

After you press F8, all the keyboard shortcuts for moving the cursor also work for selecting text. For example, press F8 and then press Ctrl+Home to select everything from the cursor to the top of the document. Later in this chapter, "Keys for getting around" describes keyboard shortcuts for getting from place to place.

Moving Around Quickly in Documents

Besides sliding the scroll bar, Word offers a handful of very speedy techniques for jumping around in documents: pressing shortcut keys, browsing in the Select Browse Object menu, using the Go To command, and navigating with the Document Map or thumbnails. Read on to discover how to get there faster, faster, faster.

Keys for getting around quickly

One of the fastest ways to go from place to place is to press the keys and key combinations listed in Table 1-2.

Table 1-2	Keys for Moving Around Documents
Key to Press	*Where It Takes You*
PgUp	Up the length of one screen
PgDn	Down the length of one screen
Ctrl+PgUp	To the previous page in the document
Ctrl+PgDn	To the next page in the document
Ctrl+Home	To the top of the document
Ctrl+End	To the bottom of the document

If pressing Ctrl+PgUp or Ctrl+PgDn doesn't get you to the top or bottom of a page, you clicked the Select Browse Object button at the bottom of the vertical scroll bar, which makes Word go to the next bookmark, comment, heading, or whatever. Click the Select Browse Object button and choose Browse By Page to make these key combinations work again.

Here's a useful keystroke for getting from place to place: Shift+F5. Press it once to go to the location of your most recent edit. Press it two or three times to go back one or two edits before that. Pressing Shift+F5 is useful when you want to return to the place where you made an edit but can't quite remember where that place is.

Navigating from page to page or heading to heading

In lengthy documents such as the one in Figure 1-5, the best way to get from place to place is to make use of the Navigation pane. Click a heading or a page in the Navigation pane and Word takes you there in the twinkling of an eye.

Click a heading   Click a page thumbnail

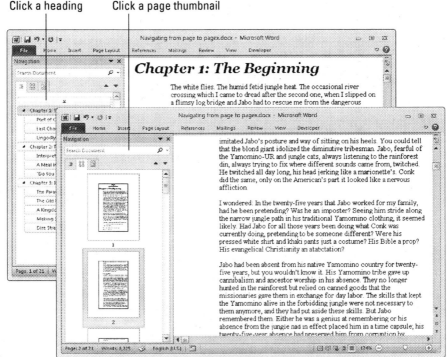

Figure 1-5: In the Navigation pane, click a heading or page thumbnail to go from place to place.

Book II
Chapter 1

Speed Techniques for Using Word

To display the Navigation pane, go to the View tab and click the Navigation Pane check box (you may have to click the Show button first). Then select a tab in the Navigation pane and go to it:

✦ **Going from heading to heading:** Select the Browse the Headings tab. Headings in your document appear (provided you assigned heading styles to headings). You can use the Navigation pane like a table of contents and click headings to get from place to place. Right-click a heading and choose a heading-level option on the shortcut menu to tell Word which headings to display. You can also right-click a heading and choose Expand All or Collapse All to see or hide lower-level headings.

✦ **Going from page to page:** Select the Browse the Pages tab. A thumbnail image of each page in the document appears. To quickly move from page to page, use the scroll bar in the Navigation pane or click a page thumbnail. Each thumbnail is numbered so that you always know which page you are viewing.

"Browsing" around a document

A really fast way to move around quickly is to click the Select Browse Object button in the lower-right corner of the screen. When you click this button (or press Ctrl+Alt+Home), Word presents 12 *Browse By* icons: Field, Endnote, Footnote, Comment, Section, Page, Go To, Find, Edits, Heading, Graphic, and Table. Select the icon that represents the element you want to go to, and Word takes you there immediately. For example, click the Browse by Heading icon to get to the next heading in your document (provided that you assigned heading styles to headings).

After you select a Browse By icon, the navigator buttons — the double-arrows directly above and below the Select Browse Object button — turn blue. Click a blue navigator button to get to the next example or the previous example of the element you chose. For example, if you selected the Browse by Heading icon, all you have to do is click the blue navigator buttons to get from heading to heading, backward or forward in your document.

Going there fast with the Go To command

Another fast way to go from place to place in a document is to use the Go To command. On the Home tab, open the drop-down list on the Find button and choose Go To (you may have to click the Editing button first). You see the Go To tab of the Find and Replace dialog box, shown in Figure 1-6. You can also open this dialog box by pressing Ctrl+G or F5.

Figure 1-6:
Using the
Go To
command.

The Go to What menu in this dialog box lists everything that can conceivably be numbered in a Word document, and other things, too. Everything that you can get to with the Select Browse Object button, as well as lines, equations, and objects, can be reached by way of the Go To tab. Click a menu item, enter a number, choose an item from the drop-down list, or click the Previous, Next, or Go To buttons to go elsewhere.

Bookmarks for hopping around

Rather than press PgUp or PgDn or click the scroll bar to thrash around in a long document, you can use *bookmarks*. All you do is put a bookmark in an important spot in your document that you'll return to many times. To return to that spot, open the Bookmark dialog box and select a bookmark name, as shown in Figure 1-7. True to the craft, the mystery writer whose bookmarks are shown in Figure 1-7 wrote the end of the story first and used bookmarks to jump back and forth between the beginning and end to make all the clues fit together.

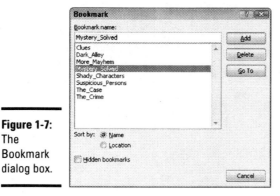

Book II
Chapter 1

Speed Techniques for Using Word

Figure 1-7:
The
Bookmark
dialog box.

Follow these instructions to handle bookmarks:

✦ **Adding a bookmark:** Click where you want the bookmark to go, visit the Insert tab, and click the Bookmark button (you may have to click the Links button first, depending on the size of your screen). Then, in the Bookmark dialog box, type a descriptive name in the Bookmark Name box, and click the Add button. Bookmarks can't start with numbers or include blank spaces. You can also open the Bookmark dialog box by pressing Ctrl+Shift+F5.

✦ **Going to a bookmark:** On the Insert tab, click the Bookmark button (you may have to click the Links button first), double-click the bookmark in the Bookmark dialog box, and click the Close button.

✦ **Deleting a bookmark:** Select the bookmark in the Bookmark dialog box and click the Delete button.

Word uses bookmarks for many purposes. For example, bookmarks indicate where cross-references are located in a document.

Entering Information Quickly in a Computerized Form

A *form* is a means of soliciting and recording information. You can use forms like the one shown in Figure 1-8 to enter data faster and to reduce data-entry errors. Instead of entering all the information by hand, you or a data-entry clerk can choose entries from combo boxes, drop-down lists, and date pickers. You save time because you don't have to enter all the information by hand, and the information you enter is more likely to be accurate because you choose it from prescribed lists instead of entering it yourself.

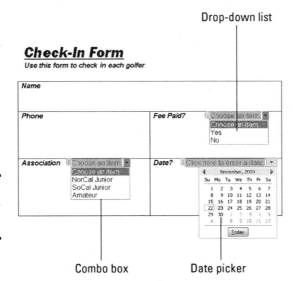

Drop-down list

Figure 1-8:
A data-entry form.

Combo box   Date picker

To create a form like the one shown in Figure 1-8, start by creating a template for your form and putting *data-entry controls* — the combo boxes, drop-down lists, and date pickers— in the form. To fill out a form, you create a document from the form template and go to it. These pages explain how to create a form and use forms to record information.

Creating a computerized form

The first step in creating a data-entry form is to create a template for holding the form. After that, you design the form itself by labeling the data fields and creating the data-entry controls. Better keep reading.

Creating a template to hold the form

Follow these steps to create a new template:

1. **On the File tab, choose New.**

You see the Available Templates window.

2. **Click the My Templates icon.**

   The New dialog box appears. It lists Word templates that are on your computer.

3. **Click the Template option button.**

   You can find this button under Create New in the lower-right corner of the dialog box.

4. **Click OK.**

5. **Click the Save button (or press Ctrl+S) to open the Save As dialog box.**

6. **Enter a descriptive name for your template and click the Save button.**

   Chapter 3 of this mini-book explains templates in detail.

Creating the form and data-entry controls

Your next task is to create the form and data-entry controls for your template. Enter labels on the form where you will enter information. The form in Figure 1-8, for example, has five labels: Name, Phone, Fee Paid?, Association, and Date. After you enter the labels, follow these steps to create the data-entry controls:

1. **Display the Developer tab, if necessary.**

   If this tab isn't showing, go to the File tab, choose Options, and on the Customize Ribbon category of the Word Options dialog box, select the Developer check box and click OK. (Book VI, Chapter 1 explains in detail how to customize the Ribbon.)

2. **Click where you want to place a control, and then create the control by clicking a Controls button followed by the Properties button on the Developer tab.**

   Here are instructions for creating three types of controls:

   * *Drop-down list:* A *drop-down list* is a menu that "drops" when you open it to reveal different options (refer to Figure 1-8). Click the Drop-Down List Content Control button and then the Properties button. You see the Content Control Properties dialog box, as shown in Figure 1-9. For each option you want to place on the drop-down list, click the Add button, and in the Add Choice dialog box, enter the option's name in the Display Name text box and click OK, as shown in Figure 1-9.

   * *Combo box:* As with a drop-down list, a *combo box* "drops" to reveal choices. However, as well as choosing an option on the drop-down list, data-entry clerks can enter information in the box (refer to Figure 1-8). Click the Combo Box Content Control button and then the Properties button. In the Content Control Properties dialog box,

enter option names the same way you enter them in a drop-down list, as shown in Figure 1-9.

- *Date picker:* A *date picker* is a mini-calendar from which data-entry clerks can enter a date (refer to Figure 1-8). Click the Date Picker Content Control button and then the Properties button. In the Content Control Properties dialog box, choose a display format for dates and click OK.

Figure 1-9: Click the Add button to create options for a drop-down list or combo box.

3. **Click the Save button to save your template.**

Now you're ready to use your newly made form to enter data.

Entering data in the form

Now that you have the template, you or someone else can enter data cleanly in easy-to-read forms:

1. **On the File tab, choose New.**

You see the Available Templates window.

2. **Click the My Templates icon.**

The New dialog box opens and shows you Word templates on your computer.

3. **Double-click the name of the template you created for entering data in your form.**

The form appears.

4. **Enter information in the input fields.**

   Press the up or down arrow, or press Tab and Shift+Tab to move from field to field. You can also click input fields to move the cursor there.

5. **When you're done, print the document or save it.**

Inserting a Whole File into a Document

One of the beautiful things about word processing is being able to recycle documents. Say that you wrote an essay on the Scissor-Tailed Flycatcher that would fit very nicely in a broader report on North American birds. You can insert the Scissor-Tailed Flycatcher document into your report document:

1. **Place the cursor where you want to insert the document.**

2. **On the Insert tab, open the drop-down list on the Object button and choose Text from File.**

   You see the Insert File dialog box.

3. **Find and select the file you want to insert.**

4. **Click the Insert button.**

Chapter 2: Laying Out Text and Pages

In This Chapter

- ✔ **Entering a section break**
- ✔ **Starting a new line and page**
- ✔ **Changing the margins**
- ✔ **Indenting text**
- ✔ **Numbering pages and handling headers and footers**
- ✔ **Adjusting the space between lines and paragraphs**
- ✔ **Handling bulleted and numbered lists**
- ✔ **Hyphenating the text**

This chapter explains how to format text and pages. A well-laid-out document says a lot about how much time and thought was put into it. This chapter presents tips, tricks, and techniques for making pages look just right.

In this chapter, you learn what section breaks are and why they are so important to formatting. You discover how to establish the size of margins, indent text, number pages, construct headers and footers, determine how much space appears between lines of text, handle lists, and hyphenate text.

Paragraphs and Formatting

Back in English class, your teacher taught you that a paragraph is a part of a longer composition that presents one idea or, in the case of dialogue, presents the words of one speaker. Your teacher was right, too, but for word-processing purposes, a paragraph is a lot less than that. In word processing, a paragraph is simply what you put on-screen before you press the Enter key.

For instance, a heading is a paragraph. If you press Enter on a blank line to go to the next line, the blank line is considered a paragraph. If you type **Dear John** at the top of a letter and press Enter, "Dear John" is a paragraph.

 It's important to know this because paragraphs have a lot to do with formatting. If you click the Paragraph group button on the Home tab and monkey around with the paragraph formatting in the Paragraph dialog box, your changes affect everything in the paragraph where the cursor is located.

To make format changes to a whole paragraph, all you have to do is place the cursor there. You don't have to select the paragraph. And if you want to make format changes to several paragraphs, all you have to do is select those paragraphs first.

Inserting a Section Break for Formatting Purposes

When you want to change page numbering schemes, headers and footers, margin sizes, and page orientations in a document, you have to create a *section break* to start a new section. Word creates a new section for you when you create newspaper-style columns or change the size of margins.

Seeing what the formats are

Sometimes seeing how text was formatted merely by looking is difficult. However, by pressing Shift+F1, you can see precisely how text and paragraphs were formatted in the Reveal Formatting task pane. It describes how the text, paragraph, and section where the cursor is located are formatted.

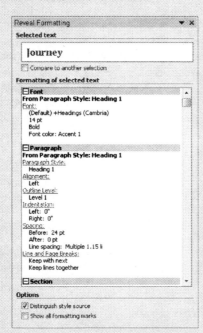

While the Reveal Formatting task pane is open, you can take advantage of these amenities:

- **Compare one part of a document to another:** Click the Compare to Another Section check box and then click another part of your document. The Reveal Formatting task pane describes how the two parts differ. Knowing how parts of a document differ can be invaluable when you're creating and modifying styles.

- **Find out which style was assigned:** Click the Distinguish Style Source check box. The task pane lists the style you assigned to the part of your document where the cursor is located.

- **See the formatting marks:** Click the Show All Formatting Marks check box. You can see where paragraphs end, where line breaks are, and where tab spaces were entered. Clicking this check box has the same results as clicking the Show/Hide¶ button on the Home tab.

Follow these steps to create a new section:

1. **Click where you want to insert a section break.**

2. **On the Page Layout tab, click the Breaks button.**

   You open a drop-down list.

3. **Under Section Breaks on the drop-down list, select a section break.**

All four section break options create a new section, but they do so in different ways:

✦ **Next Page:** Inserts a page break as well as a section break so that the new section can start at the top of a new page (the next one). Select this option to start a new chapter, for example.

✦ **Continuous:** Inserts a section break in the middle of a page. Select this option if, for example, you want to introduce newspaper-style columns in the middle of a page.

✦ **Even Page:** Starts the new section on the next even page. This option is good for two-sided documents in which the headers on the left- and right-side pages are different.

✦ **Odd Page:** Starts the new section on the next odd page. You might choose this option if you have a book in which chapters start on odd pages. (By convention, that's where they start.)

To delete a section break, make sure that you are in Draft view so you can see section breaks, click the dotted line, and press the Delete key.

In the same way that paragraph marks store formats for a paragraph, section breaks store formats for an entire section. When you delete a section break, you apply new formats, because the section is folded into the section that formerly followed it and the section you deleted adopts that next section's formats. Because it's easy to accidentally delete a section break and create havoc, I recommend working in Draft view when your document has many section breaks. In Draft view, you can tell where a section ends because Section Break and a double dotted line appear on-screen. The only way to tell where a section ends in Print Layout view is to click the Show/Hide ¶ button on the Home tab. (You can make section information appear on the status bar. Right-click the status bar and choose Section on the pop-up menu.)

Breaking a Line

To break a line of text before it reaches the right margin without starting a new paragraph, press Shift+Enter. Figure 2-1 shows how you can press Shift+Enter to make lines break better. The paragraphs are identical, but I broke lines in the right-side paragraph to make the text easier to read. Line breaks are marked with the ⏎ symbol. To erase line breaks, click the Show/Hide ¶ button to see these symbols and then backspace over them.

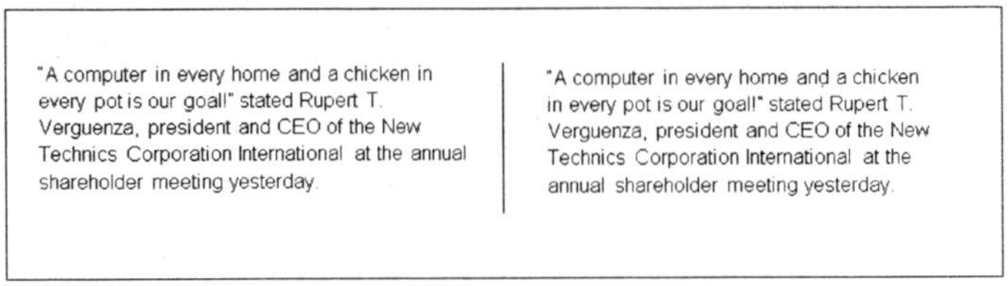

Figure 2-1:
Break lines
to make
reading
easier.

"A computer in every home and a chicken in every pot is our goal!" stated Rupert T. Verguenza, president and CEO of the New Technics Corporation International at the annual shareholder meeting yesterday.

"A computer in every home and a chicken in every pot is our goal!" stated Rupert T. Verguenza, president and CEO of the New Technics Corporation International at the annual shareholder meeting yesterday.

Starting a New Page

Word gives you another page so that you can keep going when you fill up one page. But what if you're impatient and want to start a new page right away? Whatever you do, *don't* press Enter again and again until you fill up the page. Instead, create a *hard page break* by doing one the following on the Insert tab:

✦ Click the Page Break button (or press Ctrl+Enter). Word starts a new page at the cursor position. (You can also go to the Page Layout tab, click the Breaks button, choose Page on the drop-down list.)

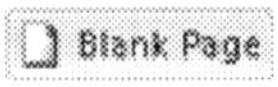

✦ Click the Blank Page button. Word enters two hard page breaks to create an empty, blank page at the cursor position.

In Draft view, you can click the Show/Hide ¶ button on the Home tab and tell where you inserted a hard page break because you see the words Page Break and a dotted line on-screen. You can't tell where hard page breaks are in Print Layout view.

To delete a hard page break, switch to Draft view, click the Show/Hide¶ button on the Home tab, click the words Page Break, and press the Delete key.

Setting Up and Changing the Margins

Margins are the empty spaces along the left, right, top, and bottom of a page, as shown in Figure 2-2. Headers and footers fall, respectively, in the top and bottom margins. And you can put graphics, text boxes, and page numbers in the margins as well. Margins serve to frame the text and make it easier to read.

Outside margin   Inside margins   Outside margin

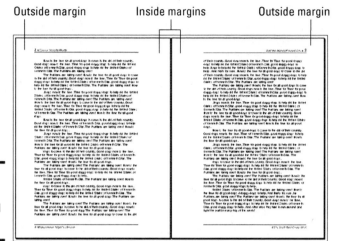

Figure 2-2:
Margins in
a two-sided
document.

When you start a new document, give a moment's thought to the margins. Changing the size of margins after you have entered the text, clip art, graphics, and whatnot can be disastrous. Text is indented from the left and right margins. Pages break on the bottom margin. If you change margin settings, indents and page breaks change for good or ill throughout your document. By setting the margins carefully from the beginning, you can rest assured that text will land on the page where you want it to land.

Don't confuse margins with indents. Text is indented from the margin, not from the edge of the page. If you want to change how far text falls from the page edge, indent it. To change margin settings in the middle of a document, you have to create a new section.

To set up or change the margins, go to the Page Layout tab and click the Margins button. You see a drop-down list with margin settings. Either choose a setting or select Custom Margins to open the Margins tab of the Page Setup dialog box and choose among these commands for handling margins:

✦ **Changing the size of the margins:** Enter measurements in the Top, Bottom, Left, and Right boxes to tell Word how much blank space to put along the sides of the page.

✦ **Making room for the gutter:** The *gutter* is the part of the paper that the binding eats into when you bind a document. Enter a measurement in the Gutter box to increase the left or inside margin and make room for the binding. Notice on the pages of this book, for example, that the margin closest to the binding is wider than the outside margin. Choose Top on the Gutter Position menu if you intend to bind your document from the top, not the left, or inside, of the page. Some legal documents are bound this way.

✦ **Using mirror margins (inside and outside margins) in two-sided documents:** In a bound document in which text is printed on both sides of the pages, the terms left margin and right margin are meaningless. What matters instead is in the *inside margin*, the margin in the middle of the page spread next to the bindings, and the *outside margin*, the margin on the outside of the page spread that isn't affected by the bindings (refer to Figure 2-2). Choose Mirror Margins on the Multiple Pages drop-down list and adjust the margins accordingly if you intend to print on both sides of the paper.

✦ **Applying margin changes:** On the Apply To drop-down list, choose Whole Document to apply your margin settings to the entire document; This Section to apply them to a section; or This Point Forward to change margins in the rest of a document. When you choose This Point Forward, Word creates a new section.

If you're in a hurry to change margins, you can change them on the ruler. Display the ruler and drag the Left Margin, Right Margin, or Top Margin marker. You can find these markers by moving the pointer onto a ruler and looking for the two-headed arrow near a margin boundary. It appears, along with a pop-up label, when the pointer is over a margin marker.

To get a good look at where margins are, go to the File tab and choose Options. In the Word Options dialog box, select the Advanced category, and click the Show Text Boundaries check box (you'll find it under "Show Document Content").

Indenting Paragraphs and First Lines

An *indent* is the distance between a margin and the text, not the edge of the page and the text. Word offers a handful of ways to change the indentation of paragraphs. You can change the indentation of first lines as well as entire paragraphs. To start, select all or part of the paragraphs you want to re-indent (just click in a paragraph if you want to re-indent only one paragraph). Then click an Indent button, fiddle with the indentation marks on the ruler, or go to the Paragraph dialog box. All three techniques are described here.

Clicking an Indent button (for left-indents)

  On the Home tab, click the Increase Indent or Decrease Indent button (or press Ctrl+M or Ctrl+Shift+M) to move a paragraph a half-inch farther away from or closer to the left margin. If you created tab stops, text is indented to the next or previous tab stop as well as to the next or previous half-inch. This is the fastest way to indent text, although you can't indent first lines or indent from the right margin this way.

"Eyeballing it" with the ruler

You can also change indentations by using the ruler to "eyeball it." This technique requires some dexterity with the mouse, but it allows you to see precisely where paragraphs and the first lines of paragraphs are indented. If necessary, display the ruler by going to the View tab and clicking the Ruler check box. Then click in or select the paragraph or paragraphs that need indenting and use these techniques to re-indent them:

✦ **Indenting an entire paragraph from the left margin:** Drag the *left-indent marker* on the ruler to the right. Figure 2-3 shows where this marker is located. Dragging the left-indent marker moves the first-line indent marker as well.

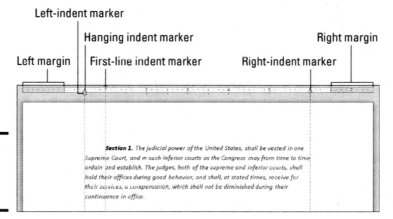

Left-indent marker

Hanging indent marker   Right margin

Left margin   First-line indent marker   Right-indent marker

Figure 2-3: Indenting with the ruler.

Section 1. *The judicial power of the United States, shall be vested in one Supreme Court, and in such inferior courts as the Congress may from time to time ordain and establish. The judges, both of the supreme and inferior courts, shall hold their offices during good behavior, and shall, at stated times, receive for their services, a compensation, which shall not be diminished during their continuance in office.*

✦ **Indenting the first line of a paragraph:** Drag the *first-line indent marker* to the right (refer to Figure 2-3). This marker determines how far the first line of the paragraph is indented.

✦ **Making a hanging indent:** Drag the *hanging indent marker* to the right of the first-line indent marker (refer to Figure 2-3). A *hanging indent* is one in which the first line of a paragraph appears to "hang" into the margin because the second and subsequent lines are indented to the right of the start of the first line. Bulleted and numbered lists employ hanging indents.

✦ **Indenting an entire paragraph from the right margin:** Drag the *right-indent marker* to the left (refer to Figure 2-3).

Notice the shaded areas on the left and right side of the ruler. These areas represent the page margins.

Indenting in the Paragraph dialog box

Yet another way to indent a paragraph or first line is to visit the Paragraph dialog box. Click in or select the paragraph or paragraphs in question, go to the Home or Page Layout tab, and click the Paragraph group button. You see the Indents and Spacing tab of the Paragraph dialog box. Change the indentation settings. If you want to indent the first line or create a hanging indent, choose First Line or Hanging on the Special drop-down list and enter a measurement in the By box.

Numbering the Pages

How do you want to number the pages in your document? You can number them in sequence starting with the number 1, start numbering pages with a number other than 1, use Roman numerals or other number formats, and include chapter numbers in page numbers. What's more, you can number the pages differently in each section of your document as long as you divided your document into sections.

When it comes to numbering pages, you can proceed in two ways, as shown in Figure 2-4:

✦ Put a page number by itself on the pages of your document.

✦ Include the page number in the header or footer.

After you enter a page number, you can format it in different ways in the Page Number Format dialog box (refer to Figure 2-4) and (Header & Footer Tools) Design tab.

To handle page numbers (as well as headers and footers), you must be in Print Layout view. Click the Print Layout view button on the status bar or go to the View tab and click the Print Layout button.

Numbering with page numbers only

Follow these steps to insert a page number by itself in the header, footer, or margin of the pages:

1. **On the Insert tab, click the Page Number button.**

2. **On the drop-down menu, choose where on the page you want to put the page number (Top of Page, Bottom of Page, or Page Margins).**

3. **On the submenu that appears, choose a page number option.**

   The farther you scroll on the submenu, the fancier the page number formats are.

Page number by itself

Page number included in a header

Choose page number format options

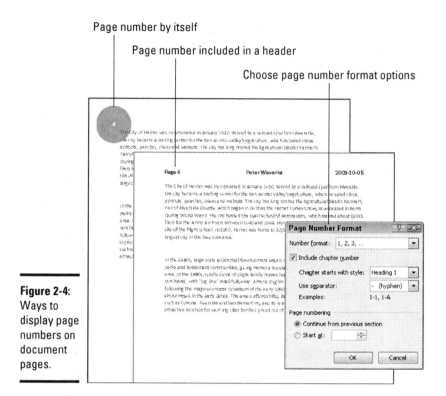

Figure 2-4:
Ways to
display page
numbers on
document
pages.

If you change your mind about the page number format you choose, switch to Print Layout view and double-click in the header or footer where the page number is displayed. The (Header & Footer Tools) Design tab opens. Click the Page Number button and make a different choice, or choose Remove Page Numbers.

Including a page number in a header or footer

To put the page number part in a header or footer, click in the header or footer where you want the page number to appear (later in this chapter, "Putting Headers and Footers on Pages" explains headers and footers). Then follow these steps to insert the page number:

1. **On the (Header & Footer Tools) Design tab, click the Page Number button.**

2. **Choose Current Position.**

You see a submenu with page number choices.

3. **Scroll through the submenu and choose a page number format.**

The "Page X of Y" option is for listing the total number of pages in a document as well as the page number. For example, page 2 of a 10-page document is numbered "Page 2 of 10."

Changing page number formats

Change page number formats in the Page Number Format dialog box (refer to Figure 2-4). To display this dialog box, make sure you're in Print Layout view and double-click your header or footer. Then use one of the following methods to change page number formats:

✦ On the Insert tab, click the Page Number button and choose Format Page Numbers.

✦ On the (Header & Footer Tools) Design tab, click the Page Number button and choose Format Page Numbers.

In the Page Number Format dialog box, make your page numbers just so:

✦ **Choosing a different number format:** Open the Number Format drop-down list and choose a page-numbering format. You can use numbers, letters, or roman numerals.

✦ **Including chapter numbers in page numbers:** If your document generates chapter numbers automatically from headings assigned the same style (a subject not covered in this book), you can include the chapter number in the page number. Click the Include Chapter Number check box, choose a style, and choose a separator to go between the chapter number and page number.

✦ **Numbering each section separately:** Click the Start At option button (not the Continue from Previous Section button) to begin counting pages anew at each section in your document. Earlier in this chapter, "Inserting a Section Break for Formatting Purposes" explains sections.

✦ **Start numbering pages at a number other than 1:** Click the Start At option button and enter a number other than 1.

To keep some pages in a document from being numbered, create a section for those pages, and then remove page numbers from the section. To paginate your document, Word skips the section you created and resumes numbering pages in the following section.

Putting Headers and Footers on Pages

A *header* is a little description that appears along the top of a page so that the reader knows what's what. Usually, headers include the page number and a title, and often the author's name appears in the header as well. A *footer* is the same thing as a header except that it appears along the bottom of the page, as befits its name.

These pages explain everything a mere mortal needs to know about headers and footers. Meanwhile, here are the ground rules for managing them:

✦ **Switching to Print Layout view:** To enter, read, edit or delete headers and footers, you must be in Print Layout view. You can't see headers and footers in the other views.

✦ **Displaying the (Header & Footer Tools) Design tab:** As shown in Figure 2-5, you manage headers and footers by way of buttons on the (Header & Footer Tools) Design tab. To display this tab after you create a header or footer, switch to Print Layout view and double-click a header or footer.

✦ **Closing the (Header & Footer Tools) Design tab:** Click the Close Header and Footer button or double-click outside the header or footer.

✦ **Placing different headers and footers in the same document:** To change headers or footers in the middle of a document, you have to create a new section. See "Inserting a Section Break for Formatting Purposes" earlier in this chapter.

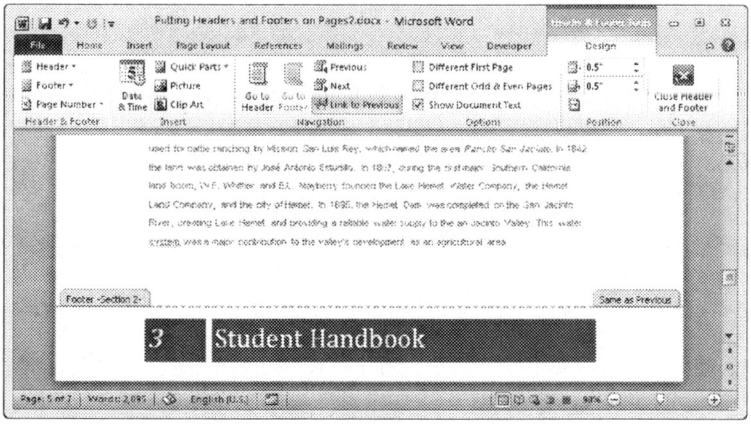

Book II
Chapter 2

Laying Out Text and Pages

Figure 2-5:
Manage headers and footers on the (Header & Footer Tools) Design tab.

Creating, editing, and removing headers and footers

Follow these instructions to create, edit, and delete headers and footers:

✦ **Creating a header or footer:** On the Insert tab, click the Header or the Footer button, and choose a header or footer on the gallery. The gallery presents headers or footers with preformatted page numbers, dates, and places to enter a document title and author's name. Click More Headers (or Footers) from Office.com to download headers or footers from Microsoft. (Later in this chapter, "Fine-tuning a header or footer" explains how to insert the date and time and change headers and footers from section to section.)

✦ **Choosing a different header or footer:** Don't like the header or footer you chose? If necessary, double-click your header or footer to display the (Header & Footer Tools) Design tab. Then click the Header or Footer button and choose a new header or footer from the gallery.

✦ **Editing a header or footer:** Click the Header or the Footer button and choose Edit Header or Edit Footer on the drop-down list. The cursor moves into the header or footer so that you can enter or format text.

✦ **Changing the appearance of a header or footer:** Click a shape or text box in a header or footer and visit the (Drawing Tools) Format tab to change the shape or text box's color, background, or size. (Book I, Chapter 8 describes the drawing tools.)

✦ **Removing a header or footer:** Click the Header or Footer button and choose Remove Header or Remove Footer on the drop-down list.

To switch back and forth between the header and footer, click the Go to Header or Go to Footer button on the (Header & Footer Tools) Design tab.

As you work away on your header and footer, you can call on most of the text-formatting commands on the Home tab. You can change the text's font and font size, click an alignment button, and paste text from the Clipboard. Tabs are set up in most headers and footers to make it possible to center, left-align, and right-align text. You can click the Insert Alignment Tab button on the (Header & Footer Tools) Design tab to insert a new tab.

Fine-tuning a header or footer

Here is advice for making a perfect header on the (Header & Footer Tools) Design tab:

✦ **Inserting a page number:** See "Including a page number in a header or footer" and "Changing page number formats" earlier in this chapter.

✦ **Inserting the date and time:** Click the Date & Time button, choose a date format in the Date and Time dialog box, and click OK. Click the Update Automatically check box if you want the date to record when you print the document, not when you created your header or footer.

🔳 Link to Previous   ✦ **Changing headers and footers from section to section:** Use the Link to Previous button to determine whether headers and footers are different from section to section (you must divide a document into sections to have different headers and footers). Deselecting this button tells Word that you want your header or footer to be different from the header or footer in the previous section of the document; selecting this button (clicking it so it looks selected) tells Word that you want your header or footer to be the same as the header or footer in the previous section of your document. To make a different header or footer, deselect the Link to Previous button and enter a different header or footer.

When the header or footer is the same as that of the previous section, the Header or Footer box reads Same as Previous (refer to Figure 2-5); when the header or footer is different from that of the previous section, the words Same as Previous don't appear. You can click the Previous or Next button to examine the header or footer in the previous or next section.

Book II
Chapter 2

Laying Out Text and Pages

✦ **Different headers and footers for odd and even pages:** Click the Different Odd & Even Pages check box to create different headers and footers for odd and even pages. As "Setting Up and Changing the Margins" explains earlier in this chapter, documents in which text is printed on both sides of the page can have different headers and footers for the left and right side of the page spread. The Header or Footer box reads Odd or Even to tell you which side of the page spread you're dealing with as you enter your header or footer.

✦ **Removing headers and footers from the first page:** Click the Different First Page check box to remove a header or footer from the first page of a document or section. Typically, the first page of letters and reports are not numbered.

Adjusting the Space between Lines

To change the spacing between lines, select the lines whose spacing you want to change, or simply put the cursor in a paragraph if you're changing the line spacing throughout a paragraph (if you're just starting a document, you're ready to go). Then, on the Home tab, click the Line and Paragraph Spacing button and choose an option on the drop-down list.

To take advantage of more line-spacing options, click the Paragraph group button on the Home or Page Layout tab or choose Line Spacing Options on the Line and Paragraph Spacing button drop-down list. You see the Paragraph dialog box. Select an option on the Line Spacing drop-down list:

✦ **At Least:** Choose this one if you want Word to adjust for tall symbols or other unusual text. Word adjusts the lines but makes sure there is, at minimum, the number of points you enter in the At box between each line.

✦ **Exactly:** Choose this one and enter a number in the At box if you want a specific amount of space between lines.

✦ **Multiple:** Choose this one and put a number in the At box to get triple-spaced, quadruple-, quintuple-, or any other number of spaced lines.

To quickly single-space text, click the text or select it if you want to change more than one paragraph, and press Ctrl+1. To quickly double-space text, select the text and press Ctrl+2. Press Ctrl+5 to put one and a half lines between lines of text.

Adjusting the Space between Paragraphs

Rather than press Enter to put a blank line between paragraphs, you can open the Paragraph dialog box and enter a point-size measurement in the Before or After text box. The Before and After measurements place a specific amount of space before and after paragraphs.

Truth be told, the Before and After options are for use with styles (a subject of the next chapter). When you create a style, you can tell Word to always follow a paragraph in a certain style with a paragraph in another style. For example, a paragraph in the Chapter Title style might always be followed by a paragraph in the Chapter Intro style. In cases like these, when you know that paragraphs assigned to one type of style will always follow paragraphs assigned to another style, you can confidently put space before and after paragraphs. But if you use the Before and After styles indiscriminately, you can end up with large blank spaces between paragraphs.

Go to the Home tab and use one of these techniques to adjust the amount of space between paragraphs:

✦ Click the Line and Paragraph Spacing button and choose Add Space Before Paragraph or Add Space after Paragraph on the drop-down list. These commands place 10 points of blank space before or after the paragraph that the cursor is in.

✦ Click the Paragraph group button to open the Paragraph dialog box, and enter point-size measurements in the Before and After boxes (or choose Auto in these boxes to enter one blank line between paragraphs in whatever your Line-Spacing choice is). The Don't Add Space between Paragraphs of the Same Style check box tells Word to ignore Before and After measurements if the previous or next paragraph is assigned the same style as the paragraph that the cursor is in.

Creating Numbered and Bulleted Lists

What is a word-processed document without a list or two? It's like an emperor with no clothes. Numbered lists are invaluable in manuals and books like this one that present a lot of step-by-step procedures. Use bulleted lists when you want to present alternatives to the reader. A *bullet* is a black, filled-in circle or other character. These pages explain numbered lists, bulleted lists, and multilevel lists.

Automatic lists and what to do about them

Word creates automatic lists for you whether you like it or not. To see what I mean, type the number 1, type a period, and press the spacebar. Word immediately creates a numbered list. In the same manner, Word creates a bulleted list when you type an asterisk (*) and press the spacebar.

Some people find this kind of behind-the-scenes skullduggery annoying. If you are one such person, do one of the following to keep Word from making lists automatically:

✔ Click the AutoCorrect Options button — it appears automatically — and choose Stop Automatically Creating Lists.

✔ On the File tab, choose Options, select the Proofing category in the Word Options dialog box, and click the AutoCorrect Options button. On the AutoFormat As You Type tab in the AutoCorrect dialog box, uncheck the Automatic Numbered Lists and Automatic Bulleted Lists check boxes.

Simple numbered and bulleted lists

  The fastest, cleanest, and most honest way to create a numbered or bulleted list is to enter the text without any concern for numbers or bullets. Just press Enter at the end of each step or bulleted entry. When you're done, select the list, go to the Home tab, and click the Numbering or Bullets button. You can also click the Numbering or Bullets button and start typing the list. Each time you press Enter, Word enters the next number or another bullet.

Meanwhile, here are some tricks for handling lists:

✦ **Ending a list:** Press the Enter key twice after typing the last entry in the list. You can also right-click the list, choose Bullets or Numbering, and choose None on the submenu.

✦ **Removing the numbers or bullets:** Select the list and click the Numbering or Bullets button.

✦ **Adjusting how far a list is indented:** Right-click anywhere in the list, choose Adjust List Indents, and enter a new measurement in the Text Indent box.

 ✦ **Resuming a numbered list:** Suppose that you want a numbered list to resume where a list you entered earlier ended. In other words, suppose that you left off writing a four-step list, put in a graphic or some paragraphs, and now you want to resume the list at Step 5. Click the Numbering button to start numbering again. The AutoCorrect Options button appears. Click it and choose Continue Numbering, or right-click and choose Continue Numbering on the shortcut menu.

✦ **Starting a new list:** Suppose that you want to start a brand-new list right away. Right-click the number Word entered and choose Restart at 1 on the shortcut menu.

Constructing lists of your own

If you're an individualist and you want numbered and bulleted lists to work your way, follow these instructions for choosing unusual bullet characters and number formats:

✦ **Choosing a different numbering scheme:** On the Home tab, open the drop-down list on the Numbering button and choose a numbering scheme. You can also choose Define New Number Format. As shown in Figure 2-6, you see the Define New Number Format dialog box, where you can choose a number format, choose a font for numbers, and toy with number alignments.

✦ **Choosing a different bullet character:** On the Home tab, open the drop-down list on the Bullets button and choose a different bullet character on the drop-down list. You can also choose Define New Bullet to open the Define New Bullet dialog box, shown in Figure 2-6, and click the Symbol button to choose a bullet character in the Symbol dialog box (Book I, Chapter 2 describes symbols). The dialog box also offers opportunities for indenting bullets and the text that follows them in unusual ways.

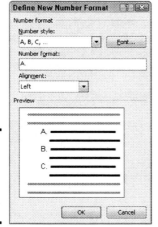

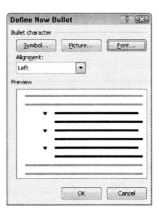

Figure 2-6:
Customizing a numbered or bulleted list.

Managing a multilevel list

A *multilevel list,* also called a *nested list,* is a list with subordinate entries, as shown in Figure 2-7. To create a multilevel list, you declare what kind of list you want, and then, as you enter items for the list, you indent the items that you want to be subordinate. Follow these steps to create a multilevel list:

1. **On the Home tab, click the Multilevel List button and choose what kind of list you want.**

If none of the lists suit you, you can choose Define New Multilevel List and create a new kind of list in the Define New Multilevel List dialog box.

2. **Enter the items for the list, pressing Enter as you complete each one.**

3. **Select a list item (or items) and click the Increase Indent button (or press Ctrl+M) to make the items subordinate in the list; click the Decrease Indent button (or press Ctrl+Shift+M) to raise their rank in the list.**

   Repeat Step 3 until the list is just so.

Figure 2-7:
Examples
of multilevel
lists.

Working with Tabs

Tabs are a throwback to the days of the typewriter, when it was necessary to make tab stops in order to align text. Except for making leaders and aligning text in headers and footers, everything you can do with tabs can also be done by creating a table — and it can be done far faster. All you have to do is align the text inside the table and then remove the table borders. (Book I, Chapter 5 explains tables.)

A *tab stop* is a point around which or against which text is formatted. As shown in Figure 2-8, Word offers five tab types for aligning text: Left, Center, Right, Decimal, and Bar (a bar tab stop merely draws a vertical line on the page). When you press the Tab key, you advance the text cursor by one tab stop. Tab stops are shown on the ruler; symbols on the ruler tell you what type of tab you're dealing with.

By default, tabs are left-aligned and are set at half-inch intervals. Display the ruler (click the Ruler check box on the View tab) and follow these steps to change tabs or change where tabs appear on the ruler:

1. **Select the paragraphs that need different tab settings.**

2. **Click the Tab box on the left side of the ruler as many times as necessary to choose the kind of tab you want.**

   Symbols on the tab box indicate which type of tab you're choosing.

3. **Click the ruler where you want the tab to go.**

   You can click as many times as you want and enter more than one kind of tab.

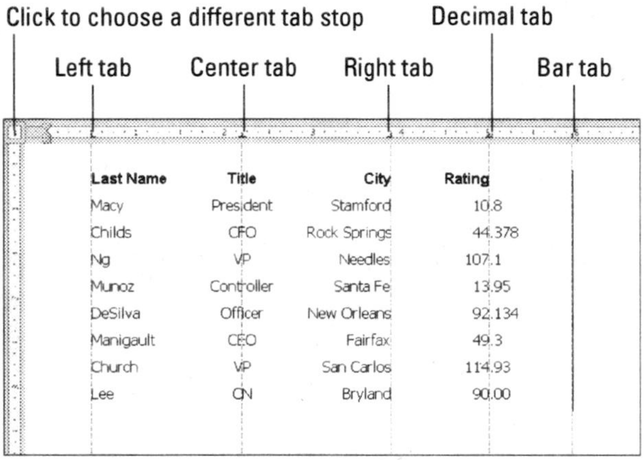

Click to choose a different tab stop   Decimal tab

Left tab   Center tab   Right tab   Bar tab

Figure 2-8: Different kinds of tab stops.

Last Name	Title	City	Rating
Macy	President	Stamford	10.8
Childs	CFO	Rock Springs	44.378
Ng	VP	Needles	107.1
Munoz	Controller	Santa Fe	13.95
DeSilva	Officer	New Orleans	92.134
Manigault	CEO	Fairfax	49.3
Church	VP	San Carlos	114.93
Lee	CN	Bryland	90.00

All about tab leaders

In my opinion, the only reason to fool with tabs and tab stops is to create tab leaders like the ones shown here. A *leader* is a series of punctuation marks — periods in the illustration — that connect text across a page. Leaders are very elegant. For the figure, I used left-aligned tab stops for the characters' names and right-aligned tab stops for the players' names. I included leaders so that you can tell precisely who played whom.

THE PLAYERS

Romeo..McGeorge Wright
Juliet..Gabriela Hernandez
Mercutio.....................................Chris Suzuki
Lady Capulet............................Mimi Hornstein

Follow these steps to create tab leaders:

1. **Enter the text and, in each line, enter a tab space between the text on the left side and the text on the right side.**

2. **Select the text you entered.**

3. **On the Home tab, click the Paragraph group button, and in the Paragraph dialog box, click the Tabs button.**

   You see the Tabs dialog box.

4. **Enter a position for the first new tab in the Tab Stop Position box.**

5. **Under Leader in the dialog box, select the punctuation symbol you want for the leader.**

6. **Click OK, display the ruler, and drag tab markers to adjust the space between the text on the left and right.**

To move a tab stop, drag it to a new location on the ruler. Text that is aligned with the tab stop moves as well. To remove a tab stop, drag it off the ruler. When you remove a tab stop, text to which it was aligned is aligned to the next remaining tab stop on the ruler or to the next default tab stop if you didn't create any tab stops of your own.

 Sometimes it's hard to tell where tabs were put in the text. To find out, click the Show/Hide ¶ button on the Home tab to see the formatting characters, including the arrows that show where the Tab key was pressed.

Hyphenating Text

The first thing you should know about hyphenating words is that you may not need to do it. Text that hasn't been hyphenated is much easier to read, which is why the majority of text in this book, for example, isn't hyphenated. It has a *ragged right margin,* to borrow typesetter lingo. Hyphenate only when text is trapped in columns or in other narrow places, or when you want a very formal-looking document.

 Do not insert a hyphen simply by pressing the hyphen key, because the hyphen will stay there even if the word moves to the middle of a line and doesn't need to be broken in half. Instead, when a big gap appears in the right margin and a word is crying out to be hyphenated, put the cursor where the hyphen needs to go and press Ctrl+hyphen. This way, you enter what is called a *discretionary hyphen,* and the hyphen appears only if the word breaks at the end of a line. (To remove a manual hyphen, press the Show/Hide ¶ button so that you can see it, and then backspace over it.)

Automatically and manually hyphenating a document

Select text if you want to hyphenate part of a document, not all of it, and use one of these techniques to hyphenate words that break on the end of a line of text:

✦ **Automatic hyphenation:** On the Page Layout tab, click the Hyphenation button and choose Automatic on the drop-down list. Word hyphenates your document (or a portion of your document, if you selected it first).

You can tell Word how to hyphenate automatically by clicking the Hyphenation button and choosing Hyphenation Options. You see the Hyphenation dialog box shown in Figure 2-9. Deselect the Hyphenate Words in CAPS check box if you don't care to hyphenate words in upper-case. Words that fall in the hyphenation zone are hyphenated, so enlarging the hyphenation zone means a less ragged right margin but more ugly hyphens, and a small zone means fewer ugly hyphens but a more ragged right margin. You can limit how many hyphens appear consecutively by entering a number in the Limit Consecutive Hyphens To box.

Figure 2-9:
Telling
Word
how to
hyphenate
(left) and
deciding
where a
hyphen
goes (right).

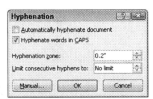

✦ **Manual hyphenation:** On the Page Layout tab, click the Hyphenation button and choose Manual on the drop-down list. Word displays a box with some hyphenation choices in it, as shown in Figure 2-9. The cursor blinks on the spot where Word suggests putting a hyphen. Click Yes or No to accept or reject Word's suggestion. Keep accepting or rejecting Word's suggestions until the text is hyphenated.

Unhyphenating and other hyphenation tasks

More hyphenation esoterica:

Em and en dashes

Here is something about hyphens that editors and typesetters know, but the general public does not know: There is a difference between hyphens and dashes. Most people insert a hyphen where they ought to use an em dash or an en dash:

✔ An *em dash* looks like a hyphen but is wider — it's as wide as the letter *m*. The previous sentence has an em dash in it. Did you notice?

✔ An *en dash* is the width of the letter *n*. Use en dashes to show inclusive numbers or time periods, like so: pp. 45–50; Aug.–Sept.

1998; Exodus 16:11–16:18. An en dash is a little bit longer than a hyphen.

To place an em or en dash in a document and impress your local typesetter or editor, not to mention your readers, press Ctrl+Alt+– (the minus sign key on the Numeric keypad) to enter an em dash, or Ctrl+– (on the numeric keypad) to enter an en dash. You can also go to the Insert tab, click the Symbol button, choose More Symbols on the drop-down list, select the Special Characters tab in the Symbol dialog box, and choose Em Dash or En Dash.

✦ **Unhyphenating:** To "unhyphenate" a document or text you hyphenated automatically, go to the Page Layout tab, click the Hyphenation button, and choose Hyphenation Options. In the Hyphenation dialog box (refer to Figure 2-9), deselect the Automatically Hyphenate Document check box and click OK.

✦ **Preventing text from being hyphenated:** Select the text and, on the Home tab, click the Paragraph group button. In the Paragraph dialog box, select the Line and Page Breaks tab, and select the Don't Hyphenate check box. (If you can't hyphenate a paragraph, it's probably because this box was selected unintentionally.)

Creating your own header or footer for the gallery

As "Putting Headers and Footers on Pages" explains earlier in this chapter, the easiest way to enter a header or footer is to go to the Insert tab, click the Header or the Footer button, and choose a header or footer from the gallery. You can create your own header or footer and place it in the gallery. For example, create a header or footer with your company logo. After you design and create your header or footer, follow these instructions to wrangle with it:

✔ **Placing a header or footer in the gallery:** Select your header or footer by dragging over it or by clicking in the margin to its left. On the (Header & Footer Tools) Design tab, click the Quick Parts button and choose Save Selection to Quick Part Gallery. You see the Create New Building Block dialog box. Enter a descriptive name for the header or footer, choose Footers or

Headers on the Gallery drop-down list, and click OK.

✔ **Inserting a header or footer you created:** On the Insert tab, click the Header or Footer button and choose your header or footer in the gallery. It is located in the Built-In or General category, depending on where you chose to put it.

✔ **Removing and editing headers or footers:** On the Insert tab, click the Quick Parts button and choose Building Blocks Organizer. The Building Blocks Organizer dialog box appears. Select your header or footer and click the Delete button to remove it from the gallery, or select the Edit Properties button to change the header or footer's name, gallery assignment, or category assignment.

Chapter 3: Word Styles

In This Chapter

- ✔ **Discovering how styles and templates work**
- ✔ **Applying a new style**
- ✔ **Creating your own styles**
- ✔ **Altering a style**
- ✔ **Creating a new template**

*W*elcome to what may be the most important chapter of this book — the most important in Book II, anyway. Styles can save a ridiculous amount of time that you would otherwise spend formatting and wrestling with text. And many Word features rely on styles. You can't create a table of contents or use the Navigation pane unless each heading in your document has been assigned a heading style. Nor can you take advantage of Outline view and the commands for moving text around in that view. You can't cross-reference headings or number the headings in a document.

If you want to be stylish, at least where Word is concerned, you have to know about styles.

All about Styles

A *style* is a collection of formatting commands assembled under one name. When you apply a style, you give many formatting commands simultaneously, and you spare yourself the trouble of visiting numerous tabs and dialog boxes to format text. Styles save time and make documents look more professional. Headings assigned the same style — Heading1, for example — all look the same. When readers see that headings and paragraphs are consistent with one another across all the pages of a document, they get a warm, fuzzy feeling. They think the person who created the document really knew what he or she was doing.

Styles and templates

Every document comes with built-in styles that it inherits from the template with which it was created. You can create your own styles to supplement styles from the template. For that matter, you can create a template, populate it with styles you design, and use your new template to create distinctive letters or reports for your company.

A simple document created with the Blank Document template — a document that you create by pressing Ctrl+N — has only a few styles, but a document that was created with a sophisticated template comes with many styles. The Oriel Report template, for example, comes with styles for formatting titles, subtitles, headings, and quotations. Figure 3-1 illustrates how choosing styles from a template changes text formatting. Notice how choosing style options in the Styles pane reformats the text.

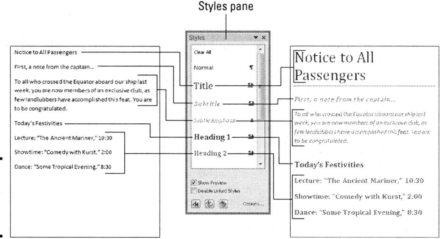

Figure 3-1: Apply styles to reformat text.

Types of styles

In the Styles pane (refer to Figure 3-1), the symbol next to each style name tells you what type of style you're dealing with. Word offers four style types:

✦ **Paragraph styles:** Determine the formatting of entire paragraphs. A paragraph style can include these settings: font, paragraph, tab, border, language, bullets, numbering, and text effects. Paragraph styles are marked with the paragraph symbol (¶).

✦ **Character styles:** Apply to text, not to paragraphs. You select text before you apply a character style. Create a character style for text that is hard to lay out and for foreign-language text. A character style can include these settings: font, border, language, and text effects. When you apply a character style to text, the character-style settings override the paragraph-style settings. For example, if the paragraph style calls for 14-point Arial font but the character style calls for 12-point Times Roman font, the character style wins. Character styles are marked with the letter *a*.

✦ **Linked (paragraph and character):** Apply paragraph formats as well as text formats throughout a paragraph. These styles are marked with the paragraph symbol (¶) as well as the letter *a*.

Applying Styles to Text and Paragraphs

Word offers several ways to apply a style, and you are invited to choose the one that works best for you. These pages explain how to apply a style and tell Word how to present style names in the various places where style names are presented for your enjoyment and pleasure.

Applying a style

The first step in applying a style is to select the part of your document that needs a style change:

✦ **A paragraph or paragraphs:** Because paragraph styles apply to all the text in a paragraph, you need only click in a paragraph before applying a style to make a style apply throughout the paragraph. To apply a style to several paragraphs, select all or part of them.

✦ **Text:** To apply a character style, select the letters whose formatting you want to change.

Next, apply the style with one of these techniques:

✦ **Styles gallery:** On the Home tab, choose a style in the Styles gallery (depending on the size of your screen, you may have to click the Styles button first). Figure 3-2 shows where the Quick Style gallery is located. The formatted letters above each style name in the gallery show you what your style choice will do to paragraphs or text. You can "live-preview" styles on the Quick Style gallery by moving the pointer over style names.

✦ **Styles pane:** On the Home tab, click the Styles group button to open the Styles pane, and select a style, as shown in Figure 3-2. Click the Show Preview check box at the bottom of the Styles pane to see formatted style names in the pane and get an idea of what the different styles are. You can drag the Styles pane to different locations on your screen. It remains on-screen after you leave the Home tab.

✦ **Apply Styles task pane:** Choose a style on the Apply Styles task pane, as shown in Figure 3-2. To display this task pane, go to the Home tab, open the Quick Style gallery, and choose Apply Styles (look for this option at the bottom of the gallery). You can drag the Apply Styles task pane to a corner of the screen. As does the Styles pane, the Apply Styles task pane remains on-screen after you leave the Home tab.

Quick Style gallery   Styles pane

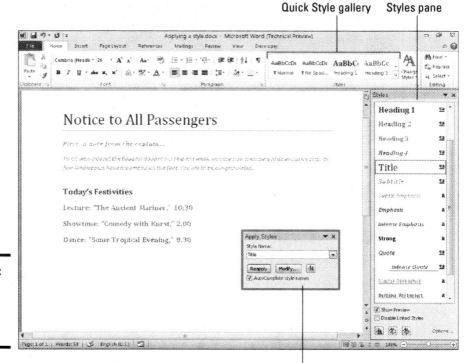

Figure 3-2:
The three
ways to
apply a
style.

Apply Styles task pane

To strip a paragraph or text of its style and give it the generic Normal style, select it and choose Clear Formatting in the Styles gallery or Clear All at the top of the Styles pane.

Keyboard shortcuts for applying styles

A handful of keyboard shortcuts can be very handy when applying paragraph styles:

- Normal: Ctrl+Shift+N

- Heading 1: Ctrl+Alt+1

- Heading 2: Ctrl+Alt+2

- Heading 3: Ctrl+Alt+3

- Next higher heading: Alt+Shift+←

- Next lower heading: Alt+Shift+→

You can assign keyboard shortcuts to styles. Book VI, Chapter 1 explains how.

Determining which style is in use

How can you tell which style has been applied to a paragraph or text? Sometimes you need to know which style is in play before you decide whether applying a different style is necessary.

Click the paragraph or text and use these techniques to find out which style was applied to it:

✔ **Glance at the Styles gallery and Styles pane to see which style is selected.** The selected style is the one that was applied to your paragraph or text.

✔ **Click the Style Inspector button at the bottom of the Styles pane.** The Style Inspector pane opens and lists the current style.

✔ **Press Shift+F1.** The Reveal Formatting task pane opens. It lists the style that was applied to the paragraph or text.

If you're especially keen to know about styles in your document, you can make style names appear to the left of the text in Outline and Draft view. On the Find tab, choose Options. In the Word Options dialog box, go to the Advanced tab and enter .5 or another measurement in the Style Area Pane Width in Draft and Outline Views box (look for this box under "Display"). You can drag the border of the Style Area pane to enlarge or shrink it.

Experimenting with style sets

A *style set* is a slight variation on the styles in the template you chose when you created your document. Style sets include Classic, Elegant, Fancy, and Modern. Choosing a style set imposes a slightly different look on your document — you make it classier, more elegant, fancier, or more modern. All templates, even those you create yourself, offer style sets. Style sets are a convenient way to experiment with the overall look of a document.

 To experiment with style sets, go to the Home tab, click the Change Styles button, choose Style Set on the drop-down list, and do one of the following:

✦ **Choose a new style set:** Select a style set on the submenu.

✦ **Use the original styles in the template:** Choose Reset to Quick Styles from Template on the submenu.

Choosing which style names appear on the Style menus

One of the challenges of applying styles is finding the right style to apply in the Styles gallery, Styles pane, or Apply Styles task pane (refer to Figure 3-2). All three can become crowded with style names. To make finding and choosing styles names easier, you can decide for yourself which names appear on the three style menus.

Styles gallery

In the Styles gallery, remove a style name by right-clicking it and choosing Remove from Styles gallery. If you regret removing style names, click the Change Styles button and choose Style Set⇨Reset to Quick Styles from Template.

Styles pane and Apply styles task pane

To decide for yourself which style names appear in the Styles pane and Apply Styles task pane, click the Styles group button, and in the Styles pane, click the Options link (you can find this link near the bottom of the pane). You see the Style Pane Options dialog box shown in Figure 3-3. Choose options to tell Word which style names appear in the Styles pane and Apply Styles task pane:

✦ **Select Styles to Show:** Choose All Styles to show all style names. The other options place a subset of names in the window and task pane. Recommended style names are those Microsoft thinks you need most often.

Figure 3-3: Deciding which names to put in the Styles pane and Apply Styles task pane.

✦ **Select How List Is Sorted:** Choose an option to describe how to list styles. Except for Based On, these options, I think, are self-explanatory. The Based On option lists styles in alphabetical order according to which style each style is based on (later in this chapter, "Creating a style from the ground up" explains how the based on setting is used in constructing styles).

✦ **Select Formatting to Show As Styles:** Choose options to declare which styles to list — those that pertain to paragraph level formatting, fonts, and bulleted and numbered lists.

✦ **Select How Built-In Style Names Are Shown:** Choose options to tell how to handle built-in styles, the obscure styles that Word applies on its own when you create tables of contents and other self-generating lists.

✦ **Apply to this document or to the template as well:** Click the Only in This Document option button to apply your choices only to the document you're working on; click the New Documents Based on This Template option button to apply your choices to your document and to all future documents you create with the template you're using.

Creating a New Style

You can create a new style by creating it from a paragraph or building it from the ground up. To do a thorough job, build it from the ground up because styles you create this way can be made part of the template you are currently working in and can be copied to other templates (later in this chapter, "Creating and Managing Templates" explains templates).

Creating a style from a paragraph

Follow these steps to create a new style from a paragraph:

1. **Click in a paragraph whose formatting you want to turn into a style.**

2. **Right-click and choose Styles⇨Save Selection As a New Quick Style.**

   You see the Create New Style from Formatting dialog box. You can also open this dialog box by opening the Styles gallery and choosing Save Selection As a New Quick Style.

3. **Enter a name for your new style.**

4. **Click OK.**

   A style you create this way becomes a part of the document you're working on; it isn't made part of the template from which you created your document.

Creating a style from the ground up

To make a style available in documents you will create in the future, make it part of a template and build it from the ground up. In the Styles pane, click the New Style button (you can find it at the bottom of the pane). You see the Create New Style from Formatting dialog box shown in Figure 3-4. Fill in the dialog box and click OK.

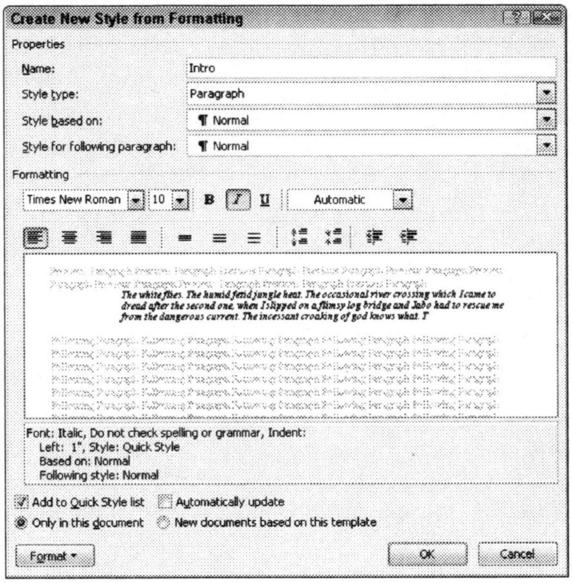

Figure 3-4:
Creating
a brand-
spanking-
new style.

Here's a rundown of the options in the Create New Style from Formatting dialog box:

+ **Name:** Enter a descriptive name for the style.

+ **Style Type:** On the drop-down list, choose a style type ("Types of Styles," earlier in this chapter, describes the style types).

+ **Style Based On:** If your new style is similar to a style that is already part of the template with which you created your document, choose the style to get a head start on creating the new one. Be warned, however, that if you or someone else changes the Based On style, your new style will inherit those changes and be altered as well.

+ **Style for Following Paragraph:** Choose a style from the drop-down list if the style you're creating is always followed by an existing style. For example, a new style called Chapter Title might always be followed by a style called Chapter Intro Paragraph. For convenience, someone who applies the style you're creating and presses Enter automatically applies the style you choose here on the next line of the document. Applying a style automatically to the following paragraph saves you the trouble of having to apply the style yourself.

+ **Formatting:** Choose options from the menus or click buttons to fashion or refine your style (you can also click the Format button to do this).

+ **Add to Quick Style List:** Select this check box to make the style's name appear in the Styles gallery, Styles pane, and Apply Styles task pane.

♦ **Automatically Update:** Normally, when you make a formatting change to a paragraph, the style assigned to the paragraph does not change at all, but the style does change if you check this box. Checking this box tells Word to alter the style itself each time you alter a paragraph to which you've assigned the style. With this box checked, all paragraphs in the document that were assigned the style are altered each time you change a single paragraph that was assigned the style.

♦ **Only in This Document/New Documents Based on This Template:** To make your style a part of the template from which you created your document as well as the document itself, click the New Documents Based on This Template option button. This way, new documents you create that are based on the template you are using can also make use of the new style.

♦ **Format:** This is the important one. Click the button and make a formatting choice. Word takes you to dialog boxes so that you can create or refine the style.

Modifying a Style

What if you decide at the end of an 80-page document that all 35 introductory paragraphs to which you assigned the Intro Para style look funny? If you clicked the Automatically Update check box in the New Style dialog box when you created the style, all you have to do is alter a paragraph to which you assigned the Intro Para style to alter all 35 introductory paragraphs. However, if you decided against updating styles automatically, you can still change the introductory paragraphs throughout your document.

Follow these steps to modify a style that isn't updated automatically:

1. **Click in any paragraph, table, or list to which you've assigned the style; if you want to modify a character style, select the characters to which you've assigned the style.**

2. **In the Styles pane or Apply Styles task pane, make sure the name of the style you want to modify is selected.**

If the right name isn't selected, select it now in the Styles pane or Apply Styles task pane.

3. **In the Styles pane, open the style's drop-down list and choose Modify; in the Apply Styles task pane, click the Modify button.**

You see the Modify Style dialog box. Does the dialog box look familiar? It is nearly identical to the Create New Style from Formatting dialog box you used to create the style in the first place (refer to Figure 3-4). The only difference is that you can't choose a style type in the Modify Style dialog box.

4. **Change the settings in the Modify Styles dialog box and click OK.**

   The previous section in this chapter explains the settings.

After you modify a style, all paragraphs or text to which the style was assigned are instantly changed. You don't have to go back and reformat text and paragraphs throughout your document.

Creating and Managing Templates

As I explain at the start of this chapter, every document you create is fashioned from a *template*. The purpose of a template is to store styles for documents. In the act of creating a document, you choose a template, and the styles on the template become available to you when you work on your document (Chapter 1 of this mini-book explains how to choose a template when you create a new document).

For example, when you double-click the Blank Template icon in the Available Templates window or press Ctrl+N, you create a document with the Blank Document template, a relatively simple template with few styles. When you create a document with a template from Office.com or a template from the New dialog box, more styles are available to you because these templates are more sophisticated.

To save time formatting your documents, you are invited to create templates with styles that you know and love. You can create a new template from scratch, create a template from a document, or create a template by assembling styles from other templates and documents. Styles in templates, like styles in documents, can be modified, deleted, and renamed.

Creating a new template

How do you want to create a new template? You can do it from scratch, create a new template from a document, or assemble styles from other templates. Read on.

To create a document from a template you created yourself, open the Available Templates window (on the File tab, choose New) and click the My Templates icon. The New dialog box opens. Select your template and click the Open button.

Creating a template from scratch

Follow these steps to create a template from scratch:

1. **On the File tab, choose New.**

   The Available Templates window opens.

2. **Click the My Templates icon to open the New dialog box.**

3. **Select the Blank Document icon.**

4. **Select the Template option button.**

    This option button is located in the lower-right corner of the dialog box.

5. **Click OK.**

    Your template appears in the Word window.

Create, modify, and delete styles as necessary (see "Creating a New Style" and "Modifying a Style" earlier in this chapter). Click the Save button to save your template, and in the Save As dialog box, enter a name for the template and click the Save button.

Creating a template from a document

If a document has all or most of the styles you want for a template, convert the document into a template so you can use the styles in documents you create in the future. Follow these steps to create a Word template from a Word document:

1. **Open the Word document you will use to create a template.**

2. **On the File tab, choose Save As.**

    The Save As dialog box appears.

3. **Enter a name for your template.**

4. **Open the Save As Type menu and choose Word Template.**

5. **Under Favorite Links, click Templates to see the folder where templates are stored.**

6. **Click the Save button.**

Probably your new templates includes text that it inherited from the document it was created from. Delete the text (unless you want it to appear in documents you create from your new template).

Assembling styles from other documents and templates

The third way to create a new template is to create a template from scratch and then gather styles from other documents and templates in your new template. Later in this chapter, "Copying styles from different documents and templates," explains how to assemble styles into a template.

Opening a template so that you can modify it

Open a template the same way you open a document. On the File tab, choose Open. You see the Open dialog box. Under Favorite Links, click Templates and then double-click the name of the template. It opens in the Word window. Style modifications you make in the template become available to all documents that were fashioned from the template.

Where templates are stored

Templates are stored in the Templates folder. To copy, move, or send templates, and to trade styles between templates, you have to know where the Templates folder is located on your computer. Where templates are stored by default depends on which version of Windows your computer runs:

- **Windows 7 and Windows Vista:** `C:\Users\`*Username*`\AppData\Roaming\Microsoft\Templates` folder.

- **Windows XP:** `C:\Documents and Settings\`*Username*`\Application Data\Microsoft\Templates` folder.

If you're having trouble finding the Templates folder, you can find out where it is located with these techniques:

- On the File tab, choose Options. In the Word Options dialog box, go to the Advanced Category and scroll to the File Locations button. Clicking this button opens the File Locations dialog box, where, under User Templates, you can see the name of the folder in which your templates are stored.

- On the File tab, choose New. In the Available Templates window, click the My Templates icon. The New dialog box appears. Right-click a template and choose Properties. The Properties dialog box lists the location of the folder where the templates are stored.

Copying styles from different documents and templates

Suppose that you like a style in one document and you want to copy it to another so that you can use it there. Or you want to copy it to a template to make it available to documents created with the template. Read on to find out how to copy styles between documents and between templates.

Copying a style from one document to another

Copy a style from one document to another when you need the style on a one-time basis. Follow these steps:

1. **Select a paragraph that was assigned the style you want to copy.**

    Be sure to select the entire paragraph. If you want to copy a character style, select text to which you have assigned the character style.

2. **Press Ctrl+C or right-click and choose Copy to copy the paragraph to the Clipboard.**

3. **Switch to the document you want to copy the style to and press Ctrl+V or click the Paste button on the Home tab.**

4. Delete the text you just copied to your document.

The style remains in the Styles pane and Styles gallery even though the text is deleted. You can call upon the style whenever you need it.

Copying styles to a template

Use the Organizer to copy styles from a document to a template or from one template to another. After making a style a part of a template, you can call upon the style in other documents. You can call upon it in each document you create or created with the template. Follow these steps to copy a style into a template:

1. Open the document or template with the styles you want to copy.

Earlier in this chapter, "Opening a template so that you can modify it" explains how to open a template.

2. In the Styles pane, click the Manage Styles button.

This button is located at the bottom of the window. The Manage Styles dialog box appears.

3. Click the Import/Export button.

You see the Organizer dialog box shown in Figure 3-5. Styles in the document or template that you opened in Step 1 appear in the In list box on the left side.

Select the styles you want to copy

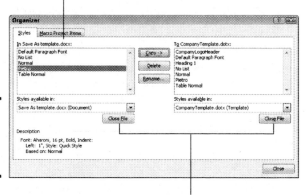

Figure 3-5: Copying styles to a template.

Click to close one template and open another

4. Click the Close File button on the right side of the dialog box.

The button changes names and becomes the Open File button.

**Book II
Chapter 3**

Word Styles

5. **Click the Open File button and, in the Open dialog box, find and select the template to which you want to copy styles; then, click the Open button.**

   You can click the Templates button (under Favorite Links) to open the Templates folder where templates are located. See the sidebar "Where templates are stored," earlier in this chapter, if you have trouble finding the Templates folder.

   The names of styles in the template you chose appear on the right side of the Organizer dialog box.

6. **In the Organizer dialog box, Ctrl+click to select the names of styles on the left side of the dialog box that you want to copy to the template listed on the right side of the dialog box.**

   As you click the names, they become highlighted.

7. **Click the Copy button.**

   The names of styles that you copied appear on the right side of the Organizer dialog box.

8. **Click the Close button and click Save when Word asks whether you want to save the new styles in the template.**

Modifying, deleting, and renaming styles in templates

Modify, delete, and rename styles in a template the same way you do those tasks to styles in a document (see "Modifying a Style" earlier in this chapter). However, in the Modify Style dialog box, select the New Documents Based on This Template option button before clicking OK.

Your style modifications will apply to all documents you create in the future with your template. For the style modifications to take effect in documents you already created with your template, tell Word to automatically update document styles in those documents. Follow these steps:

1. **Save and close your template if it is still open.**

   If any documents you fashioned from the template are open, close them as well.

2. **Open a document that you want to update with the style modifications you made to the template.**

3. **Go to the Developer tab.**

   To display this tab if necessary, open the File tab, choose Options, go to the Customize Ribbon category in the Word Options dialog box, select the Developer check box, and click OK.

Document
Template

4. **Click the Document Template button.**

   The Templates and Add-ins dialog box opens. It should list the path to the Templates folder and the template you modified. If the wrong template is listed, click the Attach button and select the correct template in the Attach Template dialog box.

5. **Select the Automatically Update Document Styles check box.**

6. **Click OK.**

Attaching a different template to a document

It happens in the best of families. You create or are given a document only to discover that the wrong template is attached to it. For times like those, Word gives you the opportunity to switch templates. Follow these steps:

1. **On the Developer tab, click the Document Template button.**

   You see the Templates and Add-Ins dialog box. If the Developer tab isn't displayed on your screen, go to the File tab, choose Options, visit the Customize Ribbon category in the Word Options dialog box, select the Developer check box, and click OK.

2. **Click the Attach button to open the Attach Template dialog box.**

3. **Find and select the template you want and click the Open button.**

   You return to the Templates and Add-ins dialog box, where the name of the template you chose appears in the Document Template box.

4. **Click the Automatically Update Document Styles check box.**

   Doing so tells Word to apply the styles from the new template to your document.

5. **Click OK.**

Chapter 4: Desktop Publishing with Word

In This Chapter

✔ **Considering ways to desktop-publish in Word**

✔ **Fine-tuning tables**

✔ **Wrapping text around graphics and other objects**

✔ **Running text in newspaper-style columns**

✔ **Putting text boxes in documents**

✔ **Putting borders on pages**

✔ **Decorating pages with drop caps and watermarks**

✔ **Printing landscape documents on various sizes of paper**

*O*nce upon a time, word processors were nothing more than glorified typewriters. They were good for typing and basic formatting, and not much else. But over the years, Microsoft Word has become a desktop publishing program in its own right. This chapter explains a few desktop publishing features that can make your documents stand out in the crowd — columns, text boxes, page borders, watermarks, and drop caps, to name a few.

Making Use of Charts, Diagrams, Shapes, Clip Art, and Photos

Figure 4-1 shows a newsletter that includes a chart, diagram, shape, clip-art image, and photo. You are invited to include these items in your Word documents, and you'll be glad to know that including them isn't very much trouble.

✦ **Charts:** A chart is an excellent way to present data for comparison purposes. The pie slices, bars, columns, or lines tell readers right away which business is more productive, for example, or who received the most votes. Book I, Chapter 6 explains how to create charts.

✦ **Diagrams:** A diagram allows readers to quickly grasp an idea, relationship, or concept. Instead of explaining an abstract idea, you can portray it in a diagram. Book I, Chapter 7 explains diagrams.

Figure 4-1:
This
newsletter
includes a
photo, chart,
diagram,
shape, and
clip-art
image.

✦ **Shapes and lines:** Shapes and lines can also illustrate ideas and concepts. You can also use them for decorative purposes in Word documents. Book I, Chapter 8 explains how to draw lines, arrows, and shapes.

✦ **Clip-art images:** Clip-art images make a document livelier. They add a little color to documents. Book VI, Chapter 4 explains how to place clip-art images in documents.

✦ **Photos:** A well-placed photo or two can make a newsletter or brochure that much more attractive. Book VI, Chapter 3 explains how to include photos in Word documents.

Constructing the Perfect Table

Create a table to present raw data to your readers or plead your case with numbers and facts. As long as the row labels and column headings are descriptive, looking up information in a table is the easiest way to find it. And tables impose order on chaos. What used to be a knotty lump of nondescript data can be turned into an orderly statement of fact if the data is presented in a table. No report is complete without one or two of them.

Book I, Chapter 5 explains how to create a table, as well as how to include mathematical calculations in Word tables. These pages explain a few table techniques that pertain strictly to Word documents — repeating the heading rows, fitting a table on a single page, and turning a list into a table.

Fitting a table on the page

Ideally, a table should fit on a single page, because studying table data that is spread across two or more pages can be difficult. Here are some suggestions for fitting a table on a single page:

✔ **Present the table in landscape mode:** In Landscape mode, a page is turned on its ear so that it is wider than it is tall and you have room for more table columns. To print in Landscape mode, however, you must create a new section for the pages in question. Later in this chapter, "Landscape Documents" explains how to switch from portrait to landscape mode.

✔ **Shrink the font size:** Sometimes shrinking the font size throughout a table shrinks the table just enough to fit it on a page. To shrink fonts throughout a table, go to the Home tab and click the Shrink Font button (or press Ctrl+[). Keep shrinking the font size until the table fits on one page.

✔ **Shrink the columns:** On the (Table Tools) Layout tab, click the AutoFit button, and choose AutoFit Contents on the drop-down list to make each column only wide enough to accommodate its widest entry.

✔ **Change the orientation of header row text:** In a top-heavy table in which the header row cells contain text and the cells below contain numbers, you can make the entire table narrower by changing the orientation of the text in the header row. To turn text on its ear, select the cells whose text needs a turn, go to the (Table Tools) Layout tab, and click the Text Direction button. Keep clicking until the text turns the direction you want.

Chances are, if your table can't fit on one page, presenting the information in a table isn't the best option. Try presenting it in bulleted or numbered lists. Or present the information in short paragraphs under small fourth- or fifth-level headings.

	Yes	*No*	*Maybe*	*Often*	*Never*
Prof. Plum in the Library	3			3	
Miss Scarlet in the Drawing Room		3	3		3
Col. Mustard in the Dining Room	3			3	

Repeating header rows on subsequent pages

Making sure that the *header row,* sometimes called the *heading row,* appears on a new page if the table breaks across pages is essential. The header row is the first row in the table, the one that usually describes what is in the columns below. Without a header row, readers can't tell what the information in a table means. Follow these steps to make the header row (or rows) repeat on the top of each new page that a table appears on:

1. **Place the cursor in the header row or select the header rows if your table includes more than one header row.**

2. **On the (Table Tools) Layout tab, click the Repeat Header Rows button (depending on the size of your screen, you may have to click the Data button first).**

   Header rows appear only in Print Layout view, so don't worry if you can't see them in Draft view.

Turning a list into a table

In order to turn a list into a table, all components of the list — each name, address, city name, state, and zip code listing, for example — must be separated from the next component by a tab space or a comma. Word looks for tab spaces or commas when it turns a list into a table, and the program separates data into columns according to where the tab spaces or commas are located. You have to prepare your list carefully by entering tab spaces or commas in all the right places before you can turn a list into a table.

Follow these steps to turn a list into a table after you've done all the preliminary work:

1. **Select the list.**

2. **On the Insert tab, click the Table button and choose Convert Text To Table on the drop-down list.**

   You see the Convert Text to Table dialog box.

   Note the number in the Number of Columns box. It should list the number of components into which you separated your list. If the number doesn't match the number of components, you misplaced a tab entry or comma in your list. Click Cancel, return to your list, and examine it to make sure each line has been divided into the same number of components.

3. **Under Separate Text At, choose the Tabs or Commas option, depending on which you used to separate the components on the list.**

4. **Click OK.**

You can turn a table into a list by clicking the Convert to Text button on the (Table Tools) Layout tab (you may have to click the Data button first, depending on the size of your screen).

Positioning and Wrapping Objects Relative to the Page and Text

"Object" is just Office's generic term for a shape, line, text box, clip-art image, photo, diagram, WordArt image, or chart that you insert in a document. Book I, Chapter 8 explains how to manipulate an object — how to change its size, shape, and other qualities. When you place an object in a Word document, you have to consider more than its size and shape. You also have to consider where to position it on the page and how to wrap text around it. In Word lingo, *wrap* refers to what text does when it butts heads with a shape, text box, photo, diagram, or other object. You must be in Print Layout view to wrap and position objects on a page.

When you insert an object, it lands *inline with text.* That means it lands against the left margin and text doesn't wrap around its side. Before you can change the position of an object, you must select it and choose a text-wrapping option apart from Inline with Text.

Wrapping text around an object

Figure 4-2 illustrates the 15 different ways you can wrap text around an object. Select the object you want to wrap text around, go to the Format tab, and use one of these techniques to wrap text around the object:

**Book II
Chapter 4**

**Desktop Publishing
with Word**

✦ Click the Wrap Text button and choose an option on the drop-down list. (You may have to click the Arrange button first, depending on the size of your screen.)

✦ Click the Wrap Text button and choose More Layout Options on the drop-down list, or click the Size group button and select the Text Wrapping tab in the Layout dialog box. Then choose a wrapping style and side around which to wrap text. Figure 4-2 shows what the different combinations of Wrapping Style and Wrap Text options do.

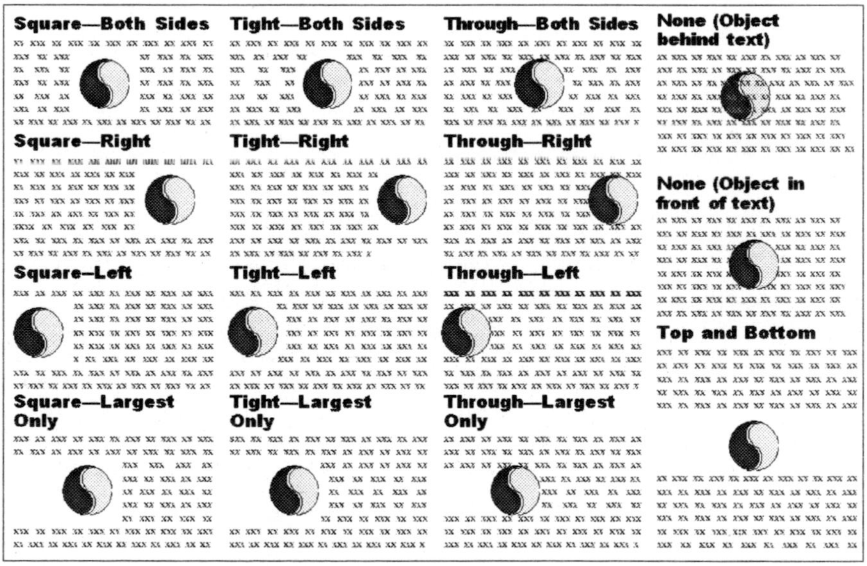

Figure 4-2:
All the ways
to wrap text
in a Word
document.

Wrapped text looks best when it is justified and hyphenated. That way, text can get closer to the object that is being wrapped.

Wrapping text with precision

You can decide for yourself how close or far text is from an object when you wrap text. Select the object, and on the Format tab, click the Wrap Text button and choose Edit Wrap Points on the drop-down list. Small black squares called *wrap points* appear around the object. Click and drag the wrap points to push text away from or bring text closer to the object in question.

Statue of Liberty

The Statue of Liberty, officially titled Liberty Enlightening the World (*la Liberté éclairant le monde*), dedicated on October 28, 1886, is a monument that commemorates the centennial of the signing of the United States Declaration of Independence. It was given to the United States by the people of France to acknowledge the friendship between the two countries established during the American Revolution. The statue represents a woman wearing a stola, a radiant crown and sandals, trampling a broken chain, carrying a torch in her raised right hand and a tabula ansata tablet, where the date of the Declaration of Independence is inscribed, in her left arm.

Positioning an object on a page

To position an object in a Word page, you can drag it to a new location. As Book I, Chapter 8 explains in torturous detail, dragging means to select the object, move the pointer over its perimeter, click when you see the four-headed arrow, and slide the object to a new location.

To make positioning objects on a page a little easier, Word also offers Position commands for moving objects. Select your object, go to the Format tab, and use one of these techniques to move your object precisely into place:

✦ Click the Position button and select a With Text Wrapping option on the drop-down list, as shown in Figure 4-3. (You may have to click the Arrange button first, depending on the size of your screen.) These options position an object squarely in a corner, a side, or the middle of the page.

✦ Click the Position button and choose More Layout Options on the drop-down list, or click the Size group button and select the Position tab in the Layout dialog box. Then choose position options. Go to the Layout dialog box when you want to place objects in the very same position on different pages.

Select the object   Choose a With Text Wrapping option

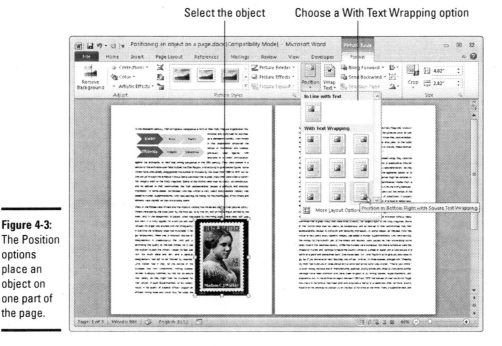

Figure 4-3:
The Position options place an object on one part of the page.

An object you position with an option on the Position drop-down list travels from page to page if you move the paragraph to which it's connected. This happens because, when you insert an object, Word attaches it to the paragraph where the cursor is located when you make the insertion. If you move that paragraph to another page or the paragraph gets moved as you edit text, the object moves right along with the paragraph. You can locate the paragraph to which an object is connected by clicking the Show/Hide ¶ button on the Home tab and then clicking the object; the anchor symbol appears beside the paragraph to which the object is connected.

Working with the Drawing Canvas

As Book I, Chapter 8 explains, shapes and lines are a great way to illustrate ideas. You can in effect doodle on the page and give readers another insight into what you want to explain. In Word, however, drawing lines and shapes is problematic unless you draw them on the drawing canvas.

The *drawing canvas* works like a corral to hold lines and shapes. After you create a drawing canvas, you can draw inside it as though you were drawing on a little page, as shown in Figure 4-4. You can treat the drawing canvas as an object in its own right. You can move it, along with the things inside it, to new locations. You can also, by way of the (Drawing Tools) Format tab, give the drawing canvas an outline shape and fill color. The drawing canvas makes working with objects on a page, especially lines and shapes, that much easier.

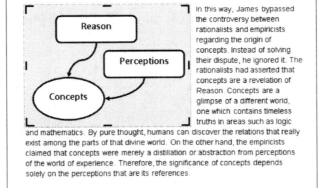

Figure 4-4:
The drawing canvas — a corral for shapes and lines.

Follow these steps to create a drawing canvas for holding lines and shapes:

1. Place the cursor roughly where you want the drawing canvas to be.

2. Go to the Insert tab.

3. Click the Shapes button and choose New Drawing Canvas.

You can find the New Drawing Canvas command at the bottom of the Shapes drop-down list. A drawing canvas appears on your screen.

The drawing canvas is an object in its own right. You can wrap text around it, give it an outline, and give it a color fill. You can drag it to a new location. To change its size, drag a handle on the side or corner.

Choosing a Theme for Your Document

When you installed Word on your computer, you also installed a dozen or more themes. A theme is a colorful, ready-made design for headings and text. Each theme imposes a slightly different look on a document. If you want to experiment with themes, more power to you, but be prepared to click the Undo button and backtrack as you rummage around for the right one.

Starting on the Page Layout tab, follow these instructions to experiment with themes:

✦ **Choosing a new theme:** Click the Themes button and choose a theme on the drop-down list.

✦ **Choosing a new set of colors for your theme:** Click the Theme Colors button, slide the pointer over the different color sets on the drop-down list, and see what effect they have on your document.

 ✦ **Changing the fonts:** Click the Theme Fonts button and choose a combination of fonts on the drop-down list for the headings and text in your document.

 ✦ **Changing theme effects:** Click the Theme Effects button and choose a theme effect on the drop-down list. A *theme effect* is a slight refinement to a theme.

Putting Newspaper-Style Columns in a Document

Columns look great in newsletters and similar documents. And you can pack a lot of words in columns. I should warn you, however, that the Columns command is only good for creating columns that appear on the same page. Running text to the next page with the Columns command can be problematic and isn't worth doing.

 Sometimes it is easier to create columns by creating a table or by using text boxes, especially when the columns refer to one another. In a two-column résumé, for example, the left-hand column often lists job titles ("Facsimile Engineer") whose descriptions are found directly across the page in the right-hand column ("I Xeroxed stuff all day long"). Creating a two-column résumé with Word's Columns command would be futile because making the columns line up is nearly impossible. Each time you add something to the left-hand column, everything *snakes* — it gets bumped down in the left-hand column and the right-hand column as well.

Doing the preliminary work

 Before you put text in newspaper-style columns, write it. Take care of the spelling, grammar, and everything else first because making text changes to words after they've been arranged in columns is difficult. Columns appear only in Print Layout view.

Running text into columns

 To "columunize" text, select it, go to the Page Layout tab, and click the Columns button. Then either choose how many columns you want on the drop-down list or choose More Columns to create columns of different widths.

You see the Columns dialog box shown in Figure 4-5 if you choose More Columns. Here are the options in the Columns dialog box:

✦ **Preset columns:** Select a Presets box to choose a preset number of columns. Notice that, in some of the boxes, the columns aren't of equal width.

Figure 4-5:
Running text in columns.

✦ **Number of columns:** If a preset column doesn't do the trick, enter the number of columns you want in the Number of Columns box.

✦ **Line between columns:** A line between columns is mighty elegant and is difficult to do on your own. Choose the Line Between check box to run lines between columns.

✦ **Columns width:** If you uncheck the Equal Column Width check box, you can make columns of unequal width. Change the width of each column by using the Width boxes.

✦ **Space between columns:** Enter a measurement in the Spacing boxes to determine how much space appears between columns.

✦ **Start New Column:** This check box is for putting empty space in a column, perhaps to insert a text box or picture. Place the cursor where you want the empty space to begin, choose This Point Forward on the Apply To drop-down list, and click the Start New Column check box.

Word creates a new section if you selected text before you columnized it, and you see your columns in Print Layout view. Chapter 2 of this mini-book explains sections.

To "break" a column in the middle and move text to the next column, click where you want the column to break and press Ctrl+Shift+Enter or go to the Page Layout tab, click the Breaks button, and choose Column on the drop-down list.

Working with Text Boxes

Put text in a text box when you want a notice or announcement to stand out on the page. Like other objects, text boxes can be shaded, filled with color, and given borders, as the examples in Figure 4-6 demonstrate. You can also lay them over graphics to make for interesting effects. I removed the borders and the fill color from the text box on the right side of Figure 4-6, but rest assured, the text in this figure lies squarely in a text box. (Book I, Chapter 8 explains how to give borders, shading, and color to objects such as text boxes.)

**Book II
Chapter 4**

**Desktop Publishing
with Word**

Figure 4-6:
Examples of
text boxes.

You can move a text box around at will on the page until it lands in the right place. You can even use text boxes as columns and make text jump from one text box to the next in a document — a nice feature, for example, when you want a newsletter article on page 1 to be continued on page 2. Instead of cutting and pasting text from page 1 to page 2, Word moves the text for you as the column on page 1 fills up.

Inserting a text box

 To create a text box, go to the Insert tab, click the Text Box button, and use one of these techniques:

+ **Choose a ready-made text box:** Scroll in the drop-down list and choose a preformatted text box.

+ **Draw a conventional text box:** Choose Draw Text Box on the drop-down list, and then click and drag to draw the text box. Lines show you how big it will be when you release the mouse button.

After you insert the text box, you can type text in it and call on all the formatting commands on the (Drawing) Format tab. These commands are explained in Book I, Chapter 8. It also describes how to turn a shape such as a circle or triangle into a text box (create the shape, right-click it and choose Add Text, and start typing).

Here's a neat trick: You can turn the text in a text box on its side so that it reads from top to bottom or bottom to top, not from left to right. Create a text box, enter the text, go to the (Drawing Tools) Format tab, click the Text Direction button, and choose a Rotate option on the drop-down list.

Making text flow from text box to text box

As I mention earlier, you can link text boxes so that the text in the first box is pushed into the next one when it fills up. To link text boxes, start by creating all the text boxes that you need. You cannot link one text box to another if the second text box already has text in it. Starting on the (Drawing Tools) Format tab, follow these directions to link text boxes:

✦ **Creating a forward link:** Click a text box and then click the Create Link button to create a forward link. The pointer changes into a very odd-looking pointer that is supposed to look like a pitcher. Move the odd-looking pointer to the next text box in the chain and click there to create a link.

✦ **Breaking a link:** To break a link, click the text box that is to be the last in the chain, and then click the Break Link button.

Sprucing Up Your Pages

You can play interior decorator with the pages of a document by putting a border around pages and splashing color on pages. Keep reading if making the pages of your document a little prettier interests you.

Decorating a page with a border

Word offers a means of decorating title pages, certificates, menus, and similar documents with a page border. Besides lines, you can decorate the sides of a page with stars, pieces of cake, and other artwork. If you want to place a border around a page in the middle of a document, you must create a section break where the page is.

Before you create your border, place the cursor on the page where the border is to appear. Place the cursor on the first page of a document if you want to put a border around only the first page. If your document is divided into sections and you want to put borders around certain pages in a section, place the cursor in the section — either in the first page if you want the borders to go around it, or in a subsequent page.

With the cursor in the right place, follow these steps to decorate your page or pages with a border:

📄 Page Borders

1. **Go to the Page Layout tab and click the Page Borders button.**

You see the Borders and Shading dialog box, as shown in Figure 4-7.

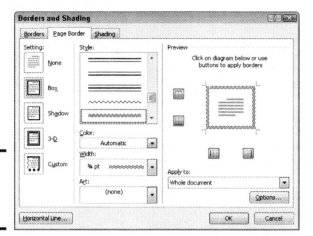

Figure 4-7:
Putting
borders on
pages.

2. **Under Setting, choose which kind of border you want.**

   The Custom setting is for putting borders on one, two, or three sides of
   the page, not four. Use the None setting to remove borders.

3. **On the Apply To drop-down list, tell Word which page or pages in the
   document get borders.**

4. **Select options to construct the border you want and then click OK.**

The Page Border tab offers a bunch of tools for fashioning a border:

✦ **Line for borders:** Under Style, scroll down the list and choose a line for
  the borders. You will find interesting choices at the bottom of the menu.
  Be sure to look in the Preview window to see what your choices in this
  dialog box add up to.

✦ **Color for borders:** Open the Color drop-down list and choose a color for
  the border lines if you want a color border.

✦ **Width of borders:** If you chose artwork for the borders, use the Width
  drop-down list to tell Word how wide the lines or artwork should be.

✦ **Artwork for borders:** Open the Art drop-down list and choose a symbol,
  illustration, star, piece of cake, or other artwork, if that is what you want
  for the borders. You will find some amusing choices on this long list,
  including ice cream cones, bats, and umbrellas.

✦ **Borders on different sides of the page:** Use the four buttons in the
  Preview window to tell Word on which sides of the page to draw borders. Click these buttons to remove or add borders, as you wish.

✦ **Distance from edge of page:** Click the Options button and fill in the
  Border and Shading Options dialog box if you want to get specific about
  how close the borders can come to the edge of the page or pages.

Putting a background color on pages

Especially if you intend to save your Word document as a Web page, you will be glad to know that putting a background color on pages is easy. You can't, however, pick and choose which pages get a background color. Putting background colors on the pages of a document is an all-or-nothing proposition.

 To grace a page with a background color or gradient color mixture, go to the Page Layout tab, click the Page Color button, and choose a color on the drop-down list. Choose Fill Effects to open the Fill Effects dialog box and apply gradient color mixtures or patterns to the pages.

Dropping In a Drop Cap

A *drop cap* is a large capital letter that "drops" into the text, as shown in Figure 4-8. Drop caps appear at the start of chapters in many books, this book included, and you can find other uses for them, too. In Figure 4-8, one drop cap marks the A side of a list of songs on a homemade music CD.

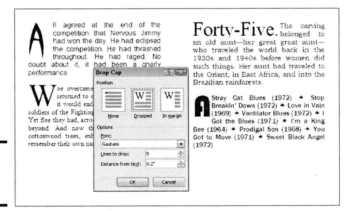

Figure 4-8: Creating a drop cap.

 To create a drop cap, start by clicking anywhere in the paragraph whose first letter you want to "drop." If you want to "drop" more than one character at the start of the paragraph, select the characters. Then go to the Insert tab, click the Drop Cap button, and choose Dropped or Drop Cap Options. Choosing Drop Cap Options opens the Drop Cap dialog box shown in Figure 4-8, where you can experiment with these options:

✦ **Position:** Choose which kind of drop-cap you want. In Margin places the drop-cap to the left of the paragraph, in the margin, not in the paragraph itself.

✦ **Font:** Choose a font from the Font drop-down list. Choose a different font from the text in the paragraph.

✦ **Lines to Drop:** Enter the number of text lines to drop the letter.

✦ **Distance from Text:** Keep the 0 setting unless you're dropping an *I, 1,* or other skinny letter or number.

Click the Drop Cap button and choose None to remove a drop cap.

Watermarking for the Elegant Effect

A *watermark* is a pale image or set of words that appears behind text on each page in a document. True watermarks are made in the paper mold and can be seen only when the sheet of paper is held up to a light. You can't make true watermarks with Word, but you can make the closest thing to them that can be attained in the debased digital world in which we live. Figure 4-9 shows two pages of a letter in which the paper has been "watermarked." Watermarks are one of the easiest formatting tricks to accomplish in Word.

Figure 4-9: Watermarks showing faintly on the page.

To create a watermark for every page of a document, go to the Page Layout tab and click the Watermark button. From the drop-down list, create your watermark:

✦ **Prefabricated text watermark:** Scroll down the list and choose an option. You will find "Confidential," "Urgent," and other text watermarks.

✦ **Picture watermark:** Choose Custom Watermark, and in the Printed Watermark dialog box, click the Picture Watermark option button. Then click the Select Picture button. In the Insert Picture dialog box, select a graphic file to use for the watermark and click the Insert button. Back in the Printed Watermark dialog box, choose or enter a size for the graphic on the Scale drop-down list. I don't recommend deselecting the Washout check box — do so and your image may be so dark it obscures the text.

✦ **Text watermark:** Choose Custom Watermark and, in the Printed Watermark dialog box, click the Text Watermark option button. Type a word or two in the Text box (or choose an entry from the drop-down list). Choose a font, size, color, and layout for the words. If you uncheck the Semitransparent check box, you do so at your peril because the watermark words may be too dark on the page.

To tinker with a watermark, reopen the Printed Watermark dialog box. To remove a watermark, click the Watermark button and choose Remove Watermark on the drop-down list.

Landscape Documents

A *landscape* document is one in which the page is wider than it is long, like a painting of a landscape, as shown on the right side of Figure 4-10. Most documents, like the pages of this book, are printed in *portrait* style, with the short sides of the page on the top and bottom. However, creating a landscape document is sometimes a good idea because a landscape document stands out from the usual crowd of portrait documents and sometimes printing in landscape mode is necessary to fit text, tables, and graphics on a single page.

Figure 4-10: A portrait document (left) and landscape document (right).

You're ready to go if you want to turn all the pages in your document into landscape pages. To turn some of the pages into landscape pages, create a section for the pages that need to appear in Landscape mode and click in the section (Chapter 2 of this mini-book explains sections). Starting on the Page Layout tab, use these techniques to change the page orientation:

✦ **Landscape pages:** Click the Orientation button and choose Landscape on the drop-down list.

✦ **Portrait pages:** Click the Orientation button and choose Portrait on the drop-down list.

Printing on Different Size Paper

You don't have to print exclusively on standard 8.5 x 11 paper; you can print on legal-size paper and other sizes of paper as well. A newsletter with an unusual shape really stands out in a crowd and gets people's attention. Go to the Page Layout tab and use one of these techniques to change the size of the paper on which you intend to print a document:

✦ Click the Size button and choose an option on the drop-down list.

✦ Click the Page Setup group button, select the Paper tab in the Page Setup dialog box, and choose a setting on the Paper Size drop-down list. If none of the settings suits you, enter your own settings in the Width and Height text boxes.

**Book II
Chapter 4**

**Desktop Publishing
with Word**

Getting Word's help with cover letters

Writing and designing a cover page for a letter or report is a chore. Word can't dictate a cover page for you, but it can provide a handsome preformatted cover page that looks nice at the front of a report or article.

Follow these steps to place a cover page at the start of a document:

1. **Go to the Insert tab.**

2. **Click the Cover Page button.**

3. **Choose a cover page predesign on the drop-down list.**

Don't forget to replace the boilerplate text on the cover page with text of your own.

If you change your mind about which cover page you want, simply click the Cover Page button again and choose a different cover page.

Chapter 5: Getting Word's Help with Office Chores

In This Chapter

✔ **Commenting on others' work**

✔ **Tracking revisions to documents**

✔ **Printing envelopes and labels**

✔ **Mail merging for form letters and bulk mailing**

*T*his chapter is dedicated to the proposition that everyone should get their work done sooner. It explains how Word can be a help in the office, especially when it comes to working on team projects. This chapter explains comments, using revision marks to record edits, and mail merging, Microsoft's term for generating form letters, labels, and envelopes for mass mailings.

Book VI, Chapter 7 explains another way to collaborate on team projects — by collaborating online with the Office Web Apps.

Highlighting Parts of a Document

In my work, I often use the Highlight command to mark paragraphs and text that need reviewing later. And on rainy days, I use it to splash color on my documents and keep myself amused. Whatever your reasons for highlighting text in a document, go to the Home tab and use one of these techniques to do it:

✦ **Select text and then choose a highlighter:** Select the text you want to highlight, and then either click the Text Highlight Color button (if it's displaying your color choice) or open the drop-down list on the button and choose a color.

✦ **Choose a highlighter and then select text:** Either click the Text Highlight Color button (if it's already displaying your color choice) or open the drop-down list on the button and choose a color. The pointer changes into a crayon. Drag across the text you want to highlight. When you're finished highlighting, click the Text Highlight Color button again or press Esc.

To remove highlights, select the highlighted text, open the drop-down list on the Text Highlight Color button, and choose No Color. Select the entire document (press Ctrl+A) and choose No Color to remove all highlights from a document.

Highlight marks are printed along with the text. To keep highlights from being printed, go to the File tab, choose Options, visit the Display category in the Word Options dialog box, and deselect the Show Highlighter Marks check box.

Commenting on a Document

In the old days, comments were scribbled illegibly in the margins of books and documents, but in Word, comments are easy to read. To show where a comment has been made on the text, Word puts brackets around text and highlights the text. Each commenter is assigned a different highlighting color so you can tell at a glance who made each comment. As shown in Figure 5-1, you can read comments in the Reviewing pane, in pop-up boxes (in Draft view and Outline view), and in balloons (in Print Layout view and Web Layout view).

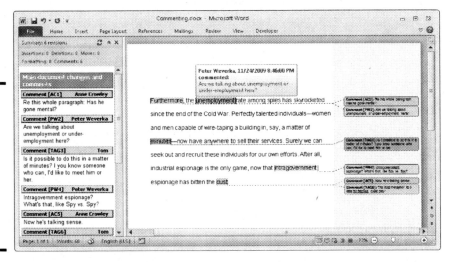

Figure 5-1: Comments appear in (left to right) the Reviewing pane, pop-up boxes, and balloons.

Entering a comment

If you're putting together a proposal, you can pass it around the office and invite everyone to comment. If someone makes an especially good comment, you can include it in the main text merely by copying and pasting it. To write a comment:

1. **Select the word or sentence that you want to comment on.**

2. **On the Review tab, click the New Comment button.**

In Draft and Outline view, the Reviewing pane opens on the left side or bottom of the screen so you can enter a comment; in Print Layout and Web Layout view, a new balloon appears on the right side of the screen so you can enter a comment. (On the Review tab, open the drop-down list on the Reviewing Pane button and choose an option to place the pane on the left side or bottom of the screen.)

3. **Type your comment in the space provided.**

In Draft and Outline view, commenters' names and initials appear beside each comment and comments are numbered. If the wrong name and initials appear beside your comments, open the drop-down list on the Track Changes button, choose Change User Name, and enter your correct name and initials in the Word Options dialog box.

**Book II
Chapter 5**

Getting Word's Help
with Office Chores

Caring for and feeding comments

Starting on the Review tab, here is a handful of tasks that deserve comment (if you'll pardon my little pun):

✦ **Editing a comment:** Right-click between the brackets and choose Edit Comment or just click in the Reviewing pane in Print Layout view. Then rewrite the comment in the Reviewing pane or the balloon.

✦ **Going from comment to comment:** Click the Previous or Next button on the Review tab. In Draft and Outline view, the Reviewing pane opens, and you can read the comment you landed on at the top of the pane. In Print Layout and Web Layout view, balloons on the right side of the screen are highlighted as you go from comment to comment.

✦ **Seeing and hiding the Reviewing pane:** Click the Reviewing Pane button to display or hide the Reviewing pane. On the button's drop-down list, choose an option to put the pane on the left side or bottom of the screen.

✦ **Temporarily removing the comments:** Click the Show Markup button and deselect Comments on the drop-down list to wipe away the comments; select Comments to see them again.

✦ **Displaying comments by a particular reviewer:** Click the Show Markup button, choose Reviewers, and deselect All Reviewers on the submenu. Then click the button again, choose Reviewers, and choose the name of a reviewer. To see all comments again, click the Show Markup button and choose Reviewers⇨All Reviewers.

✦ **Deleting a comment:** Click a comment in the Reviewing pane, click between brackets, or click a comment balloon and then click the Delete button. You can also right-click and choose Delete Comment.

✦ **Deleting all the comments in the document:** Open the drop-down list on the Delete button and choose Delete All Comments in Document.

✦ **Deleting comments made by one or two people:** First, isolate comments made by people whose comments you want to delete (see "Displaying comments by a particular reviewer" earlier in this list). Then open the drop-down list on the Delete button and choose Delete All Comments Shown.

Tracking Changes to Documents

When many hands go into revising a document, figuring out who made changes to what is impossible. What's more, it's impossible to tell what the first draft looked like. Sometimes it's hard to tell whether the changes were for good or ill. To help you keep track of changes to documents, Word offers the Track Changes command. When this command is in effect:

✦ All changes to a document are recorded in a different color, with one color for each reviewer.

✦ In Draft and Outline view, new text is underlined and deleted text is crossed out.

✦ In Print Layout and Web Layout view, new text is underlined, and deleted text appears in balloons on the right side of the window.

✦ In all views, a vertical line appears on the left side of the screen to indicate where changes were made.

By moving the pointer over a change, you can read the name of the person who made it as well as the words that were inserted or deleted. You can see changes as well in the Reviewing pane. As you review changes, you can accept or reject each change. You can also see the original document, a copy with revisions, or the final copy simply by making a choice from the Display for Review drop-down list on the Review tab.

To give you an idea of what tracking marks look like, Figure 5-2 shows the first two sentences of Vladimir Nabokov's autobiography *Speak, Memory* in Draft view, with marks showing where the author made additions and deletions to the original draft.

Telling Word to start marking changes

To start tracking where editorial changes are made to a document, turn Track Changes on. You can do that with one of these techniques:

✦ On the Review tab, click the Track Changes button (or open its drop-down list and choose Track Changes).

✦ Press Ctrl+Shift+E.

✦ On the status bar, click the words *Track Changes* so that the status bar reads "Track Changes: On." If you don't see the words *Track Changes* on your status bar and you want to see them there, right-click the status bar and select Track Changes on the pop-up menu.

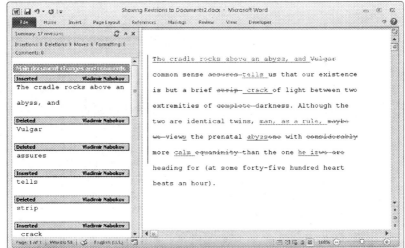

Figure 5-2: A document in Draft view with change marks and changes showing.

Book II Chapter 5

Getting Word's Help with Office Chores

To stop tracking changes to a document, click the Track Changes button again, press Ctrl+Shift+E again, or click the words *Track Changes* on the status bar so that the words read "Track Changes: Off."

Telling Word how to mark changes

To tell Word precisely how to mark changes, open the drop-down list on the Track Changes button (you may have to click the Tracking button first) and choose Change Tracking Options. You see the colorful Track Changes Options dialog box. It offers these options:

✦ **Markup options:** Declare how you want to mark insertions and deletions, and with which color you want to mark them.

✦ **Moves options:** Declare how you want to mark text that has been cut and pasted.

✦ **Table Cell Highlighting options:** When editing tables, you can mark inserted, deleted, merged, and split cells in different colors.

✦ **Formatting options:** Choose an option to mark formatting changes as well as changes to text.

✦ **Balloons:** Choose Always if you prefer to mark deleted text with balloons to the right of the text in Print Layout and Web Layout view. If you prefer not to see balloons in Print Layout and Web Layout view, choose

Never. You must display the balloons to examine revised documents in Final Showing Markup and Original Showing Markup view (see "Marking changes when you forgot to turn on change marks" later in this chapter). "Determining what revision marks look like," at the end of this chapter, explains how you can quickly hide or display balloons in Print Layout and Web Layout view.

If your name doesn't appear with the change marks you make, go to the Review tab, open the drop-down list on the Track Changes button, choose Change User Name, and enter your name and initials in the Word Options dialog box.

Reading and reviewing a document with change marks

Reading and reviewing a document with change marks isn't easy. The marks can get in the way. Fortunately, Word offers the Display for Review menu on the Review tab for dealing with documents that have been scarred by change marks. Choose options on the Display for Review drop-down list to get a better idea of how your changes are taking shape:

+ **See more clearly where text was deleted from the original document:** Choose Final: Show Markup. In Print Layout view, deleted material appears in balloons on the right side of the screen and insertions are underlined.

+ **See what the document would look like if you accepted all changes:** Choose Final. All change marks are stripped away and you see what your document would look like if you accepted all changes made to it.

+ **See more clearly where text was inserted in the document:** Choose Original: Show Markup. In Print Layout view, insertions appear in balloons on the right side of the screen and a line appears through text that has been deleted.

+ **See what the document would look like if you rejected all changes:** Choose Original. You get the original, pristine document back.

Marking changes when you forgot to turn on change marks

Suppose that you write the first draft of a document and someone revises it but that someone doesn't track changes. How can you tell where changes were made? For that matter, suppose that you get hold of a document, you change it around without tracking changes, and now you want to see what your editorial changes did to the original copy. I have good news: You can compare documents to see the editorial changes that were made to them. Word offers a command for comparing the original document to a revised edition and another for comparing two different revised editions of the same document.

After you make the comparison, Word creates a third document similar to the one shown in Figure 5-3. In the Source Document pane on the right side of the window, you can see the documents you're comparing. The Compared Document pane, meanwhile, shows who made changes and what those changes are.

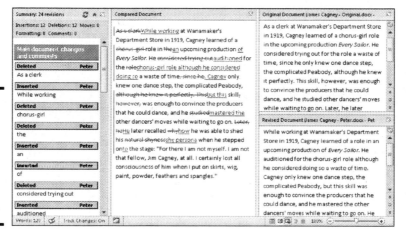

Figure 5-3:
Comparing documents to see where editorial changes are.

Follow these steps to compare an original document to its revised copy or two revised copies:

1. **On the Review tab, click the Compare button.**

   You see a drop-down list (depending on the size of your screen, you may have to choose Compare more than once to get to the drop-down list).

2. **On the drop-down list, choose Compare to compare the original document to its revised edition; choose Combine to compare two editions of the same document that were revised separately.**

   You see the Compare Documents dialog box or the Combine Documents dialog box, as shown in Figure 5-4. These dialog boxes work the same way.

3. **On the Original Document drop-down list, choose the original or a revised edition of the document; if its name isn't there, click the Browse button and select it in the Open dialog box.**

4. **On the Revised Document drop-down list, choose a revised copy, or else click the Browse button and select it in the Open dialog box.**

5. **Click the More button.**

   You see more options for comparing or combining documents.

6. **If you so desire, deselect the Comparison Settings check boxes to tell Word what you want to compare.**

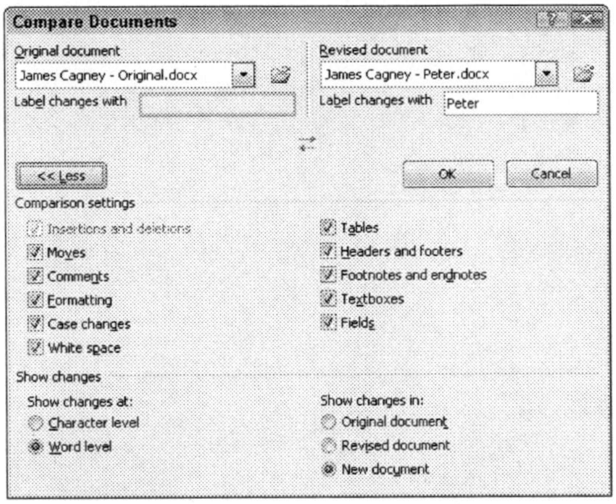

Figure 5-4:
Choosing
which
documents
to compare.

7. **Click OK.**

Word creates a new document that shows where changes were made to the original copy or where the revised copies differ (refer to Figure 5-3). You can save this document if you want to.

To help with document comparisons, you can tell Word what to display in the Source Documents pane on the right side of the screen. On the Review tab, click the Compare button, choose Show Source Documents, and choose an option on the submenu. You can hide the source documents, show the original document, show the revised edition, or show both editions.

Accepting and rejecting changes to a document

Word gives you the chance to accept or reject changes one at a time, but in my considerable experience with changes (I am a sometime editor), I find that the best way to handle changes is to go through the document, reject the changes you don't care for, and when you have finished reviewing, accept all the remaining changes. That way, reviewing changes is only half as tedious.

Whatever your preference for accepting or rejecting changes, start by selecting a change. To do so, either click it or click the Previous or Next button on the Review tab to locate it in your document. With the change selected, do one of the following:

✦ **Accept a change:** Click the Accept button or open the drop-down list on the Accept button and choose Accept Change or Accept and Move to Next. You can also right-click and choose Accept Change.

✦ **Reject a change:** Click the Reject button or open the drop-down list on the Reject button and choose Reject Change or Reject and Move to Next. You can also right-click and choose Reject Change.

✦ **Accept all changes:** Open the drop-down list on the Accept button and choose Accept All Changes in Document.

✦ **Reject all changes:** Open the drop-down list on the Reject button and choose Reject All Changes in Document.

 By way of the Accept and Reject buttons, you can also accept or reject all changes made by a single reviewer. First, isolate the reviewer's changes by clicking the Show Markup button, choosing Reviewers, and selecting a reviewer's name. Then open the drop-down list on the Accept or Reject button, and choose Accept All Changes Shown or Reject All Changes Shown.

Printing an Address on an Envelope

Printing addresses gives correspondence a formal, official look. It makes you look like a big shot. (Later in this chapter, "Churning Out Letters, Labels, and Envelopes for Mass Mailings" explains how to print more than one envelope at a time). Here's how to print an address and a return address on an envelope:

1. **To save a bit of time, open the document that holds the letter you want to send; then select the name and address of the person you want to send the letter to.**

   By doing so, you save yourself from having to type the address. However, you don't have to open a document to start with.

 2. **On the Mailings tab, click the Envelopes button (you may have to click the Create button first, depending on the size of your screen).**

   The Envelopes tab of the Envelopes and Labels dialog box appears, as shown in Figure 5-5.

3. **Enter a name and address in the Delivery Address box (the address is already there if you selected it in Step 1).**

4. **Enter your return address in the Return Address box, if you want.**

5. **Click the Omit check box if you don't want your return address to appear on the envelope.**

6. **Click the Options button, and in the Envelope Options dialog box, tell Word what size your envelopes are and how your printer handles envelopes.**

   Tell Word about your envelopes on the Envelope Options and Printing Options tabs, and click OK:

   • *Envelope Options tab:* Choose an envelope size, a font for printing the delivery and return address, and a position for the addresses. The sample envelope in the Preview shows you what your position settings do when the envelope is printed.

- *Printing Options tab:* Choose a technique for feeding envelopes to your printer. Consult the manual that came with your printer, select one of the Feed Method boxes, click the Face Up or Face Down option button, and open the Feed From drop-down list to tell Word which printer tray the envelope is in or how you intend to stick the envelope in your printer.

7. **Click the Print button.**

   All that trouble just to print an address on an envelope!

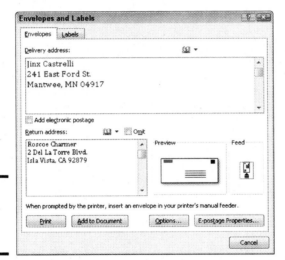

Figure 5-5:
Printing
on an
envelope.

Printing a Single Address Label (Or a Page of the Same Label)

If you need to print a single label or a sheet of labels that are all the same, you can do it. Before you start printing, however, take note of the label's Avery stock number, what size the label is, and its brand name. You are asked about label brands and sizes when you print labels. (Later in this chapter, "Churning Out Letters, Labels, and Envelopes for Mass Mailings" explains how to print multiple labels as part of a mass mailing.)

Follow these steps to print a single label or a sheet full of identical labels:

1. **On the Mailings tab, click the Labels button (you may have to click the Create button first, depending on the size of your screen).**

   You see the Labels tab of the Envelopes and Labels dialog box, as shown in Figure 5-6.

Figure 5-6:
Printing
labels.

2. **Enter the label — the name and address — in the Address box.**

3. **Either click the Options button or click the label icon in the Label box to open the Label Options dialog box.**

4. **In the Printer Information area, select either Continuous-Feed Printers or Page Printers to declare which kind of printer you have; on the Tray drop-down list, choose the option that describes how you will feed labels to your printer.**

5. **Open the Label Vendors drop-down list and choose the brand or type of labels that you have.**

    If your brand is not on the list, click the Details button, and describe your labels in the extremely confusing Information dialog box. A better way, however, is to measure your labels and see whether you can find a label of the same size by experimenting with Product Number and Label Information combinations.

6. **In the Product Number menu, select the product number listed on the box that your labels came in.**

    Look in the Label Information box on the right to make sure that the Height, Width, and Page Size measurements match those of the labels you have.

7. **Click OK to return to the Envelopes and Labels dialog box.**

8. **Choose a Print option.**

    Tell Word to print a single label or a sheet full of labels:

    *   *Full Page of the Same Label:* Select this option button if you want to print a pageful of the same label. Likely, you'd choose this option to

print a pageful of your own return addresses. Click the New Document button after you make this choice. Word creates a new document with a pageful of labels. Save and print this document on a sheet of labels.

- *Single Label:* Select this option button to print one label. Then enter the row and column where the label is located and click the Print button.

Churning Out Letters, Envelopes, and Labels for Mass Mailings

Thanks to the miracle of computing, you can churn out form letters, labels, and envelopes for a mass mailing in the privacy of your home or office, just as the big companies do. Churning out form letters, envelopes, and labels is easy, as long as you take the time to prepare the source file. The *source file* is the file that the names and addresses come from. A Word table or Excel worksheet can serve as the source.

To generate form letters, envelopes, or labels, you merge the form letter, envelope, or label document with a source file. Word calls this process *merging.* During the merge, names and addresses from the source file are plugged into the appropriate places in the form letter, envelope, or label document. When the merge is complete, you can either save the form letters, envelopes, or labels in a new file or start printing right away.

The following pages explain how to prepare the source file and merge addresses from the source file with a document to create form letters, labels, or envelopes. Then you discover how to print the form letters, labels, or envelopes after you have generated them.

Word offers a mail-merge wizard (*wizard* is Microsoft's name for a step-by-step procedure you can follow to accomplish a task). If you want to try your hand at using the wizard to complete a mail merge, go to the Mailings tab, click the Start Mail Merge button, and choose Step by Step Mail Merge Wizard on the drop-down list. Good luck to you!

Preparing the source file

If you haven't entered the addresses yet or you are keeping them in a Word table or Excel worksheet, make sure that the data is in good working order:

- ✦ **Word table:** Save the table in its own file and enter a descriptive heading at the top of each column. In the merge, when you tell Word where to plug in address and other data, you will do so by choosing a heading name from the top of a column. In Figure 5-7, for example, the column headings are Last Name, First Name, Street, and so on. (Book I, Chapter 5 explains how to construct a Word table.)

Figure 5-7:
A Word source table for a mail merge.

Last Name	First Name	Street	City	State	ZIP	Birthday
Creed	Hank	443 Oak St.	Atherton	CA	93874	July 31
Daws	Leon	13 Spruce St.	Colma	CA	94044	April 1
Maves	Carlos	11 Guy St.	Reek	NV	89201	February 28
Ng	Winston	1444 Unger Ave.	Colma	CA	94404	November 12
Smith	Jane	121 First St.	Colma	CA	94044	January 10
Weiss	Shirley	441 Second St.	Poltroon	ID	49301	May 4

✦ **Excel worksheet:** Arrange the worksheet in table format with a descriptive heading atop each column and no blank cells in any columns. Word will plug in the address and other data by choosing heading names.

A Word table or Excel worksheet can include more than address information. Don't worry about deleting information that isn't required for your form letters, labels, and envelopes. As you find out soon, you get to decide which information to include from the Word table or Excel worksheet.

Merging the document with the source file

After you prepare the source file, the next step in generating form letters, labels, or envelopes for a mass mailing is to merge the document with the source file. Follow these general steps to do so:

1. **Create or open a document.**

- *Form letters:* Either create a new document and write your form letter, being careful to leave out the parts of the letter that differ from recipient to recipient, or open a letter you have already written and delete the addressee's name, the address, and other parts of the letter that are particular to each recipient.

- *Envelopes:* Create a new document.

- *Labels:* Create a new document.

2. **On the Mailings tab, click the Start Mail Merge button.**

3. **Choose Letters, Envelopes, or Labels on the drop-down list.**

4. **Prepare the groundwork for creating form letters, envelopes, or labels for a mass mailing.**

What you do next depends on what kind of mass mailing you want to attempt:

- *Form letters:* You're ready to go. The text of your form letter already appears on-screen if you followed the directions for creating and writing it in Step 1.

- *Envelopes:* You see the Envelope Options dialog box, where, on the Envelope Options and Printing Options tabs, you tell Word what size envelope you will print on. See "Printing an Address on an Envelope," earlier in this chapter, for instructions about filling out these tabs (see Step 6). A sample envelope appears on-screen.

- *Labels:* You see the Label Options dialog box, where you tell Word what size labels to print on. See "Printing a Single Address Label (Or a Page of the Same Label)" earlier in this chapter, if you need advice for filling out this dialog box (refer to Steps 4 through 7).

5. Click the Select Recipients button and choose an option on the drop-down list to direct Word to your source file or the source of your address and data information.

Earlier in this chapter, "Preparing the source file" explains what a source file is. Your options are as follows:

- *Addresses from a Word table:* Choose Use Existing List. You see the Select Data Source dialog box. Locate the Word file, select it, and click Open.

- *Addresses from an Excel worksheet:* Choose Use Existing List. You see the Select Data Source dialog box. Locate the file, select it, and click Open. The Select Table dialog box appears. Select the worksheet that you want and click the OK button.

6. Click the Edit Recipient List button.

The Mail Merge Recipients dialog box appears, as shown in Figure 5-8.

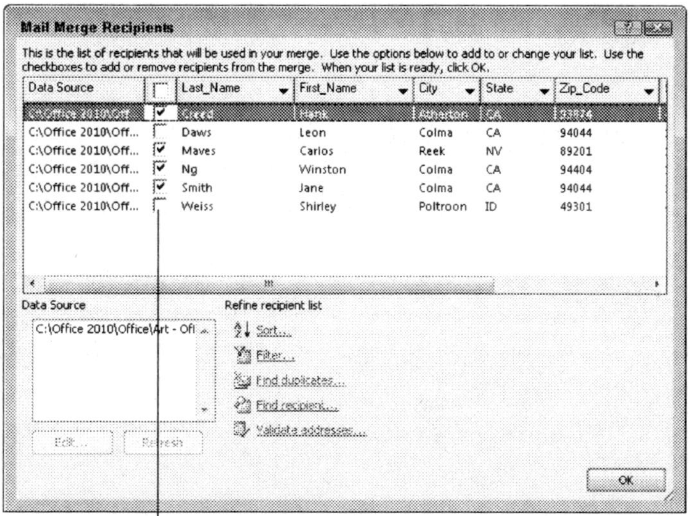

Figure 5-8: Choosing who gets mail.

Choose the names of recipients

7. **In the Mail Merge Recipients dialog box, select the names of people to whom you will send mail; then click OK.**

   To select recipients' names, check or uncheck the boxes on the left side of the dialog box.

8. **Enter the address block on your form letters, envelopes, or labels.**

   The *address block* is the address, including the recipient's name, company, title, street address, city, and ZIP Code. If you're creating form letters, click in the sample letter where the address block will go. If you're printing on envelopes, click in the middle of the envelope where the delivery address will go. Then follow these steps to enter the address block:

   a. Click the Address Block button. The Insert Address Block dialog box appears, as shown in Figure 5-9.

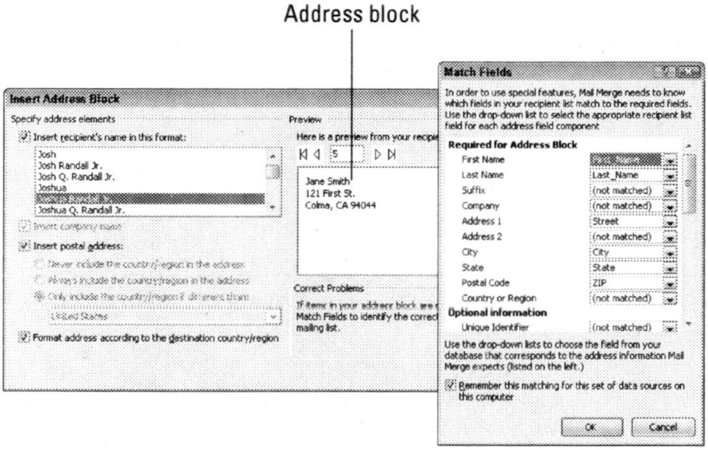

Address block

Figure 5-9: Creating the address block (left) and linking it with address fields (right).

b. Choose a format for entering the recipient's name in the address block. As you do so, watch the Preview window; it shows the actual names and addresses that you selected in Step 7.

c. Click the Match Fields button. You see the Match Fields dialog box, shown in Figure 5-9.

d. Using the drop-down lists on the right side of the dialog box, match the fields in your source file with the address block fields on the left side of the dialog box. In Figure 5-9, for example, the Street field is the equivalent of the Address 1 field on the left side of the dialog box, so Street is chosen from the drop-down list to match Address 1.

e. Click OK in the Match Fields dialog box and the Insert Address Block dialog box. The <<AddressBlock>> field appears in the document where the address will go. Later, when you merge your document with the data source, real data will appear where the field is now. Think of a field as a kind of placeholder for data.

9. Click the Preview Results button on the Mailings tab to see real data rather than fields.

Now you can see clearly whether you entered the address block correctly. If you didn't enter it correctly, click the Match Fields button (it's in the Write & Insert Fields group) to open the Match Fields dialog box and make new choices.

10. Put the finishing touches on your form letters, labels, or envelopes:

- *Form letters:* Click where the salutation ("Dear John") will go and then click the Greeting Line button. You see the Insert Greeting Line dialog box, shown in Figure 5-10. Make choices in this dialog box to determine how the letters' salutations will read.

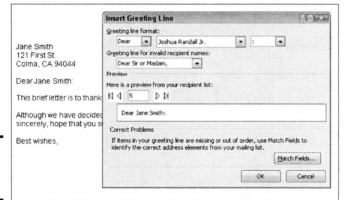

Figure 5-10: Entering the greeting.

The body of your form letter may well include other variable information such as names and birthdays. To enter that stuff, click in your letter where variable information goes and then click the Insert Merge Field button. The Insert Merge Field dialog box appears and lists fields from the source file. Select a field, click the Insert button, and click the Close button. (You can also open the drop-down list on the Insert Merge Field button and choose a field from the source file.)

If you're editing your form letter and you need to see precisely where the variable information you entered is located, click the Highlight Merge Fields button. The variable information is highlighted in your document.

- *Envelopes:* To position the address block correctly, you may have to press the Enter key and tab keys to move it to the center of the envelope. If you don't like the fonts or font sizes on the envelope, select an address, go to the Home tab, and change fonts and font sizes there.

    To enter a return address, click in the upper-left corner of the envelope and enter it there.

- *Labels:* Click the Update Labels button to enter all recipients' labels in the sample document.

11. Click the Next Record and Previous Record buttons on the Mailings tab to skip from recipient to recipient and make sure that you have entered information correctly.

These buttons are located in the Preview Results group. The items you see on-screen are the same form letters, envelopes, or labels you will see when you have finished printing. (Click the Preview Results button if you see field names rather than people's names and addresses).

If an item is incorrect, open the source file and correct it there. When you save the source file, the correction is made in the sample document.

At last — you're ready to print the form letters, envelopes, or labels. Take a deep breath and keep reading.

Printing form letters, envelopes, and labels

After you have gone to the trouble to prepare the data file and merge it with the document, you're ready to print your form letters, envelopes, or labels. Start by loading paper, envelopes, or sheets of labels in your printer:

- ✦ **Form letters:** Form letters are easiest to print. Just put the paper in the printer.

- ✦ **Envelopes:** Not all printers are capable of printing envelopes one after the other. Sorry, but you probably have to consult the dreary manual that came with your printer to find out the correct way to load envelopes.

- ✦ **Labels:** Load the label sheets in your printer.

Now, to print the form letters, envelopes, or labels, save the material in a new document or send it straight to the printer:

- ✦ **Saving in a new document:** Click the Finish & Merge button and choose Edit Individual Documents (or press Alt+Shift+N). You see the Merge to New Document dialog box. Click OK. After Word creates the document, save it and print it. You can go into the document and make changes here and there before printing. In form letters, for example, you can write a sentence or two in different letters to personalize them.

✦ **Printing right away:** Click the Finish & Merge button and choose Print Documents (or press Alt+Shift+M) to print the form letters, envelopes, or labels without saving them in a document. Click OK in the Merge to Printer dialog box and then negotiate the Print dialog box.

Save the form letters, labels, or envelopes in a new document if you intend to print them at a future date or ink is running low on your printer and you may have to print in two or more batches. Saving in a new document permits you to generate the mass mailing without having to start all over again with the merge process and all its tedium.

Determining what revision marks look like

As "Tracking Changes to Documents" explains earlier in this chapter, in Print Layout and Web Layout view, comments and revisions appear in balloons on the right side of the screen. Sometimes seeing revisions and comments in balloons is helpful; sometimes it's hard to make sense of them when they're so far to the side of the page.

To hide or display balloons in Print Layout and Web Layout view, you can click the Show Markup button on the Review tab, choose Balloons, and choose an option on the submenu:

✔ Show Revisions in Balloons displays the balloons.

✔ Show All Revisions Inline moves comments and revisions onto the page and effectively lets all the air out of the balloons.

✔ Show Only Comments and Formatting in Balloons shows comments only, not revision marks.

Chapter 6: Tools for Reports and Scholarly Papers

In This Chapter

✓ Putting a list in alphabetical order

✓ Working in Outline view

✓ Creating a table of contents

✓ Indexing and cross-referencing your work

✓ Managing footnotes and endnotes

✓ Putting together a bibliography

T his chapter is hereby dedicated to everyone who has had to delve into the unknown and write a report about it. Writing reports, manuals, and scholarly papers is not easy. You have to explore uncharted territory. You have to contemplate the ineffable. And you have to write bibliographies and footnotes and maybe an index, too. Word cannot take you directly to uncharted territory, but it can take some of the sting out of it.

This chapter explains how to handle footnotes and endnotes, generate a table of contents, index a document, include cross-references in documents, and stitch together a bibliography.

Alphabetizing a List

Which comes first in an alphabetical list, "San Jose, California" or "San José, Costa Rica"? You could research the matter on your own, delving into various dictionaries and online references, or you could rely on the Sort button for the answer. Follow these steps to quickly alphabetize a list:

1. **Select the list.**

2. **On the Home page, click the Sort button.**

   You see the Sort Text dialog box. The Then By options are for sorting tables; they don't concern you, because you're sorting a list.

3. **Click OK.**

   That was easy.

Outlines for Organizing Your Work

Outline view is a great way to see at a glance how your document is organized and whether you need to organize it differently. To take advantage of
this feature, you must have assigned heading styles to the headings in your
document (Chapter 3 of this mini-book explains styles). In Outline view, you
can see all the headings in your document. If a section is in the wrong place,
you can move it simply by dragging an icon or by clicking one of the buttons
on the Outlining tab. To change the rank of a heading, simply click a button
to promote or demote it.

 To switch to Outline view, click the Outline button on the status bar or go to
the View tab and click the Outline button. You see the Outlining tab, as
shown in Figure 6-1. Rather than see text, you see the headings in your document, as well as the first line underneath each heading. Now you get a sense
of what is in your document and whether it is organized well. By choosing an
option from the Show Level drop-down list, you can decide which headings
to see on-screen.

To leave Outline view when you're done reorganizing your document, click
the Close Outline View button or a view button apart from Outline on the
status bar.

Choose which headings to see

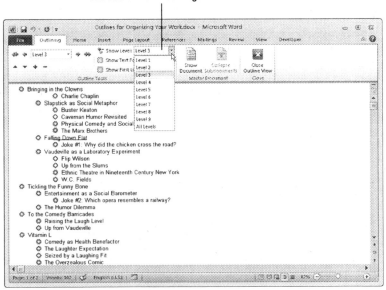

Figure 6-1:
A document
in Outline
view.

Viewing the outline in different ways

Before you start rearranging your document in Outline view, get a good look at it:

Book II
Chapter 6

Tools for Reports
and Scholarly
Papers

✦ **View some or all headings:** Choose an option from the Show Level drop-down list. To see only first-level headings, for example, choose Level 1. To see first-, second-, and third-level headings, choose Level 3. Choose All Levels to see all the headings.

✦ **View heading formats:** Click the Show Text Formatting check box. When this check box is selected, you can see how headings were formatted and get a better idea of their ranking in your document.

✦ **View or hide the subheadings in one section:** To see or hide the subheadings and text in one section of a document, select that section by clicking the plus sign beside its heading; then, click the Expand button (or press Alt+Shift+plus sign) to see the subheadings, or click the Collapse button (or press Alt+Shift+minus sign) to hide the subheadings. You can also double-click the plus sign beside a heading to view or hide its subheadings.

✦ **View or hide paragraph text:** Click the Show First Line Only check box (or press Alt+Shift+L). When this check box is selected, you see only the first line in each paragraph. First lines are followed by an ellipsis (. . .) so that you know that more text follows.

Notice the plus and minus icons next to the headings and the text. A plus icon means that the item has subheadings and text under it. For example, headings almost always have plus icons because text comes after them. A minus icon means that nothing is found below the item in question. For example, body text usually has a minus icon because body text is lowest on the Outline totem pole.

Rearranging document sections in Outline view

Outline view is mighty convenient for moving sections in a document and for promoting and demoting sections. Use these techniques to rearrange and reorganize your document:

✦ **Move a section:** To move a section up or down in the document, select it and click the Move Up or Move Down button (or press Alt+Shift+↑ or Alt+Shift+↓). You can also drag the plus sign to a new location. If you want to move the subheadings and subordinate text along with the section, be sure to click the Collapse button to tuck all the subheadings and subtext into the heading before you move it.

✦ **Promote and demote headings:** Click the heading and then click the Promote button or Demote button (or press Alt+Shift+← or Alt+Shift+→). For example, you can promote a Level 3 heading to Level 2 by clicking the

Promote button. Click the Promote To Heading 1 button to promote any heading to a first-level heading; click the Demote To Body text button to turn a heading into prose.

✦ **Choose a new level for a heading:** Click the heading and choose a new heading level from the Outline Level drop-down list.

Generating a Table of Contents

A book-size document or long report isn't worth very much without a table of contents (TOC). How else can readers find what they're looking for? Generating a table of contents with Word is easy, as long as you give the headings in the document different styles — Heading 1, Heading 2, and so on (Chapter 3 of this mini-book explains styles). The beautiful thing about Word TOCs is the way they can be updated nearly instantly. If you add a new heading or erase a heading, you can update the TOC with a snap of your fingers. Moreover, you can quickly go from a TOC entry to its corresponding heading in a document by Ctrl+clicking the entry.

Before you create your TOC, create a new section in which to put it and number the pages in the new section with Roman numerals (Chapter 2 of this mini-book explains sections and how to number pages). TOCs, including the TOC in this book, are usually numbered in this way. The first entry in the TOC should cite page number 1. If you don't heed my advice and create a new section, the TOC will occupy the first few numbered pages of your document, and the numbering scheme will be thrown off.

Creating a TOC

To create a table of contents, place the cursor where you want the TOC to go, visit the References tab, and click the Table of Contents button. On the drop-down list, choose one of Word's automatic TOC options or choose Insert Table of Contents to fashion a TOC on your own in the Table of Contents dialog box. (See "Customizing a TOC," later in this chapter, for information about fashioning a TOC in the Table of Contents dialog box.)

Suppose that you want to copy a TOC to another document? To copy a TOC, drag the pointer down its left margin to select it, and then press Ctrl+Shift+F9. Next, use the Copy and Paste commands to copy the TOC to the other document. Because Word gives the text of TOCs the Hyperlink character style, you have to change the color of the text in the TOC (it's blue) and remove the underlines. As for the original TOC, you "disconnected" it from the headings in your document when you pressed Ctrl+Shift+F9. Press the Undo button to undo the effects of pressing Ctrl+Shift+F9 and "disconnecting" your TOC from the headers to which it refers.

Updating and removing a TOC

Follow these instructions to update and remove a TOC:

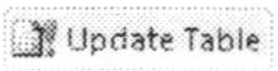

Update Table

+ **Updating a TOC:** If you add, remove, or edit a heading in your document, your TOC needs updating. To update it, go to the References tab and click the Update Table button, or click in the TOC and press F9. A dialog box asks how to update the TOC. Either update the page numbers only or update the entire table, including all TOC entries and page numbers.

+ **Removing a TOC:** On the References tab, click the Table of Contents button and choose Remove Table of Contents on the drop-down list.

Customizing a TOC

Want to tinker with your TOC? You can number the headings in different ways and tell Word to include or exclude certain headings.

To change around a TOC, click inside it, go to the References tab, click the Table of Contents button, and choose Insert Table of Contents on the drop-down list. You see the Table of Contents dialog box shown in Figure 6-2. Choose options to declare which headings you want for your TOC and how you want to format it:

+ **Showing page numbers:** Deselect the Show Page Numbers box if you want your TOC to be a simple list that doesn't refer to headings by page.

+ **Aligning the page numbers:** Select the Right Align Page Numbers check box if you want page numbers to line up along the right side of the TOC so that the ones and tens line up under each other.

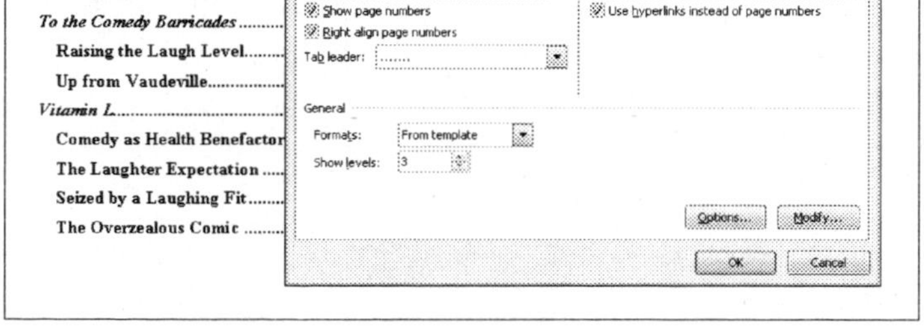

Book II
Chapter 6

Tools for Reports and Scholarly Papers

Figure 6-2:
You can decide for yourself which headings go in a TOC and how it's numbered.

✦ **Choosing a tab leader:** A *leader* is the punctuation mark that appears between the heading and the page number the heading is on. If you don't want periods as the leader, choose another leader or choose (None).

✦ **Choosing a format:** Choose a format from the Formats drop-down list if you don't care to use the one from the template. Just be sure to watch the Print Preview and Web Preview boxes to see the results of your choice.

✦ **Choosing a TOC depth:** The Show Levels box determines how many heading levels are included in the TOC. Unless your document is a legal contract or other formal paper, enter a **2** or **3** here. A TOC is supposed to help readers find information quickly. Including lots of headings that take a long time to read through defeats the purpose of having a TOC.

Changing the structure of a TOC

Sometimes the conventional TOC that Word generates doesn't do the trick. Just because a heading has been given the Heading 1 style doesn't mean that it should receive first priority in the TOC. Suppose that you created another style called Chapter Title that should stand taller in the hierarchy than Heading 1. In that case, you need to rearrange the TOC so that Heading 1 headings rank second, not first, in the TOC hierarchy.

Use the Table of Contents Options and Style dialog boxes to tinker with a TOC. These dialog boxes are shown in Figure 6-3. To open them, click, respectively, the Options button or Modify button in the Table of Contents dialog box (refer to Figure 6-2).

✦ **Assigning TOC levels to paragraph styles:** The Table of Contents Options dialog box lists each paragraph style in the document you're working in. For headings you want to appear in the TOC, enter a number in the TOC Level text box to determine the headings' rank. If headings assigned the Heading 1 style are to rank second in the TOC, for example, enter a 2 in Heading 1's TOC Level text box. You can exclude headings from a TOC by deleting a number in a TOC Level box.

✦ **Including table entry fields:** To include text you marked for entry in the TOC, select the Table Entry Fields check box in the Table of Contents Options dialog box (later in this chapter, the sidebar "Marking oddball text for inclusion in the TOC" explains how TOC fields work).

✦ **Changing the look of TOC entries:** The Style dialog box you see when you click the Modify button gives you the chance to choose new fonts, character styles, and font sizes for TOC entries if you generated your TOC from a template. Click the Modify button. Then, in the Style dialog box, choose options to format the TOC style. For example, click the Bold button to boldface TOC entries. (Chapter 3 of this mini-book explains modifying styles.)

Marking oddball text for inclusion in the TOC

Table of contents entries can refer to a particular place in a document, not just to headings that have been assigned heading styles. For example, you can include figure captions.

Use one of these techniques to mark an entry in your document for inclusion in the TOC:

- Click in the heading, figure caption, or whatnot. Next, click the Add Text button on the References tab and choose a TOC level on the drop-down list (the Do Not Show in Table of Contents option keeps text from being included in the TOC). If you choose Level 2, for example, the entry appears with other second-level headings.

- Click in a heading or text and press Alt+Shift+O. Then, in the Mark Table of Contents Entry dialog box, make sure that the words you want to appear in the TOC appear in the Entry text box (edit or enter the words if need be), and make sure that C (for Contents) appears in the Table Identifier box. In the Level box, enter a number to tell Word how to treat the entry when you generate the table of contents. For example, entering **1** tells Word to treat the entry like a first-level heading and give it top priority. A **3** places the entry with the third-level headings. Finally, click the Mark button.

When you generate the table of contents, be sure to include the oddball entries. To do that, click the Options button in the Table of Contents dialog box and, in the Table of Contents Options dialog box (refer to Figure 6-3), select the Table Entry Fields check box.

Figure 6-3:
Changing
a TOC's
structure
and
formatting.

Indexing a Document

A good index is a thing of beauty. User manuals, reference works of any length, and reports that readers will refer to all require indexes. Except for the table of contents, the only way to find information in a long document is to look in the index. An index at the end of a company report reflects well on the person who wrote the report. It gives the appearance that the author put in a fair amount of time to complete the work, even if he or she didn't really do that.

An index entry can be formatted in many ways. You can cross-reference index entries, list a page range in an index entry, and break out an index entry into subentries and sub-subentries. To help you with your index, Figure 6-4 explains indexing terminology.

Main entry

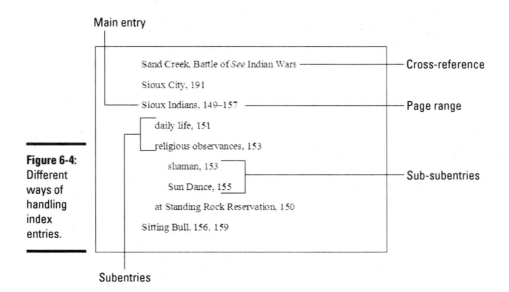

Sand Creek, Battle of *See* Indian Wars ———— Cross-reference

Sioux City, 191

Sioux Indians, 149–157 ———— Page range

daily life, 151

religious observances, 153

shaman, 153

Sun Dance, 155 ———— Sub-subentries

at Standing Rock Reservation, 150

Sitting Bull, 156, 159

Figure 6-4:
Different ways of handling index entries.

Subentries

 Writing a good index entry is as hard as writing a good, descriptive heading. As you enter index entries in your document, ask yourself how you would look up information in the index, and enter your index entries accordingly.

Marking index items in the document

The first step in constructing an index is to mark index entries in your document. Marking index items yourself is easier than it seems. After you open the Mark Index Entry dialog box, it stays open so that you can scroll through your document and make entries. (At the end of this chapter, the sidebar "Marking index entries with a concordance file" explains a quick but not very thorough method of marking index entries.)

Follow these steps to mark entries for an index:

1. **If you see a word or phrase in your document that you can use as a main, top-level entry, select it; otherwise, place the cursor in the paragraph or heading whose topic you want to include in the index.**

You can save a little time by selecting a word, as I describe shortly.

 2. **On the References tab, click the Mark Entry button (or press Alt+Shift+X).**

The Mark Index Entry dialog box appears. If you selected a word or phrase, it appears in the Main Entry box.

3. **Choose how you want to handle this index entry (refer to Figure 6-4 to see the various ways to make index entries).**

When you enter the text, don't put a comma or period after it. Word does that when it generates the index. The text that you enter appears in your index.

- *Main Entry:* If you're entering a main, top-level entry, leave the text in the Main Entry box (if it's already there), type new text to describe this entry, or edit the text that's already there. Leave the Subentry box blank.

- *Subentry:* To create a subentry, enter text in the Subentry box. The subentry text will appear in the index below the main entry text, so make sure that some text is in the Main Entry box and that the subentry text fits under the main entry.

- *Sub-subentry:* A sub-subentry is the third level in the hierarchy. To create a sub-subentry, type the subentry in the Subentry box, enter a colon (:), and type the sub-subentry without entering a space, like so: **religious observances:shaman.**

4. **Decide how to handle the page reference in the entry.**

Again, your choices are many:

- *Cross-reference:* To go without a page reference and refer the reader to another index entry, click the Cross-Reference option button and type the other entry in the text box after the word *See.* What you type here appears in your index, so be sure that the topic you refer the reader to is really named in your index.

- *Current Page:* Click this option to enter a single page number after the entry.

- *Page Range:* Click this option if you're indexing a subject that covers several pages in your document. A page range index entry looks something like this: "Sioux Indians, 149–157." To make a page range entry, you must create a bookmark first. Leave the Mark Index Entry dialog box, select the text in the page range, and press Ctrl+Shift+F5 or click the Bookmark button on the Insert tab. In the Bookmark dialog box, enter a name in the Bookmark Name box, and click the Add button. (Chapter 1 of this mini-book explains bookmarks.)

5. **You can boldface or italicize a page number or page range by clicking a Page Number Format check box.**

In some indexes, the page or page range where the topic is explained in the most depth is italicized or boldfaced so that readers can get to the juiciest parts first.

**Book II
Chapter 6**

**Tools for Reports
and Scholarly
Papers**

6. **If you selected a single word or phrase in Step 1, you can click the Mark All button to have Word go through the document and mark all words that are identical to the one in the Main Entry box; click Mark to put this single entry in the index.**

   Click outside the Mark Index Entry dialog box and find the next topic or word that you want to mark for the index. Then click the Mark Entry button on the References tab and make another entry.

A bunch of ugly field codes appear in your document after you mark an index entry. You can render them invisible by clicking the Show/Hide ¶ button on the Home tab (or pressing Ctrl+Shift+8).

Generating the index

After you mark all the index entries, it's time to generate the index:

1. **Place the cursor where you want the index to go, most likely at the end of the document.**

   You might type the word **Index** at the top of the page and format the word in a decorative way.

📄 Insert Index

2. **On the References tab, click the Insert Index button.**

   You see the Index dialog box shown in Figure 6-5.

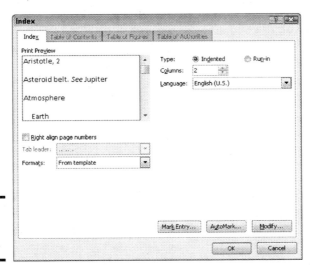

Figure 6-5:
Generating an index.

3. **Choose options in the dialog box and click OK.**

   As you make your choices, watch the Print Preview box to see what happens.

Here are the options in the Index dialog box:

✦ **Type:** Choose Run-in if you want subentries and sub-subentries to run together; choose Indented to indent subentries and sub-subentries below main entries (refer to Figure 6-4).

✦ **Columns:** Stick with 2, unless you don't have subentries or sub-subentries and you can squeeze three columns on the page or you are working on a landscape document.

✦ **Language:** Choose a language for the table, if necessary and if you have installed a foreign language dictionary. If you have installed the dictionary, you can run the spell-checker over your index and make sure that the entries are spelled correctly. (Book I, Chapter 4 explains foreign language dictionaries.)

✦ **Right Align Page Numbers:** Normally, page numbers appear right after entries and are separated from entries by a comma, but you can right-align the entries so that they line up under one another with this option.

✦ **Tab Leader:** Some index formats place a *leader* between the entry and the page number. A leader is a series of dots or dashes. If you're working with a format that has a leader, you can choose a leader from the drop-down list.

✦ **Formats:** Word offers a number of attractive index layouts. You can choose one from the list.

✦ **Modify:** Click this button if you're adventurous and want to create an index style of your own (Chapter 3 explains styles).

Update Index   To update an index after you create or delete entries, click it and then click the Update Index button or right-click the index and then choose Update Field on the shortcut menu.

Editing an index

After you generate an index, read it carefully to make sure that all entries are useful to readers. Inevitably, something doesn't come out right, but you can edit index entries as you would the text in a document. Index field markers are enclosed in curly brackets with the letters *XE* and the text of the index entry in quotation marks, like so: `{ XE: "Wovoka: Ghost Dance" }`. To edit an index marker, click the Show/Hide ¶ button on the Home tab (or press Ctrl+Shift+8) to see the field markers and find the one you need to edit. Then delete letters or type letters as you would do normal text.

Here's a quick way to find index field markers: After clicking the Show/Hide ¶ button, with the index fields showing, press Ctrl+G to open the Go To tab of the Find and Replace dialog box. In the Go to What menu, choose Field; type **XE** in the Enter Field Name box, and click the Next button until you find the marker you want to edit. You can also use the Find command on the Home tab to look for index entries. Word finds index entries as well as text as long as you click the Show/Hide ¶ button to display index fields in your document.

Putting Cross-References in a Document

Cross-references are very handy indeed. They tell readers where to go to find more information about a topic. The problem with cross-references, however, is that the thing being cross-referenced really has to be there. If you tell readers to go to a heading called "The Cat's Pajamas" on page 93, and neither the heading nor the page is really there, readers curse and tell you where to go, instead of the other way around.

Fortunately for you, Word lets you know when you make errant cross-references. You can refer readers to headings, page numbers, footnotes, endnotes, and plain-old paragraphs. And as long you create captions for your cross-references with the Insert Caption button on the References tab, you can also make cross-references to equations, figures, graphs, listings, programs, and tables. If you delete the thing that a cross-reference refers to and render the cross-reference invalid, Word tells you about it the next time you update your cross-references. Best of all, if the page number, numbered item, or text that a cross-reference refers to changes, so does the cross-reference.

Follow these steps to create a cross-reference:

1. Write the first part of the cross-reference text.

For example, you could write **To learn more about these cowboys of the pampas, see page** and then type a blank space. The blank space separates the word *page* from the page number in the cross-reference. If you are referring to a heading, write something like **For more information, see "**. Don't type a blank space this time because the cross-reference heading text will appear right after the double quotation mark.

2. On the References tab, click the Cross-Reference button.

The Cross-Reference dialog box appears, as shown in Figure 6-6.

3. Choose what type of item you're referring to in the Reference Type drop-down list.

If you're referring to a plain old paragraph, choose Bookmark. Then click outside the dialog box, scroll to the paragraph you're referring to, and place a bookmark there (Chapter 1 of this mini-book explains bookmarks.)

4. Make a choice in the Insert Reference To box to refer to text, a page number, or a numbered item.

The options in this box are different, depending on what you chose in Step 3.

- *Text:* Choose this option (Heading Text, Entire Caption, and so on) to include text in the cross-reference. For example, choose Heading Text if your cross-reference is to a heading.

- *Number:* Choose this option to insert a page number or other kind of number, such as a table number, in the cross-reference.

- *Include Above/Below:* Check this box to include the word *above* or *below* to tell readers where, in relation to the cross-reference, the thing being referred to is located in your document.

5. **If you wish, leave the check mark in the Insert as Hyperlink check box to create a hyperlink as well as a cross-reference.**

   With a hyperlink, someone reading the document on-screen can Ctrl+click the cross-reference and go directly to what it refers to.

6. **In the For Which box, tell Word where the thing you're referring to is located.**

   To do so, select a heading, bookmark, footnote, endnote, equation, figure, graph, or whatnot. In long documents, you almost certainly have to click the scrollbar to find the one you want.

7. **Click the Insert button and then click the Close button.**

8. **Back in your document, enter the rest of the cross-reference text, if necessary.**

Choose what the reference refers to

Choose how to refer to the item

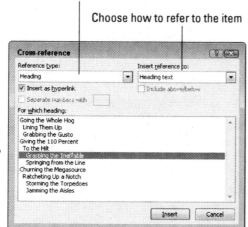

Figure 6-6:
Entering
a cross-
reference.

When you finish creating your document, update all the cross-references. To do that, press Ctrl+A to select the entire document. Then press F9 or right-click in the document and choose Update Field on the shortcut menu.

If the thing referred to in a cross-reference is no longer in your document, you see `Error! Reference source not found` where the cross-reference should be. To find cross-reference errors in long documents, look for the word *Error!* with the Find command (press Ctrl+F). Investigate what went wrong, and repair or delete errant cross-references.

Putting Footnotes and Endnotes in Documents

A *footnote* is a bit of explanation, a comment, or a reference that appears at the bottom of the page and is referred to by a number or symbol in the text. An *endnote* is the same thing, except that it appears at the end of the section, chapter, or document. If you've written a scholarly paper of any kind, you know what a drag footnotes and endnotes are.

You will be glad to know that Word takes some of the drudgery out of footnotes and endnotes. For example, if you delete or add a note, all notes after the one you added or deleted are renumbered. And you don't have to worry about long footnotes because Word adjusts the page layout to make room for them. You can change the numbering scheme of footnotes and endnotes at will. When you are reviewing a document, all you have to do is move the pointer over a footnote or endnote citation. The note icon appears, as does a pop-up box with the text of the note.

Entering a footnote or endnote

To enter a footnote or endnote in a document:

1. **Place the cursor in the text where you want the note's number or symbol to appear.**

2. **On the References tab, click the Insert Footnote button (or press Ctrl+Alt+F) or the Insert Endnote button (or press Ctrl+Alt+D).**

   If you are in Draft view, the Notes pane opens at the bottom of the screen with the cursor beside the number of the note you're about to enter. In Print Layout view, Word scrolls to the bottom of the page or the end of the document or section so that you can enter the note, as shown in Figure 6-7.

3. **Enter your footnote or endnote.**

4. **Click the Close button in the Notes pane if you're in Draft view; in Print Layout view, scroll upward to return to the main text.**

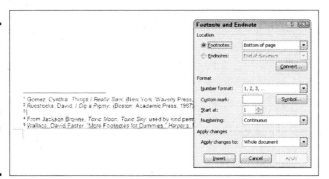

Figure 6-7:
Entering a footnote in Print Layout view (left); the Footnote and Endnote dialog box (right).

 Show Notes   Click the Show Notes button at any time to see your notes in the Notes pane, at the bottom of the page, or at the end of the section or document.

TIP   To quickly return from writing a note to the place in your document where the footnote or endnote number citation is located, double-click the number citation at the bottom of the page (in Print Layout view) or the Notes pane (in Draft view). For example, if you just finished entering footnote 3, double-click the number *3*.

Choosing the numbering scheme and position of notes

Choosing the numbering scheme and positioning of endnotes and footnotes is quite easy. On the References tab, click the Footnotes group button. The Footnote and Endnote dialog box appears (refer to Figure 6-7). Tell Word where to place your notes:

✦ **Footnotes:** Choose Bottom of Page to put footnotes at the bottom of the page no matter where the text ends; choose Below Text to put footnotes directly below the last line of text on the page.

✦ **Endnotes:** Choose End of Section if your document is divided into sections (such as chapters) and you want endnotes to appear at the back of sections; choose End of Document to put all endnotes at the very back of the document.

In the Format area, tell Word how to number the notes:

✦ **Number Format:** Choose A B C, i ii iii, or another numbering scheme, if you want. You can also enter symbols by choosing the last option on this drop-down list.

✦ **Custom Mark:** You can mark the note with a symbol by clicking the Symbol button and choosing a symbol in the Symbol dialog box. If you go this route, you have to enter a symbol each time you insert a note.

Not only that, you may have to enter two or three symbols for the second and third notes on each page or document because Word can't renumber symbols.

✦ **Start At:** To start numbering the notes at a place other than 1, A, or i, enter **2**, **B**, **ii**, or whatever in this box.

✦ **Numbering:** To number the notes continuously from the start of your document to the end, choose Continuous. Choose Restart Each Section to begin anew at each section of your document. For footnotes, you can begin anew on each page by choosing Restart Each Page.

By the way, the Convert button in the Footnote and Endnote dialog box is for fickle scholars who suddenly decide that their endnotes should be footnotes, or vice versa. Click it and choose an option in the Convert Notes dialog box to turn footnotes into endnotes, turn endnotes into footnotes, or — in documents with both endnotes and footnotes — make the endnotes footnotes and the footnotes endnotes.

Deleting, moving, and editing notes

If a devious editor tells you that a footnote or endnote is in the wrong place, that you don't need a note, or that you need to change the text in a note, all is not lost:

✦ **Editing:** To edit a note, double-click its number or symbol in the text. You see the note on-screen. Edit the note at this point.

✦ **Moving:** To move a note, select its number or symbol in the text and drag it to a new location, or cut and paste it to a new location.

✦ **Deleting:** To delete a note, select its number or symbol and press the Delete key.

Footnotes and endnotes are renumbered when you move or delete one of them.

Compiling a Bibliography

A *bibliography* is a list, usually in alphabetical order by author name, of all the books, journal articles, Web sites, interviews, and other sources used in the writing of an article, report, or book. Writing a good bibliography is a chore. Besides keeping careful track of sources, you have to list them correctly. Does the author's name or work's name come first in the citation? How do you list a Web site or magazine article without an author's name?

Word's Bibliography feature is very nice in this regard: It solves the problem of how to enter citations for a bibliography. All you have to do is enter the bare facts about the citation — the author's name, title, publication date, publisher, and so on — and Word presents this information correctly in the bibliography. You can choose among several popular bibliographical styles (APA, Chicago, and others) from the Style drop-down list, as shown in Figure 6-8. After you make your choice, Word reformats all bibliography citations. You don't have to worry about whether titles should be underlined or italicized, or how authors' names should be listed in the bibliography.

Insert a citation   Choose a bibliography style

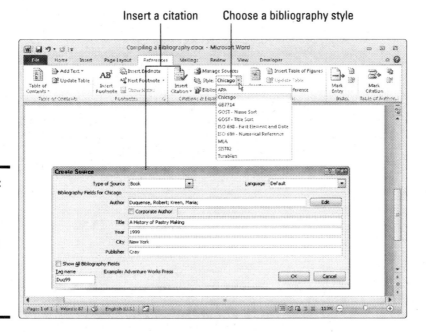

Book II Chapter 6

Tools for Reports and Scholarly Papers

Figure 6-8: Adding a citation (left) and formatting citations (right) for a bibliography.

Inserting a citation for your bibliography

An abbreviated citation appears in the text of your document in between parentheses where you enter a citation; the complete citation appears in the bibliography. After you enter the information about a citation, entering it a second time is easy because Word keeps a master list of all citations you have used in your work, both in the document you're working on and your other documents. To enter a citation, click in your document at the place that refers to the source, go to the References tab, and use one of these techniques to enter the citation:

✦ **Entering a citation you've already entered in your document:** Click the Insert Citation button and choose the citation on the drop-down list. The top of the drop-down list presents citations you've already entered.

✦ **Creating a new citation:** Click the Insert Citation button and choose Add New Source. You see the Create Source dialog box shown in Figure 6-8. Choose an option on the Type of Source drop-down list and enter particulars about the source. You can click the Show All Bibliography Fields check box to enlarge the dialog box and enter all kinds of information about the source. Whether clicking the check box is necessary depends on how detailed you want your bibliography to be.

✦ **Inserting a citation placeholder:** Click the Insert Citation button and choose Add New Placeholder if you're in a hurry and you don't currently have all the information you need to describe the source. The Placeholder Name dialog box appears. Enter a placeholder name for the source and click OK. Later, when you have the information for the source, click the citation in the text and choose Edit Source on its drop-down list. Or you can click the Manage Sources button and then, in the Source Manager dialog box, select the placeholder name (it has a question mark next to it) and click the Edit button. You see the Edit Source dialog box. Enter the information and click OK.

✦ **Inserting a citation you've entered in another document:** Click the Manage Sources button. You see the Source Manager dialog box. In the Master List, select the source you need and click the Copy button. Then click Close and enter the citation by clicking the Insert Citation button and choosing the name of the citation you copied.

Your citation appears in the text in parentheses. Move the pointer over it and you see an inline drop-down list that you can open to edit the citation as it appears in-text as well as edit it in the bibliography, as shown in Figure 6-9.

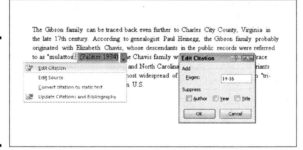

Figure 6-9:
In-text
citations
have inline
drop-down
lists.

Editing a citation

Use one of these techniques to edit a citation:

✦ Open the citation's inline drop-down list (refer to Figure 6-9) and choose Edit Source. You see the Edit Source dialog box, where you can edit the citation.

✦ Click the Manage Sources button on the References tab. The Source Manager dialog box appears. Select the citation, click the Edit button, and change around the citation in the Edit Source dialog box.

Changing how citations appear in text

Citations appear in text enclosed in parentheses. Use one of these techniques to change how a citation appears in the text of your document:

✦ **Changing what's in parentheses:** Open the citation's drop-down list and choose Edit Citation (refer to Figure 6-9). You see the Edit Citation dialog box. To suppress the author's name, year, or title from appearing inside parentheses, click the Author, Year, or Title check box (whether the citation in parentheses lists the author, year, or title depends on which citation style you choose). To make page numbers appear with the citation, enter page numbers in the Pages box.

✦ **Removing the in-text citation:** Swipe over the citation to select it and press Delete. Removing an in-text citation this way does not prevent the citation from appearing in the bibliography.

Generating the bibliography

Go to the References tab and follow these steps to generate your bibliography:

1. **Click in your document where you want the bibliography to appear.**

Probably that place is toward the end of the document.

2. **On the References tab, open the Style drop-down list and choose a style.**

If you're generating your bibliography for a paper you will submit to a journal or institution, ask the editors which style they prefer for bibliographies and choose that style from the list.

3. **Click the Manage Sources button.**

You see the Source Manager dialog box. Citations in the Current List box will appear in your bibliography.

4. **If necessary, address citations in the Current List box.**

If you entered any citation placeholders, their names appear in the list next to question marks. Select these placeholders, click the Edit button, and enter information in the Edit Source dialog box.

To keep a citation from appearing in the bibliography, select it and click the Delete button.

5. **Click the Close button in the Source Manager dialog box.**

6. **Click the Bibliography button and choose a built-in bibliography or the Insert Bibliography command on the drop-down list.**

There it is — your bibliography.

Marking index entries with a concordance file

The concordance file method of marking index entries makes for a quick-and-dirty index. The problem with the concordance file method is that you don't get to review the index entries as you mark them. You simply create a table with words and phrases to look for and tell Word to blindly include an index entry for each word or phrase in the table. However, if your index is strictly for show, if you are slaving away in a cubicle somewhere to produce a document that hardly anyone is going to read anyway, you may as well generate your index with a concordance file. You'll save time that way.

This illustration shows a concordance file, a two-column table with words to look for in the document and their corresponding index entries. The words in the left-hand column of the table are the ones Word searches for. When it finds a word that is listed in the left-hand column, it records the corresponding text in the right-hand column as the index entry along with the page number on which the word is found. For example, upon finding "dirigible" in the left column of the concordance file table shown here, Word enters "zeppelins, 6" (or some other page number) in the index. With the concordance file method of indexing, you can't include page ranges for entries or enter a cross-reference without a page number appearing beside the cross-reference, which looks kind of ridiculous.

dirigible	zeppelins
Mancini	Mancini, Henry
Eagle Steel Works	Manheim:steel manufacturing
Manini	Manini, Betsy
mangos	tropical fruit:history of
whirligig	merry-go-round
subinfeudation	land tenure:history of

Follow these steps to mark entries for an index by using a concordance file:

1. **Create a new Word document.**

2. **Create a two-column table.**

   Book I, Chapter 5 explains how to create tables.

3. **In the left-hand column, type text from your document that you want Word to find and mark for the index.**

   What you enter in the left-hand column is not the index entry itself — just the topic of the entry. For example, to make an index entry on Thomas Mann, type **Mann** in the left column to tell Word to look for all occurrences of that name.

To be indexed, words in your document must be exact matches of the words in the left column. For example, if you type **eagle steel works** in the left column of the concordance file table but the name is "Eagle Steel Works" (with each word capitalized) in your document, the topic won't be indexed because Word won't recognize it.

4. **Save the concordance file when you are finished entering the words and phrases to look for in the left column and the index entries in the right column.**

5. **Open the document that needs indexing.**

6. **On the References tab, click the Insert Index button.**

   The Index dialog box appears.

7. Click the AutoMark button.

You see the Open Index AutoMark File dialog box.

8. Select the concordance file and click the Open button.

Throughout your document, field codes appear where the concordance file marked entries for the index. Now you can generate your index (see "Generating the index," earlier in this chapter).

**Book II
Chapter 6**

**Tools for Reports
and Scholarly
Papers**

Book III

PowerPoint

Contents at a Glance

Chapter 1: Getting Started in PowerPoint 305

Getting Acquainted with PowerPoint..306
A Brief Geography Lesson 308
A Whirlwind Tour of PowerPoint 309
Creating a New Presentation...310
Advice for Building Persuasive Presentations..............................311
Creating New Slides for Your Presentation..................................314
Getting a Better View of Your Work..318
Hiding and Displaying the Slides Pane and Notes Pane 320
Selecting, Moving, and Deleting Slides 321
Putting Together a Photo Album..322

Chapter 2: Fashioning a Look for Your Presentation 327

Looking at Themes and Background Styles 327
Choosing a Theme for Your Presentation....................................329
Creating Slide Backgrounds on Your Own 330
Changing the Background of a Single or Handful of Slides 336
Using Master Slides and Master Styles for a Consistent Design...........337

Chapter 3: Entering the Text 341

Entering Text..341
Fun with Text Boxes and Text Box Shapes 344
Controlling How Text Fits in Text Frames and Text Boxes...................346
Positioning Text in Frames and Text Boxes.................................349
Handling Bulleted and Numbered Lists 350
Putting Footers (and Headers) on Slides......................................352

Chapter 4: Making Your Presentations Livelier 357

Suggestions for Enlivening Your Presentation 357
Exploring Transitions and Animations 359
Making Audio Part of Your Presentation.....................................362
Playing Video on Slides...365
Recording a Voice Narration for PowerPoint 367

Chapter 5: Delivering a Presentation 373

All about Notes 373
Rehearsing and Timing Your Presentation 374
Showing Your Presentation..375
Tricks for Making Presentations a Little Livelier 379
Delivering a Presentation When You Can't Be There in Person...........381

Chapter 1: Getting Started in PowerPoint

In This Chapter

✓ Introducing PowerPoint

✓ Finding your way around the screen

✓ Understanding what creating a presentation is all about

✓ Creating a presentation

✓ Inserting the slides

✓ Changing views of the screen

✓ Rearranging the Slides and Notes panes

✓ Manipulating slides

✓ Creating a photo album

✓ Hiding slides for use in a presentation

*I*t's impossible to sit through a conference, seminar, or trade show without seeing at least one PowerPoint presentation. PowerPoint has found its way into nearly every office and boardroom. I've heard of a man (a very unromantic man) who proposed to his wife by way of a PowerPoint presentation.

As nice as PowerPoint can be, it has its detractors. If the software isn't used properly, it can come between the speaker and the audience. In a *New Yorker* article titled "Absolute PowerPoint: Can a Software Package Edit Our Thoughts?," Ian Parker argued that PowerPoint might actually be more of a hindrance than a help in communicating. PowerPoint, Parker wrote, is "a social instrument, turning middle managers into bullet-point dandies." The software, he added, "has a private, interior influence. It edits ideas. . . . It helps you make a case, but also makes its own case about how to organize information, how to look at the world."

To make sure that you use PowerPoint wisely, this chapter shows what creating a PowerPoint presentation entails. After a brief tour of PowerPoint, you find out how to create presentations, get a better view of your work, insert slides, put together a photo album, and hide slides.

Getting Acquainted with PowerPoint

Figure 1-1 (top) shows the PowerPoint window. That thing in the middle is a *slide,* the PowerPoint word for an image that you show your audience. Surrounding the slide are many tools for entering text and decorating slides. When the time comes to show your slides to an audience, you dispense with the tools and make the slide fill the screen, as shown in Figure 1-1 (bottom).

To make PowerPoint do your bidding, you need to know a little jargon:

+ **Presentation:** All the slides, from start to finish, that you show your audience. Sometimes presentations are called "slide shows." Presentations are saved in presentation files (.pptx files).

+ **Slides:** The images you create with PowerPoint. During a presentation, slides appear on-screen one after the other. Don't be put off by the word *slide* and dreary memories of sitting through your uncle's slide show vacation memories. You don't need a slide projector to show these slides. You can plug a laptop or other computer into special monitors that display PowerPoint slides.

+ **Notes:** Printed pages that you, the speaker, write and print so that you know what to say during a presentation. Only the speaker sees notes. Chapter 5 in this mini-book explains notes.

+ **Handout:** Printed pages that you may give to the audience along with a presentation. A handout shows the slides in the presentation. Handouts are also known by the somewhat derogatory term *leave-behinds.* Chapter 5 of this mini-book explains handouts.

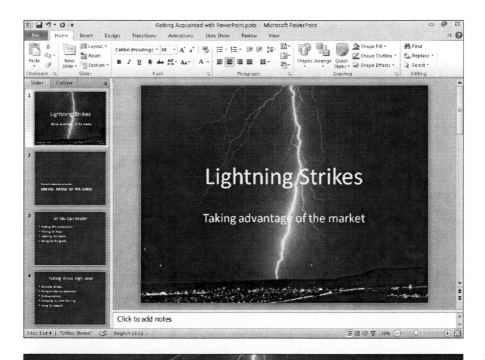

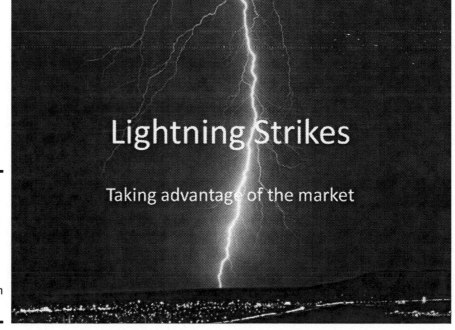

Figure 1-1:
The
PowerPoint
window
(top) and a
slide as it
looks in a
presentation
(bottom).

A Brief Geography Lesson

Figure 1-2 shows the different parts of the PowerPoint screen. I'd hate for you to get lost in PowerPoint Land. Fold down the corner of this page so that you can return here if screen terminology confuses you:

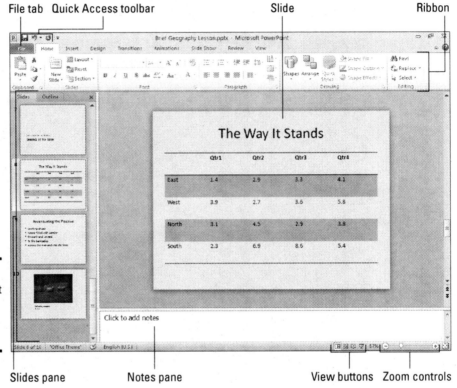

Figure 1-2:
The different parts of the PowerPoint screen.

+ *File tab* *Quick Access toolbar* *Slide* *Ribbon*
+ *Slides pane* *Notes pane* *View buttons* *Zoom controls*

The slide shown displays a table titled "The Way It Stands":

	Qtr1	Qtr2	Qtr3	Qtr4
East	1.4	2.9	3.3	4.1
West	3.9	2.7	3.6	5.8
North	3.1	4.5	2.9	3.8
South	2.3	6.9	8.6	5.4

+ **File tab:** The tab you visit to create, open, and save PowerPoint presentations, as well as do other file-management tasks.

+ **Quick Access toolbar:** A toolbar with three buttons — Save, Undo, and Repeat. You see this toolbar wherever you go in PowerPoint.

+ **Ribbon:** The place where the tabs are located. Click a tab — Home, Insert, Design, Transitions, Animations, Slide Show, Review, or View — to start a task.

+ **Slides pane:** In Normal view, the place on the left side of the screen where you can see the slides or the text on the slides in your presentation. Scroll in the Slides pane to move backward and forward in a presentation.

✦ **Slide window:** Where a slide (in Normal view) or slides (in Slide Sorter view) are displayed. Scroll to move backward or forward in your presentation.

✦ **Notes pane:** Where you type notes (in Normal view) that you can refer to when giving your presentation. The audience can't see these notes — they're for you and you alone. See Chapter 5 of this mini-book for details.

✦ **View buttons:** Buttons you can click to switch to (from left to right) Normal, Slide Sorter, Slide Show, and Reading view. See "Getting a Better View of Your Work" later in this chapter.

✦ **Zoom controls:** Tools for enlarging or shrinking a slide (in Normal and Slide Sorter view).

A Whirlwind Tour of PowerPoint

To help you understand what you're getting into, you're invited on a whirlwind tour of PowerPoint. Creating a PowerPoint presentation entails completing these basic tasks:

✦ **Creating the slides:** After you create a new presentation, your next task is to create the slides. PowerPoint offers many preformatted slide layouts, each designed for presenting information a certain way.

✦ **Notes:** As you create slides, you can jot down notes in the Notes pane. You can use these notes later to formulate your presentation and decide what you're going to say to your audience while each slide is on-screen (see Chapter 5 of this mini-book).

✦ **Designing your presentation:** After you create a presentation, the next step is to think about its appearance. You can change slides' colors and backgrounds, as well as choose a *theme* for your presentation, an all-encompassing design that applies to all (or most of) the slides (see Chapter 2 of this mini-book).

✦ **Inserting tables, charts, diagrams, and shapes:** A PowerPoint presentation should be more than a loose collection of bulleted lists. Starting on the Insert tab, you can place tables, charts, and diagrams on slides, as well as adorn your slides with text boxes, WordArt images, and shapes (see Chapter 4 of this mini-book).

✦ **"Animating" your slides:** PowerPoint slides can play video and sound, as well as be "animated" (see Chapter 4 of this mini-book). You can make the items on a slide move on the screen. As a slide arrives, you can make it spin or flash.

✦ **Delivering your presentation:** During a presentation, you can draw on the slides. You can also blank the screen and show slides out of order. In case you can't be there in person, PowerPoint gives you the opportunity to create self-running presentations and presentations that others can run on their own. You can also distribute presentations on CDs and as videos (see Chapter 5 of this mini-book).

Creating a New Presentation

When you start PowerPoint, the program creates a new, blank presentation just for you. You can make this bare-bones presentation the starting point for constructing your presentation, or you can get a more sophisticated, fully realized layout and design by starting with a template. Templates are a mixed blessing. They're designed by artists and they look very good. Some templates come with *boilerplate text* — already written material that you can recycle into your presentation. However, presentations made from templates are harder to modify. Sometimes the design gets in the way. As well, a loud or intricate background may overwhelm a diagram or chart you want to put on a slide.

File

No matter what kind of presentation you want to create, start creating it by going to the File tab and choosing New. You see the Available Templates and Themes window shown in Figure 1-3. This window offers templates for creating many types of presentations. Click a template to preview it on the right side of the window. Double-click a template (or select it and click the Create button) to create a presentation. Use one of these techniques to create a presentation:

✦ **Blank presentation:** Double-click the Blank Presentation icon. A new presentation appears. Try visiting the Design tab and choosing a theme or background style to get a taste of all the things you can do to decorate a presentation. (By pressing Ctrl+N, you can create a new, blank presentation without opening the Available Templates and Themes window.)

✦ **Recently used template:** Click the Recent Templates icon to use a template listed there.

✦ **Template on your computer:** Click the Sample Templates icon. Templates that you loaded on your computer when you installed PowerPoint appear.

✦ **Template you created (or downloaded earlier from Microsoft):** Click the My Templates icon. The New Presentation dialog box appears. Select a template and click OK.

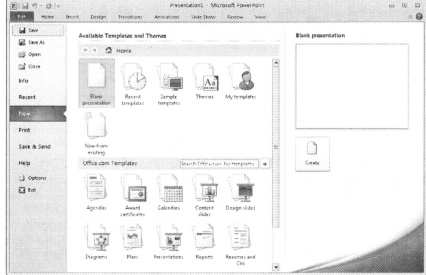

Figure 1-3:
The Available Templates and Themes window is the starting point for creating a presentation.

+ **Template available online at Office.com:** Enter a search term in the Search box, make sure your computer is connected to the Internet, and click the Start Searching button. Templates appear in the window. Double-click a template to download and use it to create a presentation.

Book III
Chapter 1

Getting Started in
PowerPoint

+ **Recycle another presentation:** If you can use another presentation as the starting point for creating a new presentation, nab slides from the other presentation. Click the New from Existing icon. In the New from Existing Presentation dialog box, select the presentation and click the Open button.

You can click the Home, Back, or Forward button in the Available Templates and Themes window to backtrack as you search for a template.

If you intend to create a presentation from photos you took of a vacation or family reunion, consider creating a photo album. See "Putting Together a Photo Album" later in this chapter.

Advice for Building Persuasive Presentations

Before you create any slides, think about what you want to communicate to your audience. Your goal isn't to dazzle the audience with your PowerPoint skills, but communicate something — a company policy, the merits of a product, the virtues of a strategic plan. Your goal is to bring the audience around to your side. To that end, here is some practical advice for building persuasive presentations:

✦ **Start by writing the text in Word.** Start in Microsoft Word, not PowerPoint, so you can focus on the words. In Word, you can clearly see how a presentation develops. You can make sure that your presentation builds to its rightful conclusion. PowerPoint has a special command for getting headings from a Word file. (See "Conjuring slides from Word document headings," later in this chapter.)

✦ **When choosing a design, consider the audience.** A presentation to the American Casketmakers Association calls for a mute, quiet design; a presentation to the Cheerleaders of Tomorrow calls for something bright and splashy. Select a slide design that sets the tone for your presentation and wins the sympathy of the audience.

✦ **Keep it simple.** To make sure that PowerPoint doesn't upstage you, keep it simple. Make use of the PowerPoint features, but do so judiciously. An animation in the right place at the right time can serve a valuable purpose. It can highlight an important part of a presentation and grab the audience's attention. But stuffing a presentation with too many gizmos turns a presentation into a carnival sideshow and distracts from your message.

✦ **Follow the one-slide-per-minute rule.** At the very minimum, a slide should stay on-screen for at least one minute. If you have 15 minutes to speak, you're allotted no more than 15 slides for your presentation, according to the rule.

✦ **Beware the bullet point.** Terse bullet points have their place in a presentation, but if you put them there strictly to remind yourself what to say next, you're doing your audience a disfavor. Bullet points can cause drowsiness. They can be a distraction. The audience skims the bullets when it should be attending to your voice and the argument you're making. When you're tempted to use a bulleted list, consider using a table, chart, or diagram instead. Figure 1-4 demonstrates how a bulleted list can be presented instead in a table, chart, or diagram.

✦ **Take control from the start.** Spend the first minute introducing yourself to the audience without running PowerPoint (or, if you do run PowerPoint, put a simple slide with your company name or logo on-screen). Make eye contact with the audience. This way, you establish your credibility. You give the audience a chance to get to know you.

✦ **Make clear what you're about.** In the early going, state very clearly what your presentation is about and what you intend to prove with your presentation. In other words, state the conclusion at the beginning as well as the end. This way, your audience knows exactly what you're driving at and can judge your presentation according to how well you build your case.

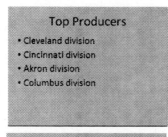
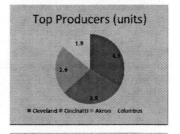
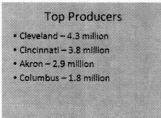
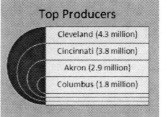

Figure 1-4:
List information presented in a table (top), chart (middle), and diagram (bottom).

✦ **Personalize the presentation.** Make the presentation a personal one. Tell the audience what *your* personal reason for being there is or why *you* work for the company you work for. Knowing that you have a personal stake in the presentation, the audience is more likely to trust you. The audience understands that you're not a spokesperson, but a *speaker* — someone who has come before them to make a case for something that you believe in.

✦ **Tell a story.** Include an anecdote in the presentation. Everybody loves a pertinent and well-delivered story. This piece of advice is akin to the previous one about personalizing your presentation. Typically, a story illustrates a problem for *people* and how *people* solve the problem. Even if your presentation concerns technology or an abstract subject, make it about people. "The people in Shaker Heights needed faster Internet access," not "the data switches in Shaker Heights just weren't performing fast enough."

✦ **Rehearse and then rehearse some more.** The better you know your material, the less nervous you will be. To keep from getting nervous, rehearse your presentation until you know it backward and forward. Rehearse it out loud. Rehearse it while imagining you're in the presence of an audience.

✦ **Use visuals, not only words, to make your point.** You really owe it to your audience to take advantage of the table, chart, diagram, and picture capabilities of PowerPoint. People understand more from words and pictures than they do from words alone. It's up to you — not the slides — as the speaker to describe topics in detail with words.

Want to see how PowerPoint can suck the life and drama out of a dramatic presentation? Try visiting the Gettysburg PowerPoint Presentation, a rendering of Lincoln's Gettysburg Address in PowerPoint. Yikes! You can find it here: `http://.norvig.com/Gettysburg`.

Creating New Slides for Your Presentation

After you create a presentation, your next step on the path to glory is to start adding the slides. To create a new slide, you start by choosing a slide layout. *Slide layouts* are the preformatted slide designs that help you enter text, graphics, and other things. Some slide layouts have *text placeholder frames* for entering titles and text; some come with *content placeholder frames* designed especially for inserting a table, chart, diagram, picture, clip-art image, or media clip.

When you add a slide, select the slide layout that best approximates the slide you have in mind for your presentation. Figure 1-5 shows the slide layouts that are available when you create a presentation with the Blank Presentation template. These pages explain how to insert slides and harvest them from Word document headings.

Inserting a new slide

Follow these steps to insert a new slide in your presentation:

1. **Select the slide that you want the new slide to go after.**

In Normal view, select the slide on the Slides pane. In Slide Sorter view, select the slide in the main window.

2. **On the Home tab, click the bottom half of the New Slide button.**

You see a drop-down list of slide layouts. (If you click the top half of the New Slide button, you insert a slide with the same layout as the one you selected in Step 1.) Figure 1-5 shows what the slide layouts look like (left), what a slide looks like right after you insert it (middle), and finished slides (right).

3. **Select the slide layout that best approximates the slide you want to create.**

   Don't worry too much about selecting the right layout. You can change slide layouts later on, as "Selecting a different layout for a slide" explains later in this chapter.

Speed techniques for inserting slides

When you're in a hurry, use these techniques to insert a slide:

✦ **Creating a duplicate slide:** Select the slide or slides you want to duplicate, and on the Home tab, open the drop-down list on the New Slide button and choose Duplicate Selected Slides. You can also open the drop-down list on the Copy button and choose Duplicate.

✦ **Copying and pasting slides:** Click the slide you want to copy (or Ctrl+click to select more than one slide) and then click the Copy button on the Home tab (or press Ctrl+C). Next, click to select the slide that you want the copied slide (or slides) to appear after and click the Paste button (or press Ctrl+V).

✦ **Recycling slides from other presentations:** Select the slide that you want the recycled slides to follow in your presentation, and on the Home tab, open the drop-down list on the New Slide button and choose Reuse Slides. The Reuse Slides task pane opens. Open the drop-down list on the Browse button, choose Browse File, and select a presentation in the Browse dialog box. The Reuse Slides task pane shows thumbnail versions of slides in the presentation you selected. One at a time, click slides to add them to your presentation. You can right-click a slide and choose Insert All Slides to grab all the slides in the presentation.

Conjuring slides from Word document headings

If you think about it, Word headings are similar to slide titles. Headings, like slide titles, introduce a new topic. If you know your way around Word and you want to get a head start creating a PowerPoint presentation, you can borrow the headings in a Word document for your PowerPoint slides. After you import the headings from Word, you get one slide for each Level 1 heading (headings given the Heading 1 style). Level 1 headings form the title of the slides, Level 2 headings form first-level bullets, Level 3 headings form second-level bullets, and so on. Paragraph text isn't imported. Figure 1-6 shows what headings from a Word document look like after they land in a PowerPoint presentation.

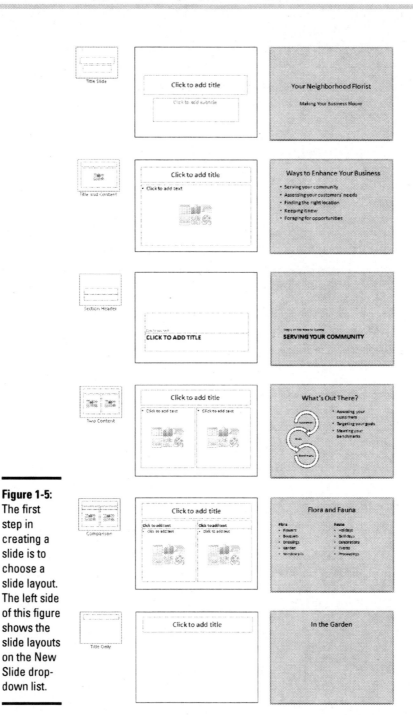

Figure 1-5:
The first step in creating a slide is to choose a slide layout. The left side of this figure shows the slide layouts on the New Slide drop-down list.

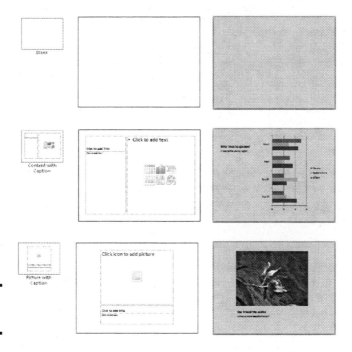

Figure 1-5:
continued.

**Book III
Chapter 1**

**Getting Started in
PowerPoint**

Each level-1 heading in the Word document becomes a slide title in PowerPoint

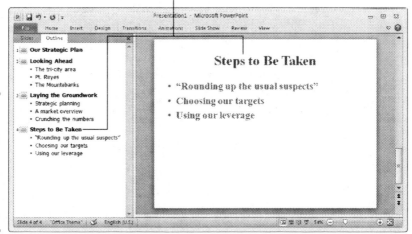

Figure 1-6:
Headings
from a Word
document
imported
into a
PowerPoint
presentation.

Follow these steps to use headings in a Word document to create slides in a PowerPoint presentation:

1. **In Normal view, click the Outline tab in the Slides pane.**

   The Outline tab displays slide text (see Figure 1-6). You get a better sense of how headings from the Word document land in your presentation by viewing your presentation from the Outline tab.

2. **Select the slide that the new slides from the Word document will follow.**

3. **On the Home tab, open the drop-down list on the New Slide button and choose Slides from Outline.**

   You see the Insert Outline dialog box.

4. **Select the Word document with the headings you want for your presentation and click the Insert button.**

   Depending on how many first-level headings are in the Word document, you get a certain number of new slides. These slides probably need work. The Word text may need tweaking to make it suitable for a PowerPoint presentation.

Selecting a different layout for a slide

If you mistakenly choose the wrong layout for a slide, all is not lost. You can start all over. You can graft a new layout onto your slide with one of these techniques:

✦ On the Home tab, click the Layout button and choose a layout on the drop-down list.

✦ Right-click the slide (being careful not to right-click a frame or object), choose Layout, and choose a layout on the submenu.

PowerPoint also offers the Reset command for giving a slide its original layout after you've fiddled with it. If you push a slide all out of shape and you regret doing so, select your slide, go to the Home tab, and click the Reset button.

Getting a Better View of Your Work

Depending on the task at hand, some views are better than others. These pages explain how to change views and the relative merits of Normal, Slide Sorter, Notes Page, Slide Show, Slide Master, Reading View, Handout Master, and Notes Master view.

Changing views

PowerPoint offers two places to change views:

✦ **View buttons on the status bar:** Click a View button — Normal, Slide Sorter, Reading View, or Slide Show — on the status bar to change views, as shown in Figure 1-7.

✦ **View tab:** On the View tab, click a button on the Presentation Views or Master Views group, as shown in Figure 1-7.

Looking at the different views

Here is a survey of the different views with suggestions about using each one:

Slides

✦ **Normal/Slides view for examining slides:** Switch to Normal view, move the pointer to the Slides pane, and select the Slides tab when you want to examine a slide. In this view, thumbnail slides appear in the Slides pane, and you can see your slide in all its glory in the middle of the screen.

Outline

✦ **Normal/Outline view for fiddling with text:** Switch to Normal view, move the pointer to the Slides pane, and select the Outline tab to enter or read text (refer to Figure 1-6). You can find the Outline tab at the top of the Slides pane. The words appear in outline form. Normal/Outline view is ideal for focusing on the words in a presentation.

Click a View button on the View tab . . .

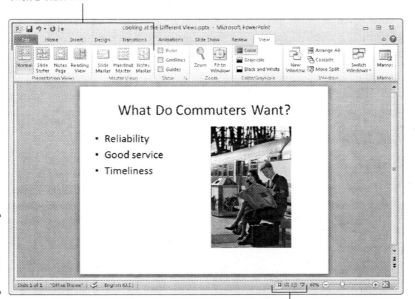

Figure 1-7:
Techniques
for changing
views.

Or click a View button on the status bar

✦ **Slide Sorter view for moving and deleting slides:** In Slide Sorter view, you see thumbnails of all the slides in the presentation (use the Zoom slider to change the size of thumbnails). From here, moving slides around is easy, and seeing many slides simultaneously gives you a sense of whether the different slides are consistent with one another and how the whole presentation is shaping up. The slides are numbered so that you can see where they appear in a presentation.

✦ **Notes Page view for reading your speaker notes:** In Notes Page view, you see notes you've written to aid you in your presentation, if you've written any. You can write notes in this view as well as in the Notes pane in Normal view. Chapter 5 of this mini-book explains notes pages.

✦ **Reading View view for focusing on slides' appearance:** In Reading View view, you also see a single slide, but it appears on-screen with the View buttons and with buttons for moving quickly from slide to slide. Switch to Reading View view to proofread slides and put the final touches on a presentation.

✦ **Slide Show view for giving a presentation:** In Slide Show view, you see a single slide. Not only that, but the slide fills the entire screen. This is what your presentation looks like when you show it to an audience.

✦ **The Master views for a consistent presentation:** The master views — Slide Master, Handout Master, and Notes Master — are for handling *master styles,* the formatting commands that pertain to all the slides in a presentation, handouts, and notes. To switch to these views, go to the View tab and click the appropriate button. Chapter 2 of this mini-book looks into master slides and master styles.

PowerPoint offers a button called Fit Slide to Current Window that you can click while you're in Normal view to make the slide fill the window. This little button is located in the lower-right corner of the screen, to the right of the Zoom controls.

Hiding and Displaying the Slides Pane and Notes Pane

In Normal view, the Slides pane with its slide thumbnails appears on the left side of the screen, and the Notes pane appears on the bottom of the screen so that you can scribble notes about slides. Sometimes these panes just take up valuable space. They clutter the screen and occupy real estate that could be better used for formatting slides. Follow these instructions to temporarily close the Slides and Notes pane:

✦ **Closing the Notes pane:** Move the pointer over the border between the pane and the rest of the screen, and after the pointer changes to a two-headed arrow, drag the border to the bottom of the screen.

✦ **Closing the Slides pane (and the Notes pane):** Click the Close button on the Slides pane. This button is located to the right of the Outline tab. Clicking it closes the Notes pane as well as the Slides pane.

 ✦ **Restoring the Slides and Notes pane:** Click the Normal button (on the status bar or View tab). You can also move the pointer to the left side or bottom of the screen and, when you see the double-headed arrow, click and start dragging toward the center of the screen.

 You can change the size of either pane by moving the pointer over its border and then clicking and dragging.

Selecting, Moving, and Deleting Slides

As a presentation takes shape, you have to move slides forward and backward. Sometimes you have to delete a slide. And you can't move or delete slides until you select them first. Herewith are instructions for selecting, moving, and deleting slides.

Selecting slides

The best place to select slides is Slide Sorter view (if you want to select several at a time). Use one of these techniques to select slides:

✦ **Select one slide:** Click the slide.

✦ **Select several different slides:** Hold down the Ctrl key and click each slide in the Slides pane or in Slide Sorter view.

✦ **Select several slides in succession:** Hold down the Shift key and click the first slide and then the last one.

✦ **Select a block of slides:** In Slide Sorter view, drag across the slides you want to select. Be sure when you click and start dragging that you don't click a slide.

✦ **Selecting all the slides:** On the Home tab, click the Select button and choose Select All on the drop-down list.

Moving slides

To move or rearrange slides, you're advised to go to Slide Sorter view. Select the slide or slides that you want to move and use one of these techniques to move slides:

✦ **Dragging and dropping:** Click the slides you selected and drag them to a new location. You see the drag pointer, and in Slide Sorter view, a vertical line shows you where the slide or slides will land when you release the mouse button. On the Slides pane, a horizontal line appears between slides to show you where the slide or slides will land when you release the mouse button.

✦ **Cutting and pasting:** On the Home tab, cut the slide or slides to the Windows Clipboard (click the Cut button, press Ctrl+X, or right-click and choose Cut). Then select the slide that you want the slide or slides to appear after and give the Paste command (click the Paste button, press Ctrl+V, or right-click and choose Paste). You can right-click between slides to paste with precision.

Deleting slides

Before you delete a slide, think twice about deleting. Short of using the Undo command, you can't resuscitate a deleted slide. Select the slide or slides you want to delete and use one of these techniques to delete slides:

✦ Press the Delete key.

✦ Right-click and choose Delete Slide on the shortcut menu.

Putting Together a Photo Album

Photo album is just PowerPoint's term for inserting many photographs into a presentation all at once. You don't necessarily have to stuff the photo album with travel or baby pictures for it to be a proper photo album. The Photo Album is a wonderful feature because you can use it to dump a bunch of photos in a PowerPoint presentation without having to create slides one at a time, insert the photos, and endure the rest of the rigmarole. Create a photo album to quickly place a bunch of photos on PowerPoint slides.

Creating your photo album

PowerPoint creates a new presentation for you when you create a photo album. To start, take note of where on your computer the photos you want for the album are. Then go to the Insert tab and click the Photo Album button. You see the Photo Album dialog box, as shown in Figure 1-8. For such a little thing, the Photo Album dialog box offers many opportunities for constructing a PowerPoint presentation. Your first task is to decide which pictures you want for your album. Then you choose a slide layout for the pictures.

Insert photos   Change the order of slides

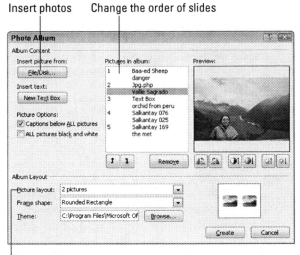

Figure 1-8:
Create a
photo album
in this dialog
box.

Choose a layout

Inserting pictures and creating slides

Here is the lowdown on choosing pictures for a photo album:

**Book III
Chapter 1**

**Getting Started in
PowerPoint**

+ **Inserting photos:** Click the File/Disk button and choose photos in the Insert New Pictures dialog box. You can select more than one photo at a time by Ctrl+clicking. The filenames of photos you selected appear in the Pictures in Album box. Slide numbers appear as well so that you know which photos are on which slides.

+ **Deciding how photos are framed:** Open the Frame Shape drop-down list and choose an option for placing borders or rounded corners on your photos. (This option isn't available if you choose Fit to Slide on the Picture Layout drop-down list.)

+ **Inserting a text box:** Insert a text box if you want to enter commentary in your photo album. In the Pictures in Album box, select the picture or text box that you want your new text box to go after and then click the New Text Box button. Later, you can go into your presentation and edit the placeholder text, which PowerPoint aptly enters as *Text Box*.

+ **Providing captions for all pictures:** To place a caption below all the pictures in your photo album, select the Captions Below ALL Pictures check box. PowerPoint initially places the picture file name in the caption, but you can delete this caption and enter one of your own. (To select this option, you must choose a picture layout option besides Fit to Slide.)

+ **Changing the order of pictures:** Select a picture in the Pictures in Album box and then click an arrow button to move it forward or backward in the presentation.

+ **Changing the order of slides:** Ctrl+click to select each picture on a slide. Then click an arrow as many times as necessary to move the slide forward or backward in the presentation.

+ **Removing a picture:** Select a picture in the Pictures in Album box and click the Remove button to remove it from your photo album. You can Ctrl+click pictures to select more than one.

Choosing a layout for slides

Your next task is to go to the bottom of the Photo Album dialog box (refer to Figure 1-8) and choose a layout for the slides in the presentation. Open the Picture Layout drop-down list to choose one of the seven picture layouts:

+ Choose Fit to Slide for a presentation in which each picture occupies an entire slide.

+ Choose a "pictures" option to fit 1, 2, or 4 pictures on each slide.

+ Choose a "pictures with" option to fit 1, 2, or 4 pictures as well as a text title frame on each slide.

Changing the look of pictures

The Photo Album dialog box (refer to Figure 1-8) offers a handful of tools for changing the look of the pictures. When you use these tools, keep your eye on the Preview box — it shows you what you're doing to your picture.

+ **Making all photos black and white:** Select the ALL Pictures Black and White check box.

+ **Rotating pictures:** Click a Rotate button to rotate a picture clockwise or counterclockwise.

+ **Changing the contrast:** Click a Contrast button to sharpen or mute the light and dark colors or shades in the picture.

+ **Changing the brightness:** Click a Brightness button to make a picture brighter or more somber.

+ **Choosing a frame shape for pictures:** If you opted for a "picture" or "picture with" slide layout, you can choose a shape — Beveled, Oval, or others — for your pictures on the Frame Shape drop-down list.

+ **Choosing a theme for your photo album:** If you selected a "picture" or "picture with" slide layout, you can choose a theme for your slide presentation. Click the Browse button and choose a theme in the Choose Theme dialog box.

At last, click the Create button when you're ready to create the photo album. PowerPoint attaches a title slide to the start of the album that says, *Photo Album* with your name below.

Putting on the final touches

Depending on the options you chose for your photo album, it needs all or some of these final touches:

✦ **Fix the title slide:** Your title slide should probably say more than the words *Photo Album* and your name.

✦ **Fill in the text boxes:** If you asked text boxes with your photo album, by all means, replace PowerPoint's generic text with meaningful words of your own.

✦ **Write the captions:** If you asked for photo captions, PowerPoint entered photo file names below photos. Replace these file names with something more descriptive.

Hidden slides for all contingencies

Hide a slide when you want to keep it on hand "just in case" during a presentation. Hidden slides don't appear in slide shows unless you shout *Ollie ollie oxen free!* and bring them out of hiding. Although you, the presenter, can see hidden slides in Normal view and Slide Sorter view, where their slide numbers are crossed through, the audience doesn't see them in the course of a presentation unless you decide to show them. Create hidden slides if you anticipate having to steer your presentation in a different direction — to answer a question from the audience, prove your point more thoroughly, or revisit a topic in more depth. Merely by right-clicking and choosing a couple of commands, you can display a hidden slide in the course of a slide show.

Follow these instructions to hide slides and show hidden slides during a presentation:

✔ **Hiding a slide:** Select the slide or slides that you want to hide, and on the Slide Show tab, click the Hide Slide button. You can also right-click a slide in the Slides pane or Slide Sorter view and choose Hide Slide. Hidden slides' numbers are boxed and crossed through in the Slides pane and the Slide Sorter window. (To unhide a slide, click the Hide Slide button again or right-click the slide and choose Hide Slide.)

✔ **Showing a hidden slide during a presentation:** Right-click the screen, choose Go to Slide, and on the submenu, select a hidden slide. To resume your presentation after viewing a hidden slide, right-click and choose Last Viewed on the shortcut menu, or choose Go to Slide and select a slide to pick up where you left off.

Editing a photo album

To go back into the Photo Album dialog box and rearrange the photos in your album, go to the Insert tab, open the drop-down list on the Photo Album button, and choose Edit Photo Album on the drop-down list. You see the Edit Photo Album dialog box. It looks and works exactly like the Photo Album dialog box (refer to Figure 1-8). Of course, you can also edit your photo album by treating it like any other PowerPoint presentation. Change the theme, fiddle with the slides, and do what you will to torture your photo album into shape.

Chapter 2: Fashioning a Look for Your Presentation

In This Chapter

- ✔ **Introducing themes and background styles**
- ✔ **Selecting and tweaking slide themes**
- ✔ **Creating a solid color, gradient, clip-art, picture, and texture slide background**
- ✔ **Selecting a theme or background for specific slides**
- ✔ **Redesigning your presentation with master slides**

From the audience's point of view, this chapter is the most important in this mini-book. What your presentation looks like — which theme and background style you select for the slides in your presentation — sets the tone. From the very first slide, the audience judges your presentation on its appearance. When you create a look for your presentation, what you're really doing is declaring what you want to communicate to your audience.

This chapter explains how to handle slide backgrounds. It examines what you need to consider when you select colors and designs for backgrounds. You also discover how to select and customize a theme, and how to create your own slide backgrounds. This chapter looks into how to change the background of some but not all of the slides in a presentation. It also explains how to use master slides and master styles to make sure that slides throughout your presentation are consistent with one another.

Looking at Themes and Background Styles

What a presentation looks like is mostly a matter of slide backgrounds, and when you select a background for slides, you start by selecting a theme. A *theme* is a "canned" slide design. Themes are designed by graphic artists. Most themes include sophisticated background patterns and colors. For each theme, PowerPoint offers several alternative theme colors, fonts, and background styles. As well, you can create a background of your own from a single color, a gradient mixture of two colors, or a picture.

Figure 2-1 shows examples of themes. Themes range from the fairly simple to the quite complex. When you installed PowerPoint on your computer, you also installed a dozen or more themes, and you can acquire more themes online from Office.com and other places. After you select a theme for your presentation, you can tweak it a little bit. You can do that by choosing a background style or by creating an entirely new background of your own.

Figure 2-1: Examples of themes.

Figure 2-2 shows examples of backgrounds you can create yourself. Self-made backgrounds are not as intrusive as themes. The risk of the background overwhelming the lists, tables, charts, and other items in the forefront of slides is less when you fashion a background style yourself.

Figure 2-2: Examples of background styles (clockwise from upper-left): plain style, gradient, solid color, customized radial gradient, clip art, and picture.

More than any other design decision, what sets the tone for a presentation are the colors you select for slide backgrounds. If the purpose of your presentation is to show photographs you took on a vacation to Arizona's Painted Desert, select light-tone, hot colors for the slide backgrounds. If your presentation is an aggressive sales pitch, consider a black background. There is no universal color theory for selecting the right colors in a design because everyone is different. Follow your intuition. It will guide you to the right background color choices.

Choosing a Theme for Your Presentation

After you initially select a theme, you can do one or two things to customize it. These pages explain how to find and select a theme for your presentation and diddle with a theme after you select it. By the way, the name of the theme that is currently in use is listed on the left side of the status bar, in case you're curious about a theme you want to replace.

Selecting a theme

Use one of these techniques to select a new theme for your presentation:

- ✦ **Selecting a theme in the Themes gallery:** On the Design tab, open the Themes gallery and move the pointer over different themes to "live-preview" them. Click a theme to select it.

- ✦ **Borrowing a theme from another presentation:** On the Design tab, open the Themes gallery, and click Browse for Themes. You see the Choose Theme or Themed Document dialog box. Locate and select a presentation with a theme you can commandeer for your presentation and click the Apply button.

Tweaking a theme

Starting on the Design tab, you can customize a theme with these techniques and in so doing alter all the slides in your presentation:

- ✦ **Choosing a new set of colors:** The easiest and best way to experiment with customizing a theme is to select a different color set. Click the Colors button, slide the pointer over the different color sets on the drop-down list, and see what effect they have on your slides.

- ✦ **Change the fonts:** Click the Fonts button and choose a font combination on the drop-down list. The first font in each pair applies to slide titles and the second to slide text. You can also choose Create New Theme Fonts on the list and select theme fonts of your own.

✦ **Change theme effects:** Click the Effects button and choose a theme effect on the drop-down list. A *theme effect* is a slight refinement to a theme.

 ✦ **Choosing background style variation:** Most themes offer background style variations. Click the Background Styles button to open the Background Styles gallery and select a style. The next topic in this chapter, "Creating Slide Backgrounds on Your Own," explains how you can create backgrounds similar to these, as well as how to create a single-color, gradient, clip-art, picture, and texture background.

 Suppose you regret customizing a theme. To get the original theme back, select it again. Make like you were selecting a theme for the first time and select it in the Themes gallery.

At the end of this chapter, the sidebar "Creating a theme" explains how to create a theme of your own for PowerPoint presentations.

Creating Slide Backgrounds on Your Own

Besides a theme or background style, your other option for creating slide backgrounds is to do it on your own. For a background, you can have a solid color, a transparent color, a gradient blend of colors, a picture, or a clip-art image.

✦ **Solid color:** A single, uniform color. You can adjust a color's transparency and in effect "bleach out" the color to push it farther into the background.

✦ **Gradient:** A mixture of different colors with the colors blending into one another.

✦ **Clip art:** A clip-art image from the Microsoft Clip Organizer.

✦ **Picture:** A photograph or graphic.

✦ **Texture:** A uniform pattern that gives the impression that the slide is displayed on a material such as cloth or stone.

How to create these kinds of slide backgrounds on your own is the subject of the next several pages.

Using a solid (or transparent) color for the slide background

Using a solid or transparent color for the background gives your slides a straightforward, honest look. Because all the slides are the same color or transparent color, the audience can focus better on the presentation itself rather than the razzle-dazzle. Follow these steps to use a solid or transparent color as the background for slides:

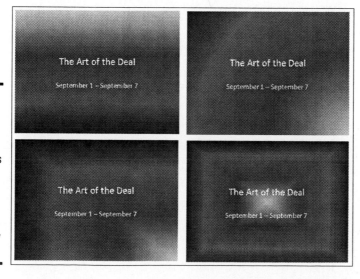

Background Styles

1. **On the Design tab, click the Background Styles button and choose Format Background on the drop-down list.**

   You see the Fill category of the Format Background dialog box.

2. **Select the Solid Fill option button.**

3. **Click the Color button and choose a color on the drop-down list.**

   The muted theme colors are recommended because they look better in the background, but you can select a standard color or click the More Colors button and select a color in the Colors dialog box.

4. **Drag the Transparency slider if you want a "bleached out" color rather than a slide color.**

   At 0% transparency, you get a solid color; at 100%, you get no color at all.

5. **Click the Apply to All button and then the Close button.**

   I sincerely hope you like your choice of colors, but if you don't, try, try, try again.

Creating a gradient color blend for slide backgrounds

Gradient refers to how and where two or more colors grade, or blend, into one another on a slide. As well as the standard linear gradient direction, you can opt for a radial, rectangular, or path gradient direction. Figure 2-3 shows examples of gradient fill backgrounds. These backgrounds look terribly elegant. Using a gradient is an excellent way to create an original background that looks different from all the other presenter's slide backgrounds.

**Book III
Chapter 2**

**Fashioning a
Look for Your
Presentation**

Figure 2-3:
Examples
of gradient
fill slide
backgrounds
(clockwise
from upper-
left): linear,
radial,
rectangular,
and path.

Follow these steps to create a gradient background for slides:

1. **On the Design tab, click the Background Styles button, and choose Format Background on the drop-down list.**

   You see the Fill category of the Format Background dialog box. Drag this dialog box to the left side of the screen so that you can get a better view of your slide.

2. **Click the Gradient Fill option button.**

   Before you experiment with gradients, try opening the Preset Colors drop-down list to see whether one of the ready-made gradient options does the job for you.

3. **On the Type drop-down list, choose what type of gradient you want — Linear, Radial, Rectangular, Path, or Shade from Title (see Figure 2-3).**

   If you choose Linear, you can enter a degree measurement in the Angle box to change the angle at which the colors blend. At 90 degrees, for example, colors blend horizontally across the slide; at 180 degrees, they blend vertically.

4. **Create a gradient stop for each color transition you want on your slides.**

   Gradient stops determine where colors are, how colors transition from one to the next, and which colors are used. You can create as many gradient stops as you want. Here are techniques for handling gradient stops:

   - *Adding a gradient stop:* Click the Add Gradient Stop button. A new gradient stop appears on the slider. Drag it to where you want the color blend to occur.

   - *Removing a gradient stop:* Select a gradient stop on the slider and click the Remove Gradient Stop button.

   - *Choosing a color for a gradient stop:* Select a gradient stop on the slider, click the Color button, and choose a color on the drop-down list.

   - *Positioning a gradient stop:* Drag a gradient stop on the slider or use the Position box to move it to a different location.

5. **Drag the Brightness slider to make the colors dimmer or brighter.**

6. **Drag the Transparency slider to make the colors on the slides more or less transparent.**

   At 0% transparency, you get solid colors; at 100%, you get no color at all.

7. **Click the Apply to All button.**

   Very likely, you have to experiment with stop colors and stop positions until you blend the colors to your satisfaction. Good luck.

Placing a clip-art image in the slide background

As long as they're on the pale side or you've made them semi-transparent, clip-art images do fine for slide backgrounds. They look especially good in title slides. Figure 2-4 shows examples of clip-art images as backgrounds. As Book VI, Chapter 4 explains, PowerPoint comes with numerous clip-art images. You're invited to place one in the background of your slides by following these steps:

1. **On the Design tab, click the Background Styles button and choose Format Background on the drop-down list.**

The Fill category of the Format Background dialog box appears.

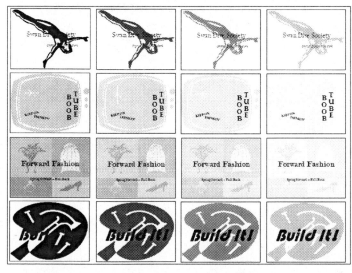

Figure 2-4:
For backgrounds, clip-art should be somewhat transparent. These slides are (from left to right) 0%, 40%, 65%, and 85% transparent.

Book III Chapter 2

Fashioning a Look for Your Presentation

2. **Click the Picture or Texture Fill option button.**

3. **Click the Clip Art button.**

You see the Select Picture dialog box.

4. **Find and select a clip-art image that you can use in the background of your slides.**

You can scroll through the clip-art images until you find a good one, enter a search term in the Search Text box and click the Go button (click the Include Content from Office Online check box to search online at Microsoft for a clip-art image), or click the Import button to get an image from your computer.

5. **In the Format Background dialog box, enter a Transparency measurement.**

    Drag the Transparency slider or enter a measurement in the box. The higher the measurement, the more transparent the image is (see Figure 2-4).

6. **Enter measurements in the Offsets boxes to make your clip-art image fill the slide.**

7. **Click the Apply to All button and then click Close.**

    There you have it. The clip-art image you selected lands in the slides' backgrounds.

Using a picture for a slide background

Figure 2-5 shows examples of pictures being used as slide backgrounds. Select your picture carefully. A picture with too many colors — and that includes the majority of color photographs — obscures the text and makes it difficult to read. You can get around this problem by "recoloring" a picture to give it a uniform color tint, selecting a grayscale photograph, selecting a photo with colors of a similar hue, or making the picture semi-transparent, but all in all, the best way to solve the problem of a picture that obscures the text is to start with a quiet, subdued picture. (Book VI, Chapter 3 explains all the ins and outs of using pictures in Office 2010.)

Figure 2-5: Examples of pictures used as slide backgrounds.

One more thing: Select a landscape-style picture that is wider than it is tall. PowerPoint expands pictures to make them fill the entire slide background. If you select a skinny, portrait-style picture, PowerPoint has to do a lot of expanding to make it fit on the slide, and you end up with a distorted background image.

Follow these steps to use a picture as a slide background:

1. **On the Design tab, click the Background Styles button and choose Format Background on the drop-down list.**

   You see the Fill category of the Format Background dialog box.

2. **Click the Picture or Texture Fill option button.**

3. **Click the File button.**

   The Insert Picture dialog box appears.

4. **Locate the picture you want, select it, and click the Insert button.**

   The picture lands on your slide.

5. **Enter a Transparency measurement to make the picture fade a bit into the background.**

   Drag the slider or enter a measurement in the Transparency box. The higher percentage measurement you enter, the more "bleached out" the picture is.

6. **Using the Offsets text boxes, enter measurements to make your picture fit on the slides.**

7. **Click the Apply to All button.**

   How do you like your slide background? You may have to open the Format Background dialog box again and play with the transparency setting. Only the very lucky and the permanently blessed get it right the first time.

Using a texture for a slide background

Yet another option for slide backgrounds is to use a texture. As shown in Figure 2-6, a *texture* gives the impression that the slide is displayed on a material such as marble or parchment. A texture can make for a very elegant slide background. Follow these steps to use a texture as a slide background:

1. **On the Design tab, click the Background Styles button and choose Format Background on the drop-down list.**

   The Fill category of the Format Background dialog box appears.

**Book III
Chapter 2**

**Fashioning a
Look for Your
Presentation**

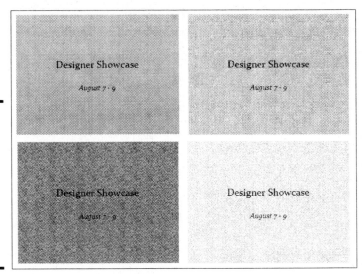

Figure 2-6:
Different
textures
(clockwise
from
upper-left):
Papyrus,
Canvas,
Newsprint,
and Cork.

2. **Click the Picture or Texture Fill option button.**

3. **Click the Texture button and choose a texture on the drop-down list.**

4. **Enter a Transparency measurement to make the texture less imposing.**

   Drag the slider or enter a measurement in the Transparency box.

5. **Click the Apply to All button and then click Close.**

Changing the Background of a Single or Handful of Slides

To make a single slide (or a handful of slides) stand out in a presentation, change their background style or theme. A different background tells your audience that the slide being presented is a little different from the one before it. Maybe it imparts important information. Maybe it introduces another segment of the presentation. Use a different background style or theme to mark a transition, indicate that your presentation has shifted gears, or mark a milestone in your presentation.

Follow these steps to change the background of one or several slides in your presentation:

1. **In Slide Sorter view, select the slides that need a different look.**

   You can select more than one slide by Ctrl+clicking slides.

2. **On the Design tab, choose a different theme or background for the slides you selected.**

    How you do this depends on whether you're working with a theme or a slide background:

    - *Theme:* In the Themes Gallery, right-click a theme and choose Apply To Selected Slides. The same goes for theme colors, fonts, and effects: To apply a theme color, font, or effect, right-click it on the drop-down list and choose Apply to Selected Slides. (See "Choosing a Theme for Your Presentation" earlier in this chapter for details.)

    - *Slide background:* Make like you're creating a background style for all the slides (see "Creating Slide Backgrounds on Your Own" earlier in this chapter) but right-click a choice on the Background Styles drop-down list and choose Apply to Selected Slides. If you're creating a background in the Format Background dialog box, click the Close button, not the Apply to All button.

When you assign a different theme to some of the slides in a presentation, PowerPoint creates another Slide Master. You may be surprised to discover that when you add a new slide to your presentation, a second, third, or fourth set of slide layouts appears on the New Slide drop-down list. These extra layouts appear because your presentation has more than one Slide Master. The next topic in this chapter, "Using Master Slides and Master Styles for a Consistent Design," explains what Slide Masters are.

Using Master Slides and Master Styles for a Consistent Design

Consistency is everything in a PowerPoint design. Consistency of design is a sign of professionalism and care. In a consistent design, the fonts and font sizes on slides are consistent from one slide to the next, the placeholder text frames are in the same positions, and the text is aligned the same way across different slides. In the bulleted lists, each entry is marked with the same bullet character. If the corner of each slide shows a company logo, the logo appears in the same position.

It would be torture to have to examine every slide to make sure it is consistent with the others. In the interest of consistency, PowerPoint offers master styles and master slides. A *master slide* is a model slide from which the slides in a presentation inherit their formats. A *master style* is a format that applies to many different slides. Starting from a master slide, you can change a master style and in so doing, reformat many slides the same way. These pages explain how master slides can help you quickly redesign a presentation.

Switching to Slide Master view

To work with master slides, switch to *Slide Master view,* as shown in Figure 2-7. From this view, you can start working with master slides:

1. **Go to the View tab.**

2. **Click the Slide Master button.**

Select the Slide Master . . .

or a layout   Change a master style

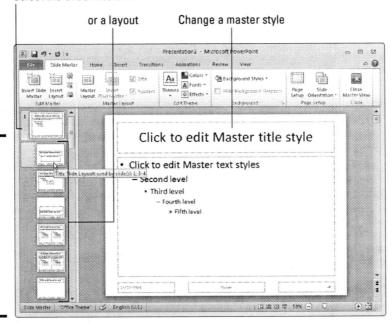

Figure 2-7: In Slide Master view, you can reformat many different slides simultaneously.

In Slide Master view, you can select a master slide in the Slides pane, format styles on a master slide, and in this way reformat many different slides. (Click the Close Master View button or a view button such as Normal or Slide Sorter to leave Slide Master view.)

Understanding master slides and master styles

Master slides are special, high-powered slides. Use master slides to deliver the same formatting commands to many different slides. Whether the commands affect all the slides in your presentation or merely a handful of slides depends on whether you format the Slide Master (the topmost slide in Slide Master view) or a layout (one of the other slides):

✦ **The Slide Master:** The *Slide Master* is the first slide in the Slides pane in Slide Master view (refer to Figure 2-7). It's a little bigger than the master slides, as befits its status as Emperor of All Slides. Formatting changes you make to the Slide Master affect all the slides in your presentation. When you select a theme for your presentation, what you're really doing is assigning a theme to the Slide Master. Because formatting commands given to the Slide Master apply throughout a presentation, the theme design and colors are applied to all slides. If you want a company logo to appear on all your slides, place the logo on the Slide Master.

✦ **Layouts:** As you know, you choose a slide layout — Title and Content, for example — on the New Slide drop-down list to create a new slide. In Slide Master view, PowerPoint provides one *layout* for each type of slide layout in your presentation. By selecting and reformatting a layout in Slide Master view, you can reformat all slides in your presentation that were created with the same slide layout. For example, to change fonts, alignments, and other formats on all slides that you created with the Title layout, select the Title layout in Slide Master view and change master styles on the Title layout. Each layout controls its own little fiefdom in a PowerPoint presentation — a fiefdom comprised of slides created with the same slide layout.

✦ **Master styles:** Each master slide — the Slide Master and each layout — offers you the opportunity to click to edit master styles (refer to Figure 2-7). The master style governs how text is formatted on slides. By changing a master style on a master slide, you can change the look of slides throughout a presentation. For example, by changing the Master Title Style font, you can change fonts in all the slide titles in your presentation.

**Book III
Chapter 2**

Fashioning a Look for Your Presentation

PowerPoint's Slide Master–layouts–slides system is designed on the "trickle down" theory. When you format a master style on the Slide Master, formats trickle down to layouts and then to slides. When you format a master style on a layout, the formats trickle down to slides you created using the same slide layout. This chain-of-command relationship is designed to work from the top down, with the master slide and layouts barking orders to the slides below. In the interest of design consistency, slides take orders from layouts, and layouts take orders from the Slide Master.

TIP

In Slide Master view, you can move the pointer over a layout thumbnail in the Slides pane to see a pop-up box that tells you the layout's name and which slides in your presentation "use" the layout. For example, a pop-up box that reads "Title and Content Layout: used by slide(s) 2-3, 8" tells you that slides 2 through 3 and 8 in your presentation are governed by the Title and Content layout.

Editing a master slide

Now that you know the relationship among the Slide Master, layouts, and slides, you're ready to start editing master slides. To edit a master slide, switch to Slide Master view, select a master slide, and change a master style. To insert a picture on a master slide, visit the Insert tab.

Changing a master slide layout

Changing the layout of a master slide entails changing the position and size of text frames and content frames as well as removing these frames:

✦ **Changing size of frames:** Select the frame you want to change, and then move the pointer over a frame handle on the corner, side, top, or bottom of the frame and drag when you see the double-headed arrow.

✦ **Moving frames:** Move the pointer over the perimeter of a frame, click when you see the four-headed arrow, and drag.

✦ **Removing a frame from the Slide Master:** Click the perimeter of the frame to select it and then press Delete.

✦ **Adding a frame to the Slide Master:** Select the slide master, and on the Slide Master tab, click the Master Layout button. You see the Master Layout dialog box. Select the check box beside the name of each frame you want to add and click OK.

Creating a theme

As "Choosing a Theme for Your Presentation" explains earlier in this chapter, a theme is a prefabricated slide design that you can choose on the Themes gallery on the Design tab. If you don't like the themes in the Themes gallery or you want to create a theme with your business's colors, you can do it. You can create a theme of your own, put it in the Themes gallery, and be able to apply it to PowerPoint presentations.

Here are ways to save, rename, and delete themes that you tweaked or customized:

✔ **Saving a theme:** On the Design tab, open the Themes gallery and choose Save Current Theme. You see the Save Current Theme dialog box. Enter a descriptive name for your theme and click the Save button.

✔ **Renaming a theme:** In Windows Explorer or Computer, go to the folder where custom theme files (`.thmx`) are kept. In Windows Vista and Windows 7, go to the `C:\Users\`*`Your Name`*`\AppData\` `Roaming\Microsoft\Templates\` `Document Themes` folder; in Windows XP, go to the `C:\Documents and` `Settings\`*`Your Name`* `(or All` `Users or Default User)\` `Application Data\Microsoft\` `Templates\Document Themes` folder. Then rename the theme file (right-click it, choose Rename, and enter a new name).

✔ **Deleting a theme:** In Windows Explorer or Computer, go to the folder where custom theme files (`.thmx`) are kept. In Windows Vista and Windows 7, go to the `C:\Users\`*`Your Name`*`\AppData\` `Roaming\Microsoft\Templates\` `Document Themes` folder; in Windows XP, go to the `C:\Documents and` `Settings\`*`Your Name`* `(or All` `Users or Default User)\` `Application Data\Microsoft\` `Templates\Document Themes` folder. Then delete the theme file (select it and press the Del key).

Chapter 3: Entering the Text

In This Chapter

✔ **Entering and changing the font, size, and color of text**

✔ **Creating text boxes and text box shapes**

✔ **Handling overflow text in text boxes and frames**

✔ **Aligning the text in text boxes and text frames**

✔ **Creating bulleted and numbered lists**

✔ **Placing footers and headers on slides**

This chapter explains how to change the appearance of text, create text boxes, and create text box shapes. I solve the riddle of what to do when text doesn't fit in a text box or text placeholder frame. You also discover how to align text, handle bulleted and numbered lists, and put footers and headers on all or some of the slides in your presentation.

By the time you finish reading this chapter, if you read it all the way through, you will be one of those people others turn to when they have a PowerPoint question about entering text on slides. You'll become a little guru in your own right.

Entering Text

No presentation is complete without a word or two, which is why the first thing you see when you add a new slide to a presentation are the words "Click to add text." As soon as you "click," those words of instruction disappear, and you're free to enter a title or text of your own. Most slides include a text placeholder frame at the top for entering a slide title; many slides also have another, larger text placeholder frame for entering a bulleted list.

As shown in Figure 3-1, the easiest way to enter text on slides is to click in a text placeholder frame and start typing. The other way is to switch to Normal view, select the Outline tab in the Slides pane (see Figure 3-1), and enter text there.

On the Slides pane in Normal/Outline view   In a text placeholder frame

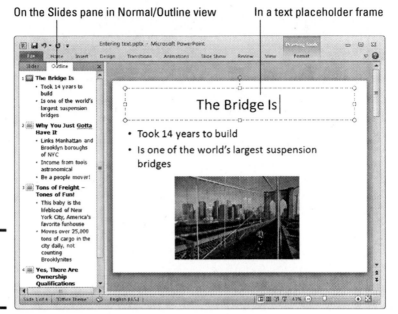

Figure 3-1:
Ways of
entering
text.

Enter text on slides the same way you enter text in a Word document — by wiggling your fingers over the keyboard. While you're at it, you can change fonts, the font size of text, and the color of text, as the following pages explain. (Chapter 1 of this mini-book describes how to get the text for slides from the headings in a Word document; Book I, Chapter 2 explains everything a sane person needs to know about handling fonts.)

Choosing fonts for text

If you aren't happy with the fonts in your presentation, you have three ways to remedy the problem:

✦ **Dig in and choose new fonts on a slide-by-slide basis.** Select the text, go to the Home tab, and choose a font from the Font drop-down list or the Font dialog box.

 ✦ **Select new theme fonts for your presentation.** Theme fonts are combinations of fonts that the designers of PowerPoint themes deem appropriate for the theme you're working in. To change theme fonts, go to the Design tab, click the Fonts button, and select a new font combination.

✦ **Choose a new font on a master slide to change fonts throughout your presentation.** Chapter 2 of this mini-book explains master slides and how you can use them to change formats simultaneously on many slides. In Slide Master view, select a master slide and change its fonts on the Home tab.

Changing the font size of text

For someone in the back row of an audience to be able to read text in a PowerPoint presentation, the text should be no smaller than 28 points. Try this simple test to see whether text in your presentation is large enough to read: Stand five or so feet from your computer and see whether you can read the text. If you can't read it, make it larger.

Go to the Home tab and select the text whose size you want to change. Then use one of these techniques to change font sizes:

✦ **Font Size drop-down list:** Open this list and choose a point size. To choose a point size that isn't on the list, click in the Font Size text box, enter a point size, and press Enter.

✦ **Font dialog box:** Click the Font group button to open the Font dialog box. Then either choose a point size from the Size drop-down list or enter a point size in the Size text box and click OK.

 ✦ **Increase Font Size and Decrease Font Size buttons:** Click these buttons (or press Ctrl+> or Ctrl+<) to increase or decrease the point size by the next interval on the Font Size drop-down list. Watch the Font Size list or your text and note how the text changes size. This is an excellent technique when you want to "eyeball it" and you don't care to fool with the Font Size list or Font dialog box.

Changing the color of text

Before you change the color of text, peer into your computer screen and examine the background theme or color you selected for your slides. Unless the color of the text is different from the theme or color, the audience can't read the text. Besides choosing a color that contributes to the overall tone of the presentation, select a color that is easy to read.

Select the text that needs touching up and then use one of these techniques to change the color of text:

 ✦ On the mini-toolbar, open the drop-down list on the Font Color button and choose a color.

✦ On the Home tab, open the drop-down list on the Font Color button and choose a color.

✦ On the Home tab, click the Font group button to open the Font dialog box, click the Font Color button in the dialog box, and choose a color on the drop-down list.

The Font Color drop-down list offers theme colors and standard colors. You are well advised to choose a theme color. These colors jive with the theme you chose for your presentation.

Fixing a top-heavy title

In typesetting terminology, a *top-heavy title* is a title in which the first line is much longer than the second. Whenever a title extends to two lines, it runs the risk of being top-heavy. Unsightly top-heavy titles look especially bad on PowerPoint slides, where text is blown up to 40 points or more.

To fix a top-heavy title, click where you prefer the lines to break and then press Shift+Enter. Pressing Shift+Enter creates a *hard line break*, a forced break at the end of one line.

(To remove a hard line break, click where the break occurs and then press the Delete key.)

The only drawback of hard line breaks is remembering where you made them. In effect, the line breaks are invisible. When you edit a title with a line break, the line break remains, and unless you know it's there, you discover the line breaking in an odd place. The moral is: If you're editing a title and the text keeps moving to the next line, you may have entered a hard line break and forgotten about it.

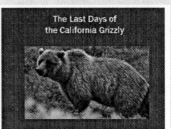

Fun with Text Boxes and Text Box Shapes

Text boxes give you an opportunity to exercise your creativity. They add another element to slides. Use them to position text wherever you want, annotate a chart or equation, or place an announcement on a slide. You can even create a vertical text box in which the text reads from top to bottom instead of left to right, or turn a text box into a circle, arrow, or other shape. Figure 3-2 shows examples of text boxes and text box shapes.

In Office terminology, a PowerPoint text box is an object. Book I, Chapter 8 explains all the different techniques for handling objects, including how to make them overlap and change their sizes. Here are the basics of handling text boxes in PowerPoint:

✦ **Creating a text box:** On the Insert tab, click the Text Box button and move the pointer to a part of the slide where you can see the *text box pointer*, a downward-pointing arrow. Then click and start dragging to create your text box, and enter the text.

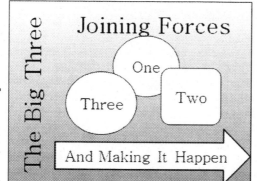

Figure 3-2:
Examples of text boxes and text box shapes.

✦ **Filling a text box with a color style:** On the (Drawing Tools) Format tab, choose a style on the Shape Styles gallery.

✦ **Rotating a text box (text included):** Use one of these techniques to rotate a text box along with the text inside it:

• Drag the rotation handle, the green circle above the text box.

• On the (Drawing Tools) Format tab, click the Rotate button and choose a Rotate or Flip command on the drop-down list.

• On the (Drawing Tools) Format tab, click the Size group button (you may have to click the Size button first) and, in the Size category of the Format Shape dialog box, enter a measurement in the Rotation box.

✦ **Turning a shape into a text box:** Create the shape, and then click in the shape and start typing. (Book I, Chapter 8 explains how to create a shape.)

✦ **Turning a text box into a shape:** Right-click the text box and choose Format Shape. In the Format Shape dialog box, go to the Text Box category and, under AutoFit, select the Do Not AutoFit option button. Then close the dialog box, go to the (Drawing Tools) Format tab, click the Edit Shape button, choose Change Shape on the drop-down list, and choose a shape on the Change Shape submenu.

Many people object to the small text boxes that appear initially when you create a text box. If you prefer to establish the size of text boxes when you create them, not when you enter text, change the AutoFit setting and then create a default text box with the new setting. The next section in this chapter explains how to change the AutoFit settings.

Controlling How Text Fits in Text Frames and Text Boxes

When text doesn't fit in a text placeholder frame or text box, PowerPoint takes measures to make it fit. In a text placeholder frame, PowerPoint shrinks the amount of space between lines and then it shrinks the text itself. When text doesn't fit in a text box, PowerPoint enlarges the text box to fit more text. PowerPoint handles overflow text as part of its AutoFit mechanism.

How AutoFit works is up to you. If, like me, you don't care for how PowerPoint enlarges text boxes when you enter the text, you can tell PowerPoint not to "AutoFit" text, but instead to make text boxes large from the get-go. And if you don't care for how PowerPoint shrinks text in text placeholder frames, you can tell PowerPoint not to shrink text. These pages explain how to choose AutoFit options for overflow text in your text frames and text boxes.

Choosing how PowerPoint "AutoFits" text in text frames

When text doesn't fit in a text placeholder frame and PowerPoint has to "AutoFit" the text, you see the AutoFit Options button. Click this button to open a drop-down list with options for handling overflow text, as shown in Figure 3-3. The AutoFit options — along with a couple of other techniques, as I explain shortly — represent the "one at a time" way of handling overflow text. You can also change the default AutoFit options for handling overflow text, as I also explain if you'll bear with me a while longer and quit your yawning.

"AutoFitting" the text one frame at a time

When text doesn't fit in a text placeholder frame, especially a title frame, the first question to ask is, "Do I want to fool with the integrity of the slide design?" Making the text fit usually means shrinking the text, enlarging the text frame, or compromising the slide design in some way, but audiences notice design inconsistencies. Slides are shown on large screens where design flaws are easy to see.

Making text fit in a text frame usually means making a compromise. Here are different ways to handle the problem of text not fitting in a text frame. Be prepared to click the Undo button when you experiment with these techniques:

✦ **Edit the text:** Usually when text doesn't fit in a frame, the text needs editing. It needs to be made shorter. A slide is not a place for a treatise. Editing the text is the only way to make it fit in the frame without compromising the design.

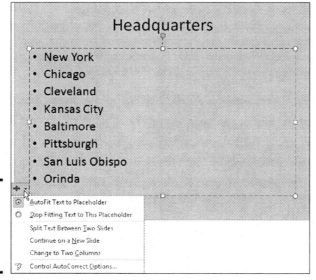

Figure 3-3:
The laundry
list of
AutoFit
options.

✦ **Enlarge the frame:** Click the AutoFit Options button and choose Stop Fitting Text to This Placeholder on the shortcut menu (see Figure 3-3). Then select the frame and drag the bottom or top selection handle to enlarge it.

✦ **Decrease the font size:** Select the text, go to the Home tab, and choose a smaller Font Size measurement. You can also click the Decrease Font Size button (or press Ctrl+<) to decrease the font size.

✦ **Decrease the amount of spacing between lines:** On the Home tab, click the Paragraph group button to open the Paragraph dialog box and decrease the After measurement under Spacing.

✦ **Change the frame's internal margins:** Similar to a page, text frames have internal margins to keep text from getting too close to a frame border. By shrinking these margins, you can make more room for text. Right-click the text frame and choose Format Shape. Then, in the Text Box category of the Format Shape dialog box, enter smaller measurements for the Internal Margin boxes.

✦ **Create a new slide for the text:** If you're dealing with a list or paragraph text in a body text frame, the AutoFit Options drop-down list offers two ways to create a new slide (refer to Figure 3-3). Choose Continue on a New Slide to run the text onto another slide; choose Split Text Between Two Slides to divide the text evenly between two slides. I don't recommend either option, though. If you need to make a new slide, do it on your own and then rethink how to present the material. Inserting a new slide to accommodate a long list throws a presentation off-track.

**Book III
Chapter 3**

Entering the Text

Choosing default AutoFit options for text frames

Unless you change the default AutoFit options, PowerPoint shrinks the amount of space between lines and then shrinks the text itself to make text fit in text placeholder frames. Follow these steps if you want to decide for yourself whether PowerPoint "auto-fits" text in text frames:

1. **Open the AutoFormat As You Type tab in the AutoCorrect dialog box.**

    Here are the two ways to get there:

    - Click the AutoFit Options button (refer to Figure 3-3) and choose Control AutoCorrect Options on the drop-down list.

    - On the File tab, choose Options to open the PowerPoint Options dialog box. In the Proofing category, click the AutoCorrect Options button.

2. **Deselect the AutoFit Title Text to Placeholder check box to prevent auto-fitting in title text placeholder frames.**

3. **Deselect the AutoFit Body Text to Placeholder check box to prevent auto-fitting in text placeholder frames apart from title frames.**

4. **Click OK.**

Choosing how PowerPoint "AutoFits" text in text boxes

PowerPoint offers three options for handling overflow text in text boxes:

- **Do Not AutoFit:** Doesn't fit text in the text box but lets text spill out

- **Shrink Text on Overflow:** Shrinks the text to make it fit in the text box

- **Resize Shape to Fit Text:** Enlarges the text box to make the text fit inside it

Follow these steps to tell PowerPoint how or whether to fit text in text boxes:

1. **Select the text box.**

2. **Right-click the text box and choose Format Shape.**

    You see the Format Shape dialog box.

3. **Go to the Text Box category.**

4. **Choose an AutoFit option: Do Not AutoFit, Shrink Text on Overflow, or Resize Shape to Fit Text.**

5. **Click the Close button.**

Some people find it easier to dispense with "auto-fitting." If you're one of those people, go to the Text Box category of the Format Shape dialog box, and under AutoFit, choose the Do Not AutoFit option or the Shrink Text on Overflow option. To make your AutoFit setting applicable to all the text boxes you create in your presentation, right-click the text box and choose Set As Default Text Box on the shortcut menu.

Positioning Text in Frames and Text Boxes

How text is positioned in text frames and text boxes is governed by two sets of commands: the Align Text commands and the Align commands. By choosing combinations of Align and Align Text commands, you can land text where you want it in a text frame or text box. Just wrestle with these two commands until you land your text where you want it to be in a text frame or box:

✦ Align commands control horizontal (left-to-right) alignments. On the Home tab, click the Align Left (press Ctrl+L), Center (press Ctrl+E), Align Right (press Ctrl+R), or Justify button.

✦ Align Text commands control vertical (up-and-down) alignments. On the Home tab, click the Align Text button and choose Top, Middle, or Bottom on the drop-down list, as shown in Figure 3-4.

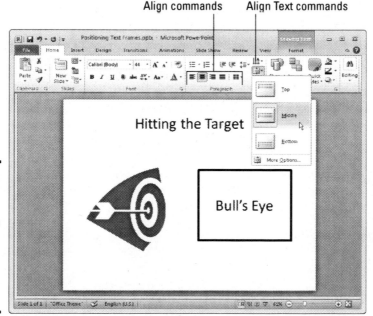

Figure 3-4:
Choose an Align Text and an Align command to position text in text frames and boxes.

Handling Bulleted and Numbered Lists

What is a PowerPoint presentation without a list or two? It's like an emperor without any clothes on. This part of the chapter explains everything there is to know about bulleted and numbered lists.

Lists can be as simple or complex as you want them to be. PowerPoint offers a bunch of different ways to format lists, but if you're in a hurry or you don't care whether your lists look like everyone else's, you can take advantage of the Numbering and Bullets buttons and go with standard lists. Nonconformists and people with nothing else to do, however, can try their hand at making fancy lists. The following pages cover that topic, too.

Creating a standard bulleted or numbered list

In typesetting terms, a *bullet* is a black, filled-in circle or other character that marks an item on a list. Many slide layouts include text frames that are formatted already for bulleted lists. All you have to do in these text frames is "click to add text" and keep pressing the Enter key while you enter items for your bulleted list. Each time you press Enter, PowerPoint adds another bullet to the list. Bulleted lists are useful when you want to present the audience with alternatives or present a list in which the items aren't ranked in any order. Use a numbered list to rank items in a list or present step-by-step instructions.

Follow these instructions to create a standard bulleted or numbered list:

+ **Creating a bulleted list:** Select the list if you've already entered the list items, go to the Home tab, and click the Bullets button. You can also right-click, choose Bullets on the shortcut menu, and choose a bullet character on the submenu if you don't care for the standard, black, filled-in circle.

+ **Creating a numbered list:** Select the list if you've already entered the list items, go to the Home tab, and click the Numbering button. You can also right-click, choose Numbering on the shortcut menu, and select a numbering style on the submenu.

+ **Converting a numbered to a bulleted list (or vice versa):** Drag over the list to select it, go to the Home tab, and then click the Bullets or Numbering button.

To remove the bullets or numbers from a list, select the list, open the drop-down list on the Bullets or Numbering button, and choose None.

Choosing a different bullet character, size, and color

As Figure 3-5 demonstrates, the black filled-in circle isn't the only character you can use to mark items in a bulleted list. You can also opt for what PowerPoint calls *pictures* (colorful bullets of many sizes and shapes) or symbols from the Symbol dialog box. While you're at it, you can change the bullets' color and size.

Figure 3-5:
Examples of characters you can use for bulleted lists.

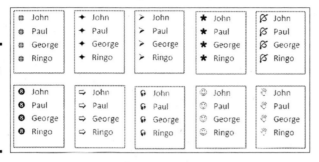

If you decide to change the bullet character in your lists, be consistent from slide to slide. Unless you want to be goofy, select the same bullet character throughout the lists in your presentation for the sake of consistency. You don't want to turn your slide presentation into a showcase for bullets, do you?

To use pictures or unusual symbols for bullets, start by selecting your bulleted list, going to the Home tab, and opening the drop-down list on the Bullets button. Do any of the bullets on the drop-down list tickle your fancy? If one does, select it; otherwise, click the Bullets and Numbering option at the bottom of the drop-down list. You see the Bulleted tab of the Bullets and Numbering dialog box. Starting there, you can customize your bullets:

✦ **Using a picture for bullets:** Click the Picture button and select a bullet in the Picture Bullet dialog box.

✦ **Using a symbol for bullets:** Click the Customize button and select a symbol in the Symbol dialog box. By opening the Font drop-down list and choosing a Wingdings font, you can choose an oddball character for bullets.

✦ **Changing bullets' size:** Enter a percentage figure in the Size % of Text box. For example, if you enter **200**, the bullets are twice as large as the font size you choose for the items in your bulleted list.

✦ **Changing bullets' color:** Click the Color button in the Bullets and Numbering dialog box and choose an option on the drop-down list. Theme colors are considered most compatible with the theme design you chose for your presentation.

Choosing a different list-numbering style, size, and color

PowerPoint offers seven different ways of numbering lists. As well as choosing a different numbering style, you can change the size of numbers relative to the text and change the color of numbers. To select a different list-numbering style, size, or color, begin by selecting your list, going to the Home tab, and opening the drop-down list on the Numbering button. If you like one of the numbering-scheme choices, select it; otherwise choose Bullets and Numbering to open the Numbered tab of the Bullets and Numbering dialog box. In this dialog box, you can customize list numbers:

✦ **Choosing a numbering scheme:** Select a numbering scheme and click OK.

✦ **Changing the numbers' size:** Enter a percentage figure in the Size % of the Text box. For example, if you enter 50, the numbers are half as big as the font size you chose for the items in your numbered list.

✦ **Changing the numbers' color:** Click the Color button and choose a color on the drop-down list. Theme colors are more compatible with the theme design you chose than the other colors are.

Putting Footers (and Headers) on Slides

A *footer* is a line of text that appears at the foot, or bottom, of a slide. Figure 3-6 shows a footer. Typically, a footer includes the date, a company name, and/or a slide number, and footers appear on every slide in a presentation if they appear at all. That doesn't mean you can't exclude a footer from a slide or put footers on some slides, as I explain shortly. For that matter, you can move slide numbers, company names, and dates to the top of slides, in which case they become *headers*. When I was a kid, "header" meant crashing your bike and falling headfirst over the handlebars. How times change.

These pages explain everything a body needs to know about footers and headers — how to enter them, make them appear on all or some slides, and exclude them from slides.

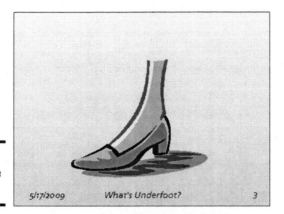

Figure 3-6:
An example
of a footer.

5/17/2009   *What's Underfoot?*   *3*

Some background on footers and headers

PowerPoint provides the Header & Footer command to enter the date, a
word or two, and a slide number on the bottom of all slides in your
presentation. This command is really just a convenient way to enter a
footer on the Slide Master without having to switch to Slide Master view. As
Chapter 2 of this mini-book explains, the Slide Master governs the formatting
and layout of all slides in your presentation. The Slide Master includes text
placeholder frames for a date, some text, and a slide number. Anything you
enter on the Slide Master, including a footer, appears on all your slides.

If a date, some text, and a slide number along the bottom of all the slides in
your presentation is precisely what you want, you've got it made. You can
enter a footer on every slide in your presentation with no trouble at all by
using the Header & Footer command. However, if you're a maverick and you
want your footers and headers to be a little different from the next guy's — if
you want the date, for example, to be in the upper-right corner of slides or
you want footers to appear on some slides but not others — you have some
tweaking to do. You may have to create a nonstandard footer or remove the
footer from some of the slides.

Putting a standard footer on all your slides

A standard footer includes the date, some text, and the page number. To put
a standard footer on all the slides in your presentation, go to the Insert tab
and click the Header & Footer button. You see the Header and Footer dialog
box. Choose some or all of these options and click the Apply to All button:

✦ **Date and Time:** Select this check box to make the date appear in the lower-left corner of all your slides. Then tell PowerPoint whether you want a current or fixed date:

- *Update Automatically:* Select this option button to make the day's date (or date and time) appear in the footer, and then open the drop-down list to choose a date (or date and time) format. With this option, the date you give your presentation always appears on slides.

- *Fixed:* Select this option button and enter a date in the text box. For example, enter the date you created the presentation. With this option, the date remains fixed no matter when or where you give the presentation.

✦ **Slide Number:** Select this check box to make slide numbers appear in the lower-right corner of all slides.

✦ **Footer:** Select this check box, and in the text box, enter the words that you want to appear in the bottom, middle of all the slides.

Creating a nonstandard footer

As "Some background on footers and headers" explains earlier in this chapter, you have to look elsewhere than the Header and Footer dialog box if you want to create something besides the standard footer. Suppose you want to move the slide number from the lower-right corner of slides to another position? Or you want to fool with the fonts in headers and footers?

Follow these steps to create a nonstandard footer:

1. **Create a standard footer if you want your nonstandard footer to include today's date and/or a slide number.**

    If you want to move the slide number into the upper-right corner of slides, for example, create a standard footer first (see the preceding topic in this chapter). Later, you can move the slide number text frame into the upper-right corner of slides.

2. **On the View tab, click the Slide Master button.**

   You switch to Slide Master view. Chapter 2 of this mini-book explains this view and how to format many slides at once with master slides.

3. **Select the Slide Master, the topmost slide in the Slides pane.**

4. **Adjust and format the footer text boxes to taste (as they say in cookbooks).**

   For example, move the slide number text frame into the upper-right corner to put slide numbers there. Or change the font in the footer text boxes. Or place a company logo on the Slide Master to make the logo appear on all your slides.

5. **Click the Close Master View button to leave Slide Master view.**

   You can always return to Slide Master view and adjust your footer.

Removing a footer from a single slide

On a crowded slide, the date, footer text, page number, and other items in the footer can get in the way or be a distraction. Fortunately, removing one or all of the footer text frames from a slide is easy:

1. **Switch to Normal view and display the slide with the footer that needs removing.**

2. **On the Insert tab, click the Header & Footer button.**

   The Header and Footer dialog box appears.

3. **Deselect check boxes — Date and Time, Slide Number, and Footer — to tell PowerPoint which parts of the footer you want to remove.**

4. **Click the Apply button.**

   Be careful not to click the Apply to All button. Clicking this button removes footers throughout your slide presentation.

Running text into columns

Text looks mighty nice when it is run into columns. Because PowerPoint slides are supposed to present text in short bursts, you don't get many opportunities to present long text passages on PowerPoint slides. Still, if you must present a long text passage, consider running it into two columns because columns look so very, very elegant.

Follow these steps to present a long text passage in two or more columns:

1. **Click in the text box or frame with the long text passage.**

2. **On the Home tab, click the Columns button.**

   A drop-down list appears.

3. **Choose Two Columns or Three Columns to run the text into two or three columns.**

   You can also choose More Columns, and in the Columns dialog box, enter how many columns you want, enter how much space in inches to put between columns, and click OK.

To cease running text in columns, click the Columns button and choose One Column on the drop-down list.

Here are some tricks worth knowing where columns are concerned:

✔ **Making columns of equal length:** If one column is longer than the other and you want the columns to be of equal length, right-click in the text frame or text box and choose Format Shape. You see the Format Shape dialog box. Go to the Text Box category, select the Resize Shape to Fit Text option button, and click Close. Then adjust the size of the text frame or text box.

✔ **Adjusting the space between columns:** Click the Columns button and choose More Columns on the drop-down list to open the Columns dialog box. Then enter a measurement in the Spacing text box and click OK.

✔ **Justifying the text:** Text that has been run into columns looks better when it is justified because the Justify command helps to define the columns. As "Aligning text in frames and text boxes" explains earlier in this chapter, justified text is aligned on both the left and right side. Aligning the text along the right side as well as the left helps define the right side of the column in text that has been run into columns. To justify text, click it and press Ctrl+J or go to the Home tab and click the Justify button.

Anti-Federalist 84

Anti-Federalist 84

Chapter 4: Making Your Presentations Livelier

In This Chapter

✔ Looking at ways to make a presentation livelier

✔ Slapping a transition or animation on a slide

✔ Making sound a part of your presentation

✔ Playing video during a presentation

✔ Recording a narration for your slide show

The purpose of this chapter is to make your presentation stand out in a crowd. It suggests ways to enliven your presentation with pictures, charts, slides, and tables. It shows how transitions and animations can make a presentation livelier. Finally, you discover how to play sound and video during a presentation, including how to record a voice narration.

Suggestions for Enlivening Your Presentation

Starting on the Insert tab, you can do a lot to make a presentation livelier. The Insert tab offers buttons for putting pictures, tables, charts, diagrams, shapes, and clip-art images on slides:

✦ **Photos:** Everyone likes a good photo, but more than that, audiences understand more from words and pictures than they do from words alone. A well-chosen photo reinforces the ideas that you're trying to put across in your presentation. (See Book VIII, Chapter 3.)

✦ **Tables:** A table is a great way to plead your case or defend your position. Raw table data is irrefutable — well, most of the time, anyway. Create a table when you want to demonstrate how the numbers back you up. (See Book I, Chapter 5.)

✦ **Charts:** Nothing is more persuasive than a chart. The bars, pie slices, or columns show the audience instantaneously that production is up or down, or that sector A is outperforming sector B. The audience can compare the data and see what's what. (See Book I, Chapter 6.)

✦ **Diagrams:** A diagram is an excellent marriage of images and words. Diagrams allow an audience to literally visualize a concept, idea, or relationship. You can present an abstract idea such that the audience understands it better. (See Book I, Chapter 7.)

✦ **Shapes:** Lines and shapes can also illustrate ideas and concepts. You can also use them as slide decorations. (See Book I, Chapter 8.)

✦ **Clip-art images:** Clip-art images bring a little more color to presentations. They make presentations friendlier and easier to look at. (See Book VIII, Chapter 4.)

The grid and drawing guides

The *grid* is an invisible set of horizontal and vertical lines to which objects — clip-art images, pictures, and shapes — cling when you move them on a slide. The grid is meant to help you line up objects squarely with one another. When you drag an object, it sticks to the nearest point on the grid.

PowerPoint also offers the *drawing guides* for aligning objects. You can drag these vertical and horizontal lines on-screen and use them to align objects with precision.

To display the grid and the drawing guides:

✔ **Displaying (and hiding) the grid:** Press Shift+F9 or go to the View tab and select the Gridlines check box.

✔ **Displaying (and hiding) the drawing guides:** Press Alt+F9 or go to the View tab and select the Guides check box.

By default, objects when you move them "snap to the grid." That means the objects stick to the nearest grid line when you move them across a slide. To control whether objects snap to the grid, right-click (but not on an object or frame), choose Grid and Guides, and in the Grid and Guides dialog box, deselect the Snap Objects to Grid check box.

Even if the Snap Objects to Grid check box in the Grid and Guides dialog box is selected, you can move objects without them snapping to a gridline by holding down the Alt key while you drag.

Select the Snap Objects to Other Objects check box if you want shapes to abut each other or fall along a common axis.

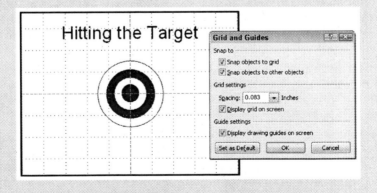

Exploring Transitions and Animations

In PowerPoint-speak, a *transition* is a little bit of excitement that occurs as one slide leaves the screen and the next slide climbs aboard. An *animation* is movement on the slide. For example, you can animate bulleted lists such that the bullet points appear on a slide one at a time when you click the mouse rather than all at one time.

Before you know anything about transitions and animations, you should know that they can be distracting. The purpose of a presentation is to communicate with the audience, not display the latest, busiest, most dazzling presentation technology. For user-run, kiosk-style presentations, however, eye-catching transitions and animations can be useful because they draw an audience. (A user-run presentation plays on its own, as I explain in Chapter 5 of this mini-book.) For audiences that enjoy high-tech wizardry, transitions and animations can be a lot of fun and add to a presentation.

Showing transitions between slides

Transitions include the Switch, Fade, and Push. Figure 4-1 shows how a transition works. For the figure, I chose the Clock transition. This slide doesn't so much arrive on-screen as it does sweep onto the screen in a clockwise fashion. You get a chance to test-drive these transitions before you attach them to slides.

Book III
Chapter 4

Making Your
Presentations
Livelier

Figure 4-1:
The Clock
transition in
action.

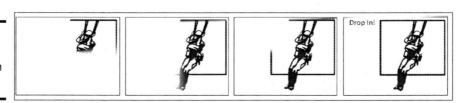

Drop In!

Assigning transitions to slides

To show transitions between slides, select the slide or slides that need transitions, go to the Transitions tab, and select a transition in the Transition to This Slide gallery. (To apply the same transition to all the slides in a presentation, click the Apply To All button after you select a transition.) The names and images in the gallery give you an idea of what the transitions are, and you can click the Preview button at any time to watch a transition you chose.

The Transitions tab offers these tools for tweaking a transition:

+ **Effect Options:** Click the Effect Options button and choose an effect on the drop-down list. For example, choose From Top or From Bottom to make a transition arrive from the top or bottom of the screen. Not all transitions offer effect options.

+ **Sound:** Open the Sound drop-down list and choose a sound to accompany the transition. The Loop Until Next Sound option at the bottom of the drop-down list plays a sound continuously until the next slide in the presentation appears.

+ **Duration:** Enter a time period in the Duration box to declare how quickly or slowly you want the transition to occur.

As I mention earlier, you can click the Apply To All button to assign the same transition to all the slides in your presentation.

Altering and removing slide transitions

In the Slides pane and Slide Sorter view, the transition symbol, a flying star, appears next to slides that have been assigned a transition. Select the slides that need a transition change, go to the Transitions tab, and follow these instructions to alter or remove transitions:

+ **Altering a transition:** Choose a different transition in the Transition to This Slide gallery. You can also choose different effect options and sounds, and change the duration of the transition.

+ **Removing a transition:** Choose None in the Transition to This Slide gallery.

Animating parts of a slide

When it comes to animations, you can choose between *animation schemes,* the pre-built special effects made by the elves of Microsoft, or customized animations that you build on your own. Only fans of animation and people with a lot of time on their hands go the second route.

Choosing a ready-made animation scheme

Follow these steps to preview and choose an animation scheme for slides:

1. **Go to the Animations tab.**

2. **Click to select the element on the slide that you want to animate.**

For example, select a text frame with a bulleted list. You can tell when you've selected an element because a selection box appears around it.

3. In the Animation Styles gallery, choose an animation effect, as shown in Figure 4-2.

You can choose Entrance, Emphasis, and Exit animation effects. As soon as you make your choice, the animation springs to life, and you can click the Preview button at any time to see your animation in all its glory.

Choose an animation   How elements are animated

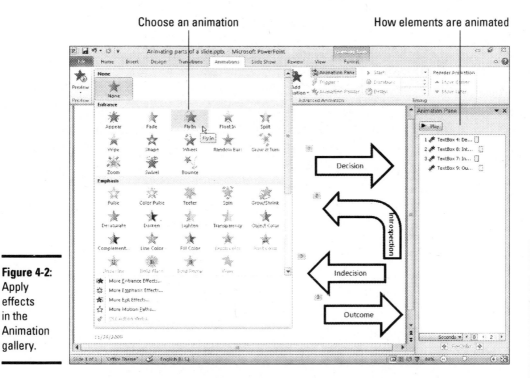

Figure 4-2: Apply effects in the Animation gallery.

4. Click the Effect Options button and experiment with choices on the drop-down list to tweak your animation.

Which options are available depends on the animation you chose.

5. If you choose a text-box or text-frame element with more than one paragraph in Step 2, click the Effect Options button and tell PowerPoint whether to animate all the text or animate each paragraph separately from the others.

- **All at Once:** All the text is animated at the same time.

- **By Paragraph:** Each paragraph is treated separately and is animated on its own. For example, each item in a bulleted list is treated as a separate element — each item fades, wipes, or flies in after the one before it, not at the same time as the one before it.

Very briefly, you see a preview of the animation choice you made. To get a good look at the animation you just chose for your slide, click the Preview button on the Animations tab.

To remove an animation, return to the Animation Styles gallery and choose None.

Fashioning your own animation schemes

To fashion your own animation scheme, go to the Animations tab and click the Animation Pane button. You see the Animation pane, as shown in Figure 4-2. It lists, in order, each animation that occurs on your slide (if animations occur). Select an element on the slide and follow these general instructions to animate it:

+ Click the Add Animation button and choose an animation.

+ On the Start drop-down list, declare whether the animation begins when you click your slide (On Click), at the same time as the previous animation (With Previous), or after the previous animation (After Previous).

+ In the Duration box, enter how long you want the animation to last.

+ In the Delay box, enter a time period to declare how soon after the previous animation in the Animation pane you want your animation to occur.

+ Select an animation in the task pane and click a Re-Order button to change the order in which animations occur, if more than one element is animated on your slide.

Making Audio Part of Your Presentation

Especially in user-run, kiosk-style presentations, audio can be a welcome addition. Audio gives presentations an extra dimension. It attracts an audience. PowerPoint offers two ways to make audio part of a presentation:

+ **As part of slide transitions:** A sound is heard as a new slide arrives on-screen. On the Transitions tab, open the Sound drop-down list and choose a sound. (See "Showing transitions between slides" earlier in this chapter.)

+ **On the slide itself:** The means of playing audio appears on the slide in the form of an Audio icon, as shown in Figure 4-3. By moving the mouse over this icon, you can display audio controls, and you can use these controls to play audio. You can also make audio play as soon as the slide arrives on-screen.

Figure 4-3:
Making
audio
part of a
presentation.

Book III
Chapter 4

**Making Your
Presentations
Livelier**

Table 4-1 describes the audio files you can use in PowerPoint presentations and whether each file type is a wave or MIDI sound. To find out what kind of audio file you're dealing with, note the file's three-letter extension; or open Windows Explorer or Computer, find the sound file, right-click it, and choose Properties.

Table 4-1	Sound File Formats	
File Type	*Extension*	*Wave/MIDI*
AIFF audio	.aif,.aiff	Wave
AU Audio	.au	Wave
Quick Time Audio	.3g2,.aac,mp4	Wave
MIDI Sequence	.midi,.mid	MIDI
MP3 audio file	.mp3	Wave
Wave audio	.wav	Wave
Windows Media Audio File	.wma	Wave

Inserting an audio file on a slide

Follow these steps to insert an audio file in a slide:

1. **Go to the Insert tab.**

2. **Click the Audio button.**

   You see the Insert Audio dialog box.

3. **Locate and select a sound file and then click Insert.**

   Earlier in this chapter, Table 4-1 lists the type of sound files that you can play in presentations.

An Audio icon appears on the slide to remind you that audio is supposed to play when your slide is on-screen. You can change the size of this icon by selecting it and dragging a corner handle or going to the (Audio Tools) Format tab and entering new Height and Width measurements. You can also drag the icon into an out-of-the-way corner of your slide.

To quit playing a sound file on a slide, select its Audio icon and then press the Delete key.

Telling PowerPoint when and how to play an audio file

To tell PowerPoint when and how to play an audio file, start by selecting the Audio icon and going to the (Audio Tools) Playback tab, as shown in Figure 4-4. From there, you can control when and how audio files play:

✦ **Controlling the volume:** Click the Volume button and choose an option on the drop-down list to control how loudly the audio plays.

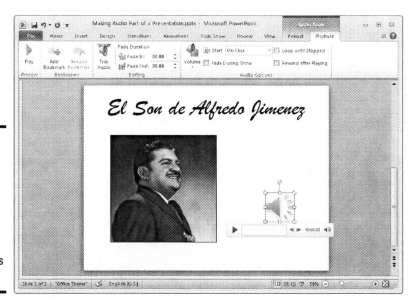

Figure 4-4:
Visit the (Audio Tools) Playback tab to control when and how sounds play.

✦ **Deciding when to start playing audio:** On the Start drop-down list, choose Automatically to make the audio play as soon as the slide appears; choose On Click to play the audio when you click the Audio icon on your slide. The Play Across Slides option plays the audio file throughout a presentation.

✦ **Hiding and unhiding the Audio icon:** Select the Hide During Show check box. If you hide the Audio icon, the file must play automatically; otherwise, you won't see the icon and be able to click it and view the audio controls.

✦ **Continuously playing audio:** Select the Loop Until Stopped check box to play the audio file over and over again or until you move to the next slide.

Click the Play button on the (Audio Tools) Playback tab to play an audio file.

Playing audio during a presentation

While an audio file is playing during a presentation, controls for starting, pausing, and controlling the volume appear onscreen (refer to Figure 4-3). They appear onscreen, I should say, if the Audio icon appears on your slide. (If you've hidden the Audio icon, you're out of luck because you can't see the Audio icon or use its audio controls.)

Follow these instructions to start, pause, and control the volume of an audio recording during a presentation:

✦ **Starting an audio file:** Move the pointer over the Audio icon, and when you see the Audio controls, click the Play/Pause button (or press Alt+P).

✦ **Pausing an audio file:** Click the Play/Pause button (or press Alt+P). Click the button again to resume playing the audio file.

✦ **Muting the volume:** Click the Mute/Unmute icon (or press Alt+U).

✦ **Controlling the volume:** Move the pointer over the Mute/Unmute icon to display the volume slider and then drag the volume control on the slider.

**Book III
Chapter 4**

**Making Your
Presentations
Livelier**

Playing Video on Slides

If a picture is worth a thousand words, what is a moving picture worth? Ten thousand? To give your presentation more cachet, you can play video on slides and in so doing, turn your presentation into a mini-movie theater.

To play video, PowerPoint relies on *Windows Media Player,* the media player that comes with Windows. Therefore, to play video on a slide, stick to formats that Windows Media Player can handle: ASF (Advanced Systems Format), AVI (Audio Visual Interleaved), MPEG (Motion Picture Experts Group), MPG (Media Planning Group), WMV (Windows Media Video), MOV (QuickTime Video), and .SWF (Adobe Flash).

Inserting a video on a slide

Follow these steps to insert a video on a slide:

1. **Open the Insert Video dialog box.**

   You can open the dialog box with one of these techniques:

   • Click the Media icon in a content placeholder frame.

   • On the Insert tab, click the Video button.

2. **Select a video file in the Insert Video dialog box and click Insert.**

   The video appears on your slide. If I were you, I would find out how (or whether) the video plays. To do that, click the Play/Pause button (or press Alt+P) or click the Play button on the (Video Tools) Playback or (Video Tools) Format tab.

Fine-tuning a video presentation

As shown in Figure 4-5, select the video and go to the (Video Tools) Playback tab to fine-tune a video presentation. The Playback tab offers all kinds of commands for making a video play the way you want it to play. Here are different ways to fine-tune a video presentation:

✦ **Controlling the volume:** Click the Volume button and choose Low, Medium, High, or Mute to control how loud the video sound is.

✦ **Playing the video automatically or when you click the Play/Pause button:** Open the Start drop-down list and choose Automatically or On Click to tell PowerPoint when to start playing the video.

✦ **Playing the video at full-screen:** Make a video fill the entire screen by selecting the Play Full Screen check box. Be careful of this one. Videos can look terribly grainy when they appear on the big screen.

✦ **Hiding the video when it isn't playing:** You can hide the video until you start playing it by selecting the Hide While Not Playing check box. Be sure to choose Automatically on the Start drop-down list if you select this check box.

✦ **Continuously playing, or looping, the video:** Play a video continuously or until you go to the next slide by selecting the Loop Until Stopped check box.

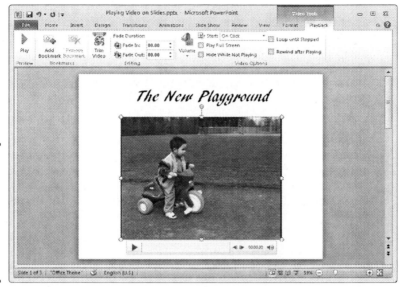

Figure 4-5:
Visit the (Video Tools) Playback tab to fine-tune a video presentation.

✦ **Rewinding the video when it's finished playing:** Rewind a video if you want to see the first frame, not the last, when the video finishes playing. Select the Rewind After Playing check box to make the start of the video appear after the video plays; deselect this option to freeze-frame on the end of the video when it finishes playing.

At the end of this chapter, the sidebar "Editing a video" explains a handful of video editing techniques.

Recording a Voice Narration for PowerPoint

A voice narration in a PowerPoint presentation is sophisticated indeed. A self-playing, kiosk-style presentation can be accompanied by a human voice such that the narrator gives the presentation without actually being there. To narrate a PowerPoint presentation, a working microphone must be attached to your computer. You record the narration for slides one slide at a time or all at one time, and the recording is stored in the PowerPoint file, not in a separate audio file.

If you think recording a voice narration is easy, think again. You need a script to read from during the recording. You need a good voice — or you need to know someone with a good voice or be able to pay an actor to read for you. You need a good sound card and a microphone. You also need disk space. A voice recording as little as 10 seconds long can add 200 KB to the size of a PowerPoint file.

The following pages explain how to test your microphone to make sure it's working. You also discover how to record a voice narration and, if the voice narration is played across several slides, how to make the slides arrive at the proper time during the voice narration.

To play voice narrations during a presentation, make sure the Play Narrations check box is selected on the Slide Show tab.

Testing your computer's microphone

Plug in and install your microphone (carefully following the manufacturer's instructions) if you haven't already plugged it in. Before recording in PowerPoint, make sure that your microphone is working. Do that by visiting the Control Panel and running Sound Recorder, the Windows software that PowerPoint relies on for recording.

Checking the Control Panel

Follow these steps to visit the Control Panel and make sure that your computer and your microphone are on speaking terms:

1. **Click the Start button and choose Control Panel.**

   The Control Panel opens.

2. **Double-click the Sound icon.**

   If you don't see this icon, open the View By drop-down list and choose Large Icons (in Windows 7) or click the Switch to Classic View link in the Control Panel (in Windows Vista and Windows XP).

   You see the Sound dialog box.

3. **Select the Recording tab, as shown in Figure 4-6.**

   The name of your microphone should appear. If it doesn't appear there, re-install your microphone and try again.

4. **Speak or blow into your microphone and notice whether the volume recording level changes.**

   If your microphone is live, the Microphone level reading on the right side of the dialog box changes (refer to Figure 4-6). If the level reading doesn't change, your microphone is not properly connected to your computer.

5. **Click OK to close the Sound dialog box.**

Figure 4-6:
Make sure that the microphone is ready to go.

Testing one, two, three . . .

PowerPoint isn't equipped with sound-recording software. To record sounds, it relies on a Windows program called Sound Recorder. Your next test is to find out whether Sound Recorder is working with your microphone and sound card. If you pass this test, you're ready to record PowerPoint voice narrations:

1. **Click the Start button and choose All Programs⇨Accessories⇨Sound Recorder.**

The Sound Recorder opens, as shown in Figure 4-7.

Figure 4-7:
Sound Recorder in action.

2. **Click the Start Recording button and start talking.**

Go ahead — talk aloud to yourself. You have a good excuse this time. If Sound Recorder and your microphone connection are working correctly, the sound level changes as you speak.

3. **Click the Stop Recording button to stop recording.**

   The Save As dialog box appears.

4. **Click Cancel and close Sound Recorder.**

   You could save your voice recording as a .WMA file in the Save As dialog box, but click Cancel for now. The object here was to test whether Sound Recorder works on your computer.

Recording a voice narration in PowerPoint

After you have determined that your microphone is working, you can begin recording a voice narration.

The best way to record voice narrations is to do it on a slide-by-slide basis. You can record across several slides, but getting your voice narration and slides to be in sync with one another can be a lot of trouble (see "Synchronizing your voice narration with the PowerPoint slides," later in this chapter). After you record a voice narration, PowerPoint inserts an audio icon on the slide.

Place your script on your desk and follow these steps to record a voice narration for a slide:

1. **Select the slide that needs a voice narration, or if you intend to record a narration across several slides, select the first slide.**

2. **Go to the Insert tab.**

3. **Open the drop-down list on the Audio button and choose Record Audio.**

   You see the Record Sound dialog box shown in Figure 4-8.

Figure 4-8:
Recording in PowerPoint.

Record Sound

Name: Recorded Sound

Total sound length: 16.4

OK

Cancel

Play | Record

Stop

4. **Click the Record button and start reading your script.**

   Click the Stop button when you want to pause recording; click the Record button to resume recording.

You can click the Play button at any time to play back what you have recorded so far. Notice that the dialog box notes how many seconds your recording lasts.

5. **Click the OK button in the Record Sound dialog box when you have finished recording the narration for your slide.**

    The Audio icon appears on your slide to show that your slide is accompanied by an audio file.

Your next task is to select the Audio icon, go to the (Audio Tools) Playback tab, and tell PowerPoint when to play the audio recording, at what volume to play it, and whether you want it to loop. See "Telling PowerPoint when and how to play an audio file," earlier in this chapter.

Synchronizing your voice narration with the PowerPoint slides

If you recorded a voice narration and want to play it across several slides, your next task is to synchronize the audio file you recorded with your slides. In other words, you must make each slide arrive on-screen at the right moment in the voice narration.

Follow these steps to synchronize your audio file and PowerPoint presentation file:

1. **Select the slide with the audio icon.**

2. **Go to the Slide Show tab.**

3. **Click the Rehearse Timings button.**

    The presentation starts and fills the screen, and the audio file starts playing.

4. **Click on-screen to advance to the next slide when you come to the appropriate place in your voice narration.**

5. **Continue to click to advance to the next slide as the voice narration file plays out.**

6. **Click Yes in the dialog box that asks whether you want to keep the new slide timings.**

    This dialog box appears at the end of the presentation rehearsal.

To play your presentation back and see whether the voice narration and slides are in sync, click the Slide Show button. As long as the Use Timings check box is selected on the Slide Show tab, the slides advance on their own.

Editing a video

To help launch your movie career, PowerPoint offers a handful of video-editing tools on the (Video Tools) Format and (Video Tools) Playback tabs. Select your video and experiment with these tools to see whether you can improve upon it:

✔ **Fading in and fading out:** To make the video fade in or out, visit the (Video Tools) Playback tab and enter a time measurement in the Fade In and Fade Out boxes. For example, entering 5.00 in the Fade In box makes the video fade in during the first 5 seconds.

✔ **Trimming the start or end from a video:** On the (Video Tools) Playback tab, click the Trim Video button to trim off the beginning or end of a video. You see the Trim Video dialog box. On the timeline bar, drag the start marker and end marker toward the center of the timeline and click OK. What is between the markers remains in the video.

To restore cuts you made to a video, click the Trim Video button and drag markers in the Trim Video dialog box.

✔ **Improving the brightness and contrast:** On the (Video Tools) Format tab, click the Corrections button and see whether you can get a better picture by selecting an option on the drop-down list. Choose Video Corrections Options if you have the wherewithal to play with the brightness and contrast settings in the Format Video dialog box.

✔ **Recoloring a video:** On the (Video Tools) Format tab, click the Color button and choose a color option on the drop-down list if doing so improves the look of your video.

Chapter 5: Delivering a Presentation

In This Chapter

↙ Writing, editing, and printing speaker notes

↙ Rehearsing a presentation to see how long it is

↙ Going from slide to slide in a live presentation

↙ Drawing on slides during a presentation

↙ Delivering a presentation when you can't be there in person

*A*t last, the big day has arrived. It's time to give the presentation. "Break a leg," as actors say before they go on stage. This chapter explains how to rehearse your presentation to find out how long it is and show your presentation. You discover some techniques to make your presentation livelier, including how to draw on slides with a pen or highlighter and blank out the screen to get the audience's full attention. The chapter describes how to handle the speaker notes and print handouts for your audience. In case you can't be there in person to deliver your presentation, this chapter shows you how to create a user-run presentation, a self-running presentation, a presentation designed to be viewed from a CD, and a video of a presentation.

All about Notes

Notes are strictly for the speaker. The unwashed masses can't see them. Don't hesitate to write notes to yourself when you put together your presentation. The notes will come in handy when you're rehearsing and giving your presentation. They give you ideas for what to say and help you communicate better. Here are instructions for entering, editing, and printing notes:

✦ **Entering a note:** To enter a note, start in Normal view, click in the Notes pane, and start typing. Treat the Notes pane like a page in a word processor. For example, press Enter to start a new paragraph and press the Tab key to indent text. You can drag the border above the Notes pane up or down to make the pane larger or smaller.

✦ **Editing notes in Notes Page view:** After you've jotted down a bunch of notes, switch to Notes Page view and edit them. To switch to Notes Page view, visit the View tab and click the Notes Page button. Notes appear in a text frame below a picture of the slide to which they refer. You may have to zoom in to read them.

✦ **Printing your notes:** On the File tab, choose Print (or press Ctrl+P). You see the Print window. Under Other Settings, open the second drop-down list and choose Note Pages. Then click the Print button.

Rehearsing and Timing Your Presentation

Slide presentations and theatrical presentations have this in common: They are as good as the number of times you rehearse them. Be sure to rehearse your presentation many times over. The more you rehearse, the more comfortable you are giving a presentation. Follow these steps to rehearse a presentation, record its length, and record how long each slide is displayed:

1. **Select the first slide in your presentation.**

2. **Go to the Slide Show tab.**

3. **Click the Rehearse Timings button.**

   The Recording toolbar appears, as shown in Figure 5-1, and you switch to Slide Show view.

Advance to the next slide

Note how long your presentation is

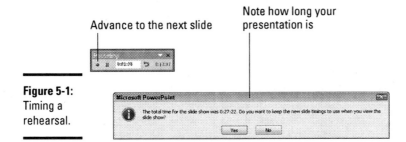

Figure 5-1: Timing a rehearsal.

4. **Give your presentation one slide at a time and click the Next button on the Recording toolbar to go from slide to slide.**

   When each slide appears, imagine that you're presenting it to an audience. Say what you intend to say during the real presentation. If you anticipate audience members asking questions, allot time for questions.

The Recording toolbar tells you how long each slide has been displayed and how long your presentation is so far. You can do these tasks from the Recording toolbar:

- *Go to the next slide:* Click the Next button.

- *Pause recording:* Click the Pause Recording button to temporarily stop the recording so that you can feed the dog or take a phone call. Click the Resume Recording button to resume recording.

- *Repeat a slide:* Click the Repeat button if you get befuddled and want to start over with a slide. The slide timing returns to 0:00:00.

5. **In the dialog box that asks whether you want to keep the slide timings, note how long your presentation is (see Figure 5-1).**

   Is your presentation too long or too short? I hope, like baby bear's porridge, your presentation is "just right." But if it's too long or short, you have some work to do. You have to figure out how to shorten or lengthen it.

6. **In the dialog box that asks whether you want to keep the new slide timings, click Yes if you want to see how long each slide stayed on-screen during the rehearsal.**

   By clicking Yes, you can go to Slide Sorter view and see how long each slide remained on-screen.

If you save the slide timings, PowerPoint assumes that, during a presentation, you want to advance to the next slide manually or after the recorded time, whichever comes first. For example, suppose the first slide in your presentation remained on-screen for a minute during the rehearsal. During your presentation, the first slide will remain on-screen for a minute and automatically yield to the second slide unless you click to advance to the second slide before the minute has elapsed. If you recorded slide timings strictly to find out how long your presentation is, you need to tell PowerPoint not to advance automatically to the next slide during a presentation after the recorded time period elapses. On the Slide Show tab, deselect the Use Timings check box.

**Book III
Chapter 5**

**Delivering a
Presentation**

Showing Your Presentation

Compared to the preliminary work, giving a presentation can seem kind of anticlimactic. All you have to do is go from slide to slide and woo your audience with your smooth-as-silk voice and powerful oratory skills. Well, at least the move-from-slide-to-slide part is pretty easy. These pages explain how to start and end a presentation, all the different ways to advance or retreat from slide to slide, and how to jump to different slides.

Starting and ending a presentation

Here are the different ways to start a presentation from the beginning:

+ On the Slide Show tab, click the From Beginning button.

+ Select the first slide and then click the Slide Show view button.

You can start a presentation in the middle by selecting a slide in the middle and then clicking the Slide Show view button or going to the Slide Show tab and clicking the From Current Slide button.

Here are the different ways to end a presentation prematurely:

+ Press Esc or – (the Hyphen key).

+ Click the Slide button and choose End Show on the pop-up menu. The Slide button is located in the lower-left corner of the screen.

+ Right-click and choose End Show in the shortcut menu.

Going from slide to slide

In a nutshell, PowerPoint offers four ways to move from slide to slide in a presentation. Table 5-1 describes techniques for navigating a presentation using the four different ways:

+ **Use the slide control buttons:** Click a slide control button — Previous, Next — in the lower-left corner of the screen, as shown in Figure 5-2. If you don't see the slide control buttons, jiggle the mouse.

+ **Click the Slide button:** Click this button and make a choice on the pop-up menu (see Figure 5-2).

+ **Right-click on-screen:** Right-click and choose a navigation option on the shortcut menu.

+ **Press a keyboard shortcut:** Press one of the numerous keyboard shortcuts that PowerPoint offers for going from slide to slide (see Table 5-1).

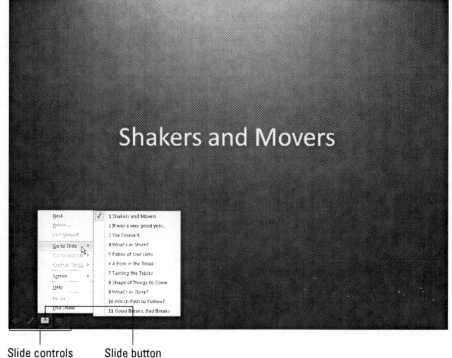

**Book III
Chapter 5**

**Delivering a
Presentation**

Figure 5-2:
Besides
using
keyboard
shortcuts,
you can
move from
slide to slide
by clicking
on-screen.

Slide controls   Slide button

Table 5-1		**Techniques for Getting from Slide to Slide**		
To go here	*Slide control button*	*Click the Slide button and choose . . .*	*Right-click and choose . . .*	*Keyboard shortcut*
Next slide*	Next	Next	Next	Enter, spacebar, N, PgDn, ↓, or →
Previous slide	Previous	Previous	Previous	Backspace, P, PgUp, ↑, or ←

(continued)

Table 5-1 *(continued)*

To go here	Slide control button	Click the Slide button and choose . . .	Right-click and choose . . .	Keyboard shortcut
Specific slide		Go To Slide⇨ *Slide number and title*	Go to Slide⇨ *Slide number and title*	*Slide number*+Enter; Ctrl+S and then select *Slide number and title*
Last viewed slide		Last Viewed	Last Viewed	
Section		Go To Section⇨ *Section name*	Go To Section⇨ *Section name*	
First slide		Go To Slide⇨ *Slide 1*	Go To Slide⇨ *Slide 1*	Home
Last slide		Go To Slide⇨ *Slide (number of last slide)*	Go To Slide⇨ *Slide (number of last slide)*	End

*If animations are on a slide, commands for going to the next slide instead make animations play in sequence. To bypass animations and go to the next slide, use a command for going forward across several slides. (See "Jumping forward or backward to a specific slide.")

Going forward (or backward) from slide to slide

To go forward from one slide to the following slide in a presentation, click on-screen. After you click, the next slide appears. If all goes well, clicking is the only technique you need to know when giving a presentation to go from slide to slide, but Table 5-1 lists other ways to go to the next slide in a presentation as well as techniques for going backward to the previous slide.

To go to the first slide in a presentation, press Home; to go to the last slide, press End.

Jumping forward or backward to a specific slide

If you find it necessary to jump forward or backward across several slides in your presentation to get to the slide you want to show, it can be done with these techniques:

✦ Either click the Slide button or right-click, choose Go to Slide, and then choose a slide in your presentation on the submenu (refer to Figure 5-2).

If you created sections for your presentation, you can choose Go to Section and then selection a section name on the submenu.

✦ Press Ctrl+S. You see the All Slides dialog box. It lists all slides in your presentation. Select the slide you want to show and click the Go To button.

✦ Press the slide number you want on your keyboard (if you can remember the slide's number) and then press the Enter key. For example, to show the third slide in your presentation, press 3 and then press Enter.

If you need to return to where you started after you make the jump to a different slide, you can do so by right-clicking and choosing Last Viewed on the shortcut menu. You can also click the Slide button and choose Last Viewed (refer to Figure 5-2). The Last Viewed command takes you to the last slide you showed, wherever it is in your presentation.

Tricks for Making Presentations a Little Livelier

To make presentations a little livelier, whip out a pen and draw on a slide or blank the screen. Draw to underline words or draw check marks as you hit the key points, as shown in Figure 5-3. Drawing on slides is an excellent way to add a little something to a presentation. Blank the screen when you want the audience's undivided attention.

Book III
Chapter 5

Delivering a Presentation

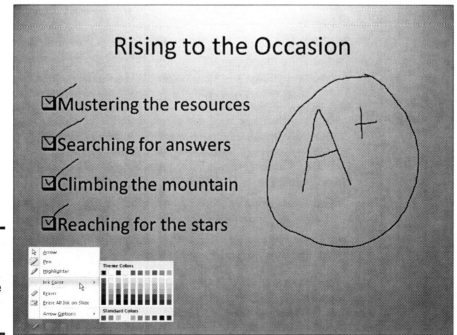

Figure 5-3:
Choose a pen and ink color on the Pen pop-up list.

Wielding a pen or highlighter in a presentation

Follow these instructions so you can draw on a slide:

✦ **Selecting a pen or highlighter:** PowerPoint offers the Pen for writing on slides and the Highlighter for highlighting text on slides. To select the Pen or Highlighter, click the Pen button and choose Pen or Highlighter (refer to Figure 5-3). You can also right-click, choose Pointer Options, and make a selection on the submenu.

✦ **Choosing a color for drawing:** After you select the Pen or Highlighter, click the Pen button, choose Ink Color, and select a color on the submenu (refer to Figure 5-3).

Press Esc when you're finished using the pen. (Just be careful not to press Esc twice because the second press tells PowerPoint to end the presentation.)

Hiding and erasing pen and highlighter markings

Follow these instructions to hide and erase pen and highlighter markings:

✦ **Temporarily showing or hiding markings:** Right-click and choose Screen⊃Show/Hide Ink Markup.

✦ **Permanently erasing markings one at a time:** Click the Pen button and choose Eraser (or right-click and choose Pointer Options⊃Eraser). The Eraser appears. Click a line to erase it. Press Esc after you're finished using the Eraser.

✦ **Permanently erasing all the markings on a slide:** Press E or click the Pen button and choose Erase All Ink on Slide (refer to Figure 5-3).

✦ **Erasing markings you told PowerPoint to keep:** As I explain shortly, PowerPoint asks at the end of a presentation that you drew on or highlighted whether you want to keep the markings. If you elect to keep them, the markings become part of your presentation, and you can't delete them by clicking with the Eraser or by choosing the Erase All Ink on Slide command. To discard these markings later, go to the Review tab, open the drop-down list on the Delete button, and choose one of these options:

   • *Delete All Markup on the Current Slide:* Deletes markings you made on a slide you selected

   • *Delete All Markup in This Presentation:* Deletes markings you made on all the slides in your presentation

Markings aren't permanent, although you can keep them. At the end of a presentation in which you have marked on slides, a dialog box asks whether you want to keep or discard your markings. Click the Keep or

Discard button. (If you prefer not to see this dialog box because you intend never to keep your markings, go to the File tab and choose Options. In the PowerPoint Options dialog box, select the Advanced category and deselect the Prompt to Keep Ink Annotations When Exiting check box.)

Blanking the screen

Here's a technique for adding a little drama to a presentation: When you want the audience to focus on you, not the PowerPoint screen, blank the screen. Make an all-black or all-white screen appear where a PowerPoint slide used to be. Every head in the audience will turn your way and listen keenly to what you have to say next. I sure hope you have something important to say.

Follow these instructions to blank out the screen during a presentation:

+ **Black screen:** Press B, the period key, or right-click and choose Screen⇨ Black Screen.

+ **White screen:** Press W, the comma key, or right-click and choose Screen⇨ White Screen.

To see a PowerPoint slide again, click on-screen or press any key on the keyboard.

Delivering a Presentation When You Can't Be There in Person

PowerPoint offers numerous ways to deliver a presentation when you can't be there in person. You can deliver your presentation in the form of a *handout,* a printed version of the presentation with thumbnail slides; create a self-running presentation; or create a user-run presentation with action buttons that others can click to get from slide to slide. The rest of this chapter explains how to do all that as well as make a video of your presentation and package your presentation so that people who don't have PowerPoint can view it.

Providing handouts for your audience

Handouts are thumbnail versions of slides that you print and distribute to the audience. Figure 5-4 shows examples of handouts. Handouts come in one, two, three, four, six, or nine slides per page. If you select three slides per page, the handout includes lines that your audience can take notes on (see Figure 5-4); the other sizes don't offer these lines.

Figure 5-4:
Examples
of handouts
(from left
to right) at
one, three,
six, and nine
slides per
page.

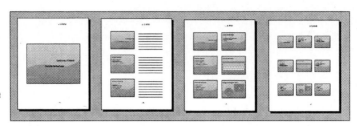

 To tell PowerPoint how to construct handouts, go to the View tab and click the Handout Master button. In Handout Master view on the Handout Master tab, you can do a number of things to make your handouts more useful and attractive. As you make your choices, keep your eye on the sample handout page; it shows what your choices mean in real terms.

+ **Handout Orientation:** Select Portrait or Landscape. In landscape mode, the page is turned on its side and is longer than it is tall.

+ **Slide Orientation:** Select Portrait or Landscape, although I can't think of a good reason to choose Portrait.

+ **Slides-Per-Page:** Open the drop-down list and choose how many slides appear on each page. Figure 5-4 shows what some of the choices are.

+ **Header:** Select the Header check box and enter a header in the text frame to make a header appear in the upper-left corner of all handout pages. Candidates for headers include your name, your company name, and the location of a conference or seminar. The point is to help your audience identify the handout.

+ **Footer:** Select the Footer check box and enter a footer in the text frame in the lower-left corner of handout pages. Candidates for footers are the same as candidates for headers.

+ **Date:** Select this check box if you want the date you print the handout to appear on the handout pages.

+ **Page Number:** Select this check box if you want page numbers to appear on the handout pages.

+ **Background Styles:** Open the Background Styles drop-down list and select a gradient or color, if you're so inclined. Chapter 2 of this mini-book explains background styles. Make sure that the background doesn't obscure the slide thumbnails or put too much of a burden on your printer.

To print handouts, go to the File tab and choose Print (or press Ctrl+P). You see the Print window. Under Settings, open the second drop-down list, and under Handouts, choose how many slides to print on each page. Then click the Print button.

Creating a self-running, kiosk-style presentation

A self-running, kiosk-style presentation is one that plays on its own. You can make it play from a kiosk or simply send it to co-workers so that they can play it. In a self-running presentation, slides appear on-screen one after the other without you or anyone else having to advance the presentation from slide to slide. When the presentation finishes, it starts all over again from Slide 1.

Telling PowerPoint how long to keep slides on-screen

PowerPoint offers two ways to indicate how long you want each slide to stay on-screen:

✦ **Entering the time periods yourself:** Switch to Slide Sorter view and go to the Transitions tab. Then deselect the On Mouse Click check box and select the After check box, as shown in Figure 5-5. Next, tell PowerPoint to keep all slides on-screen the same amount of time or choose a different time period for each slide:

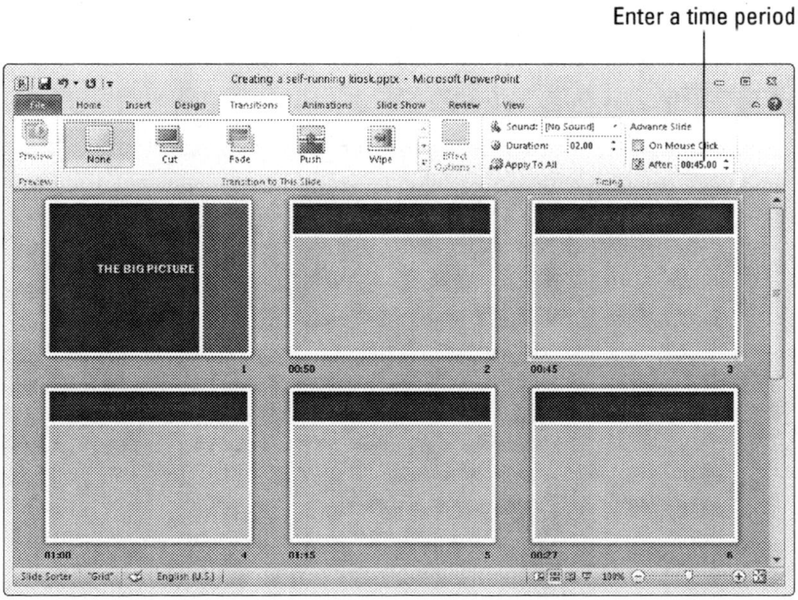

Book III
Chapter 5

Enter a time period

Figure 5-5:
Enter how long you want each slide or all the slides to remain on-screen.

Delivering a
Presentation

- *All slides the same time:* Enter a time period in the After text box and click the Apply to All button.

- *Each slide a different time:* One by one, select each slide and enter a time period in the After text box.

✦ **Rehearsing the presentation:** Rehearse the presentation and save the timings. (See "Rehearsing and Timing Your Presentation" earlier in this chapter.) Be sure to save the slide timings after you're finished rehearsing. In Slide Sorter view, you can see how long each slide will stay on-screen (see Figure 5-5).

Telling PowerPoint that your presentation is self-running

Before you can "self-run" a presentation, you have to tell PowerPoint that you want it to do that. Self-running presentations don't have the control buttons in the lower-left corner. You can't click the screen or press a key to move forward or backward to the next or previous slide. The only control you have over a self-running presentation is pressing the Esc key (pressing Esc ends the presentation).

Follow these steps to make yours a kiosk-style, self-running presentation:

1. **Go to the Slide Show tab.**

2. **Click the Set Up Slide Show button.**

You see the Set Up Slide Show dialog box.

3. **Under Show Type, choose the Browsed at a Kiosk (Full Screen) option.**

When you select this option, PowerPoint automatically selects the Loop Continuously Until 'Esc' check box.

4. **Make sure that the Using Timings, If Present option button is selected.**

5. **Click OK.**

That's all there is to it.

Creating a user-run presentation

A *user-run,* or *interactive,* presentation is one that the viewer gets to control. The viewer decides which slide appears next and how long each slide remains on-screen. User-run presentations are similar to Web sites. Users can browse from slide to slide at their own speed. They can pick and choose what they want to investigate. They can backtrack and view slides they saw previously or return to the first slide and start anew.

Self-run presentations are shown in Reading view (click the Reading View view button on the status bar to see what self-run presentations look like). A task bar appears along the bottom of the screen. On the right side of the task bar, viewers can click the Previous button or Next button to go from slide to slide. They can also click the Menu button to open a pop-up menu with commands for navigating slides.

Another way to help readers get from slide to slide is to create action buttons. An *action button* is a button that you can click to go to another slide in your presentation or the previous slide you viewed, whatever that slide was. PowerPoint provides 11 action buttons in the Shapes gallery. Figure 5-6 shows some action buttons and the dialog box you use to create them.

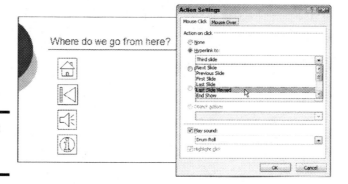

Figure 5-6:
Action
buttons.

Drawing an action button

After you draw an action button from the Shapes gallery, the Action Settings dialog box shown in Figure 5-6 appears so you can tell PowerPoint which slide to go to when the button is clicked. Select the slide (or master slide) that needs action and follow these steps to adorn it with an action button:

1. **On the Home or Insert tab, open the Shapes gallery and scroll to the Action Buttons category at the bottom.**

2. **Click an action button to select it.**

   Choose the button that best illustrates which slide will appear when the button is clicked.

3. **Draw the button on the slide.**

   To do so, drag the pointer in a diagonal fashion. (As far as drawing them is concerned, action buttons work the same as all other shapes and other objects. Book I, Chapter 8 explains how to manipulate objects.) The Action Settings dialog box shown in Figure 5-6 appears after you finish drawing your button.

4. **Go to the Mouse Over tab if you want users to activate the button by moving the mouse pointer over it, not clicking it.**

5. **Select the Hyperlink To option button.**

6. **On the Hyperlink To drop-down list, choose an action for the button.**

   You can go to the next slide, the previous slide, the first or last slide in a presentation, the last slide you viewed, or a specific slide.

   To make clicking the action button take users to a specific slide, choose Slide on the list. You see the Hyperlink to Slide dialog box, which lists each slide in your presentation. Select a slide and click OK.

7. **To play a sound when your action button is activated, select the Play Sound check box and select a sound on the drop-down list.**

   A "mouse-over" hyperlink is a good candidate for sound accompaniment. Hearing the sound helps users understand when they've activated an action button.

8. **Click OK in the Actions Settings dialog box.**

   To test your button, you can right-click it and choose Open Hyperlink.

To change a button's action, select it and then click the Action button on the Insert tab, or right-click your action button and choose Edit Hyperlink. In the Action Settings dialog box, choose a new action and click OK.

Making yours a user-run presentation

Follow these steps to declare yours a user-run presentation:

1. **Go to the Slide Show tab.**

2. **Click the Set Up Slide Show button.**

   You see the Set Up Show dialog box.

3. **Select the Browsed by an Individual (Window) option button.**

4. **Click OK.**

   Your presentation is no longer quite yours. It also belongs to all the people who view it in your absence.

Packaging your presentation on a CD

The Package for CD command copies a presentation to a CD so that you can take a presentation on the road or distribute it to others on CDs. By using the Package for CD command, you can even distribute a presentation to people who don't have PowerPoint. Someone who doesn't have PowerPoint can download the *PowerPoint Viewer,* an abridged version of PowerPoint with all the PowerPoint slide-show commands (but none of the slide-creation commands). With the Package for CD command, you don't have to be concerned whether someone to whom you give your presentation has PowerPoint or whether PowerPoint is installed on the computer where you will give your presentation.

These pages explain the ins and outs of the Package for CD command. You find out how to copy a presentation to a CD or folder and play a presentation in PowerPoint Viewer.

Packaging a presentation on a CD

Follow these steps to copy your presentation and the PowerPoint Viewer to a CD or a folder:

1. **Open the presentation you want to package.**

2. **On the File tab, choose Share.**

3. **Choose Package Presentation for CD, and click the Package for CD button.**

You see the Package for CD dialog box shown in Figure 5-7.

Figure 5-7:
Packaging
a CD to
distribute to
others.

4. **Enter a name for the CD or folder in the Name the CD text box.**

The name you enter will appear as the name of the CD if you view the CD in Windows Explorer or Computer; if you're copying your presentation to a folder, the name you enter will be given to the folder PowerPoint creates when it creates the packaged presentation file.

5. **Create the packaged presentation and copy it to a CD or to a folder on your computer.**

Copy the presentation to a folder if you want to send the presentation by e-mail rather than distribute it by CD.

- *Copying to a CD:* Click the Copy to CD button.

- *Copying to a folder:* Click the Copy to Folder button. In the Copy to Folder dialog box, click the Browse button, and in the Choose Location dialog box, select a folder for storing the folder where you will keep your packaged presentation. Then click the Select button and click OK in the Copy to Folder dialog box.

6. **Click Yes in the message box that asks if you want to include linked content in the presentation.**

    It can take PowerPoint several minutes to assemble the files and copy them to the CD or folder.

    If you're copying your presentation to a CD, PowerPoint asks whether you want to copy the same presentation to another CD. Either insert a fresh CD and click Yes, or click the No button.

Playing a packaged presentation

As shown in Figure 5-8, the AutoPlay dialog box appears when you put a CD-packaged PowerPoint presentation in the computer's CD drive. Tell the people to whom you distribute your CD that they can play the presentation starting in this dialog box whether or not PowerPoint is installed on their computers:

✦ **PowerPoint (or PowerPoint Viewer) is installed:** Click the Open Folder to View Files button in the AutoPlay dialog box. The Computer application opens to show the files on the CD. Double-click the PowerPoint presentation to play it.

✦ **PowerPoint isn't installed:** Click the Run Presentation Package button in the AutoPlay dialog box. A Web browser opens. Click the Download Viewer button to go to a Web page at Microsoft.com and download the PowerPoint Viewer. After downloading and installing PowerPoint Viewer, you can use it to play the PowerPoint presentation.

Figure 5-8:
Playing a CD-packaged presentation.

Creating a presentation video

Yet another way to distribute a video is to record it in a WMV (Windows Media Video) file and distribute the file on a CD, distribute it by e-mail, or post it on the Internet. PowerPoint offers a command for creating a WMV-file version of a presentation. Every aspect of a PowerPoint presentation, including transitions, animations, sound, video itself, and voice narrations, is recorded in the presentation video.

Figure 5-9 shows a WMV-file version of a PowerPoint presentation being played in Windows Media Player. This utility comes with the Windows operating system. Everyone with a computer that runs Windows can play WMV-file versions of your presentations by playing them in Windows Media Player.

Figure 5-9:
Viewing a WMV-file version of a PowerPoint presentation in Windows Media Player.

Book III
Chapter 5

Delivering a
Presentation

Before creating your presentation video, consider how long you want each slide to appear on-screen. You can make each slide appear for a specific length of time or make all slides appear for the same length of time. To decide for yourself how long each slide appears, switch to Slide Sorter view, go to the Transitions tab, and for each slide, select the After check box and enter a measurement in the After text box. (Earlier in this chapter, "Creating a self-running, kiosk-style presentation" explains in detail how to establish how long each slide stays on-screen.)

Follow these steps to create a WMV-file version of a PowerPoint presentation:

File

1. **On the File tab, choose Save & Send.**

2. **Choose Create a Video.**

   You see the Create a Video window.

3. **Open the first drop-down list and choose a display resolution for your video.**

4. **Open the second drop-down list and choose whether to use recorded timings and narrations.**

   Your choices are twofold. If you recorded a voice narration for your PowerPoint presentation, choose the second option if you want to preserve the voice narration in the video.

   • *Don't Use Recorded Timings and Narrations:* Each slide stays on-screen for the same amount of time. Enter a time period in the Seconds to Spend on Each Slide box to declare how long each slide stays on-screen.

   • *Use Recorded Timings and Narrations:* Each slide stays on-screen for the time period listed on the Transition tab (see the Tip at the start of this section to find out how to list slide times on the Transition tab).

5. **Open the second drop-down list and choose Preview Timings and Narrations.**

   Your presentation video plays. How do you like it? This is what your video will look and sound like after you save it in a WMV file.

6. **Click the Create Video button.**

   The Save As dialog box opens.

7. **Choose a folder for storing the WMV file, enter a name for the file, and click the Save button.**

   The status bar along the bottom of the PowerPoint screen shows the progress of the video as it is being created. Creating a video can take several minutes, depending on how large your PowerPoint presentation is and how many fancy gizmos, such as sound and animation, it contains.

Distributing your presentation to people who don't have PowerPoint

Not everyone has PowerPoint. Not everyone is so blessed. Some people live in ignorant bliss without knowing anything about PowerPoint and its slide-show capabilities.

Don't be discouraged if you want to send your PowerPoint presentation to someone who doesn't have or may not have PowerPoint. Someone who doesn't have PowerPoint on his or her computer can still play a PowerPoint presentation by way of *PowerPoint Viewer,* a software program you can download for free from Microsoft starting at this Web page (enter **PowerPoint Viewer** in the Search text box and click the Go button):

www.microsoft.com/downloads

Here are instructions for running a presentation in PowerPoint Viewer:

- ✔ **Getting from slide to slide:** Click on-screen or right-click and choose Next on the shortcut menu.

- ✔ **Retreating:** Right-click and choose Previous or Last Viewed.

- ✔ **Going to a specific slide:** Right-click, choose Go to Slide, and select a slide on the submenu.

- ✔ **Ending the show:** Press Esc or right-click and choose End Show.

**Book III
Chapter 5**

**Delivering a
Presentation**

Book IV

Excel

"No, that's not the icon for Excel, it's the icon for Excuse, the database of reasons why you haven't learned the other programs in Office."

Contents at a Glance

Chapter 1: Up and Running with Excel **395**

Creating a New Excel Workbook..395
Getting Acquainted with Excel..397
Entering Data in a Worksheet 399
Quickly Entering Lists and Serial Data with the AutoFill Command.....404
Formatting Numbers, Dates, and Time Values 406
Conditional Formats for Calling Attention to Data....................407
Establishing Data-Validation Rules 409

Chapter 2: Refining Your Worksheet **413**

Editing Worksheet Data 413
Moving around in a Worksheet..414
Getting a Better Look at the Worksheet 415
Comments for Documenting Your Worksheet..........................417
Selecting Cells in a Worksheet 419
Deleting, Copying, and Moving Data 419
Handling the Worksheets in a Workbook 420
Keeping Others from Tampering with Worksheets 421

Chapter 3: Formulas and Functions for Crunching Numbers **425**

How Formulas Work 425
The Basics of Entering a Formula..430
Speed Techniques for Entering Formulas 431
Copying Formulas from Cell to Cell..436
Detecting and Correcting Errors in Formulas...........................437
Working with Functions..440

Chapter 4: Making a Worksheet Easier to Read and Understand . . .**445**

Laying Out a Worksheet 445
Decorating a Worksheet with Borders and Colors...................450
Getting Ready to Print a Worksheet..454

Chapter 5: Analyzing Data **461**

Managing Information in Lists 461
Forecasting with the Goal Seek Command..............................464
Performing What-If Analyses with Data Tables 466

Chapter 1: Up and Running with Excel

In This Chapter

✔ Creating an Excel workbook

✔ Understanding what a worksheet is

✔ Entering text, as well as numeric, date, and time data

✔ Using the AutoFill command to enter lists and serial data

✔ Setting up data-validation rules

*T*his chapter introduces *Excel,* the official number cruncher of Office 2010. The purpose of Excel is to track, analyze, and tabulate numbers. Use the program to project profits and losses, formulate a budget, or analyze Elvis sightings in North America. Doing the setup work takes time, but after you enter the numbers and tell Excel how to tabulate them, you're on Easy Street. Excel does the math for you. All you have to do is kick off your shoes, sit back, and see how the numbers stack up.

This chapter explains what a workbook and a worksheet is, and how rows and columns on a worksheet determine where cell addresses are. You also discover tips and tricks for entering data quickly in a worksheet, and how to construct data-validation rules to make sure that data is entered accurately.

Creating a New Excel Workbook

When you start Excel, the program greets you with a brand-new workbook with the generic name "Book1" on the title bar. *Workbook* is just the Excel term for the files you create with the program. You can start working right away on the generic workbook or you can take advantage of one of Excel's templates.

A *template* is a preformatted workbook designed for a specific purpose, such as budgeting, tracking inventories, or tracking purchase orders. Creating a workbook from a template is mighty convenient if you happen to find a template that suits your purposes, but in my experience, you almost always have to start from a generic, blank workbook because your data is your own. You need a workbook you create yourself, not one created from a template by someone else.

File

Whether you want to create a new workbook from a template or from scratch, start by going to the File tab and choosing New. You see the Available Templates window shown in Figure 1-1. This window offers templates for creating many kinds of workbooks. Click a template to see, on the right side of the window, a preview of the workbook you will create. Double-click a template (or select it and click the Create button) to create a new workbook.

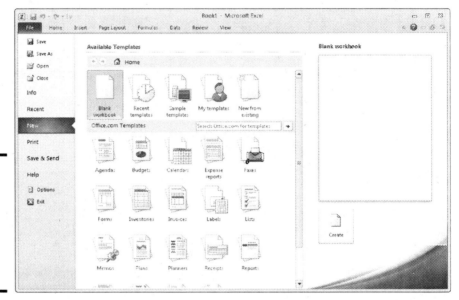

Figure 1-1:
Create a
workbook
by starting
in the
Available
Templates
window.

Use one of these techniques in the Available Templates window to create a workbook:

✦ **Create a blank workbook:** Double-click the Blank Workbook icon. (By pressing Ctrl+N, you can create a new, blank workbook without opening the Available Templates window.)

✦ **Create a workbook from a template:** Take your pick from these techniques to create a workbook from a template:

• *Use a template on your computer:* Click Sample Templates. Templates that you loaded on your computer when you installed Office appear in the window.

• *Download a template from Office.com:* Under Office.com Templates, either choose the type of template you want or make sure your computer is connected to the Internet, enter a search term in the Search box, and click the Start Searching button (or press Enter). Choose a template and click the Download button to download it to your computer.

- *Use a template you created (or downloaded earlier from Microsoft):* Click the My Templates icon. The New dialog box appears. Select a template and click OK. (Chapter 4 of this mini-book describes how to create your own template; after you create a template, its name appears in this dialog box.)

  - *Select a recently used template:* Click the Recent Templates icon and double-click a template name.

✦ **Recycle another workbook:** If you can use another workbook as the starting point for creating a new one, click the New from Existing icon. In the New from Existing Workbook dialog box, select the workbook and click the Create New button.

Book I, Chapter 1 explains how to save a workbook after you create it as well as how to open a workbook that you want to work on.

Getting Acquainted with Excel

If you've spent any time in an Office program, much of the Excel screen may look familiar to you. The buttons on the Home tab — the Bold and the Align buttons, for example — work the same in Excel as they do in Word. The Font and Font Size drop-down lists work the same as well. Any command in Excel that has to do with formatting text and numbers works the same in Excel and Word.

As I mentioned earlier, an Excel file is a *workbook.* Each workbook comprises one or more worksheets. A *worksheet,* also known as a *spreadsheet,* is a table where you enter data and data labels. Figure 1-2 shows a worksheet with data about rainfall in different counties.

A worksheet works like an accountant's ledger — only it's much easier to use. Notice how the worksheet is divided by gridlines into columns (A, B, C, and so on) and rows (1, 2, 3, and so on). The rectangles where columns and rows intersect are *cells,* and each cell can hold one data item, a formula for calculating data, or nothing at all. At the bottom of the worksheet are tabs — Sheet1, Sheet2, and Sheet3 — for visiting the other worksheets in the workbook.

Each cell has a different cell address. In Figure 1-2, cell B7 holds 13, the amount of rain that fell in Sonoma County in the winter. Meanwhile, as the Formula bar at the top of the screen shows, cell F7, the *active cell,* holds the formula =B7+C7+D7+E7, the sum of the numbers in cells — you guessed it — B7, C7, D7, and E7.

Active cell address   Formula bar

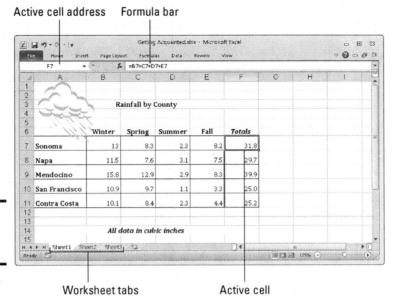

Figure 1-2:
The Excel
screen.

Worksheet tabs   Active cell

The beauty of Excel is that the program does all the calculations and recalculations for you after you enter the data. If I were to change the number in cell B7, Excel would instantly recalculate the total amount of rainfall in Sonoma County in cell F7. People like myself who struggled in math class will be glad to know that you don't have to worry about the math because Excel does it for you. All you have to do is make sure that the data and the formulas are entered correctly.

After you enter and label the data, enter the formulas, and turn your worksheet into a little masterpiece, you can start analyzing the data. For example, you can also generate charts like the one in Figure 1-3. Do you notice any similarities between the worksheet in Figure 1-2 and the chart in Figure 1-3? The chart is fashioned from data in the worksheet, and it took me about a half minute to create that chart. (Book I, Chapter 6 explains how to create charts in Excel, Word, and PowerPoint.)

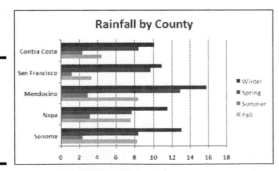

Figure 1-3:
A chart
generated
from the
data in
Figure 1-2.

Rows, columns, and cell addresses

Not that anyone except an Enron accountant needs all of them, but an Excel worksheet has numerous columns and over 1 million rows. The rows are numbered, and columns are labeled A to Z, then AA to AZ, then BA to BZ, and so on. The important thing to remember is that each cell has an address whose name comes from a column letter and a row number. The first cell in row 1 is A1, the second is B1, and so on. You need to enter cell addresses in formulas to tell Excel which numbers to compute.

To find a cell's address, either make note of which column and row it lies in, or click the cell and glance at the Formula bar (refer to Figure 1-2). The left side of the Formula bar lists the address of the *active cell*, the cell that is selected in the worksheet. In Figure 1-2, cell F7 is the active cell.

Workbooks and worksheets

When you create a new Excel file, you open a *workbook*, a file with three worksheets in it. The worksheets are called Sheet1, Sheet2, and Sheet3 (you can change their names and add more worksheets). To get from worksheet to worksheet, click tabs along the bottom of the Excel window. Why three worksheets? Because you might need more than one worksheet for a single project. Think of a workbook as a stack of worksheets. Besides calculating the numbers in cells across the rows or down the columns of a worksheet, you can make calculations throughout a workbook by using numbers from different worksheets in a calculation.

Entering Data in a Worksheet

Entering data in a worksheet is an irksome activity. Fortunately, Excel offers a few shortcuts to take the sting out of it. These pages explain how to enter data in a worksheet, the different types of data, and how to enter text labels, numbers, dates, and times.

The basics of entering data

What you can enter in a worksheet cell falls in four categories:

✦ Text

✦ A value (numeric, date, or time)

✦ A logical value (True or False)

✦ A formula that returns a value, logical value, or text

Still, no matter what type of data you're entering, the basic steps are the same:

**Book IV
Chapter 1**

**Up and Running
with Excel**

1. **Click the cell where you want to enter the data or text label.**

As shown in Figure 1-4, a square appears around the cell to tell you that the cell you clicked is now the active cell. Glance at the left side of the Formula bar if you're not sure of the address of the cell you're about to enter data in. The Formula bar lists the cell address.

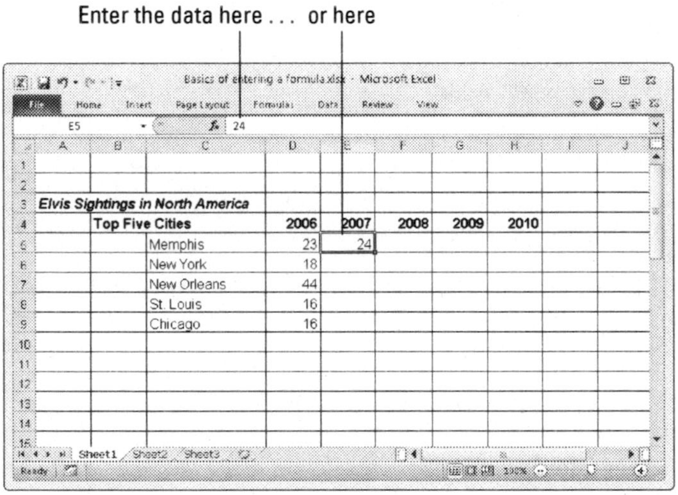

Enter the data here . . . or here

Figure 1-4:
Entering
data.

2. **Type the data in the cell.**

If you find typing in the Formula bar easier, click and start typing there. As soon as you type the first character, the Cancel button (an *X*) and Enter button (a check mark) appear beside the Insert Function button (labeled *fx*) on the Formula bar.

3. **Press the Enter key to enter the number or label.**

Besides pressing the Enter key, you can also press an arrow key (←, ↑, →, ↓), press Tab, or click the Enter button (the check mark) on the Formula bar.

If you change your mind about entering data, click the Cancel button or press Esc to delete what you entered and start over.

Chapter 3 of this mini-book explains how to enter logical values and formulas. The next several pages describe how to enter text labels, numeric values, date values, and time values.

The Paste Special command can come in very handy with worksheet data. As numbers are updated in the source file, they can be updated automatically in an Excel worksheet as well. Consider linking worksheets if your adventures in Excel enable you to keep source data in one place. Book VI, Chapter 6 explains linking files.

Entering text labels

Sometimes a text entry is too long to fit in a cell. How Excel accommodates text entries that are too wide depends on whether data is in the cell to the right of the one you entered the text in:

✦ If the cell to the right is empty, Excel lets the text spill into the next cell.

✦ If the cell to the right contains data, the entry gets cut off. Nevertheless, the text you entered is in the cell. Nothing gets lost when it can't be displayed on-screen. You just can't see the text or numbers except by glancing at the Formula bar, where the contents of the active cell can be seen in its entirety.

 To solve the problem of text that doesn't fit in a cell, widen the column, shorten the text entry, reorient the text (Chapter 4 of this mini-book explains aligning numbers and text in columns and rows), or wrap the contents of the cell. *Wrapping* means to run the text down to the next line, much the way the text in a paragraph runs to the next line when it reaches the right margin. Excel makes rows taller to accommodate wrapped text in a cell. To wrap text in cells, select the cells, go to the Home tab, and click the Wrap Text button (you can find it in the Alignment group).

Entering numeric values

 When a number is too large to fit in a cell, Excel displays pounds signs (###) instead of a number or displays the number in scientific notation. You can always glance at the Formula bar, however, to find out the number in the active cell. As well, you can always widen the column to display the entire number.

To enter a fraction in a cell, enter a 0 or a whole number, a blank space, and the fraction. For example, to enter ⅜, type a **0**, press the spacebar, and type **3/8**. To enter 5⅜, type the **5**, press the spacebar, and type **3/8**. For its purposes, Excel converts fractions to decimal numbers, as you can see by looking in the Formula bar after you enter a fraction. For example, 5⅜ displays as 5.375 in the Formula bar.

 Here's a little trick for entering numbers with decimals quickly in all the Excel files you work on. To spare yourself the trouble of pressing the period key (.), you can tell Excel to enter the period automatically. Instead of entering 12.45, for example, you can simply enter 1245. Excel enters the period for you: 12.45. To perform this trick, go to the File tab, choose Options, visit the Advanced category in the Excel Options dialog box, click the Automatically Insert a Decimal Point check box, and in the Places text box, enter the number of decimal places you want for numbers. Deselect this option when you want to go back to entering numbers the normal way.

Entering date and time values

Dates and times can be used in calculations, but entering a date or time value in a cell can be problematic because these values must be entered in such a way that Excel can recognize them as dates or times, not text.

Not that you need to know it especially, but Excel converts dates and times to serial values for the purpose of being able to use dates and times in calculations. For example, July 31, 2004, is the number 38199. July 31, 2004, at Noon is 38199.5. These serial values represent the number of whole days since January 1, 1900. The portion of the serial value to the right of the decimal point is the time, represented as a portion of a full day.

Entering date values

You can enter a date value in a cell in just about any format you choose, and Excel understands that you're entering a date. For example, enter a date in any of the following formats and you'll be all right:

m/d/yy	7/31/10
m-d-yyyy	7-31-2010
d-mmm-yy	31-Jul-10

Here are some basic things to remember about entering dates:

✦ **Date formats:** You can quickly apply a format to dates by selecting cells and using one of these techniques:

- On the Home tab, open the Number Format drop-down list and choose Short Date (*m/d/yyyy;* 7/31/2010) or Long Date (*day-of-the-week, month, day, year;* Saturday, July 31, 2010), as shown in Figure 1-5.

- On the Home tab, click the Number group button to open the Number tab of the Format Cells dialog box. As shown in Figure 1-5, choose the Date category and then choose a date format.

✦ **Current date:** Press Ctrl+; (semicolon) and press Enter to enter the current date.

✦ **Current year's date:** If you don't enter the year as part of the date, Excel assumes that the date you entered is in the current year. For example, if you enter a date in the *m/d* (7/31) format during the year 2010, Excel enters the date as 7/31/10. As long as the date you want to enter is the current year, you can save a little time when entering dates by not entering the year, as Excel enters it for you.

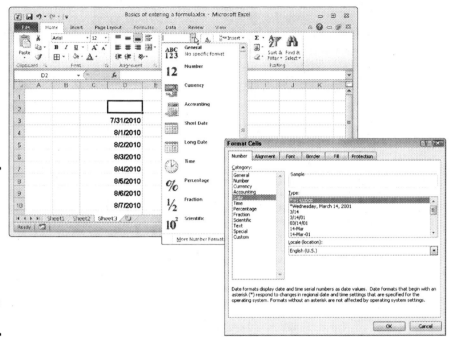

Figure 1-5:
Format
dates and
numbers on
the Number
Format
drop-down
list or
Format Cells
dialog box.

✦ **Dates on the Formula bar:** No matter which format you use for dates, dates are displayed in the Formula bar in the format that Excel prefers for dates: *m/d/yyyy* (7/31/2010). How dates are displayed in the worksheet is up to you.

✦ **20th and 21st century two-digit years:** When it comes to entering two-digit years in dates, the digits 30 through 99 belong to the 20th century (1930–1999), but the digits 00 through 29 belong to the 21st century (2000–2029). For example, 7/31/10 refers to July 31, 2010, not July 31, 1910. To enter a date in 1929 or earlier, enter four digits instead of two to describe the year: **7-31-1929**. To enter a date in 2030 or later, enter four digits instead of two: **7-31-2030**.

✦ **Dates in formulas:** To enter a date directly in a formula, enclose the date in quotation marks. (Make sure that the cell where the formula is entered has been given the Number format, not the Date format.) For example, the formula =TODAY()-"1/1/2010" calculates the number of days that have elapsed since January 1, 2010. Formulas are the subject of Chapter 3 of this mini-book.

Entering time values

Excel recognizes time values that you enter in the following ways:

h:mm AM/PM	3:31 AM
h:mm:ss AM/PM	3:31:45 PM

Here are some things to remember when entering time values:

✦ **Use colons:** Separate hours, minutes, and seconds with a colon (:).

✦ **Time formats:** To change to the *h:mm:ss* AM/PM time format, select the cells, go to the Home tab, open the Number Format drop-down list, and choose Time (see Figure 1-5). You can also change time formats by clicking the Number group button on the Home tab and selecting a time format on the Number tab of the Format Cells dialog box.

✦ **AM or PM time designations:** Unless you enter AM or PM with the time, Excel assumes that you're operating on military time. For example, 3:30 is considered 3:30 a.m.; 15:30 is 3:30 p.m. Don't enter periods after the letters *am* or *pm* (don't enter a.m. or p.m.).

✦ **Current time:** Press Ctrl+Shift+; (semicolon) to enter the current time.

✦ **Times on the Formula bar:** On the Formula bar, times are displayed in this format: *hours:minutes:seconds,* followed by the letters AM or PM. However, the time format used in cells is up to you.

Combining date and time values

You can combine dates and time values by entering the date, a blank space, and the time:

✦ 7/31/10 3:31 am

✦ 7-31-10 3:31:45 pm

Quickly Entering Lists and Serial Data with the AutoFill Command

Data that falls in the "serial" category — month names, days of the week, and consecutive numbers and dates, for example — can be entered quickly with the AutoFill command. Believe it or not, Excel recognizes certain kinds of serial data and enters it for you as part of the AutoFill feature. Instead of laboriously entering this data one piece at a time, you can enter it all at once by dragging the mouse. Follow these steps to "autofill" cells:

1. **Click the cell that is to be first in the series.**

For example, if you intend to list the days of the week in consecutive cells, click where the first day is to go.

2. **Enter the first number, date, or list item in the series.**

3. **Move to the adjacent cell and enter the second number, date, or list item in the series.**

If you want to enter the same number or piece of text in adjacent cells, it isn't necessary to take this step, but Excel needs the first and second items in the case of serial dates and numbers so that it can tell how much to increase or decrease the given amount or time period in each cell. For example, entering **5** and **10** tells Excel to increase the number by 5 each time so that the next serial entry is 15.

4. **Select the cell or cells you just entered data in.**

To select a single cell, click it; to select two, drag over the cells. Chapter 2 of this mini-book describes all the ways to select cells in a worksheet.

5. **Click the AutoFill handle and start dragging in the direction in which you want the data series to appear on your worksheet.**

The *AutoFill handle* is the little black square in the lower-right corner of the cell or block of cells you selected. Finding it can be difficult. Carefully move the mouse pointer over the lower-right corner of the cell, and when you see the mouse pointer change into a black cross, click and start dragging. As you drag, the serial data appears in a pop-up box, as shown in Figure 1-6.

Drag the AutoFill handle

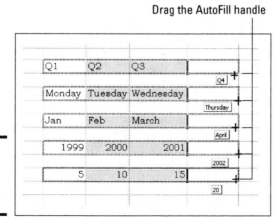

Figure 1-6:
Entering
serial data
and text.

The AutoFill Options button appears after you enter the serial data. Click it and choose an option if you want to copy cells or fill the cells without carrying along their formats.

 To enter the same number or text in several empty cells, drag over the cells to select them or select each cell by holding down the Ctrl key as you click. Then type a number or some text and press Ctrl+Enter.

At the end of this chapter, the sidebar "Creating your own AutoFill list" explains how to create a list of your own that Excel can enter automatically.

Formatting Numbers, Dates, and Time Values

When you enter a number that Excel recognizes as belonging to one of its formats, Excel assigns the number format automatically. Enter **45%**, for example, and Excel assigns the Percentage Style format. Enter **$4.25**, and Excel assigns the Currency Style format. Besides assigning formats by hand, however, you can assign them to cells from the get-go and spare yourself the trouble of entering dollar signs, commas, percent signs, and other extraneous punctuation. All you have to do is enter the raw numbers. Excel does the window dressing for you.

Excel offers five number-formatting buttons on the Home tab — Accounting Number Format, Percent Style, Comma Style, Increase Decimal, and Decrease Decimal. Select cells with numbers in them and click one of these buttons to change how numbers are formatted:

 ✦ **Accounting Number Format:** Places a dollar sign before the number and gives it two decimal places. You can open the drop-down list on this button and choose a currency symbol apart from the dollar sign.

 ✦ **Percent Style:** Places a percent sign after the number and converts the number to a percentage.

 ✦ **Comma Style:** Places commas in the number.

 ✦ **Increase Decimal:** Increases the number of decimal places by one.

 ✦ **Decrease Decimal:** Decreases the number of decimal places by one.

To choose among many formats and to format dates and time values as well as numbers, go to the Home tab, click the Number group button, and make selections on the Number tab of the Format Cells dialog box. Figure 1-7 shows this dialog box. Choose a category and select options to describe how you want numbers or text to appear.

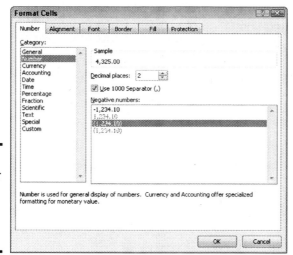

Figure 1-7:
The Number category of the Format Cells dialog box.

 To strip formats from the data in cells, select the cells, go to the Home tab, click the Clear button, and choose Clear Formats.

 Entering ZIP codes can be problematic because Excel strips the initial zero from the number if it begins with a zero. To get around that problem, visit the Number tab of the Format Cells dialog box (see Figure 1-7), choose Special in the Category list, and select a ZIP Code option.

Conditional Formats for Calling Attention to Data

A *conditional format* is one that applies when data meets certain conditions. To call attention to numbers greater than 10,000, for example, you can tell Excel to highlight those numbers automatically. To highlight negative numbers, you can tell Excel to display them in bright red. Conditional formats help you analyze and understand data better.

Select the cells that are candidates for conditional formatting and follow these steps to tell Excel when and how to format the cells:

1. **On the Home tab, click the Conditional Formatting button (you may have to click the Styles button first, depending on the size of your screen).**

2. **Choose Highlight Cells Rules or Top/Bottom Rules on the drop-down list.**

    You see a submenu with choices about establishing the rule for whether values in the cells are highlighted or otherwise made more prominent:

- *Highlight Cells Rules:* These rules are for calling attention to data if it falls in a numerical or date range, or it's greater or lesser than a specific value. For example, you can highlight cells that are greater than 400.

- *Top/Bottom Rules:* These rules are for calling attention to data if it falls within a percentage range relative to all the cells you selected. For example, you can highlight cells with data that falls in the bottom 10-percent range.

3. **Choose an option on the submenu.**

You see a dialog box similar to the one in Figure 1-8.

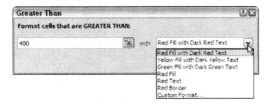

Figure 1-8:
Establishing
a condition
format for
data.

4. **On the left side of the dialog box, establish the rule for flagging data.**

5. **On the With drop-down list, choose how you want to call attention to the data.**

For example, you can display the data in red or yellow. You can choose Custom Format on the drop-down list to open the Format Cells dialog box and choose a font style or color for the text.

6. **Click OK.**

To remove conditional formats, select the cells with the formats, go to the Home tab, click the Conditional Formatting button, and choose Clear Rules➪Clear Rules from Selected Cells. You can also click the Conditional Formatting button and choose Clear Rules➪Clear Rules from Entire Sheet to remove all conditional formats from a worksheet.

Establishing Data-Validation Rules

By nature, people are prone to enter data incorrectly because the task of entering data is so dull. This is why data-validation rules are invaluable. A *data-validation rule* is a rule concerning what kind of data can be entered in a cell. When you select a cell that has been given a rule, an input message tells you what to enter, as shown in Figure 1-8. And if you enter the data incorrectly, an error alert tells you as much, also shown in Figure 1-9.

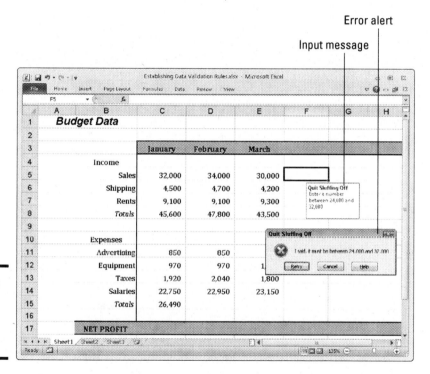

Figure 1-9: A data-validation rule in action.

Data-validation rules are an excellent defense against sloppy data entry and that itchy feeling you get when you're in the middle of an irksome task. In a cell that records date entries, you can require dates to fall in a certain time frame. In a cell that records text entries, you can choose an item from a list instead of typing it yourself. In a cell that records numeric entries, you can require the number to fall within a certain range. Table 1-1 describes the different categories of data-validation rules.

Table 1-1	Data-Validation Rule Categories
Rule	*What Can Be Entered*
Any Value	Anything whatsoever. This is the default setting.
Whole Number	Whole numbers (no decimal points allowed). Choose an operator from the Data drop-down list and values to describe the range of numbers that can be entered.
Decimal	Same as the Whole Number rule except numbers with decimal points are permitted.
List	Items from a list. Enter the list items in cells on a worksheet, either the one you're working in or another. Then reopen the Data Validation dialog box, click the Range Selector button (you can find it on the right side of the Source text box), and select the cells that hold the list. The list items appear in a drop-down list on the worksheet.
Date	Date values. Choose an operator from the Data drop-down list and values to describe the date range. Earlier in this chapter, "Entering date and time values" describes the correct way to enter date values.
Time	Time values. Choose an operator from the Data drop-down list and values to describe the date and time range. Earlier in this chapter, "Entering date and time values" describes the correct way to enter a combination of date and time values.
Text Length	A certain number of characters. Choose an operator from the Data drop-down list and values to describe how many characters can be entered.
Custom	A logical value (True or False). Enter a formula that describes what constitutes a true or false data entry.

Follow these steps to establish a data-validation rule:

1. **Select the cell or cells that need a rule.**

2. **On the Data tab, click the Data Validation button.**

   As shown in Figure 1-10, you see the Settings tab of the Data Validation dialog box.

Figure 1-10:
Creating
a data-
validation
rule.

3. **On the Allow drop-down list, choose the category of rule you want.**

   Table 1-1, earlier in this chapter, describes these categories.

4. **Enter the criteria for the rule.**

   What the criteria is depends on what rule category you're working in. Table 1-1 describes how to enter the criteria for rules in each category. You can refer to cells in the worksheet by selecting them. To do that, either select them directly or click the Range Selector button and then select them.

5. **On the Input Message tab, enter a title and input message.**

   You can see a title ("Quit Sluffing Off") and input message ("Enter a number between 24,000 and 32,000") in Figure 1-10. The title appears in boldface. Briefly describe what kind of data belongs in the cell or cells you selected.

6. **On the Error Alert tab, choose a style for the symbol in the Message Alert dialog box, enter a title for the dialog box, and enter a warning message.**

   In the error message in Figure 1-10, the Stop symbol was chosen. The title you enter appears across the top of the dialog box, and the message appears beside the symbol.

7. **Click OK.**

   To remove data-validation rules from cells, select the cells, go to the Data tab, click the Data Validation button, and on the Settings tab of the Data Validation dialog box, click the Clear All button, and click OK.

**Book IV
Chapter 1**

**Up and Running
with Excel**

Creating your own AutoFill list

As "Quickly Entering Lists and Serial Data with the AutoFill Command" explains earlier in this chapter, Excel is capable of completing lists on its own with the AutoFill feature. You can enter the days of the week or month names simply by entering one day or month and dragging the AutoFill handle to enter the others. Here's some good news: The AutoFill command can also reproduce the names of your co-workers, the roster of a softball team, street names, or any other list that you care to enter quickly and repeatedly in a worksheet.

Follow these steps to enter items for a list so that you can enter them in the future by dragging the AutoFill handle:

1. **If you've already entered items for the list on your worksheet, select the items.**

   If you haven't entered the items yet, skip to Step 2.

2. **On the File tab, choose Options to open the Excel Options dialog box.**

3. **Go to the Advanced category.**

4. **Click the Edit Custom Lists button (you have to scroll down to find it).**

   You see the Custom Lists dialog box.

5. **In the List Entries box, do one of the following:**

   If you selected the items in Step 1, click the Import button. The items you selected appear in the List Entries box.

   If you need to enter items for the list, enter them in the List Entries box, with one item on each line.

6. **Click the Add button.**

7. **Click OK.**

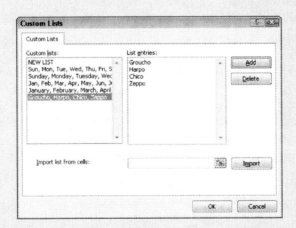

Chapter 2: Refining Your Worksheet

In This Chapter

✔ **Changing worksheet data**

✔ **Going here and there in a worksheet**

✔ **Freezing and splitting columns and rows to make data entry easier**

✔ **Documenting a worksheet with comments**

✔ **Selecting cells**

✔ **Copying and moving data**

✔ **Moving among, deleting, and renaming worksheets**

✔ **Hiding and protecting worksheets so they can't be altered**

This chapter delves into the workaday world of worksheets (say that three times fast). It explains how to edit worksheet data and move quickly here and there in a worksheet. You also discover a couple of techniques for entering data quickly, how to select cells, and how to copy and move data in cells. This chapter describes how to move, delete, and rename worksheets, as well as protect them from being edited or altered.

Editing Worksheet Data

Not everyone enters data correctly the first time. To edit data you entered in a cell, do one of the following:

✦ **Double-click the cell.** Doing so places the cursor squarely in the cell, where you can start deleting or entering numbers and text.

✦ **Click the cell and press F2.** This technique also lands the cursor in the cell.

✦ **Click the cell you want to edit.** With this technique, you edit the data on the Formula bar.

 If nothing happens when you double-click, or if pressing F2 lands the cursor in the Formula bar, not a cell, somebody has been fooling with the Options settings. On the File tab, choose Options, select the Advanced category in the Excel Options dialog box, and click the Allow Editing Directly in Cells check box.

Moving around in a Worksheet

Going from place to place gets progressively more difficult as a worksheet gets larger. Luckily for you, Excel offers keyboard shortcuts for jumping around. Table 2-1 describes these keyboard shortcuts.

Table 2-1 Keyboard Shortcuts for Getting around in Worksheets

Press . . .	To Move the Selection . . .
Home	To column A
Ctrl+Home	To cell A1, the first cell in the worksheet
Ctrl+End	To the last cell in the last row with data in it
←, →, ↑, ↓	To the next cell
Ctrl+←, →, ↑, ↓	In one direction toward the nearest cell with data in it or to the first or last cell in the column or row
PgUp *or* PgDn	Up or down one screen's worth of rows
Ctrl+PgUp *or* Ctrl+PgDn	Backward or forward through the workbook, from worksheet to worksheet

As well as pressing keys, you can use these techniques to get from place to place in a worksheet:

✦ **Scroll bars:** Use the vertical and horizontal scroll bars to move to different areas. Drag the scroll box to cover long distances. To cover long distances very quickly, hold down the Shift key as you drag the scroll box on the vertical scroll bar.

✦ **Scroll wheel on the mouse:** If your mouse is equipped with a scroll wheel, turn the wheel to quickly scroll up and down.

✦ **Name box:** Enter a cell address in the Name box and press Enter to go to the cell. The Name box is found to the left of the Formula bar.

✦ **The Go To command:** On the Home tab, click the Find & Select button, and choose Go To on the drop-down list (or press Ctrl+G or F5). You see the Go To dialog box. Enter a cell address in the Reference box and click OK. Cell addresses you've already visited with the Go To command are already listed in the dialog box. Click the Special button to open the Go To Special dialog box and visit a formula, comment, or other esoteric item.

✦ **The Find command:** On the Home tab, click the Find & Select button, and choose Find on the drop-down list (or press Ctrl+F). Enter the data you seek in the Find What box and click the Find Next button. Click the Find All button to find all instances of the item you're looking for. A list of the items appears at the bottom of the dialog box; click an item to go to it.

To scroll to the active cell if you no longer see it on-screen, press Ctrl+Backspace.

Getting a Better Look at the Worksheet

Especially when you're entering data, it pays to get a good look at the worksheet. You need to know which column and row you're entering data in. These pages explain techniques for changing your view of a worksheet so you always know where you are. Read on to discover how to freeze, split, and hide columns and rows. (On the subject of changing views, Book I, Chapter 3 explains an essential technique for changing views: zooming in and zooming out; also, the sidebar "Your own customized views," at the end of this chapter, explains how to save a view you particularly like so that you can revisit it.)

Freezing and splitting columns and rows

Sometimes your adventures in a worksheet take you to a faraway cell address, such as X31 or C39. Out there in the wilderness, it's hard to tell where to enter data because you can't see the data labels in the first column or first row that tell you where to enter data on the worksheet.

To see one part of a worksheet no matter how far you stray from it, you can *split* the worksheet or *freeze* columns and rows on-screen. In Figure 2-1, I split the worksheet so that column A (Property) always appears on-screen, no matter how far I scroll to the right; similarly, row 1 (Property, Rent, Management Fees, and so on) also appears at the top of the worksheet no matter how far I scroll down. Notice how the row numbers and column letters are interrupted in Figure 2-1. Because I split the screen, I always know what data to enter in a cell because I can clearly see property names in the first column and the column headings along the top of the worksheet.

Freezing columns or rows on a worksheet works much like splitting except that lines instead of gray bars appear on-screen to show which columns and rows are frozen, and you can't adjust where the split occurs by dragging the boundary where the worksheet is split.

**Book IV
Chapter 2**

**Refining Your
Worksheet**

Splitting the worksheet is superior to freezing columns or rows because, for one, you can drag the split lines to new locations when you split the worksheet, and moreover, you can remove a horizontal or vertical split simply by double-clicking it. However, if your goal is simply to freeze the topmost row or leftmost column in your worksheet, use a Freeze Panes command because all you have to do is go to the View tab, click the Freeze Panes button, and choose Freeze Top Row or Freeze First Column.

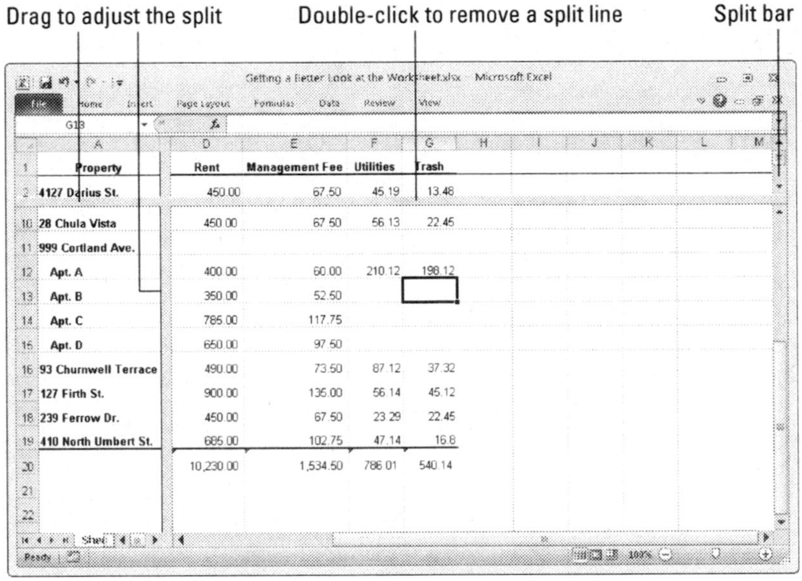

Drag to adjust the split   Double-click to remove a split line   Split bar

Figure 2-1:
Splitting a
worksheet.

	A	D	E	F	G	H	I	J	K	L	M
1	**Property**	**Rent**	**Management Fee**	**Utilities**	**Trash**						
2	**4127 Darius St.**	450.00	67.50	45.19	13.48						
10	**28 Chula Vista**	450.00	67.50	56.13	22.45						
11	**999 Cortland Ave.**										
12	**Apt. A**	400.00	60.00	210.12	198.12						
13	**Apt. B**	350.00	52.50								
14	**Apt. C**	785.00	117.75								
15	**Apt. D**	650.00	97.50								
16	**93 Churnwell Terrace**	490.00	73.50	87.12	37.32						
17	**127 Firth St.**	900.00	135.00	56.14	45.12						
18	**239 Ferrow Dr.**	450.00	67.50	23.29	22.45						
19	**410 North Umbert St.**	685.00	102.75	47.14	16.8						
20		10,230.00	1,534.50	786.01	540.14						
21											
22											

Giving the Split or Freeze Panes command

Follow these steps to split or freeze columns and rows on-screen:

1. Click the cell directly below the row you want to freeze or split, and click in the column to the right of the column that you want to freeze or split.

In other words, click where you want the split to occur.

2. On the View tab, split or freeze the columns and rows.

Go to the View tab and use one of these techniques:

- *Splitting:* Click the Split button and then click and drag the split bars to split the screen horizontally or vertically. The other way to split a worksheet is to grab hold of a *split bar,* the little division markers directly above the vertical scroll bar and directly to the right of the horizontal scroll bar (in the lower-right corner of your screen). You can tell where split bars are because the pointer turns into a double arrow when it's over a split bar.

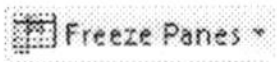

- *Freezing:* Click the Freeze Panes button and choose one of three Freeze options on the drop-down list. The second and third options, respectively, freeze the top row or first column. The first option, Freeze Panes, freezes the column(s) to the left and the row(s) above the cell you selected in Step 1.

Bars or lines appear on-screen to show which row(s) and column(s) have been frozen or split. Move where you will in the worksheet. The column(s) and row(s) you froze or split stay on-screen.

Unsplitting and unfreezing

Use one of these techniques to keep your worksheet from splitting or freezing to death:

✦ **Unsplitting:** Click the Split button again; double-click one of the split bars to remove it; or drag a split bar into the top or left side of the worksheet window.

✦ **Unfreezing:** On the View tab, click the Freeze Panes button and choose Unfreeze Panes on the drop-down list.

Hiding columns and rows

Another way to take the clutter out of a worksheet is to temporarily hide columns and rows:

✦ **Hiding columns or rows:** Drag over the column letters or row numbers of the columns or rows that you want to hide. Dragging this way selects entire columns or rows. Then go to the Home tab, click the Format button, choose Hide & Unhide, and choose Hide Columns or Hide Rows.

✦ **Unhiding columns and rows:** Select columns to the right and left of the hidden columns, or select rows above and below the hidden rows. To select columns or rows, drag over their letters or numbers. Then go to the Home tab, click the Format button, choose Hide & Unhide, and choose Unhide Columns or Unhide Rows.

It's easy to forget where you hid columns or rows. To make sure all columns and rows in your worksheet are displayed, click the Select All button (or press Ctrl+A) to select your entire worksheet. Then go to the Home tab, click the Format button and choose Hide & Unhide⇨Unhide Columns; click the Format button again and choose Hide & Unhide⇨Unhide Rows.

Comments for Documenting Your Worksheet

It may happen that you return to your worksheet days or months from now and discover to your dismay that you don't know why certain numbers or formulas are there. For that matter, someone else may inherit your worksheet and be mystified as to what the heck is going on. To take the mystery out of a worksheet, document it by entering comments here and there.

A *comment* is a note that describes part of a worksheet. Each comment is connected to a cell. You can tell where a comment is because a small red triangle appears in the upper-right corner of cells that have been commented on. Move the pointer over one of these triangles and you see the pop-up box, a comment, and the name of the person who entered the comment, as shown in Figure 2-2. Click the Show All Comments button on the Review tab to see every comment in a worksheet.

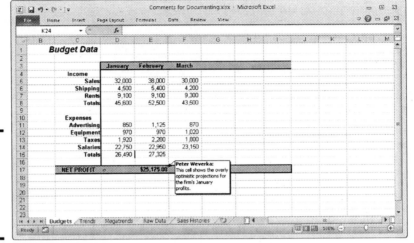

Figure 2-2:
Comments
explain
what's
what in a
worksheet.

Here's everything a mere mortal needs to know about comments:

✦ **Entering a comment:** Click the cell that deserves the comment, go to the Review tab, and click the New Comment button. Enter your comment in the pop-up box. Click in a different cell when you finish entering your comment.

✦ **Reading a comment:** Move the pointer over the small red triangle and read the comment in the pop-up box (refer to Figure 2-2).

✦ **Finding comments:** On the Review tab, click the Previous or Next button to go from comment to comment.

✦ **Editing a comment:** Select the cells with the comment, and on the Review tab, click the Edit Comment button, and edit the comment in the pop-up box. You can also right-click the cell and choose Edit Comment.

✦ **Deleting comments:** On the Review tab, click a cell with a comment, and then click the Delete button, or right-click the cell and choose Delete Comment. To delete several comments, select them by Ctrl+clicking and then click the Delete button.

✦ **Deleting all comments in a worksheet:** Select all comments and then, on the Review tab, click the Delete button. You can select all comments by clicking the Find & Select button on the Home tab, choosing Go To, and in the Go To dialog box, clicking the Special button and choosing Comments in the Go To Special dialog box.

If your name doesn't appear in the pop-up box after you enter a comment and you want it to appear there, go to the File tab, choose Options, select the General category in the Excel Options dialog box, and enter your name in the User Name text box.

You can print the comments in a worksheet. On the Page Layout tab, click the Page Setup group button, and on the Sheet tab of the Page Setup dialog box, open the Comments drop-down list and choose At End of Sheet or As Displayed on Sheet.

Selecting Cells in a Worksheet

To format, copy, move, delete, and format numbers and words in a worksheet, you have to select the cells in which the numbers and words are found. Here are ways to select cells and the data inside them:

✦ **A block of cells:** Drag diagonally across the worksheet from one corner of the block of cells to the opposite corner. You can also click in one corner and Shift+click the opposite corner.

✦ **Adjacent cells in a row or column:** Drag across the cells.

✦ **Cells in various places:** While holding down the Ctrl key, click different cells.

✦ **A row or rows:** Click a row number to select an entire row. Click and drag down the row numbers to select several adjacent rows.

✦ **A column or columns:** Click a column letter to select an entire column. Click and drag across letters to select adjacent columns.

 ✦ **Entire worksheet:** Click the Select All button, the square to the left of the column letters and above the row numbers; press Ctrl+A; or press Ctrl+Shift+Spacebar.

 Press Ctrl+Spacebar to select the column that the active cell is in; press Shift+Spacebar to select the row where the active cell is.

You can enter the same data item in several different cells by selecting cells and then entering the data in one cell and pressing Ctrl+Enter. This technique comes in very handy, for example, when you want to enter a placeholder zero (0) in several different cells.

Deleting, Copying, and Moving Data

In the course of putting together a worksheet, it is sometimes necessary to delete, copy, and move cell contents. Here are instructions for doing these chores:

 ✦ **Deleting cell contents:** Select the cells and then press the Delete key; on the Home tab, click the Clear button and choose Clear Contents; or right-click and choose Clear Contents. (Avoid the Delete button on the Home tab for deleting cell contents. Clicking that button deletes cells as well as their contents.)

✦ **Copying and moving cell contents:** Select the cells and use one of these techniques:

- *Cut or Copy and Paste commands:* When you paste the data, click where you want the first cell of the block of cells you're copying or moving to go. (Book I, Chapter 2 explains copying and moving data in detail.) Be careful not to overwrite cells with data in them when you copy or move data. After you paste data, you see the Paste Options button. Click this button and choose an option from the drop-down list to format the data in different ways.

- *Drag and drop:* Move the pointer to the edge of the cell block, click when you see the four-headed arrow, and start dragging. Hold down the Ctrl key to copy the data.

Handling the Worksheets in a Workbook

As a glance at the bottom of the worksheet tells you, each workbook comes with three worksheets named (not very creatively) Sheet1, Sheet2, and Sheet3. Follow these instructions to move among, add, delete, rename, and change the order of worksheets:

✦ **Moving among worksheets:** To go from one worksheet to another, click a worksheet tab along the bottom of the screen. If you can't see a tab, click one of the scroll arrows to the left of the worksheet tabs.

✦ **Renaming a worksheet:** Right-click the worksheet tab, choose Rename on the shortcut menu, type a new name, and press Enter. You can also go to the Home tab, click the Format button, choose Rename Sheet on the drop-down list, and enter a new name. Spaces are allowed in names, and names can be 31 characters long. Brackets ([]) are allowed in names, but you can't use these symbols: / \ : ? and * .

✦ **Selecting worksheets:** Click the worksheet's tab to select it. To select several worksheets, Ctrl+click their tabs or click the first tab and then Shift+click the last tab in the set. To select all the worksheets, right-click a tab and choose Select All Sheets on the shortcut menu.

✦ **Rearranging worksheets:** Drag the worksheet tab to a new location. As you drag, a tiny black arrow and a page icon appear to show you where the worksheet will land after you release the mouse button. You can also select a sheet, go to the Home tab, click the Format button, and choose Move or Copy Sheet on the drop-down list. The Move or Copy dialog box appears, as shown in Figure 2-3. Select the sheet in the Before Sheet list where you want the worksheet to go and click OK.

✦ **Inserting a new worksheet:** Click the Insert Sheet button (you can find it to the right of the worksheet tabs); press Shift+F11; or on the Home tab, open the drop-down list on the Insert button and choose Insert Sheet.

Figure 2-3: Besides dragging it, you can move a worksheet in this dialog box.

✦ **Deleting a worksheet:** Select the sheet, and on the Home tab, open the drop-down list on the Delete button and choose Delete Sheet. You can also right-click a worksheet tab and choose Delete. Be careful because you can't restore your deleted worksheet by pressing the Undo button.

✦ **Copying a worksheet:** Select the sheet, hold down the Ctrl key, and drag the worksheet tab to a new location.

✦ **Color-coding a worksheet:** Right-click a worksheet tab and choose Tab Color. Then select a color in the submenu, or choose More Colors and select a color in the Colors dialog box. You can also select a worksheet tab, go to the Home tab, click the Format button, choose Tab Color on the drop-down list, and choose a color on the submenu.

You can change the size of columns or apply numeric formats to the same addresses in different worksheets by selecting all the sheets first and then formatting one worksheet. The formats apply to all the worksheets that you select. Being able to format several different worksheets simultaneously comes in handy, for example, when your workbook tracks monthly data and each worksheet pertains to one month. Another way to handle worksheets with similar data is to create the first worksheet and copy it to the second, third, and fourth worksheets with the Copy and Paste commands.

Keeping Others from Tampering with Worksheets

People with savvy and foresight sometimes set up workbooks so that one worksheet holds raw data and the other worksheets hold formulas that calculate the raw data. This technique prevents others from tampering with the raw data. Furthermore, if the worksheet with raw data is hidden, the chance it will be tampered with is lower; and if the worksheet is protected, no one can tamper with it unless they have a password. These pages explain how to hide a worksheet so others are less likely to find it and how to protect a worksheet from being edited.

Hiding a worksheet

Follow these instructions to hide and unhide worksheets:

✦ **Hiding a worksheet:** Select the worksheet you want to hide, go to the View tab, and click the Hide button. You can also right-click the worksheet's tab and choose Hide on the shortcut menu. And you can also display the worksheet, go to the Home tab, click the Format button, and choose Hide & Unhide➪Hide Sheet.

✦ **Unhiding a worksheet:** On the View tab, click the Unhide button, select the name of the worksheet you want to unhide in the Unhide dialog box, and click OK. To open the Unhide dialog box, you can also right-click any worksheet tab and choose Unhide; or go to the Home tab, click the Format button, and choose Hide & Unhide➪Unhide Sheet.

Protecting a worksheet

Protecting a worksheet means to restrict others from changing it — from formatting it, inserting new rows and columns, or deleting rows and columns, among other tasks. You can also prevent any editorial changes whatsoever from being made to a worksheet. Follow these steps to protect a worksheet from tampering by others:

1. **Select the worksheet that needs protection.**

2. **On the Review tab, click the Protect Sheet button.**

   You see the Protect Sheet dialog box shown in Figure 2-4. You can also open this dialog box by going to the Home tab, clicking the Format button, and choosing Protect Sheet.

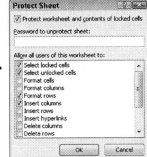

Figure 2-4: Select what you want others to be able to do.

3. **Enter a password in the Password to Unprotect Sheet box if you want only people with the password to be able to unprotect the worksheet after you protect it.**

4. On the Allow All Users of This Worksheet To list, select the check box next to the name of each task that you want to permit others to do.

For example, click the Format Cells check box if you want others to be able to format cells.

Deselect the Select Locked Cells check box to prevent any changes from being made to the worksheet. By default, all worksheet cells are locked, and by preventing others from selecting locked cells, you effectively prevent them from editing any cells.

5. Click OK.

If you entered a password in Step 3, you must enter it again in the Confirm Password dialog box and click OK.

To unprotect a worksheet that you protected, go to the Review tab and click the Unprotect Sheet button. You must enter a password if you elected to require others to have a password before they can unprotect a worksheet.

Your own customized views

Earlier in this chapter, "Getting a Better Look at the Worksheet" explains how to freeze the screen or zoom in to a position you're comfortable with. After you find this position, you can set your view of the screen as a customized view. That way, you can call upon the customized view whenever you need it. View settings, the window size, the position of the grid on-screen, and cells that are selected can all be saved in a customized view.

Follow these steps to create a customized view:

1. On the View tab, click the Custom Views button.

You see the Custom Views dialog box. It lists views you've already created, if you've created any.

2. Click the Add button.

The Add View dialog box appears.

3. Enter a name for the view and click OK.

To switch to a customized view, click the Custom Views button, select a view in the Custom Views dialog box, and click the Show button.

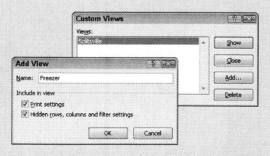

Chapter 3: Formulas and Functions for Crunching Numbers

In This Chapter

- ✔ **Constructing a formula**
- ✔ **Using cell ranges in formulas**
- ✔ **Naming cell ranges**
- ✔ **Referring to cells in other worksheets**
- ✔ **Copying formulas to other columns and rows**
- ✔ **Preventing errors in formulas**
- ✔ **Using functions in formulas**

*F*ormulas are where it's at as far as Excel is concerned. After you know how to construct formulas, and constructing them is pretty easy, you can put Excel to work. You can make the numbers speak to you. You can turn a bunch of unruly numbers into meaningful figures and statistics.

This chapter explains what a formula is, how to enter a formula, and how to enter a formula quickly. You also discover how to copy formulas from cell to cell and how to keep formula errors from creeping into your workbooks. Finally, this chapter explains how to make use of the hundred or so functions that Excel offers.

How Formulas Work

A *formula,* you may recall from the sleepy hours you spent in math class, is a way to calculate numbers. For example, 2+3=5 is a formula. When you enter a formula in a cell, Excel computes the formula and displays its results in the cell. Click in cell A3 and enter =**2+3**, for example, and Excel displays the number 5 in cell A3.

Referring to cells in formulas

As well as numbers, Excel formulas can refer to the contents of different cells. When a formula refers to a cell, the number in the cell is used to compute the formula. In Figure 3-1, for example, cell A1 contains the number 2; cell A2 contains the number 3; and cell A3 contains the formula =A1+A2. As shown in cell A3, the result of the formula is 5. If I change the number in cell A1 from 2 to 3, the result of the formula in cell A3 (=A1+A2) becomes 6, not 5. When a formula refers to a cell and the number in the cell changes, the result of the formula changes as well.

Formula in the Formula bar

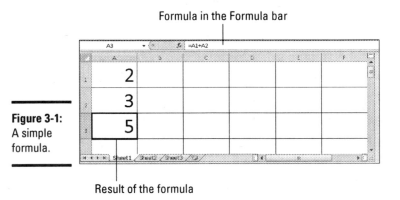

Figure 3-1:
A simple
formula.

Result of the formula

To see the value of using cell references in formulas, consider the worksheet shown in Figure 3-2. The purpose of this worksheet is to track the budget of a school's Parent Teacher Association (PTA):

		Actual Income	Projected Income	Over/Under Budget	
Income					
	Book Fair	4,876.40	5,500.00	-623.60	
	Dances	1,476.95	1,800.00	-323.05	
	Fundraising	13,175.00	5,000.00	8,175.00	
	Merchandise Sales	5,888.50	7,000.00	-1,111.50	
	Membership Fees	3,918.00	3,000.00	918.00	
Total Income		$29,334.85	$22,300.00	$7,034.85	

Figure 3-2:
Using
formulas
in a
worksheet.

✦ Column C, Actual Income, lists income from different sources.

✦ Column D, Projected Income, shows what the PTA members thought income from these sources would be.

✦ Column E, Over/Under Budget, shows how actual income compares to projected income from the different sources.

As the figures in the Actual Income column (column C) are updated, figures in the Over/Under Budget column (column E) and the Total Income row (row 8) change instantaneously. These figures change instantaneously because the formulas refer to the numbers in cells, not to unchanging numbers (known as *constants*).

Figure 3-3 shows the formulas used to calculate the data in the worksheet in Figure 3-2. In column E, formulas deduct the numbers in column D from the numbers in column C to show where the PTA over- or under-budgeted for the different sources of income. In row 8, you can see how the SUM function is used to total cells in rows 3 through 7. The end of this chapter explains how to use functions in formulas.

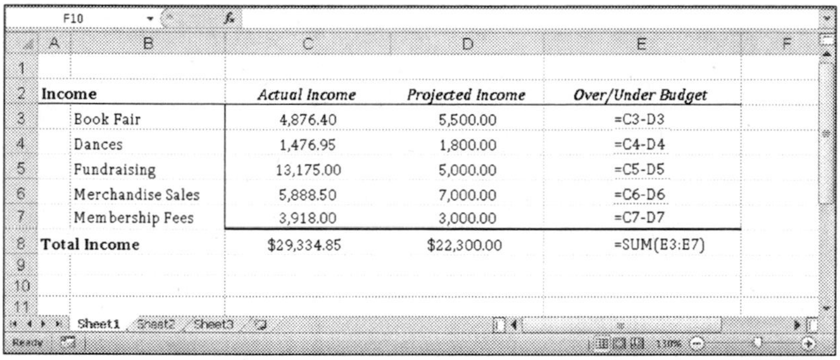

Figure 3-3:
The
formulas
used to
generate
the numbers
in Figure 3-2.

	A	B	C	D	E	F
1						
2	Income		Actual Income	Projected Income	Over/Under Budget	
3		Book Fair	4,876.40	5,500.00	=C3-D3	
4		Dances	1,476.95	1,800.00	=C4-D4	
5		Fundraising	13,175.00	5,000.00	=C5-D5	
6		Merchandise Sales	5,888.50	7,000.00	=C6-D6	
7		Membership Fees	3,918.00	3,000.00	=C7-D7	
8	Total Income		$29,334.85	$22,300.00	=SUM(E3:E7)	
9						
10						
11						

Excel is remarkably good about updating cell references in formulas when you move cells. To see how good Excel is, consider what happens to cell addresses in formulas when you delete a row in a worksheet. If a formula refers to cell C1 but you delete row B, row C becomes row B, and the value in cell C1 changes addresses from C1 to B1. You would think that references in formulas to cell C1 would be out of date, but you would be wrong. Excel automatically adjusts all formulas that refer to cell C1. Those formulas now refer to cell B1 instead.

In case you're curious, you can display formulas in worksheet cells instead of the results of formulas, as was done in Figure 3-3, by pressing Ctrl+' or clicking the Show Formulas button on the Formulas tab (you may have to click the Formula Auditing button first, depending on the size of your screen). Click the Show Formulas button a second time to see formula results again.

Referring to formula results in formulas

Besides referring to cells with numbers in them, you can refer to formula results in a cell. Consider the worksheet shown in Figure 3-4. The purpose of this worksheet is to track scoring by the players on a basketball team over three games:

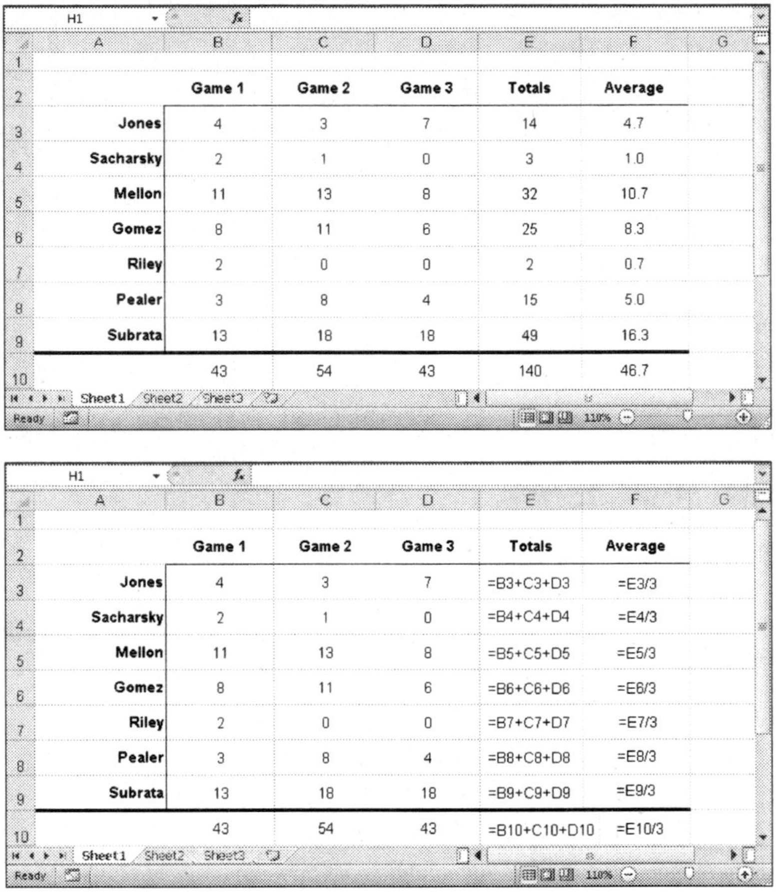

	A	B	C	D	E	F
2		Game 1	Game 2	Game 3	Totals	Average
3	Jones	4	3	7	14	4.7
4	Sacharsky	2	1	0	3	1.0
5	Mellon	11	13	8	32	10.7
6	Gomez	8	11	6	25	8.3
7	Riley	2	0	0	2	0.7
8	Pealer	3	8	4	15	5.0
9	Subrata	13	18	18	49	16.3
10		43	54	43	140	46.7

	A	B	C	D	E	F
2		Game 1	Game 2	Game 3	Totals	Average
3	Jones	4	3	7	=B3+C3+D3	=E3/3
4	Sacharsky	2	1	0	=B4+C4+D4	=E4/3
5	Mellon	11	13	8	=B5+C5+D5	=E5/3
6	Gomez	8	11	6	=B6+C6+D6	=E6/3
7	Riley	2	0	0	=B7+C7+D7	=E7/3
8	Pealer	3	8	4	=B8+C8+D8	=E8/3
9	Subrata	13	18	18	=B9+C9+D9	=E9/3
10		43	54	43	=B10+C10+D10	=E10/3

Figure 3-4: Using formula results as other formulas.

- The Totals column (column E) shows the total points each player scored in the three games.
- The Average column (column F), using the formula results in the Totals column, determines how much each player has scored on average. The Average column does that by dividing the results in column E by 3, the number of games played.

In this case, Excel uses the results of the total-calculation formulas in column E to compute average points per game in column F.

Operators in formulas

Addition, subtraction, and division aren't the only operators you can use in formulas. Table 3-1 explains the arithmetic operators you can use and the key you press to enter each operator. In the table, operators are listed in the order of precedence.

Table 3-1   Arithmetic Operators for Use in Formulas

Precedence	Operator	Example Formula	Returns
1	% (Percent)	=50%	50 percent, or 0.5
2	^ (Exponentiation)	=50^2,	50 to the second power, or 2500
3	* (Multiplication)	=E2*4	The value in cell E2 multiplied by 4
3	/ (Division)	=E2/3	The value in cell E2 divided by 3
4	+ (Addition)	=F1+F2+F3,	The sum of the values in those cells
4	– (Subtraction)	=G5-8,	The value in cell G5 minus 8
5	& (Concatenation)	="Part No. "&D4	The text *Part No.* and the value in cell D4
6	= (Equal to)	=C5=4,	If the value in cell C5 is equal to 4, returns TRUE; returns FALSE otherwise
6	<> (Not equal to)	=F3<>9	If the value in cell F3 is *not* equal to 9, returns TRUE; returns FALSE otherwise
6	< (Less than)	=B9<E11	If the value in cell B9 is less than the value in cell E11; returns TRUE; returns FALSE otherwise
6	<= (Less than or equal to)	=A4<=9	If the value in cell A4 is less than or equal to 9, returns TRUE; returns FALSE otherwise
6	> (Greater than)	=E8>14	If the value in cell E8 is greater than 14, returns TRUE; returns FALSE otherwise
6	>= (Greater than or equal to)	=C3>=D3	If the value in cell C3 is less than or equal to the value in cell D3; returns TRUE; returns FALSE otherwise

Another way to compute a formula is to make use of a function. As "Working with Functions" explains later in this chapter, a function is a built-in formula that comes with Excel. SUM, for example, adds the numbers in cells. AVG finds the average of different numbers.

Book IV
Chapter 3

Formulas and Functions for Crunching Numbers

The order of precedence

When a formula includes more than one operator, the order in which the operators appear in the formula matters a lot. Consider this formula:

=2+3*4

Does this formula result in 14 (2+[3*4]) or 20 ([2+3]*4)? The answer is 14 because Excel performs multiplication before addition in formulas. In other words, multiplication takes precedence over addition.

The order in which calculations are made in a formula that includes different operators is called the *order of precedence*. Be sure to remember the order of precedence when you construct complex formulas with more than one operator:

1. Percent (%)

2. Exponentiation (^)

3. Multiplication (*) and division (/); leftmost operations are calculated first

4. Addition (+) and subtraction (-); leftmost operations are calculated first

5. Concatenation (&)

6. Comparison (<, <=, >,>=, and <>)

To get around the order of precedence problem, enclose parts of formulas in parentheses. Operations in parentheses are calculated before all other parts of a formula. For example, the formula =2+3*4 equals 20 when it is written this way: =(2+3)*4.

The Basics of Entering a Formula

No matter what kind of formula you enter, no matter how complex the formula is, follow these basic steps to enter it:

1. **Click the cell where you want to enter the formula.**

2. **Click in the Formula bar if you want to enter the data there rather than the cell.**

3. **Enter the equals sign (=).**

You must be sure to enter the equals sign before you enter a formula. Without it, Excel thinks you're entering text or a number, not a formula.

4. **Enter the formula.**

For example, enter =B1*.06. Make sure that you enter all cell addresses correctly. By the way, you can enter lowercase letters in cell references. Excel changes them to uppercase after you finish entering the formula. The next section in this chapter explains how to enter cell addresses quickly in formulas.

5. **Press Enter or click the Enter button (the check mark on the Formula bar).**

The result of the formula appears in the cell.

Speed Techniques for Entering Formulas

Entering formulas and making sure that all cell references are correct is a tedious activity, but fortunately for you, Excel offers a few techniques to make entering formulas easier. Read on to find out how ranges make entering cell references easier and how you can enter cell references in formulas by pointing and clicking. You also find instructions here for copying formulas.

Clicking cells to enter cell references

The hardest part about entering a formula is entering the cell references correctly. You have to squint to see which row and column the cell you want to refer to is in. You have to carefully type the right column letter and row number. However, instead of typing a cell reference, you can click the cell you want to refer to in a formula.

In the course of entering a formula, simply click the cell on your worksheet that you want to reference. As shown in Figure 3-5, shimmering marquee lights appear around the cell that you clicked so that you can clearly see which cell you're referring to. The cell's reference address, meanwhile, appears in the Formula bar. In Figure 3-5, I clicked cell F3 instead of entering its reference address on the Formula bar. The reference F3 appears on the Formula bar, and the marquee lights appear around cell F3.

Get in the habit of pointing and clicking cells to enter cell references in formulas. Clicking cells is easier than typing cell addresses, and the cell references are entered more accurately.

Click a cell to enter its cell reference address in a formula

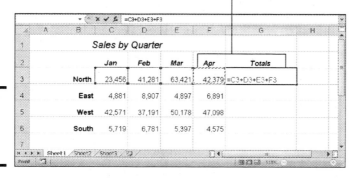

Figure 3-5:
Clicking to enter a cell reference.

Book IV
Chapter 3

Formulas and
Functions for
Crunching Numbers

Entering a cell range

A *cell range* is a line or block of cells in a worksheet. Instead of typing cell reference addresses one at a time, you can simply select cells on your worksheet. In Figure 3-6, I selected cells C3, D3, E3, and F3 to formcell range C3:F3.

This spares me the trouble of entering the cell addresses one at a time: C3, D3, E3, and F3. The formula in Figure 3-6 uses the SUM function to total the numeric values in cell range C3:F3. Notice the marquee lights around the range C3:F3. The lights show precisely which range you're selecting. Cell ranges come in especially handy where functions are concerned (see "Working with Functions" later in this chapter).

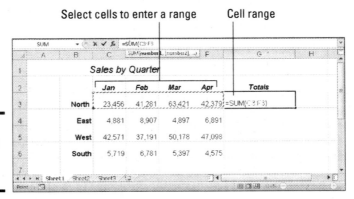

Figure 3-6:
Using a cell range in a formula.

To identify a cell range, Excel lists the outermost cells in the range and places a colon (:) between cell addresses:

✦ A cell range comprising cells A1, A2, A3, and A4 is listed this way: A1:A4.

✦ A cell range comprising a block of cells from A1 to D4 is listed this way: A1:D4.

You can enter cell ranges on your own without selecting cells. To do so, type the first cell in the range, enter a colon (:), and type the last cell.

Naming cell ranges so that you can use them in formulas

Whether you type cell addresses yourself or drag across cells to enter a cell range, entering cell address references is a chore. Entering =C1+C2+C3+C4, for example, can cause a finger cramp; entering =SUM(C1:C4) is no piece of cake, either. To take the tedium out of entering cell ranges in formulas, you can name cell ranges. Then, to enter a cell range in a formula, all you have to do is select a name in the Paste Name dialog box or click the Use in Formula button on the Formulas tab, as shown in Figure 3-7. Naming cell ranges has an added benefit: You can choose a name from the Name Box drop-down list and go directly to the cell range whose name you choose, as shown in Figure 3-7.

Choose a name to move there   Enter a named cell range in a formula

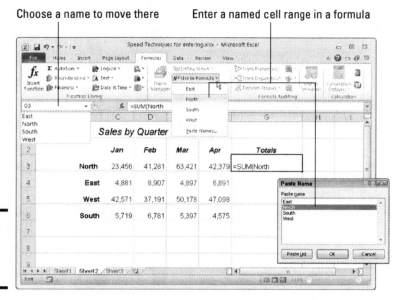

Figure 3-7:
Choosing a
named cell
range.

Naming cell ranges has one disadvantage, and it's a big one. Excel doesn't adjust cell references when you copy a formula with a range name from one cell to another. A range name always refers to the same set of cells. Later in this chapter, "Copying Formulas from Cell to Cell" explains how to copy formulas.

Creating a cell range name

Follow these steps to create a cell range name:

1. **Select the cells that you want to name.**

2. **On the Formulas tab, click the Define Name button.**

   You see the New Name dialog box.

3. **Enter a descriptive name in the Name box.**

   Names can't begin with a number or include blank spaces.

4. **On the Scope drop-down list, choose Workbook or a worksheet name.**

   Choose a worksheet name if you intend to use the range name you're creating only in formulas that you construct in a single worksheet. If your formulas will refer to cell range addresses in different worksheets, choose Workbook so that you can use the range name wherever you go in your workbook.

5. Enter a comment to describe the range name, if you want.

Enter a comment if doing so will help you remember where the cells you're naming are located or what type of information they hold. As I explain shortly, you can read comments in the Name Manager dialog box, the place where you go to edit and delete range names.

6. Click OK.

In case you're in a hurry, here's a fast way to enter a cell range name: Select the cells for the range, click in the Name Box (you can find it on the left side of the Formula bar, as shown in Figure 3-7), enter a name for the range, and press the Enter key.

Entering a range name as part of a formula

To include a cell range name in a formula, click in the Formula bar where you want to enter the range name and then use one of these techniques to enter the name:

✦ On the Formulas tab, click the Use in Formula button and choose a cell range name on the drop-down list (refer to Figure 3-7).

✦ Press F3 or click the Use in Formula button and choose Paste Names on the drop-down list. You see the Paste Name dialog box (refer to Figure 3-7). Select a cell range name and click OK.

Quickly traveling to a cell range that you named

To go quickly to a cell range you named, open the drop-down list on the Name Box and choose a name (refer to Figure 3-7). The Name Box drop-down list is located on the left side of the Formula bar.

To make this trick work, the cursor can't be in the Formula bar. The Name Box drop-down list isn't available when you're constructing a formula.

Managing cell range names

To rename, edit, or delete cell range names, go to the Formulas tab and click the Name Manager button. You see the Name Manager dialog box, as shown in Figure 3-8. This dialog box lists names, cell values in names, the worksheet on which the range name is found, and whether the range name can be applied throughout a workbook or only in one worksheet. To rename, edit, or delete a cell range name, select it in the dialog box and use these techniques:

✦ **Renaming:** Click the Edit button and enter a new name in the Edit Name dialog box.

✦ **Reassigning cells:** To assign different cells to a range name, click the Edit button. You see the Edit Name dialog box. To enter a new range of cells, either enter the cells' addresses in the Refers To text box or click the Range Selector button (it's to the right of the text box), drag across the cells on your worksheet that you want for the cell range, and click the Cell Selector button again to return to the Edit Name dialog box.

✦ **Deleting:** Click the Delete button and click OK in the confirmation box.

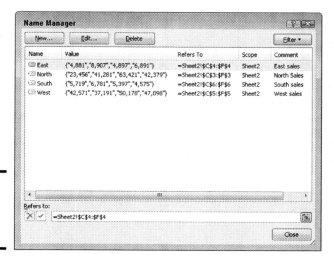

Figure 3-8:
The Name
Manager
dialog box.

Referring to cells in different worksheets

Excel gives you the opportunity to use data from different worksheets in a formula. If one worksheet lists sales figures from January and the next lists sales figures from February, you can construct a "grand total" formula in either worksheet to tabulate sales in the two-month period. A reference to a cell on a different worksheet is called a *3D reference.*

Construct the formula as you normally would, but when you want to refer to a cell or cell range in a different worksheet, click a worksheet tab to move to the other worksheet and select the cell or range of cells there. Without returning to the original worksheet, complete your formula in the Formula bar and press Enter. Excel returns you to the original worksheet, where you can see the results of your formula.

The only thing odd about constructing formulas across worksheets are the cell references. As a glance at the Formula bar tells you, cell addresses in cross-worksheet formulas list the sheet name and an exclamation point (!) as well as the cell address itself. For example, this formula in Worksheet 1 adds the number in cell A4 to the numbers in cells D5 and E5 in Worksheet 2:

```
=A4+Sheet2!D5+Sheet2!E5
```

This formula in Sheet 2 multiplies the number in cell E18 by the number in cell C15 in Worksheet 1:

```
=E18*Sheet1!C15
```

This formula in Worksheet 2 finds the average of the numbers in the cell range C7:F7 in Worksheet 1:

```
=AVERAGE(Sheet1!C7:F7)
```

Copying Formulas from Cell to Cell

Often in worksheets, the same formula but with different cell references is used across a row or down a column. For example, in the worksheet shown in Figure 3-9, column F totals the rainfall figures in rows 7 through 11. To enter formulas for totaling the rainfall figures in column F, you could laboriously enter formulas in cells F7, F8, F9, F10, and F11. But a faster way is to enter the formula once in cell F7 and then copy the formula in F7 down the column to cells F8, F9, F10, and F11.

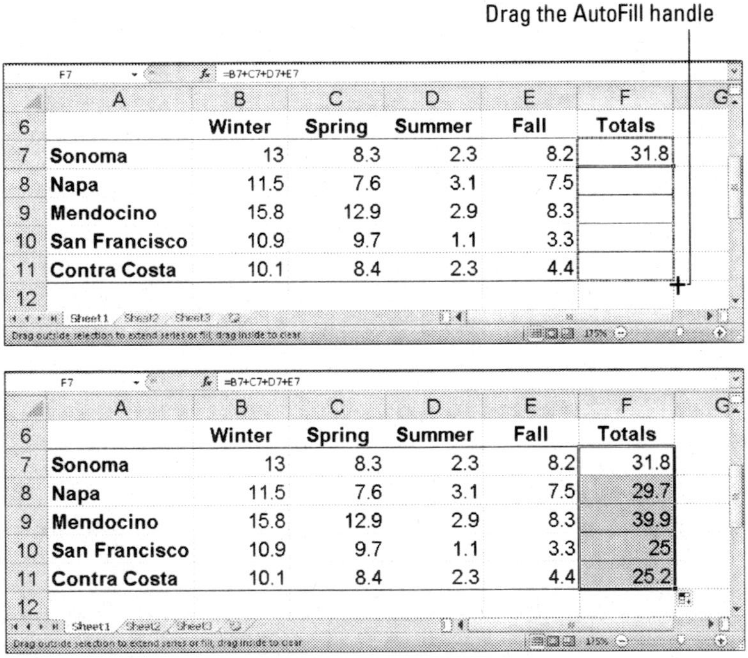

Drag the AutoFill handle

Figure 3-9:
Copying a
formula.

When you copy a formula to a new cell, Excel adjusts the cell references in the formula so that the formula works in the cells to which it has been copied. Astounding! Opportunities to copy formulas abound on most worksheets. And copying formulas is the fastest and safest way to enter formulas in a worksheet.

Follow these steps to copy a formula:

1. **Select the cell with the formula you want to copy down a column or across a row.**

2. **Drag the AutoFill handle across the cells to which you want to copy the formula.**

   This is the same AutoFill handle you drag to enter serial data (see Chapter 1 of this mini-book about entering lists and serial data with the AutoFill command). The AutoFill handle is the small black square in the lower-right corner of the cell. When you move the mouse pointer over it, it changes to a black cross. Figure 3-9 shows a formula being copied.

3. **Release the mouse button.**

   If I were you, I would click in the cells to which you copied the formula and glance at the Formula bar to make sure that the formula was copied correctly. I'd bet you it was.

You can also copy formulas with the Copy and Paste commands. Just make sure that cell references refer correctly to the surrounding cells.

Detecting and Correcting Errors in Formulas

It happens. Everyone makes an error from time to time when entering formulas in cells. Especially in a worksheet in which formula results are calculated into other formulas, a single error in one formula can spread like a virus and cause miscalculations throughout a worksheet. To prevent that from happening, Excel offers several ways to correct errors in formulas. You can correct them one at a time, run the error checker, and trace cell references, as the following pages explain.

 By the way, if you want to see formulas in cells instead of formula results, go to the Formulas tab and click the Show Formulas button (or press Ctrl+'). Sometimes seeing formulas this way helps to detect formula errors.

Correcting errors one at a time

When Excel detects what it thinks is a formula that has been entered incorrectly, a small green triangle appears in the upper-left corner of the cell where you entered the formula. And if the error is especially egregious, an *error message,* a cryptic three or four letters preceded by a pound sign (#), appears in the cell. Table 3-2 explains common error messages.

**Book IV
Chapter 3**

Formulas and
Functions for
Crunching Numbers

Table 3-2	Common Formula Error Messages
Message	*What Went Wrong*
#DIV/0!	You tried to divide a number by a zero (0) or an empty cell.
#NAME	You used a cell range name in the formula, but the name isn't defined. Sometimes this error occurs because you type the name incorrectly. (Earlier in this chapter, "Naming cell ranges so that you can use them in formulas" explains how to name cell ranges.)
#N/A	The formula refers to an empty cell, so no data is available for computing the formula. Sometimes people enter N/A in a cell as a placeholder to signal the fact that data isn't entered yet. Revise the formula or enter a number or formula in the empty cells.
#NULL	The formula refers to a cell range that Excel can't understand. Make sure that the range is entered correctly.
#NUM	An argument you use in your formula is invalid.
#REF	The cell or range of cells that the formula refers to aren't there.
#VALUE	The formula includes a function that was used incorrectly, takes an invalid argument, or is misspelled. Make sure that the function uses the right argument and is spelled correctly.

 To find out more about a formula error and perhaps correct it, select the cell with the green triangle and click the Error button. This small button appears beside a cell with a formula error after you click the cell. The drop-down list on the Error button offers opportunities for correcting formula errors and finding out more about them.

Running the error checker

 Another way to tackle formula errors is to run the error checker. When the checker encounters what it thinks is an error, the Error Checking dialog box tells you what the error is, as shown in Figure 3-10. To run the error checker, go to the Formulas tab and click the Error Checking button (you may have to click the Formula Auditing button first, depending on the size of your screen).

If you see clearly what the error is, click the Edit in Formula Bar button, repair the error in the Formula bar, and click the Resume button in the dialog box (you find this button at the top of the dialog box). If the error isn't one that really needs correcting, either click the Ignore Error button or click the Next button to send the error checker in search of the next error in your worksheet.

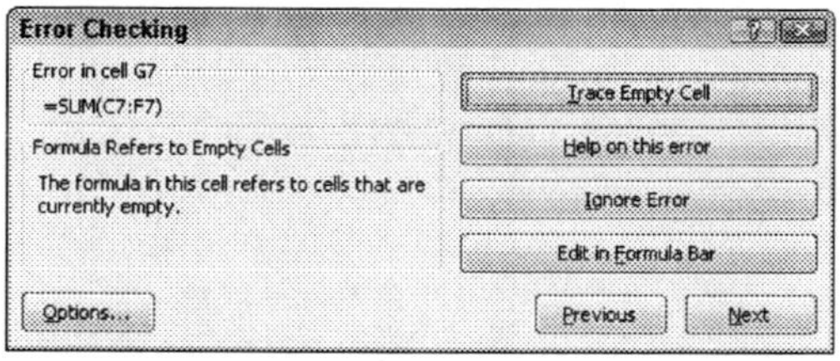

Figure 3-10:
Running
the error
checker.

Tracing cell references

In a complex worksheet in which formulas are piled on top of one another and the results of some formulas are computed into other formulas, it helps to be able to trace cell references. By tracing cell references, you can see how the data in a cell figures into a formula in another cell, or if the cell contains a formula, which cells the formula gathers data from to make its computation. You can get a better idea of how your worksheet is constructed, and in so doing, find structural errors more easily.

Figure 3-11 shows how cell tracers describe the relationships between cells. A *cell tracer* is a blue arrow that shows the relationships between cells used in formulas. You can trace two types of relationships:

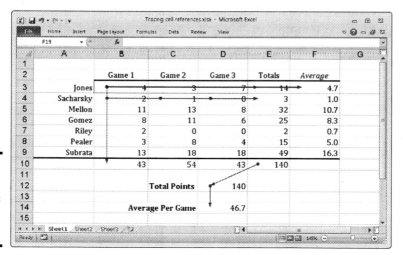

Figure 3-11:
Tracing the
relationships
between
cells.

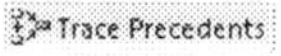

✦ **Tracing precedents:** Select a cell with a formula in it and trace the formula's *precedents* to find out which cells are computed to produce the results of the formula. Trace precedents when you want to find out where a formula gets its computation data. Cell tracer arrows point from the referenced cells to the cell with the formula results in it.

To trace precedents, go to the Formulas tab and click the Trace Precedents button (you may have to click the Formula Auditing button first, depending on the size of your screen).

 ✦ **Tracing dependents:** Select a cell and trace its *dependents* to find out which cells contain formulas that use data from the cell you selected. Cell tracer arrows point from the cell you selected to cells with formula results in them. Trace dependents when you want to find out how the data in a cell contributes to formulas elsewhere in the worksheet. The cell you select can contain a constant value or a formula in its own right (and contribute its results to another formula).

To trace dependents, go to the Formulas tab and click the Trace Dependents button (you may have to click the Formula Auditing button first, depending on the size of your screen).

To remove the cell tracer arrows from a worksheet, go to the Formulas tab and click the Remove Arrows button. You can open the drop-down list on this button and choose Remove Precedent Arrows or Remove Dependent Arrows to remove only cell-precedent or cell-dependent tracer arrows.

Working with Functions

A *function* is a canned formula that comes with Excel. Excel offers hundreds of functions, some of which are very obscure and fit only for use by rocket scientists or securities analysts. Other functions are very practical. For example, you can use the SUM function to quickly total the numbers in a range of cells. Instead of entering =C2+C3+C4+C5 on the Formula bar, you can enter =SUM(C2:C5), which tells Excel to total the numbers in cell C2, C3, C4, and C5. To obtain the product of the number in cell G4 and .06, you can use the PRODUCT function and enter =PRODUCT(G4,.06) on the Formula bar.

Table 3-3 lists the most common functions. To get an idea of the numerous functions that Excel offers, go to the Formulas tab and click the Insert Function button. You see the Insert Function dialog box shown in Figure 3-12. (Later in this chapter, I show you how you can use this dialog box to use functions in formulas.) Choose a function category in the dialog box, choose a function name, and read the description. You can click the Help on This Function link to open the Excel Help window and get a thorough description of the function and how it's used.

Table 3-3	Common Functions and Their Use
Function	*Returns*
AVERAGE(*number1,number2,. . .*)	The average of the numbers in the cells listed in the arguments.
COUNT(*value1,value2,. . .*)	The number of cells that contain the numbers listed in the arguments.
MAX(*number1,number2,. . .*)	The largest value in the cells listed in the arguments.
MIN(*number1,number2,. . .*)	The smallest value in the cells listed in the arguments.
PRODUCT(*number1,number2,. . .*)	The product of multiplying the cells listed in the arguments.
STDEV(*number1,number2,. . .*)	An estimate of standard deviation based on the sample cells listed in the argument.
STDEVP(*number1,number2,. . .*)	An estimate of standard deviation based on the entire sample cells listed in the arguments.
SUM(*number1,number2,. . .*)	The total of the numbers in the arguments.
VAR(*number1,number2,. . .*)	An estimate of the variance based on the sample cells listed in the arguments.
VARP(*number1,number2,. . .*)	A variance calculation based on all cells listed in the arguments.

Choose a function name

Choose a category

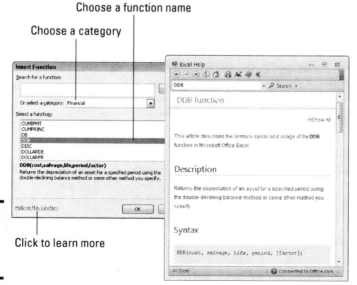

Click to learn more

Figure 3-12:
The Insert
Function
dialog box.

Using arguments in functions

Every function takes one or more *arguments*. Arguments are the cell references or numbers, enclosed in parentheses, that the function acts upon. For example, =AVERAGE(B1:B4) returns the average of the numbers in the cell range B1 through B4; =PRODUCT(6.5,C4) returns the product of multiplying the number 6.5 by the number in cell C4. When a function requires more than one argument, enter a comma between the arguments (enter a comma without a space).

Entering a function in a formula

To enter a function in a formula, you can enter the function name by typing it in the Formula bar, or you can rely on Excel to enter it for you. Enter function names yourself if you're well acquainted with a function and comfortable using it.

No matter how you want to enter a function as part of a formula, start this way:

1. **Select the cell where you want to enter the formula.**

2. **In the Formula bar, type an equals sign (=).**

   Please, please, please be sure to start every formula by entering an equals sign (=). Without it, Excel thinks you're entering text or a number in the cell.

3. **Start constructing your formula, and when you come to the place where you want to enter the function, type the function's name or call upon Excel to help you enter the function and its arguments.**

   Later in this chapter, "Manually entering a function" shows you how to type in the function yourself; "Getting Excel's help to enter a function" shows you how to get Excel to do the work.

   If you enter the function on your own, it's up to you to type the arguments correctly; if you get Excel's help, you also get help with entering the cell references for the arguments.

Manually entering a function

Be sure to enclose the function's argument or arguments in parentheses. Don't enter a space between the function's name and the first parenthesis. Likewise, don't enter a comma and a space between arguments; enter a comma, nothing more:

```
=SUM(F11,F14,23)
```

You can enter function names in lowercase. Excel converts function names to uppercase after you click the Enter button or press Enter to complete the formula. Entering function names in lowercase is recommended because doing so gives you a chance to find out whether you entered a function name correctly. If Excel doesn't convert your function name to uppercase, you made a typing error when you entered the function name.

Getting Excel's help to enter a function

Besides entering a function by typing it, you can do it by way of the Function Arguments dialog box, as shown in Figure 3-13. The beauty of using this dialog box is that it warns you if you enter arguments incorrectly, and it spares you the trouble of typing the function name without making an error. What's more, the Function Arguments dialog box shows you the results of the formula as you construct it so that you get an idea whether you're using the function correctly.

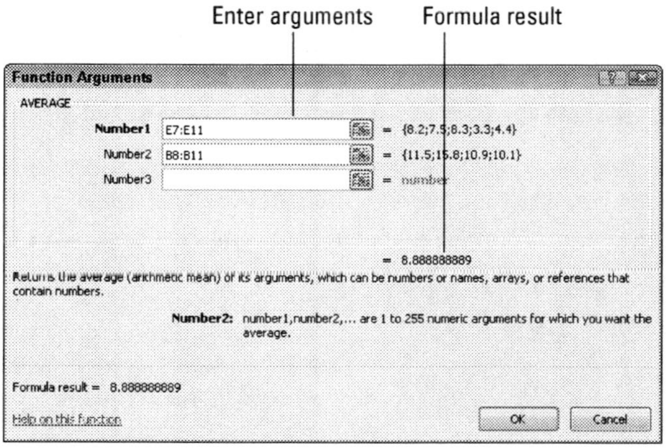

Enter arguments   Formula result

Figure 3-13: The Function Arguments dialog box.

Follow these steps to get Excel's help with entering a function as part of a formula:

1. On the Formulas tab, tell Excel which function you want to use.

You can do that with one of these techniques:

- *Click a Function Library button:* Click the button whose name describes what kind of function you want and choose the function's name on the drop-down list. You can click the Financial, Logical, Text, Date & Time, Lookup & Reference, Math & Trig, or More Functions buttons.

- *Click the Recently Used button:* Click this button and choose the name of a function you used recently.

Insert
Function

- *Click the Insert Function button:* Clicking this button opens the Insert Function dialog box (refer to Figure 3-12). Find and choose the name of a function. You can search for functions or choose a category and then scroll the names until you find the function you want.

  You see the Function Arguments dialog box (refer to Figure 3-13). It offers boxes for entering arguments for the function to compute.

2. **Enter arguments in the spaces provided by the Function Arguments dialog box.**

   To enter cell references or ranges, you can click or select cells in your worksheet. If necessary, click the Range Selector button (you can find it to the right of an argument text box) to shrink the Function Arguments dialog box and get a better look at your worksheet.

3. **Click OK when you finish entering arguments for your function.**

   I hope you didn't have to argue too strenuously with the Function Arguments dialog box.

Quickly entering a function and its arguments

To quickly total the numbers in cells, click on your worksheet where you want the total to appear, and then click the AutoSum button on the Home or Formulas tab. Excel takes an educated guess as to which cells need totaling, and the program highlights those cells. If Excel guesses correctly and highlights the cells you want to total, click the Enter button (or press Enter) and be done with it. Otherwise, select the cells you want to add up and then press Enter.

Similarly, you can use the drop-down list on the AutoSum button to quickly obtain the average, count of, maximum amount, or minimum amount of cells by clicking in a nearby cell, opening the drop-down list on the AutoSum button, and choosing Average, Count Numbers, Max, or Min.

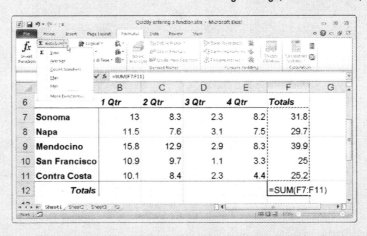

Chapter 4: Making a Worksheet Easier to Read and Understand

In This Chapter
✔ Aligning numbers and text

✔ Changing column and row sizes

✔ Applying cell styles to data in cells

✔ Splashing color on a worksheet

✔ Drawing borders between cells and titles

✔ Making worksheets fit well on the page

✔ Preparing a worksheet before you print it

This short and pithy chapter explains how to dress a worksheet in its Sunday best in case you want to print and present it to others. It explains how to align numbers and text, insert rows and columns, as well as change the size of rows and columns. You find out how to decorate a worksheet with colors and borders, as well as create and apply styles to make formatting tasks go more quickly. Finally, this chapter describes everything you need to know before you print a worksheet, including how to make it fit on one page and repeat row labels and column names on all pages.

Laying Out a Worksheet

Especially if you intend to print your worksheet, you may as well dress it in its Sunday best. And you can do a number of things to make worksheets easier to read and understand. You can change character fonts. You can draw borders around or shade important cells. You can also format the numbers so that readers know, for example, whether they're staring at dollar figures or percentages. This part of Chapter 4 is dedicated to the proposition that a worksheet doesn't have to look drab and solemn.

Aligning numbers and text in columns and rows

To start with, numbers in worksheets are right-aligned in cells, and text is left-aligned. Numbers and text sit squarely on the bottom of cells. You can, however, change the way that data is aligned. For example, you can make data float at the top of cells rather than rest at the bottom, and you can center or justify data in cells. Figure 4-1 illustrates different ways to align text and numbers. How text is aligned helps people make sense of your worksheets. In Figure 4-1, for example, Income and Expenses are left-aligned so they stand out and make it clearer what the right-aligned column labels below are all about.

Select the cells whose alignment needs changing and follow these instructions to realign data in the cells:

✦ **Changing the horizontal (side-to-side) alignment:** On the Home tab, click the Align Text Left, Center, or Align Text Right button. You can also click the Alignment group button, and on the Alignment tab of the Format Cells dialog box, choose an option on the Horizontal drop-down list. Figure 4-2 shows the Format Cells dialog box.

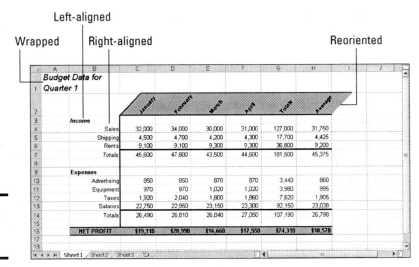

Figure 4-1:
Ways to
align data.

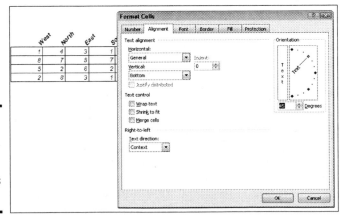

Figure 4-2:
The
Alignment
tab of the
Format Cells
dialog box.

+ **Changing the vertical (top-to-bottom) alignment:** On the Home tab, click the Top Align, Middle Align, or Bottom Align button. You can also click the Alignment group button to open the Format Cells dialog box (refer to Figure 4-2) and choose an option on the Vertical drop-down list. The Justify option makes all the letters or numbers fit in a cell, even if it means wrapping text to two or more lines.

+ **Reorienting the cells:** On the Home tab, click the Orientation button and choose an option on the drop-down list. (For Figure 4-2, I chose the Angle Counterclockwise option.) You can also click the Alignment group button, and on the Alignment tab of the Format Cells dialog box (refer to Figure 4-2), drag the diamond in the Orientation box or enter a number in the Degrees text box.

Changing the orientation of text in cells is an elegant solution to the problem of keeping a worksheet from getting too wide. Numbers are usually a few characters wide, but heading labels can be much wider than that. By changing the orientation of a heading label, you make columns narrower and keep worksheets from growing too wide to fit on the screen or page.

Inserting and deleting rows and columns

At some point, everybody has to insert new columns and rows and delete ones that are no longer needed. Make sure before you delete a row or column that you don't delete data that you really need. Do the following to insert and delete rows and columns:

+ **Deleting rows or columns:** Drag across the row numbers or column letters of the rows or columns you want to delete; then right-click and choose Delete, or, on the Home tab, open the drop-down list on the Delete button and select Delete Sheet Rows or Delete Sheet Columns.

+ **Inserting rows:** Select the row below the row you want to insert; then, on the Home tab, open the drop-down list on the Insert button and choose Insert Sheet Rows, or right-click the row you selected and choose Insert on the shortcut menu. For example, to insert a new row above row 11, select the current row 11 before choosing Insert Sheet Rows. You can insert more than one row at a time by selecting more than one row before giving the Insert Sheet Rows command.

+ **Inserting columns:** Select the column to the right of where you want the new column to be; then, on the Home tab, open the drop-down list on the Insert button and choose Insert Sheet Columns, or right-click the column you selected and choose Insert on the shortcut menu. You can insert more than one column this way by selecting more than one column before giving the Insert command.

A fast way to insert several rows or columns is to insert one and keep pressing F4 (the Repeat command) until you insert all the rows or columns you need.

**Book IV
Chapter 4**

**Making a Worksheet
Easier to Read and
Understand**

Merging and centering text across several cells

In the illustration shown here, "Sales Totals by Regional Office" is centered across four different cells. Normally, text is left-aligned, but if you want to center it across several cells, drag across the cells to select them, go to the Home tab, and click the Merge & Center button. Merging and centering allows you to display text across several columns.

To "unmerge and uncenter" cells, select the text that you merged and centered, open the drop-down list on the Merge & Center button, and choose Unmerge Cells. You can also deselect the Merge Cells check box in the Format Cells dialog box (refer to Figure 4-2).

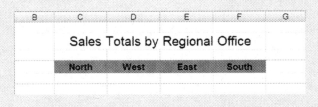

After you insert rows or columns, the Insert Options button appears. Click it and choose an option from the drop-down list if you want your new row or column to have the same or different formats as the row or column you selected to start the Insert operation.

To insert more than one row or column at a time, select more than one row number or column letter before giving the Insert command.

Changing the size of columns and rows

By default, columns are 8.43 characters wide. To make columns wider, you have to widen them yourself. Rows are 12.75 points high, but Excel makes them higher when you enter letters or numbers that are taller than 12.75 points (72 points equals one inch). Excel offers a bunch of different ways to change the size of columns and rows. You can start on the Home tab and choose options on the Format button drop-down list, as shown in Figure 4-3, or you can rely on your wits and change sizes manually by dragging or double-clicking the boundaries between row numbers or column letters.

Before you change the size of columns or rows, select them (Chapter 2 of this mini-book explains how). Click or drag across row numbers to select rows; click or drag across column letters to select columns.

Drag a boundary   Or choose a Format option

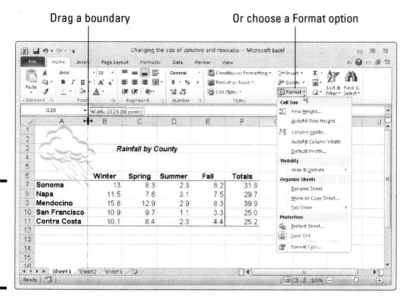

Figure 4-3:
Ways to
change
the size of
columns
and rows.

Adjusting the height of rows

Here are ways to change the height of rows:

- ✦ **One at a time:** Move the mouse pointer onto the boundary between row numbers and, when the pointer changes to a cross, drag the boundary between rows up or down. A pop-up box tells you how tall the row will be after you release the mouse button.

- ✦ **Several at a time:** Select several rows and drag the boundary between one of the rows; all rows change height. You can also go to the Home tab, click the Format button, choose Row Height, and enter a measurement in the Row Height dialog box.

- ✦ **Tall as the tallest entry:** To make a row as tall as its tallest cell entry, double-click the border below a row number (after you've selected a row), or go to the Home tab, click the Format button, and choose AutoFit Row Height.

Adjusting the width of columns

Here are ways to make columns wider or narrower:

- ✦ **One at a time:** Move the mouse pointer onto the boundary between column letters, and when the pointer changes to a cross, drag the border between the columns. A pop-up box tells you what size the column is.

✦ **Several at a time:** Select several columns and drag the boundary between one of the columns; all columns adjust to the same width. You can also go to the Home tab, click the Format button, choose Column Width, and enter a measurement in the Column Width dialog box.

✦ **As wide as their entries:** To make columns as wide as their widest entries, select the columns, go to the Home tab, click the Format button, and choose AutoFit Column Width on the drop-down list. You can also double-click the right border of a column letter. By "auto-fitting" columns, you can be certain that the data in each cell in a column appears on-screen.

To change the 8.43-character standard width for columns in a worksheet, go to the Home tab, click the Format button, choose Default Width on the drop-down list, and enter a new measurement in the Standard Width dialog box.

Decorating a Worksheet with Borders and Colors

The job of gridlines is simply to help you line up numbers and letters in cells. By default, gridlines aren't printed, and because gridlines aren't printed, drawing borders on worksheets is absolutely necessary if you intend to print your worksheet. Use borders to steer the reader's eye to the most important parts of your worksheet — the totals, column labels, and heading labels. You can also decorate worksheets with colors. This part of the chapter explains how to put borders and colors on worksheets.

Cell styles for quickly formatting a worksheet

A *style* is a collection of formats — boldface text, a background color, or a border around cells — that can be applied all at once to cells without having to visit a bunch of different dialog boxes or give a bunch of different commands. Styles save time. If you find yourself choosing the same formatting commands time and time again, consider creating a style. That way, you can apply all the formats simultaneously and go to lunch earlier. Excel comes with many built-in styles, and you can create styles of your own, as the following pages explain.

Applying a built-in cell style

By way of the Cell Styles gallery, you can choose from any number of attractive styles for cells in a worksheet. Excel offers styles for titles and headings, styles for calling attention to what kind of data is in cells, and styles to accent cells. Follow these steps to reformat cells by choosing a cell style:

1. **Select the cells that need a new look.**

2. **On the Home tab, click the Cell Styles button.**

As shown in Figure 4-4, the Cell Styles gallery opens. (Depending on the size of your screen, you may have to click the Styles button and then click the More button to open the Cell Styles gallery.)

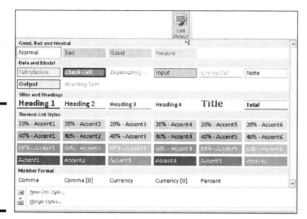

Figure 4-4:
Choosing a
new style
from the
Cell Styles
gallery.

3. Select a cell style.

The Cell Styles gallery is divided into categories. Scroll through the categories until you find a style that suits your purposes.

To remove a style from cells, select the cells, open the Cell Styles gallery, and choose Normal. (You find Normal in the "Good, Bad, and Neutral" category.)

Creating your own cell style

The names of cell styles you create on your own are placed at the top of the Cell Styles gallery under the Custom heading. Create a cell style if you're the creative type or if no built-in style meets your high standards. Follow these steps to create a cell style:

1. Apply the formatting commands you want for your style to a single cell.

For example, left-align cell data. Or apply a fill color to the cells (see "Decorating worksheets with colors" later in this chapter). Or change fonts and font sizes. Knock yourself out. Choose all the formatting commands you want for your new style.

2. On the Home tab, click the Cell Styles button open the Cell Styles gallery.

Depending on the size of your screen, you may have to click the Styles button and then click the More button first.

3. Choose New Cell Style at the bottom of the gallery.

You see the Style dialog box shown in Figure 4-5. It lists formatting specifications you chose for the cell you selected in Step 1. If these specifications aren't what you're after, or if you want to change a specification, you can click the Format button and describe your new style in the Format Cells dialog box.

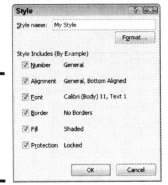

Figure 4-5:
Creating a
new style
for the
Cell Styles
gallery.

4. **Enter a descriptive name for your style in the Style Name text box.**

5. **Click OK.**

   Next time you open the Cell Styles gallery, you see the name of your
   style at the top under Custom.

To remove a style you created from the Cell Styles gallery, right-click its
name in the gallery and choose Delete on the shortcut menu.

Formatting cells with table styles

Especially if your worksheet data is arranged neatly into columns and rows
so that it looks like a conventional table, one of the easiest ways to decorate
cells is to take advantage of table styles. Excel offers many preformatted
table styles that you can apply to columns and rows on a worksheet.

Follow these steps to experiment with table styles:

1. **Select the cells you want to format as a table.**

2. **On the Home tab, click the Format As Table button and move your
   pointer over the table styles in the gallery to "live-preview" them.**

3. **Select a table style.**

   The Format As Table dialog box appears.

4. **If the cells you want to format include headers, the labels at the top of
   column rows that describe the data in the columns below, select the
   My Table Has Headers check box.**

   If you didn't select cells in Step 1, click outside the Format As Table
   dialog box and select cells on your worksheet to tell Excel which cells
   to format.

5. **Click OK in the Format As Table dialog box.**

   You can go to the (Table Tools) Design tab to refine your table. Book I,
   Chapter 5 (about tables) describes the tools on this tab.

To remove a table style from cells, select the cells, go to the (Table Tools) Design tab, and choose None in the Table Styles gallery.

Slapping borders on worksheet cells

Put borders on worksheet cells to box in cells, draw lines beneath cells, or draw lines along the side of cells. Borders can direct people who review your worksheet to its important parts. Typically, for example, a line appears above the Totals row of a worksheet to separate the Totals row from the rows above and help readers locate cumulative totals.

To draw borders on a worksheet, start by selecting the cells around which or through which you want to place borders. Then do one of the following to draw the borders:

✦ **Borders button:** On the Home tab, open the drop-down list on the Borders button (it's in the Font group) and choose a border, as shown in Figure 4-6.

✦ **Format Cells dialog box:** On the Home tab, click the Format button and choose Format Cells, or choose More Borders on the Borders button drop-down list. The Format Cells dialog box opens, as shown in Figure 4-7. On the Border tab, select a border style and either click in the Border box to tell Excel where to draw the border or click a Presets button. The Border tab offers different lines for borders and colors for borderlines as well.

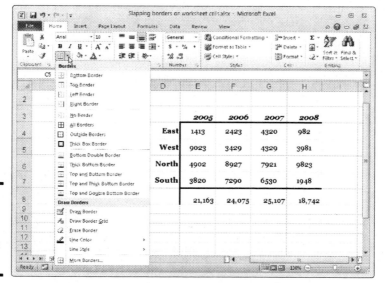

Figure 4-6: Drawing a border with the Borders button.

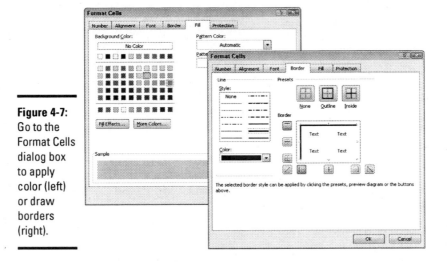

Figure 4-7:
Go to the
Format Cells
dialog box
to apply
color (left)
or draw
borders
(right).

To remove the border from cells, select the cells, open the drop-down list on the Borders button, and choose No Border.

Decorating worksheets with colors

Apply background colors to cells to make them stand out or help the people who review your worksheets understand how they are laid out. Select the cells that need a background color and use these techniques to splash color on your worksheet:

✦ On the Home tab, click the Format button and choose Format Cells on the drop-down list. You see the Format Cells dialog box. On the Fill tab, select a color and click OK. Figure 4-7 shows what the Fill tab looks like.

✦ On the Home tab, open the drop-down list on the Fill Color button and select a color.

Getting Ready to Print a Worksheet

Printing a worksheet isn't simply a matter of giving the Print command. A worksheet is a vast piece of computerized sprawl. Most worksheets don't fit neatly on a single page. If you simply click the Print button to print your worksheet, you wind up with page breaks in unexpected places, both on the right side of the page and the bottom. Read on to discover how to set up a worksheet so that the people you hand it to can read and understand it.

Making a worksheet fit on a page

Unless you tell it otherwise, Excel prints everything from cell A1 to the last cell with data in it in the southeast corner of the worksheet. Usually, it isn't necessary to print all those cells because some of them are blank. And printing an entire worksheet often means breaking the page up in all kinds of awkward places. To keep that from happening, following are some techniques for making a worksheet fit tidily on one or two pages.

 As you experiment with the techniques described here, switch occasionally to Page Layout view. In this view, you get a better idea of what your worksheet will look like when you print it. To switch to Page Layout view, click the Page Layout button on the status bar or View tab.

Printing part of a worksheet

 To print part of a worksheet, select the cells you want to print, go to the Page Layout tab, click the Print Area button, and choose Set Print Area on the drop-down list. This command tells Excel to print only the cells you selected. On the worksheet, a dotted line appears around cells in the print area. To remove the dotted lines from your worksheet, click the Print Area button and choose Clear Print Area on the drop-down list.

Printing a landscape worksheet

If your worksheet is too wide to fit on one page, try turning the page on its side and printing in landscape mode. In landscape mode, pages are wider than they are tall. Landscape mode is often the easiest way to fit a worksheet on a page.

 To make yours a landscape worksheet instead of a portrait worksheet, go to the Page Layout tab, click the Orientation button, and choose Landscape on the drop-down list.

Seeing and adjusting the page breaks

Reading a worksheet is extremely difficult when it's broken awkwardly across pages. Where one page ends and the next begins is a *page break*. Use these techniques to see where page breaks occur, adjust the position of page breaks, and insert and remove page breaks:

 ✦ **Viewing where pages break occur:** Click the Page Break Preview button on the status bar or View tab. As shown in Figure 4-8, you switch to Page Break Preview view. In this view, page numbers appear clearly on the worksheet and dashed lines show you where Excel wants to break the pages.

Insert and remove page breaks

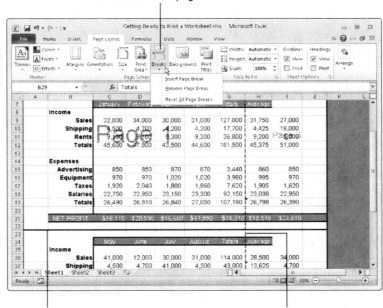

Figure 4-8:
Deciding
where
pages
break.

Manual page break   Default page break

✦ **Adjusting page break positions:** In Page Break Preview view, drag a dashed line to adjust the position of a page break. After you drag a dashed line, it ceases being a default page break and becomes a manual page break. Manual page breaks are marked by solid lines, not dashed lines (see Figure 4-8). You can drag them, too. Excel shrinks the numbers and letters on your worksheet if you try to squeeze too much data on a worksheet by dragging a page break.

✦ **Inserting a page break:** Select the cell directly below where you want the horizontal break to occur and directly to the right of where you want the vertical break to be, go to the Page Layout tab, click the Breaks button, and choose Insert Page Break (see Figure 4-8). Drag a page break to adjust its position.

✦ **Removing a page break:** Select a cell directly below or directly to the right of the page break, go to the Page Layout tab, click the Breaks button, and choose Remove Page Break (see Figure 4-8).

✦ **Removing all manual page breaks:** To remove all manual page breaks you inserted, go to the Page Layout tab, click the Breaks button, and choose Reset All Page Breaks.

Switch to Page Layout or Normal view after you're done fooling with page breaks. You can clearly see page breaks in Page Layout view. In Normal view, page breaks are marked by a dotted line.

"Scaling to fit" a worksheet

To scale the numbers and letters in a worksheet and make them a bit smaller so they fit on a page, you can experiment with the Scale to Fit options. These options are located on the Page Layout tab. Starting in Page Layout view, go to the Page Layout tab and test-drive these options to make your worksheet fit on a single page or a certain number of pages:

✦ **Scaling by width:** Open the Width drop-down list and choose an option to make your worksheet fit across one or more pages. Choose the 1 Page option, for example, to squeeze a worksheet horizontally so it fits on one page.

✦ **Scaling by height:** Open the Height drop-down list and choose an option to make your worksheet fit across on a select number of pages. For example, choose the 2 Pages option to shrink a worksheet vertically so it fits on two pages.

✦ **Scaling by percentage:** Enter a percentage measurement in the Scale box to shrink a worksheet vertically and horizontally. In order to scale this way, you must choose Automatic in the Width and Height drop-down lists.

You can also fit a worksheet on a select number of pages by going to the Page Setup dialog box shown in Figure 4-9. With this technique, you get a chance to "print-preview" your worksheet and get a better look at it after you change the scale. On the Page Layout tab, click the Page Setup group button to open the Page Setup dialog box. On the Page tab, select the Fit To option button and enter the ideal number of pages you want for your worksheet in the Page(s) Wide By and Tall text boxes. Excel shrinks the data as much as is necessary to make it fit on the number of pages you asked for. Click the Print Preview button to preview your worksheet in the Print window and find out whether shrinking your worksheet this way helps.

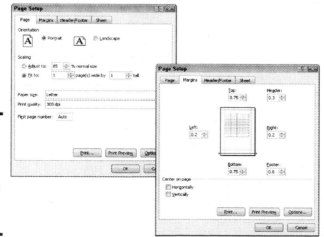

Figure 4-9: The Page (left) and Margins tab (right) of the Page Setup dialog box.

Adjusting the margins

Another way to stuff all the data onto one page is to narrow the margins a bit. Go to the Page Layout tab and use either of these techniques to adjust the size of the margins:

✦ Click the Margins button and choose Narrow on the drop-down list.

✦ Click the Page Setup group button, and on the Margins tab of the Page Setup dialog box, change the size of the margins, as shown in Figure 4-9. By clicking the Print Preview button, you can preview your worksheet in the Print window and adjust margins there by dragging them. Select the Show Margins button to display the margins. (This little button is in the lower-right corner of the Print window.)

Making a worksheet more presentable

Before you print a worksheet, visit the Page Setup dialog box and see what you can do to make your worksheet easier for others to read and understand. To open the Page Setup dialog box, go to the Page Layout tab and click the Page Setup group button. Here are your options:

✦ **Including page numbers on worksheets:** On the Page tab of the Page Setup dialog box (refer to Figure 4-9), enter **1** in the First Page Number text box. Then, on the Header/Footer tab, open the Header or Footer drop-down list and choose an option that includes a page number. Choosing the Page 1 of ? option, for example, enters the page number and the total number of pages in the worksheet in your header or footer.

✦ **Putting headers and footers on pages:** On the Header/Footer tab of the Page Setup dialog box, choose options from the Header and Footer drop-down lists. You can find options for listing the file name, page numbers, the date, and your name. By clicking the Custom Header or Custom Footer button, you can open the Header or Footer dialog box and construct a header or footer there. Figure 4-10 shows the Header dialog box.

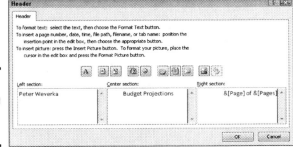

Figure 4-10: Constructing a fancy header.

✦ **Centering worksheet data on the page:** On the Margins tab, select Horizontally or Vertically to center the worksheet relative to the top or bottom or sides of the page. You can select both check boxes. The preview screen shows what your choices mean in real terms.

✦ **Printing gridlines, column letters, and row numbers:** By default, the gridlines, column letters, and row numbers that you know and love in a worksheet aren't printed, but you can print them by going to the Sheet tab of the Page Setup dialog box and selecting the Gridlines check box as well as the Row and Column Headings check box.

Repeating row and column headings on each page

If your worksheet is a big one that stretches beyond one page, you owe it to the people who view your worksheet to repeat row and column headings from page to page. Without these headings, no one can tell what the data in the worksheet means. Follow these steps to repeat row and column headings from page to page:

1. **On the Page Layout tab, click the Print Titles button.**

   You see the Sheet tab of the Page Setup dialog box.

2. **Select the Row and Column Headings check box.**

   You can find this check box under Print.

3. **To repeat rows, click the Range Selector button next to the Rows to Repeat at Top text box; to repeat columns, click the Range Selector button next to the Columns to Repeat at Left text box.**

   These buttons are located on the right side of the dialog box. The dialog box shrinks so that you can get a better look at your worksheet.

4. **Select the row or column with the labels or names you need.**

   As long as they're next to each other, you can select more than one row or column by dragging over the row numbers or column letters.

5. **Click the Range Selector button to enlarge the dialog box and see it again.**

   The text box now lists a cell range address.

6. **Repeat Steps 3 through 5 to select column or row headings.**

7. **Click OK to close the Page Setup dialog box.**

   If I were you, I would click the Print Preview button in the Page Setup dialog box first to make sure that row and column headings are indeed repeating from page to page.

To remove row and column headings, return to the Sheet tab of the Page Setup dialog box and delete the cell references in the Rows to Repeat at Top text box and the Columns to Repeat at Left text box. You can also press Ctrl+F3 and delete Print_Titles in the Name Manager dialog box.

**Book IV
Chapter 4**

**Making a Worksheet
Easier to Read and
Understand**

Saving your formats in a template

If you go to the trouble to lay out a very fine workbook, you may as well save it as a template. That way, you (or your co-workers) can call upon your newfangled workbook next time you want to create a new Excel workbook. Any workbook that could be of use to someone else is a candidate for becoming a template.

Follow these steps to save a workbook as a template and be able to call upon its formats later on:

1. **On the File tab, choose Save As.**

   You see the Save As dialog box.

2. **Enter a descriptive name for your template in the File Name text box.**

3. **In the Save As Type drop-down list, choose Excel Template.**

4. **Click the Save button.**

5. **Back in your worksheet, delete the data that you don't need when you create a file from your template and then click the Save button to save the template again.**

To call upon the template you made to create a new Excel workbook, go to the File tab, choose New, click the My Templates icon in the Available Templates window, and in the New dialog box, select your template and click OK.

Chapter 5: Analyzing Data

In This Chapter

✔ Sorting information in a worksheet list

✔ Filtering a list to find the information you need

✔ Using the Goal Seek command to produce formula results

✔ Performing what-if analyses with data tables

This chapter offers a handful of tricks for analyzing the data that you so carefully and lovingly enter in a worksheet. Delve into this chapter to find out how to manage, sort, and filter worksheet lists. You also discover how the Goal Seek command can help you target values in different kinds of analysis, and how you can map out different scenarios with data by using one- and two-input data tables.

Managing Information in Lists

Although Excel is a spreadsheet program, many people use it to keep and maintain lists — address lists, product lists, employee lists, and inventory lists, among other types of lists. These pages deal with all the different things you can do with a worksheet list. They explain the difference between a conventional worksheet and a list, constructing a list, sorting a list, and filtering a list.

Constructing a list

To sort and filter data in a worksheet, your worksheet must be constructed like a list. Make sure that your worksheet has these characteristics:

✦ **Column labels:** Enter column labels along the top row, as shown in Figure 5-1. Excel needs these labels to identify and be able to filter the data in the rows below. Each label must have a different name. The row along the top of the worksheet where the column labels are is called the *header row*.

✦ **No empty rows or columns:** Sorry, but you can't put an empty row or column in the middle of the worksheet list.

✦ **No blank columns on the left:** Don't allow any empty columns to appear to the left of the list.

✦ **A single worksheet:** The list must occupy a single worksheet. You can't keep more than one list on the same worksheet.

Product ID	Product Name	Production Cost	Packaging	Ship Cost	Sale per Unit	Profit	Warehouse	Supervisor
11100	Widget	1.19	0.14	0.46	4.11	2.33	Trenton	Munoz
11101	Gasket	2.24	0.29	0.69	4.14	0.72	Pickford	Salazaar
11102	Tappet	4.13	1.11	0.18	7.12	1.70	Trenton	Munoz
11103	Widget	8.19	3.40	0.45	14.80	2.76	LaRue	Smith
11104	Plodget	6.41	0.29	0.32	7.89	0.87	Massy	Yee
11105	Placker	7.39	0.96	1.11	12.14	2.68	Pickford	Salazaar
11106	Stacker	11.00	1.14	0.89	14.89	1.58	LaRue	Smith
11107	Knacker	14.31	3.14	0.45	20.93	3.58	Massy	Yee
11108	Tippler	2.11	0.14	0.32	5.81	3.24	Trenton	Munoz
11109	Culet	4.16	0.17	0.32	6.01	1.36	Trenton	Munoz
11110	Rooper	13.44	2.89	0.79	21.43	4.31	LaRue	Smith
11111	Knocker	23.98	2.10	0.88	32.89	6.82	Trenton	Munoz
11112	Topper	1.14	0.08	0.11	4.00	2.63	Pickford	Salazaar
11113	Rammer	2.15	0.16	0.32	5.10	2.47	Massy	Yee
11114	Cricker	3.34	0.27	0.33	8.12	2.18	LaRue	Smith
11115	Knicker	8.78	1.01	0.89	10.79	0.11	Trenton	Munoz
11116	Stamler	2.14	3.53	0.20	8.78	3.91	LaRue	Smith
11117	Doublet	9.46	1.01	0.99	14.33	2.87	Pickford	Salazaar

Figure 5-1:
A worksheet
as a list.

If you know anything about databases, the rules for constructing a worksheet list no doubt sound familiar. These are the same rules that apply to constructing a database table.

Sorting a list

Sorting means to rearrange the rows in a list on the basis of data in one or more columns. Sort a list on the Last Name column, for example, to arrange the list in alphabetical order by last name. Sort a list on the ZIP Code column to arrange the rows in numerical order by ZIP code. Sort a list on the Birthday column to arrange it chronologically from earliest born to latest born.

Starting on the Data tab, here are all the ways to sort a list:

✦ **Sorting on a single column:** Click any cell in the column you want to use as the basis for the sort, and then click the Sort Smallest to Largest or Sort Largest to Smallest button. (On the Home tab, you can get to these buttons by clicking the Sort & Filter button first.) For example, to sort item numbers from smallest to largest, click in the Item Number column and then click the Sort Smallest to Largest button.

✦ **Sort on more than one column:** Click the Sort button on the Data tab. You see the Sort dialog box, as shown in Figure 5-2. Choose which columns you want to sort with and the order in which you want to sort. To add a second or third column for sorting, click the Add Level button.

Filtering a list

Filtering means to scour a worksheet list for certain kinds of data. To filter, you tell Excel what kind of data you're looking for, and the program assembles rows with that data to the exclusion of rows that don't have the data. You end up with a shorter list with only the rows that match your filter criteria. Filtering is similar to using the Find command except that you get more than one row in the results of the filtering operation. For example, in a list of addresses, you can filter for addresses in California. In a price list, you can filter for items that fall within a certain price range.

To filter a list, start by going to the Data tab and clicking the Filter button. As shown in Figure 5-3, a drop-down list appears beside each column header.

Your next task is to open a drop-down list in the column that holds the criteria you want to use to filter the list. For example, if you want to filter the list to items that cost more than $100, open the Cost column drop-down list; if you want to filter the list so that only the names of employees who make less than $30,000 annually appears, open the Salary drop-down list.

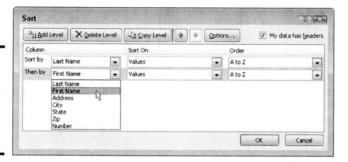

Figure 5-2:
Sort to arrange the list data in different ways.

Click the Filter button

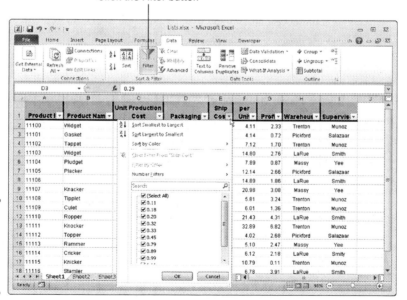

Figure 5-3:
Filter a worksheet to isolate data.

After you open the correct column drop-down list, tell Excel how you want to filter the list:

✦ **Filter by exclusion:** On the drop-down list, deselect the Select All check box and then select the check box next to each item you *don't* want to filter out. For example, to filter an Address list for addresses in Boston, Chicago, and Miami, deselect the Select All check box and then select the check boxes next to Boston, Chicago, and Miami on the drop-down list. Your filter operation turns up only addresses in those three cities.

✦ **Filter with criteria:** On the drop-down list, choose Number Filters, and then choose a filter operation on the submenu (or simply choose Custom Filter). You see the Custom AutoFilter dialog box.

Choose an operator (equals, is greater than, or another) from the drop-down list, and either enter or choose a target criterion from the list on the right side of the dialog box. You can search by more than one criterion. Select the And option button if a row must meet both criteria to be selected, or select the Or option button if a row can meet either criterion to be selected.

Click the OK button on the column's drop-down list or the Custom AutoFilter dialog box to filter your list.

 To see all the data in the list again — to *unfilter* the list — click the Clear button on the Data tab.

Forecasting with the Goal Seek Command

In a conventional formula, you provide the raw data, and Excel produces the results. With the Goal Seek command, you declare what you want the results to be, and Excel tells you the raw data you need to produce those results. The Goal Seek command is useful in analyses when you want the outcome to be a certain way and you need to know which raw numbers will produce the outcome that you want.

Figure 5-4 shows a worksheet designed to find out the monthly payment on a mortgage. With the PMT function, the worksheet determines that the monthly payment on a $250,000 loan with an interest rate of 6.5 percent and to be paid over a 30-year period is $1,580.17. Suppose, however, that the person who calculated this monthly payment determined that he or she could pay more than $1,580.17 per month? Suppose the person could pay $1,750 or $2,000 per month. Instead of an outcome of $1,580.17, the person wants to know how much he or she could borrow if monthly payments — the outcome of the formula — were increased to $1,750 or $2,000.

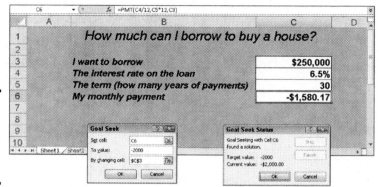

Figure 5-4:
Experimen-
ting with the
Goal Seek
command.

To make determinations such as these, you can use the Goal Seek command. This command lets you experiment with the arguments in a formula to achieve the results you want. In the case of the worksheet in Figure 5-4, you can use the Goal Seek command to change the argument in cell C3, the total amount you can borrow, given the outcome you want in cell C6, $1,750 or $2,000, the monthly payment on the total amount.

Follow these steps to use the Goal Seek command to change the inputs in a formula to achieve the results you want:

1. **Select the cell with the formula whose arguments you want to experiment with.**

2. **On the Data tab, click the What-If Analysis button and choose Goal Seek on the drop-down list.**

    You see the Goal Seek dialog box shown in Figure 5-4. The address of the cell you selected in Step 1 appears in the Set Cell box.

3. **In the To Value text box, enter the target results you want from the formula.**

    In the example in Figure 5-4, you enter 1750 or 2000, the monthly payment you can afford for the 30-year mortgage.

4. **In the By Changing Cell text box, enter the address of the cell whose value is unknown.**

    To enter a cell address, select a cell on your worksheet. In Figure 5-4, you select the address of the cell that shows the total amount you want to borrow.

5. **Click OK.**

    The Goal Seek Status dialog box appears, as shown in Figure 5-4. It lists the target value that you entered in Step 3.

**Book IV
Chapter 5**

Analyzing Data

6. **Click OK.**

   On your worksheet, the cell with the argument you wanted to alter now shows the target you're seeking. In the case of the example worksheet in Figure 5-4, you can borrow $316,422 at 6.5 percent, not $250,000, by raising your monthly mortgage payments from $1,580.17 to $2,000.

Performing What-If Analyses with Data Tables

For something a little more sophisticated than the Goal Seek command (which I describe in the preceding section), try performing what-if analyses with data tables. With this technique, you change the data in input cells and observe what effect changing the data has on the results of a formula. The difference between the Goal Seek command and a data table is that, with a data table, you can experiment simultaneously with many different input cells and in so doing experiment with many different scenarios.

Using a one-input table for analysis

In a *one-input table,* you find out what the different results of a formula would be if you change one *input cell* in the formula. In Figure 5-5, that input cell is the interest rate on a loan. The purpose of this data table is to find out how monthly payments on a $250,000, 30-year mortgage are different, given different interest rates. The interest rate in cell B4 is the input cell.

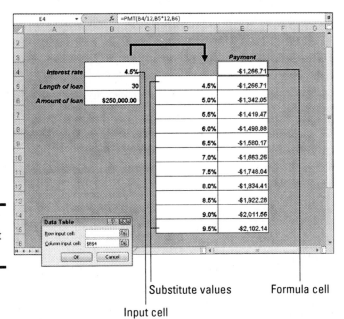

Figure 5-5:
A one-input
data table.

Substitute values   Formula cell

Input cell

Follow these steps to create a one-input table:

1. **On your worksheet, enter values that you want to substitute for the value in the input cell.**

   To make the input table work, you have to enter the substitute values in the right location:

   - *In a column:* Enter the values in the column starting one cell below and one cell to the left of the cell where the formula is located. In Figure 5-5, for example, the formula is in cell E4 and the values are in the cell range D5:D15.

   - *In a row:* Enter the values in the row starting one cell above and one cell to the right of the cell where the formula is.

2. **Select the block of cells with the formula and substitute values.**

   Select a rectangle of cells that encompasses the formula cell, the cell beside it, all the substitute values, and the empty cells where the new calculations will soon appear.

   - *In a column:* Select the formula cell, the cell to its left, as well as all the substitute-value cells and the cells below the formula cell.

   - *In a row:* Select the formula cell, the cell above it, as well as the substitute values in the cells directly to the right and the now-empty cells where the new calculations will appear.

3. **On the Data tab, click the What-If Analysis button and choose Data Table on the drop-down list.**

   You see the Data Table dialog box.

4. **In the Row Input Cell or Column Input Cell text box, enter the address of the cell where the input value is located.**

   The input value is the value you're experimenting with in your analysis. In the case of Figure 5-5, the input value is located in cell B4, the cell that holds the interest rate.

   If the new calculations appear in rows, enter the address of the input cell in the Row Input Cell text box; if the calculations appear in columns (refer to Figure 5-5), enter the input cell address in the Column Input Cell text box.

5. **Click OK.**

   Excel performs the calculations and fills in the table.

To generate the one-input table, Excel constructs an array formula with the TABLE function. If you change the cell references in the first row or plug in different values in the first column, Excel updates the one-input table automatically.

**Book IV
Chapter 5**

Analyzing Data

Using a two-input table for analysis

In a two-input table, you can experiment with two input cells rather than one. Getting back to the example of the loan payment in Figure 5-5, you can calculate not only how loan payments change as interest rates change, but how payments change if the life of the loan changes. Figure 5-6 shows a two-input table for examining monthly loan payments given different interest rates and two different terms for the loan, 15 years (180 months) and 30 years (360 months).

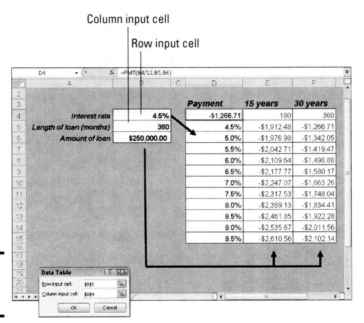

Column input cell

Row input cell

		Payment	15 years	30 years
Interest rate	4.5%	-$1,266.71	180	360
Length of loan (months)	360	4.5%	-$1,912.48	-$1,266.71
Amount of loan	$250,000.00	5.0%	-$1,976.98	-$1,342.05
		5.5%	-$2,042.71	-$1,419.47
		6.0%	-$2,109.64	-$1,498.88
		6.5%	-$2,177.77	-$1,580.17
		7.0%	-$2,247.07	-$1,663.26
		7.5%	-$2,317.53	-$1,748.04
		8.0%	-$2,389.13	-$1,834.41
		8.5%	-$2,461.85	-$1,922.28
		9.0%	-$2,535.67	-$2,011.56
		9.5%	-$2,610.56	-$2,102.14

D4 =PMT(B4/12,B5,B6)

Data Table
Row input cell: B5
Column input cell: B4
OK   Cancel

Figure 5-6: A two-input data table.

Follow these steps to create a two-input data table:

1. **Enter one set of substitute values below the formula in the same column as the formula.**

   In Figure 5-6, different interest rates are entered in the cell range D5:D15.

2. **Enter the second set of substitute values in the row to the right of the formula.**

   In Figure 5-6, 180 and 360 are entered. These numbers represent the number of months of the life of the loan.

3. **Select the formula and all substitute values.**

   Do this correctly and you select three columns, including the formula, the substitute values below it, and the two columns to the right of the formula. You select a big block of cells (the range D4:F15, in this example).

What-If Analysis

4. On the Data tab, click the What-If Analysis button and choose Data Table on the drop-down list.

The Data Table dialog box appears (see Figure 5-6).

5. In the Row Input Cell text box, enter the address of the cell referred to in the original formula where substitute values to the right of the formula can be plugged in.

In Figure 5-6, for example, the rows to the right of the formula are for length of loan substitute values. Therefore, I select cell B5, the cell referred to in the original formula where the length of the loan is listed.

6. In the Column Input Cell text box, enter the address of the cell referred to in the original formula where substitute values below the formula are.

In Figure 5-6, the substitute values below the formula cell are interest rates. Therefore, I select cell B4, the cell referred to in the original formula where the interest rate is entered.

7. Click OK.

Excel performs the calculations and fills in the table.

Conditional formats for calling attention to data

A *conditional format* is one that applies when data meets certain conditions. To call attention to numbers greater than 10,000, for example, you can tell Excel to highlight those numbers automatically. To highlight negative numbers, you can tell Excel to display them in bright red. Conditional formats help you analyze and understand data better.

Select the cells that are candidates for conditional formatting and follow these steps to tell Excel when and how to format the cells:

1. **On the Home tab, click the Conditional Formatting button (you may have to click the Styles button first, depending on the size of your screen).**

2. **Choose Highlight Cells Rules or Top/Bottom Rules on the drop-down list.**

   You see a submenu with choices about establishing the rule for whether values in

the cells are highlighted or otherwise made more prominent.

Highlight Cells Rules are for calling attention to data if it falls in a numerical or date range, or it's greater or lesser than a specific value. For example, you can highlight cells that are greater than 400.

Top/Bottom Rules are for calling attention to data if it falls within a percentage range relative to all the cells you selected. For example, you can highlight cells with data that falls in the bottom 10-percent range.

3. **Choose an option on the submenu.**

4. **On the left side of the dialog box that appears, establish the rule for flagging data.**

5. **On the With drop-down list, choose how you want to call attention to the data.**

**Book IV
Chapter 5**

Analyzing Data

(continued)

(continued)

For example, you can display the data in red or yellow. You can choose Custom Format on the drop-down list to open the Format Cells dialog box and choose a font style or color for the text.

To remove conditional formats, select the cells with the formats, go to the Home tab, click the Conditional Formatting button, and choose Clear Rules➪Clear Rules from Selected Cells.

6. Click OK.

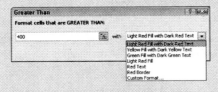
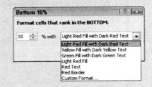

Book V

OneNote

Contents at a Glance

Chapter 1: Up and Running with OneNote 473

Introducing OneNote 473
Finding Your Way around the OneNote Screen 474
Units for Organizing Notes 475
Creating a Notebook 476
Creating Sections and Section Groups 478
Creating Pages and Subpages 479
Renaming and Deleting Groups and Pages 480
Getting from Place to Place in OneNote 480
Changing Your View of a Page 481

Chapter 2: Taking Notes 485

Notes: The Basics 485
Entering a Typewritten Note 487
Drawing on the Page 487
Converting a Handwritten Note to Text 491
Writing a Math Expression in a Note 491
Taking a Screen-Clipping Note 492
Recording and Playing Audio Notes 493
Attaching, Copying, and Linking Files to Notes 495
Formatting the Text in Notes 498
Docking the OneNote Screen 499

Chapter 3: Finding and Organizing Your Notes 501

Finding a Stray Note 501
Tagging Notes for Follow Up 503
Color-Coding Notebooks, Sections, and Pages 506
Merging and Moving Sections, Pages, and Notes 507

Chapter 1: Up and Running with OneNote

In This Chapter

✔ Getting acquainted with OneNote

✔ Understanding the OneNote screen

✔ Creating notebooks, sections, section groups, and pages

✔ Getting a better view of your notes

✔ Navigating in OneNote

Microsoft OneNote is designed for taking notes — at meetings, at conferences, or when talking on the telephone. Rather than scribble notes indiscriminately in a Word document, you can enter them in OneNote and be able to retrieve them later. You can use your notes to construct reports and white papers. You can copy them to Excel, PowerPoint, or Word. OneNote comes with all sorts of amenities for finding and filing notes. OneNote can help you brainstorm and organize your ideas.

This chapter explains what OneNote is and how you can use it to store and organize notes. It explains what sections, section groups, pages, and subpages are and why to use these items for organizing notes. You also find out how to get from place to place in OneNote and change views so that you can see your notes better.

Introducing OneNote

Everybody who has been in a classroom or participated in a business meeting knows what note taking is. What makes taking notes with OneNote special is that you can store, organize, and retrieve your notes in various ways. OneNote adds another dimension to note taking. Because notes can be copied, moved, and combined with other notes, you can use notes as building blocks for different projects.

A OneNote file is called a *notebook*. Within a notebook, you can write notes and organize your notes into sections, section groups, pages, and subpages. You can use OneNote to refine your thinking about the work you want to do and the subjects you want to tackle. OneNote helps you brainstorm, and when you finish brainstorming, it helps you organize your ideas into something coherent and useful.

OneNote is unusual among Office programs in that it doesn't have a Save button or Save command. Every 30 seconds, OneNote saves all the notes for you. You needn't concern yourself with whether notes are being saved.

Finding Your Way around the OneNote Screen

OneNote wants you to be able to enter notes and find notes quickly, and to that purpose, the screen is divided into four main areas: the Navigation bar, Section tabs, the Page window, and the Page pane. Figure 1-1 shows where these main areas are located, and the following pages explain each area in detail.

Navigation bar   Section tabs   Page window (with notes)   Page pane

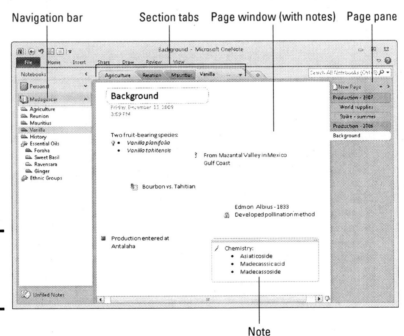

Figure 1-1: The OneNote screen.

Note

Navigation bar

Located on the left side of the screen, the Navigation bar lists the names of notebooks you created, and within each notebook, it lists sections and section groups. To go to a different notebook, section, or section group, click its name in the Navigation bar.

Click the Collapse Navigation Bar or Expand Navigation Bar button to hide or display the Navigation bar. These buttons are located on the top of the Navigation bar.

Section (and section group) tabs

Section and section group names appear in tabs above the page (refer to Figure 1-1). Click the name of a section to see its pages. (You can also click a section name in the Navigation bar.) Click the name of a section group to make its sections appear on the tabs. Later in this chapter, "Units for Organizing Notes" explains what sections and section groups are.

Page window

After you select a page in the Page pane, it appears in the Page window, and you can read notes you wrote on the page (refer to Figure 1-1). The title of the page appears at the top of the page window in the Title text box. Underneath the Title text box, you can see the date and time that the page was created.

To write a note, click in the Page window and start typing.

Page pane

The names of pages and subpages in the section you selected appear on tabs in the Page pane on the right side of the screen (refer to Figure 1-1).

To go from page to page, click a page's name. The top of the Page pane offers the New Page button for creating new pages.

 You can hide or display the Page pane by clicking its Expand or Collapse button.

Units for Organizing Notes

From largest to smallest, the program offers these units for organizing notes:

✦ **Notebook:** Create a notebook for each important project you're involved in. OneNote places one button on the Navigation bar for each notebook you create. The Navigation bar is located on the left side of the window (see Figure 1-1).

✦ **Sections:** A *section* is a subcategory of a notebook; it is used to store pages. Each notebook can have many different sections, and each section, in turn, can have many pages. In Figure 1-1, there are five sections in the Madagascar notebook: Agriculture, Reunion, Mauritius, Vanilla, and History.

✦ **Section groups:** A *section group* is a means of organizing and quickly finding sections. Although sections do not have to be stored in a section group, you can use section groups to store sections. The names of section groups appear below the names of sections on the Navigation bar and to the right of sections in the section tabs.

+ **Pages and subpages:** A *page* is for writing and storing notes. Pages are stored in sections. As shown in Figure 1-1, the names of pages appear on the Page pane (on the right side of the screen) on *page tabs*. Within a page, you can also create a *subpage*.

+ **Notes:** Write your notes on pages and subpages. To write a note, all you have to do is click a page and start typing.

Before you write your first note, give a moment's thought to organizing notes in the notebook-section-pages hierarchy. Think of descriptive names for your notebook, sections, section groups, and pages. By giving a thought to how to organize notes, you will be able to find them more easily later on.

Creating a Notebook

OneNote creates a new notebook for you called Personal the first time you start the program, but you are invited to create a notebook of your own. OneNote is kind of unusual among Office programs in that you name a notebook when you create it, not when you save it for the first time.

Follow these steps to create a new notebook:

1. **On to the File tab, choose New.**

The New Notebook window opens, as shown in Figure 1-2. You can also right-click the Notebooks pane and choose New Notebook to open this window.

Figure 1-2:
Name your
notebook
when you
create it.

2. **Under Store Notebook On, choose My Computer to store the notebook on your computer.**

   The Web option is for storing a notebook on a Windows Live site. (Book VI, Chapter 7 explains how to share files on Windows Live.) The Network option is for storing a notebook on a SharePoint Web site on a local network. SharePoint is a software program for managing and sharing files.

3. **Enter a name for the notebook.**

4. **Select the folder in which you will store the notebook.**

   To do so, click the Browse button and select a folder in the Select Folder dialog box.

5. **Click the Create Notebook button.**

   The new notebook opens on-screen. OneNote creates a section (called New Section 1) and a page (called Untitled Page) in your notebook.

6. **Change the name of the section and page.**

   Follow these instructions to change section and page names:

   - *Changing the section name:* Right-click the section name, choose Rename on the shortcut menu, and enter a descriptive name. You can also double-click a name and enter a new one.

   - *Changing the page name:* Enter a name in the Title text box at the top of the page. After you enter the name, the new name appears as well on the Page pane on the right side of the screen.

To delete a notebook, close OneNote, open Windows Explorer or Computer, go to the folder where the notebook is stored, and delete the folder. To find out where notebooks are stored by default on your computer, go to the File tab, choose Options, go to the Save & Backup category of the OneNote Options dialog box, and look for the Default Notebook Location.

Removing a notebook from the Navigation bar

Consider removing a notebook's name from the Navigation bar if the Navigation bar gets too crowded with notebooks. Follow these instructions to remove and display a notebook's name on the Navigation bar:

- **Closing a notebook:** Right-click the notebook's name and choose Close This Notebook on the shortcut menu.

- **Re-opening a notebook:** Go to the File tab and choose Open. You see the Open Notebook window. Select a notebook name under Recently Closed Notebooks. If the notebook's name doesn't appear, click the Open Notebook button and select the notebook's name in the Open Notebook dialog box.

Creating Sections and Section Groups

After the notebook, the next units in the file storage hierarchy are the section and the section group. If a notebook is a book, a section is a chapter in a book. Create a section for each subtopic in the item you're keeping notes on. A section group is a convenient way to organize groups. A group can belong to more than one section.

Creating a new section

Follow these steps to create a new section:

1. **Click the Create a New Section button.**

   This button (it looks like an asterisk) is located to the right of the section tabs. Rather than click the New Section button, you can right-click the Navigation bar or a section tab and choose New Section.

   A new section tab aptly named "New Section 1" appears.

2. **Enter a section name on the tab.**

3. **Press Enter.**

   To rename a section, right-click its name, choose Rename, and enter a new name.

After you create a new section, OneNote automatically creates a new page to go with it. This page is called "Untitled Page." To rename this page, enter a name in the Title text box at the top of the page.

Creating a section group

Follow these steps to create a section group:

1. **Right-click the Navigation bar or a section tab and choose New Section Group.**

   A section group tab appears.

2. **Enter a name for the section group.**

3. **Press the Enter key.**

   Your next task is to move or copy a section you already created into the section group.

4. **Right-click a section you want to move or copy into the group and choose Move or Copy on the drop-down list.**

   The Move or Copy Section dialog box appears, as shown in Figure 1-3.

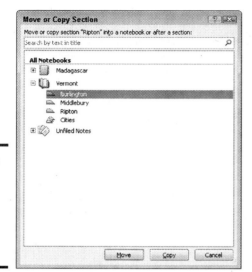

Figure 1-3:
Choose
a section
to move
or copy to
a section
group.

5. **Select the name of the section group you created.**

6. **Click the Move or Copy button.**

   You can drag a section name in the Navigation bar into a section group to move a section from one place to another.

Creating Pages and Subpages

When you create a section, OneNote automatically creates a new page for you, but that doesn't mean you can't create more pages for a section. Create a page for each subtopic you want to takes notes on. Within each page, you can create subpages, which might help you organize your notes better.

Creating a new page

Follow these steps to create a page:

1. **Click the New Page button.**

   This button is located at the top of the Page pane. A new page appears. You can also make a new page appear by pressing Ctrl+N or right-clicking the Page pane and choosing New Page.

2. **Enter a page name in the Title text box.**

   The name you enter appears on a page tab in the Page pane.

   You can rearrange pages (and subpages) in the Page pane by dragging their names higher or lower in the list of pages.

Creating a new subpage

Follow these steps to create a new subpage:

1. **Display the page under which you will create a subpage.**

   To display the page, click its name in the Page pane.

2. **Open the drop-down list on the New Page button and choose New Subpage.**

3. **Enter a name in the Title text box.**

You can create sub-subpages, and sub-sub-subpages, for that matter. To demote a page even further, right-click its name in the Page pane and choose Make Subpage on the shortcut menu that appears. Right-click and choose Promote Subpage to raise a page's standing.

Renaming and Deleting Groups and Pages

If you're like me, you'll do a lot of deleting and renaming of groups, section groups, pages, and subpages in OneNote. Making sure that these items have descriptive names is essential for locating notes and entering notes in the right places.

Luckily for all of us, OneNote makes it easy to rename and delete groups and pages. Think the words "right-click" when you want to rename or delete a group, section group, or page. To rename or delete one of these items, right-click it and choose Rename or Delete on the shortcut menu. After you choose Rename, enter a new name for your group, section group, or page.

Getting from Place to Place in OneNote

As you fill up a notebook with sections, section groups, pages, subpages, and notes, finding the place you need to be to enter or read a note gets more complicated. Here are ways to get from section to section or page to page in the OneNote window:

✦ **Going to a different notebook:** Click a notebook button on the Navigation bar. Use one of these techniques to find out where clicking a notebook button takes you:

  • *Move the pointer over a button.* You see a notebook's name and the folder where it is stored in a ScreenTip box.

- *If the Navigation bar is collapsed, click the Expand Navigation Bar button.* Now you can see the names of notebooks as well as the names of notebook sections on the Navigation bar. The Expand Navigation Bar button is located at the top of the Navigation bar.

✦ **Going to a different section or section group:** Click the name of a section or section group in the Navigation bar or along the top of the window. Section group names are listed at the bottom of the Navigation bar and to the right of section names. You can expand and collapse section groups in the Navigation bar by clicking the plus or minus sign on a section group symbol.

✦ **Go to a different page:** Click a page or subpage tab on the Page pane on the right side of the window. To make more room for page and subpage names, click the Expand Page Tabs button. You can find it to the right of the New Page button.

To return to the page you last visited, click the Back button on the Quick Access toolbar. This button works like the Back button in a browser. It takes you to where you were previously.

Changing Your View of a Page

As shown in Figure 1-4, OneNote offers two views, Normal view and Full Page view. You are encouraged to switch back and forth between these views because doing so can help you get a better view of your work. To change views, go to the View tab and click the Editing View or Reading View button:

✦ **Normal view:** For writing, editing, and organizing notes. All the tools are available to you in Normal view. To switch to Normal view, go to the View tab and click the Normal View button.

✦ **Full Page View:** For comfortably reading your notes. In Full Page view, the OneNote buttons and tools aren't there to distract you. To switch to Full Page view, go to the View tab and click the Full Page View button.

You can switch back and forth between Normal and Full Page view by pressing F11 or clicking the Full Page View button on the Quick Access Toolbar.

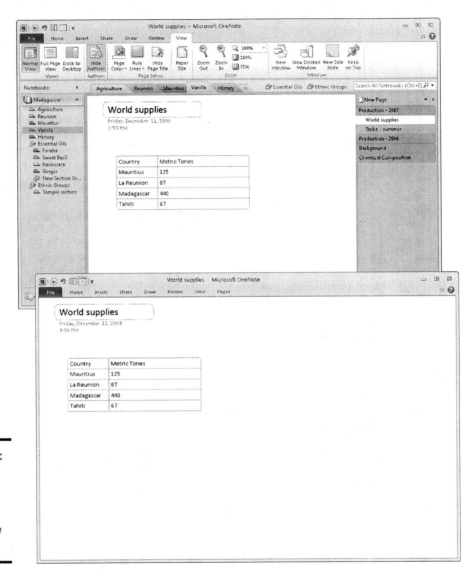

Figure 1-4:
OneNote
in Normal
view (top)
and Full
Page view
(bottom).

Revisiting (and restoring) an earlier version of a page

For each day you work on a page, OneNote saves a copy of the page in case you want to revisit or restore it. To read an earlier version of a page, follow these steps:

1. **Open the page.**

2. **Go to the Share tab.**

3. **Click the Page Versions button.**

   The names of page versions appear on the Pages pane below the name of the page you right-clicked. These page versions are dated with an author's name. You can also see page versions by right-clicking a page's name and choosing Show Page Versions on the shortcut menu.

4. **Click a page version's name to open and read an earlier version of a page.**

To make an earlier version of a page the one you want for your notes, click the top of the page to open a drop-down list with options for re-hiding, deleting, and restoring the page. Then choose Restore on the drop-down list.

To hide page versions, click the Page Versions button a second time or right-click a page's name and choose Hide Page Versions on the shortcut menu that appears.

To delete a page version, choose Delete Version on the drop-down list.

Chapter 2: Taking Notes

In This Chapter

✔ **Working with note containers**

✔ **Moving, selecting, and deleting notes**

✔ **Entering notes with the keyboard**

✔ **Drawing in OneNote**

✔ **Turning handwritten notes into text notes**

✔ **Taking screen-clipping and audio notes**

✔ **Attaching and linking notes to files**

✔ **Formatting note text**

✔ **Docking the screen to help with note taking**

To OneNote, a "note" is much more than something you scribble on a page. OneNote offers you the chance to create a variety of different notes — drawn notes, audio notes, screen clippings, and linked notes, for example.

This chapter delves into all the kinds of notes you can make with OneNote. It also shows you how to draw on a page, turn handwritten notes into text notes, write mathematical expressions, and attach and link files to notes. You also discover how to dock the OneNote window to one side of the screen so that you can take notes more easily.

Notes: The Basics

Although the program is called OneNote, you can enter many kinds of notes. You can enter typed notes, drawings, and screen clippings, for example. Moreover, if you're using a Tablet PC to scribble your notes, OneNote can (most of the time, anyway) recognize whether you're writing by hand or drawing.

Whatever kind of note you're dealing with, the basics of handling notes are the same. This section's pages look at note containers, how to select and delete notes, and how to get more room on-screen for notes.

Moving and resizing note containers

Notes appear in *containers,* as shown in Figure 2-1. Move the pointer over a note to see its container. Containers make it easier to move notes, resize notes, and arrange notes on the page so that you can read them more easily. Follow these instructions to move and resize notes:

✦ **Changing a note's position:** Move the pointer over the top of the note container, and when the pointer changes into a four-headed arrow, click and start dragging.

✦ **Changing a note's size:** Move the pointer over the right side of the note container, and when the pointer changes into a double arrow, click and drag to the left or right.

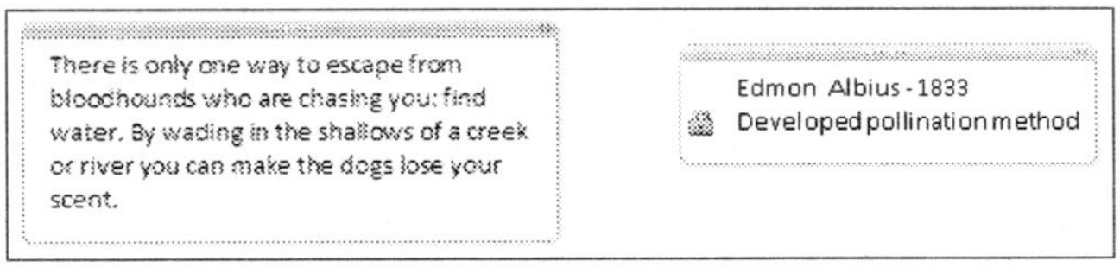

Figure 2-1:
Notes appear in note containers.

There is only one way to escape from bloodhounds who are chasing you: find water. By wading in the shallows of a creek or river you can make the dogs lose your scent.

Edmon Albius - 1833
Developed pollination method

Selecting notes

Before you can do anything to a note — move it, delete it — you have to select it. The simplest way to select a note is to click it. After you click, you see the note's container (refer to Figure 2-1). You can also use these techniques to select notes:

✦ **Ctrl+click:** Hold down the Ctrl key and click notes to select more than one.

✦ **Drag:** Click and drag across a portion of a page to select several notes.

✦ **Press Ctrl+A:** Pressing Ctrl+A selects all the notes on a page.

Deleting notes

To delete notes, select them and press the Delete key. You can also go to the Draw tab and click the Delete button.

Be careful about deleting notes, because you can't recover a note you deleted. OneNote gives you the opportunity to recover deleted sections and pages, but not notes you deleted.

Getting more space for notes on a page

How do you make room for a note on a page that is crowded with notes? You can drag notes here and there, but an easier way is to go to the Insert or Draw tab and click the Insert Space button. After you click it, drag downward on the screen where you want to make more space for notes, as shown in Figure 2-2. Notes below where you drag are pushed further down the page.

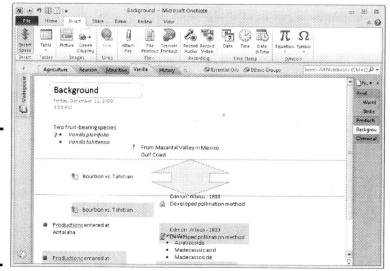

Figure 2-2: Click the Insert Space button to make more room for notes.

Entering a Typewritten Note

The simplest kind of note is the typewritten note. To type a note, simply click the page where you want the note to be and start typing. Press the Enter key to begin a new paragraph in a note. You can draw upon the commands on the Home tab to format the text or change a note's color. (Later in this chapter, "Formatting the Text on Notes," looks at ways to format text.)

The Insert tab offers the Date, Time, and Date & Time buttons in case you want to date- or time-stamp a note. If recording when you made a note is important to you, visit the Insert tab and click the Date, Time, or Date & Time button while writing your note.

 To get more room on a page for notes, try collapsing the Navigation bar and page tabs. To do so, press F11 or click the Full Page View button on the Quick Access toolbar.

Drawing on the Page

Sometimes you can't say it in words, and for those occasions, consider drawing on the page instead of writing a note. OneNote offers the Draw tab precisely for that purpose. On this tab are tools for drawing lines of different colors and widths, drawing shapes, and editing your drawings.

Drawing with a pen or highlighter

Follow these steps to draw on the page with a pen or highlighter:

1. Go to the Draw tab.

2. Choose a pen or highlighter.

Use one of these techniques to choose a pen or highlighter:

- *Tools gallery:* Open the Tools gallery and choose a pen or highlighter, as shown in Figure 2-3.

- *Color & Thickness dialog box:* Click the Color & Thickness button to open the Color & Thickness dialog box, shown in Figure 2-3. Then select the Pen or Highlighter option button, choose a line thickness, and choose a line color.

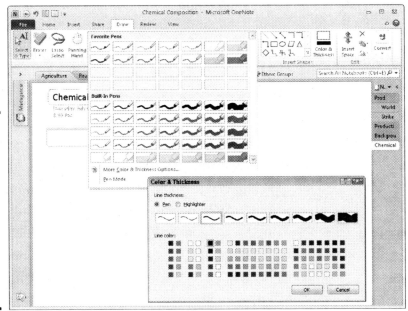

Figure 2-3: On the Draw tab, choose a pen or highlighter from the Tools gallery (top) or Color & Thickness dialog box (bottom).

3. Start drawing.

As you make your drawing, you can return to the Tools gallery or Color & Thickness dialog box and choose a different color or line type. You can also make shapes and straight lines part of your drawing. (The next topic in this chapter, "Drawing a shape," explains how.)

4. Press Esc when you finish drawing or highlighting.

Later in this chapter, "Changing the size and appearance of drawings and shapes" explains how to change a drawing's size and appearance.

Drawing a shape

As well as drawing freehand (the previous subject of this chapter), you can draw shapes and straight lines on the page. Making shapes and straight lines part of your drawings makes a drawing easier to understand, as shown in Figure 2-4. Follow these steps to draw a shape or straight line:

1. **On the Draw tab, choose a pen or highlighter.**

Your first step is to choose the color and line style you want for the shape or straight line:

- *Tools gallery:* Open the Tools gallery and choose a pen or highlighter (refer to Figure 2-3).

- *Color & Thickness dialog box:* Click the Color & Thickness button to open the Color & Thickness dialog box (refer to Figure 2-3). In the dialog box, select the Pen or Highlighter option button, choose a line thickness, and choose a line color.

2. **On the Draw tab, open the Insert Shapes gallery and choose line or shape.**

3. **Drag on-screen to draw the line or shape.**

4. **Press Esc when you finish drawing the line or shape.**

The next topic in this chapter explains how to change shapes' size and appearance.

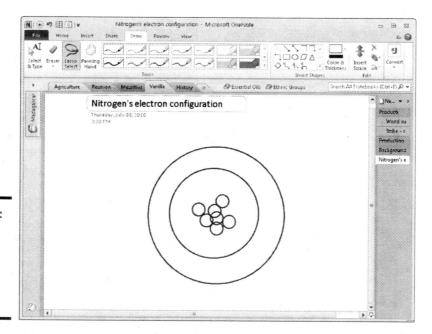

Figure 2-4:
You can draw shapes as well as draw freehand.

Changing the size and appearance of drawings and shapes

Not that you necessarily want to open this can of worms, but you can edit drawings. Starting on the Draw tab, here are instructions for changing the look and appearance of drawings:

+ **Selecting a single line or shape:** Click the Select & Type button and then click the line or shape. Dotted lines and selection handles appear around the line or shape to show it is selected.

+ **Selecting an entire drawing:** Click the Lasso Select button and drag slantwise across the drawing.

+ **Erasing:** Use the Eraser button to erase all or part of a line or shape. You can open the drop-down list on the Eraser button to choose erasers of different sizes.

  • *To erase part of a line or shape:* Click the Eraser button and drag over the part of the line or shape you want to erase.

  • *To erase entire lines and shapes:* Click the bottom half of the Eraser button to open its drop-down list, choose Stroke Eraser, and drag over or click on lines and shapes.

+ **Changing colors and line thickness:** After you select a line, shape, or drawing, click the Color & Thickness button. The Color & Thickness dialog box opens (refer to Figure 2-3). Choose a line style, choose a color, and click OK.

+ **Resizing:** After you select a line, shape, or drawing, use one of these techniques to resize it:

  • Drag a corner handle to change a shape's size and retain its symmetry.

  • Drag a side, top, or bottom handle to stretch or scrunch a shape.

+ **Moving:** After you select a line, shape, or drawing, move the pointer on top of it. When you see the four-headed arrow, click and start dragging.

+ **Rotating:** After you select a line, shape, or drawing, click the Rotate button and choose a Rotate or Flip option on the drop-down list.

+ **Arranging overlapping lines and shapes:** When lines and shapes overlap, choose an Arrange option to determine which is highest and lowest in the stack. Select a line or shape, click the Arrange button, and choose an option on the drop-down list:

  • *Bring Forward:* Moves the line or shape higher in the stack.

  • *Bring to Front:* Moves the line or shape in front of all other lines and shapes in the stack.

  • *Send Backward:* Moves the line or shape lower in the stack.

  • *Send to Back:* Moves the lines or shape behind all other lines and shapes.

✦ Deleting: After you select a line, shape, or drawing, press Delete or click the Delete button.

Converting a Handwritten Note to Text

Want proof that computers are getting smarter? In OneNote, you can write a note by hand using a stylus pen or your mouse and tell OneNote to convert it to text. In my experiments, the conversion works most of the time. OneNote is able to recognize my handwriting and render it in text, as shown in Figure 2-5.

Follow these steps to convert a handwritten note to text:

1. Select the handwritten note.

To do that, go to the Draw tab, click the Lasso Select button, and drag slantwise across the note.

2. On the Draw tab, click the Ink to Text button.

Your handwritten note, with a little luck and depending on the quality of your handwriting, is converted to text.

Figure 2-5:
A handwritten note converted to text.

Writing a Math Expression in a Note

The Insert tab offers the Equation Editor (click the Equation button) for writing mathematical equations, and you're welcome to give it a spin, but much more useful than the Equation Editor is another tool called the Ink Equation Editor. As shown in Figure 2-6, you can use it to construct mathematical expressions for notes.

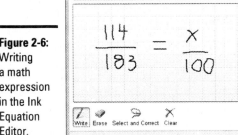

Figure 2-6:
Writing
a math
expression
in the Ink
Equation
Editor.

To open the Ink Equation Editor, go to the Draw tab and click the Ink to Math button. The Ink Equation Editor opens. Keep your eye on the Preview area while you follow these instructions to construct your equation:

✦ **Writing:** Click the Write button and drag the mouse to write your expression.

✦ **Erasing numbers and symbols:** Click the Erase button and drag to erase a number or symbol.

✦ **Correcting errors:** If the Ink Equation Editor enters the wrong number or symbol, click the Select and Correct button and then click on the part of the expression that is incorrect. A drop-down list appears. If the correct number or symbol is on the menu, select it.

✦ **Erasing the expression:** Click the Clear button to wipe the slate clean and start anew.

Click the Insert button to turn the equation into a note.

Taking a Screen-Clipping Note

In OneNote lingo, a *screen clipping* is a note with a screen shot inside it, as shown in Figure 2-7. OneNote makes it remarkably easy to take screen clippings. Take them when you want to preserve part of a screen in a note. Follow these steps to make a screen-clipping note:

1. **Go to the Web page, Word document, or other item that you need a picture of.**

2. **Switch to OneNote.**

3. **On the Insert tab, click the Screen Clipping button.**

You return to the program you were in previously.

4. **Drag the pointer to capture the portion of the screen you want for the clipping.**

   When you finish dragging, you return to OneNote, and the screen clipping you took appears in a note.

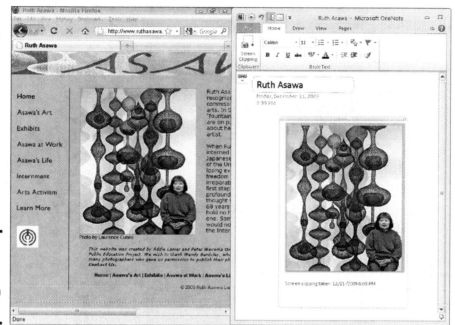

Figure 2-7:
A screen clipping taken from a Web page.

You can also take a screen clipping by starting in the Notification tray (located in the lower-right corner of the screen). Right-click the OneNote icon in the Notification tray and choose Create Screen Clipping (or press Windows key+S). Then drag the pointer on your screen to capture the part of the screen you want for the clipping. The Select Location in OneNote dialog box appears. Do one of the following:

   ✦ **Select a section in the dialog box and click the Send to Selected Location button.** OneNote creates a new page in the section you chose for the clipping and places the clipping on the page.

   ✦ **Click the Copy to Clipboard button.** Back in OneNote, right-click a page and choose Paste to paste the clipping into OneNote.

Recording and Playing Audio Notes

If you start to get sleepy in class and can no longer type notes, consider taking an *audio note*. An audio note is a recording stored in a note container.

You can take these notes as long as you have a microphone that is connected correctly to your computer. What OneNote calls an *audio note* is really a `.wma` (Windows media audio) file stored in a note container.

After you record an audio note, you can click the note's Play icon or click the Play button on the (Audio & Video) Playback tab to play the recording you made, as shown in Figure 2-8. (Book IV, Chapter 3 explains how to test your computer's microphone to make sure it is working correctly.)

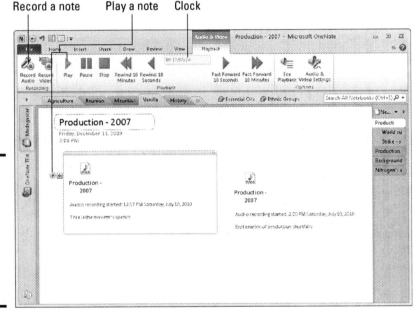

Figure 2-8:
Play and record audio notes on the (Audio & Video) Playback tab.

Recording an audio note

Make sure your microphone is connected and ready to go because OneNote begins recording audio notes as soon as you click the Record Audio button. Open the page where you want to store the note and follow these steps to record an audio note:

1. **On the Insert tab or (Audio & Video) Playback tab, click the Record Audio button.**

   As shown in Figure 2-8, you go immediately to the (Audio & Video) Playback tab (if you weren't there already), and OneNote begins recording.

2. **Direct your microphone to whatever you're recording — your own voice or someone else's.**

The clock at the top of the tab tells you how long the recording is. You can click the Pause button to suspend the recording; click Pause a second time to resume recording.

3. **Click the Stop button when you want to finish recording the audio note.**

   Notes are named for the page where they are stored. The WMA icon tells you that the note is a .wma (Windows media audio) file recording.

To help identify recordings, click in an audio note's container and enter a description.

Playing an audio note

To play an audio note, select it and do one of the following:

✦ Click the Play icon on the note (refer to Figure 2-8).

✦ Right-click the note and choose Play on the shortcut menu that appears.

✦ Go to the (Audio & Video) Playback tab and click the Play button.

The Playback group on the (Audio & Video) Playback tab offers buttons for pausing, stopping, rewinding, and fast-forwarding an audio note as it plays (refer to Figure 2-8). Glance at the clock to see how long the note is and how many seconds and minutes have played so far.

While a note is playing, you can type other notes on the page. In other words, you can take notes on the audio recording and capture the information you missed during your catnap.

On a page with more than one audio note, click the See Playback button on the (Audio & Video) Playback tab to find out which note is currently playing. The note that is playing is highlighted and selected.

Attaching, Copying, and Linking Files to Notes

OneNote endeavors to make it easier for you to take notes on files on your computer. You can attach a note to a file and be able to open the file quickly from inside OneNote, copy a file into a note, and link a Word or PowerPoint file to a OneNote section or page so that you can refer to notes you keep in OneNote while you're working in Word or PowerPoint. These tasks are described forthwith.

Attaching an Office file to a note

Attach a Word, PowerPoint, or Excel file to a note so that you can quickly open the file from inside OneNote. When you attach a file, what you really do is create a shortcut from your note to the Office file. You can click the shortcut and open the attached file right away. Follow these steps to attach an Office file to a note:

1. **Select the note.**

2. **On the Insert tab, click the Attach File button.**

    You see the Choose a File or Set of Files to Insert dialog box.

3. **Select the file or files.**

    To select more than one file, Ctrl+click their names.

4. **Click the Insert button.**

    As shown in Figure 2-9, filenames and icons appear on notes. The icons indicate what kind of file is attached to the note. To open one of these files, simply click its icon.

Figure 2-9:
Files
attached to
a note.

Copying an Office file into OneNote

Follow these steps to copy a file from Word, PowerPoint, or Excel onto a OneNote page:

1. **On the Insert tab, click the File Printout button.**

    The Choose Document to Insert dialog box opens.

2. **Select a file and click the Insert button.**

Starting in Word, Excel, or PowerPoint, you can copy a file to OneNote by going to the File tab and choosing Print. In the Print window, open the Printer drop-down list, choose Send to OneNote 2010, and click the Print button. Then switch to OneNote, and in the Select Location in One Note dialog box, choose a section or page and click OK. If you select a section, OneNote creates a new page in the section for the material from Word, Excel, or PowerPoint; if you select a page, the material lands on the page you selected.

Linking a Word or PowerPoint file to OneNote

By linking a Word or PowerPoint file to a OneNote section or page, you can open OneNote from inside Word or PowerPoint and refer right away to notes you took. Link a file to OneNote so that you can refer to notes you keep in OneNote while you're working on a Word or PowerPoint file.

Follow these steps to link a Word or PowerPoint file to a section or page in OneNote:

1. **Open the Word or PowerPoint file you want to link to notes you keep in OneNote.**

2. **On the Review tab, click the Linked Notes button.**

   OneNote opens (if it wasn't already open), and you see the Select Location in OneNote dialog box, as shown in Figure 2-10.

3. **In the dialog box, select the section or page with the notes that refer to your Word or PowerPoint file, and click OK.**

   The Linked Note icon appears in OneNote. This icon tells you that the section or page is linked to a Word or PowerPoint file.

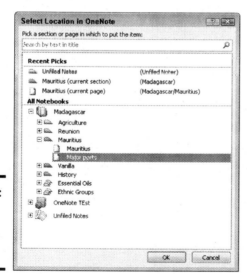

Figure 2-10: Choosing the section or page to link to.

To refer to the OneNote notes while you're working on your Word or PowerPoint file, go to the Review tab and click the Linked Notes button. OneNote opens in Dock to Desktop view. In this view, Word or PowerPoint appears on the left side of your screen, and OneNote appears on the right side. This arrangement makes it easy to work from your notes. (Later in this chapter, "Docking the OneNote Screen" explains docking to the desktop.)

Copying a note into another Office program

To copy a note into another program, use the copy-and-paste command. Select the note, right-click, and choose Copy. Then go to the other program, right-click, and choose Paste. Typed notes land in the other program in the form of text. Drawings land as Portable Network Graphics (.png) files.

Formatting the Text in Notes

On the Home and Insert tabs, OneNote offers commands for formatting the text in notes. If formatting a note's text makes reading and understanding it easier, by all means format the text. You can do so with these techniques:

✦ **Basic text formatting:** On the Home tab, you can choose a font for text, change the size and color of text, and create bulleted and numbered lists. Book I, Chapter 2 explains commands for formatting text in OneNote and the other Office programs.

✦ **Styles:** On the Home tab, styles present an easy way to format text. Click in the text you want to format, open the Styles gallery, and choose an option, as shown in Figure 2-11. Choose Heading 1, for example, to make a heading on a note stand out.

✦ **Tables:** On the Insert tab, click the Table button and choose how many columns and rows you want for your table on the drop-down list. Then enter the table data. The (Table Tools) Layout tab offers commands for laying out the table. These commands are described in Book I, Chapter 5.

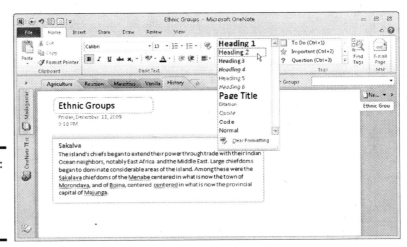

Figure 2-11: Choose a style in the Styles gallery.

Choosing your default font

By default, notes appear in Calibri font and are 11 points high (Book I, Chapter 2 explains what fonts and font size are). Does this font and font size do the job for you?

If it doesn't, you can change the default font and font size by following these steps:

1. **On the File tab, choose Options.**

The OneNote Options dialog box opens.

2. **In the General category, open the Font drop-down list and choose a font.**

3. **Open the Size drop-down list and choose a font size.**

4. **Click OK.**

Docking the OneNote Screen

In OneNote lingo, "docking" means to shunt the OneNote window to the side so that you can take notes on what is in the middle of the screen, as shown in Figure 2-12. Docking is a convenient way to be two places at one time. While looking at a Web site or report, you can also see the OneNote screen and take notes there.

Dock to Desktop button

Figure 2-12: Docking the OneNote screen makes taking notes on Web sites and documents easier.

Use these techniques to dock the OneNote screen:

✦ Click the Dock to Desktop button on the Quick Access toolbar.

✦ Press Ctrl+Alt+D.

✦ On the View tab, click the Dock to Desktop button.

While the OneNote screen is docked, you can adjust its size by dragging its left side toward or away from the center of your screen.

To "undock" the OneNote screen, click the Dock to Desktop button on the Quick Access toolbar or press Ctrl+Alt+D.

Jotting down a side note

Suppose you're brainstorming and come up with an idea that cries out to be preserved in a note. To quickly jot down your note, write a "side note" in the small but convenient Side Note window. This window works in cahoots with OneNote to help you record ideas before you forget them. When you enter a note in the window, it's entered as well in OneNote in the Unfiled Notes folder. Next time you open OneNote, you can go to the Unfiled Notes folder, locate your note, and copy or move it to another folder.

To open the Side Note window, click the OneNote icon in the Notification area or press Windows key+N. Enter your note and then click the Close button in the Side Note window.

To find your note the next time you open OneNote, click the Unfiled Notes button. You can find this button near the bottom of the Navigation bar. Your note is filed away on a page named after the note you entered.

If the OneNote icon isn't in the Notification area, go to the File tab in OneNote and choose Options. In the Options dialog box, go to the Display tab and select the Place OneNote Icon in the Notification Area of the Taskbar check box

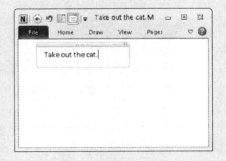

Chapter 3: Finding and Organizing Your Notes

In This Chapter

✔ Finding lost notes

✔ Tagging notes so that you can organize them better

✔ Using colors to identify notebooks, sections, and pages

✔ Moving and copying sections, pages, and notes

*I*f you're an habitual note taker, you may find yourself drowning in notes. You won't be able to find the note you're looking for. The great idea you had may be lost forever. How do you find the notes you want to review? More important, how can you organize your notes to make finding and recognizing them easier?

This chapter looks at how to organize your notes so that you can find them in a hurry. It tells you how to search for notes, tag notes to make finding them easier, color-code notebooks and sections, and merge and move sections, pages, and notes. You also discover OneNote's Recycle Bin, where sections and pages go to die unless you revive them.

Finding a Stray Note

Notes have a tendency to stray. I'm not saying they move from page to page or section by section on their own in the dead of night, but it sometimes seems that way. To track down and find a stray note, you can search by word or phrase or search by author name. Better keep reading.

Searching by word or phrase

As long as you can remember a word or two in a note, you can find it. Follow these steps to chase down a lost note:

1. **Click in the Search box.**

This box is located to the right of the Section tabs, above the Page pane, as shown in Figure 3-1. As soon as you click in the Search box, a menu opens for telling OneNote where you want to search.

Search box

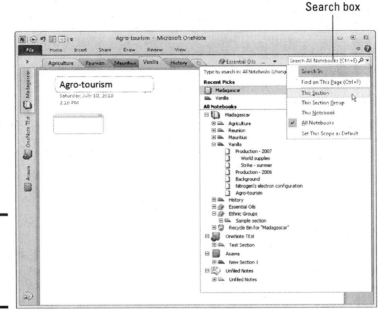

Figure 3-1:
Choosing
where to
conduct a
search.

2. **To declare where you want to search for the note, click the Change Search Scope button (it's on the right side of the Search box) and choose This Section, This Notebook, or another option on the drop-down list, as shown in Figure 3-1.**

   You can also open this drop-down list by clicking the Type to Search In hyperlink.

3. **Enter the word or phrase you're looking for in the Search box.**

4. **Click the Find button.**

   OneNote lists all notes with the text you entered.

5. **Click a note to go to the page where it is located.**

Searching by author

Another way to search is by author name. If you share your OneNote files with others, you can search for notes written by different authors by following these steps:

1. **If you want to search only in one section or section group, go to the section or section group.**

2. **On the Share tab, click the Find by Author button.**

   The Search Results pane opens. It lists notes by author name, as shown in Figure 3-2. If you see the note you're looking for, click it now.

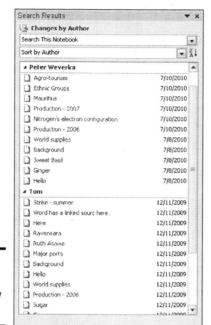

Figure 3-2:
Searching
for notes by
author.

3. **Open the first drop-down list and declare where to search.**

   If you opened a section or section group in Step 1, you can choose
   Search This Section or Search This Section Group to narrow your search
   to a group or section group.

4. **Click a note in the Search Results list.**

   OneNote opens the page with the note you clicked so that you can read
   the note.

Tagging Notes for Follow Up

The best way to keep notes from getting lost is to carefully place them in
notebooks, sections, and pages. Short of that, you can tag notes to make it
easier to follow up on them. OneNote offers numerous ways to tag notes.
After you tag a note, you can search for it by opening the Tags Summary task
pane, arranging notes according to how they were tagged, and pinpointing
the note you want, as shown in Figure 3-3.

Choose how to arrange tagged notes

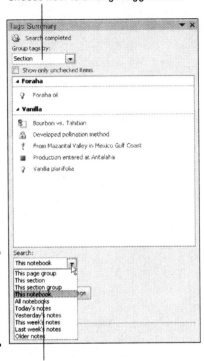

Figure 3-3:
Tag notes
so that you
can track
them better.

Choose where to look for notes

Tagging a note

Follow these steps to tag a note:

1. **Select the note.**

2. **On the Home tab, open the Tags gallery and choose a tag.**

    All options except Remember for Later and Definition place an icon on the note. The aforementioned options highlight the note text, respectively, in yellow or green. Later in this chapter, "Creating and modifying a tag" shows you how to add a tag of your own to the Tags gallery.

To remove tags from notes, select the notes and press Ctrl+0 (zero), or open the drop-down list on the Tags gallery and choose Remove Tag.

Arranging tagged notes in the task pane

Follow these steps to arrange notes that you tagged in the Tags Summary task pane:

1. **On the Home tab, click the Find Tags button.**

   You see the Tags Summary task pane (refer to Figure 3-3).

2. **Open the Group Tags By drop-down list and choose an option.**

   These options determine the order in which tagged notes appear in the task pane. Tag Name, for example, arranges notes according to which icon they're tagged with; Section arranges notes under section names; Note Text arranges notes in alphabetical order.

3. **Open the Search drop-down list and choose an option.**

   These options determine which notes appear in the task pane. This Section, for example, assembles only flagged notes from the section that appears on-screen; This Notebook gathers flagged notes from all sections in the notebook you're viewing.

   A list of notes appears in the task pane.

4. **Click the name of a note you want to visit.**

   OneNote opens the page with the note whose name you clicked and selects the note.

Creating and modifying tags

If the tags in the Tags gallery don't do the trick, you can create a tag of your own. Do so either by modifying a tag that is already there or creating a new tag from scratch. Follow these steps to create a tag:

1. **On the Home tab, open the Tags gallery and choose Customize Tags.**

   You see the Customize Tags dialog box, shown in Figure 3-4.

2. **Choose to modify a tag or create a new tag.**

   You've come to a fork in the road:

   - *Creating a new tag:* Click the New Tag button. The New Tag dialog box appears, as shown in Figure 3-4.

   - *Modifying a tag:* Select a tag you don't need in the dialog box and then click the Modify Tag button. The Modify Tag dialog box appears (it looks and works just like the New Tag dialog box shown in Figure 3-4).

3. **Enter a name for your tag in the Display Name text box.**

4. **Choose a symbol for the tag.**

5. **If you want, choose a font and highlight color.**

6. **Click OK.**

To remove a tag you created, select it in the Customize Tags dialog box and click the Remove button. To change the order of tabs in the Tags gallery, open the Customize Tags dialog box, select a tag, and click the Move Tag Up or Move Tag Down button until the tag is where you want it to be.

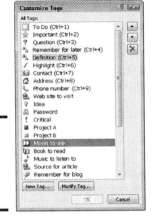
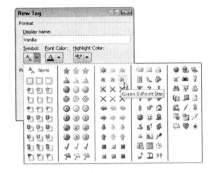

Figure 3-4:
Giving a
name and
icon to a
tag.

Color-Coding Notebooks, Sections, and Pages

If color-coding notebooks, sections, and pages helps you understand what
is in your notebooks, sections, and pages, by all means start color-coding.
Devise a color scheme for assigning colors to different topics and then
follow these instructions to color-code your notebooks, sections, and pages:

✦ **Notebook:** Right-click the notebook's name in the Navigation bar and
choose Properties. The Notebook Properties dialog box appears, as
shown in Figure 3-5. Choose a color on the Color drop-down list and
click OK.

✦ **Section:** Right-click a section's name in the Navigation bar or on a section tab and choose Section Color on the drop-down list. Then, on the
submenu, choose a color.

✦ **Page:** On the View tab, click the Page Color button and choose a color
on the drop-down list.

Figure 3-5:
Color-
coding a
notebook.

Merging and Moving Sections, Pages, and Notes

I hope that as you take notes, you find opportunities to combine sections and pages. Combining sections and pages means you're synthesizing your ideas. What used to be a sprawling mass of assorted notes is turning into a handful of rock-solid concepts. Here are instructions for merging sections, moving pages to other sections, and moving notes to different pages:

✦ **Merging one section into another:** On the Navigation bar or on a section tab, right-click the name of the section you want to merge with another section. On the shortcut menu, choose Merge into Another Section. You see the Merge Section dialog box. Choose a section and click the Merge button.

✦ **Moving a page to another section:** Right-click the page's tab and choose Move or Copy (or press Ctrl+Alt+M). You see the Move or Copy Pages dialog box. Select a section name and click the Move or Copy button.

✦ **Moving notes to another page:** Use the tried-and-true cut-and-paste method. Select the note, right-click, choose Cut, right-click the page where you want to move the note, and choose Paste.

Visiting the Recycle Bin

OneNote maintains a Recycle Bin of its own. If you mistakenly delete a section or page, you can recover it by going to the Share tab and clicking the Notebook Recycle Bin button. Sections and pages you deleted appear (deleted pages appear on the Deleted Pages tab).

Follow these steps to restore a section or page:

1. **On the Share tab, click the Notebook Recycle Bin button.**

2. **Right-click the section or page you want to restore and choose Move or Copy.**

   You see the Move or Copy dialog box.

3. **Select the notebook or section where you want to restore the deleted item.**

4. **Click the Move button.**

Book VI

Office 2010: One Step Beyond

"I hate when you bring 'Office' with you on camping trips."

Contents at a Glance

Chapter 1: Customizing an Office Program 511

Customizing the Ribbon......................511
Customizing the Quick Access
 Toolbar...516
Customizing the Status Bar...............518
Changing the Color Scheme...............519
Customizing Keyboard Shortcuts
 in Word 520

Chapter 2: Ways of Distributing Your Work 523

Printing — the Old Standby................523
Distributing a File in PDF Format.......524
Saving an Office File as a Web Page...526
Blogging from inside Word 528

Chapter 3: Handling Graphics 531

All about Picture File Formats............531
The All-Important Copyright Issue 534
Inserting a Picture in an Office File....535
Touching Up a Picture........................536
Compressing Pictures to Save
 Disk Space 543
Using Microsoft Office
 Picture Manager 544

Chapter 4: Decorating Files with Clip Art. 551

What Is Clip Art?.................................551
Inserting a Clip-Art Image...................552
Handling Media Files with
 the Clip Organizer 553

Chapter 5: Automating Tasks with Macros 561

What Is a Macro?................................561
Displaying the Developer Tab 561
Managing the Macro Security
 Problem 562
Recording a Macro..............................564
Running a Macro 567
Editing a Macro 568

Chapter 6: Linking and Embedding in Compound Files 571

What Is OLE, Anyway?.........................571
Linking to Data in a Source File..........574
Embedding Data from
 Other Programs 577

Chapter 7: Office Web Apps 581

Introducing the Office Web Apps.......581
Storing and Sharing Files on
 the Internet...................................582
Office Web Apps: The Big Picture......583
Getting Ready to Use the
 Office Web Apps 584
Signing In to Windows Live.................584
Navigating to the SkyDrive
 Window 584
Managing Your Folders 585
Creating an Office File in SkyDrive.....589
Opening and Editing Office
 Files Stored on SkyDrive................590
Managing Your Files on SkyDrive 594
Ways of Sharing Folders:
 The Big Picture 597
Making Friends on Windows Live 598
Understanding the Folder Types 601
Establishing a Folder's
 Share With Permissions.................604
Sharing on a Public or
 Shared Folder................................606
Writing File Comments
 and Descriptions 610
Coauthoring Files Shared
 on SkyDrive 611

Chapter 1: Customizing an Office Program

In This Chapter

✔ **Personalizing the Ribbon**

✔ **Changing around the Quick Access toolbar**

✔ **Choosing what appears on the status bar**

✔ **Choosing a new color scheme**

✔ **Devising keyboard shortcuts in Word**

This short chapter describes a handful of things you can do to customize Office 2010 programs. Don't be afraid to make like a software developer and change a program to your liking. Many people are wary of retooling Office programs, but you can always reverse the changes you make if you don't like them, as I explain throughout this chapter.

This chapter shows how to put your favorite button commands on the Ribbon and Quick Access toolbar. Instead of fishing around for your favorite commands, you can assemble them on the Ribbon or Quick Access toolbar and locate them right away. You also discover how to change around the status bar, dress up an Office program in a new set of clothes, and designate your own keyboard shortcuts in Word.

Customizing the Ribbon

As you surely know by now, the Ribbon is the stretch of ground across the top of all Office programs. The Ribbon is composed of tabs. On each tab, commands are arranged by group. To undertake a task, you visit a tab on the Ribbon, find the group with the command you want, and choose the command. If you are so inclined, you can customize the Ribbon. You can place the tabs and commands you know and love where you want to find them on the Ribbon. And you can remove tabs and commands that aren't useful to you.

To customize the Ribbon, open the Customize Ribbon tab of the Options dialog box with one of these techniques:

✦ On the File tab, choose Options, and select the Customize Ribbon cate-
      gory in the Options dialog box.

   ✦ Right-click a tab or button and choose Customize the Ribbon.

You see commands for customizing the Ribbon, as shown in Figure 1-1. The
right side of the dialog box ("Customize the Ribbon") lists the names of tabs,
groups within tabs, and commands within groups that are currently on the
Ribbon. To customize the Ribbon, you arrange the right side of the dialog
box to your liking. You list the tabs, groups, and commands that you want
for the Ribbon on the right side of the dialog box.

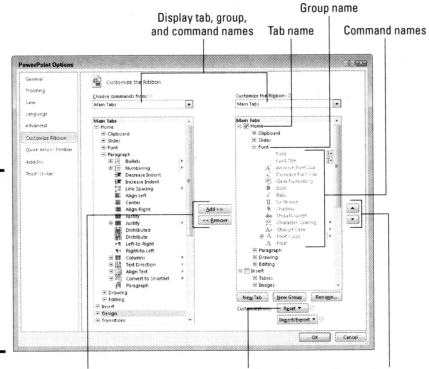

Figure 1-1:
Starting
in the
Customize
Ribbon
category of
the Options
dialog box,
you can
customize
the Ribbon.

The left side of the dialog box ("Choose Commands From") presents every
tab, group, and command in your Office program. To customize the Ribbon,
you select a tab, group, or command on the left side of the dialog box and
move it to the right side.

Keep reading to find out how to display tabs, groups, and commands in the
Options dialog box and how to do all else that pertains to customizing the

Ribbon. In case you make a hash of the Ribbon, you also find instructions for restoring the Ribbon to its original state.

Displaying and selecting tab, group, and command names

To customize the Ribbon, you need to display and select tab names, group names, and command names in the Options dialog box (refer to Figure 1-1). Start by opening the drop-down lists and choosing a display option:

✦ **Choose Commands From:** Choose an option to locate the tab, group, or command you want to add to the Ribbon. For example, choose All Commands to see an alphabetical list of all the commands in the Office program you're working in; choose Main Tabs to see a list of tabs.

✦ **Customize the Ribbon:** Choose an option to display the names of all tabs, main tabs, or tool tabs. Tool tabs are the context-sensitive tabs that appear after you insert or click something. For example, the Table Tools tabs appear when you construct tables.

After you choose display options on the drop-down lists, display the names of groups and commands (refer to Figure 1-1):

✦ **Displaying group names:** Click a plus sign icon next to a tab name to see the names of its groups. You can click the minus sign icon to fold group names back into a tab name.

✦ **Displaying command names in groups:** Click the plus sign icon next to a group name to see the names of its commands. You can click the minus sign icon to collapse command names.

After you display the tab, group, or command name, click to select it.

Moving tabs and groups on the Ribbon

To change the order of tabs on the Ribbon or groups on a tab, go to the Customize Ribbon category of the Options dialog box (refer to Figure 1-1) and select the name of a tab or group on the right side of the dialog box. Then click the Move Up or Move Down button. Click these buttons as necessary until tabs or groups are in the order that you see fit.

Be careful about moving groups by clicking the Move Up or Move Down button. Clicking these buttons too many times can move a group to a different tab on the Ribbon.

Adding, removing, and renaming tabs, groups, and commands

In the Options dialog box (refer to Figure 1-1), display and select the tab, group, or command you want to add, remove, or rename. Then proceed to add, remove, or rename it. (Earlier in this chapter, "Displaying and selecting tab, group, and command names" explains how to display items in the Options dialog box.)

Adding items to the Ribbon

Follow these steps to add a tab, group, or command to the Ribbon:

1. **On the left side of the Customize Ribbon tab of the Options dialog box, select the tab, group, or command you want to add.**

   For example, to add the Tables group to the Home tab, select the Tables group.

2. **On the right side of the dialog box, select the tab or group where you want to place the item.**

   If you're adding a tab to the Ribbon, select a tab. The tab you add will go after the tab you select.

3. **Click the Add button.**

Removing items from the Ribbon

Follow these steps to remove a tab, group, or command from the Ribbon:

1. **On the right side of the Customize Ribbon tab of the Options dialog box, select the tab, group, or command you want to remove.**

2. **Click the Remove button.**

   Except for tabs you create yourself, you can't remove tabs from the Ribbon. And you can't remove a command unless you remove it from a group you created yourself.

Renaming tabs and groups

Sorry, you can't rename a command. As for tabs and groups, you can rename them, but only if you created them yourself. Tabs and groups that came with Office can't be renamed. Follow these steps to rename a tab or group:

1. **On the right side of the Customize Ribbon tab of the Options dialog box, select the tab or group you want to rename.**

2. **Click the Rename button.**

   You see the Rename dialog box.

3. **Enter a new name and click OK.**

Creating new tabs and groups

Create new tabs and groups on the Ribbon for commands that are especially useful to you. Follow these steps on the Customize Ribbon tab of the Options dialog box (refer to Figure 1-1) to create a new tab or group:

1. **On the right side of the dialog box, display and select the name of a tab or group.**

   Earlier in this chapter, "Displaying and selecting tab, group, and command names" explains how to select items in the Options dialog box.

   - *Tab:* If you're creating a tab, select a tab name. The tab you create will appear after the tab you select.

   - *Group:* If you're creating a group, select a group name. The group you create will appear after the group you select.

2. **Click the New Tab or New Group button.**

   Your Office program creates a new tab or group called "New Tab (Custom)" or "New Group (Custom)." If you created a tab, Office also creates a new group inside your new tab.

3. **Click the Rename button to give the tab, group, or both a name.**

   In the Rename dialog box, enter a descriptive name and click OK. If you're naming a group, the Rename dialog box gives you the opportunity to select an icon to help identify the group.

4. **Add groups, commands, or both to your newly made tab or group.**

   For instructions, see "Adding items to the Ribbon," earlier in this chapter.

Resetting your Ribbon customizations

If you make a hash of the Ribbon, all is not lost because you can restore the original settings. In the Options dialog box, click the Reset button (refer to Figure 1-1) and choose one of these commands on the drop-down list:

- **Reset Only Selected Ribbon Tab:** Select a tab name on the right side of the Options dialog box and choose this command to restore a tab to its original state.

- **Reset All Customizations:** Choose this command to restore the Ribbon in its entirety. All changes you made are reversed.

You can also remove tabs and groups you created if you discover you don't need them. See "Removing items from the Ribbon," earlier in this chapter. At the end of this chapter, the sidebar "Exporting and importing program customizations" explains how you can trade your customizations with others.

Customizing the Quick Access Toolbar

No matter where you go in Office, you see the Quick Access toolbar in the upper-left corner of the screen. This toolbar offers the Save, Undo, and Repeat buttons. However, which buttons appear on the Quick Access toolbar is entirely up to you. You can put your favorite buttons on the toolbar to keep them within reach. And if the Quick Access toolbar gets too big, you can move it below the Ribbon, as shown in Figure 1-2. Adding buttons to and removing buttons from the Quick Access toolbar is, I'm happy to report, a piece of cake. And moving the toolbar below the Ribbon is as easy as pie.

Right-click a button to add it to the toolbar

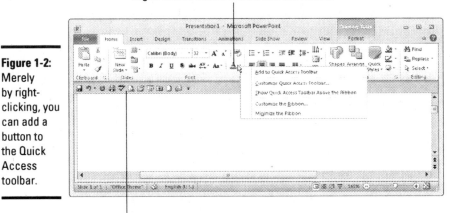

Figure 1-2:
Merely
by right-
clicking, you
can add a
button to
the Quick
Access
toolbar.

The Quick Access toolbar below the Ribbon

Adding buttons to the Quick Access toolbar

Use one of these techniques to add buttons to the Quick Access toolbar:

✦ Right-click a button you want to see on the toolbar and choose Add to Quick Access Toolbar on the shortcut menu (refer to Figure 1-2). You can add all the commands in a group to the Quick Access toolbar by right-clicking the group name and choosing Add to Quick Access Toolbar.

✦ Click the Customize Quick Access Toolbar button (this button is located to the right of the Quick Access toolbar) and choose a button on the drop-down list. The list offers buttons deemed most likely to be placed on the Quick Access toolbar by the makers of Office.

✦ On the File tab, choose Options, and go to the Quick Access Toolbar category in the Options dialog box (or right-click any button or tab and choose Customize Quick Access Toolbar on the shortcut menu). You see the Quick Access Toolbar category of the Options dialog box, as shown in Figure 1-3. On the Choose Commands From drop-down list, select the name of the tab with the button you want to add to the Quick Access toolbar. Then select the button's name and click the Add button.

Select a tab   Select a button and click Add

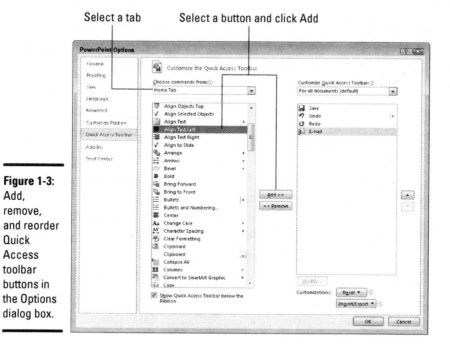

Figure 1-3:
Add,
remove,
and reorder
Quick
Access
toolbar
buttons in
the Options
dialog box.

To restore the Quick Access toolbar to its original buttons, click the
Reset button in the Options dialog box (see Figure 1-3) and choose Reset
Only Quick Access Toolbar on the drop-down list. Choosing Reset All
Customizations resets Ribbon customizations as well as Quick Access tool-
bar customizations.

Changing the order of buttons on the Quick Access toolbar

Follow these steps to change the order of buttons on the Quick Access toolbar:

1. **Click the Customize Quick Access Toolbar button and choose More
   Commands on the drop-down list.**

   The Quick Access Toolbar category of the Options dialog box appears
   (see Figure 1-3). You can also open this dialog box by right-clicking any
   button or tab and choosing Customize Quick Access Toolbar.

2. **Select the name of a button on the right side of the dialog box and
   click the Move Up or Move Down button.**

3. **Repeat Step 2 until the buttons are in the right order.**

4. **Click OK.**

Removing buttons from the Quick Access toolbar

Use one of these techniques to remove buttons from the Quick Access toolbar:

✦ Right-click a button and choose Remove from Quick Access Toolbar on the shortcut menu.

✦ Right-click any button or tab and choose Customize Quick Access Toolbar. You see the Quick Access Toolbar category of the Options dialog box (refer to Figure 1-3). Select the button you want to remove on the right side of the dialog box and click the Remove button.

You can click the Reset button in the Options dialog box (refer to Figure 1-3) to remove all the buttons you placed on the Quick Access toolbar.

Placing the Quick Access toolbar above or below the Ribbon

The Ribbon is the stretch of ground along the top of the screen where the tabs and buttons are found. If your Quick Access toolbar contains many buttons, consider placing it below the Ribbon, not above it (refer to Figure 1-2). Follow these instructions to place the Quick Access toolbar above or below the Ribbon:

✦ **Quick Access toolbar below the Ribbon:** Right-click the toolbar, and on the shortcut menu, choose Show Quick Access Toolbar Below the Ribbon.

✦ **Quick Access toolbar above the Ribbon:** Right-click the toolbar, and on the shortcut menu, choose Show Quick Access Toolbar Above the Ribbon.

The Options dialog box offers a check box called Show Quick Access Toolbar Below the Ribbon (refer to Figure 1-3). You can select this check box as well to move the toolbar below the Ribbon.

Customizing the Status Bar

The status bar along the bottom of the window gives you information about the file you're working on. The Word status bar, for example, tells you which page you're on and how many pages are in your document, among other things. In PowerPoint, the status bar tells you which slide you're looking at and the theme you chose for your presentation. The status bar also presents the view buttons and Zoom controls.

To choose what appears on the status bar, right-click the status bar. You see a drop-down list similar to the one in Figure 1-4. By selecting and deselecting items in this list, you can decide what appears on the status bar.

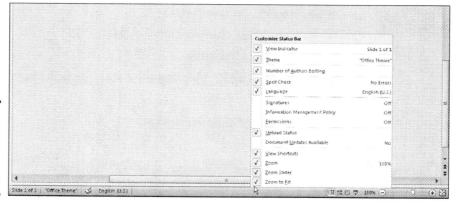

Figure 1-4:
Right-click
the status
bar to
customize it.

Changing the Color Scheme

Figure 1-5 shows three color schemes with which you can dress up Excel, Word, OneNote, and PowerPoint: Blue, Silver, and Black. Which do you prefer? Follow these steps to choose a color scheme:

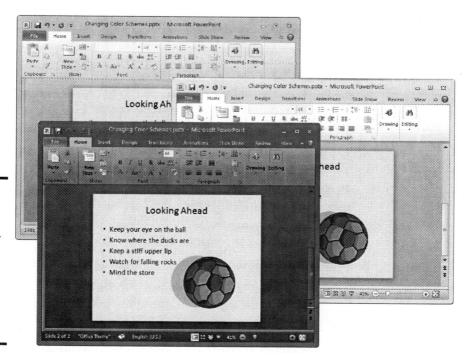

Figure 1-5:
Take your
choice of
these color
schemes:
Blue (top),
Silver
(middle),
or Black
(bottom).

File

1. **On the File tab, choose Options.**

   You see the Options dialog box.

2. **Select the General category.**

3. **Open the Color Scheme drop-down list and choose Blue, Silver, or Black.**

4. **Click OK.**

   How do you like your new get-up?

Customizing Keyboard Shortcuts in Word

In Microsoft Word, you can change the keyboard shortcuts. A *keyboard short-cut* is a combination of keys that you press to give a command. For example, pressing Ctrl+P opens the Print window; pressing Ctrl+S gives the Save command. If you don't like a keyboard shortcut in Word, you can change it and invent a keyboard shortcut of your own. You can also assign keyboard short-cuts to symbols, macros, fonts, AutoText entries, and styles.

Follow these steps to choose keyboard shortcuts of your own in Microsoft Word:

File

1. **On the File tab, choose Options.**

   You see the Word Options dialog box.

2. **Go to the Customize Ribbon category.**

3. **Click the Customize button (you can find it at the bottom of the dialog box next to the words "Keyboard Shortcuts").**

   You see the Customize Keyboard dialog box, as shown in Figure 1-6.

4. **In the Categories list, choose the category with the command to which you want to assign the keyboard shortcut.**

   At the bottom of the list are the Macros, Fonts, AutoText, Styles, and Common Symbols categories.

5. **Choose the command name, macro, font, AutoText entry, style, or symbol name in the Commands list.**

6. **In the Press New Shortcut Key box, type the keyboard shortcut.**

   Press the actual keys. For example, if the shortcut is Ctrl+8, press the Ctrl key and the 8 key — don't type out C-t-r-l+8.

   If you try to assign a shortcut that has already been assigned, the words "Currently assigned to" and a command name appear below the Current Keys box. You can override the preassigned keyboard assignment by entering a keyboard assignment of your own.

Exporting and importing program customizations

You can preserve your Ribbon and Quick Access toolbar customizations for posterity in a special file called an Import Customization file; these files have the `.exportedUI` file extension. Keep the file on hand for when you need it, or distribute the file to co-workers. For that matter, a co-worker who is proud of his or her customizations can send them to you in a file and you can load the customizations into your Office program.

To save your Ribbon and Quick Access toolbar customization settings in a file, go to the File tab, choose Options, and visit to the Customize Ribbon or Quick Access Toolbar category of the Options dialog box. Then click the Import/Export button and choose Export All Customizations on the drop-down list. The File Save dialog box opens. Give the customizations file a name and click the Save button.

To load customizations from a file into your Office program, return to the Customize Ribbon or Quick Access Toolbar category of the Options dialog box, click the Import/Export button, and choose Import Customization File. You see the File Open dialog box. Select the file and click the Open button.

**Book VI
Chapter 1**

Customizing
an Office Program

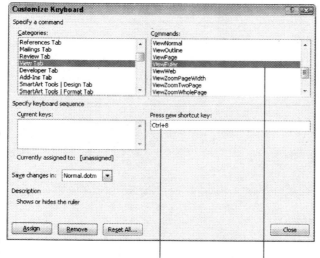

Figure 1-6:
Assigning
keyboard
shortcuts
to Word
commands.

Enter the shortcut   Select a command

7. **If you want the keyboard shortcut changes you make to apply to the document you're working on, not to all documents created with the template you're working with, open the Save Changes In drop-down list and choose your document's name.**

8. **Click the Assign button.**

9. **When you finish assigning keyboard shortcuts, close the Customize Keyboard dialog box.**

To delete a keyboard shortcut, display it in the Current Keys box, select it, and click the Remove button.

You can always get the old keyboard shortcuts back by clicking the Reset All button in the Customize Keyboard dialog box.

Chapter 2: Ways of Distributing Your Work

In This Chapter

✔ **Printing files**

✔ **Saving files so that others can read them in Adobe Acrobat Reader**

✔ **Saving a file so that it can be viewed in a Web browser**

✔ **Writing and keeping a blog from inside Word**

This chapter explains how to distribute your work to co-workers and friends. You'll be glad to know that people who don't have Office 2010 can still read and review an Office 2010 file you created. You can print it for them, save it so that it can be read in Adobe Acrobat Reader, or save it as a Web page. This chapter explains all that as well as how to write and post blog entries from inside Word.

By the way, Book III, Chapter 5 describes other ways to distribute PowerPoint presentations. You can provide audience handouts, ship presentations on CDs, and save presentations as video files.

Printing — the Old Standby

In spite of predictions to the contrary, the paperless office is still a pipe dream. The day when Johnny at his computer is completely digitized and communicating with his colleagues without having to print anything on paper has yet to materialize. As for Jane, she can hardly go a day without printing reports, spreadsheets, and brochures. The office is still awash in paper, and all Jane and Johnny can do for consolation is try their best to recycle.

File

To print a file, preview a file before you print it, and do all else that pertains to printing, go to the File tab and choose Print (or press Ctrl+P). You land in the Print window, as shown in Figure 2-1. From here, you can choose how many copies to print, choose a part of a file to print, and get a look at your file before you print it. Notice that the Print window offers Zoom control buttons and buttons for going from page to page (or slide to slide).

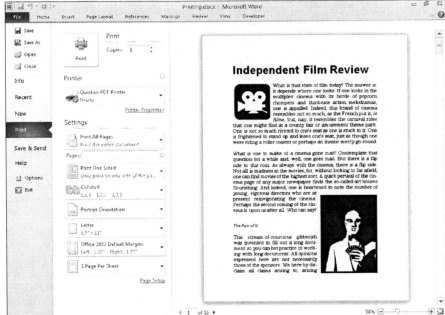

Figure 2-1:
Starting in
the Print
window, you
can preview
and print
files.

Distributing a File in PDF Format

As shown in Figure 2-2, you can save and distribute a file in the PDF
(Portable Document File) format if the person to whom you want to give
the file doesn't have the program with which it was created. For example,
someone who doesn't have Excel can still view your Excel file in PDF format.
Moreover, you can post PDF files on the Internet so that others can view
them there.

About PDF files

PDF files are designed to be viewed and printed in a program called Adobe
Reader. This program is very good at acquiring data from other programs
and presenting it so that it can be read and printed easily. Nearly every computer has Adobe Reader. If someone to whom you sent a PDF file doesn't
have the program, they can download it for free at this Web page:

```
http://get.adobe.com/reader/
```

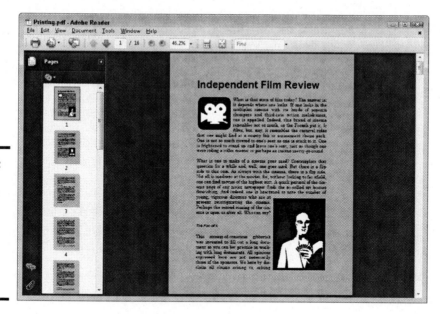

Figure 2-2:
A Word
document
as seen
through
the eyes
of Adobe
Acrobat
Reader.

Saving an Office file as a PDF

Follow these steps to save an Office file as a PDF file:

File

1. **Go to the File tab and choose Save & Send to open the Save & Send window.**

2. **Choose Create PDF/XPS Document.**

3. **Click the Create a PDF/XPS button.**

   The Publish as PDF or XPS dialog box appears. If your goal is to create an XPS file, not a PDF file, open the Save As Type drop-down list and choose XPS Document (*.xps). Microsoft created the XPS format to compete with the PDF format. As are PDF files, XPS files are meant to present data from different programs, in this case in Internet Explorer. However, the XPS format is not nearly as well known or frequently used as the PDF format.

4. **Select a folder for storing your PDF (or XPS) file, give it a name, and click the Publish button.**

   The Adobe Reader program opens and you see your file. (If you created an XPS file, Internet Explorer opens.)

Later in this chapter, "Saving an Office File as a Web Page" explains another way to distribute Office files to people who don't have Office — by saving the files as Web pages.

Saving an Office File as a Web Page

Figure 2-3 shows what a Word document looks like after it is saved as a Web page and displayed in a Web browser. Looks like a normal Word document, doesn't it? Anyone with a Web browser can view a Word document or other Office file after it's saved as a Web page. Save an Office file as a Web page and post it on the Internet so that people who don't have Office can view it.

These pages explain the different ways to save an Office file as a Web page, as well as how to save your Office file as a Web page and open a Web page you created in a Web browser.

Choosing how to save the component parts

When you save an Office file as a Web page, you have the choice of saving it as a Single File Web Page (.mht, .mhtml) or Web Page (.htm, .html).

✦ **Single File Web Page (**.mht, .mhtml**):** All component parts of the file — graphics, separate pages, and sounds, for example — are bundled into a single file. Keeping all the component parts in one file makes moving, copying, and sending the file easier. However, only the Internet Explorer browser can open and read .mht and .mhtml files. The popular Mozilla Firefox and Opera browsers can't handle them.

✦ **Web Page (**.htm, .html**):** All the component parts of the file are kept in separate files and are saved in the same folder. Keeping the component parts in separate files is the standard way to present pages on the Internet. Handling the half-dozen or more files that are needed to display the Web page can be troublesome, but you can be certain that the Web page displays properly in all browsers.

Turning a file into a Web page

Before you save your file as a Web page, create a folder on your computer or computer network for storing the page if you intend to save it in several files in the .htm format. Unless you create a folder for storing all the files, you'll have a hard time locating them later, and you must be able to locate them to transfer them to a Web server for display on the Internet or to send them to someone else.

Follow these steps to save an Office file as a Web page:

1. Go to the File tab and choose Save & Send.

The Save & Send window opens.

2. Choose Change File Type.

Change File Type options appear on the right side of the window.

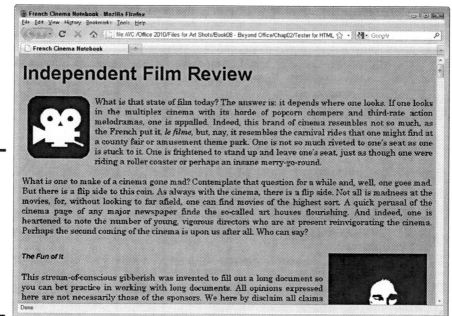

Figure 2-3:
A Word
document
saved as a
Web page,
as seen
through
the eyes
of a Web
browser.

3. **Save your file as a single file Web page or Web page.**

   The previous topic in this chapter, "Choosing how to save the component parts," explains the difference between the two.

   - *Single file Web page:* Choose the Single File Web Page option and click the Save As button. The Save As dialog box opens.

   - *Web page:* Choose the Save as Another File Type option, click the Save As button, and in the Save As dialog box, open the Save as Type drop-down list and choose Web Page.

4. **In the Save As dialog box, click the Change Title button, enter a descriptive title in the Enter Text dialog box, and click OK.**

   The title you enter will appear in the title bar along the top of the Web browser window.

5. **Choose a folder for storing your new Web page.**

   If you followed my advice about creating a Web page, choose the folder you recently created for storing the page and its attendant files.

6. **Click the Save button.**

   If your file includes features that can't be displayed in a Web browser, the Compatibility Checker dialog box tells you what those features are. Click the Continue button to create your Web page.

Opening a Web page in your browser

To open a Web page you fashioned from an Office file, open the folder where you stored the Web page in Computer or Windows Explorer and double-click the .htm or .mht file. For example, if your file is called Sales Projections, double-click the Sales Projections.htm or Sales Projections.mht file to open the Web page.

Blogging from inside Word

The word *blog* is shorthand for *Web log.* A typical blog is a hodgepodge of commentary and links to online news sources and often other blogs where topics of concern to the blogger are discussed. Many blogs are online diaries. You get a daily picture of what the blogger is interested in — dating, technology, politics, and just about anything else under the sun.

To make it easier to keep a blog, Word offers special commands for writing blog entries and posting them immediately with a blogging service. Figure 2-4 shows the blogging feature in action. The title and the blog entry in the Word document are transported *in toto* to the blog without your having to enter a password or even visit a blogging service. What's more, Word offers a special Blog Post tab for posting blog entries and managing accounts with your blogging service. To take advantage of Word's blogging feature, you must already have an account with a blogging service.

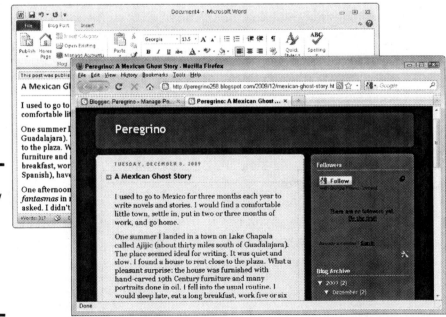

Figure 2-4:
A blog entry written in Word (left) and posted to a blogging service (right).

Describing a blog account to Word

Word can't post entries to a blog unless you tell it where the blog is located, what your password is, and some other juicy tidbits. As of this writing, Word is compatible with these blogging services: Blogger, Community Server, Sharepoint Blog, TypePad, and WordPress.

Follow these steps to register your blogging account with Word so that Word can upload blog entries:

File

1. **Go to the File tab and choose Share.**

   The Share window opens.

2. **Choose Publish as Blog Post.**

3. **Click the Publish as Blog Post button.**

   You see the Register a Blog Account dialog box.

4. **Click the Register Now button and answer questions in the dialog box to describe the blogging service you use.**

   Which questions you are asked depends on which blogging service you use. You're asked for a username and password, and also perhaps an http or ftp address for publishing pictures on your blog.

After you finish describing your blogging service, you will be pleased to discover a new tab in Word — the Blog Post tab (refer to Figure 2-4). You can use this tab to post blog entries and manage your blog accounts.

Posting an entry to your blog

When you're ready to share your thoughts with the world, follow these steps to write and post an entry to your blog from inside Word:

1. **In Word, write the entry from scratch or open a document you've already written.**

   You can start from a new document, or if you've written the entry, open the Word document with the entry.

File

2. **Go to the File tab, choose Share, choose Publish as Blog Post, and click the Publish as Blog Post button.**

   You land in the Blog Post tab (refer to Figure 2-4). It offers all the character styles and proofing tools that you find in Word. Go to the Insert tab to enter a hyperlink. (Book I, Chapter 2 explains hyperlinks.)

3. **Enter a title for your blog entry in the space provided.**

4. **When you're finished writing and preparing your blog entry, click the Publish button on the Blog Post tab.**

   If all goes well, Word informs you that your post has been published on your blogging service, and it lists the time and date it was published. This information appears in the Word document itself.

Instead of publishing your blog entry right away, you can open the drop-down list on the Publish button and choose Publish as Draft. Doing so uploads the blog entry to your blogging service without posting it. The entry lands on the Editing page, where you can select it, click the Editing button, and edit it online before publishing it.

Taking advantage of the Blog Post tab

By clicking buttons on the Blog Post tab, you can manage blog entries:

+ **Go to your blog page:** Click the Home Page button to open your browser and display the home page of your blog.

+ **Edit a blog entry:** Click the Open Existing button, and in the Open Existing Post dialog box, select a blog entry and click OK. The entry appears in Word. Edit it and click the Publish button to post it on your blog.

+ **Manage accounts:** Click the Manage Accounts button to describe a new account to Word, change a blog account, or remove a blog account. Word provides the Blog Accounts dialog box for doing these activities.

Sending Office files by e-mail

Yet another way to distribute Office files is to distribute them by e-mail. Every e-mail program worth its salt offers commands for sending files along with e-mail messages. In e-mail parlance, sending a file with a message is called "attaching a file."

The only problem with sending Office files by e-mail is that the recipient can't open the file unless he or she has the right Office software. If you're sending a Word or Excel file, you can get around this problem by saving the file in a neutral file format that non-Office programs can read. Follow these steps in Word or Excel to save a file in a different format:

1. **On the File tab, choose Save As to open the Save As dialog box.**

2. **Open the Save As Type drop-down list and choose a neutral file format.**

   In Word, you can choose Rich Text Format (RTF) or Plain Text. Most word processors can open RFT files and all can open plain-text files (although formatting is lost in the plain-text format). In Excel, you can choose Text (Tab Delimited) or CSV (Comma Delimited). All spreadsheet programs can open and read files in the tab- and comma-delimited format.

3. **Click the Save button.**

As for PowerPoint, you needn't worry about sending a PowerPoint presentation to someone who doesn't have PowerPoint. As Book III, Chapter 5 explains, you can save a PowerPoint presentation as a WMV video file or save it so that others can view it with the PowerPoint Viewer.

And OneNote? Sorry, OneNote doesn't translate to a neutral file format. Only people with OneNote can view OneNote files in their native habitat.

Chapter 3: Handling Graphics

In This Chapter

✔ **Understanding the different graphic file formats**

✔ **Placing a graphic in a Word document, PowerPoint slide, Excel worksheet, or OneNote notebook**

✔ **Recoloring, cropping, and otherwise altering a picture**

✔ **Compressing graphics**

✔ **Handling graphics with Office Picture Manager**

A picture, so they say, is worth a thousand words. Whether it's worth a thousand words or merely 950 is debatable. What is certain is that visuals help people remember things. A carefully chosen image in a PowerPoint presentation, Word document, Excel worksheet, or OneNote notebook helps others understand you better. The image reinforces the ideas or information that you're trying to put across.

This chapter explains how you can make pictures — photographs and graphics — part of your Word documents, PowerPoint presentations, Excel worksheets, and OneNote notebooks. It looks into graphic file formats, copyrights, and other issues pertaining to graphics as well as how to touch up graphics in an Office program and in an auxiliary program called Office Picture Manager.

By the way, Chapter 4 of this minibook looks at another way to decorate your work with images — that is, with images called clip art.

All about Picture File Formats

Graphics and photographs come in many different file formats, and as far as Office 2010 is concerned, some are better than others. These pages explain what you need to know about graphic files to use them wisely in Office files. Here, you find out what bitmap and vector graphics are, what resolution and color depth are, and how graphic files are compressed.

Bitmap and vector graphics

All graphic images fall in the bitmap or vector category:

✦ A *bitmap graphic* is composed of thousands upon thousands of tiny dots called *pixels* that, taken together, form an image (the term pixel comes from "picture element").

✦ A *vector graphic* is drawn with the aid of computer instructions that describe the shape and dimension of each line, curve, circle, and so on.

The major difference between the two formats is that vector graphics do not distort when you enlarge or shrink them, whereas bitmap graphics lose resolution when their size is changed. Furthermore, vector images do not require nearly as much disk space as bitmap graphics. Drop a few bitmap graphics in a file and soon you're dealing with a file that is close to 750k in size.

Table 3-1 describes popular bitmap graphic formats; Table 3-2 lists popular vector graphic formats.

Table 3-1	**Bitmap Graphic File Formats**		
Extension	*File Type*	*Color Depth*	*Compression*
BMP, BMZ, DIB	Microsoft Windows Bitmap	To 24-bit	None
GFA, GIF	Graphics Interchange Format	To 8-bit	Lossy
JPEG, JPG, JFIF, JPE	JPEG File Interchange Format	To 24-bit	Lossy
PICT	Macintosh PICT	To 32-bit	None
PNG	Portable Network Graphics	To 48-bit	Lossless
RLE	Bitmap File in RLE Compression Scheme	To 24-bit	None
TIF, TIFF	Tagged Image File Format	To 24-bit	Lossless

Table 3-2	**Vector Graphic File Formats**
Extension	*File Type*
CDR	CorelDRAW
CGM	Computer Graphics Metafile
EMF	Enhanced Windows Metafile
EMZ	Windows Enhanced Metafile
EPS	Encapsulated PostScript
PCT	Macintosh PICT
WMF	Windows Metafile
WPG	WordPerfect Graphics

Resolution

Resolution refers to how many pixels comprise a bitmap image. The higher the resolution, the clearer the image is. Resolution is measured in *dots per inch* (dpi), sometimes called *pixels per inch* (ppi). Images with more dots (or pixels) per inch are clearer and display more fineness of detail. When you scan an image, your scanner permits you to choose a dots-per-inch setting.

High-resolution images look better but require more disk space than low-resolution images. Figure 3-1 illustrates the difference between a high- and low-resolution photograph.

Book VI
Chapter 3

Handling Graphics

Figure 3-1:
A high-resolution photo (left) and the same photo at low resolution (right).

Compression

Compression refers to a mathematical algorithm by which bitmap graphic files can be made smaller. In effect, compression enables your computer to store a bitmap graphic with less disk space. Some bitmap graphic types can't be compressed; the other bitmap graphic types are compressed using either lossless or lossy compression:

+ **Lossless compression:** To maintain the picture's integrity, the same number of pixels is stored in the compressed file as in the original. Because the pixels remain intact, you can change the size of a file that has undergone lossless compression without losing picture quality.

+ **Lossy compression:** Without regard for the picture's integrity, pixel data in the original picture is lost during compression. Therefore, if you try to enlarge a picture that has undergone lossy compression, the picture loses quality.

Choosing file formats for graphics

One of the challenges of using graphics and photographs in Office files is keeping file sizes to a minimum. A file that is loaded down with many photographs can take a long time to load and send over the Internet because graphics and photographs make files that much larger. The trick is to find a balance between high-quality, high-resolution graphics and the need to keep files sizes low. Here are some tips for choosing graphic file formats:

✦ Consider sticking with vector graphics if you're including graphics in your file strictly for decoration purposes. As Chapter 4 of this mini-book explains, Office provides vector clip-art images. These images are easy to come by, don't require very much disk space, and can be edited inside Word, PowerPoint, and Excel.

✦ For photographs, make JPEG your first choice for graphics. JPEG images have a fairly high resolution. If you intend to post your file on the Internet, you can't go wrong with JPEGs; they are the de facto photograph standard on the Internet.

✦ If you're dealing with black-and-white photos or resolution doesn't matter, use GIF files. These files eat up the least amount of disk space.

The All-Important Copyright Issue

To save any image on the Internet to your computer, all you have to do is right-click it and choose Save Picture As. By starting from Google Image Search (www.images.google.com), you can scour the Internet for any image you need. Never before has it been easier to obtain images for your own use.

Still, obtaining images and using them legally are two different matters. Would it surprise you to know that the vast majority of graphics can't be used without the owner's permission? The copyright laws have a "fair use" provision for borrowing written words. You can quote others' words as long as you cite the author and work and you don't quote passages longer than 250 to a thousand words (the "fair use" provision is vague on this point). The copyright law regarding graphics is quite straightforward. Unless you have the owner's permission, you can't legally use a graphic.

Sometimes it's hard to tell who owns a graphic. The artist or photographer (or his or her estate) doesn't necessarily own the copyright because artists sometimes relinquish their copyrights when they create works for hire. The only way to get permission to use a graphic is to ask. Contact the owner of the Web site with the image you want, the publisher if the image is in a book, or the museum if the work is owned by a museum. You will be asked to write a letter describing precisely how you intend to use the image, reproduce it, and distribute it. Your letter should also say how long you intend to use it and at what size you intend to reproduce it.

Inserting a Picture in an Office File

After you've weighed the merits of different kinds of graphics and decided which one is best for you, you can insert it. Inserting a picture is as simple as choosing it in the Insert Picture dialog box. Follow these steps to insert a picture on a PowerPoint slide, Word document, Excel worksheet, or OneNote page:

1. **Go to the Insert tab.**

2. **Click the Picture button.**

   You see the Insert Picture dialog box, as shown in Figure 3-2. In PowerPoint, you can also open this dialog box by clicking the picture icon in a content placeholder frame.

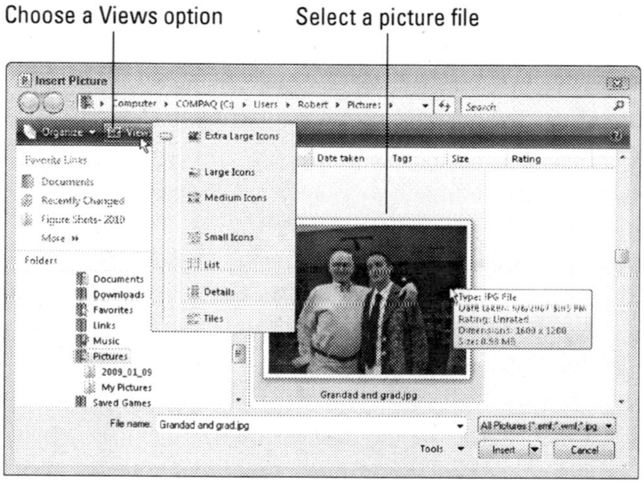

**Book VI
Chapter 3**

Handling Graphics

Choose a Views option   Select a picture file

Figure 3-2:
You can
preview a
picture file
before you
insert it.

3. **Select a file in the Insert Picture dialog box.**

   As Figure 3-2 shows, you can open the drop-down list on the Views button and choose an option to see what a graphic looks like.

   You can click the File Types button to open a drop-down list and choose a file type to locate files of a certain type in the dialog box. Move the pointer over a picture in the dialog box to get information about its file type, dimensions, and size.

4. **Click the Insert button.**

   Go to the (Picture Tools) Format tab to see all the different ways you can manipulate a picture after you insert it.

After a picture lands on a file, it becomes an object. Book I, Chapter 8 explains how to manipulate objects — how to move them, change their size, and change their borders. Later in this chapter, "Touching Up a Graphic" looks into various ways to change the appearance of graphics.

 If you chose the wrong picture, don't fret because you can exchange one picture for another. On the (Picture Tools) Format tab, click the Change Picture button and select a different picture in the Insert Picture dialog box.

Touching Up a Picture

Every picture can be a collaboration. You can do the following to make a picture your own as well as the work of the original artist:

+ **Softening and sharpening:** Mute or polish a picture. See "Softening and sharpening pictures," later in this chapter.

+ **Changing the brightness and contrast:** Adjust a picture's tone. See "Correcting a picture's brightness and contrast."

+ **Recoloring:** Give your picture a brand-new set of colors or gray shades. See "Recoloring a picture."

+ **Choosing an artistic effect:** Take your picture for a walk on the wild side. See "Choosing an artistic effect."

+ **Choosing a picture style:** Present your picture in an oval fame, soft-edged frame, or other type of frame. See "Selecting a picture style."

+ **Cropping:** Cut out the parts of a picture that you don't want. See "Cropping off part of a picture."

+ **Removing picture areas:** Keep the essentials of a picture and remove the rest. See "Removing the background."

To touch up a picture, visit the (Picture Tools) Format tab. As shown in Figure 3-3, you can also open the Format Picture dialog box and choose settings in these categories: Picture Corrections, Picture Color, Artistic Effects, and Crop. To open the Format Picture dialog box, right-click a picture and choose Format Picture on the shortcut menu.

 If you regret experimenting with your picture and you want to start all over, go to the (Picture Tools) Format tab and click the Reset Picture button. Clicking this button restores a picture to its original condition.

 PowerPoint, Word, Excel, and OneNote offer only a handful of tools for changing a picture's appearance. If you have the time and the inclination, alter a graphic's appearance in a program designed especially for that purpose. You can find many more options for editing graphics in Photoshop, Paint Shop Pro, and Corel Photo-Paint, for example. Later in this chapter, "Using Microsoft Office Picture Manager" describes a nifty program that comes with Office for editing pictures.

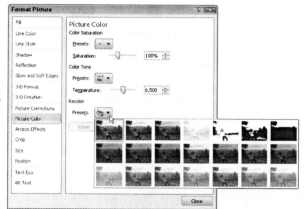

Figure 3-3:
Touching up
a photo in
the Format
Picture
dialog box.

Softening and sharpening pictures

Figure 3-4 shows the effects of the softening/sharpening settings. These settings mute a picture or make it look more succinct. To soften or sharpen a picture, select it and use one of these techniques:

✦ On the (Picture Tools) Format tab, click the Corrections button and choose a Sharpen and Soften option on the drop-down list.

✦ Open the Format Picture dialog box to the Picture Corrections category and drag the Soften-Sharpen slider or enter a negative or positive number in the text box. Negative numbers soften the picture; positive numbers sharpen it. To open the Format Picture dialog box, right-click your picture and choose Format Picture.

Figure 3-4:
Effects
of the
softening/
sharpening
settings.

Correcting a picture's brightness and contrast

Figure 3-5 shows a picture that has been made over several times with the Brightness and Contrast settings. Brightness settings govern the overall brightness of a picture; contrast settings determine how distinguishable the different parts of the picture are from one another. Change a picture's brightness and contrast to make it fit better on a page or slide. Select your picture and use one of these techniques:

✦ On the (Picture Tools) Format tab, click the Corrections button and choose a Brightness and Contrast option on the drop-down list.

✦ Open the Format Picture dialog box to the Picture Corrections category and change the Brightness and Contrast settings. Negative Brightness settings make a picture darker; positive settings make it brighter. Negative Contrast settings mute the differences between the parts of a picture; positive settings heighten the differences. To open the Format Picture dialog box, right-click your picture and choose Format Picture.

Figure 3-5:
Effects of the Brightness and Contrast settings.

Recoloring a picture

Recolor a picture to give it a makeover. Figure 3-6 shows examples of Recolor options. As well as recoloring a picture, you can change its color saturation and color tone settings. *Color saturation* refers to the purity and intensity of the colors; *color tone* determines the degree of lightness and darkness. Recoloring is useful for giving a picture a uniform appearance. Select your picture and use these techniques to recolor it:

✦ On the (Picture Tools) Format tab, click the Color button and choose a Color Saturation, Color Tone, or Recolor option on the drop-down list. You can choose More Variations at the bottom of the list and choose a color on the sublist.

✦ Open the Format Picture dialog box to the Picture Color category and change the Color Saturation and Color Tone settings. Change the Saturation setting to mute or bring out the colors; change the Temperature setting to make the color tones darker or lighter. To open the Format Picture dialog box, right-click your picture and choose Format Picture.

Figure 3-6:
Examples of Recolor options.

Making a color transparent

The (Picture Tools) Format tab offers the Set Transparent Color command for making one color in a picture transparent and thereby allowing the background to show through in certain parts of a picture. The Set Transparent Color command works by making all the pixels in a picture that are the same color transparent. In a picture in which one color predominates, you can make this color transparent and get some interesting effects.

To experiment with the Set Transparent Color command:

1. Select the picture.

2. On the (Picture Tools) Format tab, click the Color button and choose Set Transparent Color on the drop-down list.

3. Click in your picture on the color that you want to be transparent.

You can choose the Set Transparent Color command again and make another color in your picture transparent.

TIP Live-previewing really comes in handy when you're recoloring a graphic. Move the Format Picture dialog box to the side of your picture and watch what happens when you change the Picture Color settings.

Choosing an artistic effect

Figure 3-7 demonstrates four of the 23 artistic effects that you can apply to a picture: Pencil Sketch, Glow Diffused, Glass, and Glow Edges. To experiment with the artistic effects and maybe find one to your liking, select your picture and use one of these techniques:

Artistic Effects ▾

✦ Go to the (Picture Tools) Format tab, click the Artistic Effects button, and choose an effect on the drop-down list.

✦ Open the Format Picture dialog box to the Artistic Effects category and choose an artistic effect. To open the Format Picture dialog box, right-click your picture and choose Format Picture.

Figure 3-7:
Examples
of artistic
effects.

Selecting a picture style

A *picture style* is way of presenting or framing a picture. Figure 3-8 shows examples of picture styles. Picture styles include Simple Frame, Soft Edge Rectangle, Perspective Shadow, and Reflected Bevel. To choose a picture style for a picture, select it, go to the (Picture Tools) Format tab, open the Picture Styles gallery, and choose a style.

If you don't like the picture style you chose (or you don't care for any change you made to a picture), click the Reset Picture button to reverse all your format changes and start over.

If you like the picture styles, you may be enamored as well with the picture effects. On the (Picture Tools) Format tab, click the Picture Effects button and experiment with the options on the drop-down list and sublists.

Cropping off part of a picture

Cropping means to cut off part of a picture. I'm afraid you can't use the Office cropping tool like a pair of scissors or an Xacto knife to zigzag cut around the edges of a picture or cut a hole in the middle. You can, however, cut strips from the side, top, or bottom. In Figure 3-9, the cropping tool is being used to cut off extraneous parts of a picture.

Figure 3-8:
Examples of picture styles.

Figure 3-9:
Cropping off
parts of a
picture.

Select your picture, go to the (Picture Tools) Format tab, and use one of these techniques to crop it:

✦ **Crop manually:** Crop the picture by dragging its cropping handles. Click the Crop button. Cropping handles appear around the picture, as in Figure 3-9. Drag cropping handles to lop off a part or parts of the picture. Click the Crop button again or press Esc after you finish cropping.

✦ **Crop to a shape:** Crop the picture to a rectangle, circle, or other shape. Open the drop-down list on the Crop button, choose Crop to Shape, and select a shape in the Shapes gallery.

✦ **Crop to proportions:** Crop the picture to a proportional size setting. Open the drop-down list on the Crop button, choose Aspect Ratio, and choose a ratio. For example, choose 1:1 to crop to a perfect square with the width and height the same size.

✦ **Crop by filling:** For placing an image in a picture placeholder, crop the image to make it fit in the placeholder box.

✦ **Crop by fitting:** For placing an image in a picture placeholder, shrink the picture to make it fit.

With the cropping handles showing, you can drag the picture left, right, up, or down to determine where it is cropped.

Another way to crop pictures is to click the Size group button on the (Picture Tools) Format tab and enter measurements in the Crop category of the Format Picture dialog box (Word doesn't allow cropping this way). Use this method if you need to crop several different pictures in the same manner.

When you crop a picture, you don't cut off a part of it — not as far as your computer is concerned. All you do is tell Office not to display part of a graphic. The graphic is still whole. You can, however, compress a graphic after you crop it, and in so doing truly shave off a part of the graphic and thereby decrease the size of the file you're working with, as "Compressing Graphics to Save Disk Space" explains later in this chapter.

Removing the background

Yet another way to diddle with pictures is to use the Remove Background command. This command endeavors to locate the unessential parts of a picture so that you can remove them, which sometimes means removing the foreground or the background, as shown in Figure 3-10 (in the figure, I exchange the background sky for a clip-art rainbow). Select a picture and follow these steps to test-drive the Remove Background command:

1. **On the (Picture Tools) Format tab, click the Remove Background button.**

The Background Removal tab opens and the parts of your picture that Office wants to remove turn a lurid shade of magenta, which you could see in Figure 3-10 if this book were in color.

Figure 3-10:
Removing parts of a picture (in this case the sky).

2. **On the Background Removal tab, indicate what you want to keep and remove.**

Keep your eye on what's magenta and what's not as you use these techniques, and consider zooming to 200 percent or more so that you can get a good look at your picture:

- *Changing the size of the box:* Drag the side and corner handles of the box to capture what you want to keep or remove.

- *Marking what you want to keep:* Click the Mark Areas to Keep button. The pointer changes into a pencil. Click your picture to indicate what you want to keep. Each time you click, a keep mark (a plus sign icon) appears on your picture.

- *Marking what you want to remove:* Click the Mark Areas to Remove button. The pointer changes to a pencil. Click your picture to indicate what you want to remove. When you click, a remove mark (a minus sign) appears.

- *Deleting keep and remove marks:* Click the Delete Mark button and then click a keep or remove mark to remove a mark and change what is and isn't removed from the picture.

Of course, you can click the Undo button to backtrack as you work. If you get thoroughly lost on the Background Removal tab, click the Discard All Changes button and start all over.

3. **Click the Keep Changes button when you finish marking what you want to keep and remove.**

How do you like your picture now? If it needs more work, click the Remove Background button again and diddle some more on the Background Removal tab. Click the Discard All Changes button if you want your original picture without the background removed.

Compressing Pictures to Save Disk Space

By compressing pictures, you reduce their file size and consequently the size of the file you're working on. Not all pictures can be compressed, as "Compression" explains earlier in this chapter, and some types of graphics lose their integrity when they're compressed. You can't resize lossy-compressed graphics without their looking odd.

Compress pictures to make files load faster and make e-mail messages with file attachments travel faster over the Internet. Compressing a picture file reduces its pixels per inch (ppi) setting. Follow these steps to compress pictures:

1. **Optionally, select the picture or pictures you want to compress if you want to compress only one or two.**

The Compress Pictures command compresses all the graphics in a file unless you select graphics first.

2. **Go to the (Picture Tools) Format tab.**

3. **Click the Compress Pictures button.**

You see the Compress Pictures dialog box.

4. **Select the Apply to Selected Pictures Only check box if you selected graphics in Step 1 and you want to compress only a couple of graphics.**

5. **Click the Delete Cropped Areas of Pictures check box if you want to delete the unused portions of pictures you cropped.**

As "Cropping off part of a picture" explains earlier in this chapter, Office crops graphics in name only. It retains the cropped part of the graphic in case you want it back, but you can remove the cropped part as well by selecting this check box.

6. **Choose a target output for the pictures.**

These options tell Office which pixels per inch (ppi) setting to use when compressing graphics. Which setting you choose depends on where you intend to show your graphics. Graphics to be shown on a computer monitor need be no more than 72 ppi. If you intend to print your graphics, choose a setting in the 600-3000 ppi range. To print for an offset publication, choose an even higher setting.

7. **Click OK.**

Using Microsoft Office Picture Manager

You may not know it, but you installed a program for managing and editing pictures when you installed Office. The program is called Microsoft Office Picture Manager, and you can use it to organize graphics and touch up graphics before inserting them in a PowerPoint, Word, Excel, or OneNote file. As shown in Figure 3-11, Picture Manager displays graphics so that you can see precisely what your editorial changes do to them. The program makes it easy to find and organize graphic files on your computer. It also provides tools for editing graphics.

To open Picture Manager, click the Start button and choose All Programs➪ Microsoft Office➪Microsoft Office 2010 Tools➪ Microsoft Office Picture Manager. You see the window shown in Figure 3-11. Starting there, you can display a graphic on your computer and change its appearance in several different ways.

Select a folder Change views Edit a graphic Zoom in or out

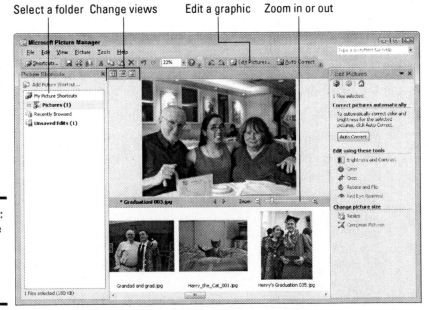

Figure 3-11: The Picture Manager window in Filmstrip view.

Mapping the graphic files on your computer

The first step in using the Picture Manager is to point to the folders on your computer where important graphic files are located. After you tell Picture Manager which folders graphic files are kept in, shortcuts to the folders appear in the Picture Shortcuts pane on the left side of the window (see Figure 3-11). By clicking one of these shortcuts, you can open a folder, view its contents, and edit a graphic file.

Follow these steps to create shortcuts to folders in the Picture Shortcuts pane:

1. **Choose File⇨Add Picture Shortcut or click the Add Picture Shortcut link in the Picture Shortcuts pane (click the Shortcuts button to see this pane).**

   The Add Picture Shortcut dialog box opens.

2. **Select a folder where you store graphics that you want to work with.**

3. **Click the Add button.**

   Repeat these steps until you've created shortcuts to folders where you store important graphics.

 Instead of pointing to folders one at a time, you can choose File⇨Locate Pictures and have Picture Manager scour your computer or network for the graphic file types you select in the File Types dialog box. Shortcuts to folders with those file types appear in the Picture Shortcuts task pane. If you go this route, however, you'll likely discover many, many folders on your computer where graphic files are kept, and shortcuts to these folders will crowd the Picture Shortcuts task pane.

Click the Shortcuts button (or choose View⇨Shortcuts) to display the Picture Shortcuts task pane. To remove a shortcut from the task pane, right-click it and choose Remove Shortcut.

Displaying the graphic file you want to work with

After you've created shortcuts to the folders where you keep graphic files, you can display a graphic file by following these steps:

1. **Click the Shortcuts button, if necessary, to display the Picture Shortcuts task pane.**

2. **Click a shortcut to a folder.**

   Graphic files in the folder appear in the middle window (refer to Figure 3-11).

3. **Scroll to or choose a different view to pinpoint the file.**

   Picture Manager offers three views: Thumbnails, Filmstrip, and Single Picture. Choose an option on the View menu or click a View button to change views (refer to Figure 3-11).

Double-click a thumbnail image to see a graphic in Single Picture view. To zoom in and out, drag the Zoom slider.

Editing a picture

With the graphic you want to edit on display, you're ready to start editing. Your next task is to display the editing tools you need on the right side of the window. Picture Manager offers two ways to get the editing tools you need:

✦ Click the Edit Pictures button to display the Edit Pictures task pane. It lists the names of editing tools. Click the link that represents the kind of editing you want to do. For example, to crop a graphic, click the Crop link.

✦ Open the Picture menu and choose Brightness and Contrast, Color, Crop, Rotate and Flip, Red Eye Removal, Resize, or Compress Pictures. For example, choose Picture➪Crop to cut off part of a graphic.

To let Picture Manager try its hand at improving your graphic, click the AutoCorrect button, choose Picture➪AutoCorrect, or press Ctrl+Q.

If you regret making changes to a graphic, choose Edit➪Discard Changes. All changes you made are reversed and you get your original graphic back.

Click the Save button (or press Ctrl+S) to save your graphic after you finish editing it. For that matter, choose File➪Save As before you start editing and save the file under a new name so that you have the original in reserve.

If you edit one picture and go to another without saving the first one, Picture Manager takes notice. Copies of unsaved files are kept in the Unsaved Edits folder. To see the contents of this folder, click Unsaved Edits in the Picture Shortcuts task pane. Unsaved graphics appear on-screen so that you can select and save them, if you so choose.

Adjusting the brightness and contrast

Select a graphic and choose Picture➪Brightness and Contrast or click the Brightness and Contrast hyperlink in the Edit Pictures task pane to adjust a graphic's tonal intensity. You see a Brightness, Contrast, and Midtone slider on the Brightness and Contrast task pane. Without going into too much detail, here is what these sliders do:

✦ **Brightness:** Adjusts the inherent brightness value in each pixel. Increasing the brightness makes the image lighter; decreasing it makes the image darker.

✦ **Contrast:** Increasing the contrast, in the words of a laundry detergent manufacturer, "makes your whites whiter and your darks darker," whereas decreasing the contrast making the tones more similar.

+ **Midtone:** Redefines the *midtones,* or tonal values between light and shadow, of an image. Dragging the slider to the right brightens the image.

If dragging the sliders doesn't provide the results you want, say the heck with it and just click the Auto Brightness button to let Picture Manager adjust the brightness and contrast for you.

Balancing the colors

Select a graphic and choose Picture⇨Color or click the Color hyperlink in the Edit Pictures task pane to fine-tune a graphic's colors.

You can have Picture Manager do the fine-tuning for you. Click the Enhance Color button and then click a part of the graphic that is supposed to be white. If you don't like the results, try balancing the colors in the graphic yourself by dragging these three sliders:

+ **Amount:** Increasing this value magnifies the hue and saturation settings; decreasing this value minimizes them.

+ **Hue:** Increasing this value further distinguishes the colors from one another; decreasing this value makes the colors blend.

+ **Saturation:** Increasing it makes colors more luminous; decreasing this value makes colors grayer.

Cropping a graphic

Select a graphic and choose Picture⇨Crop or click the Crop hyperlink in the Edit Pictures task pane to cut off parts of a graphic. Picture Manager shows precisely how much of the graphic you will crop when you click OK. The Crop task pane is especially useful if you want your graphic to be a certain size. Under Picture Dimensions, you can see exactly how many pixels high and wide your graphic is. By dragging the selected part of the graphic — the part that isn't grayed out — you can be very precise about what part of the graphic remains after you crop.

The Crop task pane offers two ways to crop a graphic:

+ **Crop at will:** In the Aspect Ratio drop-down list, choose None and then drag a corner or side cropping handle.

+ **Maintain symmetry when you crop:** Choose an option from the Aspect Ratio drop-down list and select the Landscape or Portrait option button before you drag a corner or side cropping handle. *Aspect ratio* proportionally describes the relationship between a graphic's width and height. For example, at the 4 x 6 aspect ratio, the graphic in Portrait mode is a third taller than it is wide (⅔); in Landscape mode, the graphic is a third wider than it is tall. Choose an aspect ratio setting when you want your graphic to have symmetry.

**Book VI
Chapter 3**

Handling Graphics

Cropping a graphic doesn't reduce its file size. To reduce a graphic's file size after you've cropped it, compress the graphic. See "Compressing a graphic" later in this chapter.

Rotating and flipping graphics

Select a graphic and choose Picture⇨Rotate and Flip, or click the Rotate and Flip hyperlink in the Edit Pictures task pane to rotate or flip graphics. The Rotate commands turn the graphic on its side; the Flip commands provide mirror images of the original graphic. You can rotate a graphic by degrees by entering a value in the By Degree text box. The Formatting toolbar also offers Rotate buttons for rotating graphics.

Removing "red eyes" from a graphic

Sometimes the subject of a photo appears to have *red eyes,* not because the subject didn't get enough sleep, but because the camera flash made the subject's irises turn red. Follow these steps to remove red eye from a digital flash photograph:

1. **Choose Picture⇨Red Eye Removal or click the Red Eye Removal hyperlink in the Edit Pictures task pane.**

2. **Drag the Zoom slider to the right so that you get a good look at the red eyes in the photo.**

3. **Click each red eye to select it.**

4. **Click the OK button.**

   You can click the Reset Selected Eyes button to start all over, if you need to do that.

Resizing a graphic

To change the size of a graphic, select it and choose Picture⇨Resize or click the Resize hyperlink in the Edit Pictures task pane. You land in the Resize task pane. It offers three ways to change the size of a graphic:

✦ **Predefined Width x Height:** Select this option button, and on the drop-down list, choose the setting that best describes the graphic's size. For example, if you intend to post the graphic on a Web page, choose Web - Large or Web - Small.

✦ **Custom Width x Height:** Select this option button and enter pixel measurements for the width and height of the graphic. Be careful with this option because the graphic doesn't maintain its original proportions unless you calculate the proportions yourself, and when a resized graphic loses its original proportions, it can be skewered or blurred.

✦ **Percentage of Original Width x Height:** Select this option button and enter the percentage by which you want to enlarge or shrink the graphic.

The bottom of the task pane tells you how many pixels wide and high your graphic was to start with and how wide and high it is after resizing.

Compressing a graphic

Near the beginning of this chapter, "Compression" explains what compressing a graphic entails. Compress a graphic to reduce its file size. Compressing a graphic file reduces its pixels per inch (ppi) setting. Some graphic types, however, can't be compressed.

To compress a graphic, select it and choose Picture⇨Compress Pictures or click the Compress Pictures hyperlink in the Edit Pictures task pane. You see the Compress Pictures task pane. The bottom of the task pane tells you how much the graphic shrinks in size after you compress it. Choose a Compress For option button and click OK.

Before you compress a graphic, save a copy. After you compress graphics, you can't get the high-resolution originals back.

Book VI
Chapter 3

Handling Graphics

Shooting a screenshot

Word, PowerPoint, Excel, and OneNote make it easier than ever to take a picture of a screen on your computer and insert it in a document, slide, worksheet, or e-mail message. Follow these steps to take a picture of a screen:

1. **If you want to capture a portion of one screen, open the screen.**

2. **On the Insert tab, click the Screenshot button.**

   A drop-down list shows you thumbnail images of each screen that is open on your computer.

3. **Choose a thumbnail image to shoot an entire screen, or choose Screen Clipping and drag on screen to shoot a portion of a screen.**

A picture of the screen or a portion of the screen lands in your document, slide, worksheet, or e-mail message.

Here are a couple of other tried-and-true techniques for capturing screens:

- Press PrtScn (the key to the right of F12) to capture an entire screen to the Clipboard.

- Press Alt+PrScn to capture the active part of the screen to the Clipboard. For example, to capture a dialog box, select the dialog box and press Alt+PrScn.

After the screen capture is on the Clipboard, you can paste it where you will.

Chapter 4: Decorating Files with Clip Art

In This Chapter

✔ **Understanding what clip art is**

✔ **Placing a clip-art image on a page, slide, or worksheet**

✔ **Changing the look of a clip-art image**

✔ **Using the Clip Organizer to store, organize, and insert clip art**

This chapter explains how you can use clip art to decorate Word documents, PowerPoint slides, and Excel worksheets (sorry, but you can't put clip-art images in a OneNote note except by copying and pasting). You also find a treatise on how to use the *Microsoft Clip Organizer,* an auxiliary program for storing clip art and other kinds of media files so that you can find the files in a hurry. If you often use media files in your work, you owe it to yourself to look into the Clip Organizer.

What Is Clip Art?

In the old days, long before the invention of computers, people would buy clip-art books. They would literally cut, or clip, images from these books and paste them into posters, letters, and advertisements. Today's clip art is the digital equivalent of old-fashioned clip art. You can paste clip art into computer programs such as Word, PowerPoint, and Excel. You can resize clip-art images without the images losing their integrity. The clip art that comes with Office 2010 isn't encumbered by licensing restrictions; it's in the public domain, and you can use it as you please.

Figure 4-1 shows examples of some clip-art images that come with Office. Use images like these to decorate your files. Use them to help illustrate an idea or simply to add a little liveliness to your work. In my experience, the hardest task where clip art is concerned is finding the right image. You can choose from so many images that finding the right one is a chore.

Figure 4-1:
Examples
of clip-art
images.

Inserting a Clip-Art Image

To insert a clip-art image, you open the Clip Art task pane, search in the Clip Organizer for the image you want, and insert the image. The trick to finding the right image is knowing your way around the Clip Organizer. The majority of this chapter explains how to organize the art on your computer so that you can get it by way of the Clip Organizer. For now, you can follow these basic steps to insert a clip-art image in a page, slide, or worksheet:

1. **Go to the Insert tab.**

2. **Click the Clip Art button.**

You see the Clip Art task pane, as shown in Figure 4-2. In PowerPoint, you can also click the Clip-Art icon to insert a clip-art image in a content placeholder frame.

The Clip Art task pane is actually an entrée into the *Clip Organizer,* the Microsoft program for organizing and quickly inserting clip art. (The Clip Organizer is explained in more detail later in "Handling Media Files with the Clip Organizer.")

3. **In the Search For text box, enter a keyword that describes the clip-art image you need.**

Later in this chapter, "Searching for a media file in the Search pane" explains how keywords work.

4. **Select the Include Office.com content check box (and make sure your computer is connected to the Internet) to search for images online as well as on your computer.**

5. **In the Results Should Be drop-down list, choose Illustrations, and if you want to search for photos as well, choose Photographs (see Figure 4-2).**

6. **Click the Go button.**

The bottom of the task pane shows the clip-art images found in your search. You may have to scroll through the task pane to see all the images.

7. **Double-click an image or open its drop-down list and choose Insert to place it in your Word document, PowerPoint slide, or Excel worksheet.**

   Your next task is to move the image into position and perhaps change its size. Book I, Chapter 8 explains how to manipulate clip-art images and other objects.

Enter a keyword   Choose what to search for

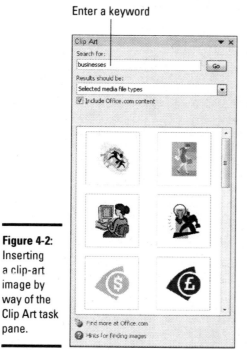
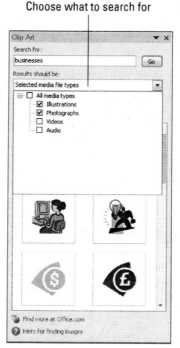

Figure 4-2: Inserting a clip-art image by way of the Clip Art task pane.

Handling Media Files with the Clip Organizer

As computers get faster and better, media files — clip art, graphics, video clips, and audio files — will play a bigger role in computing. Dropping a clip-art image in a Word document or PowerPoint slide won't be a big deal. Playing video clips on PowerPoint slides will be commonplace.

Well aware that the future is closing in on us, Microsoft created the Clip Organizer to help you manage the media files on your computer. By using the Clip Organizer, you can place graphics, video clips, and audio files in Word documents, PowerPoint presentations, and Excel worksheets. More important, the Clip Organizer is the place to organize media files in your computer so that you can find them and make good use of them. These pages explain how to manage the Clip Organizer.

To open the Clip Organizer, click the Start button and choose All Programs⇨ Microsoft Office⇨Microsoft Office 2010 Tools⇨Microsoft Clip Organizer.

Knowing your way around the Clip Organizer

As shown in Figure 4-3, the Clip Organizer is divided in two parts, with a pane on the left and a window for displaying files on the right. The Clip Organizer offers two panes: Collection List and Search.

✦ **Collection List task pane:** Use the Collection List task pane to organize your media files and to quickly locate and insert a media file. To display the Collection List task pane, click the Collection List button or choose View⇨Collection List.

✦ **Search task pane:** Use the Search task pane to locate a media file on your computer. Notice that this task pane is similar to the Clip Art task pane in Office programs (refer to Figure 4-2). To display the Search task pane, click the Search button or choose View⇨Search.

Click to display a different task pane   Search results

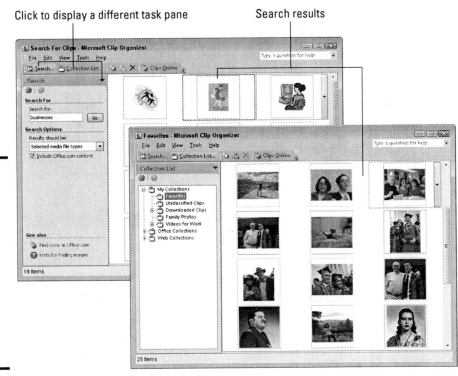

Figure 4-3: The Clip Organizer window with the Search pane displayed (left) and Collection List pane displayed (right).

Locating the media file you need

The Clip Organizer presents two ways to find a media file you need. Starting from the Search pane, you can conduct a keyword search; starting from the Collection List pane, you can select folders and subfolders to display clip art and other media files on the right side of the window.

Searching for a media file in the Search pane

By entering a keyword in the Search For text box, telling the Clip Organizer where to look, and telling it what kind of files to look for, you can pinpoint the clip-art image you need:

✦ **Search For text box:** Enter a keyword that describes what kind of clip-art image you want. As Figure 4-4 shows, each clip-art image has been assigned descriptive keywords. If the keyword you enter matches a keyword assigned to a clip-art image, the image appears in the search results. (To view an image's keywords, open its drop-down list and choose Preview/Properties.)

✦ **Results Should Be:** Choose which type of media you're seeking — illustrations, photographs, videos, or audio.

✦ **Include Office.com Content:** Select this check box (and make sure your computer is connected to the Internet) to search for images online as well as on your computer.

Figure 4-4:
For searching purposes, each clip-art image has been assigned keywords.

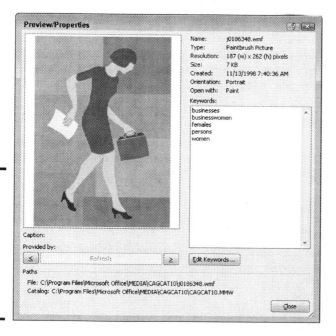

Preview/Properties

Name:	j0186348.wmf
Type:	Paintbrush Picture
Resolution:	187 (w) x 262 (h) pixels
Size:	7 KB
Created:	11/13/1998 7:40:36 AM
Orientation:	Portrait
Open with:	Paint

Keywords:
businesses
businesswomen
females
persons
women

Caption:
Provided by:

<   Refresh   >   Edit Keywords...

Paths
File: C:\Program Files\Microsoft Office\MEDIA\CAGCAT10\j0186348.wmf
Catalog: C:\Program Files\Microsoft Office\MEDIA\CAGCAT10\CAGCAT10.MMW

Close

Click the Go button when you're ready to conduct the search. The results of the search appear on the right side of the window (refer to Figure 4-3).

Locating a media file in the Collection List

If you know that the media file you want is stored on your computer, you can find it by starting with the Collection List.

The folders in the Collection List pane work just the same as folders in Windows Explorer or Computer. Click a folder name to display its contents on the right side of the screen. Display or hide subfolders by clicking the plus sign (+) or minus sign (−) next to folder names.

When you select a folder (or subfolder) in the Collection List pane, its contents appear on the right side of the Clip Organizer window (refer to Figure 4-3). These are the top-level folders in the Collection List pane:

✦ **My Collections:** Includes the Favorites subfolder (where you can store media files you use most often), subfolders you create yourself for different projects, and the Downloaded Clips subfolder (where clip art you downloaded from Office.com is stored). How to store a file in the Favorites folder or a folder you create yourself is explained later in this chapter in "Creating your own My Collections subfolder for the Clip Organizer."

✦ **Office Collections:** Includes many subfolders, each named for a clip-art category. Select a subfolder to view clip art in a category. You installed these clip-art images when you installed Office. The clip-art images are located on your computer.

✦ **Web Collections:** Includes many subfolders, each named for a clip-art category. To see these clip-art images, your computer must be connected to the Internet.

Inserting a media file

After you've found the media file you want, either by searching in the Search pane or browsing among the folders in the Collection List pane, you can insert it by following these instructions:

✦ **Clip Organizer:** Open the file's drop-down list and choose Copy. Then click in your file, go to the Home tab, and click the Paste button (or right-click and choose Paste).

✦ **Clip Art task pane in an Office program:** Either double-click the image or open its drop-down list and choose Insert.

Getting clip art from Microsoft

Microsoft permits users of Office to get clip art, photos, audio files, and video clips from a Microsoft Web site. To see what kind of media Microsoft offers online, use one of these techniques:

✔ **Clip Art task pane:** Connect your computer to the Internet and click the Find more at Office.com link (you can find it at the bottom of the Clip Art task pane).

✔ **Clip Organizer:** Click the Clips Online button.

You come to a Microsoft Web site where you can download collections of clip art and other media files to your computer.

When you find a file you like, move your pointer over the file and choose Add to Collection. To download the files to your computer, click the Unsaved Collection link (you can find this link on the upper-right corner of the window) and choose Download. In the Clip Organizer, you can find files you downloaded from Microsoft in the `My Collections\Downloaded Clips` subfolder.

Storing your own files in the My Collections folders

The Collection List pane in the Clip Organizer is a convenient place to go when you need a media file. Wouldn't it be nice if you could go to the Clip Organizer when you want a file of a family photo, graphics that pertain to your work, or a video you're involved with?

It so happens that you can use the Clip Organizer for your own media files, not just the media files that come from Office. You can arrange it so that the media files you need are available to you simply by selecting the Favorites subfolder in the Collection List pane. For that matter, you can create a subfolder of your own in the Collection List and keep your media files there.

Adding your own media files to the Clip Organizer

If you're a fan of the Clip Organizer — if you think it's a convenient place to store and get media files — place your own files in the Clip Organizer. This way, you can open the Clip Organizer and get right to work making graphics or videos for a project you're working on.

Follow these steps to put your own media files in the Clip Organizer:

1. **Click the Collection List button, if necessary, to see the Collection List.**

2. **Choose File⇨Add Clips to Organizer⇨On My Own.**

The Add Clips to Organizer dialog box appears, as shown in Figure 4-5.

Select files   Select a subfolder

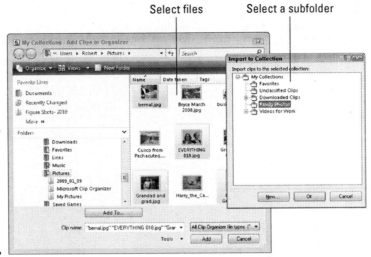

Figure 4-5:
Making your
favorite
media files
available
in the Clip
Organizer.

3. **Select the file or files whose names you want to store in the Clip Organizer.**

   For example, open your My Pictures folder and select the graphic files that you often work with. You can select more than one file by Ctrl+clicking.

4. **Click the Add To button.**

   The Import to Collection dialog box appears, as shown in Figure 4-5. It lists subfolders of the My Collections folder.

5. **Select the subfolder where you want to store your file or files and click OK.**

6. **Click the Add button in the Add Clips to Organizer dialog box.**

When you add media files to the Clip Organizer, you don't move the files to a new location on your computer, although it may appear that way. Truth be told, the folders in the Clip Organizer don't really exist on your computer. The folders actually represent categories. Inside each category are shortcuts similar to the shortcuts on the Windows desktop that tell your computer where the files are located on your computer. When you place a file in the Clip Organizer, what you're really doing is placing a shortcut to a file located somewhere on your computer or network.

Organizing media files in the My Collections subfolders

The My Collections subfolders in the Collection List pane — Favorites and the others — are excellent places for storing the media files you use often. All you have to do to get them is select the Favorites subfolder or another subfolder in the Collection List. Follow these steps to copy or move a media file to the Favorites subfolder or another subfolder in the Clip Organizer (the next section in this chapter explains how to make subfolders of your own):

1. **Find the media file or files you want to store in a subfolder.**

   Earlier in this chapter, "Locating the media file you need," explains how to locate a media file.

2. **Select the file or files on the right side of the Clip Organizer window.**

   To select more than one file, Ctrl+click the files; choose Edit⇨Select All to select them all.

3. **Give the Copy to Collection or Move to Collection command.**

   You can give these commands two different ways:

   - Open the file's drop-down list and choose Copy to Collection or Move to Collection.
   - Open the Edit menu and choose Copy to Collection or Move to Collection.

   You see the Copy to Collection or Move to Collection dialog box.

4. **Select a folder in the dialog box.**

   If necessary, click a plus sign (+) beside a folder to display its subfolders.

5. **Click OK.**

To remove a file from a subfolder, select it and then press the Delete key, or open its drop-down list and then choose Delete from Clip Organizer. Deleting a file this way doesn't remove it from your computer; it just takes its name out of the Clip Organizer.

Creating your own My Collections subfolder for the Clip Organizer

If you work with a number of media files, organize them into My Collections subfolders. Put photographs in a Photographs subfolder. Put audio files in a Music subfolder. That way, you can find media files simply by going to the subfolder where you place them. Follow these steps to create a new subfolder in the Clip Organizer:

1. **Click the Collection List button, if necessary, to display the Collection List task pane.**

2. **Choose File⇨New Collection.**

   The New Collection dialog box appears.

3. **Select the folder in which to place your new subfolder.**

   Selecting My Collections is probably the best choice, but place your new subfolder wherever you want.

4. **Enter a name for the subfolder in the Name box.**

5. **Click OK.**

If you need to rename a folder, select it in the Collection List, choose Edit⇨ Rename Collection, and enter a new name. To remove it, choose Edit⇨ Delete.

Tinkering with a clip-art image's appearance

Sometimes a clip-art image doesn't sit well with the rest of the page, slide, or worksheet. The image is too bright or too dark. It clashes with the other images. When an image clashes, you don't have to abandon it in favor of another image. As Figure 4-3 shows, you can alter a clip-art image's appearance in different ways.

Select your image, go to the (Picture Tools) Format tab, and change the image's appearance. Chapter 3 of this mini-book describes the different ways to touch up a picture or clip-art image.

Chapter 5: Automating Tasks with Macros

In This Chapter

✔ Understanding what a macro is

✔ Displaying and hiding the Developer tab

✔ Examining macro security issues

✔ Recording, running, and editing a macro

This brief chapter explains how macros can make your work a little easier. I describe how to display the Developer tab on the Ribbon, record a macro, run a macro, and edit a macro. I also look into macro security issues and show you how to place a macro button on the Quick Access toolbar.

You can run macros in Word, Excel, and PowerPoint, but not OneNote.

What Is a Macro?

A *macro* is a set of command instructions recorded under a name. When you activate a macro, the program you're working in carries out the instructions in the macro. Macros help automate repetitive and complex tasks. Instead of entering commands yourself, the macro does it for you — and it enters the commands faster and more efficiently. Instead of reaching into several dialog boxes to get a task done, you can run a macro and let it do the work.

Not that you necessarily need to know it, but playing a macro involves running command sequences in *Visual Basic for Applications* (VBA), a programming language built into all the major Office 2010 applications. Behind the scenes, the application you're working in executes VBA code when you run a macro.

Displaying the Developer Tab

Before you can run a macro or do anything in the wonderful world of macros, you must display the Developer tab. Figure 5-1 shows the Developer tab in PowerPoint. Follow these steps to display or remove this tab:

Figure 5-1:
The
Developer
tab (in
PowerPoint).

File

1. **On the File tab, choose Options.**

   You see the Options dialog box.

2. **Go to the Customize Ribbon category.**

3. **On the right side of the dialog box, select the Developer check box.**

4. **Click OK.**

Managing the Macro Security Problem

A macro is a little (and sometimes not so little) computer program in its own right. As such, macros can contain computer viruses. When you run a macro in a PowerPoint presentation, Word document, Excel workbook, or any other file, you run the risk of infecting your computer with a virus.

To help protect you against macro viruses, Office gives you the opportunity to decide how you want to handle files that contain macros. You can disable all macros, disable some macros, or enable all macros. (If you're working in an office on a network, the network administrator may have decided for you whether you can run macro files on your computer. Network administrators can disable all files that contain macros.)

Follow these steps to tell Office how you want to handle macros:

1. **On the Developer tab, click the Macro Security button.**

   You see the Macro Settings category of the Trust Center dialog box, as shown in Figure 5-2.

2. **Under Macro Settings, declare how you want to handle Office files that contain macros.**

   Your choices are as follows:

   • *Disable All Macros without Notification:* You can't run macros, and moreover, you're not alerted to the fact that your file contains macros or given the opportunity to enable the macros.

- *Disable All Macros with Notification:* When you open a file with macros, you see the panel shown in Figure 5-3. It tells you that macros have been disabled, but gives you the opportunity to enable the macros by clicking the Enable Content button.

- *Disable All Macros Except Digitally Signed Macros:* You can run only macros that have been certified with a digital signature. Developers can apply for digital signatures that deem their macros safe to run. When you open a file with digitally signed macros, a dialog box tells you who developed the macros and gives you the opportunity to decide whether you want to allow them. However, you can't run macros that don't have a digital signature.

- *Enable All Macros:* You can run all macros, no matter where they came from and who made them. Choosing this option is a risky proposition. Choose it only if you get Office files from people or parties you know and trust.

3. **Click OK.**

Book VI Chapter 5

Figure 5-2:
Choosing how to handle macro security.

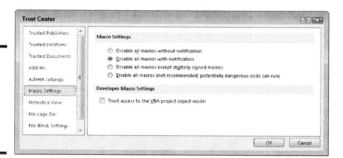

Figure 5-3:
Choose whether to run macros.

Excel, PowerPoint, and Word files that contain macros have a file extension that ends in the letter *m* (the *m* stands for "macro"). Excel files have the extension .xlsm, PowerPoint files the extension .pptm, and Word files the extension .docm. Even if you disable macros, you can glance at a file's extension letters to tell whether it includes macros.

Recording a Macro

Recording a macro in an Office application is a matter of turning on the Macro Recorder and giving commands. The Macro Recorder is modeled after a tape recorder. You turn on the recorder, choose commands, and turn the thing off. Following are ground rules and instructions for recording macros.

Unless you want to construct them on your own using VBA code, you can't record your own macros in PowerPoint. (You can record macros in Word and Excel.) To make use of macros in PowerPoint, you have to obtain them from a developer or have them already in your files.

Enabling your files for macros

To record macros, you must make sure that the file in which you record them is *macro enabled*. Macro-enabled files have file extensions that end in *m* (the *m* stands for "macro"). Excel files have the extension `.xlsm`, PowerPoint files the extension `.pptm`, and Word files the extension `.docm`.

Follow these steps to macro-enable a file so that you can record and run macros in it:

File

1. **On the File tab, choose Save As.**

2. **In the Save As dialog box, open the Save As Type drop-down list and choose the macro-enable option.**

   For example, to macro-enable a Word document, choose Word Macro-Enabled Document (*.docm).

3. **Click the Save button.**

Ground rules for recording macros

Before you record a macro, observe these ground rules:

✦ Plan ahead. If the actions you intend to record in the macro are complex, write them down beforehand so that you can execute the commands without making any mistakes.

✦ Set up the program the way it will be when you play back the macro. Before creating a macro that manipulates information in a worksheet, for example, open a worksheet that is typical of the kind of worksheet on which you'll run the macro. Unless you prepare yourself this way, you may have to pause the Macro Recorder (you can do that in Word) as you record, or you may have to edit the macro in the Visual Basic Editor later.

✦ Toggle commands that you can switch on and off have no place in macros because when the macro starts running, the Macro Recorder can't tell whether the command is on or off.

✦ Close open files that might get in the way. For example, before creating a macro that copies information from one file to another, close any open files that might confuse the issue.

✦ If you intend to include a Find or a Find-and-Replace operation in a Word macro, open the Find dialog box in Word before you start recording the macro, click the More button, and then click Cancel. This way, you can get to all the find-and-replace options when you open the dialog box as part of recording the macro.

✦ In Excel, click the Use Relative References button on the Developer tab if you want to record cell references as relative, not absolute, references.

Recording the macro

Having read and followed the ground rules, follow these steps to record a macro in Word or Excel:

📇 Record Macro

1. On the Developer tab, click the Record Macro button.

The Record Macro dialog box, shown in Figure 5-4, opens.

Figure 5-4:
The Macro
Recorder
dialog box in
Word (left)
and Excel
(right).

If you can't find the Record Macro button, chances are an administrator removed it to prevent you from using or recording macros. Depending on which version of Windows you have, administrators can remove all macro and VBA functionality from Office by not installing the VBA component, or they can install the component but prevent individuals from accessing macros and VBA.

2. In the Macro Name text box, enter a name for your macro.

Macro names can be 80 characters long, must begin with a letter, and can include numbers and underscores. Blank spaces, symbols, and punctuation are not allowed in macro names.

3. **If you so desire, assign a toolbar button or keyboard shortcut to the macro.**

   In Word, you can click the Button or the Keyboard icon and assign a button or keyboard shortcut for activating the macro. Later in this chapter, the sidebar "Running a macro from a button on the Quick Access toolbar" explains how to put a macro on the Quick Access toolbar. Chapter 1 of this mini-book explains how to assign a keyboard shortcut to a Word macro.

   In Excel, you can assign a Ctrl+key combination to a macro by entering a key in the Ctrl+ text box.

4. **In the Store Macro In drop-down list, decide where to store the macro you're about to record.**

   In Word, you can store macros in the document you're working on, the template the document is attached to, or the Normal template (the global template that's always loaded). Store a macro with a template if you'd like to be able to run the macro in all documents you create with your template.

   In Excel, you can store macros in the workbook you're working on (choose the This Workbook menu item), a new workbook, or the Personal.Macro Workbook. The Personal.Macro Workbook is designed expressly for storing macros. It is created automatically the first time you choose Personal.Macro Workbook. The workbook is called `Personal.xlsb`, and it's stored in this folder if your machine runs Windows 7 or Windows Vista:

   ```
   C:\Users\Your Name\AppData\Roaming\Microsoft\Excel\XLStart
   ```

   The `Personal.xlsb` workbook is stored in this folder if your machine runs Windows XP:

   ```
   C:\Documents and Settings\Your Name\Application Data\Microsoft\Excel\
       XLSTART
   ```

5. **In the Description text box, enter a concise description of what the macro does.**

6. **Click OK.**

   The Record Macro dialog box closes.

7. **Perform the actions you want to record in the macro.**

   The Macro Recorder records every action you take, but it doesn't record actions in real time. Take your time when recording a macro. Concentrate on taking the actions in the right order so that you don't need to adjust the code afterward.

   Word offers the Pause Recording button. You can click it to suspend recording. Click it again to resume recording.

Avoid using the mouse as you record a macro (although you can use it to open menus and select menu commands). The Macro Recorder interprets some mouse actions ambiguously. Select data by using key presses. (In Excel, you can select cells with the mouse because the Macro Recorder is able to recognize cell addresses.)

When you visit a dialog box as part of recording your macro, take into account all the dialog box settings. For example, if you visit the Font dialog box and choose 12 points on the Font Size drop-down list, the Macro Recorder duly records the 12-point font size, but it also records the Times Roman font in the macro if Times Roman happens to be the font that is chosen in the Font dialog box. The moral: Take account of all the settings in a dialog box when you visit it while recording a macro.

In dialog boxes with tabs, you can't click tabs to switch from tab to tab and choose commands. Instead, click OK to close the dialog box, reopen it, click a different tab, choose a command on the tab, and close the dialog box again.

 8. **Click the Stop Recording button.**

That's all she wrote — your macro is recorded. I suggest you test it to see how well it runs.

To delete a macro, click the Macros button on the Developer or View tab, and in the Macros dialog box, select the macro you want to delete and then click the Delete button.

Running a Macro

Before you run a macro, take note of where the cursor is located. The macro may require the cursor to be in a certain place to run properly. Follow these steps to run a macro:

1. **On the Developer or View tab, click the Macros button (or press Alt+F8).**

The Macros dialog box, shown in Figure 5-5 appears.

2. **Select the macro that you want to run.**

Macros have cryptic names, but you can usually tell what they do by glancing at their descriptions.

If you don't see the macro you want, make a new selection in the Macro In drop-down list.

3. **Click the Run button.**

If your macro is a long one and you need to stop it from running, press Ctrl+Break. (On most keyboards, the Break key is located along with the Pause key on the right side of the keyboard, to the right of the F12 key.)

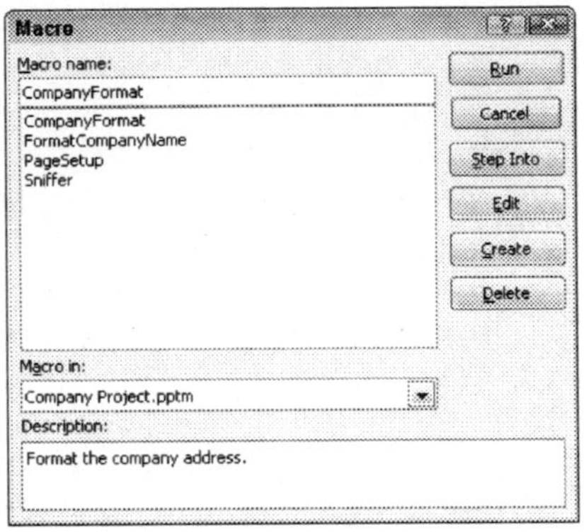

Figure showing Macro dialog box with Macro name field containing "CompanyFormat", a list showing CompanyFormat, FormatCompanyName, PageSetup, Sniffer, and buttons Run, Cancel, Step Into, Edit, Create, Delete. Macro in: Company Project.pptm. Description: Format the company address.

Figure 5-5:
The Macros
dialog box.

Editing a Macro

Editing a macro entails opening the Visual Basic Editor and editing Visual Basic codes, which is not for the faint of heart. If your macro is an uncomplicated one, you're better off re-recording it. This book isn't a developer's guide, so it can't go into the details of using the Visual Basic Editor. However, the following pages explain the basics of reading a macro in the Visual Basic Editor, deleting parts of a macro, and editing the text in a macro.

Opening a macro in the Visual Basic Editor

Follow these steps to view a macro in the Visual Basic Editor window:

1. On the Developer tab, click the Macros button (or press Alt+F8).

You see the Macro dialog box (refer to Figure 5-5).

2. Select the name of the macro that needs editing.

3. Click the Edit button.

You see the Visual Basic window, shown in Figure 5-6.

4. Choose File⇨Save (or press Ctrl+S) after you finish editing your macro.

Macro names appear in the Procedure box on the right side of the window. Those computer codes in the Code window are scary, aren't they? You can find one line of code for each command in your macro. Edit computer codes the same way that you edit text in a Word document. For example, click to the left of a line to select it and then press Delete to delete a line. Or type in the Code window to add commands or change the text that the macro enters in documents.

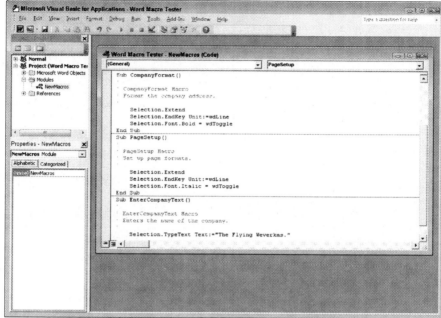

Figure 5-6:
Edit macros
in the Visual
Basic Editor
window.

Reading a macro in the Code window

Before you can do any editing in the Visual Basic Editor, you have to know
how to read the codes in the Code window. Observe these attributes of the
Code window:

✦ **Sub and End Sub line:** A macro begins with the Sub line and ends with
the End Sub line.

✦ **Apostrophes (') at the beginning of lines:** Lines that begin with an apostrophe (') are descriptive comments and aren't part of the macro except
insofar as they help you understand what it does. Notice, for example,
that the description line (the one you wrote before recording the macro)
near the top of the macro appears after an apostrophe. Enter blank lines
and lines of commentary to make macros easier to read and understand.

✦ **Text enclosed in double quotation marks ("):** Text that is typed in as
part of the macro is enclosed in double quotation marks ("). If you need
to edit the text in your macro, edit the text inside double quotation marks.

✦ **With and End With lines:** Codes that pertain to choices made in a dialog
box begin with the With line and end with the End With line.

✦ **All dialog box options are recorded:** Even if you select only a single
option in a dialog box, the macro records all the options in the dialog
box. A visit to the Font dialog box, for example, adds more than 20 lines
to a macro, one for every option in the dialog box. However, you can
edit out lines that your macro does not require.

Running a macro from a button on the Quick Access toolbar

Any macro that you run often is a candidate for the Quick Access toolbar. As Chapter 1 of this mini-book explains, you can place your own buttons on the Quick Access toolbar and move the toolbar below the Ribbon as well. Follow these steps to assign a macro to a button and place the button on the Quick Access toolbar:

1. **Right-click any button or tab and choose Customize Quick Access Toolbar on the shortcut menu.**

   You see the Quick Access Toolbar category of the Options dialog box.

2. **In the Choose Commands From drop-down list, choose Macros (you can find it near the top of the list).**

   The cryptic names of macros in your file appear in the dialog box.

3. **Select the macro you want to assign to a button and click the Add button.**

   The macro's name appears in the right side of the dialog box alongside the names of buttons already on the Quick Access toolbar.

4. **Make sure that your macro is still selected and click the Modify button.**

   The Modify Button dialog box appears. It offers symbols you can place on your macro button.

5. **Select a symbol and click OK.**

6. **Click OK in the Options dialog box.**

   A button representing your macro appears on the Quick Access toolbar. You can click this button to run your macro. If you want to remove the button, right-click it and choose Remove from Quick Access Toolbar.

Editing the text that a macro enters

As I mention earlier, text that is typed during a macro procedure is enclosed in double quotation marks (") in the Code window. To edit the text in a macro, you can edit the text between double quotation marks in the Code window. Edit this text as though you were editing it in Word.

Deleting parts of a macro

Delete part of a macro when you want to remove a command or command sequence. For that matter, you may delete parts of a macro if they are unnecessary. Deleting unnecessary lines makes a macro easier to read and run faster. As I mention in the preceding section of this chapter, a visit to a dialog box, such as the Font dialog box, adds many lines to a macro, most of which are unnecessary. Your macro requires only the lines that pertain to changing settings.

To delete part of a macro, delete the lines as though they were text in a Word document: Click or click and drag in the left margin and then press the Delete key.

Chapter 6: Linking and Embedding in Compound Files

In This Chapter

↙ Understanding what object linking and embedding (OLE) is

↙ Embedding foreign data in a file

↙ Linking to foreign data in another file

A compound file is a computer file that brings together data created in different programs. A year-end report is a classic example of a compound file. Typically, a year-end report includes word-processed text, worksheet tables, and graphics. Thanks to object linking and embedding (OLE), you can create compound files. They can include data from different sources — Excel worksheets, Word text, or Paint graphic files. What's better, you can copy and continuously update material from other programs without leaving the Office 2010 program you're working in.

All this magic is accomplished with something called object linking and embedding (OLE). This chapter explains OLE, tells you how to embed data from another file, and explains how to link data from another file so that your files are updated automatically.

OLE is available in Word, Excel, and PowerPoint, but not OneNote.

What Is OLE, Anyway?

Object linking and embedding (OLE) is a means of putting more than one program to work on the same file. You can think of OLE as a high-powered version of the standby Copy and Paste commands. As you probably know, the Copy and Paste commands are for copying material from one place or program to another. For example, with the Copy and Paste commands, you can copy text from an Excel worksheet into a Word document. You can copy columns and rows from a Word table and paste them straight into a PowerPoint table.

Linking and embedding

Object linking takes the copy-and-paste concept a step further. When you copy text from a Word document to a PowerPoint slide, you can *link* the Word file and PowerPoint slide so that changes made to the Word text are made as well to the same text on your PowerPoint slide. In effect, linking means you can run the Copy and Paste commands in the background without having to actually choose Copy or Paste. Linking establishes a connection between the two objects, in this case the text in the Word document and the text in the PowerPoint slide, so that the one automatically updates the other.

Similarly, *embedding* enables you to keep, or embed, foreign data from another program in the file you're working on. The program you're working in understands that the data is foreign. When you click the data, the program's tabs and buttons disappear to be replaced by tabs and buttons belonging to the program designed to handle the data. For example, when you click an Excel worksheet embedded in a Word document, you see Excel tabs and buttons for handling the worksheet data. In effect, you can open a second program inside the first program and use the second program to create data without having to copy the data from the second program. The object — the Word document or Excel worksheet — isn't connected to another file but is contained within the file.

Figure 6-1 shows an Excel worksheet embedded in a PowerPoint slide. Notice the Excel tabs and buttons in the window. The tabs and buttons are at the ready. After you finish using them, you can click outside the embedded object — you can click outside the Excel worksheet — and go back to using the PowerPoint tabs and buttons. Although the table data was made in Excel, it looks like a PowerPoint table. Embedding an object spares you from having to open a different program, construct material there, and copy it into the file you're working on.

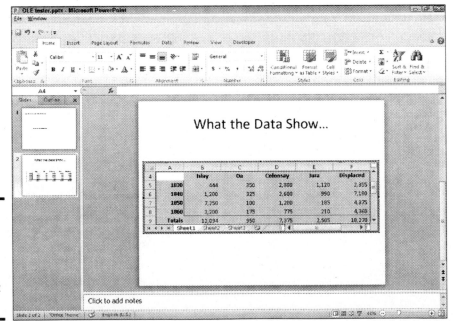

Figure 6-1:
An Excel
worksheet
embedded
in a
PowerPoint
slide.

A *linked object* is a little bit different from an embedded object. In the linked relationship, the program you're currently using shouts out to the program where the material was created to find out whether the material was edited or altered in any way. If the material was updated, you can tell Office to gather the updated material and incorporate it into your current file. Linking is an opportunity for you to keep your files up to date. You can fold the work that you or a co-worker did to the original file into your file without having to go outside the program you're using, and then copying and pasting it.

Uses for linking

Linking was designed to let files dynamically share information. The object — the Excel worksheet or Word file, for example — remains connected to its source. As the source file is updated, the files to which it is linked can be updated, too.

Book VI
Chapter 6

Linking saves you the trouble of updating files that often change. Co-workers can maintain a library of source files and use them to update the files to which the source files are linked. Here are some examples of object linking coming in handy:

- ✦ Your PowerPoint presentation contains sales data, and you want the data to be up to date. You create a link to the Excel worksheet where the sales data is stored so that your PowerPoint slide remains up to date as sales data changes.

- ✦ A co-worker has created an Excel worksheet with demographic data that often changes. In your Word report, you create a link to your co worker's worksheet so that demographic data appears in your report and is always up to date.

- ✦ Your company maintains a Word file with a list of branch office addresses and telephone numbers, and you want this list to be available to employees. You link your Word file to the company's Word file. Your address and telephone list document stays up to date as addresses and telephone numbers change.

Uses for embedding

Embedding enables you to work inside an Office program on data that the program isn't equipped to handle or display. Embed an Excel worksheet in a Word document if you want to have a table with complex mathematical formulas. Embed a Word document in an Excel worksheet if you want to write paragraphs of explanatory text and be able to call upon Word formatting commands. Consider embedding an object if you want to attempt something that you can't normally do in the program you're working in.

Pitfalls of linking and embedding

Linking and embedding aren't for everybody. Here are some OLE pitfalls:

✦ **File size:** Including embedded objects in a file makes the file grow in size — and I mean really grow. A large file can be unwieldy and hard to store. It takes longer to load on-screen. By linking, you solve the file-size problem because the item has to be stored only once — in its original location.

✦ **Carrying charges:** Links are broken if you move your file or you or someone else moves a file to which your file is linked. A file with links can't be sent over the Internet or copied to a laptop without the links being broken. Linking is out of the question in the case of files that travel to other computers. If you link to files over a network, establish a scheme for storing files with your co-workers so that files aren't moved inadvertently.

✦ **Formatting embedded and linked objects:** Unfortunately, linked and embedded objects are often hard to format. Selecting the same fonts and colors as the fonts and colors in your file can be difficult because you have to rely on the commands in the source file to do the formatting. The end result is that linked and embedded objects sometimes look out of place.

Before you undertake any activity regarding object linking and embedding, save the file you're working on. The program with which you're working needs to know precisely where OLE objects go in order to execute OLE commands. Therefore, your file must be completely up to date for OLE commands to work.

Linking to Data in a Source File

Link a slide, document, or worksheet to another file so that changes made to the other file are made automatically to your slide, document, or worksheet. Earlier in this chapter, "Uses for linking" explains the benefits of linking to another file. These pages explain how to establish the link between your files, how to update the link, how to break a link, and how to mend broken links.

Links are broken when files are renamed or moved to different folders. Linking files is more trouble than it's worth if you often move or rename files. Very carefully create or choose folders for storing linked files so that you don't have to move them.

Before you link one file to another, save the file you're working on. Your program needs to know precisely where OLE objects go in order to execute OLE commands. Therefore, your file must be completely up to date — and saved — for OLE commands to work.

Establishing the link

For the purposes of linking, the original file with the data you will link to is the *source*. Follow these steps to establish a link between your file and the source file so that your file can be updated whenever the source file is changed:

1. **Open the source file with the data that you'll link to your file.**

2. **Select the data you need and copy it to the Windows Clipboard.**

   You can do that by right-clicking and choosing Copy or pressing Ctrl+C.

3. **Click in the file where you want the linked data to appear.**

4. **Click the Save button.**

   As I explain earlier, all files must be saved and up to date for links to be successfully made.

5. **On the Home tab, establish the link between the source file and your file.**

   How you do this depends on the Office program you are working in. Do one of the following:

   - *Link and use styles:* Open the drop-down list on the Paste button and choose Link & Use Destination Styles on the drop-down list. You can also choose Link & Keep Source Formatting in the unlikely event that you want the text formatting in the source file to be retained in your file.

   - *Paste Special dialog box:* Open the drop-down list on the Paste button and choose Paste Special. You see the Paste Special dialog box.

     If you're pasting data between different programs as well as different files, the Paste Special dialog box has an As list that shows what kind of data is being transferred. Make sure the correct option is chosen in the As list and click OK in the Paste Special dialog box.

     If you're pasting data between files created in the same program, the Paste Special dialog box offers options for choosing whether to copy formats and other things. For example, to copy data between Excel worksheets, you can copy the formulas or values only. Choose options and click the Paste Link button.

6. **Save your file by clicking the Save button.**

   Congratulations. The link is established.

In some Office programs, you can open the source file from inside your file by right-clicking the linked data and choosing Linked Object⇨Open (or Open Link). The Linked Object command is named for the kind of data being linked. For example, if the link is to an Excel worksheet, the command is called Linked Worksheet Object.

To change the size of a linked object, click it, move the pointer over a selection handle, and drag. To move a linked object, move the pointer over the object and drag when you see a four-headed arrow. (To be able to move an object in Word, go to the Page Layout tab, click the Wrap Text button, and choose an option other than In Line with Text on the drop-down list.)

Updating a link

Each time you open and a file with data linked to a source file, the program you're working in asks whether you want to update your file from the source file, as shown in Figure 6-2. Click the Yes, Update, or Update Links button in the dialog box to get new, up-to-the-minute data from the source file.

In some Office programs, you can update a link after you open a file. To do so, right-click the linked data and choose Update Link on the shortcut menu.

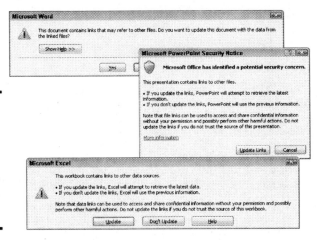

Figure 6-2:
Click Yes,
Update,
or Update
Links to
update your
file from the
source file.

Editing data in the source file

Suppose, while staring at the linked data in your file, you notice something wrong. The numbers in the table aren't accurate. There's a misspelling in the list. In some Office programs, you can open the source file and edit the data:

1. **Right-click the linked data and choose Linked Object⇨Edit (if the linked data is in an Office program) or Linked Object⇨Open (if the linked data is not in an Office program).**

   The program in which the source file was created and the source file itself open.

2. **Edit the data in the source file.**

   Changes you make are transferred immediately from the source file to your file.

3. **Click the Save button in the source file to save the editorial changes you made there.**

   When you return to your file, you see the changes you made.

Embedding Data from Other Programs

By embedding data, you can enter and edit foreign data without leaving the program you're working in. An Excel worksheet, for example, can be embedded on a PowerPoint slide (refer to Figure 6-1). When you double-click the embedded object, the computer program with which it was created opens so that you can start editing.

Embedding foreign data

How you embed data that is foreign to the program you're working in depends on whether the data has already been created. You can get a head start embedding data if you or someone else has already created it. Following are instructions for embedding an object so you can enter the data on your own and embedding data that has already been created.

Creating an embedded object from scratch

Create an embedded object from scratch if the data you need hasn't been created yet. Follow these steps:

1. **Go to the Insert tab.**

   If your aim is to create an Excel table, click the Table button, choose Excel Spreadsheet, and be done with it.

2. **Click the Object button.**

   You see the Object (or Insert Object) dialog box, as shown on the left side of Figure 6-3.

Figure 6-3:
Creating
space for
embedding
data
(left) and
embedding
an entire file
(right).

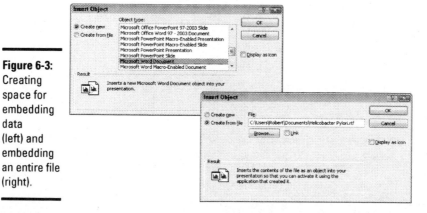

3. **Click the Create New option tab (or option button).**

4. **In the Object Type list, choose the name of the program that handles the kind of data you want to embed.**

   For example, to insert a space for Word text, choose Microsoft Word Document.

5. **Click OK.**

   Where your program's tabs and buttons used to be, you see different tabs and buttons. Use them to create and edit data.

Click outside the data when you're finished working on it.

Embedding data that has already been created

If the data you want to embed has been created already in another program, you can embed the data in your file by following these steps:

1. **Open the file with the data you want to embed.**

   Open the file in the program with which it was created.

2. **Copy the portion of the file you want to embed with the Copy command.**

   Select the data, right-click, and choose Copy in the shortcut menu.

3. **Return to the program where you want to embed the data.**

4. **Go to the Home tab.**

5. **Open the drop-down list on the Paste button and choose Paste Special.**

   You see the Paste Special dialog box, as shown in Figure 6-4.

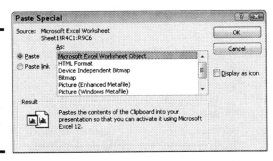

Figure 6-4:
Choose the program where the embedded data comes from.

6. **Select the Paste option button.**

7. **In the As list, choose an option with the word *Object* in its name.**

Which options appear in the list depends on which type of object you're embedding. The options without Object in their names are for pasting the data in picture format.

8. **Click OK.**

The data lands in your file.

Embedding an entire file

You can embed an entire file in the file you're working on by following these steps:

1. **In the Insert tab, click the Object button.**

You see the Object (or Insert Object) dialog box.

2. **Select the Create from File tab (or option button).**

You see the version of the Object (or Insert Object) dialog box, as shown on the right side of Figure 6-3 (shown previously).

3. **Click the Browse button.**

The Browse dialog box opens.

4. **Select the file you want to embed in your file and click OK (or Insert).**

5. **Click OK in the Object (or Insert Object) dialog box.**

That's all there is to it.

Editing embedded data

To edit an embedded object, double-click it. Where your program's tabs and buttons used to be, you see a new set of tabs and buttons — ones belonging to the program normally used to edit the type of object you're editing. When you finish editing the foreign data, click outside it.

To change the look of embedded data, right-click it and choose Format Object. Then choose formatting commands in the Format Object dialog box.

The techniques for changing the size and position of embedded objects are the same as the techniques for resizing and repositioning shapes, graphics, clip-art images, and other objects (Book I, Chapter 8 enumerates these techniques). To reposition an embedded object, move the pointer onto its perimeter and drag. To resize an embedded object, move the pointer over a selection handle and then drag.

Converting a linked object to an embedded object

As the start of this chapter explains in torturous detail, "embedded object" is Microsoft's term for data in a file that you create and manipulate with a program other than the one you are working in. In a Word document, for example, you can embed Excel data in a file and be able to edit the Excel data without leaving Word.

Suppose that the linked data in a file would serve you better if it were embedded. Rather than go to the source file to edit the data, you can put the data in your file by embedding it. For these occasions, convert your linked object into an embedded object by following these steps:

1. **Right-click the linked data and choose Linked Object⇨Convert.**

   The Convert dialog box appears.

2. **Select the Convert To option.**

3. **If necessary, select what type of data you are dealing with in the list.**

4. **Click OK.**

   There is a drawback to converting a linked object to an embedded object. The link to the source is broken, and you can no longer update the data from its original source.

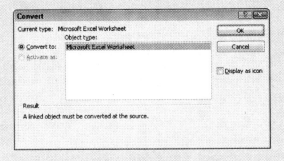

Chapter 7: Office Web Apps

In This Chapter

✔ Understanding how the Office Web Apps work

✔ Using Windows Live SkyDrive to store files online

✔ Creating, opening, and closing files in an Office Web App

✔ Maintaining folders on SkyDrive

✔ Sharing files with coworkers on SkyDrive

✔ Coauthoring files in an Office Web App

This chapter looks into Office Web Apps, the online versions of Word, Excel, PowerPoint, and OneNote. Respectively, these applications are called Word Web App, Excel Web App, PowerPoint Web App, and OneNote Web App. Anyone can use these applications. You don't have to pay a fee of any kind or install Office 2010. All you need is an Internet connection and an account with Windows Live, a Microsoft Web site. Moreover, users of the Office Web Apps can collaborate online with one another to create Word documents, Excel worksheets, PowerPoint presentations, and OneNote notebooks. As long as both of you are connected to the Internet and have a Windows Live account, you and your colleagues can work together on the same file simultaneously, even if some of you are in Maine and others in Montana.

This chapter describes how the Office Web Apps work and how to use them to collaborate with others at Windows Live. You find out how to get a Windows Live account, create files with Office Web Apps, and store files in folders at Windows Live. This chapter also explains how to manage folders and determine who can and can't get into your folders.

Introducing the Office Web Apps

The "Web App" portion of the name "Office Web Apps" stands for *Web application*. A Web application is a software program that runs from a Web site on the Internet. Web applications are sometimes called *online applications* because the software to run them isn't stored on individuals' computers, but rather on a Web server on the Internet.

The Office Web Apps are online versions of Excel, PowerPoint, Word, and OneNote. Figure 7-1 shows Excel Web App. The Office Web Apps are stripped-down versions of Excel, PowerPoint, Word, and OneNote. As a user of the Office 2010 Home and Student edition software, the Office Web Apps will be familiar to you.

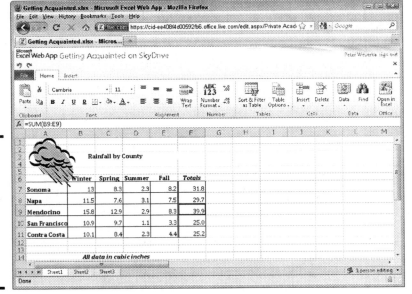

Figure 7-1:
Web appli-
cations —
Excel Web
App in this
case — are
run inside
a browser
window.

Using the Office Web Apps doesn't cost anything. Microsoft provides the Office Web Apps for free. Notice in Figure 7-1 how Excel Web App appears inside the browser window. Wherever you go and whatever you do with an Office Web App, you do it inside a browser window. When you give commands to run an Office Web App, the commands are transmitted by your browser over the Internet to the Office Web App.

To run a Web application, you start from your computer and open Internet Explorer, Firefox, or another Web browser. Then, using your browser to sign in to Windows Live, you go to a Web site where you can start the Web application. From there, you open a file and get to work. Files you work on are, like the Web application itself, stored on the Internet, not on your computer.

Storing and Sharing Files on the Internet

Here's something else that is unique about computing with the Office Web Apps: The files you work on aren't stored on your computer, but rather on Web servers on the Internet.

Storing files on the Internet makes sharing files on the Internet possible. The files aren't kept on one person's computer. They're kept on the Internet, on a Web server, where everyone with an Internet connection and permission to edit the files can edit them.

SharePoint 2010: The other way to use the Office Web Apps

In this book, I describe how to run the Office Web Apps from a server located at Windows Live, a Microsoft Web site, but you can also run Office Web Apps without keeping your files at Windows Live. Using a software product called SharePoint 2010, you can run the Office Web Apps from a SharePoint Web site on a local network. For example, you can run the applications from and store your files on a server that is owned and operated by the company you work for.

Keeping files on a network server close to home helps solve the privacy problem. Meddlers and spies who want to steal files have a harder time getting them from a server on a closed network than they do from a Windows Live server on the Internet. To maintain a SharePoint 2010 Web site, however, you need a fair amount of technical expertise. If SharePoint 2010 interests you, see *SharePoint 2010 For Dummies,* by Vanessa L. Williams.

Using an Office Web App, two or more people can work on the same file at the same time. For that matter, a dozen or a hundred people can work on the same file using an Office Web App.

This ability to share files — Microsoft uses the term *coauthor* to describe what happens when two or more people work on the same file — is one of the great advantages of the Office Web Apps. In fact, being able to share files is the greatest advantage. By themselves, the Office Web Apps aren't anything to crow about, but being able to share files, and being able to work on a shared file in an Office Web App or an Office 2010 program, is what makes the Office Web Apps special.

Office Web Apps: The Big Picture

The good news is that you can get up and running with the Office Web Apps in a matter of minutes if you have an Internet connection and a Windows Live account. Testing the waters doesn't require any special software or high-tech gadgetry on your part.

To use the Office Web Apps, start by setting up an account with Windows Live, a Microsoft Web site that offers Web-based applications and services. One of these services is called SkyDrive. Using SkyDrive, you can store and share Word, Excel, PowerPoint, and OneNote files.

Starting in SkyDrive, you can also create Word, Excel, PowerPoint, and OneNote files with Word Web App, Excel Web App, PowerPoint Web App, and OneNote Web App. SkyDrive provides folders for storing and sharing files. You can invite other people to access your SkyDrive folders, open your Office files, and collaborate with you.

Getting Ready to Use the Office Web Apps

To start using the Office Web Apps, complete these tasks:

1. **Make sure you have the right Web browser.**

   The Office Web Apps work with Internet Explorer, Firefox, Safari, and Chrome. For all occasions, I recommend using Firefox, and you can download and install it starting at this address:

   `www.mozilla.com/firefox`

2. **Install Microsoft Silverlight.**

   Silverlight is an application that improves the delivery of media over the Internet. Installing Silverlight isn't mandatory, but Microsoft recommends it because the Office Web Apps work better and faster when Silverlight is installed. To download and install Silverlight, go to this address:

   `www.silverlight.net`

3. **Sign up with Windows Live.**

   Go to the address listed here to sign up. If you intend to share files with your coworkers, be sure to get an account with Hotmail when you sign up. You will need your Hotmail account to send invitations to share files.

   `http://home.live.com`

Signing In to Windows Live

After you create an account with Windows Live, you can begin creating Office files and storing your files in SkyDrive at Windows Live.

Sign in to Windows Live by going to the address listed here, entering your ID and password, and clicking the Sign In button:

`http://home.live.com`

Click the Sign Out link when your visit to Windows Live is finished. This link is located in the upper-right corner of the window below your username.

Navigating to the SkyDrive Window

After you sign in to Windows Live, you land in the Home window, which is fine and dandy, but to use the Office Web Apps and store files on SkyDrive, you need to start at the SkyDrive window. The SkyDrive window is the place where you keep the folders that store your files.

As shown in Figure 7-2, follow these steps to go to the SkyDrive window:

1. **Move the pointer over the Windows Live link on the Windows Live taskbar.**

   The Windows Live taskbar is located along the top of the screen. It includes the Windows Live, Hotmail, Messenger, Office, and Photos links.

2. **On the drop-down list that appears, choose SkyDrive.**

   You land in the SkyDrive window. It lists top-level folders you created. If you just started using SkyDrive, you see one folder in the window — My Documents. Windows Live creates this folder for you. You can create folders of your own here, as "Creating a folder" explains shortly.

Windows Live taskbar

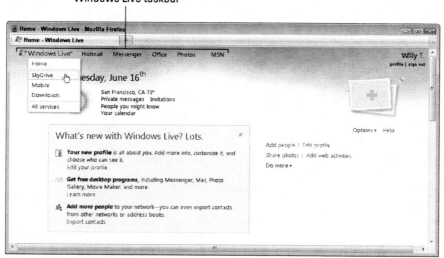

Figure 7-2:
Going to the
SkyDrive
window at
Windows
Live.

Managing Your Folders

All folders you create for storing files are kept in SkyDrive. SkyDrive can store up to 25GB of files. The measurement bar on the right side of the SkyDrive window tells you how many gigabytes (GB) remain available for storing files.

To begin with, SkyDrive gives you one folder called My Documents for storing files. These pages explain how to create folders of your own, get from folder to folder in SkyDrive, and do folder-management tasks such as renaming, deleting, and moving folders.

Creating a folder

How you create a folder depends on whether you create a top-level folder or a subfolder of another folder. When you create a top-level folder, you are asked about folder permissions and given the opportunity to upload files to the folder. These pages explain how to create top-level folders and subfolders.

Creating a top-level folder

Follow these steps to create a top-level folder for storing files:

1. **Go to the SkyDrive window.**

   The previous section in this chapter explains how to open this window (click Windows Live on the Windows Live taskbar and choose SkyDrive).

2. **Click the New button and choose Folder on the drop-down list, as shown in Figure 7-3.**

   The Create a Folder window opens.

3. **In the Name box, enter a descriptive name for the folder.**

4. **Click the Change link.**

   Options for sharing the folder and inviting others to visit it appear, as shown in Figure 7-3.

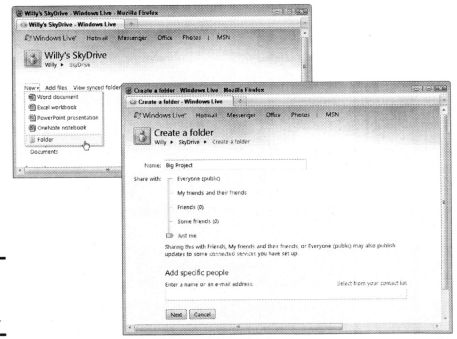

Figure 7-3:
Creating a new top-level folder.

5. **Using the Share With slider, choose an option to make the folder public, shared, or private.**

   The Share With options matter if you intend to share and coauthor files in your new folder with other people. "Establishing a Folder's Share With Permission," later in this chapter, explains the Share With settings in detail and how to change a folder's Share With settings.

   For now, choose Just Me, the default setting, to create a private folder that only you can open. You can change Share With settings later (as "Establishing a Folder's Share With Permission" explains in detail).

6. **Click the Next button.**

   The Add Documents window appears in case you want to upload files from your computer to the new folder. See "Uploading files to a folder on SkyDrive," later in this chapter, if you want to upload files.

7. **Return to the SkyDrive window (click Windows Live and choose SkyDrive on the drop-down list).**

   Your new folder appears in the SkyDrive window. Congratulations, you just created a new top-level folder.

Creating a subfolder inside another folder

A *subfolder* is a folder inside of another folder. Create a subfolder by starting inside a folder you already created or by starting inside the default My Documents that SkyDrive created for you. A subfolder inherits Share With permissions from its parent folder. This is why, when you create a subfolder, you aren't asked to choose a Share With setting for sharing files in the folder with others.

Follow these steps to create a subfolder:

1. **Open the folder that your new folder will go inside.**

   To open a folder, click its name. The next topic in this chapter describes how to navigate from folder to folder.

2. **Click the New button and choose Folder on the drop-down list.**

   You see the Create a New Folder window.

3. **In the Name box, enter a name for the folder.**

4. **Click the Create Folder button.**

   If you want to upload files from your computer to the subfolder you created, see "Uploading files to a folder on SkyDrive," later in this chapter.

Going from folder to folder in SkyDrive

After you accumulate a few folders on SkyDrive, getting to the folder you want to open can be an arduous, interminable journey. To help you on your way, SkyDrive offers different techniques for going to a folder:

✦ **The drill-down method:** Starting in the SkyDrive window (move the pointer over the Windows Live link and choose SkyDrive), click a top-level folder to display its subfolders. If necessary, keep drilling down this way until you reach the folder you want to open.

✦ **The Office link method:** On the Windows Live taskbar, move the pointer over the Office link and choose Recent Documents or Your Documents on the drop-down list. The Office window opens. This window is a convenient entré into the folders on SkyDrive:

  • *Recent Documents:* Lists documents you recently opened as well as, on the left side of the window, your top-level folders organized under the headings "Personal" and "Shared." Click the name of a folder to display its files and subfolders.

  • *Your Documents:* Lists all top-level folders under the headings "Personal" and "Shared." Click the name of a folder to display its files and subfolders.

✦ **The SkyDrive Navigation bar method:** The *SkyDrive navigation bar* — located below the folder name — lists the path to the folder that is currently open. To backtrack, click the name of a folder on the path, as shown in Figure 7-4.

✦ **The browser button method:** Click the Back or Forward button in your browser to open a folder you previously opened.

SkyDrive navigation bar

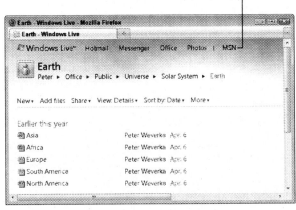

Figure 7-4: Click a folder name on the SkyDrive Navigation bar to open a folder.

By bookmarking a folder in your browser, you can go straight to a folder without having to navigate to it in Windows Live. After you choose the bookmark (and enter your Windows Live ID and password if you haven't yet signed in to Windows Live), the folder opens.

Deleting, moving, and renaming folders

To delete, move, or rename a folder, start by opening it. Then, in the Folder window, use these techniques:

✦ **Moving a folder:** Click the More link and choose Move on the drop-down list. You see a list of your folders on SkyDrive. Select a folder and then choose Move This Folder Into command. You can move only subfolders, not top-level folders.

✦ **Deleting a folder:** Click the More link and choose Delete on the drop-down list. Then click OK in the confirmation dialog box to delete the folder and all its contents.

✦ **Renaming a folder:** Click the More link and choose Rename on the drop-down list. Then enter a name in the New Name text box and click the Save button. You can't rename the My Documents folder.

Creating an Office File in SkyDrive

I'm happy to report that creating an Office file — a Word, Excel, PowerPoint, or OneNote file — in SkyDrive is quite easy. Follow these steps to create a file with an Office Web App:

1. **Open the folder where you want to store the file.**

Earlier in this chapter, "Going from folder to folder in SkyDrive" explains how to open folders and subfolders.

2. **Click the New button or move the pointer over the Office link on the Windows Live taskbar.**

3. **Choose an option on the drop-down list, as shown in Figure 7-5.**

Choose among these options:

• **Word Document:** Create a letter, report, or other word processing document.

• **Excel Workbook:** Create a worksheet for crunching numbers.

• **PowerPoint Presentation:** Create a presentation for showing slides to an audience.

• **OneNote Notebook:** Create a notebook for storing and organizing notes.

The New window opens.

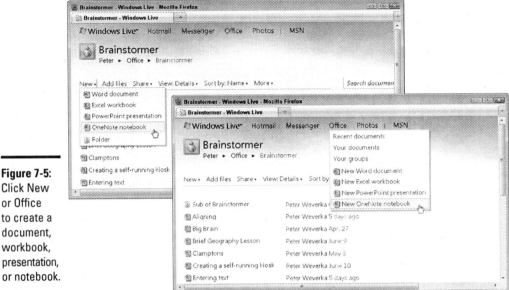

Figure 7-5:
Click New
or Office
to create a
document,
workbook,
presentation,
or notebook.

4. **In the Name text box, enter a name for your document, workbook, presentation, or notebook.**

5. **Click the Save button.**

   Your new Office file opens.

Opening and Editing Office Files Stored on SkyDrive

Opening a Word, Excel, PowerPoint, or OneNote file that you store on SkyDrive is a tad different from opening an Office file stored on a computer. You have the choice of viewing a file before you open it, opening it in your browser, or opening it in an Office 2010 program. These pages explain how to open an Office file. I also tell you what's what in the File window, which is the window you can open to preview your file.

Opening and editing a file in an Office Web App

Follow these steps to open and edit a Word, Excel, PowerPoint, or OneNote file in an Office Web App:

1. **In SkyDrive, open the folder where the file is stored.**

   Earlier in this chapter, "Going from folder to folder in SkyDrive" explains how to open folders and subfolders.

2. **Click the name of the file you want to open and edit.**

As shown in Figure 7-6, the file opens in a preview window if you clicked a Word, Excel, or PowerPoint file (OneNote files open right away without appearing first in the preview window).

You can't edit the file, but you can scroll through it to see what it's all about. If this isn't the file you want to edit, click the Close button (the *X* on the right side of the window) or go to the File tab and choose Close.

You can bypass the preview window and open a file right away in an Office Web App by switching to Details view in the folder window and selecting the Edit in Browser link beside a file's name.

3. **Click the Edit in Browser button to open the file in an Office Web App and begin editing.**

Whether you can edit a file that is kept in a folder that you share with others depends on whether you are the owner of the file, or else on the permissions you have been given for opening the file.

When you finish editing a file, click the Close button (the *X* on the right side of the window) or visit the File tab and choose Close.

To open more than one file at the same time, rather than click a file's icon, right-click it and choose Open Link in New Window or Open Link in New Tab. A new window or tab opens. (In Internet Explorer, the commands are called Open in New Window and Open in New tab.)

Open the file in an Office 2010 program

Open the file in an Office Web App

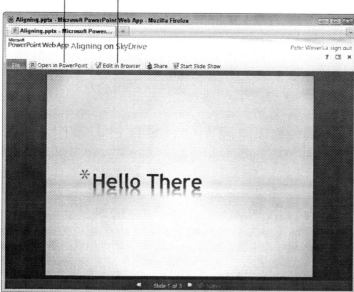

Figure 7-6:
You can examine the file in a preview window before opening it.

Opening and editing a SkyDrive file in an Office 2010 program

As anybody who has spent more than five minutes with an Office Web App knows, the Office Web Apps don't offer nearly as many features and doo-dads as their Office 2010 counterparts. If you want to create or edit a chart in Word Web App, for example, you're out of luck because Word Web App doesn't provide charts. You can, however, open a Word file that you keep on SkyDrive in Word 2010 and edit the file with your Word 2010 software.

If you get frustrated editing a file with the measly number of commands available in an Office Web App, you can open the file in Word 2010, Excel 2010, PowerPoint 2010, or OneNote 2010 and edit it there by using the techniques I explain forthwith.

Opening a file on SkyDrive in an Office 2010 program

Starting in an Office Web App, you can open an Office file from the preview window or the Home tab:

1. **Click the Open In button.**

    This button is found in the preview window and on the Home tab in all four Office Web Apps. The button is named after the Office Web App you are working in. For example, in PowerPoint Web App, the button is called Open In PowerPoint.

    *   **Preview window:** Click the Open In button (refer to Figure 7-6). To open a file's preview window, click the file's name in a folder. (See "Opening and editing a file in an Office Web App," earlier in this chapter.

    *   **Office Web App:** On the Home tab, click the Open In button, or visit the File tab and choose Open In.

    The Open Document dialog box appears.

2. **Click OK to affirm that although the file is located on the Internet, opening it is okay.**

    Word, Excel, PowerPoint, or OneNote 2010 opens on your computer, and you see the Connecting To dialog box.

3. **Enter your Windows Live ID and password; then click OK.**

    You see your file in an Office 2010 program. Depending on your Windows settings, you may have to click the Enable Editing button before you can start editing the file.

Although the file looks as though it is located on your computer, the file is located on a Web server at SkyDrive. All editorial changes you make are saved to the file on the Web server, not to a file located on your computer's hard drive.

Notice that the Save button (in Word, Excel, and PowerPoint) looks a little different from the usual Office file Save button when you open a SkyDrive-stored file in an Office 2010 program. (OneNote doesn't have a Save button.) The Save button looks different to remind you that your editorial changes, when you save your file, are sent to a server on the Internet at SkyDrive, and that changes made by others are downloaded to your file. When you click the Save button, notice the message on the status bar that says "Uploading to Server."

Editing an Office file on SkyDrive with an Office 2010 program has one big disadvantage if the file is being shared. Editing the file in Word, Excel, and PowerPoint 2010 (not OneNote) shuts out all others from editing the file at the same time in an Office Web App.

Saving a file from Office 2010 to SkyDrive

Sharing is caring, and you can save a Word, Excel, PowerPoint, or OneNote 2010 file on your computer to a SkyDrive folder starting in Word, Excel, PowerPoint, or OneNote and thereby share your file with other people. Others who have access to the folder on SkyDrive can open the file in an Office Web App or an Office 2010 program (if Office 2010 is installed on their computers).

Follow these steps to save a file to a SkyDrive folder by starting in an Office 2010 program:

1. **In Word, Excel, PowerPoint, or OneNote 2010, open the file you want to share with others on a SkyDrive folder.**

2. **On the File tab, choose Save & Send.**

   The Save & Send window opens.

3. **Choose Save to Web.**

   Save to Windows Live options appear.

4. **Click the Sign In button, enter your Windows Live ID and password, and click OK.**

   A list of folders you keep on Windows Live appears in the Save & Send window.

5. **Select the folder where you want to store the Office 2010 file.**

6. **Click the Save As button.**

   The Save As dialog box appears. In the top of the dialog box, notice the path to the folder where the file will be saved. The path shows a Web address followed by the name of the folder you selected in Step 5. You are about to save the file to a SkyDrive folder on the Internet.

7. **Click the Save button.**

Although the file appears in Excel, Word, PowerPoint, or OneNote 2010 and looks to be stored on your computer, it is stored in a SkyDrive folder. The Save button looks a little different than what you're used to in an Office file because clicking the Save button saves your editorial changes to a SkyDrive folder, not to a folder on your computer's hard drive. In fact, when you click the Save button, a message on the status bar says "Uploading to Server."

When you save an Excel, Word, PowerPoint, or OneNote 2010 file on SkyDrive, you create a second copy of the file. The original remains on your computer. Try this experiment: After saving an Office 2010 file to SkyDrive, go to the File tab and click Recent. You see a list of files you recently opened. Notice that the name of the file you saved to SkyDrive appears twice: once at a Web address on SkyDrive and once at a folder on your computer.

Later in this chapter, "Uploading files to a folder on SkyDrive" explains another way to place an Office 2010 file from your computer on SkyDrive — by uploading it.

Managing Your Files on SkyDrive

SkyDrive is first and foremost a means of organizing and managing files. You can take advantage of commands in SkyDrive to upload files, download files from SkyDrive to your computer, and delete, rename, move, and copy files. Better keep reading.

Making use of the Properties window

As shown in Figure 7-7, the Properties window is the place to go when you want to do this, that, or the other thing to a file. The window offers commands for downloading, editing, deleting, moving, renaming, and copying files.

Opening the Properties window

To open a file's Properties window, use one of these techniques:

✦ In an Office Web App or the preview window (the window you see when you click a file's name in a folder), go to the File tab and choose Properties.

✦ In a folder in Details view (click the View link and choose Details on the drop-down list), move the pointer over a file, click the file's More link, and choose Properties on the drop-down list.

✦ In the Office window (on the Windows Live taskbar, move the pointer over the Office link and choose Recent Documents), move the pointer over a file, click the file's More link, and choose Properties on the drop-down list.

Do file-related tasks   Open different file in the folder

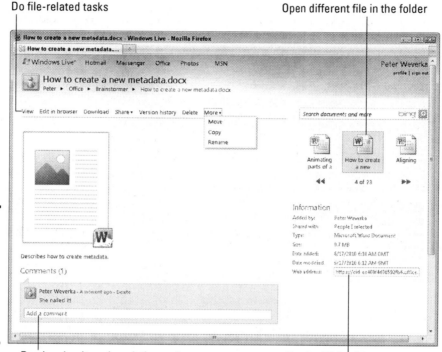

Figure 7-7:
The
Properties
window,
where you
do all things
relating to a
file.

Read and write a description and comments   Get the Web address

Properties window activities

Take heed of the activities you can do in the Properties window:

✦ **View or edit the file:** On the taskbar, click View to examine the file in the preview window; click Edit in Browser to open the file in an Office Web App.

✦ **Do other file-related tasks:** Visit the File window taskbar to download, share, delete, move, copy, or rename a file.

✦ **Read and enter a description and comments:** Especially if you share the file with others, enter a description of the file so that others know what it is. You can also enter and read comments about the file.

✦ **Examine a different file in the folder:** Click the Scroll Back or Scroll Forward button in the upper-right corner of the window to see the names of other files in the folder. Click a file's icon to open to it in the Properties window.

✦ **Get file information:** Glance at the right side of the File window to see who created the file, whether it is shared, and other information (you may have to scroll down to see this information).

✦ **Copy the file's Web address:** One way to share a file is to copy its Web address and send it to other people. Under Information, you can copy the file's address from the Web Address box. For more information, see "Sending out e-mail invitations," later in this chapter.

✦ **Copy code for embedding:** You can also share a public file by embedding code on a Web page so that others can click a hyperlink and go to the file on SkyDrive. See "Posting hyperlinks on the Internet," later in this chapter, for more information.

Uploading files to a folder on SkyDrive

A file must be smaller than 50MB to upload it to a folder on SkyDrive. Follow these steps to upload files from your computer to a folder you keep on SkyDrive:

1. **On SkyDrive, open the folder where you want to store the files.**

2. **Click the Add Files link.**

The Add Documents window appears.

3. **Upload files by dragging and dropping or selecting files in the Open dialog box.**

Choose which technique suits you best:

- *Dragging and dropping:* Open Windows Explorer, drag its window to the right side of the screen, locate the files you want to upload, and select them. You can select more than one file. Then drag and drop the files into the Add Documents window.

- *Choosing files in the Open dialog box:* Click the Select Documents from Your Computer link. The Open dialog box appears. Select files and click the Open button.

The Add Documents window lists the files you want to upload.

4. **Click the Continue button.**

The file or files are uploaded to the folder you selected in SkyDrive.

You can also upload an Excel 2010, Word 2010, PowerPoint 2010, or OneNote 2010 file by opening it in an Office 2010 program and saving it to a SkyDrive folder. See "Saving a file from Office 2010 to SkyDrive," earlier in this chapter.

Downloading files from SkyDrive to your computer

SkyDrive gives you the choice of downloading files one at a time or downloading all the files in a folder in a zip file.

◆ **Downloading a file:** In the file's Properties window, click the Download link. You see the standard dialog box for downloading files from the Internet. Choose to open or save the file after you download it and click OK. (Earlier in this chapter, "Making use of the Properties widow" explains how to open the Properties window.)

◆ **Downloading all the files in a folder:** Open a folder and click the Download as .Zip File link. In the standard dialog box for downloading files, click the Save File option button and click OK.

Moving, copying, renaming, and deleting files

Starting in a Properties window (see "Making use of the Properties window" and Figure 7-7 earlier in this chapter), use these techniques to move, copy, rename, or delete a file:

◆ **Moving a file:** Click the More link and choose Move on the drop-down list. You see a window that lists your SkyDrive folders. Select a folder name and then choose the Move This File command.

◆ **Copying a file:** Click the More link and choose Copy on the drop-down list. Then select a folder name and choose the Copy This File command.

◆ **Renaming a file:** Click the More link and choose Rename on the drop-down list. Then enter a name in the New Name text box and click the Save button.

◆ **Deleting a file:** Click the Delete link and then click OK in the confirmation dialog box.

Ways of Sharing Folders: The Big Picture

This is the first thing you need to know if you want to share and coauthor files with others on SkyDrive: Only people who have signed up with Windows Live can edit files.

Here is the second thing you need to know: The owner of a folder decides whether the folder is public, shared, or private, and for anyone besides the owner to work on a file, it must be in a public or shared folder.

Here is the third thing: The owner of a folder can choose between different ways of sharing a folder and files inside it:

◆ **Sharing with friends on Windows Live:** The owner makes the folder available to her friends on Windows Live. These friends can go to the owner's profile page, where they see all public and shared folders. Friends can open these folders, view the files, and if they have permission, edit the files. (See "Making Friends on Windows Live," the next topic in this chapter, for information about making friends.)

✦ **Sending out e-mail invitations:** The owner decides that she doesn't want to fool around with making friends on Windows Live. When she wants to share a file, she sends an e-mail invitation to visit the folder. A guest who gets the e-mail can go to the owner's SkyDrive page, where she sees the owner's public folders and the shared folders that she was invited to open. The guest can open the owner's public folders or shared folder and see a file's contents. If the guest wants to edit a file, she must sign in with Windows Live. (See "Sending out e-mail invitations," later in this chapter.)

✦ **Posting hyperlinks on the Internet:** The owner creates a hyperlink to a folder and posts it on a Web page or blog. Anyone who clicks the hyperlink goes, after signing in to Windows Live, to the owner's SkyDrive page, where all public folders and the shared folder are visible. The guest can open all public folders and open the shared folder targeted by the hyperlink, if the guest has permission to enter the shared folder. (See "Posting hyperlinks on the Internet," later in this chapter.)

Kind of confusing, isn't it? And it's not as though you have to choose one of the methods described here. You can use a combination of folder-sharing methods or use all three methods. Get together with the people with whom you will share folders and decide which folder-sharing method or methods are best for you.

Making Friends on Windows Live

As the previous topic in this chapter, "Ways of Sharing Folders," explains, one way to share folders in SkyDrive is to rely on friends you make in Windows Live. Using this method, your circle of Windows Live friends can visit your profile page, open public and shared folders if you give them permission to do that, and open the files in those folders.

If you want to use the friends method of sharing files, you need to know what a Windows Live friend is, how to choose your friends, and how to reply when someone asks to be your friend. Heave a deep sigh and keep reading.

Friend invitations on Windows Live are sent with Hotmail, the Windows Live e-mail service. If you want to share folders and files with friends, your friends on Windows Live must sign up to use Hotmail. Moreover, you must get their e-mail addresses so that you can send them invitations to be your friend.

The two types of friends

It used to be that a friend in need was a friend indeed, but Facebook, MySpace, and now Windows Live have changed the meaning of "friend." Now a friend is something less intimate. A friend is somebody you designate as your friend on a social networking Web site on the Internet.

To muddy the waters even further as to what a friend is, Windows Live makes a distinction between two types of friends:

+ **Limited-access friend:** This friend can't send you instant messages, see your photo files, or get your contact information, but this friend can get information about your activities on Windows Live. As shown in Figure 7-8, when someone on Windows Live asks to be your friend, you can select the Limit the Access This Person Has to My Stuff and My Info check box to make your newfound friend a limited-access friend.

+ **Friend:** This friend has full privileges to your Windows Live information and will be your friend till your dying day, through thick or thin.

For the purposes of sharing files, the two types of friends matter in that you can admit friends into a shared folder but keep limited-access friends out of it, as "Establishing a Folder's Share With Permissions" explains later in this chapter.

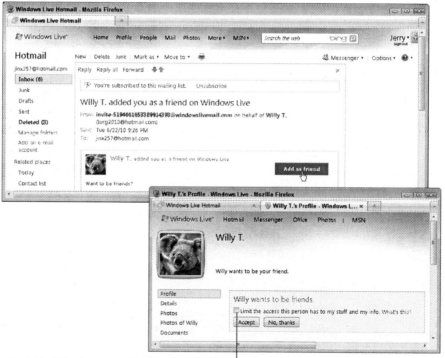

Figure 7-8: Befriending someone on Windows Live.

Click Limit the Access to This Person to make yourself a limited-access friend

Fielding an invitation to be someone's friend

As shown at the top of Figure 7-8, invitations to be friends with someone else arrive in the form of e-mail messages. (To make friends on Windows Live, you must sign up for Hotmail, the Windows Live e-mail service.) To open the Inbox, click the Hotmail link on the Windows Live taskbar. Accept or decline the invitation by following these steps:

1. **Click the "Added you as a friend on Windows Live" message to open it.**

   The message window opens.

2. **Click the Add As Friend button.**

   Click this button whether or not you want a new friend. A profile window for the person who sent the invitation appears, as shown at the bottom of Figure 7-8. You can click the Details button in this window to discover more about the person who wants to be your friend.

3. **Click the Accept button to accept the invitation, or the No Thanks button to decline it (or simply ignore the invitation altogether).**

   To be a limited-access friend, select the Limit the Access This Person Has to My Stuff and My Info check box. The previous topic in this chapter, "The Two Types of Friends," explains what a limited-access friend is.

And if you don't want to be friends with someone anymore? Click the Profile link to go to your Profile page and then click the Your Friends link to see a list of your friends. Then select your friend's name and click the Delete link.

Inviting someone to be your friend

To add a friend, get his or her Hotmail e-mail address and send an invitation by following these steps:

1. **Click the Profile link.**

   This link is located in the upper-right corner of the screen below your name. You land on your Profile page.

2. **Click the Your Friends link to see your list of friends.**

3. **On the left side of the window, under "Your Network," click the Add People link.**

4. **Enter your prospective friend's e-mail address in the text box and click the Next button.**

5. **In the window that appears, jot down a note to your prospective friend.**

6. **Click the Invite button.**

   If your friend accepts your invitation, you are alerted by e-mail in your Hotmail account.

To see a list of your friends, click the Profile link (located below your name in the upper-right corner of the window). The names of your friends appear on the right side of your Profile page. You can click a friend's name to go to his or her Profile page.

Understanding the Folder Types

Whether coworkers can open a folder in SkyDrive, view its files, and edit its files depends on what kind of folder it is. In some types of folders, you can do tasks such as renaming and deleting files.

These pages explain the different types of folders. They also spell out which tasks you can do in private, public, shared, and linked folders. You need to know about folder types if you intend to collaborate with others on files that are stored in SkyDrive folders.

Types of folders

Table 7-1 describes the four types of folder — private, shared, public, and linked. Which Share With permission is assigned to a folder determines what kind of folder it is. Later in this chapter, "Establishing a Folder's Share With Permissions" explains how to assign a Share With permission to a folder.

Table 7-1	Types of SkyDrive Folders
Folder Type	*Description*
Private	Only the folder's owner — its creator — sees the folder in SkyDrive and can open the folder, view its files, and edit its files. The default My Documents folder is an example of a private folder.
	Store files in a private folder if you don't want anybody else to be able to see or open the files.
Shared	Friends on Windows Live and guests whom the owner invites to a shared folder can see the shared folder, open the folder to see the names of files inside it, open the files, and edit the files. Friends and guests can do other file-management tasks as well.
	Store files in a shared folder to collaborate with others online.
Public	Friends on Windows Live and guests whom the owner invites to his or her SkyDrive page can see and open all public folders and view the files in all public folders. However, guests can't edit files or do most file-management tasks.
	Don't store files in a public folder unless you don't care at all whether anybody sees them.

continued

Table 7-1 *(continued)*

Folder Type	Description
Linked	Anybody who has been invited to open the folder can open it, whether or not they have a Windows Live account. Invitations to open the folder are sent by e-mail. After opening the folder, a guest can see the names of files in the folder, open a file, and view the contents of a file. To edit a file after opening it, however, the guest must have a Windows Live account.
	Store files in a Linked folder to allow people who don't have Windows Live accounts to view files' contents.

Knowing what kind of folder you're dealing with

You can tell which type of folder you're dealing with by glancing at its icon in the SkyDrive window. As shown in Figure 7-9, private folders have the lock symbol, shared folders the people symbol, public folders the globe symbol, and linked folders the e-mail symbol.

Figure 7-9:
Left to right:
A private
folder,
shared
folder,
public
folder,
and linked
folder.

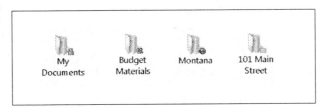

As Figure 7-10 shows, you can also tell whether a folder is private, shared, public, or linked by opening its Folder window (click a folder's icon to open its Folder window). Next to the words "Shared With," these words tell you what type of folder you're dealing with:

"Just Me"	Private folder
"Friends"	Shared folder
"Everyone (public)"	Public folder
"People with a link"	Linked folder

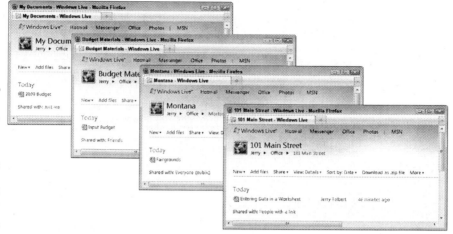

Figure 7-10:
In the Folder window, the "Shared With" words tell you what type of folder it is.

You can click the words next to "Shared With" to open the Permissions window and find out who owns the folder as well as who is sharing it (if anybody is allowed to share it).

Public and shared folder tasks

Table 7-2 lists tasks that Windows Live friends and guests of public folders and shared folders can do. The owner of a public folder or shared folder — the person who created the folder in the first place — can do all the tasks listed in Table 7-2.

Table 7-2	Tasks in Public and Shared Folders	
Task	**Public Folder**	**Shared Folder**
View Office files	Yes	Yes
Create new Office files	No	Yes
Edit an Office file with an Office Web App	No	Yes
Edit an Office file with an Office 2010 program (Word, Excel, PowerPoint, or OneNote)	No	Yes*
Establish permissions (decide who can view and edit files)	No	No
View permissions (see who owns and who can view and edit files)	Yes	Yes
Do folder-management tasks (delete, rename, and move the folder)	No	No

continued

Table 7-2 *(continued)*

Task	Public Folder	Shared Folder
Do subfolder-management tasks (create, delete, rename, and move a subfolder within the folder)	No	Yes
Upload files to the folder	No	Yes
Download an individual file from the folder	Yes	Yes
Download all the files in the folder in a .ZIP file	No	Yes
Delete files	No	Yes
Rename files	No	Yes
Move files to a subfolder within the folder	No	Yes
Copy files to a subfolder within folder	No	Yes

* To edit an Office file stored in SkyDrive with Word 2010, Excel 2010, PowerPoint 2010, or OneNote 2010, those programs must be installed on your computer.

Establishing a Folder's Share With Permissions

When you create a new top-level folder, SkyDrive asks you to choose a Share With option to determine whether the folder is private, shared, or public (see "Understanding the Folder Types" earlier in this chapter for a description of private, shared, and public folders). At any time, however, you can follow these steps to establish or change a top-level folder's Share With permissions:

1. **Open the folder.**

To open a folder window, click its name in the SkyDrive window.

2. **Click the Share With link and choose Edit Permissions on the drop-down list.**

You see the Edit Permissions window shown in Figure 7-11.

3. **Drag the Who Can Access This slider up or down to determine the folder's Share With permissions.**

Choose whether to make the folder public, shared, or private. Earlier in this chapter, "Types of folders" explains the three folder types.

- *Public folder:* Choose Everyone (Public).

- *Shared folder:* Choose one of the Friends settings:

  My Friends and Their Friends allows your Windows Live friends and friends you have in common with your Windows Live friends to access the folder.

Friends allows all your Windows Live friends, including your limited-access friends, to access the folder. Earlier in this chapter, "The two types of friends" explains the difference between friends and limited-access friends.

Some Friends allows your Windows Live friends but not friends with limited-access to access the folder.

- *Private folder:* Choose Just Me.

As "Ways of Sharing Folders" explains earlier in this chapter, you can share files on SkyDrive without having Windows Live friends. With this method, you invite colleagues by e-mail to share the files in a folder. If you want to use this method of sharing files, choose the Friends setting in the Edit Permissions window (and see "Sending out e-mail invitations," later in this chapter).

Be careful about making a folder public. Anyone who comes to your SkyDrive profile page or who is invited to share a folder with you can open any public folders you have and see their contents. Your public folders are exposing themselves! I just thought you'd like to know.

4. **Optionally, if you choose Friends or Some Friends, you can open the drop-down list and choose Can View Files if you want your friends to be able to view the files in the folder but not edit them.**

If you choose Can View Files, friends who visit your shared folder have the same privileges as visitors to a public folder. In other words, they have a narrower set of privileges. For example, they can't edit files in Office 2010 programs. Table 7-2, earlier in this chapter, describes tasks you can do in public and private folders.

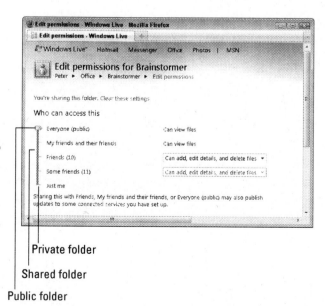

Figure 7-11:
The Edit
Permissions
window.

Private folder

Shared folder

Public folder

5. Click the Save button.

Share With permissions are assigned to top-level folders in SkyDrive. Subfolders inside these top-level folders inherit their permissions from their parent folders. For example, if a top-level folder called Planner is a shared folder, all subfolders that you or others create inside the Planner folder are shared folders as well.

Sharing on a Public or Shared Folder

Earlier in this chapter, "Ways of Sharing Folders" explains the different methods of sharing top-level folders on SkyDrive. You can create a circle of friends and share folders with them, bring others to a SkyDrive folder by invitation, or post hyperlinks that colleagues can click to get to a shared SkyDrive folder. All three techniques are explained forthwith.

Sharing with friends on Windows Live

Earlier in this chapter, "Making Friends on Windows Live" shows you how to invite people on Windows Live to be your friend. It also explains how to field invitations from others who want to make friends with you. If a friend on Windows Live is sharing his or her folders, how do you get to your friend's folders? Good question. Follow these steps to navigate to a friend's folders:

1. Click the Profile link to open your Profile page.

This link is located in the upper-right corner of the window. The right side of the Profile page lists your friends.

2. Click the name of the friend who is sharing folders.

You land in your friend's Profile page, as shown at the top of Figure 7-12.

3. Click the Documents link (it's on the left side of the screen).

Folders that your friend is sharing appear in Details view in the Documents window, also shown in Figure 7-12.

4. Click a folder name to open a folder.

5. Click a file name to open a file.

Whether you can edit as well as open a file in the folder depends on the Share With settings its owner, your friend, chose for the folder.

Figure 7-12:
Click the
Documents
link to see
a list of
folders your
friend is
sharing.

Sending out e-mail invitations

To share folders on Windows Live without making friends on the site, you
can send out e-mail invitations to folders. The left side of Figure 7-13 shows
an e-mail invitation to visit a SkyDrive folder. By clicking the View Folder
button in the invitation, also shown in Figure 7-13, the recipient of the e-mail
can go straight to a folder on SkyDrive. These invitations can be sent to
people who are enrolled in Windows Live as well as people who aren't members of that exclusive club.

Follow these steps to send an e-mail invitation to someone to collaborate at
a public or shared SkyDrive folder:

1. **Open the public or shared folder with the files that you want to share.**

2. **On the taskbar, click the Share link and choose Send a Link on the
   drop-down list.**

   The Send a Link window opens, as shown on the left side of Figure 7-13.

3. **Enter the e-mail address of the person you want to invite.**

   If you maintain a Contacts List at Windows Live, you can click the To
   button and select names from your Contacts List. To enter more than
   one address, separate the addresses with a colon or semicolon.

4. **If you want, enter a note to accompany the invitation.**

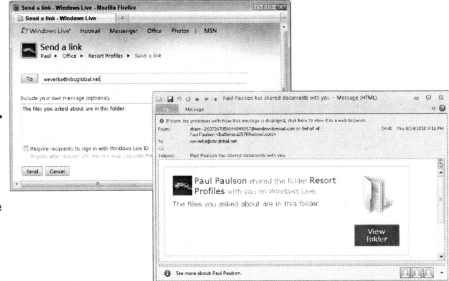

Figure 7-13:
Composing
an e-mail
invitation
to a folder
(left) and the
invitation
after it
arrives
(right).

I suggest telling recipients to bookmark the folder after they visit it the first time. Except by keeping the e-mail invitation on hand and clicking the View Folder button to visit the folder (refer to Figure 7-13), recipients won't be able to visit the folder without bookmarking it. By bookmarking the folder, they can select the bookmark in their browsers and go to the folder without having to reopen the e-mail message.

5. **Optionally, select the Require Recipients to Sign In with Windows Live ID check box if you want to share this folder only with people who have a Windows Live account.**

   If you don't select the check box, guests can open the folder without first signing in to Windows Live. They can open and view files in the folder, but they can't edit the files unless they provide a Windows Live ID.

   If you select the check box, guests have to enter their Windows Live ID before they can see, much less open, the folder.

6. **Click the Send button.**

If you don't select the Require Recipients to Sign In with Windows Live ID check box, your folder becomes a linked folder. Anybody who has the link can see its files. Linked folders are marked with the e-mail icon (see "Understanding the Folder Types," earlier in this chapter, for a detailed explanation of linked folders). If you prefer that your linked folder be another kind of folder, open the folder, click the Share With Link on the toolbar, and choose Edit Permissions on the drop-down list to go to the Edit Permissions page. Then deselect the Don't Require Sign-In to View This Folder check box.

Posting hyperlinks on the Internet

Yet another way to attract people to a SkyDrive folder with files you want to share is to obtain the folder's hyperlink and either give the hyperlink to other people or make it part of a Web page by pasting it into the Web page's HTML code.

Obtaining a folder's URL link

To direct guests to a public or shared folder, you can obtain the folder's Web address, copy it, and send it to guests or use it to create a hyperlink. Guests who follow the link go to the folder. Follow these steps to obtain the Web address of a public or shared folder:

1. **Open the folder with the files you want to share.**

2. **In the Folder window, click the Share link on the toolbar and choose Get a Link on the drop-down list.**

The Get a Link window opens. It offers two hyperlinks if your folder is shared (or one if it is private).

People who click the first hyperlink have to enter their Windows Live ID to view the folder you want to share.

People who click the second hyperlink (or the first and only link, if your folder is public) can open the folder without providing a Windows Live ID, but they can only view the files, not edit them. (Click the Create Link button to create the second hyperlink.)

Your folder becomes a linked folder when you create a hyperlink to a Public folder or click the Create Link button to create a hyperlink to a shared folder such that people can visit the folder without entering a Windows Live ID. Anyone who has its hyperlink can visit a linked folder. (Earlier in this chapter, "Understanding the Folder Types" describes linked folders.) To turn a linked folder into another kind of folder, open the folder, click the Share With Link on the toolbar, choose Edit Permissions on the drop-down list, and deselect the Don't Require Sign-In to View This Folder check box on the Edit Permissions page.

3. **Click in a Web Address box to select its hyperlink.**

The text in the box is highlighted.

4. **Right-click and choose Copy.**

The hyperlink is copied to the Clipboard. Now you can paste the address in an e-mail message or use it to create a hyperlink that directs guests to the folder.

5. **Click the Done button.**

Obtaining HTML code for a public folder hyperlink icon

If you know your way around HTML codes, you can obtain code that creates a hyperlink icon that directs users to a public folder, and you can embed the code in a Web page or blog. Guests can click the hyperlink icon on the Web page or blog to open the public folder without having to enter a Windows Live ID. The icon appears in form of a folder icon that looks just like a folder icon in the SkyDrive window.

Follow these steps to obtain the HTML code:

1. **Open the public folder with the files you want to share.**

2. **In the Folder window, click the Share link and choose Embed on the drop-down list.**

   The Share window opens. The code you see in this window, after it is embedded in a Web page or blog, creates the icon hyperlink shown on the right side of the window.

3. **Click the code to select it.**

   The code is highlighted.

4. **Right-click and choose Copy.**

   The HTML code is copied to the Clipboard. Now you can paste the code in a Web page or blog.

5. **Click the Done button.**

   You return to the Folder window.

Writing File Comments and Descriptions

If you share a file with others, be sure to enter comments and a description in the file's Properties window. Comments are the only way to record when changes were made and what the changes were. You owe it to the people with whom you share files to describe your editorial changes. While you're at it, you can also enter a description of the file in the Properties window to help your collaborators understand what the file is all about.

Figure 7-14 shows a Properties window with a description and comments. To open the Properties window, open the folder where the file is located and switch to Details view (click the View link and choose Details). Then move the pointer over the file's name, click More on the toolbar, and choose Properties.

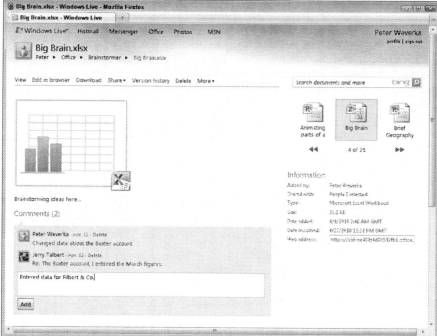

**Book VI
Chapter 7**

Office Web Apps

Figure 7-14:
The
Properties
window
offers
places for
writing a
description
and
comments.

Follow these instructions to enter a description or comments in the
File window:

✦ **A description:** Click where the description or the words "Add a
Description" are and enter a description. You can change a file's description at any time by clicking the description, which makes the description
box appear, and entering a new description.

✦ **Comments:** Enter a comment in the Add a Comment box and click the
Add button. Along with the commenter's name and the time of the comment, comments appear below the Comments box. You can delete a
comment by clicking its Delete link.

Coauthoring Files Shared on SkyDrive

Microsoft uses the word *coauthor* to describe what happens when two
people work on the same file simultaneously. Depending on which Web
App you're working in, it isn't always possible to work on the same file with
someone else. Sometimes you have to open the file in an Office 2010 program, not a Web App, to coauthor a file. These pages explain how you can
coauthor files that are stored on SkyDrive and find out who else is coauthoring a file. You also discover what to do when you get locked out of a file.

When you can and can't coauthor

Whether and how you coauthor files depends on the Office Web App you're working in. Sometimes you can't coauthor a file in an Office Web App and have to coauthor it an Office 2010 program instead. Table 7-3 describes when you can and can't coauthor files in Office Web Apps and Office 2010 programs.

Table 7-3	Coauthoring Files Stored on SkyDrive		
User #1	*User #2*	*Description*	*Coauthoring?*
Word			
Word Web App	Word Web App	More than one person can't coauthor the same document in Word Web App.	No
Word Web App	Word 2010	One person in Word Web App and the other in Word 2010 can't coauthor the same document.	No
Word 2010	Word 2010	Two people both working in Word 2010 can coauthor the same document.	Yes
Excel			
Excel Web App	Excel Web App	More than one person can coauthor the same worksheet in PowerPoint Web App.	Yes
Excel Web App	Excel 2010	One person in Excel Web App and the other in Excel 2010 can't coauthor the same worksheet.	No
Excel 2010	Excel 2010	Two people, both editing in Excel 2010, can't coauthor the same worksheet.	No

User #1	User #2	Description	Coauthoring?
PowerPoint			
PowerPoint Web App	PowerPoint Web App	Two people can't coauthor the same presentation in PowerPoint Web App.	No
PowerPoint Web App	PowerPoint 2010	One person in PowerPoint Web App and the other in PowerPoint 2010 can't coauthor the same presentation.	No
PowerPoint 2010	PowerPoint 2010	Two people, both working in PowerPoint 2010, can coauthor the same presentation.	Yes
OneNote			
OneNote Web App	OneNote Web App	More than one person can coauthor the same notebook in OneNote Web App.	Yes
OneNote Web App	OneNote 2010	One person in OneNote Web App and the other in OneNote 2010 can coauthor the same notebook.	Yes
OneNote 2010	OneNote 2010	Two people, both working in OneNote, 2010 can coauthor the same workbook.	Yes

Book VI
Chapter 7

Office Web Apps

Finding out who your coauthors are

Except when you're working in OneNote Web App or OneNote 2010, it's easy to find out who is coauthoring a file with you. Follow these instructions to see who is coauthoring a file:

+ **In Excel Web App:** The lower-right corner of the Office Web App window tells you how many people are coauthoring a file. As shown in Figure 7-15, you can click this notice to see a pop-up window that lists the Windows Live IDs of the other coauthors.

✦ **In Word 2010 and PowerPoint 2010:** On the status bar, the number next to the Authors icon tells you the number of coauthors. Click the Authors icon to see a pop-up list with coauthors' names. You can also go to the File tab, choose Info, and see your coauthors' names in the Information About window.

You can't find out who is currently editing a OneNote notebook, but you can get the names of people who wrote notes. In OneNote Web App, go to the View tab and choose Show Authors to see who authored notes. The name of its author appears beside each note. In OneNote 2010, authors' initials appear beside their notes. (Go to the View tab and click the Hide Authors button if you don't see authors' initials.) By moving the pointer over initials, you can read the author's name and when the note was written or edited last.

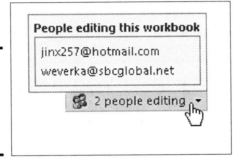

Figure 7-15:
Seeing who else is editing a file in Excel Web App.

Getting locked out of a shared file

As Table 7-3 (earlier in this chapter) explains, you can coauthor files in Excel Web App and OneNote Web App, but not in Word Web App or PowerPoint Web App. And you can coauthor files in Word 2010, PowerPoint 2010, and OneNote 2010, but not Excel 2010.

Here are scenarios for what happens if you try to open a file on SkyDrive that is already open in an incompatible program:

✦ **Want to open in Word, Excel, or PowerPoint Web App; already open in Word, Excel, or PowerPoint 2010:** In this scenario, the file you want to open in an Office Web App is already open in an Office 2010 program. You see the message box at the top of Figure 7-16. All you can do is click OK in the message box and come back later when your colleague finishes working on the file in Word, Excel, or PowerPoint 2010.

✦ **Want to open in Word 2010, Excel 2010, or PowerPoint 2010; already open in Word Web App, Excel Web App, or PowerPoint Web App:** In this scenario, the file you want to open in an Office 2010 program is already open in an Office Web App, and you can't open it in an Office 2010 program.

If the file is already open in your browser window and you try to open it by clicking the Open In button, you see the message box in the middle of Figure 7-16. All you can do is click OK and keep editing in your browser.

If you try to open the file in an Office 2010 from the get-go, you see the File In Use message box shown at the bottom of Figure 7-16. Choose an option and click OK:

• *View a Read-Only Copy:* The file opens in read-only mode. You can examine but not edit the file unless you click the Save As button and save it under a different name.

• *Save and Edit a Copy of the File:* The Save As dialog box opens so that you can save a copy of the file to work on. The copy is saved in the same SkyDrive folder as the original.

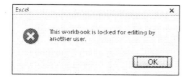

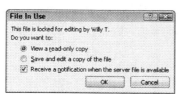

Figure 7-16: Locked out! What's a person to do?

Retrieving an earlier version of a file

For your convenience and to rescue you when a coworker has made hash out of a file, SkyDrive keeps copies of earlier versions of files and gives you the opportunity to revisit an earlier version and restore it as the official version if you so desire. Each time you close a file, a new version is created and kept on hand.

To examine older versions of a file, click the file's icon to open it in the preview window; then go to the File tab and choose Properties.

You land in the Properties window. From there, click the Version History link. The preview window opens the latest version of the file and lists older versions.

To examine an older version of a file, click its date and time designation on the left side of the window. The older version appears in the preview window. To restore an older version and make it once again the official version of the file, click the Restore link.

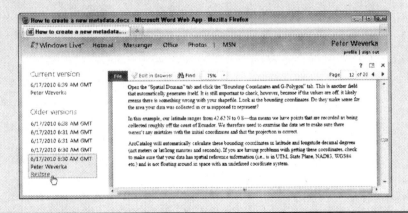

Index

A

Access, 10
Accounting Number Format button, Excel, 406
action button, PowerPoint, 385–386
Action Settings dialog box, PowerPoint, 385–386
active cell, Excel worksheet, 397–400, 415, 419
Add Assistant command, 150
Add Choice dialog box, Word, 203
Add Clips to Organizer dialog box, Clip Organizer, 557–558
Add Custom Dictionary dialog box, 72
Add Documents window, SkyDrive, 587, 596
Add Picture Shortcut dialog box, Picture Manager, 545
Add Shape commands, 147–150
Add View dialog box, Excel, 423
address, printing on envelope, 271–272
address block, in Word, 277, 279
address label, printing in Word, 272–274
adjacent cells, selecting in Excel, 419
Adjust List Indents option, Word, 221
Adobe Reader, 524–525

Advanced Find option, 48
Advanced Properties option, 28
After style, Word, 220
Align commands, 87, 175–177, 349
Align Text commands, PowerPoint, 349
aligning
  objects, 171, 175–176, 358
  text, 87, 356
Alignment button, Layout tab, 87, 97
Alignment group, Word, 87
All Caps text effect, 41
All Programs option, Start menu, 10–11
All Slides dialog box, PowerPoint, 379
alphabetizing list, in Word, 281
Alt key, 20, 358
Analysis button, Layout tab, 123
analyzing data, in Excel, 461–470
angle, line, 162
animation, PowerPoint, 309, 359–362
annotating chart, 139
antonym, 78
Any Value data-validation rule, Excel, 410
Apply Styles task pane, Word, 231, 233–235, 237
area chart, 108, 111, 113–115, 123
arguments, Excel function, 442, 444

arithmetic operators, 429–430
Arrange All button, 62
Arrange button, 102, 125, 176–177, 179–181, 249–250, 490
arrow keys, 400
arrows, 17, 160–165
artistic effect, 536, 539
ascending sorts, 100
aspect ratio, 174, 547
Aspect Ratio crop option, 541
Attach File button, OneNote, 496
Attach Template dialog box, Word, 243
attaching
  file to e-mail, 530
  Office file to notes, in OneNote, 495–496
audio, PowerPoint presentation, 362–365
Audio icon, PowerPoint, 362, 364–365, 371
audio note, OneNote, 493–495
Audio Tools, PowerPoint, 364–365, 371
author, searching for OneNote notes by, 502–503
Auto Brightness button, Picture Manager, 547
AutoCorrect feature, 62–65, 70, 221, 348, 546
AutoFill command, Excel, 404–406, 412
AutoFill handle, Excel, 405, 437

AutoFit mechanism, 86,
90, 247, 346–349,
449–450
AutoPlay dialog box,
PowerPoint, 388
AutoRecovery file,
24–25
AutoSum button, Excel,
444
Available Templates and
Themes window,
PowerPoint, 310–311
Available Templates
window, 191–192,
202, 204, 238, 240,
396–397, 460
AVERAGE function,
Excel, 429, 441
axes, chart, 105,
129–130
Axes button, Layout
tab, 129, 140
Axis Titles button,
Layout tab, 128

B

background,
PowerPoint slide
changing, of single
or multiple slides,
336–337
clip art image in,
333–334
gradient color blend,
331–332
overview, 327–329
pictures as, 334–335
solid color for, 330–331
style variation,
choosing, 330
texture as, 335–336
transparent color for,
330–331
background, removing
from picture, 536,
542–543

background color, Word
document, 258
Background Removal
tab, 542
Background Styles
gallery, PowerPoint,
330
balancing color, in
Picture Manager, 547
balloon, revision, in
Word, 267–268, 280
banded columns and
rows, table, 93
bar chart, 108, 110,
113–114
bar of pie chart, 113,
121–122
Bar tab, Word, 223–224
Based On option, style,
234, 236
baseline, chart, 130
Before style, Word, 220
bibliography, Word
document, 296–301
Bing research site, 75
bitmap graphic, 533
Black color scheme, 519
Blank Document
template, Word, 192,
230, 238
blanking screen,
during PowerPoint
presentation, 381
block of cells, selecting
in Excel, 419
Blog Accounts dialog
box, Word, 530
Blog Post tab, Word,
528–530
Blue color scheme, 519
boilerplate text, 310
bold font style, 4, 37,
39–40, 286
Bookmark dialog box,
Word, 201, 289
bookmarks, 201, 289,
292, 589, 608

border
Excel worksheet cell,
453–454
table, 84, 93–94
in Word documents,
256–257
Border and Shading
Options dialog box,
Word, 257
Borders and Shading
dialog box, Word,
94, 256–257
Break key, 567
breaking
columns, in Word
document, 254
lines in PowerPoint, 344
lines in Word, 209–210
links between text
boxes, in Word, 256
pages, 210
sections, 208–209
brightness, 324, 332, 372,
536–538, 546–547
Brightness and Contrast
task pane, Picture
Manager, 546–547
Bring commands, 102,
178–179, 490
Browse By icons, Word,
198, 200
Browse dialog box, 579
Browse the Headings
tab, Word, 199
Browse the Pages tab,
Word, 199
browser, Web, 584
bubble chart, 108, 116,
118–120
Building Blocks
Organizer dialog
box, Word, 227
bullet, 220, 222, 312, 350
bulleted list, 152–153,
220–223, 350–352
Bullets and Numbering
dialog box,
PowerPoint, 351–352

C

Calibri font, 499
callout shape, 139
cap, line, 162, 163
capitalization, 42–44, 65
Caps Lock key, 65
caption, PowerPoint photo album, 323, 325
categories, chart, 105
category axis, chart, 105
CD, packaging PowerPoint presentation on, 386–388
cell, Excel worksheet
  AutoFill command, 404–405
  borders on, 453–454
  clicking to enter cell references, 431
  color in, 454
  copying contents of, 420
  deleting contents of, 419
  entering data in, 400
  formulas, copying from cell to cell, 436–437
  moving contents of, 420
  raw data for chart, entering, 124
  referring to in different worksheets, 435–436
  referring to in formulas, 425–427
  selecting, 419
  text, merging and centering across, 448
  text labels, 401
  tracing cell references, 439–440
cell, table, 83, 86

cell address, Excel worksheet, 397–399, 435
cell range, Excel, 431–435
Cell Size group button, Word, 89
cell style, for Excel worksheet, 450–452
Cell Styles gallery, Excel, 450–452
cell tracer, Excel, 439–440
Center tab, Word, 223–224
Change Chart Type dialog box, 126, 137
changes, tracking. *See* tracking changes to Word document
Chapter Intro style, Word, 220
chapter number, in page number, 216
Chapter Title style, Word, 220, 286
character style, Word, 230–231
Chart dialog box, 106
Chart Elements drop-down list, 122, 131–133, 135–138
chart floor, 133
Chart group, Excel, 106
Chart Layouts gallery, 136
Chart Styles gallery, 17–18, 126–127
Chart Title button, Layout tab, 128
Chart Tools tabs, 125
chart wall, 133
charts. See also *specific types of chart by name*
  annotating, 139
  changing type of, 126
  Chart Styles gallery, 126–127
  choosing type of, 108

  combination, 121–123
  creating, 105–107
  drop lines, 123
  elements, appearance of, 132–133
  error bars, 123
  Excel, 398
  gridlines, 130–132
  layout, 127–130
  parts of, 103–105
  picture, decorating with, 135
  positioning in, 124–125
  in PowerPoint presentations, 357
  raw data, displaying alongside, 136
  raw data, providing for, 124
  shape, 126
  size, 126
  template, saving as, 133–134
  trendline, 122–123, 137–138
  troubleshooting, 138–140
  types of, 108–109
  up/down bars, 123
  in Word documents, 245–246
Charts folder, 134
Charts group button, Excel, 106
Choose a File or Set of Files to Insert dialog box, OneNote, 496
Choose a SmartArt Graphic dialog box, 141, 143–145, 153
Choose Document to Insert dialog box, OneNote, 496
Choose Location dialog box, PowerPoint, 388
Choose Theme dialog box, PowerPoint, 324

Choose Theme or Themed Document dialog box, PowerPoint, 329

citation, Word document bibliography, 297–299

clip art, 245–246, 358, 551–553. *See also* Clip Organizer

clip art slide background, PowerPoint, 328, 330, 333–334

Clip Art task pane, 552–553, 556–557

Clip Organizer, 10, 552–560

Clipboard, 35–36, 575

Clock transition, PowerPoint, 359

coauthoring files, 583, 611–615

Code window, Visual Basic Editor, 568–570

Collapse All option, Word, 199

Collapse button, 283, 475

Collapse Navigation Bar button, OneNote, 474

Collection List pane, Clip Organizer, 554, 556–560

color
  background, in Word documents, 258
  balancing in Picture Manager, 547
  bullet, 352
  chart gridline, 131
  diagram shape, 156–158
  for drawing in PowerPoint, 380
  Excel worksheet, decorating with, 454
  gridline, changing, 131

of letters in WordArt image, 170

object outline, 185

in OneNote drawings, 490

for PowerPoint slide background, 329–332

recoloring items, 98, 372, 536, 538–539

shape fill, 182–183

in tables, 94–95

text, changing, 42

of text in PowerPoint, 343–344

of text in text box shapes, 168

transparent, 183–184, 539

for Word page borders, 257

for Word themes, 253

Color & Thickness dialog box, OneNote, 488–490

color saturation, 538

color scheme, customizing, 519–520

color style, PowerPoint text box, 345

color tone, 538

color-coding, 421, 506

Colors dialog box, 331, 421

column chart, 108–111, 113, 114

column label, Excel worksheet, 461

column letter, Excel worksheet, 459

Column Width dialog box, Excel, 450

columns
  Excel worksheet, 415–417, 419, 447–450, 459–460, 467
  running text into in PowerPoint, 356

table, 87, 89–93, 247

Word document, 253–254

Columns dialog box, 253–254, 356

combination chart, 121

Combine Documents dialog box, Word, 269–270

combo box, for Word forms, 203–204

Comma Style button, Excel, 406

commands, 4, 513

comments
  Excel worksheet, 417–419
  in Properties window, 595
  SkyDrive file, 610–611
  Word document, 264–266, 280

comparing documents, in Word, 268–270

Compatibility Checker dialog box, 527

compatibility mode, 23

compound file. *See* object linking and embedding

Compress Pictures command, 543–544, 549

compression, 533, 543–544, 549

Computer, 27–29, 477

concordance file, 300–301

conditional format, Excel, 407–409, 469–470

Confirm Password dialog box, 30, 423

Connecting To dialog box, Office Web App, 592

connector, 161–165

constant, 427

container, OneNote note, 486
Content Control Properties dialog box, Word, 203, 204
content placeholder frame, slide layout, 314
context-sensitive group button, 17
contrast, 324, 372, 536–538, 546–547
Control Panel, 368–369
Controls button, Word, 203
Convert dialog box, 580
Convert Notes dialog box, Word, 296
Convert Text to Table dialog box, Word, 85, 248
Copy command
  Clipboard, 35
  embedding data, 578
  Excel, 420
  Home tab, PowerPoint, 315
  Move or Copy Pages dialog box, 507
  Move or Copy Section dialog box, 479
  versus object linking and embedding, 571–572
  Office shortcut menus, 35
  OneNote, 478, 498, 507
  Organizer dialog box, 242
  Source Manager dialog box, 298
  Word, 240
Copy Here option, 35
Copy This File command, SkyDrive, 597
Copy to Collection command, Clip Organizer, 559

Copy to Folder dialog box, PowerPoint, 388
copying
  Excel worksheet data, 419–421
  files on SkyDrive, 597
  with Format Painter, 37
  HTML code for public folder hyperlink icon, 610
  Office file into notes, on OneNote, 496
  OneNote notes into another Office program, 498
  from Properties window, 596
  slides, in PowerPoint, 315
  source file data, for OLE, 575
  styles in templates, Word, 240–242
  table of contents in Word, 284
  text, 35
copyright, picture, 534
correcting errors, 437–440, 492
Corrections button, 372, 537–538
COUNT function, Excel, 441
cover page, creating in Word, 261
Create a Folder window, SkyDrive, 586–587
Create a Video window, PowerPoint, 390
Create Chart dialog box, 134
Create Custom Dictionary dialog box, 72
Create New Building Block dialog box, Word, 227
Create New Style from Formatting dialog box, Word, 235, 236

criteria, filtering Excel lists with, 464
cropping pictures, 536, 540–541, 547–548
cross-reference, 288–289, 292–294
Ctrl key, 172, 175, 321, 406, 419–420, 486
curved connector, 164–165
Custom AutoFilter dialog box, Excel, 464
Custom data-validation rule, Excel, 410
Custom Dictionaries dialog box, 71–73
Custom Lists dialog box, Excel, 412
Custom Views dialog box, Excel, 423
Customize Keyboard dialog box, Word, 520–522
Customize Quick Access Toolbar option, 516–518, 570
Customize Tags dialog box, OneNote, 505–506
customized view, Excel, 423
customizing
  color scheme, 519–520
  Import Customization files, 521
  keyboard shortcuts in Word, 520–522
  Quick Access toolbar, 516–518
  Ribbon, 511–515
  SmartArt diagrams, 143
  status bar, 518–519
  table of contents in Word, 285–286
Cut command, 35, 91, 322, 420, 507
cycle diagram, 142, 147–148

D

Data button, 100, 247–248
data cluster, 115, 119
data label, chart, 105
Data Labels dialog box, 128
data marker, chart, 104–105, 135, 138
data point, chart, 105
data range, 124
data series, chart, 104–105
Data tab, Excel, 462–463
data table, 104, 136, 466–470
Data Table dialog box, Excel, 467, 469
Data Validation dialog box, Excel, 410–411
data-entry controls, 202–204
data-entry form. *See* forms, Word
data-validation rule, Excel, 409–412
date
  entering values in Excel worksheet, 402–404
  formatting, chart, 138
  formatting in Excel, 406–407
  inserting in Word header or footer, 218
  in notes, 487
  on PowerPoint handouts, 382
  on PowerPoint slides, 354
Date & Time button, 217, 487

Date and Time dialog box, Word, 218
date axis, chart, 129–130
Date data-validation rule, Excel, 410
date picker, for Word forms, 204
Decimal data-validation rule, Excel, 410
Decimal tab, Word, 223–224
decimals, in Excel worksheets, 401
Define New Bullet dialog box, Word, 222
Define New Multilevel List dialog box, Word, 222
Define New Number Format dialog box, Word, 222
Delete key, 36, 90, 107, 124, 146, 153, 419, 570
Delete Shortcut dialog box, 12
deleted material, viewing in Word document, 268
Deleted Pages tab, OneNote, 507
deleting
  AutoCorrect entry, 64–65
  background removal marks, 543
  bookmarks in Word, 201
  bulleted items from diagram, 153
  cell range names, Excel, 435
  in Clip Organizer, 559–560
  columns in table, 90
  comments in Excel worksheet, 418
  comments in Word documents, 265–266

cropped areas of pictures, 543
Excel worksheet, completely, 421
Excel worksheet data, 419–420
Excel worksheet rows and columns, 447–448
files on SkyDrive, 597
in-text bibliography citations in Word, 299
keyboard shortcuts in Word, 522
macro parts in Visual Basic Editor, 570
macros, 567
markings on PowerPoint slides, 380
OneNote drawings, 491
OneNote groups and pages, 480
OneNote notebooks, 477
OneNote notes, 486
page version, OneNote, 483
PowerPoint themes, 340
repeated words, in Word, 68, 70
rows in table, 90
shortcut icons, 12
SkyDrive folders, 589
slides, PowerPoint presentation, 322
style from Cell Styles gallery, 452
styles in templates, Word, 242–243
text, 36
Word document header or footer, 218
worksheet cells, 124
dependents, tracing in Excel, 440

descending sort, 100
description, SkyDrive file, 595, 610–611
Design tab
  charts, 107, 128
  Excel, 125, 452–453
  PowerPoint, 38, 125, 329–330, 337
  table, 85
  Table Tools, 15–16
  Word, 125, 214, 217
desktop publishing, Word
  background color, adding, 258
  border, adding to page, 256–257
  charts, 245–246
  clip art, 245–246
  diagrams, 245–246
  drawing canvas, working with, 251–252
  drop cap, 258–259
  landscape documents, 260–261
  newspaper-style columns, 253–254
  objects, 248–251
  photos, 245–246
  printing on different size paper, 261
  shapes, 245–246
  tables, 246–248
  text boxes, 255–256
  theme, choosing, 252–253
  watermarks, 259–260
desktop shortcut icon, 11–12, 28
Details view, 26, 591
Developer tab, 203, 242–243, 561–562, 567
diagonal lines, drawing on table, 99–101

diagrams
  appearance, 154–155
  creating, 144, 158
  direction, changing, 153–154
  position of, changing, 145
  in PowerPoint presentations, 357
  shapes, 145–151, 155–158
  size of, changing, 145
  SmartArt, creating, 141–143
  starting from sketch, 144
  swapping for another, 144–145
  three-dimensional, 157
  turning bulleted list into, 153
  in Word documents, 245–246
dialog box launcher, 16–17
dictionaries, spell checker, 67, 70–73
digital signature, macro, 563
discretionary hyphen, 225
distributing
  objects, 171, 176–177
  work, 523–530
Dock to Desktop view, OneNote, 497
docking OneNote screen, 499–500
Document Inspector dialog box, 29
Document Properties panel, 28
Document Recovery task pane, 24
Document Views group, Word, 193

documents, Word.
  See also desktop publishing, Word; reports; styles, Word
  breaking lines, 209–210
  commenting on, 264–266
  creating, 191–193
  defined, 9, 191
  footers, 216–219
  hard page breaks, 210
  headers, 216–219
  highlighting parts of, 263–264
  hyphenating text, 225–227
  indentation, 212–214
  inserting files into, 205
  lists, 220–223
  margins, 210–212
  mass mailings, 274–280
  moving around in, 198–201
  numbering pages, 214–216
  paragraphs and formatting, 207–208
  PowerPoint slides, from headings, 315–318
  section breaks, inserting, 208–209
  space between lines, adjusting, 219–220
  space between paragraphs, adjusting, 220
  tabs, working with, 223–225
  templates, switching, 243
  tracking changes to, 266–271
  viewing, 193–195

Documents folder, 21
dots per inch (dpi), 533
double strikethrough, 41
double-space text, 220
doughnut chart, 109,
  113, 119
Downloaded Clips
  subfolder, 556
downloading
  clip art from Microsoft,
  557
  files to computer from
  SkyDrive, 596–597
Draft view, Word, 194–196,
  209–210, 233, 247,
  264–267, 294–295
Draw Borders button,
  85, 94, 101
Draw tab, OneNote, 487
Draw Table option, 84,
  88, 101
Draw Text Box option,
  Word, 255
drawing
  in OneNote, 487–491
  on tables, 101–102
  text boxes, in Word, 255
drawing canvas, Word,
  164, 166, 251–252
drawing commands. *See*
  also objects
  arrows, 160–165
  connectors, 161–165
  drawing process,
  160–161
  lines, 160–165
  overview, 159
  shapes, 165–168
  WordArt images,
  169–170
drawing guide,
  PowerPoint, 358
Drawing Tools,
  PowerPoint, 345
drop cap, in Word
  documents, 258–259
drop lines, in line and
  area charts, 123
drop-down list, 17, 203

E

Edit Citation dialog box,
  Word, 299
Edit Hyperlink dialog
  box, 56
Edit Name dialog box,
  Excel, 434–435
Edit Permissions
  window, SkyDrive,
  604–605, 608–609
Edit Photo Album dialog
  box, PowerPoint,
  326
Edit Pictures task pane,
  Picture Manager,
  546–547
Edit Source dialog box,
  Word, 298–299
editing
  blog entries online, 530
  comments in Excel
  worksheet, 418
  comments in Word
  documents, 265
  custom dictionary,
  72–73
  embedded data, 579
  Excel worksheet
  data, 413
  index, in Word
  document, 291–292
  macros, 568–570
  master slides,
  PowerPoint
  presentation, 339
  photo albums,
  PowerPoint, 326
  in Picture Manager,
  546–549
  text frame text,
  PowerPoint, 346
  text in text box
  shapes, 168
  three-dimensional
  diagrams, 157
  videos in PowerPoint,
  372

Word document
  header or footer, 218
Effects button,
  PowerPoint, 330
elbow connector,
  164–165
em dash, 226
e-mail, 56, 530, 598,
  607–608
embedded object,
  580. *See also*
  object linking and
  embedding
en dash, 226
Encarta dictionaries, 75
Encrypt Document
  dialog box, 29–31
endnote, Word
  document, 294–296
Enter key, 124, 379, 400
Enter Text dialog box,
  527
Envelope Options dialog
  box, Word, 271, 275
envelopes, printing,
  279–280. *See also*
  mass mailings, Word
Envelopes and Labels
  dialog box, Word,
  271–272
Equalize character
  height text effect,
  PowerPoint, 41
Equation Editor,
  OneNote, 491
Eraser tool, 85, 88, 380
Error Alert tab, Data
  Validation dialog
  box, 411
error bar, in chart, 123
Error Checking dialog
  box, Excel, 438–439
error message, Excel,
  437–438
errors, 294, 492
Esc key, 376, 380, 391,
  400

Excel. *See also* charts; customizing; formulas, Excel; Office Web Apps; text; worksheet, Excel
attaching file from to OneNote note, 495–496
AutoFill command, 404–406
cell addresses, 399
coauthoring files, 612–615
columns, 399
conditional formats, 407–409
copying file into OneNote, 496
data-validation rules, 409–412
defined, 9
earlier versions of files, 23
e-mail, sending files by, 530
formatting data, 404–407
Goal Seek command, 464–466
lists, managing information in, 461–464
macros, 563, 565–566
overview, 29, 395
preparing to merge worksheet in Word, 275
rows, 399
save options, adjusting, 21
screen, 397–398
SmartArt diagrams, 141–143
table, constructing from worksheet, 85
templates, saving formats in, 460

what-if analyses with data tables, 466–470
Window buttons, 62
workbooks, creating new, 395–397
workbooks, defined, 399
Zoom commands, 62
Excel Help window, 440
Excel Options dialog box, 401, 412–413, 418
exclusion, filtering Excel lists by, 464
exploded doughnut chart, 119
exploded pie chart, 113

F

F2 key, 413
F3 key, 434
F4 key, 447
F7 key, 68
F8 key, 198
Factiva iWorks research site, 76
Favorite Links, 26, 30, 239
Favorites list, 30
Favorites subfolder, 556, 557
file formats, 363, 366, 531–534
File In Use message box, 615
File Locations dialog box, Word, 240
File Open dialog box, 521
File Save dialog box, 521
File tab, 28–29, 31, 190, 308, 396, 476
File Types dialog box, Picture Manager, 545

files. *See also* distributing work; object linking and embedding
closing, 28
coauthoring files shared on SkyDrive, 611–615
creating in SkyDrive, 589–590
Document Recovery task pane, 24
hyperlinks to another place in, 54–56
inserting into Word documents, 205
managing on SkyDrive, 594–597
opening, 26–28
password for, 29–31
properties of, reading and recording, 28–29
saving, 20–25
sending by e-mail, 530
sharing on Internet, 582–583
stored on SkyDrive, opening and editing, 590–594
storing on Internet, 582–583
writing comments and descriptions for, on SkyDrive, 610–611
fill, diagram shape, 156–158
fill, object, 171
Fill Color button, Excel, 454
Fill Effects dialog box, 183, 258
filling, cropping picture by, 541
Filmstrip view, Picture Manager, 544
filtering lists, in Excel, 462–464

Find & Select button, 45, 52, 172, 414, 418
Find and Replace dialog box, 47–48, 52, 200, 291
Find command, 45, 200, 291, 294, 414, 502
Find dialog box, 52, 565
Find Format dialog box, Excel, 47
Find Options dialog box, 47–48
finding
  Excel worksheet comments, 418
  and replacing text, 45–53
Firefox Web browser, 584
first-line indent marker, Word, 213
Flip commands, 180, 490, 548
flipping
  graphics, in Picture Manager, 548
  objects, 171, 179–180
floor, chart, 133
flow chart type diagram, 142
Folder window, 589, 602–603, 609
folders, SkyDrive
  creating, 586–587
  deleting, 589
  e-mail invitations, sending out, 607–608
  going from one to another, 588–589
  moving, 589
  overview, 585
  posting hyperlinks on Internet, 609–610
  renaming, 589
  Share With permissions, 604–606
  sharing, 597–598

types of, 601–604
Windows Live, sharing with friends on, 606–607
Folders bar, 26
font
  choosing, 38
  default OneNote, 499
  defined, 37
  diagram shape, 158
  installing, 57
  in PowerPoint presentation, 329
  removing, 57
  table, 86, 97
  of text in PowerPoint, 342
  of text in text box shapes, 168
  for Word themes, 253
Font Color drop-down list, 42, 343
Font dialog box, 38–42, 168, 192, 342–343
Font drop-down list, 38, 342, 397
Font group button, 40, 192
font size
  changing, 39
  chart, changing, 132
  diagram shape, 158
  fitting text in text frame, 347
  table, 86, 247
  of text in PowerPoint, 343
  of text in text box shapes, 168
Font Size drop-down list, 39, 343, 397
font style, 37, 39–40
Fonts icon, Control Panel, 57
footers, 214–219, 227, 352–356, 458
footnote, Word document, 294–296

forecasting, in Excel, 464–466
foreign characters, 44–45
foreign language text, 79–81
form letters, 279–280. *See also* mass mailings, Word
Format As Table dialog box, Excel, 452
Format Axis dialog box, 129–130, 138, 140
Format Background dialog box, PowerPoint, 331–336
Format Cells dialog box, Excel, 402–404, 406–408, 446–448, 451, 453–454, 470
Format Data Table dialog box, 136
Format dialog box, 132, 173, 175, 180, 185
Format Gridlines dialog box, 131
Format Object dialog box, 579
Format Painter, 37
Format Picture dialog box, 536–539, 541
Format Plot Area dialog box, 132
Format Selection button, 132, 136, 138
Format Shape dialog box, 162–163, 168, 184, 345, 347–349, 356
Format tab
  charts, 107, 125, 132
  drawing objects, 161
  Picture Tools, 535–543, 560
  PowerPoint, 345, 372
  WordArt image, 169
Format Trendline dialog box, 123, 137

Format Video dialog box, PowerPoint, 372
formatting. *See also* file formats
data, Excel, 404–407
date, in Excel, 402
Excel worksheet, 421
finding and replacing, 47–48
heading, viewing in Word Outline view, 283
as OLE pitfall, 574
paragraph storage of, in Word, 207–208
section break storage of, 209
table, 91–95
time, in Excel worksheet, 404
formatting marks, 208
Formatting toolbar, Picture Manager, 548
forms, Word, 202–205
Formula bar, Excel, 124, 399–400, 403–404, 413, 430, 434–435, 442
Formula dialog box, Word, 95–96
formulas, Excel
basics of entering, 430
cell range, entering, 431–432
cell range, naming, 432–435
cell references in, 425–427
cells, clicking to enter cell references, 431
copying from cell to cell, 436–437
correcting errors one at time, 437–438
dates in, 403
error checker, running, 438–439

errors in, detecting and correcting, 437–440
functions, working with, 440–444
operators in, 428–430
overview, 425
referring to cells in different worksheets, 435–436
referring to formula results in, 427–428
tracing cell references, 439–440
Formulas tab, Excel, 434, 443–444
fractions, in Excel worksheets, 401
Freeze Panes commands, Excel, 415–417
friends, Windows Live, 598–601
Full Page view, OneNote, 481–482
Full Screen Reading view, Word, 194–195
full-screen video, in PowerPoint presentation, 366
Function Arguments dialog box, Excel, 443–444
Function Library buttons, Excel, 443
functions, Excel, 429, 440–444

G

Gettysburg PowerPoint Presentation, 314
Glass artistic effect, 539
Glow Diffused artistic effect, 539

Glow Edges artistic effect, 539
Go To command, 200, 414, 418
Go To Special dialog box, Excel, 414, 418
Goal Seek command, Excel, 464–466
Goal Seek Status dialog box, Excel, 465
Google Image Search, 534
gradient color slide background, 328, 330–332
gradient shape fill, 183
gradient stops, PowerPoint, 332
grammar checker, Word, 73–74
graphics. *See* clip art; pictures
grid, 171, 173, 358
Grid and Guides dialog box, PowerPoint, 358
gridlines
chart, 104, 130–132
Excel worksheet, printing, 459
table, 84
Group command, 181–182
grouping objects, 171, 181–182
groups
OneNote, 480
Ribbon, 513–515
Guides check box, PowerPoint, 358
gutter, Word document, 211

H

Handout Master view, PowerPoint, 382

handouts, PowerPoint presentation, 306, 381–383

handwritten note, converting to text, 491

hanging indent, Word document, 213–214

hanging relationship, Organization Chart diagram, 149, 150–151

hard line break, 344

hard page break, 210

header
Excel worksheet, 458
PowerPoint slide, 352–356
Word document, 214–219, 227

Header and Footer dialog box, PowerPoint, 353–355

Header dialog box, Excel, 458

header row, 84, 92–93, 96–97, 100, 247, 461

heading
cases for, 43
Excel worksheet column and row, 459–460
Word document, 199, 282–287

Help window, Excel, 440

hidden format symbols, 51, 197

hiding
Audio icon, PowerPoint, 365
chart gridlines, 131
columns and rows, in worksheet, 417
Excel worksheet, 421–422
page version, OneNote, 483
slides, PowerPoint, 326
video, PowerPoint, 366

hierarchy diagram, 142, 144, 148–149, 151

HighBeam Research site, 76

highlighter, 263–264, 380, 488–489

Home button, Word, 193

Home Page button, Word, 530

Home tab
Excel, 16, 397, 406
hybrid buttons on, 17
Office, 40, 42, 86, 158, 575, 578
OneNote, 498
PowerPoint, 176–177, 343
Ribbon, 14

horizontal (side-to-side) alignment, in Excel cells, 446

Horizontal Align button, PowerPoint, 87

horizontal axis, chart, 105, 129–130

Hotmail, 584, 598, 600

HTML code, for public folder hyperlink icon, 610

Hue slider, Picture Manager, 547

hyperlink, 53–57, 293, 598, 609–610

Hyperlink character style, Word, 284

hyphen key, 225

hyphenating text, Word document, 225–227

1

icons, 5, 602

images. *See* clip art; drawing commands; pictures; WordArt image

Import Customization file, 521

Import to Collection dialog box, Clip Organizer, 558

In Line with Text option, Word, 179

Indent buttons, Word, 212

indentation, 211–214, 221, 291

index, Word document, 287–292, 300–301

Info option, File tab, 23

Information window, 28–31

Ink Color option, PowerPoint, 380

Ink Equation Editor, OneNote, 491–492

Ink to Math button, OneNote, 492

Ink to Text button, OneNote, 491

input cell, Excel, 466

Insert Address Block dialog box, Word, 277–278

Insert Audio dialog box, PowerPoint, 364

Insert Chart dialog box, 106, 134

Insert File dialog box, Word, 205

Insert Function dialog box, Excel, 440–441

Insert Greeting Line dialog box, Word, 278

Insert Hyperlink dialog box, 53, 55–56

Insert Merge Field dialog box, Word, 278

Insert New Pictures dialog box, PowerPoint, 323

Insert Object dialog box, 577, 579

Insert Outline dialog box, PowerPoint, 318

Insert Picture dialog box, 99, 135, 183, 259, 335, 535–536
Insert Shapes gallery, 160–161, 489
Insert tab, 14, 357–358, 487, 498, 577
Insert Table dialog box, 84
Insert Video dialog box, PowerPoint, 366
insertions, viewing in Word documents, 268
interactive PowerPoint presentation, 384–386
interface, Office, 13–20
Internet, 76, 534, 582–583. *See also* Office Web Apps; SkyDrive
Invite button, Windows Live, 600
italics, 37, 39–40

J

justifying text, 356, 447

K

keyboard shortcuts. *See also* shortcut commands
applying font styles to text, 40
applying styles in Word, 232
assigning to macro, 566
in book, 4
closing file, 28
jumping around in documents in Word, 198

moving around in Excel worksheet, 414
moving cursor in table, 86
opening files, 26
opening thesaurus, 78
PowerPoint navigation, 376–378
saving files, 20
selecting text, 34, 197
undoing actions, 36
Word, 198, 520–522
KeyTips, 20
keyword, clip art, 555
kiosk-style PowerPoint presentation, 383–384

L

Label Options dialog box, Word, 273, 276
labeling
axes, chart, 129–130
chart element, 128–129
labels, printing in Word, 279–280. *See also* mass mailings, Word
Landscape mode, 247, 260–261, 335, 455, 547
Language button, Review tab, 73, 79–80
Language dialog box, 73, 80–81
Lasso Select button, OneNote, 490–491
Last Viewed option, PowerPoint, 325, 379, 391
layout
chart, 127–130
Excel worksheet, 445–450
master slide, 340

PowerPoint slide, 318, 339
table, 88–91
Layout dialog box, 173, 175, 180, 249–250
Layout tab, 85–86, 107, 125, 128, 132
Layouts gallery, 145
leader, tab, 224, 286, 291
Left Hanging option, Layout drop-down list, 150
Left Margin marker, Word, 212
Left tab, Word, 223–224
left-aligned data, in Excel, 446
left-indent marker, Word, 213
legend, chart, 105, 128, 138
limited-access friend, Windows Live, 599
line chart, 109, 111–113, 115, 117, 123
Line Spacing Options, Word, 219
Line Weight drop-down list, Word, 94
Linear Forecast trendline option, 123
linear gradient fill background, PowerPoint, 331–332
linear trendline, 122
lines
adjusting space between, in Word, 219–220
breaking in PowerPoint, 344
breaking in Word, 209–210
in chart, width of, 132
drawing, 160–161, 489–490
handling, 161–165

lines *(continued)*
  in PowerPoint
    presentations, 358
  style of, 94, 131, 163,
    185
  for Word page borders,
    257
Lines button, Layout
  tab, 123
Link to Previous button,
  Word, 218
linked notes, 497
linked object, 575–576,
  580. *See also*
    object linking and
    embedding
linked SkyDrive folder,
  602, 608–609
linked style, Word, 231
linking worksheets,
  Excel, 400
Links button, Word, 201
List data-validation rule,
  Excel, 410
list diagram,
  142, 147–148
lists
  AutoFill, in Excel, 412
  Excel, 461–464
  PowerPoint, 350–352
  text of, converting into
    table, 85
  Word, 220–223, 281
live-previewing, 539
locked aspect ratio,
  89, 174
lossless compression,
  533
lossy compression, 533
lowercase, 43

M

Macro dialog box,
  567–568
Macro Recorder,
  564–567

macros, 561–570
Mail Merge Recipients
  dialog box, Word,
  276
Mailings tab, Word, 271
main entry, index,
  288–289
Manage Accounts
  button, Word, 530
Manage Sources button,
  Word, 288–289
Manage Styles dialog
  box, Word, 241
margins
  Excel worksheet,
    adjusting, 458
  PowerPoint text frame,
    347
  setting up and
    changing, in Word,
    210–212
Mark Index Entry dialog
  box, Word, 288–290
Mark Table of Contents
  Entry dialog box,
  Word, 287
mass mailings, Word,
  274–280
Master Layout dialog
  box, PowerPoint,
  340
master slide,
  PowerPoint,
  337–340, 342
master style,
  PowerPoint, 320,
  338–339
Master view,
  PowerPoint, 320
Match Fields dialog box,
  Word, 277–278
math expression, in
  note, 491–492
math formula, in Word
  table, 95–96
matrix diagram, 142,
  147–148
MAX function, Excel, 441

Media icon, PowerPoint,
  366
Merge Section dialog
  box, OneNote, 507
Merge to New Document
  dialog box, Word,
  279
Merge to Printer dialog
  box, Word, 280
merging, in Word,
  274–279
merging cells, in tables,
  87–88
Message Alert dialog
  box, Excel, 411
microphone, testing,
  368–370
Microsoft clip art Web
  site, 557
Microsoft Clip
  Organizer. *See* Clip
  Organizer
Microsoft Office Picture
  Manager, 10, 544–549
Microsoft Office
  submenu, Start
  menu, 10–11
Microsoft Product
  Information
  Center, 79
Microsoft Silverlight, 584
MIN function, Excel, 441
Mini Translator
  command, 80
Minimize the Ribbon
  button, 14
mini-toolbar,
  38–40, 42, 343
mirror margins, Word
  document, 212
misspellings. *See*
  AutoCorrect feature;
  spell checker
Modify Button dialog
  box, 570
Modify Location dialog
  box, 21
Modify Style dialog box,
  Word, 237–238, 242

mouse
  scroll wheel, 61, 414
  using in Macro
    Recorder, 567
Move Chart dialog box,
    Excel, 125
Move or Copy dialog
    box, 420–421, 507
Move or Copy Pages
    dialog box,
    OneNote, 507
Move or Copy Section
    dialog box,
    OneNote, 478–479
MSN Money Stock
    Quotes site, 76
multilevel list, Word,
    222–223
Mute/Unmute icon,
    PowerPoint, 365
My Collections folder,
    556, 557–560
My Documents folder, 21
My Templates icon, 192,
    203–204, 238, 240,
    310, 397, 460

N

Name Manager dialog
    box, Excel, 434–435,
    459
named cell ranges,
    Excel, 432–435
narration. *See*
    voice narration,
    PowerPoint
Navigation bar,
    OneNote, 474–475,
    477–478, 480
Navigation pane, 26,
    45–46, 48, 199–200
navigator buttons,
    Word, 200
nested list, 222–223

New Collection dialog
    box, Clip Organizer,
    559–560
New dialog box, 192,
    203–204, 238, 397,
    460
New Drawing Canvas
    command, Word,
    164, 252
New from Existing
    Document dialog
    box, Word, 192
New from Existing
    Workbook dialog
    box, Excel, 397
New Name dialog box,
    Excel, 433–434
New Notebook window,
    OneNote, 476
New Presentation dialog
    box, PowerPoint, 310
New Style dialog box,
    Word, 237
New Tag dialog box,
    OneNote, 505–506
New Yorker, 305
Normal style, Word, 232
Normal template,
    Word, 566
Normal view, 456,
    481–482
Normal/Outline view,
    PowerPoint, 319
Normal/Slides view,
    PowerPoint, 319
notebook, OneNote,
    473, 475–477,
    480–481, 506–507
notes, OneNote
  attaching Office file to,
    495–496
  audio, 493–495
  containers, moving
    and resizing, 486
  copying into another
    Office program, 498
  copying Office file into,
    496

defined, 476
deleting, 486
drawing on page,
    487–491
formatting text in,
    498–499
getting more space for
    on page, 486–487
handwritten,
    converting to text,
    491
linking Word or
    PowerPoint file to,
    497
math expression,
    writing in, 491–492
merging and moving,
    507
overview, 485
screen-clipping,
    492–493
searching for, 501–503
selecting, 486
tagging, 503–506
typewritten, 487
units for organizing,
    475–476
notes, PowerPoint
    presentation, 306,
    309, 373–374
Notes Page view,
    PowerPoint, 320, 374
Notes pane, 294, 309,
    320–321, 373
Notification tray,
    OneNote, 493
Nudge commands, 175
Number Format drop-
    down list, 96, 216,
    295, 402–404
numbered list, 220–223,
    350, 352
numbering pages, in
    Word, 214–216
numbering scheme,
    Word list, 222

numbers
  in charts, formatting, 138
  in charts, displaying large, 130
  in Excel worksheet, aligning text and, 445–447
  in Excel worksheet, displaying large, 124
  formatting in Excel, 406–407
  tables, entering on, 86
numeric values, in Excel worksheet, 401
numerical axis, chart, 129–130

O

Object dialog box, 577–579
object linking and embedding (OLE)
  converting linked object to embedded object, 580
  editing embedded data, 579
  embedding, uses for, 573
  embedding data from other programs, 577–579
  linking, uses for, 573
  linking to data in source file, 574–577
  overview, 571–573
  pitfalls of, 574
objects
  aligning, 175–176
  default style, declaring, 185
  distributing for equidistance, 176–177
  flipping, 179–180
  grid, hiding and displaying, 173
  grouping, 181–182
  moving, 174–175
  overlapping, 178–179
  overview, 170–171
  positioning, 174–175
  PowerPoint tools for handling, 358
  regrouping, 182
  rotating, 179–180
  rulers, hiding and displaying, 173
  selecting, 172
  shape, changing, 173–174
  shape fill colors, 182–183
  shape outline, 184–185
  size, changing, 173–174
  transparent colors, 183–184
  ungrouping, 182
  in Word documents, 248–251
Office 2010 Home and Student edition
  overview, 1–5
  programs included in, 9–10
  starting programs, 10–12
Office 97–2003, 22
Office Collections folder, 556
Office link, Windows Live taskbar, 588–589
Office Web Apps. *See also* SkyDrive
  file comments and descriptions, 610–611
  Office file, creating, 589–590
  overview, 581–582
  SharePoint 2010, 583
  sharing files on Internet, 582–583
  starting with, 583–584
  storing files on Internet, 582–583
  Windows Live friends, 598–601
  Windows Live, signing in to, 584
Office window, Windows Live, 588
Office.com diagram, 142
Office.com templates, 192, 311, 396
Oganization chart diagram, 149–151
OLE. *See* object linking and embedding
100% charts, 115
one-input data table, 466–467
OneNote. *See also* customizing; notes, OneNote; Office Web Apps
  coauthoring files, 612–615
  color-coding in, 506
  defined, 9
  deleting groups and pages, 480
  docking screen, 499–500
  e-mail, sending files by, 530
  getting from place to place in, 480–481
  groups, renaming and deleting, 480
  languages, choosing, 79
  notebook, creating, 476–477
  overview, 473–474
  pages, 479–480, 507
  preventing text from being spell checked, 73
  Recycle Bin, 507
  renaming groups and pages, 480
  screen, 474–475

searching, 501–503
section, creating, 478
section, merging and moving, 507
section group, creating, 478–479
Side Note window, 500
subpages, creating, 480
Symbol dialog box, 44–45
table, creating, 84–85
views, 481–483
OneNote Options dialog box, 477, 499
online applications, 581. *See also* Office Web Apps
Open dialog box, 21, 25–30, 239, 242, 269, 596
Open Document dialog box, Office Web App, 592
Open Existing Post dialog box, Word, 530
Open Index AutoMark File dialog box, Word, 301
Open Notebook dialog box, OneNote, 477
operators, in Excel formulas, 428–430
Options dialog box
AutoCorrect dialog box, opening, 63
Check Spelling As You Type check box, 68
color scheme, choosing, 520
customizations, exporting and importing, 521
Developer tab, displaying or removing with, 562
earlier versions of files, 23
language, choosing, 79

macro, running from Quick Access toolbar button, 570
metric system, choosing, 173
OneNote, 500
overview, 13
Paste Options button, 34
preferred place to save files, choosing, 21
Quick Access toolbar, customizing, 516–518
Recent Documents list, 27
Ribbon, customizing, 511–515
saving AutoRecovery information, 25
order of precedence, Excel operator, 430
Organization Chart diagram, 150
Organizer dialog box, Word, 241–242
Oriel Report template, Word, 230
orientation, PowerPoint handout, 382
Orientation button, 261, 447, 455
outline
of letters in WordArt image, 170
object, 171
shape, 156–158, 182–185
Outline tab, PowerPoint, 318–319, 341–342
Outline view, Word, 194–196, 233, 264–266, 282–284
Outlining tab, Word, 282
Outlook, 10
Oval shape option, 101
overlapping objects, 171, 178–179, 490

overlay chart, 136–137
owner, folder, 597–598

p

Package for CD command, PowerPoint, 386–388
page break, 210, 455–456
Page Color button, 258, 506
Page Layout tab, 14, 38, 176–177, 419, 457–458
Page Layout view, Excel, 173, 455–456
page numbers
on Excel worksheets, 458
for index entries, 288–289
on PowerPoint handouts, 382
in Word, 214–216, 284–285
Page pane, OneNote, 474–477, 479–480
Page Setup dialog box, 192, 211, 261, 419, 457–459
page tabs, OneNote, 476
Page window, OneNote, 474–475
pages
charts, positioning in, 124–125
moving from one to another in Word, 199–200
OneNote, 476–481, 483, 506–507
Paragraph dialog box, 207, 212, 214, 219–220, 224, 227, 347
paragraph style, Word, 230–232, 286

paragraphs
  animating in
    PowerPoint, 361
  Word document,
    207–208, 220, 251,
    283
Parker, Ian, 305
password, 29–31, 422–423
Paste command
  Excel, 420
  Office, 17, 35, 91,
    571–572, 575, 578
  OneNote, 493, 498, 507
  PowerPoint, 315
  Word, 240
Paste Name dialog box,
  Excel, 432–434
Paste Special command,
  400, 575, 578–579
pasting slides in
  PowerPoint, 315, 322
path gradient fill
  background,
  PowerPoint, 331
PDF (Portable
  Document File)
  format, 524–525
Pen Color button,
  Design tab, 85, 88,
  94, 101
Pen Style dropdown list,
  PowerPoint, 94
pen tool, 380, 488–489
Pen Weight drop-down
  list, PowerPoint, 94
Pencil Sketch artistic
  effect, 539
pencil tool, 85
Percent Style button,
  Excel, 406
percentage, scaling
  worksheet by, 457
Permissions window,
  SkyDrive, 603
Personal notebook,
  OneNote, 476
personalizing
  PowerPoint
  presentation, 313

Personal.Macro
  Workbook, Excel,
  566
PgDn key, 198
PgUp key, 198
photo album,
  PowerPoint, 311,
  322–326
photos. *See* pictures
phrase, searching for
  notes by, 501–502
Picture Bullet dialog
  box, PowerPoint, 351
picture diagram, 142
Picture Dimensions,
  Picture Manager, 547
Picture Manager. *See*
  Microsoft Office
  Picture Manager
Picture menu, Picture
  Manager, 546
Picture Shortcuts pane,
  Picture Manager, 545
picture slide
  background,
  PowerPoint, 330
picture style, 536, 540
Picture Styles gallery,
  540
Picture Tools, 535–543,
  560
picture watermark,
  259–260
pictures
  as bullets in lists, 351
  in charts, 135
  compressing, 543–544
  copyright, 534
  file formats, 531–534
  inserting in Office file,
    535–536
  overview, 531
  photo album,
    PowerPoint, 311,
    322–326
  Picture Manager,
    544–549
  in PowerPoint
    presentations, 357

as slide background,
    334–335
  as table background,
    97–99
  touching up, 536–543
  in Word documents,
    245–246
pie chart, 109, 112–113,
  119, 121–122
Pin to Start Menu
  option, 11
Pin to Taskbar option, 12
pixel, 531
pixels per inch (ppi),
  533, 544
placeholder,
  bibliography
  citation, 298
plain text format, 530
Playback tab, 364–367,
  371–372, 494
plot area, chart, 104,
  132, 135
points, font size, 39
Portable Document
  File (PDF) format,
  524–525
Portrait mode, 260–261,
  335, 547
Position commands,
  Word, 125, 250–251
posting entry to blog,
  Word, 529–530
PowerPoint. *See also*
  charts; customizing;
  delivering
  PowerPoint
  presentation;
  diagrams; Office
  Web Apps; shortcut
  commands; tables;
  text
  aligning objects, 175
  animation, 360–362
  attaching file from
    to OneNote note,
    495–496
  audio, 362–365

AutoFit mechanism, 346–349
basic tasks, 309–310
coauthoring files, 612–615
copying file into OneNote, 496
defined, 9
earlier versions of files, 23
e-mail, sending files by, 530
enlivening presentations, 357–358
footers, 352–356
headers, 352–356
Insert Picture dialog box, 535
language, checking, 79
linking file to OneNote notes, 497
lists, bulleted and numbered, 350–352
macros, 563–564
master slides, 337–340
moving objects, 175
Notes pane, hiding and displaying, 320–321
overview, 29, 305–307
persuasive presentations, 311–314
photo albums, 322–326
presentation, creating new, 310–311
save options, adjusting, 21
screen, 308–309
slide backgrounds, 330–336
slides, 314–319, 321–322
Slides pane, hiding and displaying, 320–321
text boxes, 344–345
themes, 327–330

transitions, 359–360
video, 365–367
views, 318–320
voice narration, 367–372
PowerPoint Options dialog box, 348, 381
PowerPoint Viewer, 386–388, 391
ppi (pixels per inch), 533, 544
precedence, Excel operator, 429–430
precedents, tracing in Excel, 439–440
presentation, PowerPoint
animation, 360–362
audio, 362–365
AutoFit mechanism, 346–349
creating new, 310–311
defined, 9, 306
enlivening, 357–358
footers, 352–356
headers, 352–356
lists, bulleted and numbered, 350–352
master slides, 337–340
overall process for making, 309–310
persuasive, 311–314
PowerPoint Viewer, 391
slide backgrounds, 330–336
slides, 314–319, 321–322
text, entering, 341–344
text, positioning in frames and text boxes, 349
text boxes, 344–345
themes, 327–330
transitions, 359–360
video, 365–367
voice narration, 367–372
Preview area, Ink Equation Editor, 492

preview window, Office Web App, 591
Preview window, Word, 257, 277
Print dialog box, Word, 280
Print Layout view, Word, 190, 193–194, 214. *See also* Word
Print window, 374, 383, 457–458, 496, 523–524
Printed Watermark dialog box, Word, 259–260
printing
address labels, in Word, 272–274
address on envelope, in Word, 271–272
comments, in Excel worksheet, 419
envelopes, in Word, 279–280
form letters, in Word, 279–280
labels, in Word, 272–274, 279–280
landscape worksheet, Excel, 455
Office projects, 523–524
part of Excel worksheet, 455
PowerPoint handouts, 383
PowerPoint notes, 374
Word documents, 261
private SkyDrive folder, 601, 605
process diagram, 142, 147–148
PRODUCT function, Excel, 440, 441
Profile page, Windows Live, 600–601, 606–607

programs, Office, 9–12.
See also *specific
programs by name*
proofing tools
for foreign language
text, 79–81
grammatical errors,
checking for in
Word, 73–74
Research task pane,
74–77
spell checker, 67–73
thesaurus, 77–79
properties, file, 28–29
Properties dialog box,
28–29, 240
Properties window,
594–597, 610–611,
616
proportions, cropping
to, 541
Protect Document
button, File tab,
29, 31
Protect Sheet dialog
box, Excel, 422–423
PrtScn key, 549
public SkyDrive folder,
601, 603–610
Publish as PDF or XPS
dialog box, 525
Publish button, Word,
529–530
Publisher, 10
punctuation, 48, 50–51
pyramid diagram, 142,
147–148

Q

Quick Access toolbar,
189, 308, 481,
516–518, 521, 570
Quick Launch toolbar, 12
Quick Style gallery,
Word, 231

R

radar chart, 109, 120–121
radial gradient fill
background,
PowerPoint, 331
ragged right margin, 225
Range Selector button,
Excel, 411, 435, 444,
459
raw data, chart, 124, 136
Reading View button,
OneNote, 481
Reading view,
PowerPoint, 320, 385
Recent Documents list,
27, 588
recoloring, 98, 372, 536,
538–539
Record Macro dialog
box, 565–566
Record Sound dialog
box, 370–371
recording
audio notes, OneNote,
494–495
file properties, 28–29
macros, 564–567
Recording toolbar,
PowerPoint, 374–375
rectangular gradient
fill background,
PowerPoint, 331
Recycle Bin, OneNote,
507
Red Eye Removal
command, Picture
Manager, 548
Register a Blog Account
dialog box, Word, 529
Regroup command, 182
regular font style, 39
Rehearse Timings
button, PowerPoint,
371, 374
rehearsing PowerPoint
presentation, 314,
374–375, 384

relationship diagram,
142, 147–148
Remember icon, 5
Remove Background
command, 542
Remove from Quick
Access Toolbar
option, 518, 570
Rename dialog box,
514–515
renaming
cell range names in
Excel, 434
Clip Organizer
folder, 560
Excel worksheet, 420
files on SkyDrive, 597
groups and pages,
OneNote, 480
OneNote items,
477–478, 480
PowerPoint themes, 340
styles in templates,
Word, 242–243
Re-Order buttons,
PowerPoint, 362
repairing hyperlinks,
56–57
Repeat command, 60,
375, 447
replacing text, 45–53
reports
alphabetizing lists, 281
bibliography, 296–301
cross-references,
292–294
endnotes, 294–296
footnotes, 294–296
index, 287–292
Outline view, 282–284
searching for elements
of, 51
table of contents,
284–287
Reroute Connectors
option, 165
Research button,
Review tab, 76

Research Options dialog box, 77
Research task pane, 74–80
Resize task pane, Picture Manager, 548–549
resizing
  graphic, in Picture Manager, 548–549
  OneNote drawings, 490
  shapes to fit text, 168, 348, 356
resolution, file format, 533
Reuse Slides task pane, PowerPoint, 315
Reveal Formatting task pane, Word, 208, 233
Review tab, 69, 417–418
Reviewers option, Word, 265, 271
Reviewing pane, Word, 264–266
revision marks, Word, 280
rewinding video, PowerPoint, 367
Ribbon, 4, 15–16, 190, 308, 511–515, 518, 521
Right Hanging option, Layout drop-down list, 150
Right Margin marker, Word, 212
Right tab, Word, 223–224
Right to Left button, Design tab, 154
right-alignment, 285, 291, 446
right-indent marker, Word, 213
rotating
  axis title, 128
  graphics, in Picture Manager, 548
  objects, 171, 179–180
  OneNote drawings, 490

picture, 324
text box text, 256
text boxes, in PowerPoint, 345
rotation handle, 180, 345
Row Height dialog box, Excel, 449
row label, table, 84
rows
  Excel worksheet, 399, 415–417, 419, 447–449, 459–460, 467
  table, 86–87, 89–93, 97
ruler, 173, 212–213, 223, 225
running macros, 567–568

S

sample templates, 192, 310, 396
saturation, color, 538, 547
Save & Send option, PowerPoint, 390
Save & Send window, 22, 525, 526, 593
Save As dialog box
  e-mail, sending files by, 530
  Excel, 460
  Favorites list, 30
  macro-enabling files, 564
  navigating, 25–26
  Office 97–2003, saving file for use in, 22
  preferred place to save files, choosing, 21
  presentation video, PowerPoint, 390
  saving files, 20–21
  SkyDrive folder, saving file to, 593
  Sound Recorder, 370
  Web page, turning file into, 527
  Word, 203, 239

Save As Template button, Design tab, 134
Save Chart Template dialog box, 134
Save Current Theme dialog box, PowerPoint, 340
saving
  AutoRecovery file, 24–25
  choosing location to save to, 21
  edited graphics, 546
  file for first time, 20–21
  file for use in earlier versions of program, 21–24
  file from Office 2010 to SkyDrive, 593–594
  keyboard shortcut changes, 521
  mass mailings, in Word, 279
  in OneNote, 474
  overview, 20
  paragraph formatting to creat style, 235
  PowerPoint themes, 340
  in preparation for OLE, 574
scale, chart, 129–131, 140
Scale to Fit options, Excel, 457
scatter (XY) chart, 109, 115–118, 120
scholarly papers. *See* reports
screen-clipping note, OneNote, 492–493
screen shot, 3, 549
ScreenTip box, OneNote, 481
scroll bars, 47, 190, 414
scroll wheel, mouse, 414

Search box
  Available Templates
    window, 192, 396
  OneNote, 501
Search Document text
  box, Word, 47
Search drop-down list,
    Tags Summary task
    pane, 505
Search For text box
  Clip Organizer, 552, 555
  Research task pane,
    76–78
Search pane, Clip
    Organizer, 554–556
Search Results pane,
    OneNote, 502–503
searching
  Clip Organizer for
    media file, 555–556
  for notes, OneNote,
    501–503
section
  OneNote, 475, 477–478,
    481, 506–507
  Word document, 216,
    218–219, 256,
    283–284
section break, inserting
    in Word, 208–209
Section Color option,
    OneNote, 506
section group, OneNote,
    475, 478–479, 481
section tabs, OneNote,
    474–475
security problem, with
    macros, 562–563
See Playback button,
    OneNote, 495
Select & Type button,
    OneNote, 490
Select and Correct
    button, Ink Equation
    Editor, 492
Select Browse Object
    button, Word, 198,
    200

Select button, 34, 93,
    172, 197
Select Data button,
    Design tab, 138
Select Data Source
    dialog box, 138, 276
Select Folder dialog
    box, OneNote, 477
Select Location in
    OneNote dialog box,
    493, 496–497
Select Picture dialog
    box, PowerPoint, 333
Select Row command,
    86–87
Select Table command,
    86–87, 93, 99
Select Table dialog box,
    Word, 276
Select Text with Similar
    Formatting option,
    Word, 34, 197
selecting
  diagram shapes, 146
  Excel worksheets, 420
  in OneNote, 490
  parts of tables, 86–87
  slides, PowerPoint,
    314, 321
  text, 33–34
Selection and Visibility
    pane, 172, 179
selection handles, 165,
    172, 173
self-running PowerPoint
    presentation,
    383–384
Send a Link window,
    SkyDrive, 607
Send commands, 99,
    178–179, 490
sentence case, 43
serial values, in Excel,
    402
services, blogging,
    528–529
Set Hyperlink ScreenTip
    dialog box, 54–55

Set Up Slide Show dialog
    box, PowerPoint,
    384, 386
Shading button, Design
    tab, 94, 99
shape, of object, 171
shape effect, diagram,
    157
shape fill, 182–183
Shape Fill button,
    Format tab, 101, 132,
    135, 157, 182–183
Shape Height box,
    Format tab, 126
shape outline, 182–185
Shape Outline button,
    Format tab, 101–102,
    131, 157, 162–163,
    182, 184
Shape Styles gallery,
    156, 163, 182, 345
Shape Width box,
    Format tab, 126
shapes. *See also* shapes,
    diagram
  cropping pictures
    to, 541
  drawing, 160–161,
    166–167, 489–491
  overview, 165–166
  in PowerPoint
    presentations, 358
  symmetry, changing,
    167
  using as text box,
    167–168
  in Word documents,
    245–246
shapes, diagram
  adding, 143, 147–149
  appearance of,
    changing, 155–158
  color, changing,
    156–158
  demoting in hierarchy
    diagrams, 151
  exchanging for
    another, 156
  fill, changing, 156–158

fonts and font sizes, changing, 158

moving to different positions, 146

Oganization charts, adding to, 149–151

outline, changing, 156–158

overview, 145–146

promoting in hierarchy diagrams, 151

removing, 146

selecting, 146

size of, changing, 155–156

text on, 151–153

when resizing diagram, 145

Shapes button, 101, 139, 160, 164, 166, 252

Shapes gallery, 156, 161, 164, 166–168, 385, 541

Share window, 529, 610

Share With permissions, 604–606

shared SkyDrive folder, 597–598, 601, 603–610

SharePoint 2010, 477, 583

sharing files on Internet, 582–583

sharpening picture, 536–537

Shift key, 65, 166, 173, 174, 180, 414

Short Date option, Excel, 402

shortcut commands

AutoCorrect feature, 62–65

Clip Organizer, 558

Repeat command, 60

Undo command, 59–60

Window group options, 62

Zoom controls, 61–62

shortcut icon, 11–12, 28

shortcut menu, 19

Shortcuts button, Picture Manager, 545

Shrink Font button, Word, 247

Shrink Text on Overflow option, 348–349

Side Note window, OneNote, 500

side selection handle, 173

side-to-side (horizontal) alignment, 446

Silver color scheme, 519

Silverlight, 584

Single File Web Page option, 526–527

Single Picture view, Picture Manager, 546

single-space text, 220

Size button

Format tab, 99, 126, 145, 173, 175

Page Layout tab, 261

Size group button, Format tab, 126, 173–175, 249–250, 345, 541

sketch, starting diagram from, 144

SkyDrive. *See also* folders, SkyDrive

coauthoring files, 611–615

defined, 583

earlier versions of files, 616

file comments and descriptions, 610–611

files, managing on, 594–597

Office files, creating, 589–590

Office files, opening and editing, 590–594

public folder tasks, 603–604

shared folder tasks, 603–604

window, navigating to, 584–585

SkyDrive navigation bar, Windows Live, 588

Slide button, PowerPoint, 376–379

slide control buttons, PowerPoint, 376–378

slide layout, PowerPoint, 314–316, 318, 339

Slide Master, PowerPoint, 337–340, 353, 355

Slide Master view, PowerPoint, 338–339, 342, 355

Slide Orientation option, PowerPoint, 382

slide show. *See* presentation, PowerPoint

Slide Show tab, PowerPoint, 371, 374, 384

Slide Show view, PowerPoint, 320, 374, 376

Slide Sorter view, PowerPoint, 46, 320–322, 325, 336, 375, 383–384, 389

Slide window, PowerPoint, 309

slides, PowerPoint

audio, 362–364

backgrounds, 327–337

charts, positioning in, 124–125

creating new, for text, 347

defined, 306–307

deleting, 322

hidden, 326

inserting, 314–315

layout for, selecting different, 318

slides, PowerPoint
(continued)
  moving from slide to
    slide, 376–379
  moving in
    presentation, 322
  overview, 314
  recording voice
    narration for, 370
  selecting, 321
  transitions, 359–360
  video, inserting on, 366
  voice narration,
    synchronizing with,
    371–372
  from Word document
    headings, 315–318
Slides from Outline
  option, PowerPoint,
  318
Slides pane, PowerPoint,
  308, 319–322, 325
Slides tab, PowerPoint,
  319
Slides-Per-Page
  drop-down list,
  PowerPoint, 382
Small caps text effect, 41
SmartArt diagram,
  141–143. *See also*
  diagrams
SmartArt Styles gallery,
  154–155, 157
softening picture,
  536–537
solid color slide
  background,
  PowerPoint, 328,
  330–331
Sort dialog box, 99–100,
  462–463
Sort Text dialog box,
  Word, 281
sorting
  lists, Excel, 462
  tables, 100
Sound dialog box,
  368–369
sound file formats, 363

Sound icon, Control
  Panel, 368
Sound Recorder, 368–370
sounds, PowerPoint,
  360, 362, 386
Source Document pane,
  Word, 269–270
source file, 274–279,
  400. *See also*
  object linking and
  embedding
Source Manager dialog
  box, Word, 298–299
spacing between lines,
  PowerPoint text
  frame, 347
special characters,
  searching for, 50–51
specialty document, 192
spell checker, 67–73. *See
  also* AutoCorrect
  feature
Spelling and Grammar
  dialog box, 69, 71,
  73–74
Spelling dialog box, 65,
  68–69, 71
spider chart, 120–121
Split Cells dialog box, 88
splitting
  cells, table, 87–88
  Excel worksheet,
    415–417
  screen, Word, 195–196
  text between slides, 347
spreadsheet. *See*
  worksheet, Excel
stacked area chart,
  114–115
stacked bar chart,
  113–114
stacked column chart,
  109–110
stacked line chart,
  112, 115
Standard Width dialog
  box, Excel, 450

Start menu, placing
  Office program on,
  10–11
starting programs,
  10–12
Startup folder, 12
status bar
  customizing, 518–519
  PowerPoint, 79, 319,
    390
  Word, 79, 190, 267
STDEV function,
  Excel, 441
STDEVP function,
  Excel, 441
Step by Step Mail Merge
  Wizard option,
  Word, 274
stock chart, 109, 111, 117
Store Notebook On box,
  OneNote, 477
straight connector,
  164–165
strikethrough, 41
Stroke Eraser option,
  OneNote, 490
Style Area pane,
  Word, 233
Style dialog box,
  286–287, 451–452
Style Inspector pane,
  Word, 233
style menus, Word,
  233–235
Style Pane Options
  dialog box, Word, 234
style set, Word, 233
styles, OneNote, 498
styles, Word
  applying, 231–233
  creating new, 235–237
  defined, 220, 229
  modifying, 237–238
  names appearing
    on style menus,
    233–235
  overview, 208, 229
  seeing which is in use,
    233

style sets, 233
templates, 229–230, 238–243
types of, 230–231
Styles gallery, 231–234, 498
Styles group button, Word, 231
Styles pane, Word, 230–235, 237
Sub line, in Visual Basic Editor, 569
subentry, index, 288–289
subfolder, 558–560, 587
subheadings, Word document, 283
subpages, OneNote, 476, 480–481
Subscript text effect, 41
sub-subentry, index, 288–289
suffix, 48
SUM function, Excel, 429, 432, 440–441
Superscript text effect, 41
surface chart, 109, 116–118
Switch Row/Column button, chart, 105
Switch Windows button, 62
Symbol dialog box, 44–45, 222, 226, 295, 351
symbols, 44–45, 51, 197
symmetry, shape, 167
Synchronous Scrolling button, 62
synonym, 77–79
system tray, 36

T

Tab box, ruler, 223
Tab Color option, Excel, 421
Tab key, 85, 86, 90, 124, 223, 373, 400
Tab leader drop-down list, 286, 291
tab stop, 223–225
Table button, Insert tab, 248, 498, 577
Table Cell Highlighting options, 267
Table drop-down list, Insert tab, 85
TABLE function, Excel, 467
Table icon, PowerPoint, 84
Table menu, 84
Table of Contents dialog box, Word, 284–285, 287
Table of Contents Options dialog box, Word, 286–287
table of contents (TOC), Word, 284–287
Table Properties dialog box, Word, 89
table style, 91–92, 452–453
Table Style Options group, Design tab, 91–92
Table Styles gallery, 91–92, 98, 453
Table Tools tabs, Ribbon, 15–16, 85
tables
aligning text, 87
creating, 84–85
diagonal lines on, 99–101
drawing on, 101–102
from Excel worksheet, 85
fitting on page, 247
formatting, 91–95
header row text direction, 96–97
layout, 88–91
math formulas, in Word, 95–96
merging cells, 87–88
numbers, entering, 86
in OneNote, 498
picture background, 97–99
in PowerPoint, 357
selecting parts of, 86–87
sorting, 100
splitting cells, 87–88
terminology related to, 83–84
text, entering, 86
in Word documents, 246–248, 274–275
tabs
Excel worksheet, 397–398, 420
Ribbon, 14–15, 513–515
working with in Word, 223–225
Tabs dialog box, Word, 224
tagging notes, OneNote, 503–506
Tags gallery, OneNote, 504–505
Tags Summary task pane, OneNote, 503–505
taskbar, starting program from, 12
Technical Stuff icon, 5
templates
charts, saving as, 133–134
Excel, 395, 460
PowerPoint, 310
Word, 191–192, 202–203, 229–230, 238–243
Templates and Add-ins dialog box, Word, 243
Templates folder, 240, 242–243

text. *See also* proofing tools; Word
animating in PowerPoint, 361
appearance, changing, 36–42
AutoCorrect feature, entering with, 64
capitalization, 42–44
case, 42–44
Clipboard task pane, 35–36
copying, 35
deleting, 36
in diagram shapes, 151–153
entering in diagram, 143
in Excel, merging and centering, 448
in Excel, aligning, 445–447
finding and replacing, 45–53
foreign characters, 44–45
foreign language, proofing, 79–81
handwritten notes, converting to, 491
hyperlinks, 53–57
macros, 570
moving, 35
OneNote note, formatting, 498–499
Paste options, 34
in PowerPoint, 312, 341–356
selecting, 33–34, 196–198
symbols, 44–45
in tables, aligning, 87
in tables, entering, 86
in text box shapes, 168
text attribute, 37
text axis, chart, 129

text box
PowerPoint, 323, 325, 344–345, 346–349
turning into text box shape, 168
in Word documents, 255–256
text box pointer, PowerPoint, 344
text box shape, 167–168
Text Direction button, Word, 97, 247, 256
text effect, 37, 40–41
Text Fill button, Format tab, 170
text frame, PowerPoint, 346–349
Text from File option, Word, 205
Text Highlight Color button, Word, 263–264
Text Indent box, Word, 221
text label, Excel worksheet, 401
Text Length data-validation rule, Excel, 410
Text Outline button, Format tab, 170
Text pane, 152–153
text placeholder frame, 314, 341–342
text watermark, 260
text wrapping, 98, 179, 248–250, 401, 446–447
Texture option, Shape Fill drop-down list, 183
texture slide background, PowerPoint, 330, 335–336
theme
photo album, 324
PowerPoint, 309, 327–330, 337, 340

Word document, 252–253
theme colors, 42, 253, 343, 352
theme effect, 253, 330
theme font, PowerPoint, 342
Theme Fonts button, 38, 253
Themes button, Word, 252
Themes gallery, PowerPoint, 329–330, 337, 340
thesaurus, 75, 77–79
third-party dictionary, 72
Thomas Gale Company Profiles site, 76
3D reference, Excel, 435–436
three-dimensional chart, 110, 118, 138
three-dimensional diagrams, 157
tick marks, chart, 130
time
entering in Excel worksheet, 402, 404
formatting in Excel, 406–407
inserting in Word header or footer, 218
Time button, OneNote, 487
Time data-validation rule, Excel, 410
timing PowerPoint presentation, 374–375
Tip icon, 5
title bar, 22, 189
title slide, PowerPoint photo album, 325
Title text box, OneNote, 475, 477–480
titles, 43, 344
TOC (table of contents), Word, 284–287

tOGGLE cASE option, 44
toggle commands, 565
tone, color, 538
tool tabs, 513
Tools gallery, OneNote, 488–489
Top Border command, 94
Top Margin marker, Word, 212
Top/Bottom Rules option, Excel, 407–408, 469
top-heavy title, PowerPoint, 344
top-level folder, SkyDrive, 586–587
topographical map, 118
top-to-bottom (vertical) alignment, Excel, 447
Total Row check box, Word and PowerPoint, 92–93
touching up pictures, 536–543
tracing cell references, Excel, 439–440
tracking changes to Word document, 266–271
Transition to This Slide gallery, PowerPoint, 359–360
transitions, PowerPoint, 359–360, 362
Transitions tab, PowerPoint, 359–360, 362, 383–384, 389
translation, 75, 80
Translation Language Options dialog box, 80
Transparency slider, 184, 331–332, 334–336
transparent color, 183–184, 330–331, 539

transparent object, 179
trendline, chart, 117, 122–123, 137–138
Trim Video dialog box, PowerPoint, 372
troubleshooting charts, 138–140
Trust Center dialog box, 562–563
Two Pages button, Word, 193
two-digit years, in Excel worksheets, 403
two-input data table, 468–470
two-sided Word document, 212
Type group, Design tab, 134
typewritten note, OneNote, 487
typos. *See* AutoCorrect feature; spell checker

U

underlining text, 40–41
Undo command, 36, 59–60, 126, 145, 151, 154
Unfiled Notes folder, OneNote, 500
Unfreeze Panes option, Excel, 417
Ungroup command, 182
Unhide Columns option, Excel, 417
Unhide dialog box, Excel, 422
Unhide Rows option, Excel, 417
Unhide Sheet option, Excel, 422
unlocked aspect ratio, 174

Unmerge Cells option, Excel, 448
Unpin This Program from Taskbar option, 12
Unprotect Sheet button, Excel, 423
Unsaved Collection link, 557
Unsaved Edits folder, Picture Manager, 546
Update Field option, Word, 291, 294
Update Index button, Word, 291
Update Labels button, Word, 279
Update Link option, 576
Update Table button, Word, 285
updating
cross-references, in Word, 294
files, through linking, 573
up/down bars, in line chart, 123
uploading files to SkyDrive folder, 596
uppercase, 43
user-run PowerPoint presentation, 384–386

V

value axis, chart, 105
values, chart, 104
VAR function, Excel, 441
VARP function, Excel, 441
VBA (Visual Basic for Applications), 561
vector graphics, 531–532, 534

vertical (top-to-bottom) alignment, in Excel, 447

Vertical Align button, PowerPoint, 87

vertical axis, chart, 105, 129–130

video, PowerPoint, 365–367, 389–391

Video Tools, PowerPoint, 366–367, 372

View Gridlines button, Layout tab, 84

View option, 24, 595

View Ruler button, Word, 196

View Side by Side button, 62

View tab, 319, 416, 567

views
Excel, customized, 423
Insert Picture dialog box, 535
OneNote, 481–483
Open dialog box, 26
Picture Manager, 545
PowerPoint, 309, 318–320
Save As dialog box, 26
Word document, 193–195

viruses, macro, 562

Visual Basic Editor, 568–570

Visual Basic for Applications (VBA), 561

voice narration, PowerPoint, 367–372, 390

volume, PowerPoint audio, 365

Volume button, PowerPoint, 364, 366

W

wall, chart, 133

Warning icon, 5

watermark, Word documents, 259–260

Web address, SkyDrive file, 596

Web application, 581. *See also* Office Web Apps

Web browser, 584

Web Collections folder, Clip Organizer, 556

Web Layout view, Word, 194–195, 264–267, 280

Web page, 53–54, 493, 526–528

what-if analysis, 466–470

White Screen option, PowerPoint, 381

white space, 49

Whole Number data-validation rule, Excel, 410

wildcard operator, 49–50

Window group options, 62

Windows 7, 12, 240, 340, 566

Windows Clipboard, 575

Windows Explorer, 27–29, 477

Windows Live, 477, 583–585, 597–601, 606–607. *See also* SkyDrive

Windows Live taskbar, 585, 588–589

Windows Media Player, 366, 389

Windows Vista, 12, 26, 240, 340, 566

Windows XP, 12, 240, 340, 566

Word. *See also* charts; customizing; desktop publishing, Word; drawing commands; Office Web Apps; proofing tools; reports; shortcut commands; styles, Word; tables; text
attaching file to note, 495–496
blogging from, 528–530
breaking lines, 209–210
coauthoring files, 612, 614–615
commenting on document, 264–266
copying file into OneNote, 496
defined, 9
document, creating, 191–193
earlier versions of files, 23
e-mail, sending files by, 530
footers, 216–219
forms, 202–205
grammar checker, 73–74
hard page breaks, 210
headers, 216–219
highlighting parts of document, 263–264
hyphenating text, 225–227
indentation, 212–214
indexes, 300–301
keyboard shortcuts, 520–522
linking file to OneNote notes, 497
lists, 220–223
macros, 563, 565–566
margins, 210–212
mass mailings, 274–280

moving around in documents, 198–201
moving linked objects in, 576
numbering pages, 214–216
overview, 29
paragraphs and formatting, 207–208
PowerPoint slides, from headings, 315–318
PowerPoint text, working on in, 312
printing address labels, 272–274
printing address on envelope, 271–272
save options, adjusting, 21
screen, 189–190
searching, 45–51
section breaks, inserting, 208–209
SmartArt diagrams, 141–143
space between lines, 219–220
space between paragraphs, 220
splitting screen, 195–196
tabs, working with, 223–225
text, selecting, 196–198
tracking changes to documents, 266–271
viewing documents, 193–195
Word Options dialog box, 74, 203, 212, 221, 233, 240, 242–243, 264–265, 268, 520
WordArt image, 169–170

WordArt Styles gallery, Format tab, 170
words, searching for notes by, 501–502
workbook, Excel
charts, positioning in, 124–125
creating new, 395–397
defined, 9, 395
handling worksheets in, 420–421
saving as template, 460
worksheets in, 399
worksheet, chart, 104
worksheet, Excel
borders on cells, 453–454
cell addresses, 399
cell styles for formatting, 450–452
cells, selecting in, 419
chart, positioning, 125
colors, decorating with, 454
columns, 399
comments, 417–419
copying data, 419–420
defined, 397–398
deleting data, 419–420
editing data, 413
entering data in, 399–404
freezing columns and rows, 415–417
getting ready to print, 454–460
handling in workbook, 420–421
hiding columns and rows, 417
hiding entire worksheet, 421–422
layout, 445–450
lists, 461–464

moving around in, 414–415
moving data, 419–420
preparing to merge in Word, 275
protecting, 422–423
raw data for chart, entering, 124
rows, 399
splitting columns and rows, 415–417
table styles, 452–453
in workbook, 399
wrap points, Word, 250
wrapping text, 98, 125, 248–250, 401, 576
Write & Insert Fields group, Word, 278
writing, in Ink Equation Editor, 492

X

x axis, chart, 105
XY (scatter) chart, 109, 115–118, 120

y

y axis, chart, 105
year, in Excel worksheet, 402–403

Z

Zoom controls, 61–62, 190, 309, 523, 546, 548

Printed in the United States of America
ED-12-05-12